I0759658

ECCLESIASTES

Volume 18C

THE ANCHOR BIBLE is a fresh approach to the world's greatest classic. Its object is to make the Bible accessible to the modern reader; its method is to arrive at the meaning of biblical literature through exact translation and extended exposition and to reconstruct the ancient setting of the biblical story, as well as the circumstances of its transcription and the characteristics of its transcribers.

THE ANCHOR BIBLE is a project of international and interfaith scope: Protestant, Catholic, and Jewish scholars from many countries contribute individual volumes. The project is not sponsored by any ecclesiastical organization and is not intended to reflect any particular theological doctrine. Prepared under our joint supervision, THE ANCHOR BIBLE is an effort to make available all the significant historical and linguistic knowledge which bears on the interpretation of the biblical record.

THE ANCHOR BIBLE is aimed at the general reader with no special formal training in biblical studies; yet, it is written with the most exacting standards of scholarship, reflecting the highest technical accomplishment.

This project marks the beginning of a new era of cooperation among scholars in biblical research, thus forming a common body of knowledge to be shared by all.

William Foxwell Albright
David Noel Freedman
GENERAL EDITORS

THE ANCHOR BIBLE

ECCLESIASTES

♦

A New Translation
with Introduction and Commentary

C. L. SEOW

THE ANCHOR BIBLE
Doubleday
New York   London   Toronto   Sydney   Auckland

THE ANCHOR BIBLE
PUBLISHED BY DOUBLEDAY
a division of Bantam Doubleday Dell Publishing Group, Inc.
1540 Broadway, New York, New York 10036

THE ANCHOR BIBLE, DOUBLEDAY, and the portrayal of an anchor with
the letters A and B are trademarks of Doubleday, a division
of Bantam Doubleday Dell Publishing Group, Inc.

Library of Congress Cataloging-in-Publication Data
Bible. O.T. Ecclesiastes. English. Seow. 1997.
Ecclesiastes: a new translation with introduction and commentary
/ Choon-Leong Seow.
p.   cm. — (The Anchor Bible; v. 18C)
Includes bibliographical references and index.
1. Bible.   O.T.   Ecclesiastes. — Commentaries.   I. Seow, C. L.
(Choon-Leong)   II. Title.   III. Series: Bible.   English.
Anchor Bible.   1964; v. 18C.
BS192.2.A1   1964.G3   vol. 18C
[BS1473]
223'.8077 — dc20   96-8214
                                                                                         CIP

ISBN 0-385-41114-6

Copyright © 1997 by Doubleday, a division of Bantam
Doubleday Dell Publishing Group, Inc.
All Rights Reserved
Printed in the United States of America
March 1997
First Edition

1 3 5 7 9 10 8 6 4 2

To
Lai-King

כבר רצה האלהים את-מעשיך

"God has already favored what you have done"
(Eccl 9:7)

CONTENTS

◆

Contents

INDEXES

PREFACE

◆

There is perhaps no book in the Bible that is the subject of more controversies than Ecclesiastes. From the start, its place in the canon was called into question largely because it was perceived to be internally inconsistent and partly because it appears to be unorthodox. Down at least to the fifth century of the common era, there were voices of doubt regarding the canonicity of the book. Even in modern times there have been some who have wondered about its authority. Nevertheless, through the ages the book has fascinated interpreters and inspired writers, even musicians. Hundreds of commentaries, both ancient and modern, have been written on it. Indeed, the book has rightly been regarded as one of the most remarkable little books in world literature.

There has been little on which commentators agree, however. The book has been dated anywhere from the tenth century B.C.E. to the first century C.E. Interpreters have variously judged the author of the book to be utterly pessimistic or thoroughly optimistic; some say he is the quintessential skeptic, while others perceive him to be a paragon of piety. Some have detected commonalities between Ecclesiastes and Greek philosophy, others find affinities with Mesopotamian, Egyptian, or even Buddhist thought. A majority of scholars find absolutely no structure to the book, although in recent years some have discerned evidence of a careful, even intricate, structure. Perhaps there are some things about the book that will always remain elusive and incomprehensible — a veritable testimony to the message of Ecclesiastes that everything is *hebel* "vanity," literally "a breath."

Despite its elusive nature, however, there are profound and ever-timely insights in this enigmatic book. This commentary rests on the assumption that the traditional, if sometimes shaky, place of Ecclesiastes in the canon implies that it has meaning for the community of faith. Hence, we seek to clarify the message of the book as well as we can, even if our interpretations may soon be challenged and corrected by others. In this effort I readily acknowledge the contributions of all those who have gone before me — commentators both ancient and modern, Jewish and Christian. On the shoulders of all these scholars I stand. For practical reasons, however, I do not present alternative proposals on every point. There are commentaries that discuss more fully the history of interpretation and survey the alternatives. What I have endeavored to do, rather, is to consolidate and advance the discussions, if only with tentative steps.

In accordance with the format of the ANCHOR BIBLE, each unit begins with a translation of the text. Every translation, however, is necessarily interpretive.

No matter how literalistic one tries to be, it is inevitable that one interprets the intent of the author and conveys that interpretation through the words and punctuation. I have, therefore, tried to stay faithful to the intent of the text without being literalistic. Inasmuch as the author of the book appears to be concerned with the plight of humankind, I have generally translated Hebrew 'ādām inclusively as "a person," "humanity," "one," or even with the plural "human beings," or the like. Accordingly, I have also translated the pronouns associated with 'ādām inclusively, even when the Hebrew pronouns are masculine and singular. Thus in 1:2, I translate, "What advantage does one have in all the toil, at which one toils under the sun?" Some may argue that the Hebrew may be more precisely rendered: "What advantage is there for the human being in all *his* toil, at which *he* toils under the sun?" The pronouns in Hebrew are, after all, clearly masculine. Yet, there can be no doubt that the text intends 'ādām to refer generically to any human being, whether male or female. The point of the book as a whole is that all people, male and female, are under this burden of toil — not only men. The inclusive language translation in this case more accurately represents what the author intended. In other instances, however, where it seems clear that the author has in mind a specific man, my translation is gender-specific.

This commentary is written with two audiences in mind: the specialist and the general reader. The Notes include fairly detailed and technical discussions of text-critical and philological matters, some of which may be of interest only to scholars. The Comment sections contain exposition of the literary and theological issues that should be easily accessible to the general reader. Accordingly, I have reduced references to foreign words to a bare minimum, referring the reader to the Notes for fuller discussions. Those who use the commentary for reference, who are interested in specific words and phrases, may turn to the appropriate Notes. Most other users of the commentary may want to begin with the Comment and refer to the pertinent Notes only as the need arises. My hope is that this will be a helpful resource to all researchers, pastors, rabbis, students, and, indeed, anyone who is curious about the teachings of Ecclesiastes.

It is my pleasure to acknowledge my debt to the editor of the ANCHOR BIBLE, Professor David Noel Freedman, for his invitation to write this commentary and for the expert editorial work that only he can do. I cannot imagine anyone else who would be as thorough, insightful, and prompt in giving editorial critiques. Princeton Theological Seminary has been generous in providing me with a sabbatical leave to complete this book. I have also been privileged to have several fine research assistants over the years, including Gregory Glover, Gerald Bilkes, and David Janzen. These have all rendered invaluable help to me and I look forward to their own contributions to scholarship. I wish to thank Professors Richard J. Clifford, Richard E. Whitaker, Harold C. Washington, Douglas M. Miller, all of whom read portions or all of my manuscript and offered constructive criticisms.

No one in the last three years could have heard as many sermons or attended as many lectures on Ecclesiastes as my wife, Lai-King. Without her support and understanding, this book would not have seen the light of day. Her efficiency and resourcefulness have made it possible for me to concentrate on this project. It is to her, therefore, that this book is dedicated with gratitude.

C. L. Seow
Princeton Theological Seminary
Princeton, New Jersey
Sukkot 1995

LIST OF MAPS

◆

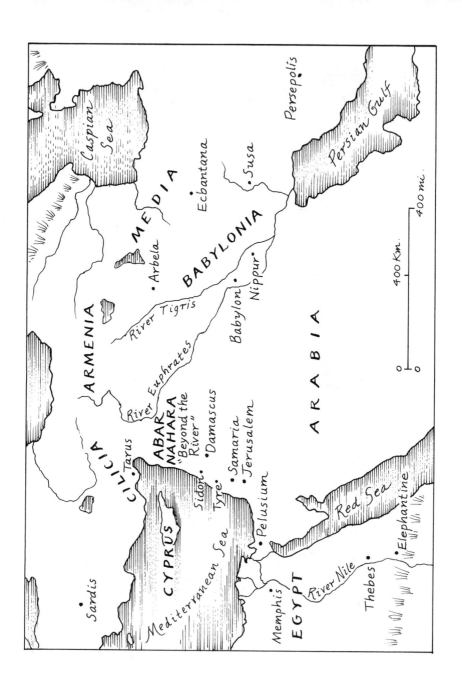

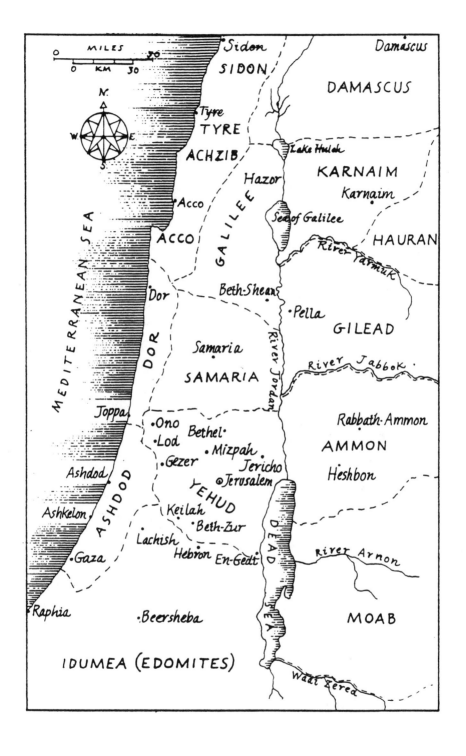

PRINCIPAL ABBREVIATIONS AND SIGNS

◆

1QH	*Hōdāyôt (Thanksgiving Hymns)* from Qumran Cave 1
1QS	*Serek hayyaḥad (Rule of the Community)* from Qumran Cave 1
1QSa	Appendix A to 1QS
1QSb	Appendix B to 1QS
4QMMT	*Miqṣat Maʿaseh Torah* from Qumran Cave 4
4QQohᵃ	Qohelet fragments from Qumran Cave 4
4QQohᵇ	Qohelet fragments from Qumran Cave 4
11QTemple	*Temple Scroll* from Qumran Cave 11
ÄAT	Ägypten und Altes Testament
AB	Anchor Bible
ABD	D. N. Freedman, ed. *Anchor Bible Dictionary.* 6 Volumes. New York: Doubleday, 1992.
ABL	R. F. Harper, ed. *Assyrian and Babylonian Letters.* 14 Volumes. London and Chicago: University of Chicago, 1892–1914.
ABRL	Anchor Bible Reference Library
Adv. Indoctum	Lucian, *Adversus Indoctum*
AEL	A. Lichtheim, ed. *Ancient Egyptian Literature.* 3 Volumes. Berkeley: University of California, 1971–80.
AfO	*Archiv für Orientforschung*
AHW	W. von Soden, ed. *Akkadisches Handwörterbuch.* 3 Volumes. Wiesbaden: Harrassowitz, 1965–81.
AJBA	*Australian Journal of Biblical Archaeology*
AJSL	*American Journal of Semitic Languages and Literatures*
ALASP	Abhandlungen zur Literatur Alt-Syrien-Palästinas und Mesopotamiens
Anab.	Xenophon, *Anabasis*
AnBib	Analecta Biblica
ANET³	J. B. Pritchard, ed. *Ancient Near Eastern Texts Relating to the Old Testament.* 3d ed. with supplement. Princeton, N.J.: Princeton University, 1969.
ANETS	Ancient Near Eastern Texts and Studies
AnOr	Analecta Orientalia
AOAT	Alter Orient und Altes Testament

APOT	R. H. Charles, ed. *Apocrypha and Pseudepigrapha of the Old Testament*. 2 Volumes. Oxford: Clarendon, 1913.
Aq	Aquila
ARAB	D. D. Luckenbill, ed. *Ancient Records of Assyria and Babylonia*. 2 Volumes. Chicago: University of Chicago, 1926–27. Reprinted 1989.
ARMT	Archives royals de Mari: transcriptions et traductions
AS	Assyriological Studies
ASOR	American Schools of Oriental Research
ASTI	*Annual of the Swedish Theological Institute*
ASV	American Standard Version
ATD	Das Alte Testament Deutsch
AUSS	*Andrews University Seminary Studies*
BA	*Biblical Archaeologist*
BASOR	*Bulletin of the American Schools of Oriental Research*
BAW	Die Bibliothek der alten Welt
BBB	Bonner biblische Beiträge
BBET	Beiträge zur biblischen Exegese und Theologie
BDB	F. Brown, S. R. Driver, and C. A. Briggs, eds. A *Hebrew and English Lexicon of the Old Testament*. Oxford: Clarendon, 1907.
BeO	*Bibbia e oriente*
Beth Mikra	Beth Mikra
BETL	Bibliotheca ephemeridum theologicarum lovanensium
BHK	R. Kittel, ed. *Biblia Hebraica*. 3d ed. Stuttgart: Württembergische Bibelanstalt, 1937.
BHS	*Biblia Hebraica Stuttgartensia*
Bib	*Biblica*
BibOr	Biblica et orientalia
Bij	*Bijdragen: Tijdschrift voor Filosofie en Theologie*
BK	*Bibel und Kirche*
BKAT	Biblischer Kommentar: Altes Testament
BL	H. Bauer and P. Leander. *Historische Grammatik der hebräischen Sprache*. Halle: Niemeyer, 1922. Reprinted 1991.
BLS	Bible and Literature Series
BN	*Biblische Notizen*
BO	*Bibliotheca Orientalis*
BOT	De Boeken van het Oude Testament
Brockelmann	C. Brockelmann. *Hebräischen Syntax*. Neukirchen: Neukirchener, 1956.
BT	*Bible Translator*
BTB	*Biblical Theology Bulletin*
BWANT	Beiträge zur Wissenschaft vom Alten und Neuen Testament

BWL	W. G. Lambert, ed. *Babylonian Wisdom Literature.* Oxford: Clarendon, 1960.
BZ	*Biblische Zeitschrift*
BZAW	Beihefte zur ZAW
CAD	*Chicago Assyrian Dictionary*
CahRB	Cahiers de la Revue biblique
CBC	Cambridge Bible Commentary
CBQ	*Catholic Biblical Quarterly*
CBQMS	Catholic Biblical Quarterly Monograph Series
CBS	tablets in the collections of the University Museum of the University of Pennsylvania ("Catalogue of the Babylonian Section")
CBSC	Cambridge Bible for Schools and Colleges
CChr	Corpus Christianorum
CD	Cairo (Genizah text of the) Damascus Document
CIJ	J. B. Frey, ed. *Corpus inscriptionum iudaicarum.* Citta del Vaticano: Pontifico istituto di archeologia cristiania, 1936–52.
CIS	*Corpus inscriptionum semiticarum*
CJT	*Canadian Journal of Theology*
ConBOT	Coniectania biblica, Old Testament
Copt	Coptic version
CT	*Cuneiform Texts from Babylonian Tablets in the British Museum*
CTM	*Concordia Theological Monthly*
CurTM	*Currents in Theology and Mission*
Cyr	J. N. Strassmaier, ed. *Inschriften von Cyrus.* Leipzig: Pfeiffer, 1890.
Cyrop.	Xenophon, *Cyropaedia*
DJD	Discoveries in the Judean Desert
DNWSI	J. Hoftijzer and K. Jongeling, eds. *Dictionary of the Northwest Semitic Inscriptions.* 2 Volumes. New York/Leiden: Brill, 1995.
DSB	Daily Study Bible
EA	Tell el-Amarna tablets
EBib	Études bibliques
ECarm	*Ephemerides Carmeliticae*
EI	*Eretz Israel*
ETL	*Ephemerides Theologicae Lovanienses*
ÉTR	*Études theologiques et Religieuses*
EuntDoc	*Euntes Docete*
EvQ	*Evangelical Quarterly*
EvT	*Evangelische Theologie*
ExpTim	*Expository Times*
Fs.	Festschrift

Gilg	Gilgamesh Epic
	M = Meissner Fragment
	P = Pennsylvania Tablet
	Y = Yale Tablet
GKC	E. Kautzsch, trans. A. E. Cowley. *Gesenius Hebrew Grammar*. 2d ed. Oxford: Clarendon, 1910.
HALAT	W. Baumgartner et al., eds. *Hebräisches und aramäisches Lexikon zum alten Testament*. Leiden: Brill, 1967–90.
HAR	*Hebrew Annual Review*
HAT	Handbuch zum Alten Testament
Hist. Eccl.	Eusebius, *Historia Ecclesia*
HKAT	Handkommentar zum Alten Testament
HS	*Hebrew Studies*
HSAT	Die heilige Schrift des Alten Testaments
HSM	Harvard Semitic Monographs
HSS	Harvard Semitic Studies
HTR	*Harvard Theological Review*
HUCA	*Hebrew Union College Annual*
IBS	*Irish Biblical Studies*
ICC	International Critical Commentary
IDB	G. A. Buttrick, ed. *Interpreter's Dictionary of the Bible*. 4 Volumes. Nashville, Tenn.: Abingdon, 1962.
IEJ	*Israel Exploration Journal*
Int	*Interpretation*
ITC	International Theological Commentary
ITQ	*Irish Theological Quarterly*
ITS	*Indian Theological Studies*
JAAR	*Journal of the American Academy of Religion*
JAOS	*Journal of the American Oriental Society*
Jastrow, *Dictionary*	M. Jastrow, ed. A *Dictionary of the Targumim, the Talmud Babli and Yerushalmi, etc.* Brooklyn, N.Y.: Traditional Press, 1903.
JB	Jerusalem Bible
JBL	*Journal of Biblical Literature*
JBR	*Journal of Bible and Religion*
JCS	*Journal of Cuneiform Studies*
JEA	*Journal of Egyptian Archaeology*
JETS	*Journal of the Evangelical Theological Society*
JJS	*Journal of Jewish Studies*
JNES	*Journal of Near Eastern Studies*
JNSL	*Journal of Northwest Semitic Languages*
Joüon-Muraoka	P. Joüon, trans. and rev. T. Muraoka. A *Grammar of Biblical Hebrew*. Rome: Pontificio Istituto Biblico, 1991 [1922].
JQR	*Jewish Quarterly Review*

JSOT	*Journal for the Study of the Old Testament*
JSOTSup	Journal for the Study of the Old Testament Supplement Series
JSS	*Journal of Semitic Studies*
JTS	*Journal of Theological Studies*
KAI	H. Donner and W. Röllig, eds. *Kanaanäische und aramäische Inschriften.* 3 Volumes. Wiesbaden: Harrassowitz, 1962–64.
KAT	Kommentar zum Alten Testament
KBL	L. Koehler and W. Baumgartner, eds. *Lexicon in Veteris Testamenti Libros.* Leiden: Brill, 1958.
KHC	Kurzer Handkommentar zum Alten Testament
KJV	King James Version
KPG	Knox Preaching Guides
KTU	M. Dietrich, O. Loretz, and J. Sanmartín, eds. *The Cuneiform Alphabetic Texts from Ugarit, Ras Ibn Hani and Other Places (KTU: second, enlarged edition).* ALASP 8. Münster: Ugarit-Verlag, 1995.
KUB	Keilschrifturkunden aus Boghazköi
Lane	E. W. Lane, ed. *An Arabic-English Lexicon.* 8 Parts. London: Williams & Norgate, 1863–93. Reprinted 1980.
LCL	Loeb Classical Library
LD	Lectio divina
Leš	*Lešonenu*
Life	Josephus, *The Life of Josephus*
LXX	Septuagint
LXX^A	Codex Alexandrinus
LXX^B	Codex Vaticanus
LXX^C	Codex Ephraemi
LXX^P	Hamburg Papyrus (Greek) Codex
LSS^S	Codex Sinaiticus
LXX^V	Codex Venetus
MPL	*Patrologia latina*, ed. J. P. Migne
MT	Masoretic Text
MVAG	Mitteilungen der vorder-asiatisch-ägyptischen Gesellschaft
NAB	New American Bible
NASB	New American Standard Bible
NCBC	New Century Bible Commentary
NEAEHL	E. Stern, ed. *New Encyclopedia of Archaeological Excavations in the Holy Land.* 4 Volumes. Jerusalem: Israel Exploration Society, 1993.
NEB	New English Bible
NIV	New International Version
NJPS	New Jewish Publication Society Version

NRSV	New Revised Standard Version
OBO	Orbis biblicus et orientalis
OIP	Oriental Institute Publications
OL	Old Latin
OLA	Orientalia Lovaniensia Analecta
OLP	*Orientalia lovaniensia periodica*
OLZ	*Orientalische Literaturzeitung*
Or	*Orientalia* (Nova Series)
OTL	Old Testament Library
OTM	Old Testament Message
OTS	*Oudtestamentische Studiën*
OTWSA	*De Ou Testamentiese Werkgemeenskap in Suid-Afrika*
PAAJR	*Proceedings of the American Academy for Jewish Research*
Pap.	papyrus
PBS	*Publications of the Babylonian Section*
PEQ	*Palestine Exploration Quarterly*
PN(N)	personal name(s)
PRU	C. F. A. Schaeffer and J. Nougayrol, eds. *Le Palais Royal d'Ugarit.* 3 Volumes. Paris: Imprimerie Nationale, 1955–57.
PS	Proto-Semitic
PSB	*Princeton Seminary Bulletin*
RA	*Revue d'Assyriologie et d'Archéologie orientale*
RB	*Revue biblique*
RES	*Repertoire d'épigraphie sémitiques* [cited by number]
RevistB	*Revista Biblica*
RHPR	*Revue d'histoire et de philosophie religieuses*
RIH	*Ras Ibn Hani*
RN	royal name
RSP	L. R. Fisher and Stan Rummel, eds. *Ras Shamra Parallels.* 3 Volumes. AnOr 49–51. Rome: Pontifical Biblical Institute, 1972–81.
RSR	*Recherches de science religieuse*
RSV	Revised Standard Version
SB	La Sacra Bibbia
SBLASP	Society of Biblical Literature Abstracts and Seminar Papers
SBLDS	Society of Biblical Literature Dissertation Series
SBLSCS	Society of Biblical Literature: Septuagint and Cognate Studies
SBT	Studies in Biblical Theology
Sef	*Sefarad*
SFEG	Suomen Eksegeettisen Seuran julkaisuja
SJT	*Scottish Journal of Theology*

Sokoloff, *Dictionary*	M. Sokoloff, ed. A *Dictionary of Jewish Palestinian Aramaic*. Ramat-Gan, Israel: Bar Ilan University, 1990.
SP	Samaria Papyrus
STU	*Schweizerische theologische Umschau*
SubBib	Subsidia Biblica
Symm	Symmachus
Syr	Syriac (Peshitta)
SyrH	Syro-Hexaplar
TAD	*Textbook of Aramaic Documents from Ancient Egypt*. 3 Volumes. B. Porten and A. Yardeni, eds. Jerusalem: Israel Academy of Sciences and Humanities, 1986–93.
TAPA	*Transactions of the American Philological Association*
TAPS	*Transactions of the American Philosophical Society*
Targ	Targum
TBT	*The Bible Today*
TCL	*Textes cunéiforms du Musée du Louvre*
TD	*Theology Digest*
TDOT	*Theological Dictionary of the Old Testament*
Theod	Theodotion
TGl	*Theologie und Glaube*
ThQ	*Theologische Quartalschrift*
ThStK	*Theologische Studien und Kritiken*
TLZ	*Theologische Literaturzeitung*
TOB	Traduction Oecuménique de la Bible
TOTC	Tyndale Old Testament Commentaries
TRev	*Theologische Revue*
TSFB	*Theological Student Fellowship Bulletin*
TTZ	*Trierer theologische Zeitschrift*
TWAT	*Theologisches Wörterbuch zum Alten Testament*
TZ	*Theologische Zeitschrift*
UET	Ur Excavations Texts
UF	*Ugarit-Forschungen*
UM	tablets in the collections of the University Museum of the University of Pennsylvania, Philadelphia
UT	Cyrus Gordon, *Ugaritic Textbook*
VAB	Vorderasiatische Bibliothek
VAS	Vorderasiatische Schriftdenkmäler
VS	Verbum salutis
VT	*Vetus Testamentum*
VTSup	Vetus Testamentum Supplements
Vulg	Vulgate
War	Josephus, *The Wars of the Jews*
WbÄS	A. Erman and E. Grapow, eds. *Wörterbuch der ägyptischen Sprache*. 7 Volumes. Leipzig: Akademie Verlag, 1926–31. Reprinted 1982.

WBC	Word Bible Commentary
WO	*Die Welt des Orients*
WTJ	*Westminster Theological Journal*
WUNT	Wissenschaftliche Untersuchungen zum Neuen Testament
YOS	Yale Oriental Series
ZAH	*Zeitschrift für Althebräistik*
ZAW	*Zeitschrift für die alttestamentliche Wissenschaft*
ZDMG	*Zeitschrift der deutschen morgenländischen Gesellschaft*
ZDPV	*Zeitschrift des deutschen Palästina-Vereins*
ZTK	*Zeitschrift für Theologie und Kirche*
*	hypothetical form
< >	text emended
{ }	text does not belong or text transposed

INTRODUCTION

◆

I. Title of the Book

The Hebrew title of the book is *Qōhelet*, the supposed name or title of its author (1:1, 2, 12; 7:27; 12:8, 9, 10). This name has been transliterated in various Greek sources as *kōeleth* or *kōelth* and in Latin as *Coeleth* (see Notes at 1:1). "Ecclesiastes" is the Latinized form of the Greek translation of the Hebrew word, which the Greek translators interpreted to mean *ekklēsiastēs*, a member of the citizen's assembly. Although it has been argued that Qohelet is only the persona of the real author (see Comment at 1:2), it is convenient to refer to the author by the Hebrew name, Qohelet. The book itself, however, will be referred to by the name Ecclesiastes.

II. Canonicity and Order

It is commonly believed that the so-called "Council of Jamnia" convened around 90 C.E. in order to establish the Hebrew canon once and for all. Indeed, it was in conjunction with the issue of the canonicity of Ecclesiastes that Heinrich Graetz first referred to the "Council of Jamnia" as the event that led to the closing of the Hebrew canon (*Kohelet*, pp. 165–66). The term "council" often leads one to imagine that there was a major convocation summoned to take a binding vote on the limits of the canon. In truth, however, the meeting in question was nothing like the ecumenical councils of later Christianity. It was, rather, a particular session of the rabbinic academy at Jamnia, where a debate took place. Moreover, the issue at the session in question was not the canon in general, but whether certain books — particularly Ecclesiastes — "defile the hands," a technical expression of obscure origin meaning that the document was regarded as inspired scripture. The conclusion of the session was not a ruling but a determination of the consensus of that time.

It appears that the rival schools of Shammai and Hillel were divided over the question of Ecclesiastes. The more conservative House of Shammai rejected it as an inspired book, but the House of Hillel approved it (*m. Yad* 3:5, *'Ed.* 5:3; *b. Meg.* 7a). The position of the Hillelites was confirmed during the session, but the decision was apparently nonbinding. The dispute persisted for some time. According to Jerome as late as the fourth century C.E., some Jewish scholars maintained that the book ought to be suppressed because of its radical thoughts ("Commentarius in Ecclesiasten," *MPL* 23, p. 1172).

There were two primary arguments against the book. The first was that it was not internally coherent (*b. Šabb.* 30b; see also *Lev. Rabb.* 28.1). The second was that some of the views expressed were too heretical (so Jerome reports in his commentary; see also *Qoh. Rabb.* 1:3; 11:9; *Num. Rabb.* 161b). But the book won support, in part because of the authority of the Solomonic name, although that could not have been the primary reason, since the Wisdom of Solomon and the Odes of Solomon were excluded from the canon despite their claims to Solomonic authorship. The most important reason for the acceptance of the book was that the early interpreters found it possible somehow to interpret the document as orthodox (see Dell, "Ecclesiastes as Wisdom," pp. 301–29). No doubt the addition of the orthodox-sounding statement at the end of the book helped its case (*b. Šabb.* 30b).

At all events, by the end of the first century C.E., Ecclesiastes was included in the Hebrew canon — at least according to the majority in the Jamnia academy. Josephus, the Jewish historian writing in the last decade of the first century C.E., refers to twenty-two books that were accepted, including the five "books of Moses," thirteen books of the prophets, and four books that contained "hymns to God and precepts for the conduct of human life" (*Contra Apionem* 1.38–41). The book of "hymns to God" no doubt refers to the Psalter, while the books of precepts for life probably are Proverbs, Ecclesiastes, and Song of Songs. Ecclesiastes clearly appears on other twenty-two-book lists, including the so-called "Byrennios List" (second century), the lists of Epiphanius (possibly dating back to the second century), Origen (third century), and Jerome (fourth century). It is also included in the list of Melito of Sardis from the second century (see Eusebius, *Hist. Eccl.* 4.26.13–14), as well as other Christian canonical lists. Already by late third century, we have a paraphrase of Ecclesiastes by Gregory Thaumaturgos, indicating something of the status of the book among Christians. It appears that Theodore of Mopsuestia (fifth century) rejected the divine inspiration of Ecclesiastes. Theodore's predisposition must have influenced his disciple Nestorius, for Ecclesiastes does not appear in the Nestorian canon.

Ecclesiastes was clearly a book on the margins of the canon, but in the end its authority was acknowledged by the majority of Jews and Christians.

ORDER

Josephus seems to have known a tripartite canon in which the "four books" — presumably Psalms, Proverbs, Job, Ecclesiastes — belonged to the third division of the Hebrew Bible, namely, *Ketubim* "Writings" (*Contra Apionem* 1:38–41). This is the order followed by the Babylonian Talmud, where Ecclesiastes also appears in the third division (*b. B. Bat.* 14b).

In most Christian canonical lists, the books are arranged first according to their literary content and supposed authorship. They then are ordered according to a broad chronological principle. In the Eastern church, the poetical books typically appear after the historical writings but before the prophets because of the historical priority of David and Solomon over the prophets. This is the order reflected in Codex Vaticanus. The Christians may also have preferred to place the prophets immediately before the gospels for theological reasons. A number of lists coming from the Western church, however, place the poetical books after the prophets. This is the order found in Codex Sinaiticus and Codex Alexandrinus.

In most modern printed editions of the Hebrew Bible, Ecclesiastes is found in the subdivision known as *Megillot* "scrolls," a reference to five scrolls, including also the Song of Songs, Ruth, Lamentations, and Esther. As evident in the listings of Josephus and the Talmud, however, this is a relatively late grouping. In most cases Ecclesiastes appears as the fourth book—after Song of Songs, Ruth, and Lamentations, but before Esther. This order was determined by the order of the festivals during which the various books were read in the Ashkenazic synagogues. Thus, the Song of Songs was read during the Passover, Ruth was read during Pentecost (that is, the Feast of Weeks, Shavuot), Lamentations was read on the Ninth of Ab (when the destruction of the temple was commemorated), Ecclesiastes was read during Sukkot, and Esther was read at Purim. Ecclesiastes may have been associated with Sukkot because of the calls for enjoyment in the book. The feast of Sukkot is known in liturgy as *zĕmān śimḥātēnû* "the season of our rejoicing."

III. Texts and Versions
Masoretic Texts

In this commentary the abbreviation "MT" refers to the Tiberian Masoretic Text as preserved in the Leningrad Codex, Ms B 19ᴬ, completed in 1008 C.E. This codex is the basis of *BHK³* and *BHS*, in which editions F. Horst was responsible for Ecclesiastes. The formidable S. R. Driver edited Ecclesiastes in *BHK¹* (1905) and *BHK²* (1913), which were based on the second Rabbinic Bible produced by Jacob ben Chayyim ("the Bomberg Edition"). Driver's notes in these editions are still enormously helpful and will be cited from time to time in this commentary. Hebrew variants are listed by Kennicott (*Vetus Testamentum Hebraicum cum variis lectionibus* II, pp. 549–61) and de Rossi (*Variae lectionibus Veteris Testamenti librorum* III, pp. 247–64), as well as in Baer's *Quinqua Volumina* (pp. 20–31, 60–70). The Hebrew University Bible Project currently underway in Israel is based on the highly regarded Aleppo Codex from the tenth century, but Ecclesiastes belongs to a portion of that codex that has been lost.

In general, the Hebrew text is in good order, there being relatively few textual corruptions. In a few places, however, the scribes seem to have misdivided the words. Thus, *m'śrh šlyṭym* "(more than) ten proprietors" is read instead of *m'šr hšlyṭym* "(more than) the wealth of the proprietors" (7:19), *'mrh qhlt* (Qohelet being mistaken to be a feminine noun) instead of *'mr hqhlt* "(the) Qohelet said" (7:27), *khhkm* "like the wise" instead of *kh hkm* "so wise" (8:1), and *zbwby mwt* "flies of Death" instead of *zbwb ymwt* "a fly that dies" (10:1). There are also a number of *Ketib-Qere* readings in MT. These have been studied by A. Schoors ("Ketibh-Qere in Ecclesiastes," pp. 215–22), who has concluded that the *Qere* is superior in most cases. Except in 9:4 and 12:6, however, the *Ketib-Qere* variants do not affect the meaning of the text.

QUMRAN FRAGMENTS

There are Hebrew fragments of two Ecclesiastes manuscripts found in Cave IV at Qumran. The first and larger one, known as 4QQoh[a], was published by James Muilenburg ("Qoheleth Scroll," pp. 20–28). Dated on paleographic grounds to 175–150 B.C.E., this manuscript preserves portions of Eccl 5:13–17 (Eng vv 14–18); 6:1?, 3–8, 12; 7:1–10, 19–20. Apart from the standard orthographic variants that one might expect of Qumran manuscripts (*plene* spellings; e.g., *ky'* for *ky*), one notes the reading *nwht* instead of *nht* in MT (6:5) and *g'rwt* instead of *g'rt* (7:5). Significant variants include *wy'wh* instead of *y'bd* (7:7), *t'zr* instead of *t'z* (7:19), *hnpl mmnw* instead of *mmnw hnpl* (6:3), and *[byt š]mhh* instead of *byt mšth* (7:2). In the first of these, the reading of 4QQoh[a] (*wy'wh*) is unique, but MT (*wy'bd*) is supported by the Septuagint (LXX) and the Old Latin (OL). In the second instance, the reading of 4QQoh[a] (*t'zr*) is probably supported by LXX. In 6:12, 4QQoh[a] seems to reflect a shorter reading than MT, although it is uncertain what the reading is. Interestingly, there is an erasure of several words just before 7:7, precisely where scholars have posited a missing line of several words (see Notes at 7:7).

The smaller manuscript, known as 4QQoh[b], has been published by E. Ulrich ("Ezra and Qoheleth Manuscripts," pp. 139–57). This manuscript is dated by Ulrich to "around the middle of the first century BCE, though possibly as late as the early first century CE" (p. 148). The fragments preserve portions of 1:10–14, but the variants are of little text-critical value.

LXX

Of the various ancient translations, the most important is the Greek (LXX). The Greek text is preserved in six uncial MSS. They are, in order of reliability: (1) Codex Vaticanus (LXX[B]) from the fourth century, (2) Codex Sinaiticus (LXX[S]) also from the fourth century, (3) Codex Alexandrinus (LXX[A]) from the fifth century, (4) Hamburg Papyrus Codex (LXX[P]), a bilingual MS including a Greek and a Coptic text of Ecclesiastes, dating to the end of the third century, (5) Codex Ephraemi (LXX[C]), a fifth-century palimpsest, and (6) Codex Venetus (LXX[V]), usually dated to the eighth or ninth century. LXX[B] is, by all accounts, the most reliable of the MSS. LXX[P] was discovered in 1929 but was only published sixty years later by B. J. Diebner and R. Kasser (*Hamburger Papyrus*). This fragmentary MS most often agrees with LXX[B] but is somewhat less literalistic. It confirms a number of known variants but does not offer significant new readings. In addition to the uncials, there are fifteen cursive MSS, the most important of which is MS 68 from the fifteenth century C.E.

The translation technique of LXX Ecclesiastes is unique among the books in the Bible, so that one may say with a reasonable amount of certainty that the translator is not the same as for any other books. The translation shows a number of features that are typical of the works of Aquila of Pontus, a second-century (C.E.) gentile convert to Judaism. Aquila, a pupil of the famous Rabbi Aqiba, is best known for his translation of the Hebrew Bible into literalistic Greek, among other reasons, to provide Jews who spoke Greek but did not read Hebrew or Aramaic with a translation that would reflect the Hebrew as much as possible. Thus, the Hebrew word order is rigidly adhered to and all details in Hebrew are represented, even when they seem awkward or even nonsensical in Greek. Most notably, where the Hebrew has the *nota accusativi* ('t) + a direct definite object marked by the definite article, Aquila translated the Hebrew with the Greek preposition *syn* + accusative, contrary to Greek usage, where *syn* typically takes the dative. This technique is evident also in LXX Ecclesiastes (e.g., 1:14). Other features identified as typical of Aquila's style include: Hebrew *gm* and *wgm* translated by Greek *kai ge* — to distinguish the Hebrew from the simple conjunction *w* "and" (e.g., in 2:14); Hebrew *l* + infinitive rendered by Greek *tou* + infinitive (e.g., 1:8); Hebrew *l* + noun translated by the article + noun, the article merely indicating the presence of the preposition in the Hebrew (e.g., 4:11; 9:4). The presence of these and other "Aquilan" features has led some scholars to posit that in LXX we have a preliminary draft or first edition of Aquila's translation and that the material in the third column of Origen's *Hexapla*, the place normally reserved for Aquila's revision, was in fact Aquila's "second edition."

It was Heinrich Graetz who first argued that LXX Ecclesiastes was actually the work of Aquila (*Kohelet*, pp. 173–79), although others before him had noticed the similarities between LXX and Aquilan style. A. H. McNeile, too, maintained that LXX was the work of Aquila (*Introduction to Ecclesiastes*, pp. 115–68). McNeile argued that it was Aquila himself who revised the first edition of his work, because that first edition was made from a text of which his teacher Aqiba did not approve. So McNeile called LXX "the Pre-Aqiban version" of Aquila.

D. Barthélemy has furthered this discussion by a careful study of both LXX and the third column of Origen's *Hexapla* (*Les devanciers d'Aquila*). He maintained, however, that LXX Ecclesiastes is not simply a draft or a first edition; it *is* the original and final work of Aquila. Accordingly, the third column of Origen's *Hexapla* belongs to another author, not Aquila. Thus, Barthélemy notes that the materials in the third column of the *Hexapla* are more like Symmachus than Aquila. In this view, Aquila's version has supplanted the Old Greek (Alexandrian) version, that is now lost, much in the same way that Theodotion supplanted the Old Greek version for the book of Daniel and became the only Greek version of Daniel that was known until the twentieth century. This view (that LXX Ecclesiastes is the work of Aquila) has been widely accepted by scholars. It is stated as a matter of fact in a number of commentaries, as well as in various handbooks on textual criticism of the Hebrew Bible.

Barthélemy's hypothesis, however, has been seriously undermined by the work of K. Hyvärinen (*Die Übersetzung von Aquila*, pp. 88–99) and by J. Jarick ("Aquila's Koheleth," pp. 131–39). It is observed, on the one hand, that the third column of Origen's *Hexapla* (which Barthélemy says is not Aquilan) is, in fact, Aquilan; there is nothing in its style or vocabulary that proves that it is not from Aquila. On the other hand, LXX Ecclesiastes (which Barthélemy and others say is Aquila's work) betrays numerous characteristics that are *not* Aquilan. For instance, the name of the author is translated in LXX as *ekklēsiastēs*, whereas the third column of the *Hexapla* transliterates the name as *kōleth*, as Aquila surely would have done. LXX, too, interprets *hebel* as *mataiotēs* "vanity," whereas the third column of Origen translates the term literally as *atmos* "breath." There are also places where LXX is a little more free in its translation than is the case in the third column of the *Hexapla*: e.g., *hml'k* "the angel/messenger" is interpreted in LXX as *tou theou* "God," but it is rendered literally by *tou aggelou* "the angel/messenger" in the third column (5:5); the impersonal pronoun in *hwldw* "his being born" = "one's being born" (7:1) is mechanically reproduced in the translation of the third column of the *Hexapla*, whereas it is omitted in the free rendering of LXX; *'m* "people" is rendered by *anthrōpon* in LXX, but in the third column of the *Hexapla* we have *laon* (12:9).

It seems, then, that LXX is not Aquila's work after all but a version that, like Aquila, is motivated by the desire to facilitate certain kinds of exegesis promoted by the rabbis (see Salters, *The Book of Ecclesiastes*, pp. 12–30). Indeed, there is some indication in LXX of significant interpretive moves (e.g., 2:15; 11:9). Thus, the style of LXX Ecclesiastes may be better explained as "Proto-Aquilan" or "Aquilanic" (i.e., comparable to Aquila), but it is not strictly Aquilan — not by Aquila himself. The third column of the *Hexapla* was probably correctly designated by Origen as the work of Aquila, an even more literalistic version than the Aquilanic translation of LXX Ecclesiastes. In short, LXX Ecclesiastes is merely Aquilanic; the third column of the *Hexapla* is Aquilan.

As for the Old Greek (that is, the Alexandrian Greek translation that we find in most of the Bible), there is no evidence that there ever was such a translation, although that possibility cannot be ruled out. From all the available evidence, it seems that the Aquilanic translation is all that was known in antiquity as LXX Ecclesiastes. This is the version of the Greek text of Ecclesiastes quoted by the so-called "church fathers." This is the version translated into Coptic in the third century, as evident in the Hamburg Papyrus Codex from the third century. It is also on the basis of this version of the Greek text that Gregory Thaumaturgos made his paraphrase in the same century.

There is, unfortunately, still no standard critical edition of the Greek texts for Ecclesiastes. The major project of the so-called "Cambridge Septuagint" edited by A. E. Brooke, N. McLean, and H.St.J. Thackeray ceased publication in 1940, before Ecclesiastes was completed. The Göttingen edition of Ecclesiastes has yet to appear. In their stead, one must rely on their respective manual editions. The *editio princeps* of the Hamburg Papyrus Codex (LXX^P) also includes a valuable critical apparatus. Besides these, one must rely on the outdated but still important edition of J. Parsons (*Vetus Testamentum Graecum*) and the indispensable work of F. Fields (*Origenis Hexaplarum*, pp. 302–405).

TRANSLATIONS OF THE GREEK

There are several "daughter translations" of the Greek — that is, translations of the Greek text in Latin, Syriac, and Coptic. With the possible exception of the Latin, these translations witness only to the Greek parent; they do not reflect a Hebrew original. The first of these is the Vetus Latina or Old Latin (OL), a collective designation for various early Latin translations of the Greek text that are preserved only in fragmentary manuscripts, Patristic quotations, liturgical books, letters, and so forth. These are collected in P. Sabatier's *Bibliorum sacrorum latinae versiones antiquae* (Rheims: Reginald Florentain, 1743). The multivolume critical edition of the Vetus Latina edited by B. Fisher duly records all the readings of OL, but the volume on Ecclesiastes has yet to appear. The Syro-Hexaplar text (SyrH) is a translation of Origen's *Hexapla* that Paul of Tella made in the seventh century. This translation is preserved in the eighth-century Codex Ambrosianus Syrohexaplaris (see Ceriani, *Translatio Syra Pescitto*). The Coptic version (Copt) is a translation of the Greek traceable to the third century. A full list of the various Coptic MSS is provided in Diebner and Kasser's edition of the bilingual Hamburg Papyrus Codex (*Hamburger Papyrus Bil. 1*, pp. 145–46). There the Hamburg Papyrus version of Coptic Ecclesiastes has been edited carefully with a critical apparatus. The editors also reproduced an eclectic Coptic text based on currently available MSS, including several hitherto unpublished ones.

HEXAPLARIC RECENSIONS

Origen's *Hexapla* included the revisions of Aquila (Aq), Symmachus (Symm), and Theodotion (Theod) in columns 3, 4, and 6, respectively. These Greek translations of the Hebrew text were intended to reflect the Hebrew more accurately than the other Greek translations of that time. Of these, Aquila is the most literalistic. Symmachus attempts to render the Hebrew accurately but also in good Greek idiom. The work attributed to Theodotion is, like LXX Ecclesiastes, a "*kaige* recension" — it is a revision of the Greek using *kai ge* for Hebrew *wgm*. Some scholars have argued that the material attributed to "Aquila" in the third column of the *Hexapla* is really the work of Symmachus (so Barthélemy) or that Symmachus (the fourth column of Origen's *Hexapla*) really belongs to some other version (see Beckwith, *Old Testament Canon*, pp. 472–77). These arguments have not been convincing. Pending further research, I assume the correctness of Origen's attributions in his *Hexapla*. The readings of Aquila, Symmachus, and Theodotion are collected in the works of B. de Montfaucon (*Hexaplorum Origenis quae supersunt* II, pp. 55–75) and F. Field (*Origenis Hexaplorum*).

SYRIAC

The Syriac version (Syr) is commonly known as the Peshitta ("the simple"), a term used to distinguish it from the Syro-Hexaplar. The oldest dated MS is from

9

the fifth century, but the original version may have been earlier, perhaps as early as the third century c.e. The Syriac version of Ecclesiastes is probably a translation of the Hebrew, although it appears to be dependent on the Greek at many points (see Kamenetsky, "Die P'sita zu Koheleth," pp. 181–239; Schoors, "The Peshitta of Koheleth," pp. 345–57). The standard critical edition by D. J. Lane (*The Old Testament in Syriac* II/5) is based on Codex Ambrosianus from the sixth or seventh century, with the text emended where it seems to be in error.

ARAMAIC

The Targum (Targ) of Ecclesiastes has been characterized as "translation and midrash completely fused together" (Sperber). It is, as one might expect of the Targum, both paraphrastic and interpretive. Yet it is not quite as free as the midrash. At times it offers a straight translation of the Hebrew, with little or no commentary. It is, therefore, still a valuable witness to the original text of Ecclesiastes, although one must be extremely cautious in differentiating the translation from the paraphrase. There are a number of MSS and editions of the Targum. All these are conveniently collocated in the dissertation of P. S. Knobel. The earliest citation of the Targum of Ecclesiastes is in the 'Aruk, the dictionary of Nathan ben Yehiel completed in 1101 c.e. The version no doubt was produced much earlier, probably after the completion of the Babylonian and Palestinian Talmuds, but before the Arab conquest of Palestine — somewhere in the sixth or seventh century. The important critical editions are by de Lagarde, Levy, Sperber, Levine, and Dîez Merino. Unless otherwise indicated, citations of the Targum in this commentary are taken from the Sperber edition.

VULGATE

As Jerome got further and further into the translation of the Latin Bible, first on the basis of the Greek text, he became more and more convinced that he had to return to the original Hebrew in order to recover what he called the *hebraica veritas* "the true Hebrew" — the more reliable Hebrew original. So he set out to work on a new translation that became the Vulgate, the vernacular translation for the Latin-speaking world. By his own account, the books of Proverbs, Job, and Ecclesiastes were completed in three days. The date was probably around 398 c.e. The translation was made from the Hebrew, but Jerome made full use of Origen's *Hexapla* and other Greek translations. The readings of Ecclesiastes in the Vulgate generally coincide with MT, although there are suggestive differences here and there.

Several critical editions of the Vulgate are available. Ecclesiastes is found in the large edition known as *Biblia Sacra iuxta latinam Vulgatam versionem* 11 (Rome: Polyglott Vaticanis, 1957). This edition, based on an eclectic text, is especially valuable for its collection of variants. More readily accessible and in many ways more reliable is the smaller Stuttgart edition by R. Weber.

ETHIOPIC

Although the Ethiopic version of the Old Testament probably dates to the middle of the seventh century, the oldest known Ethiopic MS containing Ecclesiastes is dated no earlier than the fifteenth century. The first and only attempt at a critical edition of the Ethiopic text of Ecclesiastes was by S. A. B. Mercer in 1931 (*The Ethiopic Text of the Book of Ecclesiastes*). According to Mercer, the Ethiopic translation was made from some version of LXX, although the translator probably had various Hebrew MSS available, as well as the Syriac and Vulgate. In some eighteen instances, by Mercer's count, the Ethiopic version sides with MT against LXX. In a few instances, however, the translator exercised a great deal of independence.

ARABIC

There is an Arabic version published in the *London Polyglot* (1656) and *Paris Polyglot* (1630). The work is commonly attributed to Saadia Gaon of Egypt (d. 942 C.E.), who is reputed to have written a commentary on Ecclesiastes. Others, however, think the translation is the work of Isaac ben Judah Ibn Ghiyyat, who lived a century after Saadia. Although the version is apparently based on a Hebrew text, it is not reliable for textual criticism. The version is now more readily accessible, thanks to the efforts of H. Zafrani and A. Caquot (*La version arabe de la Bible de Sa'adya Gaon*).

IV. LANGUAGE

There is perhaps no other book in all of the Hebrew Bible where the language has received more attention of scholars than Ecclesiastes. Beginning with Grotius in the seventeenth century, scholars have scrutinized and debated the linguistic peculiarities in the book, with a significant majority of them concluding that the language of the book makes a Solomonic date well-nigh impossible (see Bianchi, "Language of Qohelet," pp. 210–11). The judgment of Franz Delitzsch on this matter reflects the opinion of most: "If the Book of Koheleth were of old Solomonic origin, then there is no history of the Hebrew language" (*Song of Songs and Ecclesiastes*, p. 190).

Scholars have variously attempted to explain the aberrant character of Qohelet's Hebrew in terms of a foreign origin (i.e., the book was originally composed in Aramaic), heavy foreign influences (of Aramaic, Canaanite, Phoenician, Greek), a late date (with traces of "Mishnaisms"), dialectal origins (i.e., it was composed in northern Hebrew or a dialect like it), specialized vocabulary (i.e., the author used philosophical jargon), or vernacular elements (i.e., reflecting the Hebrew of everyday speech). Within the past decade alone, three major monographs have appeared on the subject by B. Isaksson in 1987 (*Language of Qoheleth*), D. Fredericks in 1988 (*Qoheleth's Language*), and A. Schoors in 1992 (*Pleasing Words*). The whole topic deserves careful consideration, for despite the difficulties, the linguistic clues remain the most compelling for the dating of the book. There are, after all, no reliable historical references within the book and no external evidence for its date of origin apart from the existence of 4QQohᵃ, whose date (between 175–150 B.C.E.) provides us only with the *terminus ante quem.*

ORTHOGRAPHY

If MT is a reliable witness to the book's original orthography, Qohelet's spelling convention is quite consistent with what one might expect in the exilic or postexilic period. At the same time, it is far more conservative than the orthography of the Qumran scrolls and fragments, where internal vowel letters are much more common, occurring in as much as 90 percent of all forms that might possibly have them. In the Qumran documents, the imperfect forms are typically *yqtwl*, the active participles are *qwtl*, and the infinitive construct forms are *qtwl* or *qwtl* (one of the possible developments from original *qutl or *qutul). Moreover, the negative particle is also typically spelled with a vowel letter (*lwʾ*), as are the forms that are original *qull or *qutl. So, too, in 4QQohᵃ we find *kwl* instead of *kl* in MT, *lwʾ* instead of *lʾ*, and *ḥwšk* instead of *ḥšk*. Whereas MT has *mśḥq* (7:3), *lšmʿ* (7:5), *śḥq* (7:6), 4QQohᵃ has *mśḥwq*, *lšmwʿ*, and *śḥwq*, respectively. And whereas MT has *lʿlmym* in 1:10, 4QQohᵇ has *lʿwlmym*. The orthography of Qumran Hebrew represents a later stage than what we have in Ecclesiastes. Thus, Schoors certainly is correct to state that Ecclesiastes "represents a somewhat middle stage in the development of *plene* writing" (*Pleasing Words*, p. 32). In terms of orthographic conventions, therefore, Ecclesiastes is to be placed somewhere between the beginning of the sixth century and the end of the third century B.C.E.

FOREIGN INFLUENCES

1. Persianisms

There are two widely recognized Persian loanwords in Ecclesiastes: *pardēs* (2:5) and *pitgām* (8:11). This datum is important, since there is no clear evidence of Persianisms prior to the Achaemenid period. All Persian loanwords and Persian names in the Bible are dated to the postexilic period. Indeed, it may be observed that there are no Persian words or names in the texts that are clearly associated with the first major wave of returnees, namely, in the books of Haggai, Zechariah, and Malachi, nor in any other texts prior to the fifth century. Persian names in the Bible are found in the books of Chronicles, Ezra, Nehemiah, Esther, and Daniel; they are not in earlier documents.

2. Aramaisms

Most scholars recognize an unusually high frequency of Aramaisms in Ecclesiastes—Aramaic loanwords and Aramaic syntactical features. Indeed, the presence of Aramaisms is so strongly felt that F. C. Burkitt, F. Zimmermann, C. C. Torrey, and H. L. Ginsberg have argued that the book originally was composed in Aramaic and only later translated imperfectly into Hebrew. Proponents of this theory maintained that the inconsistent use of the definite article, as well as a number of texts that are problematic in Hebrew, can be explained once the Hebrew is retroverted to Aramaic. The theory has been so effectively demolished by R. Gordis, C. F. Whitley, and others that it hardly is taken seriously anymore. Nevertheless, many scholars recognize that there are a number of morphological, syntactical, or lexical Aramaisms in the book (see especially M. Wagner, *Aramäismen*, pp. 17–121; W. C. Delsman, "Sprache des Buches Koheleth," pp. 345–48).

To be sure, the presence of isolated Aramaisms in any book says nothing of its provenance; Aramaisms are attested sporadically in preexilic works, as well, particularly those texts coming from the north (see Hurvitz, "Chronological Significance," pp. 234–40). Yet, a high frequency of Aramaic expressions in a book is a likely indication of a late date, probably in the postexilic period, when Aramaic became the vernacular in administration and commerce. Fredericks observes correctly that a number of these Aramaisms occur already in preexilic texts, while others are attested only in Jewish Aramaic — too late to be diagnostic, as far as the date of Ecclesiastes is concerned (*Qoheleth's Language*, pp. 217–41). It is significant, however, that a number of terms in Ecclesiastes are paralleled by their Aramaic equivalents specifically in Persian period texts. For instance, one notes that Aramaic *ytrn* "surplus" (*TAD* III, 3.11.6), *hsrn* "deficit" (*TAD* I, 4.3.9, 10), *hšbn* "account" (*TAD* III, 3.28.79), and *nksyn* "assets" (*TAD* II, 2.8.4, 9.6; III, 1.1.66, 74, etc.) all occur as economic terms in Egyptian Aramaic texts from the fifth century. These terms are not attested in Aramaic or Hebrew prior to the Persian period.

A few other Aramaisms, too, may be dated to the Persian period. The noun *zĕmān* "appointed time," for example, is first attested in an Aramaic document from North Saqqara in the fifth century (Segal, *Aramaic Texts*, 2.4; 18.6; 80.4). All occurrences of the root *zmn* in the Hebrew Bible are late: the noun in Esth 9:27, 31; Neh 2:6; Sir 43:7; the denominative verb in Ezra 10:14; Neh 10:35; 13:51. The *qĕṭāl* pattern of the Hebrew noun (*zĕmān*) suggests that it is borrowed from Aramaic. This noun came into Late Biblical Hebrew from Aramaic no earlier than 500 B.C.E. Early Biblical Hebrew uses the noun *môʿēd* with the same meaning. It is also in the Persian period that one finds the expression *khd*, the Aramaic equivalent of Hebrew *k'hd* used with the meaning "one and the same, equally" (*TAD* II, 3.1.7).

The noun *ṭaḥănâ* "mill" in 12:4 is a Hebrew *hapax legomenon*. The normal word for "mill" in Hebrew is *rēḥayim* (Exod 11:5; Num 11:8; Deut 24:6; Isa 47:2; Jer 25:10), although the masculine noun *ṭĕḥôn* is attested once (Lam 5:13). Now an Aramaic parallel for Hebrew *ṭaḥănâ* is attested in a text from the Persian period (see Segal, *Aramaic Texts*, No. 20.5). We cannot be sure if the Hebrew word should be termed an "Aramaism," but one notes again that the Hebrew has an Aramaic cognate in a fifth-century text. Similarly, the verb *lwh* "to accompany" (8:15) is also attested in a fifth-century Aramaic text (see *TAD* III, 1.1.100), although there is insufficient evidence to allow one to call the verb an "Aramaism."

The verb *šlṭ* ("to have right, power") occurs in Ecclesiastes in reference to the control of inheritance and assets (see Notes at 2:19; 5:18 [Eng v 19]; 6:2), and related to the verb are the nouns *šallîṭ* "proprietor" (see Notes at 7:19; 8:9) and *šilṭôn* "authority, right" (8:4, 8). Except for the last, all these terms recur in Aramaic legal documents from the Persian period concerning transferable rights over various sorts of property.

The verb is used here in the technical sense meaning "to have the right of disposal." It refers to the legal and transferable right over property and income. This same sense of the verb is found in Neh 5:15, a text from the fifth century: "The former governors who were before me laid a heavy burden upon the people, and they took from them food and wine, along with forty shekels of silver. Even their retainers exercised proprietorship (*šālĕṭû*) over the people." It appears that the subordinates of Nehemiah's predecessors used their legal authority to exploit the resources of the populace — that is, by taxation. The verb is not used in the same way after the Persian period. Thus, in the book of Daniel, the verb *šlṭ* simply means "to rule, overpower" (Dan 2:38, 39, 48; 3:27; 5:7, 16; 6:25 [Eng v 24]) but not "to have right of disposal," as in the Persian period. By the same token, the noun *šallîṭ* in Ezra 4:20 and 7:24 refers to one with the right of taxation, whereas in Daniel it refers simply to one with power (Dan 2:10, 15; 4:14, 22, 23, 29 [Eng vv 17, 25, 26, 32]; 5:21, 29). The term *šlyṭ* is, likewise, used in the technical sense of "right of disposal" in the legal documents from Elephantine and Wadi Daliyeh.

In a careful study of the *šlyṭ*-clause in Aramaic, D. M. Gropp observes that this legal terminology is not continued beyond the Persian period ("The Origin and Development of the Aramaic *šallîṭ* clause," p. 34). It is not found in the documents from Wadi Murabbaʿat and Naḥal Ḥever. After the Persian period, according to Gropp, "the form *raššay* generally replaced *šallîṭ* in legal contexts" (ibid.). Instead of *šlyṭ*, the term *ršy* is found in the deeds from Murabbaʿat and Naḥal Ḥever and in Nabatean tomb inscriptions. After the Persian period, the term *šallîṭ* was increasingly used in the sense of one having power, particularly a ruler, but it no longer referred to one having a legal right over property and income. The noun *šlṭn* occurs only once, in an Aramaic ostracon from Egypt, where it means "authority to dispose," an economic term (*Neue Ephemeris für semitische Epigraphik* III, p. 48, lines 12–13). This meaning of the noun is different from its usage in Nabatean and Palmyrene, where the word refers to political power, rather than legal right (*DNWSI*, p. 1142). In the Hellenistic period, we find the Aramaic noun *šlṭn* attested fourteen times in the book of Daniel, always in the political sense. One may observe also that in Sir 3:22, a text dated to the Hellenistic period, the verb *ršh* is used instead of *šlṭ* for the right of disposal. At Qumran, too, the verb *ršh* is found in place of *šlṭ* used in the legal sense (see CD 11.20). Thus, the usage of the root *šlṭ* in Ecclesiastes is typical of the fifth and fourth centuries B.C.E. This datum, in fact, supports an argument made long ago by D. S. Margoliouth, who maintained that if Ecclesiastes had been written in the third century, one should expect *hiršâ* instead of *hišlîṭ* for "to authorize, give right" (see "Ecclesiastes," in *Jewish Encyclopedia* V, pp. 32–33). Margoliouth's characterization of these forms as Phoenicianisms, however, is open to question.

In sum, the high frequency of Aramaisms suggests a postexilic date, a fact confirmed by the cluster of common Hebrew and Aramaic terms all from the fifth and fourth centuries. The technical usage of the root *šlṭ*, too, suggests a date no later than the Persian period.

3. Phoenicianisms

In a series of articles, Mitchell Dahood has argued that Qohelet was a Jewish resident of Phoenicia, who wrote in Hebrew but with Phoenician orthography and heavy Canaanite-Phoenician influences in morphology, syntax, and vocabulary. The argument from orthography is based, however, on selected verses in the book, reconstructed from various witnesses, including questionable retroversions from the Greek, Latin, and Syriac. If anything, the orthographic evidence (as far as we can tell from MT) contradicts the claim that the orthography of Ecclesiastes is according to the Phoenician convention: the vowel letters are fully utilized, contrary to the practice in Phoenician (see above).

As for the grammatical elements, Dahood cites the use of the masculine plural suffix -*hem* for feminine plural antecedents, the feminine demonstrative *zōh*, the alleged nonsyncopation of the definite article (but see Notes at 8:1), the feminine noun ending -*at* (instead of -*â* in standard Hebrew), supposedly peculiar uses of various prepositions, the use of the infinitive absolute followed by the independent pronoun, and the presence of asyndetic relative clauses. But most of the features cited by Dahood are found in Biblical Hebrew, notably in Late Biblical Hebrew. Otherwise they are attested in Mishnaic Hebrew, which may have included traces of a northern Hebrew dialect, as well as vernacular elements (see Davila, "Northern Hebrew," pp. 73–74).

To be sure, one cannot rule out the possibility of some Phoenician influences on Late Biblical Hebrew and in various Hebrew dialects, but Dahood has not succeeded in proving his hypothesis. Some of the alleged parallels have been found to be untenable: e.g., *šiddâ*, which is supposedly found in the Amarna letters to mean "concubine" is now shown to be based on a misreading of the cuneiform signs (see Notes at 2:8); *yḥwš*, which is thought to be related to Ugaritic *ḫšt* must be called into question because of Dahood's misunderstanding of the Ugaritic word (see Notes at 2:25). So, too, the presence of several putative Canaanite grammatical features has been denied, not only in Ecclesiastes but in the whole Hebrew Bible: e.g., the third-person masculine suffix -*y* (see Notes at 2:25), the *taqtul*-imperfect (see Notes at 10:15), the Yiphil infinitive construct (see Schoors, *Pleasing Words*, pp. 78–79). Dahood also finds the enclitic-*mem* (a "Canaanite" feature) appearing a few times in the book, but his examples are not compelling (see Notes at 4:6). One may also point to many manifestly *unphoenician* traits in the book: the first independent pronoun is *'ny* (not *'nk*, as is always the case in Phoenician), the marker of direct definite object is *'t* not Phoenician *'yt*, the relative particle is *š* or *'šr* not Phoenician *'š*, and so on.

Dahood's thesis of a book written with Phoenician orthography and reflecting heavy Phoenician influences in grammar and vocabulary must be rejected. Nevertheless, he has succeeded in pointing to some illuminating parallels between

Ecclesiastes and general "Canaanite" or Phoenician: e.g., the use of the infinitive absolute followed by the independent pronoun (see Notes at 4:1), the parallelism of *ymk* "collapses" and *ydlp* "crumbles" in 10:18, the possibility that *'šr* in 6:10 may be a noun meaning "destiny" (see Notes at 6:10), the term *šmn rwqḥ* "perfumer's oil" in 10:1, the term *'spwt* "assemblies" in 12:11, and many others. Most suggestive of all is the expression *tḥt hšmš* "under the sun." The phrase occurs twenty-nine times in Ecclesiastes, but nowhere else in Hebrew, where the idiom *tḥt hšmym* "under the heavens" is preferred. The same expression — *tḥt šmš* "under the sun" — is found twice in Phoenician, in the inscriptions of Kings Tabnit and Eshmunazor of Sidon.

To summarize: the possibility that some idioms in Ecclesiastes are a result of Phoenician influences cannot be ruled out (see Piotti, "La lingue dell'Ecclesiaste," pp. 185–95), even though that possibility cannot be demonstrated convincingly. It is suggestive that the idiom *tḥt šmš* "under the sun" occurs also in Phoenician inscriptions from the fifth century. The idiom in Ecclesiastes may have been borrowed from Phoenician, although the expression in Phoenician itself may have come from elsewhere.

4. Grecisms

The superficial affinities between Ecclesiastes and certain Greek philosophical notions have prompted a considerable number of scholars to date the book to the Hellenistic period or later. This late dating, however, does not rest on linguistic grounds. There are no clear instances of Greek loanwords or Greek constructions in the book. Admittedly, this datum is of questionable significance, since there are no grecisms in the Qumran scrolls and fragments either. Yet, the Qumran materials are self-consciously conservative; the scribes of that community deliberately tried to imitate standard Biblical Hebrew. The same cannot be said of Ecclesiastes, which is clearly not a book that tries to sound conservative. Despite the Solomonic disguise of the author, and apart from the royal fiction 1:12–2:11, there is no attempt to sound archaic or to look to the past. Moreover, scholars who want to date the book to the Hellenistic period commonly speak of Hellenistic influences in Qohelet's thought, and some speak of an overwhelming Hellenistic feel about the book. The author is frequently assumed to be conversant with contemporary Greek thought, if he is not directly dependent on it. If all that were true, it is all the more odd that there should be no trace of linguistic grecisms in the book. One may observe that among the many epigraphic finds from Persian period Palestine, there is none written in Greek and none that shows any grecism. By contrast, Greek loanwords are well attested in Hellenistic period inscriptions from Palestine.

DICTION

Scholars nowadays recognize that there are significant differences between the standard Biblical Hebrew of the preexilic period and Late Biblical Hebrew — the language of the postexilic era. Already in 1875, Delitzsch presented a long list of *hapax legomena,* as well as idioms and forms in Qohelet that belonged to the late period (*Ecclesiastes,* pp. 190–96). Included in this list are twenty-six expressions that occur elsewhere only in postexilic texts. A few of these deserve elaboration.

1. Frequency of *še-*.

    One of the features in the language of Ecclesiastes that stands out is the use of *še-* along with *'ăšer*. Of the 136 occurrences of *še-* in the Hebrew Bible, half are in Ecclesiastes. The next highest concentration is the Song of Songs, where the particle is found 30 times. The 68 occurrences of *še-* in Ecclesiastes make it one of the most frequently attested lexemes in the book. With the exception of Gen 6:3, *še-* occurs in either texts of probable northern provenance or texts that are late. Not counting Ecclesiastes, *še-* occurs 62 times in passages that are probably exilic or postexilic, and 6 times in passages of northern origin. It is attested in epigraphic Hebrew only in late texts (see *DNWSI,* p. 1091). The particle seems to have been a feature of northern Hebrew that was used more frequently after the exile. This is not to say that northern Hebrew uses *še-* to the exclusion of *'ăšer*, but *še-* does seem to be used more commonly in the north. It may be observed, too, that *še-* is used in Ecclesiastes in a variety of ways, including as a conjunction introducing a subject of an object clause, or even a purpose clause (1:7; 2:13, 14, 15, 24; 3:13, 14; 5:14, 15 [Eng vv 15, 16]; 8:14; 9:5; 12:9). This wide and varied use of *še-* is characteristic of Late Biblical Hebrew; *še-* is used as a relative particle in the older texts but not to introduce an object or a purpose clause.

2. Exclusive use of *'ănî*.

    It has long been recognized that the independent pronoun *'ănōkî* is more conservative than the shorter form *'ănî*. Indeed, the greater frequency of the shorter form has been identified by a number of scholars as a trait of Late Biblical Hebrew. If this is correct, the usage of the first person independent pronoun is suggestive. The form in Ecclesiastes is always *'ănî* (twenty-nine times), never the longer form *'ănōkî*.

3. The use of *'ēt/'et-*.

    As a rule, *'ēt/'et-* is used in classical Hebrew to mark the direct definite object, and it may appear with pronominal suffixes to indicate the personal object. In Ecclesiastes, however, *'ēt/'et-* is also used with an apparently indefinite noun (*'et-nirdāp* in 3:15; *'et-kol-'āmāl* in 4:4; *'et-lēb* in 7:7), and it is used in a nominative clause, that is, as a subject (4:3). Both of these are characteristic of the use of *'ēt/'et-* in Late Biblical Hebrew.

4. The feminine demonstrative *zōh*.

    The feminine demonstrative in Ecclesiastes is always *zōh*, never *zō't* (2:2, 24; 5:15, 18 [Eng vv 16, 19]; 7:23; 9:13). It appears, then, that the form *zōh/ zô* in Hebrew is a dialectal element that became common only in the later period. The precise nature of that dialect is, however, difficult to define. The form is probably derived from some dialect or other, and it became common in written compositions only from the postexilic period on. The epigraphic evidence also suggests that *zōh/zô* became common only in the later period.

5. The 3 mp pronominal suffix for feminine plural antecedents.

In several cases, the masculine plural (mp) pronominal suffix is used for the feminine plural (fp) noun:

With Pronominal Suffix	Antecedent	
mēhem "from them"	*bĕrēkôt* "pools"	2:6
mēhem "from them"	*'ênê* "eyes"	2:10
bāhem "by them"	*'ăbānîm* "stones"	10:9
kullām "all of them"	*šānîm* "years"	11:8
bāhem "in them"	*šānîm* "years"	12:1

Such a lack of coordination between the pronominal suffix and the antecedent noun is not unknown elsewhere in Biblical Hebrew (see GKC §135.o). Its sporadic occurrence in Early Biblical Hebrew may be explained as a colloquialism. Nevertheless, it is in Late Biblical Hebrew that the 3 mp pronominal suffix is regularly used in place of the 3 fp. This is simply a case where an earlier colloquialism becomes accepted as normative in later literary works. Thus in Chronicles, a work dated probably to the end of the fifth century, the 3 mp suffix is consistently used instead of the 3 fp. Such a consistency may be regarded as a trait of Late Biblical Hebrew (see Polzin, *Late Biblical Hebrew*, pp. 52–54). It is noteworthy that in the later Hebrew of Qumran, Wadi Murabba'at, and the Bar Kochba letters, as well as in Mishnaic Hebrew, the third-person plural suffix is not infrequently marked by -*n* instead of -*m* (even for the masculine plural!), perhaps as a result of Aramaic influence (see Qimron, *Hebrew of the Dead Sea Scrolls* §200.142; Segal, *Mishnaic Hebrew Grammar* §71; Polzin, *Late Biblical Hebrew*, p. 53). In short, Qohelet's language is typical of Late Biblical Hebrew but not of later dialects.

6. The negation of the infinitive with *'ên*.

In Eccl 3:14 one finds the construction *'ên lĕhôsîp* . . . *'ên ligrôa'*, literally, "not to add . . . not to take away." The construction indicates prohibition or impossibility. The infinitive construct forms are negated by *'ên*, instead of *lĕbiltî* as one might expect. The awkward construction signals a technical usage. This *'ên liqtōl* construction (meaning "it is not permitted . . .") is attested in the postexilic texts of Ezra (9:15), Chronicles (1 Chron 23:26; 2 Chron 5:11; 14:10; 20:6; 22:9; 35:15), and Esther (4:2; 8:8). It is also found in the late book of Ben Sira (Sir 10:23 [twice]; 39:21; 40:26) and in the Qumran texts (see Qimron, *Hebrew of the Dead Sea Scrolls*, pp. 78–79). Early Biblical Hebrew uses *lō' tiqtōl* for the same purpose. The difference between the idiom in Late Biblical Hebrew (*'ên liqtōl*) and that in Early Biblical Hebrew is evident when one compares the similar formula in the book of Deuteronomy, where we get *lō' tiqtōl*, instead of *'ên/lō' liqtōl*: *lō' tōsîpû* "you shall not add" . . . *lō' tigrĕ'û* "you shall not take away"

(Deut 4:2); *lōʾ tōsēp* "you shall not add" . . . *lōʾ tigraʿ* "you shall not take away" (Deut 13:1). Thus, whereas Deuteronomy (representing preexilic Hebrew) has *lōʾ tōsīpû* . . . *lōʾ tigrĕʿû*, Ecclesiastes (representing Late Biblical Hebrew) has *ʾên lĕhôsîp* . . . *ʾên ligrōaʿ* (3:14). Fredericks cites 1 Sam 9:7 and, on the basis of that text, concludes that the *ʾên liqtōl* construction is as much a feature of Early Biblical Hebrew as it is of Late Biblical Hebrew (*Qoheleth's Language*, pp. 132–33). But *ʾên-lĕhābîʾ lĕʾîš hāʾĕlōhîm* in 1 Sam 9:7 has nothing to do with prohibition; it means "there is nothing to bring to the man of God." That is not a *ʾên liqtōl* construction. Thus, the use of the *ʾên liqtōl* construction in the prohibitive sense is found only in Late Biblical Hebrew, beginning with texts from the fifth century B.C.E.

After a thorough study of the language, Schoors concludes that there are thirty-four features in Ecclesiastes that are typical of Late Biblical Hebrew (*Pleasing Words*, pp. 221–24). The language of the book appears to have greatest affinities with the postexilic works of Chronicles, Ezra, Nehemiah, and Esther. Indeed, one may observe that a number of expressions in the book can be dated to the fifth century and beyond. A. Hurvitz has demonstrated, for instance, that the expression *kōl ʾăšer ḥāpēṣ ʿāśâ* "he does everything he desires" (see 8:2) belonged originally to the domain of jurisprudence and is found only after 500 B.C.E. ("The History of a Legal Formula, pp. 257–67). Hurvitz argues that the Hebrew expression was influenced by Aramaic legal terminology. In Early Biblical Hebrew and in Old Aramaic, the expression is not "he does all that he desires" but "he does whatever is good in his sight" (see Josh 9:25; 2 Sam 10:12; 2 Kgs 10:5; Sefire, KAI 223.C.1–3). Thus, the expression "he does whatever is good in his sight" is the standard idiom before 500 B.C.E., whereas "he does everything he desires" is the expression of choice after 500 B.C.E. By the same token, one may note that the repeated idiom *nātan lēb* "to pay attention" occurs only in Late Biblical Hebrew, whereas Early Biblical Hebrew uses *śām lēb* or *šāt lēb* for the same thing (see Notes at 1:13).

Not all the linguistic features in the book may be explained merely as reflexes of Late Biblical Hebrew, however. There are some traits in Ecclesiastes that are attested only exceptionally in other Late Biblical Hebrew writings (e.g., *zōh/zô*; *ʾillû*) and others that do not appear at all in other late biblical texts (e.g., *ḥûṣ min* meaning "except, outside of," 2:25; *siklût* in 10:5). It has been assumed traditionally that those differences between the Hebrew of Ecclesiastes and other Late Biblical Hebrew texts are evidence that Ecclesiastes is linguistically more advanced than Late Biblical Hebrew, since a number of these features seem to be more typical of Postbiblical Hebrew than they are of Biblical Hebrew. Some would even characterize the language of the book as something that stands midway between classical Biblical Hebrew and Mishnaic Hebrew (so Gordis, Crenshaw). Yet, as has been demonstrated in a number of recent studies, the Hebrew of Ecclesiastes cannot be identified with what we find in the Hebrew of Ben Sira, Qumran, Wadi Murabbaʿat, Naḥal Ḥever, and the Bar Kochba letters (see Fredericks, *Qoheleth's Language*, pp. 110–24). The truth is that a number of the linguistic features may have no chronological significance whatsoever. They are, rather, evidence of the extensive use of colloquialisms in the book. Thus, the relatively infrequent use of the *waw-consecutive* imperfects (only in 1:17; 4:1, 7), the anticipatory pronominal suffix (e.g., in 2:21; 4:12), the inconsistent use of the definite article (e.g., 2:8; 3:17; 4:4, 9–12; 7:25; 10:19, 20; 12:1, 4, 6), the discordance of subject and predicate (1:10; 2:7; 10:12, 15), the use of masculine plural pronominal suffix for the feminine plural antecedent (2:6, 10; 10:9; 11:8; 12:1) may all be explained as vernacular elements. Moreover, the possibility that the Hebrew of Ecclesiastes reflects a non-Judean dialect cannot be ruled out (so Davila, Rainey), although it is difficult to identify the dialect specifically (see Piotti, "La lingua dell'Ecclesiaste," pp. 185–95). These features in the Hebrew of Ecclesiastes — the vernacular and non-Judean dialectal elements — are also found in Mishnaic Hebrew, which has been described as "a vernacular elevated to a literary level" (Greenfield, "Lexicographical Notes," p. 204). One should not, however, speak of "Mishnaic influence" on Ecclesiastes. Nor should one even refer to the features as "proto-Mishnaic." As Fredericks has shown, there are in fact more discontinuities between the language of Ecclesiastes and Mishnaic Hebrew than there are continuities (*Qohelet's Language*, pp. 51–109). The Hebrew of Ecclesiastes is like Mishnaic Hebrew only inasmuch as both languages are the literary deposits of popular speech. In terms of Qohelet's vocabulary, only two words, *'ăbiyyônâ* "caper-berry" and *siklût* "folly," are unique in Ecclesiastes and Postbiblical Hebrew.

On the basis of its language, then, the book should be dated to the postexilic period. The presence of two Persian loanwords should place the language no earlier than the fifth century. The number of Aramaisms also suggests a date in the postexilic period, when Aramaic was used as the *lingua franca* in administration and commerce. Specifically, one finds a number of economic and legal terms that are at home in the socioeconomic world of the Persian empire in the fifth and fourth centuries B.C.E. The verb *šlṭ* is used in a legal sense in the book, a sense it does not have after the Persian period, when the term meant only "to rule, to have dominion." Other terms that may not be Aramaisms, too, belong to the socioeconomic vocabulary of this period: *ḥēleq* "portion, lot," *taḥănâ* "mill," *ḥōpen* "handful," *kap* "hand" used as a measure (see Notes at 4:6), *bêt hāsûrîm* "prison" (see Notes at 4:14). This dating is corroborated by the number of idioms that are typical of Late Biblical Hebrew, especially those that are found only in postexilic texts. Even the *qōṭelet* pattern of the author's name, *qōhelet*, finds parallels precisely in the Persian period in the names *sōperet* (Ezra 2:55; Neh 7:57; 1 Esdr 5:33) and *pōkeret* (Ezra 2:57; Neh 7:59; 1 Esdr 5:34). In no other period in the Hebrew Bible do we have masculine names of this precise pattern (see Notes at 1:1).

In terms of a typology of language, then, Ecclesiastes belongs in the Persian period. The language of the book reflects not the standard literary Hebrew of the postexilic period, however. Rather, it is the literary deposit of a vernacular, specifically the everyday language of the Persian period, with its large number of Aramaisms and whatever jargons and dialectal elements one may find in the marketplace.

V. SOCIOECONOMIC CONTEXT

The linguistic evidence in Ecclesiastes indicates a date in the Persian period for the book, specifically between the second half of the fifth and the first half of the fourth centuries B.C.E. This long has been considered a "dark age" in the history of Israel on account of the paucity of information on it. Our knowledge of the socioeconomic environment of the period has been significantly enriched in recent decades by a wealth of epigraphic finds, however, despite the many gaps in political history that still remain. These disparate epigraphic sources, together with the results of archaeological surveys and excavations of Persian period sites, allow us to catch a few glimpses of the socioeconomic world in which Qohelet lived and taught.

MONETARY AND COMMERCIAL ECONOMY

One of the most important features of the economy during the postexilic period is the prominent role of money. The Achaemenid government instituted a highly efficient system of taxation throughout the empire, according to which imperial taxes were to be paid in precious metal. Moreover, to facilitate both trade and the payment of taxes, the government began minting coins and standardizing currency. Thus, under Darius I, a gold coin known as the "Daric" was first struck by the central government around the year 515 B.C.E., but silver *sigloi* (to be distinguished from weighed silver pieces) were also minted by the satraps. Coins began appearing in Palestine during the Achaemenid period, and they became common from the second half of the fifth century onwards. Numerous hoards have been found in various sites in Israel, all dating to the fifth century and later.

It is not that "money" was unknown in earlier periods, for silver pieces in various forms and sizes already were used as a medium of exchange in earlier times. Yet, the introduction of coinage by the Persians democratized the usage of money and radically transformed the economy of the Levant. Not surprisingly, therefore, the epigraphic materials from this era show a great deal of concern with money. Contemporaneous inscriptions are replete with references to money, most frequently mentioned in connection with taxes, wages, rent, loans, fines, inheritance, and the prices of goods and services. Money was used in everyday business transactions both large and small, given as gifts and bribes, and hoarded. Money had become not just a convenient medium of exchange; it had become a commodity.

The development and growth of this monetary economy may provide a specific socioeconomic context within which to interpret a number of sayings in Ecclesiastes. Qohelet says: "One who loves money will not be satisfied with money, nor whoever loves abundance with yield" (5:10 [Heb v 9]). When bounty increases, the author notes, the consumers "increase" — in every sense of the word (see Notes at 5:11 [Heb v 10]). Qohelet observes that the *'ōbēd* "worker" sleeps well, whether that one has consumed little or much, while the surfeit of the rich permits them no rest (5:12 [Heb v 11]). Those greedy consumers cannot get rest, either because of indigestion (overconsumption of food) or anxiety about their investments (overconsumption of wealth). While Qohelet clearly draws on timeless wisdom teachings, he also addresses people facing a new world of money and finance. Hence, he uses the vocabulary of his day to subvert the preoccupations of his contemporaries. In a couple of instances, the author alludes to popular sayings about the power of money. Thus, in 7:12 he seems to have turned a popular notion about money into an instruction about its ephemerality. In this text, the Hebrew saying *bĕṣēl haḥokmâ bĕṣēl hakkāsep* may be interpreted either to mean "wisdom is a protection, money is a protection" (the original intended meaning) *or* "wisdom is a shadow, money is a shadow" (see Notes at 7:12). Whereas the saying could be taken — perhaps had been taken — to mean that wisdom and money both provide protection (*ṣēl*), Qohelet means to say that neither wisdom nor money is reliable as real protection after all. Contrary to popular notions, money is *ṣēl* only in the sense of a shade, a temporary shelter (see Comment at 7:12). The people whom Qohelet addressed were preoccupied with the acquisition of money; they believed in its power, thinking that "money answers everything" (*wĕhakkesep ya'ăneh 'et-hakkōl*, 10:19).

There can be no doubt that Ecclesiastes presumes an audience that is deeply concerned with economic matters. Besides general terms like *kesep* "money," *'ōšer* "riches," *'āšîr* "rich," *sĕgullâ* "private possession," *śākār* "salary, reward, compensation," *naḥălâ* "inheritance," and *kišrôn* "success, accomplishments," one finds a number of terms in the book that suggest a lively economic environment: *yitrôn* "surplus, advantage," *ḥesrôn* "deficit, what is lacking," *ḥešbôn* "account," *nĕkāsîm* "assets," *tĕbû'â* "yield," *hămôn* "abundance, wealth," *'inyān* "preoccupation, venture, business," *'āmāl* "toil, fruit of toil," *'ôkēl* "consumer," *'ōbēd* "worker," *ḥēleq* "lot, portion." Indeed, at times Qohelet sounds like a pragmatic entrepreneur ever concerned with the "bottom line." Here, again, he is borrowing from the vocabulary of his generation to make his point. Thus, regarding the value of labor, his question is always this: *mah-yitrôn* "what is the advantage?" (1:3; 3:9; 5:16 [Heb v 15]). He repeatedly uses the Hebrew word *yitrôn* "advantage, surplus," which is related to Aramaic *ytrn*, a term found on an accounting document from the late fifth century (*TAD* III, 3.11.6). Thus, Qohelet is talking about the *net gain* of labor, as it were. And any merchant would understand his point. If there is no advantage — no net gain — in a particular investment, one should not waste one's resources. Moreover, when Qohelet speaks of humanity's desperate search for wisdom, he draws on the image of a merchant or an accountant frantically checking a ledger to explain some discrepancy, examining the account item by item — *'aḥat lĕ'aḥat limṣō' ḥešbôn* "one by one to find an accounting" (7:27). The word *ḥešbôn* ("accounting") is, again, a commercial term found among the Aramaic documents of the Persian period. The author makes the point that those who seek to clarify the distinction between wisdom and folly

22

will be frustrated. They will not be able to find a clear accounting of it all. There will always be discrepancies in this confusing *ḥešbôn* (account) of wisdom and folly (see Notes and Comment at 7:25–29).

Ecclesiastes reflects a monetary and commercial economy, an environment that is different from the largely subsistence agrarian culture of preexilic Judah. In the fifth century, commerce was democratized and privatized; it was no longer primarily a royal enterprise (see J. P. Weinberg, "Bemerkungen zum Problem 'Der Vorhellenismus im Vorderen Orient'," *Klio* 58 [1976] 11). Indeed, the Persian period is distinguished from the preceding epochs by the widespread use of money and the democratization of commerce.

Jerusalem in the fifth century was a thriving cosmopolitan marketplace where the Judeans, even on the Sabbath day, worked in the winepresses, brought in heaps of grain, loaded the animals with goods, and hawked their agricultural products — grain, wine, grapes, figs, and "all kinds of loads" — and sold food, while Tyrians brought fish and all kinds of merchandise (Neh 13:15–16). Competition from the gentiles living in the city probably prompted the Jews to disregard the Sabbath injunction; the merchants must have felt that they could not afford to take a day off a week. Indeed, when Nehemiah ordered the city gates to be closed for Sabbath, "traders and the sellers of all kinds of merchandise" camped outside the city to wait for the market to open (Neh 13:20). That was the kind of competitive commercial atmosphere that existed in fifth-century Jerusalem. Ecclesiastes presumes such a lively and competitive economic environment. For Qohelet the silencing of the mill — perhaps he is referring to the commercial mill (see Notes at 12:4) — and the closing of the doors leading to the street-bazaar (*šûq*) was an ominous sign of the end of human existence (see Comment at 12:4). Certainly, an urbane audience is presumed in the book. For the author and his audience, it was axiomatic that only the fool would not know the way to the city (10:15).

ECONOMIC OPPORTUNITIES AND RISKS

The Persians instituted a system of property grants under which rights over various properties were given to favored individuals, military personnel, or temple communities. Most generous were the royal grants that were given outright to relatives and friends of the crown. The recipients of such grants had the responsibility for collecting the taxes from their domains, but the grant meant that they were also entitled to retain a portion of the revenues. The grantees sometimes further divided grant portions of their fiefs to those whom they favored, in return for annual taxes and military services as needed.

One recipient of royal grants was Arsham, the satrap of Egypt. In a letter from the satrap dated to the end of the fifth century, one learns that a grant had been given to a certain Egyptian named Aḥḥapi, an administrator of the satrap's estates in Egypt (see *TAD* I, 6.4). The grant is said to have been given by the king and by Arsham, probably meaning that it was given by Arsham from a part of his own royal grant. When Aḥḥapi died, he was succeeded in his position by his son,

Psamshek, who wrote to the satrap, requesting that the grant be transferred to him. So Arsham, who was in Babylon at that time, sent this letter to his representative in Egypt, giving Psamshek the legal authority (*šlyṭ*) to assume the grant (*TAD* I, 6.4.4). From this text it is clear that a grant was not automatically transferable to one's heirs. The heir had to be given the legal right of proprietorship (*šlyṭ*). Psamshek did not presume that he had the right to the property as the legal heir of his father; he had to appeal to the satrap's goodwill to have the grant renewed.

The Persian system of royal grants provides a backdrop against which to interpret Eccl 5:18–6:2 (Heb 5:17–6:2). Qohelet affirms that it is appropriate to enjoy the fruit of one's toil, for God has authorized one to do so:

> Here is what I have observed is good: that it is appropriate (for people) to eat, drink, and to enjoy good in all their toil that they toil under the sun, during the few days of their lives, which God has given them, for this is their portion. Indeed to all people God has given wealth and assets, and he has authorized them to partake of them, to take up their portion, and to have pleasure in their toil. This is the gift of God.
>
> (Eccl 5:18–20 [Heb vv 17–19])

Several terms in this passage echo the language of the royal grant: *nātan* "give," *šālaṭ* "to have right," *nāśā'* "to take up," *mattat 'ĕlōhîm* "gift/grant of God" (see Szubin and Porten, "Royal Grants in Egypt," p. 47). Qohelet presents life's possibilities in terms of such grants. The deity has granted humanity certain gifts, including wealth (*'ōšer*) and assets (*nĕkāsîm*), and the recipients of this favor are authorized to exercise proprietorship (*hišlîṭ*) over this divine grant (*mattat 'ĕlōhîm*).

Qohelet uses the word *ḥēleq* "portion" a couple of times in this passage: "this is their portion" (v 18 [Heb v 17]), "to take up their portion" (v 19 [Heb v 18]). This word is used once in an Aramaic contract in reference to a royal grant or a part thereof: *'tnnhy lk m[n] ḥlqy lmlk* "I shall give to you fr[om] my portion from the king" (*TAD* II, 1.1.11). The term is used elsewhere of a share of property, whether movable or immovable.

Qohelet refers to life as a portion given by God, and he says that human beings have been authorized to "take up" this portion that has been granted. In this view, life is like a portion that one receives as a grant from the divine sovereign. It is like a lot that is limited in time and space. In this lot the grantee toils, but it is also possible to enjoy the fruits of one's toil from that lot (5:18 [Heb v 17]). In this grant from God there is both the inevitability of toil and possibility of enjoyment. So when one has a portion, however imperfect that portion may be, one had better make the most of it, for that portion can be enjoyed only when one is alive. No one can take the portion along with him or her when death comes. No one has a portion that lasts forever (9:6).

The divine sovereign may be just as arbitrary as the Persian ruler who issues royal grants, however. Qohelet speaks of the case of someone who somehow is not permitted to enjoy the grant (6:2). In this instance, the right to enjoy the wealth and assets seems to have been given to an outsider, an *'îš nokrî*. The grant is given to someone else and not to the rightful heir. Again, one may understand Qohelet's sentiments in the light of the administration of royal grants during the Persian period. There is another Aramaic letter written by the satrap Arsham to the manager of his estates in Egypt (*TAD* I, 6.11). It seems that a steward of Arsham named Petosiri had written a letter to the satrap. Petosiri's father Pamun had been given the rights over a piece of property of a certain size. The land was abandoned when Pamun died during an unrest of some sort, perhaps during one of the several Egyptian rebellions against Persian rule. So the son, Petosiri, asked to be considered for the grant that his father had received: "Let him (that is, Arsham) take thought of me, let him give (the land) to me. Let me hold it as heir." The satrap then ordered his manager in Egypt to investigate the case. If the property in question had not been given already to someone else, Arsham wrote, then it should be given to Petosiri, but Petosiri must pay the appropriate taxes, as his father had done. The fact that Pamun had received the grant from Arsham and the fact that Petosiri was Pamun's heir did not mean that Petosiri was automatically allowed to enjoy the benefits. The grant had been issued to an individual, but the giver of the grant must still give the authorization for the grant to be assumed by the heir of the grantee. We do not know the outcome of the investigation of this particular case. Arsham's letter makes clear, however, that there was no guarantee that Petosiri would receive the authorization. It was entirely possible that the property had, in fact, been given to someone else — to an outsider.

There was a considerable amount of arbitrariness in the Persian system of royal grants. The great king gave grants to his relatives, friends, and favorite subordinates, but others were left out. The king's powerful relatives and allies who received the large grants also parceled out their assets to their friends and favorites, apparently with the same arbitrariness. It must have appeared to the "have-nots" that what one received was entirely dependent on the whim of the giver. There were fortunate people who fared extremely well, and there were the unfortunate ones who received little or nothing. Life is like that to Qohelet: people receive whatever portion the divine sovereign chooses to give them. One does not have a choice in the matter. So Qohelet speaks of those who are favored by God (*ṭôb lĕpānāyw; ṭôb lipnê hā'ĕlōhîm*) and those who are not so fortunate — the *ḥôṭe'* "the offender" (see Notes and Comment at 2:24–26). The former are lucky enough to be favored with the good life; the latter are plain unlucky. The former are given wisdom, knowledge, and joy, but the latter are given the task of collecting and gathering for others to enjoy: "For to the person who is good before him, God has given wisdom, knowledge, and pleasure; but to the offender he has given a preoccupation of gathering and collecting to give to the one who is good before God. This is also vanity and a pursuit of wind" (2:26). God is seen here to be like the human sovereign, the great king of the Persian empire or the powerful satrap, who arbitrarily gives grants to favorite friends and courtiers, while others are left out. Divine grants, like royal grants, created a distinction between the "haves" and "have-nots."

Besides the royal grants given by the king to family, friends, and other favorites, there were also grants given to various people on condition of military service and/or payment of an annual tax. The lands so acquired were initially not alienable, but in time the proprietors were permitted to sublet or pawn their lands. These fiefs were sometimes shared by a number of coproprietors, with the rights of proprietorship being transferable in each case by inheritance. And through the division of inheritances, the average size of properties available for economic exploitation became smaller and smaller. To meet the demand for taxes paid in silver, fiefs were often converted into cash-producing rental properties. In all cases, taxes and services remained obligatory. The tenant farmers and workers paid their dues to the smallholders whose property they rented, and the smallholders in turn paid those above them, and so forth. Through this elaborate system of land grant, then, the Persian rulers were able to control and exploit the provinces.

Along with the potential for economic exploitation there were economic opportunities. There were ample opportunities for people to climb the socioeconomic ladder, as it were. Neo-Babylonian documents from this period show that there were slaves who borrowed substantial sums of money or otherwise accumulated enough wealth to buy their own slaves, trade independently, participate in all kinds of business ventures, hold various assets, rent property, and even acquire expensive real estate (see M. A. Dandamaev, *Slavery in Babylonia* [trans. by V. A. Powell; DeKalb, Illinois: North Illinois University Press, 1984], pp. 320–97). Slaves could borrow money for investment. Some bought or leased real estate, which could then be rented out or subleased. Others leased storehouses. Still others owned or leased workshops, farms, orchards, and livestock. It was possible, thus, for slaves to become quite rich. From the Murashu archive, for instance, we know of a certain Ribat, a slave of Rimut-Ninurta of the business firm of Murashu and Sons. This slave, or former slave, paid taxes for an office that he held, loaned large sums of money and amounts of grain and dates to various individuals, leased out several workers and 416 head of sheep and goats in the space of a single day, rented land to others, leased access to a canal with other assets that went with it, and served as a guarantor for various debtors. Ribat had become a rich entrepreneur. He is an example of a poor person who managed to become quite economically and socially successful. In one text (PBS 2/1, 106) we learn that Ribat, together with Raḥim the son of Bel-ab-uṣur, another slave of Rimut-Ninurta, subleased from their master a piece of land for three years, together with livestock, equipment, and seed. Thus, Rimut-Ninurta, who had the land rented or mortgaged to him, subleased it to his slaves, who later sub-subleased part of that land, together with some livestock, equipment, and seed to their own slaves (PBS 2/1, 123). Certainly the opportunities were there during the Achaemenid period for people to climb the ladder of success, but they were also easily exploited.

In a tantalizing but textually problematic passage, Qohelet seems to allude both to the economic exploitation and the opportunities in such a society:

If you see the oppression of the poor and the violation of justice and right in the province, do not be surprised over the matter—for an arrogant one is above an arrogant one, (and) arrogant ones have watched over them all.

(Eccl 5:8–9 [Heb vv 7–8])

The arrogant ones keep climbing the ladder, but no matter how high they climb, there are always people higher up than they, who look down on them. The text goes on to speak of the insatiability of the greedy: "the one who loves money will not be satisfied with money, and whoever loves abundance will not be satisfied with yield." These people keep consuming more and more, but they never seem to have enough. They permit themselves no rest. Elsewhere in the book, Qohelet says it is envy that drives people to vain pursuits (4:4). For them the advice is that it is better to have the smallest amount of anything with rest than to have twice as much with "toil and pursuit of wind" (4:6). The author addresses those whose "eyes are not satisfied with wealth," who toil and toil even though they have neither descendants nor kinfolks with whom to share their wealth (4:7–8). The fear of poverty and the possibility of wealth prompted people to be excessively driven and to be ever discontented with what they had. And so they were unable to enjoy their present lot, because they were trying to move ahead and up the socioeconomic pyramid. Qohelet's repeated exhortation, however, is to enjoy what is before one's eyes and consume the fruit of one's toil. For him, the grant that one receives from God is meant to be enjoyed. That is humanity's lot. Qohelet's attitude in fact parallels a saying in the contemporaneous wisdom text known as the (Aramaic) *Proverbs of Ahiqar*. In the latter text, dated to the second half of the fifth century, one finds the following advice to be content:

[Do not despise the littl]e that is your lot,
And do not covet the plenty that is withheld from you.
[Do not accumulate] wealth,
And do not mislead your heart.

(see *TAD* III, 1.1.136–37)

Like the audience of this wisdom text in Persian period Egypt, who apparently also had opportunities to accumulate wealth, Qohelet's audience does not seem secure with what they have. Rather, they are constantly toiling to acquire more and more, and they are worried about the possibility of losing what they have. They do not appear to be among the most wealthy of society. They are paranoid about disparaging remarks that their subordinates may be making about them (7:21). At the same time, they themselves are making disparaging remarks about their bosses—the rich and powerful (10:20). They have subordinates, but they themselves are subordinate to others. They are people who are socially and economically in the middle. Qohelet distinguishes them from the nobles, the princes, and the rich (10:16–20), but he never implies that they are poor. The recipients of Qohelet's instructions are commoners — smallholders, homesteaders, and people of the middle classes. They are susceptible to the various occupational hazards that the ordinary workers face: they are perfumers whose precious products could be contaminated by a single dead fly (10:1); they are hunters who dig pits to trap animals, farmers who remove stones from old fences in order to build new ones, wood-cutters and quarry workers (10:8–10). They are ordinary citizens facing the vagaries of a rapidly changing social world. They are people of the middle classes who are trying to scale the socioeconomic pyramid without sliding down into poverty. They are people caught between the impulse to protect and conserve whatever they have (see 5:13–17 [Eng vv 12–16]; 11:1–2) and the desire to get rich (4:4–6). They are a people caught between the opportunities and risks of a volatile economy.

Among the various social classes mentioned in the book are the *šallîṭîm*. Most commentators have assumed that these *šallîṭîm* were political figures of some sort and, hence, the word is usually translated as "rulers." But the term *šallîṭîm* probably refers to the wealthy land barons of the time (so NJPS: "magnates"), people who have been given the right of disposal over movable and immovable property. A *šallîṭ* is a proprietor — someone who has the right over property. This meaning is evident in various texts from the Persian period (see *TAD* II, 2.3.9–10; 2.6.17–22). The *šallîṭîm* were rich and powerful landowners who no doubt exacted taxes from the tenant farmers, part of which they paid to higher authorities. The proprietors were required to pay annual taxes and render military service as needed. In many cases, however, they hired substitutes to fulfill their military obligations. This practice is well documented in contemporaneous texts from Mesopotamia. In one instance, a certain Abi-Yaqari requested a home-born slave named Tirakam to be his substitute: "Bear the responsibility of my obligation" (see G. Cardascia, *Les archives des Murašû, une famille d'hommes d'affaires babyloniens à l'époque perse (455–403 av. J.-C)*. [Paris: Imprimerie Nationale, 1951] 165–66). In return for that service, Abi-Yaqari promised to pay his substitute 20 *kurs* of barley (roughly 3600 liters) annually, a payment large enough to allow the slave to start his own small business.

From the private records of a certain Kuṣur-Ea, a barber from the city of Ur, one finds the following:

Nidintu-Sin the son of Sin-aḫḫē-iddina said to Kuṣur-Ea the son of Sin-aḫḫē-bulliṭ: Give me money, provisions, (and) all the equipment according to (the rates) of the dispatches (^{LÚ}AL.LAK^{MEŠ}) of the citizens of Ur. Let me go to the muster of the king in the eighth year of King Artaxerxes (i.e., 397 B.C.E.). Whenever the king gives an order regarding your obligation, let me fulfill (it). Also the mission of the king, whenever he gives an order regarding your obligation (I will fulfill).

(UET 4, 109)

Kuṣur-Ea accepted the offer and Nidintu-Sin, the volunteer-substitute, was paid according to the standard "going rates." We learn from other texts in the archive that Kuṣur-Ea had acquired the infantry fief (*bīt qišti*) along with four other coproprietors. The partners were able to buy the fief, probably from a financially insolvent soldier. But instead of performing the military service himself, Kuṣur-Ea decided to pay Nidintu-Sin to be his substitute.

A variety of such contracts is found in texts from the Achaemenid period. Although the sending of substitutes into battle was explicitly forbidden in earlier Babylonian laws (see *Code of Hammurabi*, Laws 26, 33; ANET[3], p. 167), the existence of such laws suggests that the practice must have been common. Otherwise there would have been no need to legislate. In the freewheeling economic environment of the Persian empire, it became a common practice for the rich to hire substitutes whom they could send to do their military duty for them and perhaps to die on their behalf. The poor were willing to bear the responsibilities for a chance to get out of poverty. The long-standing Babylonian laws were disregarded in favor of economic pragmatism under the new regime, with its policy of "free enterprise."

In light of this background we are better able to understand Qohelet's polemic against the rich and powerful. He says:

There is no one who is proprietor (*šallîṭ*) over the spirit (or life-breath), to detain (*liklô'*) the spirit, and there is no proprietorship (*šilṭôn*) over the day of death. There is no substitution in the battle, and wickedness will not deliver those who practice it.

(Eccl 8:8)

The medieval Jewish commentator Rashbam was correct in understanding the battle in the context to be a reference to the day of death (see Notes and Comment at 8:8). In the decisive battle that is death, no one can send a substitute. As *Qoh. Rabb.* puts it: "No one can say to the Angel of Death . . . let my son, or my slave (*'bdy*), or my home-born slave (*bn byty*) go in place of me." The point that Qohelet makes is that proprietors may be rich and powerful, but no one has proprietorship over the *rûaḥ* "life-breath." No one can detain the life-breath, as one might detain a poor debtor. No one owns the day of Death. When the time comes for one to fight the battle with Death, no one can hire a substitute. Thus, this passage is a social commentary of sorts.

The economy provided opportunities for the ambitious. Poorer people could begin by borrowing, or by hiring themselves out to acquire capital, as Tirakam the home-born slave did. They could begin with smaller lots or with rental property. Or they could pool their capital with others in various joint ventures, as Kuṣur-Ea the barber and his partners did.

Along with the economic opportunities, however, there were risks. Usually the smallholders had to pay a very high price for their investments. In one case, three brothers approached the Murashu firm for a business loan (H. V. Hilprecht and A. T. Clay, *Business Documents of Murashu Sons of Nippur* [CT IX; Philadelphia: University of Pennsylvania, 1898], pp. 39–40). The brothers needed two trained oxen together with equipment for irrigation for a three-year period, and seven *kurs* (about 1260 liters) of barley for sowing. They had to go into a joint venture and also to borrow for their investment. The brothers had to pay seventy-five *kurs* (about 13,500 liters) of barley annually for their "seed money." Of course, the animals, equipment, and initial amount of barley had to be returned at the end of the loan-period. In another example, an individual agreed to pay one of the Murashus sixty *kurs* of dates by a certain time. It was stipulated that penalty for failure to meet the obligation on time was the doubling of the amount due.

From Egypt of this period we have a number of documents dealing with loans of various sorts—cash and grain (see *TAD* II, 3.1; 3:13; 4.1; 4.2; 4.7). In general the amount of the loan was small, averaging only about 4–6 shekels. These were consumer loans, procured by the average citizen for consumption. The interest rate for such loans was high and the penalty for default severe. In one instance, a woman secured a loan of 4 shekels at the compound rate of 5 percent *per mensem*, that is, 60 percent *per annum* (*TAD* II, 3.1). According to another contract, failure to repay the loan by the stipulated deadline meant that the loan (with its interest) was doubled: the interest would be 10 percent *per mensem* and 120 percent *per annum* (*TAD* II, 4.2). The extremely high interest rate is startling. Clearly the demand for money was great and it was easy to fall into debt. Some people went into debt to get rich or to improve their condition, but others did so merely to survive. The smallholder was extremely vulnerable in such an economic environment. This environment is reflected in an instruction in the *Proverbs of Ahiqar* found in Elephantine in Egypt, a text dated to the second half of the fifth century:

Borrow the grain and the wheat that you may eat
and be satisfied and give to your children with you.
[Do not take] a heavy [l]oan;
Do not borrow from an evil person.
Moreover, [i]f you do take a loan,
Do not give yourself rest until [you repay] the [l]oan,
[. . .] the loan is nice whe[n there is a need],
But its repayment is a houseful.

(see *TAD* III, 1.1.129–31)

The text assumes that many people had no choice but to borrow merely to survive. People had to borrow to eat. The advice, however, is to keep debts to a bare minimum and not to delay the repayment. Although not explicitly stated, one may assume that the saying here alludes to the extremely high interest rates. Loans are nice when there is a need, the text says, but the payment of the debt will be terribly exorbitant: it is a "houseful." In the event of a default, the creditor is entitled to seize the debtor's entire estate, including the debtor's house, slaves, grain, food, and even the children. And the liability is extended to the children if the debtor dies without paying the debt.

In Palestine, the Jews faced a similar environment when they returned from Babylon. Their plight is recorded in the book of Nehemiah (Neh 5:3–5). There was no letup of the imperial taxes. So people had to borrow to eat and to meet their financial obligations. And when they defaulted on their debts, their properties were foreclosed and their children taken into custody or sold into slavery. That was the situation in Judah during the time of Nehemiah in the second half of the fifth century. With the end of the famine and the social reform initiated by Nehemiah, the conditions presumably improved. Nevertheless, the experience of extreme poverty must have remained in the memory of Qohelet's audience.

It should hardly be surprising, then, that people in Qohelet's time should be toiling endlessly to accumulate as much wealth as possible. Whatever improvements there might have been, the dangers were still present. What happened in an earlier generation could happen again. The economy was volatile. With the high interest rates, the smallholder became extremely vulnerable. Those who were unable to pay their debts were seized and put in prisons, which were not penitentiaries (as they are supposed to be today) but workhouses where the poor worked to pay off their debts. In the Achaemenid period some powerful private entrepreneurs also had their own prisons for insolvent debtors and, sometimes, the debtor's children. From several Aramaic fragments from North Saqqâra, we learn of prisoners being registered and put to work in the *byt 'srn* "prison" (Segal, *Aramaic Texts*, 3.1; 8.10; 50.9).

The Aramaic term for prison (*byt 'srn*) is comparable to Hebrew *bêt hāsûrîm* (from *bêt hā'ăsûrîm*) found in Eccl 4:12. The text in Ecclesiastes contrasts a poor but wise individual with an old but stupid king; the former went forth from prison (*bêt hāsûrîm*) to become king, while the latter was born a king but became poor (*rāš*). This rags-to-riches/riches-to-rags story may be a common wisdom *topos*. Form-critically it may be classified as a *Beispielerzählung* "example story" (so Murphy). At the same time, however, Qohelet's usage of it may reflect the volatile economy of the Persian period, a time when there were tremendous economic opportunities but also significant risks. So his audience could certainly relate to this *Beispielerzählung*. It was an unreliable world in which Qohelet and his audience lived, for those who were rich and powerful could suddenly find themselves impoverished, while those who were poor might suddenly come into great wealth and prestige. Elsewhere in the book, Qohelet describes a world turned upside down:

There is an evil that I have observed under the sun, a veritable mistake stemming from the proprietor. The simpleton is set in great heights, but the rich abide in low estate. I have seen slaves on horses, but princes walk on foot like slaves.

(Eccl 10:5–7)

31

This description of a topsy-turvy world is commonly identified as another wisdom *topos* (so Murphy). And that is indeed correct. This is another instance, however, where literature also reflects social reality. The allusion to the downfall of a certain *šallîṭ* "proprietor" (see Comment at 10:5–7) has a historical ring to it. Perhaps the author has in mind a wealthy individual who has lost everything because of an inadvertent error (see 5:13–15 [Heb vv 12–14]). In any case, Qohelet goes beyond the particular case to reflect on an unpredictable world where events seem to spin out of control and social order is completely disrupted. Individuals are vulnerable to all kinds of dangers in the rapidly changing economic world, it seems. At a macrolevel, there are social, economic, and political forces at work that are beyond the control of individuals (see Comment at 10:5–7). At a microlevel, professionals face everyday occupational hazards: the hunter who digs a pit to trap animals is liable to fall into such a pit, the farmer who removes rocks from fences is vulnerable to snakes that lurk in the nooks and crannies, one who quarries stones is susceptible to certain industrial accidents, as is the one who splits wood (10:8–9). There is also the perfumer, whose precious product may be ruined by the presence of a single fly (10:1). There are risks everywhere and at every level in the new economic world.

Qohelet's characterization of this world is not a figment of his imagination. It is drawn from the wisdom tradition, but it is not merely rhetoric. His use of the tradition reflects the volatile economy of his time. Here, again, the Murashu archive is a valuable resource. Stolper points out that in the first year of the reign of Darius II Ochos (423–404 B.C.E.), the number of texts dealing with mortgages rose by more than 300 percent (*Entrepreneurs and Empire*, pp. 104–24). The number of lands pawned as well as the number of loans rose dramatically. One may observe, too, that a large number of texts mentioning "prison" are dated to the years 423–422 B.C.E. It appears that something was happening in the period of political transition that suddenly caused people to lose their holdings. Those who once possessed property had to give it up and many found themselves imprisoned for debt or enslaved. One wonders if these people were not losing their fiefs and other assets because they happened to be on the wrong side of the struggle. Certainly we expect some of the royal grants to have been revoked for political reasons, with consequences for all the dependents of the former grantees and their tenants. Whatever the explanation, it seems clear that land tenure and its privileges were somehow susceptible to the unpredictable wind of political change. The already volatile economy was made even more volatile by the fortunes of the various levels of proprietors who issued the grants. Given such uncertainties, it is no wonder that we find in the book a concern with ephemerality. Nothing seems permanent, nothing seems reliable in such a world. Even those who have their grants given to them could not count on having their assets forever.

Qohelet speaks of the person who was so afraid of losing his wealth that he hoarded it (Eccl 5:13–15 [Heb vv 12–14]). We do not know what that terrible business was that caused the man to lose all his wealth. Lohfink speculates that the man had deposited his money in a bank, but the bank became insolvent and so the poor fellow lost all his money (see Notes at 5:14 [Heb 13]). The point is that the man did not enjoy his wealth while he was able to do so. Somehow he had made a bad financial decision and, in consequence, lost everything for which he had toiled. Whatever Qohelet's intent in telling this story, it illustrates the volatility of the economy that his audience knew. They were cognizant of the fact that what they had one day might be gone the next.

Elsewhere in the book, Qohelet urges people not to be too tightfisted with their money. People should take the risk to be generous, even though tragedies — surely he includes economic tragedies — may happen in the future. People should take a chance and throw away a good deed:

> Release your bread upon the waters,
>   after many days you will find it.
> Give a portion to seven, or even eight
>   you do not know what misfortune may come about.

(Eccl 11:1–2)

This text goes on to note that people cannot watch for the perfect conditions. The farmer who watches the wind will never sow, those who watch the clouds will not harvest. Qohelet urges spontaneity instead: sow at any time (11:6). Or, as the Aramaic *Proverbs of Ahiqar* have it, "Harvest any harvest and do any work. Then you will eat and be satisfied and give to your children" (*TAD* III, 1.127). Both Ecclesiastes and the *Proverbs of Ahiqar* must be read in the light of the volatility of the economy in the last hundred and eighty years of the Achaemenids, a time of great economic opportunities and equally great risks.

SOCIAL PROBLEMS

Until recently, historians of the Persian period have often assumed that heavy taxation by the imperial government drained the economy of cash to the point that it was in stagnation, if not decay. This view has now been challenged (see Stolper, *Entrepreneurs and Empire*, pp. 143–51 and the literature cited there). Certainly the economic texts from Mesopotamia, Egypt, and Palestine indicate that there were eager entrepreneurs who were more than willing to extend credit and supply cash. Indeed, the evidence points to an environment of investment and overall economic growth throughout the empire. The economic growth, however, did not benefit all people equally. Land was easily available and cheap, but other expenses — like draft animals, equipment, water — were costly. Such a situation was generally favorable to the rich proprietors who could afford significant capital outlays, but the smallholders who had only limited access to capital were at a disadvantage. Small plots of land could not be exploited efficiently enough to yield adequate profits for the tenant farmers, but the landlords continued to receive their revenues. Rents and taxes still had to be paid. To be sure, there were opportunities, and it was possible to break out of the cycle of poverty, as Ribat the slave of Rimut-Ninurta and other slaves did. But the odds were against the smallholder.

33

A fifth-century Aramaic ostracon from Elephantine provides a glimpse of the economic uncertainties that many families faced. The text is a letter from a man who has been away from home for some reason. He writes to his wife and instructs her to sell his possessions so that the family may survive: "If you will sell all my valuables, (then) the babies may eat. There are no more coins left!" (*KAI* 270). People in such dire straits were forced to sell and borrow just to get by, as the *Proverbs of Ahiqar* suggest: "Borrow the grain and the wheat that you may eat and be satisfied and give to your children with you" (*TAD* III, 1.1.129).

The economic environment favored the political elite and the most influential entrepreneurs. In consequence, the gap between the rich and the dependent classes widened. The rich became exceedingly powerful, but the nonrich were vulnerable to exploitation. This social condition is reflected in the *Proverbs of Ahiqar*. It was axiomatic that the average person could not easily challenge the rich:

> With one who is more exalted than you,
>   do not initiate a dis[pute];
> With one who is impude[nt] and mightier than you,
>   [do not . . .].
> [. . . for he will take] from your portion
>   And he will ad[d it] to his own.

(TAD III, 1.1.142–44)

The vulnerability of the commoner is evident in other texts from Elephantine. In one instance (*TAD* I, 5.2) a farmer complains of a miscarriage of justice. He had apparently worked on a field but was not paid. The matter was brought before the "judges of the province" (*dyny mdnt'*), but the petitioner feels that "indeed injustice was done" (*k'šq 'byd*, literally, "indeed an oppression was done," lines 5, 8, 9). We do not know the details because the text is fragmentary. Perhaps the judges had taken a bribe. In any case, the petitioner appeals to a higher authority. Unfortunately, we do not know the eventual outcome of the appeal, or if the plaintiff was satisfied that justice was done eventually. We also do not know how long the process took. It is clear only that the poor man had already lost in the first stage of the legal process because the provincial judges were not on his side.

A comparable social environment is reflected in Ecclesiastes. The author complains of injustices being done (*'ăsūqîm 'ăšer na'ăśîm*) and he observes that those who have been treated unjustly have no one on their side (4:1–3). The problem seems to be the competitive economic culture, in which people are driven by envy to strive for success and they cannot seem to be satisfied (4:4–8). In that environment the poor could not count on the legal system to protect them (see 3:16), no doubt because of corruption in the courts (see Notes and Comment at 3:16). In 5:8 (Heb v 7), Qohelet speaks of oppression (*'ōšeq*) of the poor and the taking away of justice in the province (*mĕdînâ*), while "arrogant ones are above arrogant ones, and arrogant ones are above them" (5:8–9 [Heb vv 7–8]). There, again, the problem is that people are driven by greed and ambition, and the evil of their greed is portrayed in terms reminiscent of the gaping mouth of personified Death, attempting to swallow up the whole cosmos (see Comment at 6:7–9). In 7:7, Qohelet alludes to injustice (*hāʿōšeq*) and the taking of a bribe (*mattānâ*). The impression one gets is that there are people who are willing to do anything in order to get ahead in that competitive economic environment, and the rich are somehow circumventing the law at the expense of others. Moreover, even though it was possible to appeal the decision of a lower court, as we see in the petition from Elephantine, a drawn-out legal process would certainly have favored the rich. Indeed, according to Qohelet, the slow legal process encouraged people to act wickedly: "Since sentence for evil work is not executed quickly, people dare to do evil; an offender does the evil of hundreds but endures" (8:11–12a). In context, it seems likely that the author has in mind the rich proprietors who seem to think that they can exercise their power at will (see Comment at 8:7–9).

The ordinary citizen was at the mercy of the rich and powerful proprietors, the provincial judges and other officials, and the government, with its host of spies. Hence, Qohelet warns his audience to be careful with what they say: "Even in your intimacy do not disparage a king, nor in the bedroom disparage a rich person, for a bird of the sky may carry the utterance and a winged-creature may report any matter" (10:20). The instruction here echoes a passage in the *Proverbs of Ahiqar*, a text dated to the second half of the fifth century:

[My] son, do not c[ur]se the day until you have seen [nig]ht,
Do n[ot] let it come upon your mind,
since their e[yes] and their ears are everywhere.
As regards your mouth, watch yourself;
Let it not be [their] prey.
Above all watchfulness, watch your mouth,
and against him who [is listening] harden (your) heart;
for a word is a bird and one who releases it is without sens[e].

(see *TAD* III, 1.1.80–82)

Both Ecclesiastes and the sage of Ahiqar are probably alluding to the network of spies that the Persian government instituted. The Greek sources refer to secret agents of the Persian empire known as "the king's eyes" and "the king's ears" (see Notes at 10:20).

Elsewhere in the book, Qohelet paints a picture of a citizenry terrified of the arbitrary power of the rulers (Eccl 8:2–5). Commentators sometimes suppose that this passage reflects the conditions of the Ptolemaic period. But the best parallel in fact comes from the Aramaic *Proverbs of Ahiqar*, a literary text found among the Aramaic papyri at Elephantine (see *TAD* III, 1.1.84–90).

Qohelet taught at a time when the average citizen felt vulnerable and powerless before the rich and the political elite. So when the author speaks of humanity's helplessness before the whim of the sovereign deity, he draws on the social experiences of his audience: "Whatever happens has already been designated; the course of human beings is known, and they cannot dispute with the one who is stronger than they" (6:10).

Such was the social world of Qohelet and his audience. It was an unpredictable epoch, a period full of opportunities and risks. Theirs was a world of money, commerce, and investment. It was also a world of loans, mortgages, and foreclosures. For the ordinary citizen — the smallholder, the homesteader, the worker — there was much about which to worry, but not much about which one could be certain. No doubt the many success stories of those who went from rags to riches — like the case of Ribat the slave in Nippur who became rich, or the case of the poor man who went forth from prison to be king — must have given hope to multitudes. As Qohelet saw it, envy drove people to toil and "the pursuit of wind" (see 4:4–6). The reality of the Persian period economy is that individuals were caught in the tides of swift political and economic changes, and most people were helpless in the face of all that was happening.

The discoveries at Mugharet Abu Shinjeh, a cave in Wadi Daliyeh, provide us with an unforgettable vignette. Archaeologists have uncovered in that cave the skeletons of some two hundred men, women, and children, along with scores of bullae, exquisite gold signet rings, personal jewelry, remnants of fine linen, and an assemblage of coins that must have been part of a much larger hoard. There were also found the now famous papyri, all dating to the period 375–335 B.C.E., all of which are legal and administrative documents recording various economic transactions. These are the remains of a group of wealthy Samarians who had participated in a conspiracy against Alexander the Great when he moved on from Palestine to Egypt. When Alexander's army returned, this group of rebels fled to the cave, where they were eventually hunted down and massacred. These Samarian proprietors brought their families and all their money, jewelry, various title deeds to movable and immovable assets to this cave. And there they perished with all their wealth — a veritable testimony to the truth of what Qohelet taught in their generation or a little before: no one is a proprietor over death and no one can send a substitute to that decisive "battle." Wealth is to be enjoyed in the present and people cannot bring their wealth with them when they die. Indeed, "everything is vanity."

VI. AUTHORSHIP, INTEGRITY, AND STRUCTURE
AUTHORSHIP

The superscription attributes the book to "Qohelet, the Davidide, a king in Jerusalem" (1:1). Since Hebrew *ben-Dāwīd* may be most readily interpreted as "the son of David" and since Solomon is said to have been a patron and author of wisdom materials (1 Kgs 4:32–34 [Heb 5:12–14]; Prov 1:1; 10:1; 25:1), it is easy to see why the book traditionally has been attributed to him. Moreover, there are several allusions to Solomon in the fictional royal autobiography in 1:12–2:11

(see Comment at 1:1 and 1:12). It is probably the intent of the author to evoke memory of Solomon, the wise king *par excellence* and the best example of one who has it all.

The language of the book does not permit a Solomonic date, however. Indeed, it is precisely in the royal autobiography that one finds a Persian loanword, *pardēsîm* "parks" (2:5). This means that the book can be dated no earlier than the mid-fifth century B.C.E., for there are no clear examples of Persian loanwords in the Hebrew Bible prior to that time. Furthermore, the fiction of kingship is not continued beyond the second chapter. In fact, it is clear from a number of passages that the author looks at kingship from a distance and not as an insider of the royal court (4:13–16); he gives advice on how to behave before the king, rather than how to be king (8:1–6; 10:16–20). It is also unlikely, given the understanding of kingship in the ancient Near East, that a king would point to injustice in the land (3:16; 4:1–2; 5:8 [Heb v 7]) or to the prevailing social instability (10:4–7). The author seems to speak more as an observer and a critic of society than as a ruler. Solomonic authorship of the book is simply implausible.

The epilogue (12:9–14) refers to the author not as a king but as a *ḥākām* "a sage" (12:9). Accordingly, the author was a teacher, concerned with articulating his message felicitously and truthfully (12:10). He was among the *ḥăkāmîm* "sages" whose words were like goads and implanted pricks (12:11).

Beyond that fact, we know practically nothing about the author personally. We can only speculate if being *ḥākām* "a sage" meant that he was a professional teacher in some sort of wisdom "school." There is no mention of his pupils anywhere. Instead, he is said to have taught "the people," but we are not told of the specific context in which he taught. Certainly it is difficult to know anything about Qohelet's social background. We do not know if he was an aristocrat (so Gordis, Crüsemann, Whybray) or if he was a middle-class individual (Harrison). Wisdom is not the prerogative of a particular economic or social status. As Qohelet himself tells us, "bread does not belong to the wise, nor wealth to the intelligent, nor favor to the clever" (9:11). There are sages even among the lower classes, people who are despised (9:13–16). Wisdom knows no social class. Or as it is said in *The Instruction of Ptahhotep*: "Good speech is more hidden than greenstone, yet it may be found among the maids at the grindstones" (AEL I, p. 63). It has been suggested that 7:21 shows that Qohelet was a slave-owner and the saying there is believed to betray an arrogant upper-class attitude (so Crüsemann, Crenshaw). But the text may indicate only the background of the audience, not the author, and, in any case, slavery is not the issue in that passage (see Notes at 7:21). So we do not know anything about Qohelet's socioeconomic status. In fact, we are not even sure if *qōhelet* is the real name of the author (see Notes at 1:1) or if it is merely an epithet, as the form *haqqōhelet* "*the* Qohelet" may suggest (7:27 [emended text]; 12:8).

There has been some debate about where the author might have composed the work. Although Egypt has been proposed as a possible candidate for that honor (notably by Humbert), there is something of a consensus in more recent commentaries that the author wrote in Palestine. The rapidly changing weather conditions (1:6; 11:4; 12:2) make sense for Palestine but not for Egypt. The allusion to the north-south direction of the winds, too, is appropriate in reference to Palestine (see Song 4:16; Prov 25:23; Job 37:9, 17; Sir 43:20; Luke 12:55). Moreover, the text refers to reservoirs (2:6) and wells (12:6). These are typical of Palestine but not of Egypt. Importantly, the mention of "almond" presupposes familiarity with the tree (see Notes at 12:5), which makes the Palestinian setting probable. The almond tree was foreign to Egypt, but almonds were recognized as one of the choice products of Palestine (Gen 43:11). The traditional assumption that the book was composed in Palestine, thus, seems correct (see Hertzberg, "Palästinische Bezüge im Buche Kohelet," pp. 113–24; Bishop, "A Pessimist in Palestine," pp. 33–41).

The author of Ecclesiastes was an unknown sage who took the pen name Qohelet, a name that may have meant "Gatherer" (see Notes at 1:1). He probably composed his work in Palestine some time between the second half of the fifth and the first half of the fourth centuries B.C.E.

INTEGRITY

Related to the question of authorship is the issue of the book's integrity. A sensitive critic will no doubt notice that the author usually refers to himself in the first person, except in 1:1, 1:2, 7:27, and in 12:9–14. For most scholars the voice that refers to Qohelet in the third person is editorial. The epilogue not only refers to Qohelet in the third person, but also commends him and his work and, some say, adds a corrective or two to balance the author's supposedly radical point of view. In short, with the exception of 7:27, the first-person accounts are framed by third-person remarks. M. V. Fox has pointed out that similar framing techniques are found in other ancient Near Eastern texts ("Frame-Narrative," pp. 85–106). These parallels indicate that the third-person retrospective style in the epilogue is not necessarily indicative of a perspective that is different from the rest of the book. This is the point that Fox makes. Indeed, in the view of Fox, the voice in the "frame-narrative" is that of the author of the book, although the author elsewhere assumes the character of "Qohelet." Accordingly, it is one and the same person who produced the first-person accounts and the third-person "frame-narrative" (essentially 1:1–2; 7:27; 12:9–14). This conclusion is plausible but not necessary. It is equally plausible that in Ecclesiastes, as in the parallel texts from Egypt, an editor was responsible for collocating the materials and putting at the end a stamp of authenticity or an apology for reading the book in question.

Whether Qohelet is the actual author of the book, or only the persona of the author, as Fox would have it, the perspective of the book is one and the same as the framework. The only exception is the very end of the epilogue, 12:13b–14, where we have a call to obey God's commandments and an allusion to eschatological judgment—both new elements in the book. Indeed, 12:13a sounds decisively final: "end of the matter; everything has been heard." This may have been the original ending of the book to which an additional text (12:13b–14) was tacked on (see Notes at 12:13).

Beyond the tension between the third-person and first-person accounts, the most serious questions concerning the integrity of Ecclesiastes revolve around the contradictions. Indeed, the apparent internal inconsistencies almost caused the book to be rejected as a canonical work: "the sages sought to withdraw the book of Qohelet because its words are mutually contradictory" (*b. Šabb.* 30b). It may be argued that for most of this century the integrity of the book has been the essential question in the study of Ecclesiastes (Crenshaw, "Qohelet in Current Research," p. 43). The problem is that there seem to be a number of inconsistent, even diametrically opposite, points of view within the book: wisdom is denigrated (1:17–18; 2:15–16), but it is also affirmed as an advantage in some instances (2:13; 7:11, 19; 9:16–18); the significance of pleasure is questioned (2:2–3, 10–11), but pleasure is repeatedly commended (2:24–26; 5:18–20 [Heb vv 17–19]; 8:15); Qohelet says he hates life (2:17), but other passages affirm life (9:4–6; 11:7); God does not seem to intervene in human affairs (8:10, 14, 17; 9:2–3), but there are texts that speak of divine retribution (3:17; 5:6 [Heb v 5]; 8:12–13; 11:9). Positive and negative attitudes seem to exist side by side.

To many scholars, the inconsistencies may be explained as evidence of multiple sources, interpolations, expanded annotations, and the like. In this view, the radical and pessimistic message of the "original Qohelet" has been countered later by more orthodox glossators. There is no agreement, however, as to the number of editorial hands involved. An extreme position is represented by C. G. Siegfried (*Prediger und Hoheslied*, pp. 2–12), who discerned several glossators adding to the work of the "original Qohelet," whom he designated as Q[1]: a Sadducee who had come under the influence of Epicureanism (Q[2]), a sage (Q[3]), a *ḥāsîd* (Q[4]), and a number of others responsible for various insertions (Q[5]). In addition, Siegfried maintained that there were two epilogists (E[1] and E[2]) and two editors (R[1] and R[2]). Thus, there are no fewer than nine different strands in the book. Similar, though more moderate, theories have undergirded the work of many modern commentators, notably McNeile, Barton, Podechard, Ellermeier, and Lauha. This is clearly an influential approach. Yet it is strange that a book that at its core is supposedly so problematic to the orthodox would not have been suppressed. Instead, such theories assume, the glossators sought to make it more acceptable by their repeated corrections. But if so, the glossators were clumsy and largely unsuccessful. As Fox observes: (a) the elimination of the putative additions more often than not leaves syntactical and logical gaps in the text, (b) the supposed glosses do not fulfill their alleged purposes, (c) the glossators have failed inasmuch as the skeptical or pessimistic character remains blatant, and (d) excising does not result in consistency (*Contradictions*, pp. 24–25).

Moreover, the dissonance between these putative conservative statements and the central teachings of the book is frequently exaggerated. The modern interpreter may be inclined to classify the statements in the book as either positive or negative, either optimistic or pessimistic. But those are categories that the interpreter imposes on the text. For Qohelet, pleasure is regrettably ephemeral, and so it must be enjoyed whenever one has the opportunity. Wisdom is not always reliable and it does not always give one advantage, but it is appropriate to apply wisdom whenever possible (10:10). Life in general, too, is imperfect; it may even be miserable. For Qohelet, however, one still has the possibility for pleasure in life, whereas death is the end of all possibilities. Qohelet does not think of these issues in terms of "either-or" propositions. As one learns from the Chinese concept of *yin-yang*, life can be like that: sometimes there is too much *yin*, sometimes too much *yang*, but both are ever present.

In some cases, there are inconsistencies only when the text is read a certain way. For instance, 3:17, 8:12b–13, and 11:9c are commonly attributed to orthodox glossators on the grounds that Qohelet never speaks of *future* judgment, since he repeatedly insists that no one knows what will happen in the future. Yet it is not necessary to assume that Qohelet is thinking of the certainty of judgment in the eschatological sense. It is true that divine judgment is in view, but the time for it is not specified. Thus, *yišpōṭ hā'ĕlōhîm* "God will judge" (3:17) conveys no more the certainty of future divine action than *yĕbaqqēš hā'ĕlōhîm* "God will seek" (3:15) or *ya'ăśeh hā'ĕlōhîm* "God does" (3:13). In fact, *yišpōṭ hā'ĕlōhîm* "God will judge" may be compared with *yiqṣōp hā'ĕlōhîm* "God will be angry" in 5:5 (Eng v 6), in a text that refers to divine retribution and one that is generally accepted as original to Qohelet. The point of 3:17 is not the outcome of eschatological judgment but the freedom of God to act whenever it is appropriate. By the same token, 11:9c is not so much about a certain outcome in the future, as it is about human accountability to God. Qohelet never denies divine oversight and judgment, although he believes that no one can tell precisely what will happen in the hereafter. The message conveyed in 11:9 is in fact entirely consistent with Qohelet's emphasis elsewhere in the book: it is the lot of human beings to enjoy themselves whenever possible and, hence, God calls people into account for living according to that divine will for enjoyment (see Comment at 11:9).

In the case of 8:12–13, the author seems to be quoting a standard view (as indicated by the words "for even though I know that . . .") only to show that reality often contradicts what mortals believe to be normative or self-evident. This is a good example of what Hertzberg calls a *zwar-aber Aussage*, a "yes-but" argumentation (*Prediger*, pp. 30–31). That is, Qohelet admits for the purpose of argument that a certain proposition is true (*zwar*), but (*aber*) he proceeds to qualify it, showing how the truth applies only in a limited context or in exceptional cases. The *aber*-situation shows the inadequacy of the *zwar*-proposition. This kind of argumentation Hertzberg finds in numerous passages in the book.

In a variation of the *zwar-aber* approach, a number of scholars maintain that Qohelet sometimes quotes traditional sayings or cites an opponent, whether real or imaginary, and then goes on to refute their positions (so Gordis, Michel) or to radically reinterpret them (so Whybray). An even more specific version of this approach maintains that the book actually contains dialogues between Qohelet and some unnamed dialogue partner (so Perry). Fox objects that the quotation hypothesis is too facile a solution, for in most cases it is impossible to prove that a quotation is in place ("Identification of Quotations"). Fox demands, therefore, that there be stricter controls in identifying quotations. Accordingly, one should expect the mention of another person, a shift in grammatical number or person, some reference to speech, or the like. Fox's own approach is to deal with the contradictions head-on and to come to terms with the terrain of the text "with all its bumps and clefts, for they are not mere flaws, but the essence of the landscape" (*Contradictions*, p. 28).

Concerning the nature of the book, it is perhaps not amiss to observe that pessimistic literature in the ancient Near East often explores contradictory viewpoints deliberately, sometimes by means of dialogues. Thus, the Akkadian *Dialogue of Pessimism* is presented in the form of an exchange between a master and his slave, in the course of which the master changes his mind over and over again (*BWL*, pp. 139–50). The consideration of various alternatives leads eventually to utter despair at the futility of life. In the *Babylonian Theodicy*, various positions are explored through cycles of speeches by various individuals (*BWL*, pp. 63–91). Such texts were no doubt occasioned by the inadequacy of the standard explanations for human experiences of anomie. Hence these texts give voice to various points of view.

Since in Ecclesiastes different voices are not identified, however, one should perhaps find better parallels in the Egyptian wisdom text known as *The Dispute Between a Man and His Ba*, where conflicting points of view are presented in the form of a dialogue between a man and his inner-self (see *AEL* I, pp. 163–69). Essentially the man is engaged in a debate with himself. In another text, *The Complaints of Khakheperre-Sonb*, one reads of conversations that a man has with his heart (*AEL* I, pp. 145–49). This kind of inner exploration may provide some clue to the interpretation of some of Qohelet's contradictions. As in the Egyptian texts, Qohelet refers to his conversations with his heart or to his heart's perspective, as if the heart were an independent entity: "I spoke with my heart" (1:16; 2:1; 3:17, 18); "and my heart observed" (1:16). If the book as a whole is any reflection of the author's inner struggles, his debates with himself, one should not be surprised that various perspectives are considered at once, even contradictory ones.

Be that as it may, it is evident that to Qohelet there are all sorts of inconsistencies in the world. That, indeed, is one of his main points: that the real world is full of inconsistencies and even flagrant contradictions that cannot be explained away. The world is not an orderly place, and meaning is not always discernible, despite the best human efforts. So Qohelet frequently speaks of what he observes or knows to be true, but he quickly points out that there are inconsistencies, even outright contradictions. In many instances, he sets the reader up for the main point in his argument, namely, the very fact of contradiction. In this connection one notes that he sometimes uses typical setup phrases: "I have observed that . . ." (2:13), "for even though I know that . . ." (8:12), and "I thought . . ." (9:16). In 2:13, the setup phrase "and I have observed that . . ." is immediately countered by "but I also know that . . ." (see Notes at 2:14). Qohelet's observation that the wise have advantage over fools (2:13) is contradicted by his own recognition that in death the wise and the fool are equal (2:14). The first observation refers to what is generally true (that the wise are generally better off than fools), but the second statement maintains that there are exceptions to the rule, at least inasmuch as death is a leveler. Here the author seems to be engaged in a disputation in his own mind—a dispute with his inner-self. So he concludes in his heart—perhaps he means literally *with* his heart—that this matter is elusive. It is *hebel* "vanity" precisely because of the irreconcilable contradiction; the situation cannot be grasped.

The contrary view is sometimes clearly enough marked, as in 2:14 ("but I also know"), but sometimes the counterpoint is discernible only in context, as in 8:12–14 and 9:16–17. In 8:12–14, the contradiction is indicated by the mere assertion: "there is *hebel*." In this case *hebel* ("vanity") is, again, referring to something that is elusive, something that cannot be grasped. Life is like that to Qohelet: it is full of inconsistencies that mortals cannot resolve. Hertzberg is correct to recognize that we have a *zwar-aber Aussage* here. Yet the purpose of the "yes-but" formulation is not to resolve the contradiction and show consistency. On the contrary, the intent is to call attention to the contradiction. Qohelet does not mean to say that there is no contradiction, even though he may have wished that were the case. He is not merely quoting someone else's point of view to refute it. As Fox observes, what Hertzberg regards as the *zwar*-element (what Qohelet grants to be true) is as much Qohelet's own belief as anyone else's: "The 'aber'—the recognition of anomalies—*imposes* itself on Qohelet, who would prefer to retain the rule" (*Contradictions*, p. 22). Contradictions in life and in the world are a reality to Qohelet.

In 9:16, Qohelet introduces an axiom: "so I thought, wisdom is better than might." Then he immediately relativizes the saying with no indication in Hebrew that his thought has shifted: "but (*wĕ-*) the wisdom of the commoner is despised and [the sage's] words are not heeded." By the same token, the statement "wisdom is better than weapons of war" in 9:18 is apparently a traditional saying or a self-evident truth that Qohelet accepts, although he points to a contradiction: "but (*wĕ-*) a single offender destroys much good." In such cases, the interpreter desires clear indicators of direct quotations or allusions, and one looks for linguistic indicators of shifts in thought. But there are hardly any markers. Still there are enough cues from the text that one should not merely assume contradictory viewpoints within the book as secondary accretions or signs of editorial tampering. Rather, it may indeed be the intention of the author for the reader to wrestle with the contradictions, as one does with life itself. For Qohelet, the realities of the world are not easy to grasp. They are contradictory and incomprehensible. Everything is ephemeral and illusory—like *hebel* ("vanity"), literally, "a breath, whiff, puff, vapor." Moreover, Qohelet seems to make the point that any apparent orderliness of the world is only an impression, for upon closer examination one finds evidence to the contrary. So there are certain literary setups throughout the book. He sometimes gives the impression of saying one thing, leads the reader down an expected path, only to show that all is not as one might expect. Already in the introductory poem (1:3–11) one sees how he constructs a poem with a series of active participles, and develops his argument as if making the case that there are significant activities going on in the universe, but then the reader is led to the surprising conclusion that "there is nothing new under the sun."

The impression of significant activities is only that: an impression that quickly disappears. Through such a rhetorical device, then, he leads his reader to recognize that what one perceives at first glance may not necessarily be the reality. It is as if one experiences *hebel* itself. One's initial impression quickly dissipates like mist.

STRUCTURE

Scholarly opinion regarding the structure of the book falls between two poles. There are those who find no order whatsoever, and those who discern a carefully constructed structure (see Schoors, "La structure littéraire de Qoheleth," pp. 91–93). An extreme example of the first position is the elaborate reconstruction of G. Bickell (*Prediger*, pp. 1–45). For Bickell, Ecclesiastes cannot be understood as it stands. He posits that what we have now is originally part of a larger collection of Qohelet's thoughts written on separate fascicles consisting of separate pages (*Blätter*), each containing 525 letters. Some of the fascicles fell out when the string that held them together broke, and the loose pages were then picked up by someone who did not know how to put them back together. The resulting inconsistency then prompted various insertions later on. Hence, we now have an authentic but disorderly collection. Bickell's reconstruction has found few supporters, and rightly so. Apart from the fact that it is anachronistic to think of Qohelet writing on loose pages rather than on a scroll (leaf-books were first used in the first centuries of the common era), and the fact that the Ecclesiastes fragments found at Qumran clearly belonged to scrolls, one wonders why anyone would have preserved a document that is as utterly incomprehensible as Bickell suggests. But Bickell is by no means alone in seeing disorder in the book. Other scholars, too, believe that Ecclesiastes is without any structure. For Galling, the book is a loose collection of twenty-seven separate units ("Prediger," pp. 76–77). Lauha takes the same view, identifying thirty-six discrete units (*Koheleth*, pp. 4–7). Still others agree that there are larger units loosely held together, but they find no deliberate ordering of the material.

Of those who discern an overarching structure, there are some who argue for a basically logical development (e.g., Coppens, Schoors) and others who find an architectonic design (e.g., Wright, Rousseau, Lohfink). The difficulty in most cases, however, is that one must find the right labels to place on each literary unit and, if the labels are appropriately suggestive, then one may speak of a structure. J. A. Loader's analysis of the book's "polar structures" is particularly susceptible to this criticism. Apart from the acceptance of all that he calls "pole" or "contrapole," one must further accept his labels for each of the units in order to find his overall structure compelling (*Polar Structures*, p. 112). Despite the many new insights that one gains from Loader's analysis, the resulting structure — with its series of interlocking brackets at several levels — must give one pause. One wonders why any author, ancient or modern, would construct a work that is so structurally complex.

Lohfink proposes a simpler structure (*Kohelet*, p. 10). In his view, Qohelet was influenced by the philosophical diatribes of the Cynics and, consequently, appropriates the Greek rhetorical device known as the palindrome. The resulting structure consists of balanced elements, allowing one to read from either the beginning or the end of the document and still arrive at the same point. The structure is, thus, basically chiastic. Here, again, the persuasiveness of the proposal depends largely on the acceptability of the rubrics.

Probably the most ambitious and influential study of the structure of Ecclesiastes is the series of articles by A. G. Wright ("The Riddle of the Sphinx," pp. 313–34; "The Riddle of the Sphinx Revisited," pp. 38–51; "Additional Numerical Patterns," pp. 32–43). In these essays, Wright highlights numerous signs of a deliberate design, notably the division of the book into two halves, the use of inclusions, and the strategic placement of key phrases and catchwords. But arguably the most ingenious of his proposals is the possible use of employment of numerological patterns. Among his arguments, one notes the following:

1. The word *hbl* ("vanity"), whose numerical value in Hebrew is 37, is found 37 times in the book, if one omits the "textually dubious" occurrence of *hblym* in 5:6 (Eng 5:7) or the second occurrence of *hbl* in 9:9, a text that may contain a dittography. It is unclear why Wright regards 5:6 (Eng 5:7) as textually dubious, but the case for a shorter text in 9:9 is supported by some ancient textual witnesses. If he is correct, the significance of this observation is heightened by the fact that *hbl* is the key word in Ecclesiastes.
2. The phrase *dbry* "words of" in 1:1 has the numerical value of 216. This is the number of verses in the book, excluding the epilogue (12:9–14). The word is significant because the editor uses it three times in the epilogue (12:10 [twice], 11).
3. The word *hbl* occurs in the singular three times in the motto of the book — 1:2 and in 12:8. The total numerical value of the three is 111, which is the number of verses at the midpoint of the entire book (222 verses, including the epilogue).
4. The phrase *hbl hblym hkl hbl* "vanity of vanities, all is vanity" in the second half of 1:2 has the total numerical value of 216. There are precisely 216 verses in the book, not counting the epilogue (12:9–14).
5. The *wytr* in 12:9, 12 is important because the letter *w* has the numerical value of 6 and the number of verses in the epilogue is also 6. Thus, *wytr* may be interpreted as "six additional."

The numerology is clever, but finally unconvincing. Even if one grants that the ancients (who did not mark their verses) happened to have had the same ideas about versification as in the medieval period (when the verses were first marked), one must question what Wright chooses to count and what he does not. In number 2 above, Wright takes only *dbry* to be coded, but not the rest of 1:1. To be sure *dbry* "words of" appears thrice in the epilogue, but the name Qohelet appears twice. Why is the first datum significant but not the second? In number

4, Wright counts only the second half of 1:2, but not the first. To arrive at the figure of 111 (number 3), he includes the *hbl* in the beginning of the verse (which is not included in number 4), excludes the two plural forms (*hblym*), and includes the epilogue (not included in number 4) in the count of verses in the book. The six additional verses of the epilogue are included in number 3 (111 is half of 222), but not for numbers 2 and 4. As for *wytr* (number 5), Wright counts only *w* as a numeral, but not *ytr*. In short, the numerical patterns proposed are not compelling for the lack of methodological controls.

Despite the problems posed by the various proposals, there are clues that the book was not merely a loose collection of aphorisms. Most of these have been noted by Wright. Indeed, the epilogue commends Qohelet as a sage who had been very careful in his work: "he listened and deliberated; he edited many proverbs. Qohelet tried to find felicitous words and he wrote words of truth rightly." Moreover, the motto of the book is stated in 1:2 and repeated almost verbatim in 12:8. Thus, apart from the superscription (1:1) and the epilogue (12:9–14), the sweeping *hebel*-judgment marks the beginning and the end of the book. The opening poem (1:3–11) is also matched at the end by a concluding poem (12:3–7). Furthermore, it is clear that 6:10 is the midpoint of the book, as the Masoretes note in the margins and at the end of the book. Wright and others have observed that there are 222 verses in the book, 111 in 1:1–6:9 and 111 in 6:10–12:14. Whether the ancients had conceived of the verses in the same way is beside the point. The fact is that the book is divided into two halves of more or less the same lengths. D. N. Freedman has pointed out to me that 6:9b may be the precise midpoint or pivot of the entire book, for apart from the five Hebrew words *gam-zeh hebel ûrĕʿût rûaḥ* "this, too, is vanity and pursuit of wind" (an appropriate phrase for a pivot!), we have precisely the same number of words in the first half of the book as in the second: 1,491 words in the first half (1:1–6:9a) and 1,491 words in the second (6:10–12:14). This is a remarkable coincidence, but only that. I do not believe it was the author's or the editor's intention to produce the exact number of words in each half: the twofold structure is deliberate, but the matching numbers that Freedman notices are a coincidence. One does not need to prove numerological pattern or demonstrate mathematical precision in order to have a structure.

Wright points out that the first half is marked by the recurrence of the expressions "(this is) *hebel*" and "a pursuit of wind." This is certainly true for the phrase "a pursuit of wind" (*rĕʿût rûaḥ/raʿyôn rûaḥ*), which appears a total of seven times, all in the first half of the book (1:14; 2:11, 17, 26; 4:4, 6; 6:9). The *hebel*-judgment is not as consistent, however, for it appears also in the second half: 7:6; 8:10, 14. Wright also observes that the second half is dominated by expressions of not finding (*lōʾ māṣāʾ* "not find") and not knowing (*lōʾ yādaʿ, ʾên yôdēaʿ*). According to him, the first ("not find") is concentrated in 6:10–8:17 (7:14, 24, 28 [twice]; 8:17 [thrice]), the second ("not know") in 9:1–11:6 (9:1, 5; 10:12, 14, 15; 11:2, 5, 6). But the occurrences of these expressions are not so strictly confined: *lōʾ māṣāʾ* "not find" also appears in 3:11, *lōʾ yādaʿ* "not know" is in 4:13; 6:5; 8:5; *ʾên yôdēaʿ* "not know" is in 4:17 (Eng 5:1); 8:7. It is also peculiar that Wright should count the rhetorical question *mî yimṣā'ennû* "who can find it?" (7:24) as an expression of not finding, but not *mî yôdēaʿ* "who knows?" in 6:11 as an expression of not knowing. Wright is no doubt correct that there are strong clues that there is a structure in the book, but the book probably does not have the intricate design that he and others proffer.

The most thorough and generally persuasive analysis of the literary structure, in my judgment, is the work of F. J. Backhaus (*"Denn Zeit und Zufall trifft sie alle,"* pp. 1–332). On formal, semantic, and contextual grounds, Backhaus argues that the body of Ecclesiastes may be divided into four compositions: (1) 1:3–3:22, (2) 4:1–6:9, (3) 6:10–8:17, and (4) 9:1–12:8. Despite differences in detail, this is the structure that I follow, except that I would argue that the first block includes 1:2–4:16 and the second block includes 5:1–6:9 (Heb 4:17–6:9). The change in tone, from the indicative to the imperative, marks the transition from the first block to the second.

The book is divided into two halves of roughly equal length (1:2–6:9; 6:10–12:8). Each half includes two large blocks of material (Part I: 1:2–4:16 and 5:1–6:9 [Heb 4:17–6:9]; Part II: 6:10–8:17; 9:1–12:8). The first block in each half presents a certain situation that people face, while the second contains mostly practical advice on how to cope with that situation. Reflection is followed by ethics. Thus, 1:2–4:16 makes the case that everything is ephemeral and nothing is ultimately reliable. Human beings cannot hope to change the nature of things, for everything is in the hand of a sovereign deity. All that people strive to attain is *hebel* "vanity" and a pursuit of wind. Then, in 5:1–6:9 (Heb 4:17–6:9), one finds advice on how to cope with the situations where human beings are not in control. Clearly 1:2–11 serves as the introduction to the first block, the first half of the book, as well as for the entire book.

Like the first half, the second begins with an extended presentation of a situation. The case is made that wisdom is elusive and no one knows what is good. Righteousness, too, is elusive and human beings are left vulnerable in an arbitrary world. Then, in the second block, advice is given on how one should live when there are forces in the world beyond one's control.

The book of Ecclesiastes may, therefore, be analyzed as follows:

1:1 Superscription

Part I

I.A. Reflection: Everything Is Ephemeral and Unreliable
I.A.1.	1:2–11	Preface
I.A.2.	1:12–2:26	Nothing Is Ultimately Reliable
I.A.3.	3:1–22	Everything Is in the Hand of God
I.A.4.	4:1–16	Relative Good Is Not Good Enough

I.B. Ethics: Coping with Uncertainty
I.B.1.	5:1–7 (Heb 4:17–5:6)	Attitude Before God
I.B.2.	5:8–6:9 (Heb 5:7–6:9)	Enjoyment, Not Greed

Part II

II.A. Reflection: Everything Is Elusive
    II.A.1   6:10–7:14   No One Knows What Is Good
    II.A.2.   7:15–29   Righteousness and Wisdom Are Elusive
    II.A.3.   8:1–17   It's an Arbitrary World

II.B. Ethics: Coping with Risks and Death
    II.B.1.   9:1–10   *Carpe Diem*
    II.B.2.   9:11–10:15   The World Is Full of Risks
    II.B.3.   10:16–11:6   Living with Risks
    II.B.4.   11:7–12:8   Conclusion

12:9–13a Epilogue
12:13b–14 Additional Material

VII. MESSAGE

In presenting the message of a biblical book, there is always a temptation to over-systematize. One is inclined to organize the materials around a central theme (e.g., "all is vanity") and show how that theme is the point of the author. Alternatively, commentators sometimes choose key concepts to discuss: e.g., vanity, toil, joy, wisdom, death, and so forth. This approach avoids the imposition of a theological system on the book. Yet it is not entirely satisfactory, for the author's message becomes overly fragmented. It seems preferable, therefore, first to consider the content of Ecclesiastes more or less as it is presented. That is to say, we give priority to the book's own order of discussion before we step back to reevaluate its message systematically.

CONTENT

The obvious starting point in the consideration of Qohelet's content is the notion of *hebel*, traditionally translated as "vanity." The importance of this term is indicated by the fact that it is part of the thematic statements that frame the main body of the book: "absolute vanity . . . everything is vanity" (1:2; 12:8). The word is the first that one encounters after the superscription (1:1). It appears thirty-eight times in the book. Its literal meaning is "breath, whiff, puff, steam," or the like, a meaning that one should certainly keep in mind as one interprets Ecclesiastes. It refers to anything that is superficial, ephemeral, insubstantial, incomprehensible, enigmatic, inconsistent, or contradictory. Something that is *hebel* cannot be grasped or controlled. It may refer to something that one encounters or experiences for only a moment, but it cannot be grasped — neither physically nor intellectually.

The preface (1:2–11) introduces the book. It paints a picture of a universe that is full of activities by the elements of nature — the sun, the wind, the streams — and by human beings. The author uses a lively style to convey the vigor of all that seems to be going on in the cosmos. But in the end, nothing new happens. The world is an unchanging stage on which the drama of natural and human activities is taking place. No advantage is gained despite all the activities, for everything is "vanity." Here one is introduced to two key concepts in the book: "toil" and "advantage" (1:3). The first refers generally to physical or intellectual struggle to achieve some end or other. The second concept refers to the additional "edge" or "surplus" that one may expect as a return for the investment of one's resources, including the investment of labor (toil), or for the possession of certain "capital," like wisdom. The preface, thus, answers the thematic question in 1:3 in the negative: the mortal toils but does not gain any advantage. This is one sign for Qohelet that "all is vanity."

The theme of "vanity" is continued in 1:12–2:26. Here the author adopts the ancient Near Eastern literary genre of the fictional royal autobiography, the purpose of which typically was to exalt certain rulers as superior to all their contemporaries and predecessors. Such fictional royal autobiographies tended to call attention to the extraordinary statures of these rulers and to preserve their fame forever. Given the Israelite context, the author of Ecclesiastes chooses to evoke the memory of Solomon, a consummate wise king who had seen it all, knew it all, and had it all. Hence we have the traditional association of the entire book with his name (1:1). But the genre is only a rhetorical device employed ironically to show that everything is in fact "a vanity and a pursuit of wind" (see 1:14, 17; 2:1, 11, 15, 17, 19, 21, 23, 26). The genre, which must have been familiar to Qohelet's audience, heightens expectations that some exceptional people may be able to have it all. But the reader is, in the end, brought to the surprising conclusion that there are in fact no exceptions to the rule that "all is vanity and a pursuit of wind." Even a king, a wise and powerful ruler, is subject to the truth that nothing is permanent. Everything is ephemeral and nothing is ultimately reliable (1:12–2:11). Wisdom may give the wise some advantage, but the advantage is only a limited one. In the face of death, all mortals, whether wise or foolish, are equal, proving once again that nothing is finally reliable (2:12–17). Like wisdom, toil is also limited by the reality of death (2:18–23). Whatever material gain one may acquire through human efforts — that is, the fruit of one's toil — one cannot control it when one dies. Whatever one has acquired through toil must be left to others, who have not labored or may not be deserving. In fact, one's successor and heir may turn out to be a fool. Thus, the possibility of passing one's wealth to posterity is no way to have control over what one has. Immortality of any sort is impossible, for death is the fate of every mortal. Nothing that human beings may possess — wisdom, pleasure, success, progeny — can change that fact. Everything is ephemeral and is ultimately unreliable. In the face of this, then, people can only enjoy life's goodness as the opportunity presents itself. Even in this, however, human beings have no control. The possibility for joy is not determined by mortals: it is a gift of God, who decides who should have it and who should not (2:24–26). Human beings are caught in such a situation where they are not in control; only God is in charge — just like a sovereign ruler who alone determines who should be favored and who should be left out.

Continuing the thought of God's determination of events, the author introduces a catalogue on times and seasons (3:1–8). The rhythmic character of the catalogue gives the initial impression of a discernible pattern. Yet the pattern, if there ever was one, escapes most interpreters. Indeed, it may be the point of the poem that order in the world is elusive, despite the impressions to the contrary. The text is not about moments that people choose. It concerns events that people encounter in life, those that just happen whether one is ready or not. A prose commentary in 3:9–15 makes plain that it is God who determines the timing of events. The deity has imbued humanity with a recognition of the eternal (ʿôlām) — that which is not limited by time — but mortals can only respond moment by moment. So, again, enjoyment of the moment is urged. People are inclined to pursue that which they cannot grasp, but that is not their place so to do. Instead, it is God who will seek what is pursued (3:15). That is, all the vain pursuits that occupy human minds should be left to God.

By the same token, humanity may face anomie: there is no justice where justice ought to be found (3:16). To this situation, Qohelet's response is that judgment belongs to God alone: "God will judge" (3:17). So, too, the fate of humanity is entirely in the hand of God: God will judge (3:17), as God will seek (3:15). People cannot know what will happen to the human spirit after they die, for God has not given them to know such things (3:18–22). All that humanity can do, therefore, is to accept their divinely given portion and enjoy themselves whenever they can (3:22).

The series of "better-than" sayings (Tôb-Sprüche) in 4:1–16 is somewhat surprising because it comes at the heels of the conclusion in the preceding unit that there is "nothing better" for humanity but to find pleasure in all that they do. The initial impression created is that there are principles that one can learn better to cope with life. But by the time one gets to the end of the passage, the initial impression that there is relative good quickly disappears. One realizes that relative good, too, is nothing but "a vanity and a pursuit of wind" (4:4, 9, 16). Those things that are supposed to be better prove not to be reliable after all.

Given the situation that is described at length in 1:3–4:16, namely, that human beings are caught in a world where everything is ephemeral and nothing is reliable, Qohelet turns to give some advice on how one should conduct oneself in the face of such a situation (5:1–6:9 [Heb 4:17–6:9]). The tone changes. The predominantly descriptive language in 1:2–4:16 gives way to the language of instruction and direct command and exhortation. The author moves, thus, from reflection (1:2–4:16) to ethics (5:1–6:9 [Heb 4:17–5:9]). First, he speaks of proper attitude before God, emphasizing divine transcendence and counseling caution and restraint (5:1–7 [Heb 4:17–5:6]). Then, in a passage that is arranged chiastically, he advises people to enjoy themselves but not to be too greedy (see Comment at 5:8–6:9 [Heb 5:7–6:9]). This literary unit consists of matching elements: the insatiability of certain people (5:8–12 [Heb vv 7–11] // 6:7–9), people who cannot enjoy the present (5:13–17 [Heb vv 12–16] // 6:3–6), the good and bad of divine arbitration (5:18–19 [Heb vv 17–18] // 6:1–2). All of this leads to the pivotal exhortation in 5:20 (Heb v 19) about how people should behave in a world that is so unreliable and so full of contradictions: "Indeed, they should not much call to mind the days of their lives, for God gives a preoccupation through the joy of their hearts!" People must not brood over all their days of misery because God, like a sovereign ruler, has given them a grant. And that grant comes with the authorization to enjoy all that they have received. To be sure, God has given humanity a preoccupation that is terrible, as if to deliberately bother them (see Notes at 1:12; 3:10). But the same God has also given humanity a positive preoccupation through joy. Here is, as it were, an *answer* (*ma'ăneh*) to the implicit question of how human beings may cope in an uncertain world, a world over which they have no control. The only response possible to the fact that all is vanity is to accept the gift of joy whenever it is possible to do so. Thus ends Part One of the book.

Part Two begins with a reflection on God's determination of all that happens in the world and humanity's place in it (6:10–7:14). Again, God alone is in control. As for human beings, they are not in a position to challenge the divine. That point is made at the beginning (6:10–12) and the end of the literary unit (7:12–14): mortals can neither challenge what God has decided nor change the nature of things that God has made. The increase of human words only increases *hebel* "vanity" (6:11). The author means either that they increase nothing of significance, or that they only add to the contradictions. It is not the place of humanity to control, for no human knows what is good for all. Yet, sandwiched between the two parts of the theological framework (6:10–12 // 7:12–14), with its emphasis on human ignorance, is a series of "better-than" sayings (*Ṭôb Sprüche*) that appears to give guidance on what is good (7:1–12). Following the insistence that no one knows what is good (6:10–12), these "better-than" sayings are surely to be interpreted as a parody of all the many vain ramblings in which people indulge, as if they are in control of what would turn out right and what would not. In truth, people can only accept what the deity does, whether good or bad (7:13–14). They cannot know what will happen. Knowledge eludes humanity.

By the same token, wisdom and righteousness are elusive (7:15–29). The traditional doctrine of retribution is contradicted in reality. The righteous and the wicked do not always get what they deserve; sometimes the results are contrary to human expectations. Thus, the point is the same as in the preceding unit: no one knows what is good, no one knows what will happen in the future. The rules do not work. No amount of righteousness or wisdom will avert disaster. So one must not try to be too righteous or too wise. At the same time, one must not be too wicked or foolish. Extreme righteousness and wisdom are impossible, and wickedness and folly are realities from which human beings cannot escape. The only alternative is to accept human limitations: the one who fears God goes forth with both of them (7:18). The fear of God that accepts the reality of *both* righteousness-wisdom and wickedness-folly is the very opposite of the hubris that leads one to believe that one can find perfect righteousness and wisdom. No one can escape the grasp of wickedness-folly, for "there is no one on earth so righteous, who does only good and does not err" (7:20).

As righteousness is elusive, so is wisdom (7:23–24). Just as it is difficult to escape the hold of wickedness, so it is difficult to avoid folly. One may seek an accounting (*ḥešbôn*) of it all, as if wisdom and folly can easily be clearly identified on a ledger, but it is impossible to find the right balance. Qohelet seems to mix metaphors here, using the language of commerce and accounting, but also the language of a lover's pursuit. As other wisdom teachers have done (so Proverbs 1–9), he depicts folly and wisdom in terms of two women, the one a pernicious seductress and the other the elusive virtuous bride. For Qohelet, humanity is caught in a crazy game of seeking and finding. People are constantly chased by Folly, a dangerous "woman" from whose deadly snares they must try to escape; but only those favored by God can do so, while others inevitably are caught (7:26). At the same time, one tries desperately to find Wisdom, the "woman" who could save one from danger, but she is elusive (7:24, 28).

Inadequately equipped though people are (since wisdom eludes them), they live in an arbitrary world dominated by powerful people who impose their will on and exercise their power over others (8:1–9). In this world, the traditional doctrine of retribution does not seem to apply. Things do not always turn out as expected. The wicked are properly buried when they die, and even honored, while those who have acted justly are ignominiously abandoned when they die (8:10). Moreover, even if justice might be carried out, it is often so delayed that the wicked dare to keep doing evil (8:11). This situation poses a problem for those who believe in a doctrine of retribution (8:12–15). One may follow the traditions and say that things will turn out all right, that everyone will have their just recompense, but the truth is that reality contradicts the doctrine. The inexplicable fact — a *hebel* situation — is that there are righteous people who are treated as if they are wicked, and there are wicked people who are treated as if they are righteous (8:14). It is a ridiculous situation, one that Qohelet cannot grasp. He does not resolve the problem, however. Instead, he commends joy. He counsels enjoyment of life's pleasures, even amidst one's toil (8:15). He readily admits that the situation is beyond human control. Though one may struggle to understand the situation, one cannot discover anything. Observing all that happens, all that God has done, one realizes that no human can discern the rationale of it all (8:16–17). So this is the situation in which mortals find themselves. They live in an arbitrary world over which they have no control and about which they do not understand.

Qohelet says that everything is in the hand of God: the righteous and the wise and all their works, including all their love and hate (9:1). It is true that no one knows what is to come, except that all mortals suffer the same fate. Death is the fate that all mortals must face, regardless of their character: the righteous and the wicked, the good and the bad, the clean and the unclean, those who are religious and those who are not (9:2–3). It is unfair that the same fate comes to all, no matter how one has led one's life, but death does have this leveling effect. This may lead one to despair over life. But Qohelet says that life, for all its uncertainties, still provides one with some possibilities, whereas in death all is gone. In death there will no longer be hope, indeed, no longer any possibilities at all (9:3–6). For this reason, he counsels people to live fully — eat, drink, celebrate, and enjoy one's family — for this is humanity's assigned portion in life. One should vigorously do all that one is able, for in death one will no longer have opportunities to do anything (9:7–10).

Qohelet paints a picture of a world fraught with uncertainties and risks (9:11–10:15). It is a world in which there are no guarantees; what is expected may not happen (9:11–12). Success is not guaranteed for the swiftest, bravest, wisest, most intelligent, or most experienced. Everything is precarious. Everything in life is subject to chance. People do not control time and they do not determine their fate. Death may come suddenly, falling like a net or springing like a trap, without distinguishing the species or the readiness of its victims. No one is safe from the danger of that fate.

By the same token, there is no formula that will guarantee success (9:13–10:4). Even if it is true that wisdom is better than might, there are cases where wisdom will not be used and, therefore, cannot be effective (9:13–16). Likewise, wisdom may be better than the weapons of war, but all it takes is for one fool or one foul-up to destroy all the good that wisdom may have accomplished (9:17–18; 10:1–3). There are no fail-safe formulas in life. Yet, Qohelet does not leave the reader with the impression that wisdom is of no use whatsoever. True, it does not guarantee results, but there are times when it still may make a difference (10:4). Practical wisdom is not a formula for success, but it yet may do some good. It yet may win one some favor.

There are all kinds of risks in society (10:5–11). All sorts of political, social, and economic forces are at work, the results of which may be devastating. And they are beyond the individual's control. Social order may be completely disrupted (10:5–7). At the microlevel, too, one is vulnerable to all sorts of dangers, including everyday occupational hazards (10:8–9). In all these situations, there are no rules that one can follow that will guarantee one safety. To be sure, the practical application of wisdom may reduce the risks. Thus, one sharpens one's implements before taking on a task that requires the sharp tools (10:10). It is good, perhaps even necessary, to apply wisdom in order to navigate through the dangers that are part of life. Even so, there are problems that cannot be solved even with all the precautions and with the assistance of experts. Some accidents may be attributed to the lack of wisdom, such as the failure to prepare adequately. But other accidents cannot be explained in this way. People must do their best to cope with life's vicissitudes, but risks can never be eliminated altogether. So it is when a snake bites before it is charmed, or if the particular snake is of the variety that cannot be charmed even by the best "charmer" — the *ba'al hallāšôn* "master of the tongue" (10:11). Here, by calling the snake charmer the "master of the tongue," Qohelet may be making innuendos about all those "wise" people, who are really fools. They talk a lot and are recognized as the experts who have all the antidotes to life's problems, but they really do not know that much (10:12–15).

The sense of danger and uncertainty depicted in 9:11–10:15 is continued in the next unit, 10:16–11:6. The author speaks of risks in the political and economic realms. The first section of the literary unit (10:16–20) is exceedingly difficult to interpret. It is probably a warning to avoid political subversion, whether overt or covert. The second section (11:1–6) urges liberality despite economic uncertainties. In the face of political and economic dangers, caution is necessary (so 10:16–20), but too much caution is unnecessary (so 11:1–6). There are risks that one must avoid, but there are also times when one must take risks. Those who are too cautious will never do anything that needs to be done: "One who watches the wind will not sow; and one who looks at the clouds will not reap" (11:4). Interestingly, the text moves from the unpredictability of the *rûaḥ* "wind" (11:4), to the mystery of the *rûaḥ* "life-breath" entering the human body (11:5), and finally to the mystery of divine action (11:5). In the face of life's mysteries and the mystery of what God might do, Qohelet counsels spontaneity: sow at anytime, in the morning or in the evening (11:6). From a literary point of view, one sees the spontaneity (11:6) as a balance to the call for responsibility (10:16–18).

In the final literary unit of the second half of the book, 11:7–12:8, the author returns to the subject of enjoyment, even as he does in the final literary unit of the first half (5:8–6:9 [Heb 5:7–6:9]). However, whereas the call at the end of the first half is *not to remember* the days to come (5:20 [Heb v 19]), the message at the conclusion of the second half is *to remember* the days to come (11:8). The contrast is just as stark as in Deutero-Isaiah's call on the one hand *not to remember* the former days (Isa 43:18) and, on the other hand, *to remember* (Isa 46:8). There is no more contradiction in Ecclesiastes than there is in Deutero-Isaiah. The issue in both cases is correct remembering. For Deutero-Isaiah, correct remembering of the days gone by brings hope in the present. It is not the same as brooding. In Ecclesiastes, correct remembering of the days to come prompts one to enjoy. If remembering the days to come brings only misery, one must *not* remember the days to come (5:20 [Heb v 19]). Yet, if one remembers that there may be days of misery still to come, then one may enjoy while there is the possibility of doing so (11:3). In any case, the message is clear: people should enjoy life while they are able, for there will come a time when they will not be able to do so anymore (11:7–12:1). The reader is addressed as a youth (11:9), and the text moves from the days of one's youth ("the days of your prime") to the days of old age, which are said to be "the days of unpleasantness" (12:1).

Then, beginning in 12:2, the author speaks not of a period (*yāmîm* "days"), but of a coming time, a particular day (*yôm*). The language in 12:2 sounds ominously eschatological; it seems to be referring not just to the end of a person's life but to the end of human existence altogether, although there are hints within the poem itself that old age may lie in the background of the text. Apparently the author has reused an old poem about the travails of old age and infused it with eschatological allusions. He depicts a scene of the end-time: the skies darken, people are terrified, economic activities and social intercourse cease, unsavory creatures enter devastated human habitations, and nature comes to an end (12:3–5a). Then, at the climax of the poem, one sees a vision of a funeral and recognizes that it is humanity that is going to the grave (12:5b). It becomes clear, then, that it is not merely the end of the human life span of which the author speaks, but the end of human life in general. The text is not about the demise of an individual, but the end of humanity. The decisiveness of the end is depicted by various symbolisms of life being crushed and shattered: a durable lamp-stand is destroyed (see Notes at 12:6), pottery is smashed and cast into the grave. Then the text ends, picking up on the symbolic return of clay to the ground: "Dust returns to the earth where it had been, and the life-breath returns to God who gave it." The conclusion that one is meant to draw is that nothing is permanent. When humanity goes to the *bêt 'ôlām*, literally "eternal house" (12:5b), it is the end. So the poem, indeed, the words of Qohelet are given an appropriate conclusion, which is the thematic statement of the book: "Vanity of vanities, says Qohelet, everything is vanity" (12:8).

Finally there is an epilogue that endorses the teachings of the book (12:9–13a). The reader is assured that Qohelet the sage has been careful and deliberate. Qohelet has spoken rightly, the reader is told, although it may be difficult to hear his words and those of other sages. The epilogue certifies that the book is authentic and complete: there should be no more additions, for all has been said and heard.

THEOLOGICAL ANTHROPOLOGY

It is a commonplace to treat Ecclesiastes not as a theological work but as a philosophical treatise. R. B. Y. Scott's assessment on this issue is representative of the majority opinion: "What we have before us here is primarily a philosophical work rather than a book of religion" (*Proverbs, Ecclesiastes*, p. 196). It is ironic, indeed, that a book that is so skeptical and critical about wisdom should be regarded as "philosophy," a term which etymologically means "love of wisdom." At the same time, even though God is mentioned explicitly some forty times and implied in other passages, commentators are reluctant to refer to Qohelet's thoughts as "theology."

To some extent the reticence in labeling Ecclesiastes as "theology" is understandable. Certainly the author did not set out to write a treatise about God. The deity is not mentioned in the thematic statements that frame the book (1:2; 12:8), nor does God appear in the preface (1:2–11). Moreover the text has more references to humanity than to God: *'ādām* "humanity, human, person" is mentioned 48 times, as opposed to 40 times for *'ĕlōhîm* "God." Immediately after the superscription and the thematic statement of the book, it is the *'ādām* who is mentioned, not God. So the book is arguably better characterized as an "anthropology," a discourse about humanity. But that, too, is not a satisfactory label, for the deity's presence is pervasive in the book. Qohelet thinks of humanity in relation to what God has done in the universe. Indeed, Qohelet seems to be reflecting on the human condition in a world where God is undeniably in control, although the cosmos and God are both still a mystery. True to the tendency of the wisdom tradition, the sage's starting point in his reflection is not God, but the cosmos, society, and humanity. If Qohelet's thought may be called a "theology," then it is a "theology from below." It begins with humanity, but it also reflects on the fate of humanity in God's hands and it speaks of the mysterious ways of God.

The author begins not with divine revelation, nor with divine demands, but with the cosmos that the deity has brought into being, a complex web in which mortals are inevitably caught. It is a world with no discernible design, no order. Everything seems to be in the power of the deity who determines it all. In such a world and before such a God the mortal lives. This is Qohelet's "theological anthropology."

The deity is mentioned first in 1:13, after the preface (1:2–11). The priority in Qohelet's "theology from below" is to set forth the human condition first. Yet, even before that first mention of God, the role of the deity is implicitly raised. There exists a cosmos full of activities, a cosmos where the elements of nature and generations of humanity move and have their being. P. P. Chia perceives that Qohelet is thinking of the Creator and, perhaps, even has Genesis in mind as he writes the preface ("Wisdom, Yahwism, Creation," pp. 22–23). The specific linkage with Genesis is both difficult to prove (the vocabulary is dissimilar) and unnecessary. It is safe to say that the ancients probably knew other cosmologies besides the Genesis accounts. Yet Chia is no doubt right about the rhetorical effect of the passage; in reading the preface of Ecclesiastes, one is inevitably led to the question of the Creator. The text itself anticipates the first explicit mention of God, for the passive "whatever has been done" in 1:9 leads one to "all that has been done" in 1:13, where there can be no doubt that the actor is God. In this cosmos, the mortal toils — just as everything and everyone else on earth does — without being able to get ahead.

It is clear that for Qohelet toil is burdensome (2:18–23; 4:6, 8; 9:9). Toil is an inevitable and inconvenient fact of life (4:4; 6:7; 8:15, 17). Yet that does not mean that toil does not bear fruit. Toil does bear fruit. In fact, the same word for toil is used for the fruit of toil, something that may be enjoyed (2:10, 24; 3:13; 5:18–19 [Heb v 17–18]). But the benefit of toil is limited. Toil is not something that would give one an advantage (1:3; 3:9; 5:16 [Heb v 15]). Whatever pleasure it yields is ephemeral.

In Qohelet's view, humanity is set in a world over which mortals have no control. It is a world that is full of inconveniences, inconsistencies, and contradictions. Nothing that human beings do or have is ultimately reliable: not wealth, not pleasure, not wisdom, not toil, not life itself. There are no fail-safe rules, no formulas that guarantee success. Justice may not be found where one might expect it. People may not get what they deserve. There is no telling who will have a good life and who will not. And even if one has a good life one moment, it may be gone the next. It is an arbitrary world in which human beings live, one that is full of risks but no guarantees. Social, economic, and political forces are at work, creating uncertainties to which everyone is subjected. There are dangers in daily life, too, as accidents happen even amid life's routines. Some amount of wisdom may help reduce the risks, but accidents happen nonetheless. This is what it is like "under the sun."

Above all there looms the specter of death, the one thing of which people can be certain. Death is the one fate that comes to all mortals whether wise or foolish, righteous or wicked, human or beast. It is a certain fate, but its timing is uncertain. Death may come at any time, without regard for one's readiness. For Qohelet, death marks the end of all hopes, all possibilities that one may have in life. In death there can be no enjoyment, no wisdom, no knowledge, no memory. Speculation of what may happen after death is entirely moot, for no one knows what will come about. Finally, lest anyone should entertain the thought that death is only an issue that people face individually, and that the succession of human generations is a defiant testimony to the persistent return of life, Qohelet points ominously to an end-time, when life as humanity knows it will cease altogether. The only eternity of which one may speak is the march of humanity to the grave, called *bêt 'ôlām*, literally "eternal house." The earthly body returns to the earth, and the life-breath returns to God.

Although it is the human condition on which Qohelet reflects, his thoughts are not on mortals alone. His reflection on humanity's plight is theological, inasmuch as he wonders about the role of the deity in all that is happening. It has rightly been observed that God is very active in Ecclesiastes (Murphy). The deity is always giving/permitting (*ntn*; 1:13; 2:26; 3:10, 11; 5:17–18 [Eng vv 18–19]; 6:2; 8:15; 9:9; 12:7) and doing/making (*'śh*; 3:11, 14; 7:14, 29; 8:17; 11:5). This God judges the wicked and the righteous (3:17), is angry at the violation of religious proprieties (5:6 [Heb v 5]), and calls people into account for not enjoying themselves (11:9). This deity has not withdrawn from the world after having created it. Yet, it is not an immanent deity of whom Qohelet speaks. This deity does not relate personally with anyone. In Ecclesiastes, God does not enter into a covenant with anyone. Indeed, this God is wholly transcendent, and the distance between God and humanity is stressed: "God is in heaven, but you are on earth" (5:2 [Eng v 1]). Qohelet appears to be so intent on avoiding any reference to divine immanence that he does not risk even the language of divine omnipresence. He does not say, as we read elsewhere in the Bible, that God is "in heaven above *and on earth beneath*" (Deut 4:39). Rather, he speaks only of God being in heaven, as contrasted with human beings on earth. The deviation may be deliberate, since Qohelet appears to have been familiar with Deuteronomy (so Eccl 5:4 [Heb v 3] // Deut 23:21 [Heb v 22]; Eccl 3:14b // Deut 4:1–2; 13:1). He insists that before this deity one must show due reverence (5:1, 7 [Heb 4:16; 5:6]; 7:18; 8:13). People should not bring forth every matter before God (5:2 [Heb 1]), nor utter promises they do not mean (5:4 [Heb v 3]).

Qohelet's God is an inscrutable deity who brings about both pleasant and unpleasant deeds on earth (7:13–14). Thinking probably of social injustices, the author insists that there are things that are distorted, even distorted by God (*'iwwĕtô*), that no human can straighten (7:13). In this he shares the honest perspective of Job. Even though Bildad and Elihu both insist that God never distorts justice (*yĕ'awwēt*, Job 8:3; 34:12), Job believes otherwise (*'iwwĕtanî*, Job 19:6) and he insists on an explanation. He demands that injustice be corrected. Qohelet, too, accepts that there are distortions for which God must ultimately be responsible. But unlike Job, he does not insist that these distortions be straightened out. He speaks of divine foreknowledge and predetermination, insisting in so doing that the mortal is in no position to dispute with God (6:10). Here he may be alluding to the case of Job (see Job 9:4–5; 14:20). The abundance of human words are so much hot air or emptiness (*hebel*), says Qohelet, again probably with Job in mind (Job 13:22–28; 35:14–16). No one can challenge God and no one can explain the ways of the divine being.

There are two poles, then, in Qohelet's theological anthropology: one "in heaven" and the other "on earth." On the one hand there is God, a transcendent deity who determines all things, but whose ways are utterly mysterious to humankind. On the other hand, there is ʾādām, mortals who have no control over their own destiny. Yet the two poles are not unconnected. The relationship between God and humankind is not one of equals, but one does relate to the other. Despite the apparent lack of order in the world and inconsistencies of life, humankind must live in knowledge of its place in relation to the deity. This is, indeed, what Qohelet means by the "fear of God."

As Qohelet sees it, people try to cope with the situation in various ways. They toil. They fret. They are never content with what they have. They accumulate wealth and hoard it. They long for more wisdom and understanding. They endeavor to give an accounting of all that is happening. They desire to straighten out everything that is crooked, correct every injustice, and fill every void. They strive to gain an immortality of sorts through fame, through their wealth, or their accomplishments. They try to be without offense whatsoever. In short, they try everything conceivable to take a hold of the situation and gain some control. But nothing really works, since all is *hebel*.

The only alternative is to accept the fact that nothing can be controlled. No outcome is predictable. In this connection, his most persistent counsel is to find pleasure in all that one does, even in toil. Indeed, it has been observed that there is a total of seven explicit exhortations to enjoy, and they all occur in key passages (so Rousseau, "Structure de Qohelet," pp. 200–17). One should enjoy whenever there is the opportunity, because this is the "portion" that God has assigned to humanity. It is, as it were, an antidote given by God to counter life's miseries (5:20 [Heb v 19]). The point is not that one must go through life looking for joy everywhere. Nowhere in the book does the author say one should seek pleasure or pursue joy. The issue is, rather, acceptance of the fact that human beings have no control over what will happen. So when the possibility of joy presents itself, one must not fail to be in it, see it, and experience it.

This ethic of joy is nowhere more clearly elaborated than in 5:8–6:9 [Heb 5:8–6:9], the denouement of the first half of the book. The exhortation to enjoy in 5:20 (Heb v 19) is the pivot of the entire literary unit. Revolving around this center are reflections on human greed and discontentment. There is oppression and injustice in the world because there are ambitious and greedy people who simply cannot have enough (5:8–12 [Heb vv 7–11] // 6:7–9). So society, even the entire cosmos, is endangered by this lack of contentment (see especially Comment at 6:7–9). There are individuals who, even when they have opportunities before their eyes, are not able to see them (5:13–17 [Heb vv 12–16] // 6:3–6). Because of their discontent, they live in perpetual gloom. God has given humanity wealth and other assets, although some are able to enjoy but others are not

(5:18–19 [Heb vv 17–18] // 6:1–2). The possibility of joy is a gift of God. At the heart of this literary unit, then, is the call to forget human miseries and to enjoy (5:20 [Heb v 19]). It is evident from the structure that the issue is contentment with what one has at the moment. The joy of the moment should be that which preoccupies one's heart. This is what one accepts as a gift of God (5:19 [Heb v 18]). This is the appropriate response to the fact that human beings do not control what is happening in the universe. One cannot determine or explain — for all is *hebel* "vanity" — but one may still experience good.

Unlike the prophets, Qohelet's ethic does not explicitly call for social transformation and the elimination of injustice. Yet his ethic requires radical change — not of social and political structures, but of attitude toward everything that humanity may want: material possessions, wisdom, esteem, and passion. As emphatic as Qohelet is about the good of joy when one has it, his ethic is not so much about joy as it is about acceptance and spontaneity: "When times are good, enjoy (literally 'be in good'); when times are bad, see. Yes, God has made the one just like the other so that people will not discover anything after them" (7:14). His ethic calls for acceptance of the fact that humanity lives before a sovereign God who alone decides what will happen and when. Hence he says that everything is in the hand of God: who will enjoy and who will glean, who will be favored by God or who will be an offender (2:24–26). So is the fate of every mortal in the hand of God (3:18–22; 9:1–6). Whatever will be will be.

Enjoyment is possible only when people accept that God has made the world just so and that mortals have been given a *ḥēleq* "portion." A portion is something that is only a part. It is not whole. It is not perfect. A portion is always limited, but there is the possibility of enjoyment even from the portion. The recipient of the grant has no say about the quality or quantity of the portion. The recipient is not in a position to determine which portion to take. Moreover, the possession of a portion entails toil. Yet there is always the possibility of enjoyment of one's portion — the fruit of one's toil. Qohelet emphasizes that people must enjoy their portion while it is still possible, for in Sheol all that seems important to mortals will not matter anymore: not reward, not reputation, not passion, not accomplishments, not reason, not knowledge, and not wisdom (9:5–10). When people die, says Qohelet, "they will never again have a portion in all that is done under the sun" (9:6). So one must seize the day and enjoy before it is too late and do everything wholeheartedly (9:7–8, 10).

It is important to observe that for Qohelet enjoyment is not simply the best option under the circumstances. Rather, he repeatedly emphasizes that enjoyment is the gift of God (2:24–26; 3:12; 5:19 [Heb 18]), that God has shown favor to one who enjoys (9:7), and that God calls one to account for not enjoying (11:9). Enjoyment of the present — contentment — is always interpreted theologically in Ecclesiastes. Qohelet's ethic is a theological one. It is based on his understanding of the nature of God and God's relation to humanity.

This ethic in his theological anthropology is evident in his admonition regarding the elusiveness of wisdom and righteousness and the inevitability of folly and wickedness (7:14–22). He does not regard righteousness and wisdom as sure virtues, the possession of which will help one avert disasters. People can be wise and righteous and still suffer the fate of wicked fools. Indeed, in his judgment no mortal can be correct on every score. No one can be so perfect that offense is avoided altogether: "For there is no one on earth so righteous, who does only good and does not err" (7:20). Wickedness and folly are inevitable.

There are people, it seems, who believe that perfect wisdom and righteousness are attainable and that the attainment of perfect righteousness and wisdom will help bring a good life and avert negative consequences. Qohelet's counsel, however, is that one should neither be too righteous or too wise, nor too wicked or foolish. Significantly, he puts it in theological terms once again: "It is good that you grasp the one but also not let go of the other, for the one who fears God goes forth with both of them" (7:18). The fearer of God is the one who recognizes the distance between God and humanity. Such a one does not imagine that it is possible only to hold on to one reality. It is one who does not fear God who believes that mortals can be so wise and so righteous that they can avert negative consequences. No one is that good. This is an entirely consistent motif in Qohelet's theological anthropology. Human beings are simply not in control of anything, including wisdom and righteousness. Therefore, they must live as fearers of God — people who go forth in life, knowing that righteousness and wisdom are elusive and that wickedness and folly are inevitable realities of life.

The theological content of Qohelet's ethic is also evident in his call for liberality even in the face of uncertainty (11:1–6). He admonishes people to cast their bread upon the waters — to throw away a good deed (11:1) — and to give generously even though they may not know what disasters may strike. He recognizes that mortals live in a world full of risks and uncertainty, and he urges that people take the necessary precautions (9:16–20). At the same time, he asserts that one ought not be hampered by being overly cautious. Those who constantly watch the weather conditions will never sow or reap. The wind (*rûaḥ*) is completely unpredictable, so one must not always second guess the weather (11:4). Similarly, no one knows when and how the life-breath (*rûaḥ*) enters a human body, for life's origin is a mystery (11:5a). There is a movement in the passage from the uncertainty of events to the uncertainty of wind (*rûaḥ*), to the mystery of the life-breath (*rûaḥ*), and finally to the mystery of God's action (11:5b). No one knows the mystery of God's will, so one should be spontaneous and sow at any time (11:6). Thus, Qohelet's ethic is thoroughly grounded in his theological anthropology.

In sum, Qohelet always begins his reflection with humanity and the human condition. He concludes at every turn that mortals are not in control of the things that happen in the world. They are not in control of their destiny. This is why Qohelet says that everything is *hebel*. He does not mean that everything is meaningless or insignificant, but that everything is beyond human apprehension and comprehension. But in thinking about humanity, Qohelet also speaks of God. People are caught in this situation where everything is *hebel* — in every sense of the word. God is transcendent and wholly other, but humanity is "on earth." Yet God is related to humanity, and God has given humanity the possibilities of each moment. Hence people must accept what happens, whether good or bad. They must respond spontaneously to life, even in the midst of uncertainties, and accept both the possibilities and limitations of their being human.

VIII. QOHELET AMONG THE WISE

The epilogue tells us that Qohelet was a *ḥākām* "sage" (12:9), and it implies that he was among the wise (*ḥăkāmîm*), whose words are like goads and pricks deliberately applied by a herder (12:11). It is important, therefore, to consider the ancient Near Eastern and Israelite sapiential contexts of the book.

ANCIENT NEAR EASTERN WISDOM LITERATURE

Several texts from Egypt, Mesopotamia, and Ras Shamra (ancient Ugarit) have been given the label "wisdom" because they correspond in form, subject matter, and attitudes to their biblical counterparts, especially the books of Proverbs, Job, and Ecclesiastes. The word "wisdom" rarely appears in the extrabiblical texts, but the affinities are sufficiently clear that scholars recognize that they belong to the same type of literature as the wisdom books of the Bible. Indeed, the similarities are sometimes thought to be so compelling that from time to time scholars have argued for literary influence of the other ancient Near Eastern texts on the biblical material.

In the case of Ecclesiastes, the debate has raged for much of this century over the possibility of either Egyptian or Mesopotamian influence. So P. Humbert argues for Egyptian influence on Ecclesiastes, while O. Loretz maintains the priority of the Mesopotamian sources. The possibility that Qohelet might have been familiar with wisdom and other traditions from elsewhere in the ancient Near East certainly cannot be ruled out. Israelite wisdom is, after all, characterized by an international outlook and it was fostered early in the court of Solomon (see Day, "Foreign Semitic Influence," pp. 55–70). Our purpose for surveying the ancient Near Eastern wisdom texts, however, is not so much to establish influence, for "that, too, is vanity." Rather, it is to gain a sense of Ecclesiastes as literature and, perchance, to discover a few insights regarding the genres that are employed in the book.

From Egypt comes a large number of didactic texts known as *sebayit* "instruction." These texts typically are presented in the form of instructions of a parent to a child and the reader is frequently addressed as "my child." This feature is present also in Mesopotamian instructional literature, where the reader is also addressed as "my child." Although the best biblical examples for these are in the book of Proverbs (so in Prov 1:8, 10, 15; 2:1; 3:1), one may note that the reader of Ecclesiastes is also addressed as a youth (11:9) and is in fact called *bĕnî* "my child" in the epilogue (12:12). By addressing the reader as a youth and "my child," therefore, Ecclesiastes is assuming the typical didactic posture of wisdom literature.

One of the oldest of the Egyptian didactic texts is *The Instruction of Ptahhotep*

(*AEL* I, pp. 61–80). This work consists of thirty-seven maxims framed by a prologue and a long epilogue. Among the maxims in this text one finds an instruction that reminds us of parts of Ecclesiastes, especially the admonition to enjoy
oneself when young and to "follow the ways of your heart and what your eyes
see" (11:9):

> Follow your heart as long as you live,
> Do no more than is required,
> Do not shorten the time of "follow-the-heart,"
> Trimming its moment offends the *ka*.
> Don't waste your time on daily cares
> Beyond providing for your household;
> When wealth has come, follow your heart,
> Wealth does no good if one is glum.

(AEL I, p. 66)

In the same text is a description of old age, elements of which faintly echo the
final poem in Ecclesiastes, although the travails of old age seem no longer to be
the focus of Qohelet in that passage (see Notes and Comment at 12:3–6).

Another old didactic text is *The Instruction to Kagemni*, composed by a sage
whose name is lost (*AEL* I, pp. 59–61). The book ends with an epilogue that
certifies that the book was written as the sage had intended. It also warns the
reader not to go beyond what has been set down. The epilogue of Ecclesiastes,
too, may have served similar purposes: the reader is assured that the sage Qohelet
deliberately had taught what he taught, and one is warned not to go beyond
the teachings.

The Instruction of Anii also includes an epilogue that, like the epilogues of
Kagemni and Ecclesiastes, looks retrospectively at the work of the sage (*AEL* II,
pp. 135–46). The epilogue takes the form of a dialogue between a father and his
son, in the course of which the son is urged to pay attention to the words of the
sage even though they may be difficult to understand and to obey. The sage is
also praised as someone who has carefully chosen his words. The son is asked to
be "like all the beasts" and listen and learn what to do. One may recall that the
epilogue of Ecclesiastes also concedes that the words of the sages — presumably
including the sage who wrote the book — are difficult; they are like goads and
pricks applied by a herder. Those subjected to the instructions of the wise are,
therefore, like beasts being deliberately prodded on by herders. The epilogue of
Anii serves as an apology for the sage. This epilogue thus sheds some light on
how an epilogue of a difficult wisdom text might function.

The Instruction of Papyrus Insinger is a late text (first century C.E.) that has a
few thematic and verbal affinities with Ecclesiastes (*AEL* III, pp. 184–217). The
concern with fate and the emphasis on moderation in this text are frequently
cited by scholars. Yet, as Lichtheim observes, "Qohelet's point of view is quite
different from Papyrus Insinger's" ("Observations on Papyrus Insinger," p. 301).
Likewise, the few links that scholars have made between Ecclesiastes and *The*

61

Instruction of Ankhsheshonq (AEL III, pp. 159–84) are too general and superficial
to be helpful (see B. Gemser, "Instruction of 'Onchsheshonqy"). A proverb in
the Egyptian text about liberality, however, does offer a suggestive parallel for
Eccl 11:1, indeed clarifying what throwing "bread" upon the water might mean
in Ecclesiastes:

> Do a good deed and throw it in the water;
> when it dries you will find it.
>
> (19,1; see AEL III, p. 174)

Of the Egyptian pessimistic texts, the one most commonly cited is *The Dispute
Between A Man and His Ba* (AEL I, pp. 163–69). In this text, a man who has
become disillusioned with life contemplates death. He longs for death, but does
not go so far as to consider suicide. Different points of view are given voice
through the dialogue that the man has with his *ba*, his "soul." The *ba* tries to
convince the man that life, for all its limitations and troubles, is better than death.
So the man is urged to stop worrying and to enjoy life while he still has a chance
to do so: "Follow the feast day, forget worry!" (see AEL I, p. 165).

Also suggestive are the so-called "Harpers' Songs," a genre of tomb inscriptions
that reflect on death and call for the enjoyment of life. These texts typically lament the transitory nature of human existence and question the possibility of life
after one dies. In the face of death, the living are admonished to enjoy themselves
while they still can (see AEL I, pp. 196–97).

Finally, one may also consider *The Complaints of Khakheperre-Sonb*, a text
about a man's conversation with his heart regarding the troubles in the land (AEL
I, pp. 145–49). The inquirer seeks to understand what is happening around him,
but he finds no answers for "none is wise enough to know it."

As in Egypt, there are a number of practical texts from Mesopotamia, such as
the *Instructions of Shuruppak*, attributed to a survivor of the Flood (BWL, pp.
92–95), and the *Counsels of Wisdom* (BWL, pp. 96–107). To this group belongs
The Counsels of Shube-awilum found at Ras Shamra (*Ugaritica* V, text 163), a
text that may be related to the *Instructions of Shuruppak*, and a fragmentary bilingual text, also found at Ras Shamra (BWL, p. 116). The last of these, written in
Hurrian and Akkadian, concerns proper attitudes before a god:

> One who acknowledges no guilt rushes to his god,
> Without thinking he raises his hands (in prayer) to the god.
> . . . his guilt. . . . .
> A man in ignorance rushes to his god.
>
> (BWL, p. 116, lines 10–13)

This warning concerning religious attitude finds a parallel in the teachings of
Qohelet (5:1–7 [Heb 4:17–5:6]).

The admonitions associated with the name Ahiqar, preserved in several versions in several languages, are believed to have originated in Mesopotamia, al-

though the earliest version is the Aramaic text found at Elephantine, a text dating to the fifth century B.C.E. (*TAD* III, 1.1). Portions of this text echo Qohelet's teaching in 8:1–5 (see *TAD* III, 1.1.84–90).

It is also in this text that one finds a good parallel for Qohelet's call not to be too wise nor too foolish (7:15–16). The Aramaic text reads: 'l tstkl kbyr [w']l yd'k h[. . .] "do not be overly clever, lest . . . be extinguished" (*TAD* III, 1.1.147). In light of this parallel, there is no longer any need to trace this call for moderation to Greek philosophy, as some commentators have done.

Finally, an interesting passage in Ahiqar warns against sedition in words and images that are reminiscent of Eccl 10:20:

[My] son, do not c[ur]se the day until you have seen [nig]ht,
Do n[ot] let it come upon your mind,
since their e[yes] and their ears are everywhere.
As regards your mouth, watch yourself;
Let it not be [their] prey.
Above all watchfulness, watch your mouth,
and against him who [is listening] harden (your) heart;
for a word is a bird and one who releases it is without sens[e].

(see *TAD* III, 1.1.80–82)

We know that the Jewish community in Elephantine corresponded with their kinfolk in Palestine and so it is entirely possible that a sage writing in the Achaemenid period, as Qohelet probably did, might have been familiar with the Aramaic *Proverbs of Ahiqar*. Certainly the book of Tobit, which probably originated in the same period, shows that this wisdom text was in circulation in Palestine (Tobit 1:21–22; 2:10; 11:18; 14:10–12; see Greenfield, "The Wisdom of Ahiqar," p. 46).

Besides the practical wisdom texts, there are also reflective texts from Mesopotamia. In *I Will Praise the Lord of Wisdom* (*ludlul bēl nēmeqi*), a text whose story line is reminiscent of the book of Job, the precarious nature of human existence and the mystery of divine behavior are highlighted (*BWL*, pp. 21–62). To account for the senselessness of the world's affairs, the text suggests that perhaps all human values are inverted for the gods, so that what is considered good by mortals is bad to the gods and *vice versa* (*BWL*, p. 41, lines 34–38).

The Babylonian Theodicy (*BWL*, pp. 63–91) is an acrostic poem recording a dialogue between a sufferer who complains about social injustice and an orthodox friend who defends the traditional viewpoints. The apparent contradictions in the universe cannot be explained, it is argued, because of the limitation of human knowledge (*BWL*, p. 87, lines 256–57).

The text known as *Counsels of a Pessimist* (*BWL*, pp. 107–9) is similar to Ecclesiastes inasmuch as it speaks of the transitory nature of human life. Human accomplishments are ephemeral and so one is urged: "Banish misery and suffering from your side." This advice is comparable to what Qohelet says: "Remove vexation from your heart, and banish unpleasantness from your body" (11:10).

In *The Dialogue of Pessimism,* a master and his slave explore what is right to do, and they end up in utter despair (*BWL,* pp. 139–49). The answer to the question "what is good" is death; beyond that, no one really knows what is good. The question is also raised rhetorically by Qohelet, who despairs that no one knows (6:12). Yet, the perspective of Qohelet is different from the *Dialogue* in that Ecclesiastes does not point to death as an alternative. To Qohelet, it is still possible for people to "see good" in life — to enjoy themselves whenever there is the opportunity to do so.

Arguably the most compelling of the parallels come from the *Gilgamesh Epic,* an ancient tale that goes back to the Sumerian period in the third millennium B.C.E. and one that survives in many versions. This was apparently a classic of the "fertile crescent," widely circulated and even translated into different languages. Fragments of the epic have been found in Palestine itself, lending credibility to the suggestion of some scholars that the author of Ecclesiastes might have known at least the broad outline or various aspects of the story. Commentators have pointed to several affinities between the *Gilgamesh Epic* and Ecclesiastes (see Loretz, *Qohelet,* pp. 116–22). First of all, the dominant theme of the *Gilgamesh Epic* is the mortality of human beings, which is also a primary concern of Qohelet. Not only that, the words used in the *Gilgamesh Epic* to convey the transitory nature of human life are remarkably similar to the words of Qohelet: "only the gods l[ive] forever with the sun; as for human beings their days are numbered; whatever they achieve is but wind" (Gilg Y iv 5–8). Life with the sun, the numbered days of human life, and the reference to the insubstantial nature of human accomplishments all are echoed in Ecclesiastes. Moreover, the usage of "wind" is quite similar to Qohelet's usage of *hebel* "vanity" — literally, "breath, whiff, puff, wind."

In 4:12, Qohelet cites a proverb: "the three-ply cord will not readily snap." This is widely recognized as the same proverb that one finds in the *Gilgamesh Epic,* best attested in a Sumerian version: "Two men will not die; the towed boat will not sink. A three-ply cord cannot be cut" (see Notes and Comment at 4:12). Most scholars also concede that the *carpe diem* passage in 9:7–9 is somehow related to the exhortation of Šiduri the tavern-keeper in the *Gilgamesh Epic:*

The life you pursue you shall not find.
When the gods created humanity,
Death for humanity they set aside,
Retaining life in their own hands.
As for you, Gilgamesh, let your belly be full,
Enjoy yourself day and night.
Find enjoyment every day,
Dance and play day and night.
Let your garments be clean,
Let your head be washed; bathe in water.

Look upon the little one who holds your hand,
Let your spouse enjoy herself in your embrace!

(Gilg Me iii 2–14; see ANET³, p. 90)

Lambert has recently pointed out that this Šiduri is identified in an incantation text (Šurpu II 173) as ᵈIštar nēmeqi "the goddess of wisdom" ("Some New Babylonian Wisdom Literature," pp. 31–32).

The association of the *Gilgamesh Epic* with wisdom literature is, in fact, not surprising. W. L. Moran detects a "strong didactism" in the standard version of the epic, especially in the new prologue and epilogue ("Gilgamesh," in *The Encyclopedia of Religion* V, p. 558). The new framework of the epic emphasizes all that Gilgamesh has seen and learned. Tablet I of that version also calls attention to the legendary successes of Gilgamesh, the renowned king of Uruk, including his various building projects, as well as to his "toils" (*mānaḫtu*) and "troubles" (*marṣātu*). According to Moran, "[b]y a tissue of allusions to a genre of pseudo-autobiography in which the kings made lessons of their lives and recorded them for posterity, these lines also imply that Gilgamesh did the same." The epic now addresses the reader directly ("you"), and through this didactism "becomes part of wisdom literature" (ibid.).

It has been argued that Ecclesiastes, too, begins with such a "pseudoauto-biography," a genre of text that imitates the royal inscriptions (Seow, "Qohelet's Autobiography"). Ironically the allusions to the king's many accomplishments only serve to underscore the ephemerality of these successes, for ultimately even the most famous heroes cannot overcome the limitation of death. This, too, is the point that Gilgamesh's "pseudoautobiography" makes in context. The walls of Uruk that Gilgamesh built, the very walls that the reader of the epic is invited to view at the end of the text, mark the extent of immortality that Gilgamesh had attained. No more may be expected of mortals. As the story develops, one learns that it was the reality of death — the death of Enkidu — that brought home the ephemerality of human accomplishments, proving conclusively that "all human achievements are but wind." Gilgamesh, the illustrious and wise king, who has succeeded in all his kingly deeds is, in the final analysis, just like any mortal. That same movement — from the accomplishments of the king to the stark reality of death — is also evident in Ecclesiastes. Following the fictional royal autobiography (1:12–2:11), Qohelet proceeds immediately to speak of the leveling effect of death (2:12–17). In the face of death, there is no advantage for anyone. Everything is but *hebel* and a pursuit of wind.

ECCLESIASTES AND ISRAELITE WISDOM

The affinities between the Israelite wisdom tradition and other wisdom texts of the ancient Near East are strong. Indeed, wisdom stands out from all other parts of the Hebrew Bible on account of its significant continuities with other Near Eastern texts. At the same time, there are also noticeable discontinuities between wisdom literature and other parts of the Bible. To begin with, the main themes that one finds elsewhere in the canon are absent in the wisdom books. In this biblical corpus one finds no reference to the promise to the ancestors, the exodus, the election of a particular people, the giving of the law on Mount Sinai, or the guidance of God in the wilderness. Neither salvation history nor covenant—two themes that modern scholars have identified as critical to the understanding of Old Testament theology—figures prominently. It seems that the tradition is much more concerned with universal human experience, with life that "everyone" faces, rather than it is with the particularistic theology of a nation. This is perhaps why God is always 'ĕlōhîm in Ecclesiastes (forty times), never YHWH, the distinctive name of Israel's God.

Moreover, some perceive in the wisdom texts a certain reticence in speaking of divine intervention, despite the presence of a doctrine of retribution. Simply stated, this doctrine assumes that good acts bring good consequences, evil acts bring evil consequences. In the wisdom tradition the consequence is thought to be intrinsically related to the act: the act mechanically generates the consequence. This is not to say that there are no manifestations of an act-consequence mentality anywhere else in the Bible. Certainly one finds a strong doctrine of retribution in Deuteronomistic theology, foundationally stated in the farewell discourse of Moses (see Deut 30:15–20). Yet wisdom's presentation of the doctrine is different. Whereas in Deuteronomistic theology YHWH is clearly responsible for bringing about the consequences, in the wisdom tradition there is no mention of the deity as the originator of reward or punishment. The divergence in perspectives between the wisdom tradition and other parts of the Bible is evident when one compares an injunction against vows stated in Ecclesiastes over against that stated in Deuteronomy. The version in Deuteronomy is theologically dogmatic: "When you make a vow to YHWH your God, do not be slack in fulfilling it; for YHWH your God will certainly require it of you and it shall be an offense against you [if you do not fulfill it]" (Deut 23:21 [Heb v 22]). By contrast, Ecclesiastes states the matter in neutral terms: "When you make a vow to God, do not be slack to fulfill it, for there is no delight in fools" (Eccl 5:4 [Heb v 3]). Apart from the fact that the more generic name "God" is preferred over the more particularistic "YHWH your God," the admonition in Ecclesiastes resorts to circumlocution instead of using the language of divine retribution: "there is no delight in fools." To be sure, the sages do not deny that God is *sometimes* responsible for the consequences of human action. It is even likely that Qohelet has in mind God's retribution in this passage, as the reference to God's anger in 5:6 (Heb v 4) suggests. Still, there is a reticence in wisdom in attributing all things to God's direct intervention. Wisdom, it appears, leaves more room for other explanations of events. It does not explain all things in terms of divine intervention in the realm of the mundane. By the same token, the wisdom tradition seems to derive its authority not from any claim of divine revelation (there is no "thus saith the LORD" formula), but from the authority of human observation and experience. The sayings are set forth and passed on as what people know to be true from what they have seen and what they have experienced.

Ecclesiastes belongs to this tradition. There may be sporadic allusions to Genesis 1–11, as some scholars have argued (so Chia, Forman), but there can be no doubt that the strongest ties are between Ecclesiastes and other wisdom books. Qohelet's chief concerns are with the plight of humanity and with the quest for what is good for humanity. Apart from the grammatical particles (the prepositions, definite article, and the like) and the word *kōl* "all," the word that is most frequently attested in the book is *ṭôb* "good" (51 times) and the next most frequent is *ʾādām* "human being, person." Qohelet's methodology, too, is true to the wisdom tradition. Hence he appeals repeatedly to human observation. The verb *rāʾâ* "to see, observe" appears 47 times; in 26 of those times the author refers to what he himself or his heart sees.

Wisdom and knowledge are common motifs in the book. Thus, the noun *ḥokmâ* "wisdom" is found 28 times, *ḥākām* "wise, wise one" appears 21 times, while the verb *ḥākam* "to be wise, act wisely" is used thrice. The verb *yādaʿ* "to know" appears 36 times, while the noun *daʿat* "knowledge" is attested 7 times. In short, the vocabulary of Qohelet is typical of an Israelite wisdom text. He also uses typical wisdom forms — sayings, admonitions, example stories, and the like.

This does not mean, however, that Qohelet is uncritical of the tradition. Although he does give much attention to what is good, as do other sages, his conclusion is that people do not know what is good except to enjoy what is before them whenever they are able to do so (2:1–3, 24–26; 3:12, 13, 22; 5:18 [Heb v 17]; 6:11). Indeed, in a number of instances he seems to employ "better-than" sayings (*Ṭôb Sprüche*) ironically to show that human beings really do not know what is better. In 4:1–16 and 7:1–12 the "better-than" sayings are relativized by a preemptive statement in each case insisting that no one knows what is good (3:22; 6:11). In 9:16a and 18a, the "better-than" sayings are contradicted by specific exceptions (9:16b, 18b). The point that Qohelet appears to be making in these subversions of the "better-than" sayings is that the rules that people formulate are, at best, only relatively reliable. They do not guarantee results.

By the same token, observation of the world reveals not the order and reasonable conduct that one might desire to find, but inconsistencies, contradictions, and inexplicable situations. There is, in fact, much that one sees in life that does not make sense, much that does not seem reasonable. Qohelet observes that there are righteous people and wicked people who get the opposite of what they deserve (7:15; 9:10), that the swiftest, strongest, and wisest people do not always get ahead (9:11, 13), and that the rich and the poor may suddenly trade places (10:7). The doctrine of retribution often does not seem to work. Observation does not lead one to discern that there is order in the universe, as a doctrine of retribution presumes.

Qohelet stands in the wisdom tradition inasmuch as he recognizes wisdom's benefits. Wisdom has clear advantage over folly — as stark as the advantage of light over darkness (2:13). It is as good as an inheritance and an advantage to those who are alive (7:12). Indeed, wisdom may help one to act appropriately and, in so doing, keep one alive (8:1). The application of wisdom may help one prevent accidents (10:1). Wisdom is more precious to the wise than wealth is to the proprietors (7:19, emended text). Thus wisdom is regarded positively by Qohelet, unlike folly, which is never commended. Yet, it is equally clear that wisdom has its limits and is subject to failure (see Fox, "Wisdom in Qohelet," pp. 123–26).

On account of Qohelet's skepticism regarding wisdom, commentators sometimes present Ecclesiastes as an essentially heterodox work within the wisdom tradition, or even as antiwisdom. In the judgment of some scholars, the positive views in the book about wisdom come from the hand of a ḥākām-glossator, someone from the traditional wisdom school-of-thought. Others speak of Ecclesiastes and Job as reflecting a "crisis" in wisdom, representing views that arose because traditional wisdom teachings became inadequate (so H. Gese, H. H. Schmid). That view, however, defines sapiential orthodoxy in terms of what is found in Proverbs, which is only part of a larger tradition. It also assumes that reflective texts (like Job, Ecclesiastes, and other pessimistic literature from the ancient Near East) are always developed after and in reaction to the practical texts (like Proverbs and other didactic collections). Of this chronological development one cannot be certain.

It should be emphasized that in the book of Proverbs wisdom is not easy to find. The simpletons who have not heeded Woman Wisdom's call soon enough will seek her but they will not find her: "they will call upon me, but I will not answer; they will seek me, but they will not find me" (Prov 1:28). Indeed, Woman Wisdom is portrayed as the desirable lover whom one must diligently seek, even though she is difficult to find: "happy is the one who finds wisdom . . . she is more precious than jewels" (Prov 3:13, 15). Similar language is found in the portrayal of the extraordinary wife and mother, the ultimate symbol of Woman Wisdom:

'ēšet-ḥayil mî yimṣā'
wěrāḥôq mippěnînîm mikrāh
The woman of quality who can find?
Her price is more unattainable than jewels.

(Prov 31:10)

Qohelet develops the motif of seeking Wisdom. Though he is a sage who has investigated many things through Wisdom, he finds Wisdom elusive: "I said, 'I would be wise,' but that is beyond me (*hî' rěḥôqâ mimmennî*). All that happens is inaccessible (*rāḥôq*) and utterly unfathomable; who can discover it (*mî yimṣā'ennû*)?" (7:23b–24). Using the language of a lover's pursuit, Qohelet says he has sought but cannot find. Presumably this lover, Woman Wisdom, eludes him (see Notes and Comment at 7:28). At the same time, another woman, no doubt Folly herself, seeks to ensnare him. This is the one woman that he has found: "the woman more bitter than death, inasmuch as she is a trap, her heart is a net, her hands are fetters" (7:26). The language echoes the portrayal of Folly in Proverbs (see Proverbs 1–9). This "other" woman is pernicious. Qohelet's depiction of his own plight — also the plight of humanity in general — is comical. Woman

Folly chases the individual, even as the individual is desperately seeking Woman Wisdom, who could deliver from Folly's grasp, but who could not be found. Only the one who is favored by God (*ṭôb lipnê hā'ĕlōhîm*) will be able to escape Folly's snare, while the offender (*ḥôṭe'*) is sure to be captured by her. Elsewhere Qohelet says the one who is favored by God is given wisdom, but the offender is given the task of gathering for the favored to enjoy (2:26). But who is the one who is favored by God? Who is the offender? No one knows, for everything is in the hand of God.

In other ways, as well, Ecclesiastes shows continuity with the sapiential mainstream. Thus Qohelet emphasizes the fear of God, a concept that is prominent in Proverbs, although there it is the "fear of YHWH" rather than "fear of God" (Prov 1:7, 29; 2:5; 8:13; 9:10; 10:27; 14:26, 27; 15:16, 33; 16:16; 19:23; 22:4; 23:17). This fear of God motif, which is present in both biblical and extrabiblical wisdom texts, emphasizes the place of humanity in relation to God. For Qohelet, God has placed limitations on humanity in order that they might have this "fear" (3:14; 5:7 [Heb v 6]). The fear of God is the recognition of those limitations. Hence, the one who fears God does not behave as if it is possible to be perfectly righteous and wise. Rather, one does not try to be too righteous or wise, nor too foolish or wicked. The fearer of God in fact goes forth with "both of them" (7:18). In this emphasis on the fear of God, Qohelet stands with others in the wisdom tradition.

The assessment of Qohelet in the epilogue is correct. He was a sage. He stood in the wisdom tradition. He used wisdom's methodologies and forms. However, he also made his own distinctive contributions, often in agreement with most of the tradition but at times in criticism of it. Qohelet "taught the people knowledge," the epilogue tells us (12:9). We gather that he did so as one who knew the wisdom tradition well. Yet, the lessons that Qohelet taught from the wisdom tradition were not conveyed without specific reference to the context of the audience. He did not merely impart wisdom teachings as timeless propositions. Like any wise teacher, Qohelet was keenly aware of the environment in which his audience found themselves. So he did not only draw on the wisdom tradition, he brought the tradition to bear on the experiences of his generation. He employed the vocabulary of his day to address the concerns of his audience. His audience was apparently preoccupied with all sorts of social and economic issues — the volatility of the economy, the possibility of wealth, inheritance, social status, and so forth. Qohelet drew on these concerns and employed idioms that were familiar to his audience in order to subvert their preoccupation. Although they lived in a new environment, with new economic possibilities and dangers, the real issues that they faced were nothing new: "there is nothing new under the sun" (1:9). Others had already wrestled with the issues of life's inconsistencies, contradictions, and absurdities — as is evident in other reflective wisdom texts. Mortals in every generation had always been and will always be caught in a world that is beyond human control. Life is just so: "everything is vanity."

A SELECT
BIBLIOGRAPHY

◆

I. TEXTS AND VERSIONS OF ECCLESIASTES

Baer, S. and F. Delitzsch, eds. *Quinqua Volumina*. Leipzig: Tauchnitz, 1886.

Ceriani, A. M., ed. *Translatio Syra Pescitto Veteris Testamenti ex codice ambrosiani sec. fere VI*. Mediolani: Pogliani, 1876.

Diebner, B. J. and R. Kasser, eds. *Hamburger Papyrus Bil. 1*. Geneva: Cramer, 1989.

Dîez Merino, L., ed. *Targum de Qohelet*. Edición Principe del Ms. Villa-Amil No. 5 de Alfonso de Zamora. Biblioteca Hispana Biblica 13. Madrid: Consejo Superior de Investigaciones Cientificas, 1987.

Elliger, K. and W. Rudolph, eds. *Biblia Hebraica Stuttgartensia*. Stuttgart: Deutsche Bibelstiftung, 1977.

Field, F., ed. *Origenis Hexaplorum*. Oxford: Clarendon, 1875.

Kennicott, B., ed. *Vetus Testamentum Hebraicum cum variis lectionibus*. Vol. 2. Oxford: Clarendon, 1780.

Kittel, R., ed. *Biblia Hebraica*. 16th ed. Stuttgart: Württembergische Bibelanstalt, 1971.

Knobel, P. S. *Targum Qohelet: A Linguistic and Exegetical Inquiry*. Unpublished dissertation, Yale University, 1976.

————. "The Targum of Qohelet," in *The Aramaic Bible*. Vol. 15. Collegeville, Minn.: Liturgical, 1991.

Lagarde, P. de, ed. *Hagiographa Chaldaice*. Osnabrück: Zeller, 1967 [1873].

Lane, D. J., ed. "Qoheleth," in *The Old Testament in Syriac*. Vol. 2/5. Leiden: Brill, 1979.

Levine, E., ed. *The Aramaic Version of Qohelet*. New York: Sepher-Hermon, 1978.

Levy, A., ed. *Das Targum zu Kohelet nach südarabischen Handschriften herausgegeben*. Breslau: Fleishmann, 1905.

Mercer, S. A. B., ed. *The Ethiopic Text of the Book of Ecclesiastes*. The Oriental Society Research Series 6; London: Luzac, 1931.

Montfaucon, B. de., ed. *Hexaplorum Origenis quae supersunt*. Vol. 2. Paris: Nicolaum Simart, 1714.

Muilenburg, J. "A Qoheleth Scroll from Qumran," *BASOR* 135 (1954) 20–28.

Parsons, J., ed. *Vetus Testamentum Graecum.* Vol. 3. Oxford: Clarendon, 1823.

Rahlfs, A., ed. *Septuaginta.* Vol. 2. Stuttgart: Württembergische Bibelanstalt, 1935.

Rossi, J. B. de, ed. *Variae lectionibus Veteris Testamenti librorum.* Vol. 3. Amsterdam: Philo, 1970 [1786].

Sperber, A. *The Bible in Aramaic.* Vol. 4A. Leiden: Brill, 1968.

Swete, H. B., ed. *The Old Testament in Greek According to the Septuagint.* Vol. 2. 3rd ed. Cambridge: Cambridge University, 1907.

Ulrich, E. "Ezra and Qoheleth Manuscripts From Qumran (4QEzra, 4Q-Qoh^{A,B})," in *Priests, Prophets and Scribes (Fs. J. Blenkinsopp).* JSOTSup 149. Ed. E. Ulrich, et al. Sheffield: JSOT, 1992. Pp. 139–57.

Weber, R., ed. *Biblia Sacra iuxta Vulgatam versionem.* Vol. 2. 3d ed. Stuttgart: Deutsche Bibelgesellschaft, 1983.

Zafrani, H. and A. Caquot, eds. *L'Ecclesiaste et Son Commentaire: Le Livre de L'ascese: La Version Arabe de la Bible de Sa'adya Gaon.* Collection Judaisme en terre d'Islam 4. Paris: Maisonneuve & Larose, 1989.

II. COMMENTARIES ON ECCLESIASTES

Aalders, G. Ch. *Het Boek de Prediker.* Commentaar op het Oude Testament. Kampen: Kok, 1948.

Alonso-Schökel, L. *Eclesiastes y Sabiduria.* Los Libros Sagrados 17. Madrid: Ediciones Cristiandad, 1974.

Barton, G. A. *A Critical and Exegetical Commentary on the Book of Ecclesiastes.* ICC. Edinburgh: T. & T. Clark, 1908.

Barucq, A. *Ecclésiaste.* VS 3. Paris: Beauchesne, 1968.

Beek, M. A. *Prediker. Hooglied.* De Prediking van het Oude Testamen. Nijkerk: Callenbach, 1984.

Crenshaw, J. L. *Ecclesiastes: A Commentary.* OTL. Philadelphia: Westminster, 1987.

Delitzsch, F. *Commentary on the Song of Songs and Ecclesiastes.* Trans. M. G. Easton. Edinburgh: T. & T. Clark, 1877 [German edition 1875; reprint of English edition, Grand Rapids: Eerdmans, 1982].

Galling, K. "Der Prediger," in *Die fünf Megilloth.* HAT 18. 2d ed. Tübingen: Mohr, 1969.

Ginsberg, H. L. *Koheleth.* Jerusalem: Newman, 1961.

Ginsburg, C. D. *Coheleth, Commonly Called the Book of Ecclesiastes: Translated from the Original Hebrew, with a Commentary, Historical and Critical.* London: Longman, 1861 [Reprint. New York: KTAV, 1970].

Glasser, E. *Le procès du bonheur par Qohelet.* LD 61. Paris: Cerf, 1970.

Gordis, R. *Koheleth — the Man and His World.* 3d ed. New York: Schocken, 1968.

Graetz, H. *Kohelet.* Leipzig: Winter, 1871.

Hertzberg, H. W. *Der Prediger.* KAT 17/4. Gütersloh: Mohn, 1963.

Hitzig, F. *Der Prediger Salomo's*. Leipzig: Hirzel, 1883.

Ibn Ezra. *El Comentario de Abraham Ibn Ezra Al Libro del Eclesiastes: Introduccion, Traduccion y Edicion Critica*. Textos y estudios "Cardenal Cisneros" 56. Ed. M. Gómez Aranda. Madrid: Instituto de Filologia del CSIC, 1994.

Jastrow, M. *A Gentle Cynic*. Philadelphia: Lippincott, 1919.

Jerome. "Commentarius in Ecclesiasten," in *S. Hieronymi Presbyteri Opera*. Ed. M. Adrianen. CChr (Series Latina) 72/1. Turnholti: Brepols, 1959. Pp. 249–361.

Kroeber, R. *Der Prediger*. Schriften und Quellen der Alten Welt 13. Berlin: Akademie, 1963.

Lauha, A. *Kohelet*. BKAT 19. Neukirchen-Vluyn: Neukirchener, 1978.

Levy, L. *Das Buch Qoheleth*. Leipzig: Hinrich's, 1912.

Loader, J. A. *Ecclesiastes: A Practical Commentary*. Text and Interpretation. Grand Rapids, Michigan: Eerdmans, 1986.

Lohfink, N. *Kohelet*. Die Neue Echter Bibel. Würzburg: Echter, 1980.

Luther, M. "Notes on Ecclesiastes," in *Luther's Work*. Vol. 15. Ed. J. Pelikan. St. Louis: Concordia, 1972. Pp. 3–187.

Lys, Daniel. *L'Ecclésiaste ou que vaut la vie?* Paris: Letouzey et Ané, 1977.

Maillot, A. *La Contestation: Commentaire de l'Ecclésiaste*. Lyon: Cahiers de Reveil, 1971.

Michel, D. *Qohelet*. Erträge der Forschung 258. Darmstadt: Wissenschaftliche Buchgesellschaft, 1988.

Murphy, R. E. *Ecclesiastes*. WBC 23A. Dallas: Word Books, 1992.

Nötscher, F. *Kohelet*. Echter Bibel 4. Würzburg: Echter, 1954.

Ogden, G. *Qoheleth*. Sheffield: JSOT, 1987.

Ploeg, J. van der. *Prediker*. BOT 8. Roermond: Romen & Zonen, 1952.

Plumptre, E. H. *Ecclesiastes*. CBSC. Cambridge: Cambridge University, 1887.

Podechard, E. *L'Ecclésiaste*. EBib. Paris: Gabalda, 1912.

Rashbam. *The Commentary of R. Samuel Ben Meir Rashbam on Qoheleth*. Ed. S. Japhet and R. Salters. Jerusalem/Leiden: Magnes/Brill, 1985.

Ravasi, G. *Qohelet*. Milano: Edizioni Paoline, 1988.

Scott, R. B. Y. *Proverbs. Ecclesiastes*. AB 18. Garden City, N.Y.: Doubleday, 1965.

Siegfried, C. G. *Prediger und Hoheslied*. HKAT 2:3,2. Göttingen: Vandenhoeck & Ruprecht, 1898.

Strobel, A. *Das Buch Prediger (Kohelet)*. Die Welt der Bibel. Düsseldorf: Patmos, 1967.

Whybray, R. N. *Ecclesiastes*. NCBC. Grand Rapids, Mich.: Eerdmans, 1989.

Wildeboer, G. "Der Prediger," in *Die fünf Megilloth*. KHC 17. Freiburg: Mohr [Paul Siebeck], 1898. Pp. 109–68.

Zapletal, V. *Das Buch Kohelet*. Freiburg: Gschwend, 1905.

Zimmerli, W. *Das Buch des Predigers Salomo*. ATD 16/1. Göttingen: Vandenhoeck & Ruprecht, 1962. Pp. 123–253.

III. ARTICLES, MONOGRAPHS, AND SPECIAL STUDIES

Ackroyd, P. R. "Two Hebrew Notes," *ASTI* 5 (1966/67) 82–86.

Alderini, G. "Qohelet 5,7–8: Note linguistiche ed esegetische," *BeO* 183 (1995) 13–32.

Alonso-Schökel, L. A *Manual of Hebrew Poetics*. SubBib 11. Rome: Pontifical Biblical Institute, 1988.

Anat, M. A. "The Lament on the Death of Humanity in the Scroll of Qohelet," *Beth Mikra* 15 (1970) 375–80 [Hebrew].

Armstrong, J. F. "Ecclesiastes in Old Testament Theology," *PSB* 94 (1983) 16–25.

Audet, J.-P. "A Hebrew-Aramaic List of Books of the Old Testament in Greek Transcription," *JTS* 1 (1950) 135–54.

Auffret, P. "'Rien du tout de nouveau sous le soleil'. Étude stucturelle de Qoh 1,4–11," *Folia Orientalia* 26 (1989) 145–66.

Backhaus, F. J. *"Denn Zeit und Zufall trifft sie alle": Studien zur Komposition und zum Gottesbild im Buch Qohelet*. BBB 83. Frankfurt am Main: Anton Hain, 1993.

———. "Die Pendenskonstruktion im Buch Qohelet," *ZAH* 8 (1995) 1–30.

Baltzer, K. "Women and War in Qohelet 7,23–8,1a," *HTR* 80 (1987) 127–32.

Barthélemy, D. *Les devanciers d'Aquila*. VTSup 10. Leiden: Brill, 1963.

Baumgärtel, F. "Die Ochsenstachel und die Nägel in Koh 12,11," *ZAW* 81 (1969) 98.

Bianchi, R. "'Essi non hanno chi li consoli' (Qoh 4:1)," *Rivista Biblica* 40 (1992) 299–307.

———. "The Language of Qohelet: A Bibliographical Survey," *ZAW* 105 (1993) 210–23.

Bickell, G. *Der Prediger über den Wert des Daseins: Wiederherstellung des Bisher zerstückelten Textes*. Innsbruck: Wagner, 1884.

Bickerman, E. J. *Four Strange Books of the Bible: Jonah, Daniel, Koheleth, Esther*. New York: Schocken, 1967.

Bishop, E. F. F. "A Pessimist in Palestine," *PEQ* 100 (1968) 33–41.

Blenkinsopp, J. "Ecclesiastes 3.1–15: Another Interpretation," *JSOT* 66 (1995) 55–64.

Bonora, A. *Il Libro Di Qohelet*. Guide spirituali all'antico testamento. Roma: Citta Nuova Editrice, 1992.

Bons, E. "Zur Gliederung und Kohärenz von Koh 1,12–2,11," *BN* 24 (1984) 73–93.

———. "*šiddā w-šiddōt*: Überlegungen zum Verständnis eines Hapaxlegomenons," *BN* 36 (1987) 12–16.

Braun, R. *Kohelet und die frühhellenistische Popularphilosophie*. BZAW 130. Berlin/New York: de Gruyter, 1973.

Brenner, A. "M Text Authority in Biblical Love Lyrics: The Case of Qoheleth

3:1–9 and Its Textual Relatives," in *On Gendering Texts: Female and Male Voices in the Hebrew Bible*. Biblical Interpretation 1. Ed. A. Brenner and F. van Dijk-Hemmes. Leiden/New York: Brill, 1993. Pp. 133–63.

Broznick, N. M. "Of the Making of Books There is No End," *Beth Mikra* 82 (1979/80) 213–18 [Hebrew].

Bruns, J. E. "The Imagery of Eccles 12,6a," *JBL* 84 (1965) 428–30.

Burkitt, F. C. "Is Ecclesiastes a Translation?" *JTS* 23 (1922) 22–28.

Busto Saíz, J. R. "Estructura métrica y estrófica del 'poema sobre la juventud y la vejez': Qohelet 11,7–12,7," *Sef* 43 (1983) 17–25.

———. "בוראיך (Qoh 12,1): Reconsiderado," *Sef* 46 (1986) 85–87.

Butting, K. "Weibsbilder bei Kafka und Kohelet. Eine Auslegung von Prediger 7,23–29," *Texte und Kontexte* 14 (1991) 2–15.

Buzy, D. "Le portrait de la vieillesse (Ecclésiaste XII, 1–7)," *RB* 41 (1932) 329–40.

———. "La notion du bonheur dans l'Ecclésiaste," *RB* 43 (1934) 494–511.

———. "Les auteurs de l'Ecclésiaste," *L'Année Theologique* 11 (1950) 317–36.

Castellino, G. "Qohelet and His Wisdom," *CBQ* 30 (1968) 15–28.

Ceresko, A. R. "The Function of Antanaclasis (*mṣ'* 'to find' // *mṣ'* 'to reach, overtake, grasp') in Hebrew Poetry, Especially in the Book of Qoheleth," *CBQ* 44 (1982) 551–69.

Chia, P. P. "Wisdom, Yahwism, Creation: In Quest of Qoheleth's Theological Thought," *Jian Dao* 3 (1995) 1–32.

Chopineau, J. *Hèvèl en hébreu biblique: Contribution à l'étude des rapports entre sémantique et exégèse de l'Ancien Testament*. Doctoral dissertation, University of Strasbourg, 1971.

———. "Une image de l'homme. Sur Ecclésiaste 1/2," *ÉTR* 53 (1978) 366–70.

———. "L'Image de Qohelet dans l'Exégèse Contemporaine," *RHPR* 59 (1979) 595–603.

Coppens, J. "La structure de l'Ecclésiaste," in *La sagesse de l'Ancien Testament*. Ed. M. Gilbert. BETL 51. Gembloux: Leuven University, 1979. Pp. 288–92.

Corré, A. D. "A Reference to Epipasm in Koheleth," *VT* 4 (1954) 416–18.

Crenshaw, J. L. "The Eternal Gospel (Eccl. 3:11)," in *Essays in Old Testament Ethics (Fs. J. P. Hyatt)*. Ed. J. L. Crenshaw and J. T. Willis. New York: KTAV, 1974. Pp. 23–55.

———. "The Shadow of Death in Qoheleth," in *Israelite Wisdom (Fs. S. Terrien)*. Ed. J. G. Gammie. Missoula, Mont.: Scholars, 1978.

———. "The Birth of Skepticism," in *The Divine Helmsman (Fs. L. H. Silberman)*. Ed. J. L. Crenshaw and S. Sandmel. New York: KTAV, 1980. Pp. 1–19.

———. "Qoheleth in Current Research," *HAR* 7 (1983) 41–56.

———. "The Expression *mî yôdēaʿ* in the Hebrew Bible," *VT* 36 (1986) 274–88.

———. "Youth and Old Age in Qoheleth," *HAR* 11 (1987) 1–13.

Cross, F. M. "Papyri of the Fourth Century B.C. from Dâliyeh," in *New Directions in Biblical Archaeology*. Ed. D. N. Freedman and J. C. Greenfield. Garden City, N.Y.: Doubleday, 1969. Pp. 45–69.

————. "Samaria Papyrus I: An Aramaic Slave Conveyance of 335 B.C.E.," *EI* 18 (1985) 7–17.

————. "A Report on the Samaria Papyri," in *Congress Volume, Jerusalem 1986*. VTSup 40. Ed. J. A. Emerton. Leiden: Brill, 1988. Pp. 17–26.

Crüsemann, F. "The Unchangeable World: The 'Crisis of Wisdom' in Koheleth," in *The God of the Lowly*. Ed. by W. Schottroff and W. Stegemann. Trans. by M. J. O'Connell. Maryknoll, N.Y.: Orbis, 1984 [1979]. Pp. 57–77.

Dahood, M. "Canaanite-Phoenician Influence in Qoheleth," *Bib* 33 (1952) 30–52, 191–221.

————. "The Language of Qoheleth," *CBQ* 14 (1952) 227–32.

————. "Qoheleth and Recent Discoveries," *Bib* 39 (1958) 302–18.

————. "Qoheleth and Northwest Semitic Philology," *Bib* 43 (1962) 349–65.

————. "Canaanite Words in Qoheleth 10,20," *Bib* 46 (1965) 210–12.

————. "The Phoenician Background of Qoheleth," *Bib* 47 (1966) 264–82.

————. "Scriptio Defectiva in Qoheleth 4,10a," *Bib* 49 (1968) 243.

————. "Three Parallel Pairs in Eccl. 10:18. A Reply to Prof. Gordis," *JQR* 62 (1971) 84–87.

————. "Northwest Semitic Philology and Three Biblical Texts," *JNSL* 2 (1972) 17–22.

D'Alario, Vittoria. *Il Libro del Qohelet: Struttura Litteraria e Retorica*. Supplementi alla Rivista Biblica 27. Bologna: Dehoniane, 1992.

Davila, J. R. "Qoheleth and Northern Hebrew," *Maarav* 5–6 (1990) 69–87.

Day, J. "Foreign Semitic Influence on the Wisdom of Israel and Its Appropriation in the Book of Proverbs," in *Wisdom in Israel (Fs. J. A. Emerton)*. Ed. J. Day et al. Cambridge: Cambridge University, 1995. Pp. 55–70.

Dell, K. J. "Ecclesiastes as Wisdom: Consulting Early Interpreters," *VT* 44 (1994) 301–29.

Dell'Aversano, C. "משפט in Qoh 11:9c," in *Biblische und Judaistische Studien (Fs. P. Sacchi)*. Ed. A. Vivian. Franfurt am Main: Peter Lang, 1990. Pp. 121–34.

Delsman, W. C. "Zur Sprache des Buches Koheleth," in *Von Kanaan bis Kerala (Js. J. van der Ploeg)*. AOAT 211. Ed. W. C. Delsman et al. Neukirchen-Vluyn: Kevelaer/Neukirchener, 1982. Pp. 341–65.

Dohmen, C. "Der Weisheit letzter Schluß? Anmerkungen zur Übersetzung und Bedeutung von Koh 12,9–14," *BN* 63 (1992) 12–18.

Dohmen, C. and M. Oeming. *Biblischer Kanon, worum und wozu? Eine Kanontheologie*. Questiones disputate 137. Freiburg: Herder, 1992.

Driver, G. R. "Problems and Solutions," *VT* 4 (1954) 225–45.

Duesberg, H. and I. Fransen. "La critique de la sagesse par le Qoheleth," in *Les scribes inspirés*. Maredsous: Editions de Maredsous, 1969. Pp. 537–92.

Ehrlich, A. B. *Randglossen zur hebräischen Bibel*. Vol. 7. Leipzig: Hinrich's, 1914. Pp. 55–108.

Eissfeldt, O. "Alles Ding währt seine Zeit," in *Kleine Schriften*. Vol. 5. Ed. R. Sellheim and F. Maass. Tübingen: Mohr, 1973. Pp. 174–78.

Ellermeier, F. "Die Entmachung die Weisheit im Denken Qohelets: zu Text und Auslegung von Qoh 6,7–9," *ZTK* 60 (1963) 1–20.

———. "Das Verbum חוש in Koh. 2,25. Eine exegetische, auslegungsgeschichtliche und semasiologische Untersuchung," *ZAW* 75 (1963) 197–217.

———. *Qohelet I/1. Untersuchungen zum Buche Qohelet.* Herzberg: Jungfer, 1967.

———. *Qohelet I/2. Einzelfrage Nr. 7: Das Verbum חוש in Qoh. 2,25. Akkadisch ḫâšu(m) 'sich sorgen' im Lichte neu veröffentlicher Texte.* 2d ed. Herzberg: Jungfer, 1970.

Euringer, S. *Der Masorahtext des Koheleth.* Leipzig: Hinrich's, 1890.

Fernández, E. "Es Ecclesiastes una Versión?" *Bib* 3 (1922) 45–50.

Fischer, A. "Beobachtungen zur Kompositionen von Kohelet 1,3–3,15," *ZAW* 103 (1991) 72–86.

Foresti, F. "*ʿāmāl* in Koheleth: 'Toil' or 'Profit'," *ECarm* 31 (1980) 415–30.

Forman, C. G. "The Pessimism of Ecclesiastes," *JSS* 3 (1958) 336–43.

———. "Koheleth's Use of Genesis," *JSS* 5 (1960) 256–63.

Fox, M. V. "Frame-Narrative and Composition in the Book of Qohelet," *HUCA* 48 (1977) 83–106.

———. "A Study of Antef," *Or* 46 (1977) 393–423.

———. "The Identification of Quotations in Biblical Literature," *ZAW* 92 (1980) 416–31.

———. "The Meaning of *Hebel* for Qohelet," *JBL* 105 (1986) 409–27.

———. "Qoheleth 1.4," *JSOT* 40 (1988) 109.

———. "Aging and Death in Qoheleth 12," *JSOT* 42 (1988) 55–77.

———. *Qohelet and His Contradictions.* BLS 18. Sheffield: Almond, 1989.

———. "Wisdom in Qoheleth," in *In Search of Wisdom: Essays in Memory of John G. Gammie.* Ed. L. G. Perdue et al. Louisville: Westminster/John Knox, 1993. Pp. 115–31.

Fox, M. V. and B. Porten. "Unsought Discoveries: Qohelet 7:23–8:1a," *HS* 19 (1979) 26–38.

Fredericks, D. C. "Chiasm and Parallel Structure in Qoheleth 5:6–6:9," *JBL* 108 (1989):17–35.

———. "Life's Storms and Structural Unity in Qoheleth 11:1–12:8," *JSOT* 52 (1991):95–114.

———. *Qoheleth's Language: Re-evaluating Its Nature and Date.* ANETS 3. Lewiston, N.Y.: Mellen, 1988.

———. *Coping with Transience: Ecclesiastes on Brevity in Life.* The Biblical Seminar 18. Sheffield: JSOT Press, 1993.

Frendo, A. "The 'Broken Construct Chain' in Qoh 10,10b," *Bib* 62 (1981) 544–45.

Galling, K. "Koheleth-Studien," *ZAW* 50 (1932) 276–99.

———. "Stand und Aufgabe der Kohelets-Forschung," *TRev* 9 (1934) 355–73.

———. "Das Rätsel der Zeit im Urteil Kohelets (Koh. 3,1–15)," *ZTK* 58 (1961) 1–15.

Gelio, R. "Osservazioni critiche sul *māšāl* di Qoh. 7,5–7," *Lateranum* 54 (1988) 1–15.

Gemser, B. "The Instruction of 'Onchsheshonqy and Biblical Wisdom Literature," in *Congress Volume, Oxford, 1959*. VTSup 7. Leiden: Brill, 1960. Pp. 102–28.

Gese, H. "The Crisis of Wisdom in Koheleth," in *Theodicy in the Old Testament*. Issues in Religion and Theology 4. Ed. J. L. Crenshaw. Philadelphia/London: Fortress/SPCK, 1983. Pp. 141–53 [1963].

Gilbert, M. "La description de la vielliesse en Qohelet XII 1–7 est-elle allégorique?" in *Congress Volume, Vienna, 1980*. Ed. J. A. Emerton. VTSup 32. Leiden: Brill, 1981. Pp. 96–109.

Ginsberg, H. L. *Studies in Koheleth*. Texts and Studies of the Jewish Theological Seminary of America 17. New York: Jewish Theological Seminary of America, 1950.

———. "Koheleth 12,4 in the Light of Ugaritic," *Syria* 33 (1951) 99–101.

———. "Supplementary Studies in Kohelet," *PAAJR* (1952) 35–62.

———. "The Structure and Contents of the Book of Koheleth," in *Wisdom in Israel and in the Ancient Near East*. Ed. M. Noth and D. Winton Thomas. VTSup 3. Leiden: Brill, 1955. Pp. 138–49.

———. "The Quintessence of Koheleth," in *Biblical Motifs*. Ed. A. Altmann. Philip W. Lown Institute of Advanced Judaic Studies. Studies and Texts 3. Cambridge, Mass.: Harvard University, 1966. Pp. 47–59.

Glender, S. "The Book of Ecclesiastes: A Collection Containing 'Diverse' Sayings or a Unified and Consistent World-View," *Beth Mikra* 26 (1981) 378–87 [Hebrew].

Gómez Aranda, M. "Ecl 12,7 Interpretado por Abraham Ibn 'Ezra," *Sef* 52 (1992) 13–21.

Good, E. M. "The Unfilled Sea: Style and Meaning in Ecclesiastes 1:2–11," in *Israelite Wisdom* (*Fs. S. Terrien*). Ed. J. G. Gammie et al. Missoula, Mont.: Scholars, 1978. Pp. 59–73.

———. *Irony in the Old Testament*. 2d ed. Sheffield: Almond, 1981.

Gordis, R. "Eccles. 1:17: Its Text and Interpretation," *JBL* 56 (1937) 323–30.

———. "Quotations in Wisdom Literature," *JQR* 30 (1939/40) 123–47.

———. "The Social Background of Wisdom Literature," *HUCA* 18 (1943/44) 77–118.

———. "The Original Language of Qohelet," *JQR* 37 (1946/47) 67–84.

———. "Quotations as a Literary Usage in Biblical, Oriental, and Rabbinic Literature," *HUCA* 22 (1949) 157–219.

———. "The Translation Theory of Qohelet Re-examined," *JQR* 40 (1949/50) 103–16.

———. "Koheleth — Hebrew or Aramaic?" *JBL* 71 (1952) 93–109.

———. "Was Koheleth a Phoenician?" *JBL* 71 (1955) 103–14.

———. "Qohelet and Qumran — A Study of Style," *Bib* 41 (1960) 395–410.

Gorsen, L. "La cohérence de la conception de Dieu dans l'Ecclésiaste," *ETL* 46 (1970) 282–324.

Greenberg, M. "נסה in Exodus 20:20 and the Purpose of the Sinaitic Theophany," *JBL* 79 (1960) 273–76.

Greenfield, J. C. "Lexicographical Notes I," *HUCA* 29 (1958) 203–38.

———. "The Wisdom of Ahiqar," in *Wisdom in Israel (Fs. J. A. Emerton)*. Ed. J. Day et al. Cambridge: Cambridge University, 1995. Pp. 43–52.

Gropp, D. M. "The Origin and Development of the Aramaic *šallīṭ* Clause," *JNES* 52 (1993) 31–36.

Harrison, C. R. *Qoheleth in Social-historical Perspective*. Unpublished dissertation, Duke University, 1991.

Hermann, W. "Zu Koheleth 3,14," *Wissenschaftliche Zeitschriftliche Leipziger Universität* 3 (1953/54) 293.

Hertzberg, H. W. "Palästinische Bezüge im Buche Kohelet," *ZDPV* 73 (1957) 13–24.

Hessler, B. "Der verhüllte Gott. Der heilstheologische Sinn des Buches Ecclesiastes (Kohelet)," *TGl* 43 (1953) 347–59.

Holm-Nielsen, S. "On the Interpretation of Qoheleth in Early Christianity," *VT* 24 (1974) 168–77.

———. "The Book of Ecclesiastes and the Interpretation of It in Jewish and Christian Theology," *ASTI* 10 (1975/76) 38–96.

Horton, E. "Koheleth's Concept of Opposites as Compared to Samples of Greek Philosophy and Near and Far Eastern Wisdom Classics," *Numen* 19 (1972) 1–21.

Humbert, P. *Recherches sur les source égyptiennes de la littérature sapientiale d'Israël*. Neuchâtel: Delachaux & Niestlé, 1929.

Hurvitz, A. "The Chronological Significance of 'Aramaisms' in Biblical Hebrew," *IEJ* 18 (1968) 234–40.

———. "The History of a Legal Formula: *kōl ʾăšer ḥāpēṣ ʿāśāh* (Psalms CXV 3, CXXXV 6)," *VT* 32 (1982) 257–67.

Hutter, M. "Adam als Gärtner und König (Gen 2,8.15)," *BZ* 30 (1986) 258–62.

Hyvärinen, K. *Die Übersetzung von Aquila*. ConBOT 10. Lund: Gleerup, 1977.

Irwin, W. A. "Ecclesiastes 3,18," *AJSL* 56 (1939) 298–99.

———. "A Rejoinder," *AJSL* 58 (1941) 100–1.

———. "Eccles. 4:13–16," *JNES* 3 (1944) 255–57.

———. "Ecclesiastes 8:2–9," *JNES* 4 (1945) 130–31.

Isaksson, B. *Studies in the Language of Qoheleth: With Special Emphasis on the Verbal System*. Studia Semitica Upsaliensia 10. Stockholm: Almqvist & Wiksell, 1987.

Jarick, J. *Gregory Thaumaturgos' Paraphrase of Ecclesiastes*. SBLSCS 29. Atlanta: Scholars, 1990.

———. "Aquila's Koheleth," *Textus* 15 (1990) 131–39.

Jasper, F. N. "Ecclesiastes: A Note for Our Time," *Int* 21 (1967) 259–73.

Johnson, R. E. *The Rhetorical Question as a Literary Device in Ecclesiastes*. Unpublished dissertation, Southern Baptist Theological Seminary, 1986.

Johnson, R. F. *A Form Critical Analysis of the Sayings in the Book of Ecclesiastes*. Unpublished dissertation, Emory University, 1973.

Johnston, R. K. "Confessions of a Workaholic: A Reappraisal of Qoheleth," *CBQ* 38 (1976) 14–28.

Jones, B. W. "From Gilgamesh to Qoheleth," in *The Bible in the Light of Cuneiform Literature: Scripture in Context III.* Ed. W. W. Hallo et al. ANETS 8. Lewiston, N.Y.: Edwin Mellen, 1990. Pp. 349–79.

Joüon, P. "Sur le nom de Qohéleth," *Bib* 2 (1921) 53–54.

———. "Notes de syntaxe hébraïque: 2. L'emploi du participe et du parfait dans L'Ecclésiaste," *Bib* 2 (1921) 225–26.

———. "Notes philologiques sur le texte hébreu d'Ecclésiaste," *Bib* 11 (1930) 419–25.

Kaiser, C. W. "Integrating Wisdom Theology into Old Testament Theology: Ecclesiastes 3:10–15," in *A Tribute to Gleason Archer.* Ed. W. C. Kaiser and R. F. Youngblood. Chicago: Moody, 1986. Pp. 197–209.

Kaiser, O. "Die Sinnkreise bei Kohelet," in *Rechtfertigung, Realismus, Universalismus in biblischer Sicht (Fs. A. Köberle).* Ed. G. Müller. Darmstadt: Wissenschaftliche Buchgesellschaft, 1978. Pp. 3–21.

———. *Der Mensch unter der Schicksal.* BZAW 161. Berlin: de Gruyter, 1985.

———. "Qoheleth," in *Wisdom in Ancient Israel (Fs. J. A. Emerton).* Ed. J. Day et al. Cambridge: Cambridge University, 1995. Pp. 83–93.

———. "Die Botschaft des Buches Kohelet," *ETL* 71 (1995) 48–70.

Kamenetzky, A. S. "Die Pšita zu Koheleth textkritisch und ihrem Verhältnis zu dem masoretischen Text, der Septuaginta und den andern alten griechischen Versionen," *ZAW* 24 (1904) 181–239.

———. "Die Rätselname Koheleth," *ZAW* 34 (1914) 225–28.

———. "Die ursprünglich beabsichtigte Aussprache der Pseudonyms קהלת," *OLZ* (1921) 11–15.

Klein, C. *Kohelet und die Weisheit Israels: Eine Formgeschichtliche Studie.* BWANT 132. Stuttgart/Berlin: Kohlhammer, 1994.

Klopfenstein, M. A. "Die Skepsis des Qohelet," *TZ* 28 (1972) 97–109.

Knoph, C. S. "The Optimism of Koheleth," *JBL* 49 (1930) 195–99.

Kottsieper, I. "Die Bedeutung der Wz. 'ṣb und skn in Koh 10,9," *UF* 18 (1986) 213–22.

Kroeber, C. S. "'Der Prediger': Ein Werk der altjüdischen Weisheitsliteratur," *Altertum* 11 (1965) 195–209.

Krüger, T. "'Frau Weisheit' in Koh 7,26?" *Bib* 73 (1992) 394–403.

Kugel, J. "Qohelet and Money," *CBQ* 51 (1989) 32–49.

Lambert, W. G. "Some New Babylonian Wisdom Literature," in *Wisdom in Israel (Fs. J. A. Emerton).* Ed. J. Day et al. Cambridge: Cambridge University, 1995. Pp. 30–42.

Lamparter, H. *Das Buch der Weisheit: Prediger und Spruche.* Botschaft des Alten Testaments 16. Stuttgart: Calwer, 1959.

Lang, B. "Ist der Mensch hilflos? Das biblische Buch Kohelet, neu und kritisch gelesen," *ThQ* 159 (1979) 109–24.

Lange, A. *Weisheit und Torheit bei Kohelet und in Seiner Umwelt.* Frankfurt am Main/Bern/New York: Peter Lang, 1991.

Lauha, A. "Die Krise des religiösen Glaubens bei Kohelet," in *Wisdom in Israel and in the Ancient Near East*. Ed. M. Noth and D. Winton Thomas. VTSup 3. Leiden: Brill, 1955. Pp. 83–91.

———. "Kohelets Verhältnis zur Geschichte," in *Die Botschaft und die Boten* (*Fs. H. W. Wolff*). Ed. J. Jeremias and L. Perlitt. Neukirchen-Vluyn: Neukirchener, 1981. Pp. 393–401.

———. "Omnia Vanitas: Die Bedeutung von *hbl* bei Kohelet," in *Glaube und Gerechtigkeit* (*Fs. R. Gyllenberg*). SFEG 38. Ed. J. Kiilunen et al. Helsinki: Suomen Eksegeettisen Seura, 1983. Pp. 19–25.

Leahy, M. "The Meaning of Ecclesiastes 10,15," *ITQ* 18 (1951) 297–300.

———. "The Meaning of Ecclesiastes 12,1–5," *ITQ* 19 (1952) 297–300.

Leanza, S. "Eccl 12,1–7: L'interpretazione escatologica dei Padri e degli esegeti medievali," *Augustianum* 18 (1978) 191–208.

Levine, B. A. "The Semantics of Loss: Two Exercises in Biblical Hebrew Lexicography," in *Solving Riddles and Untying Knots* (*Fs. J. C. Greenfield*). Ed. Z. Zevit, et al. Winona Lake, Ind.: Eisenbrauns, 1995. Pp. 137–58.

Levine, E. "Qohelet's Fool: A Composite Portrait," in *On Humor and the Comic in the Hebrew Bible*. Ed. Y. T. Radday and A. Brenner. JSOTSup. 92. Sheffield: Almond, 1990. Pp. 277–94.

Lévy, I. "Rien de nouveau sous le soleil," *Nouvelle Clio* 5 (1953) 326–28.

Lichtheim, M. "Observations on Papyrus Insinger," in *Studien zu altägyptischen Lebenslehren*. Ed. E. Hornung and O. Keel. OBO 28. Freiburg/Göttingen: Vandenhoeck & Ruprecht, 1979. Pp. 283–305.

Loader, J. A. "Qohelet 3:2–8 — A 'Sonnet' in the Old Testament," *ZAW* 81 (1969) 240–42.

———. "Different Reactions of Job and Qoheleth to the Doctrine of Retribution," *OTWSA* 15/16 (1972/73) 43–48.

———. *Polar Structures in the Book of Qohelet*. BZAW 152. Berlin/New York: de Gruyter, 1979.

Lohfink, N. "War Kohelet ein Frauenfeind? Ein Versuch, die Logik und den Gegenstand von Koh., 7,23–8, 1a herauszufinden," in *La Sagesse de l'Ancien Testament*. BETL 51. Ed. M. Gilbert. Gembloux: Leuven University, 1979. Pp. 259–87.

———. "*melek, šallîṭ* und *môšēl* bei Kohelet und die Abfassungszeit des Buchs," *Bib* 62 (1981) 535–43.

———. "Warum ist der Tor unfähig, böse zu handeln? (Koh 4,17)," in *Augewählte Vorträge*. ZDMG Supplement 5. Ed. F. Steppat. Wiesbaden: Steiner, 1983. Pp. 113–20.

———. "Die Wiederkehr des immer Gleichen: Eine frühe Synthese zwischen griechischem und jüdischem Weltgefühl in Kohelet 1,4–11," *Archivo di Filosofia* 53 (1985) 125–49.

———. "Gegenwart und Ewigkeit: die Zeit im Buch Kohelet," *Geist und Leben* 60 (1987) 2–12.

———. "Kohelet und die Banken: zur Übersetzung von Kohelet V 12–16," *VT* 39 (1989) 488–95.

————. "Koh 1,2 'Alles ist Windhauch' — universale oder anthropologische Aussage?" in *Der Weg zum Menschen* (*Fs. A. Deissler*). Ed. R. Mosis and L. Ruppert. Freiberg: Herder, 1989. Pp. 201–16.

————. "Technik und Tod nach Kohelet," in *Strukturen christlichen Existenz: Beiträge zur Erneuerung des geistlichen Lebens* (*Fs. F. Wulf*). Ed. H. Schlier et al. Würzburg: Echter, 1989. Pp. 27–35.

————. "Qoheleth 5:17–19 — Revelation by Joy," *CBQ* 52 (1990) 625–35.

————. "Zur Philosophie Kohelets: Eine Auslegung von Kohelet 7,1–10," *BK* 45 (1990) 20–25.

————. "Grenzen und Einbindung des Kohelet-Schlußgedichts." In *Altes Testament: Forschung und Wirkung* (*Fs. H. G. Reventlow*). Ed. P. Mommer and W. Thiel. Frankfurt: Lang, 1994. Pp. 33–46.

————. "Freu Dich, Jüngling — doch nicht, weil du jung bist zum Formproblem im Schlußgedicht Kohelets (Koh 11,9–12,8)," *Biblical Interpretation* 3/2 (1995) 158–89.

Longman, T. III. "Comparative Methods in Old Testament Studies: Ecclesiastes Reconsidered," *TSFB* 7/4 (March–April 1984) 5–9.

————. *Fictional Akkadian Autobiography: A Generic and Comparative Study.* Winona Lake, Ind.: Eisenbrauns, 1991.

Loretz, O. "Zur Darbietungsform der 'Ich-Erzählung' im Buche Qohelet," *CBQ* 25 (1963) 46–59.

————. *Qohelet und der alte Orient: Untersuchungen zu Stil und theologischer Thematik des Buches Qohelet.* Freiburg: Herder, 1964.

————. "Gleiches Los trifft alle! Die Antwort des Buches Qohelet," *BK* 20 (1965) 6–8.

————. "Altorientalische und kanaanäische Topoi im Buche Kohelet," *UF* 12 (1980) 267–78.

————. "Anfänge jüdischer Philosophie nach Qoheleth 1,1–11 und 3,1–15," *UF* 23 (1991) 223–44.

————. "'Frau' und griechisch-jüdische Philosophie im Buch Qohelet (Qoh 7,23–8,1 und 9,6–10)," *UF* 23 (1991) 245–64.

Luder, E. "Gott und Welt nach dem Prediger Salomo," *STU* 28 (1958) 105–14.

Lux, R. "'Ich, Kohelet bin König . . .': Die Fiktion als Schlüssel zur Wirklichkeit in Kohelet 1, 12–2, 26," *EvT* 50 (1990) 331–42.

————. "Der 'Lebenskompromiß' — ein Wesenszug im Denken Kohelets? Zur Auslegung von Koh 7,15–18," in *Alttestamentlicher Glaube und Biblische Theologie* (*Fs. H. Dietrich*). Ed. J. Hausmann and H.-J. Zobel. Stuttgart: Kohlhammer, 1992. Pp. 268–78.

Machinist, P. "Fate, *miqreh*, and Reason: Some Reflections on Qohelet and Biblical Thought," in *Solving Riddles and Untying Knots* (*Fs. J. C. Greenfield*). Ed. Z. Zevit et al. Winona Lake, Ind.: Eisenbrauns, 1995. Pp. 159–75.

McNeile, A. H. *An Introduction to Ecclesiastes.* Cambridge: Cambridge University, 1904.

Michel, D. "Vom Gott, der im Himmel ist (Reden von Gott bei Qohelet)," *Theologia Viatorum* 12 (1973/74) 87–100.

———. "Qohelet-Probleme: Überlegungen zu Qoh 8,2–9 und 7,11–14," *Theologia Viatorum* 15 (1979/80) 81–103.

———. *Untersuchungen zur Eigenart des Buches Qohelet.* BZAW 183. Berlin/New York: de Gruyter, 1989.

Middendorp, T. *Die Stellung Jesu Ben Siras zwischen Judentum und Hellenismus.* Leiden: Brill, 1973.

Moore, G. F. "The Caper-plant and Its Edible Products, with Reference to Eccles. XII,5," *JBL* 10 (1891) 56–64.

Mulder, J. S. M. "Qoheleth's Division and Also Its Main Points," in *Von Kanaan bis Kerala* (*Fs. J. P. M. van der Ploeg*). Ed. W. C. Delsman et al. Neukirchen-Vluyn: Kevelaer/Neukirchener, 1982. Pp. 341–65.

Müller, H.-P. "Wie sprach Qohälät von Gott?" *VT* 18 (1968) 507–21.

———. "Neige der althebräischen 'Weisheit.' Zum Denken Qohäläts," *ZAW* 90 (1978) 238–64.

———. "Theonome Skepsis und Lebensfreude zu Koh 1,12–3,15," *BZ* 30 (1986) 1–19.

———. "Der unheimliche Gast. Zum Denken Kohelets," *ZTK* 84 (1987) 440–64.

Murphy, R. E. "The Pensées of Coheleth," *CBQ* 17 (1955) 304–14.

———. "A Form-critical Consideration of Ecclesiastes VII," in *SBLASP* 1. Ed. G. MacRae. Missoula, Mont.: Scholars, 1974. Pp. 77–85.

———. "Koheleth, der Skeptiker," in *Leiden und christlicher Glaube.* Concilium 12/11 (1976) 567–70.

———. "Qoheleth's 'Quarrel' with the Fathers," in *From Faith to Faith* (*Fs. D. G. Miller*). Ed. D. Y. Hadidian. Pittsburgh: Pickwick, 1981. Pp. 235–45.

———. "Qohelet Interpreted: The Bearing of the Past on the Present," *VT* 32 (1982) 331–37.

———. "The Faith of Qoheleth," *Word and World* 7 (1987) 253–60.

———. "The Sage in Ecclesiastes and Qoheleth the Sage," in *The Sage in Israel and the Ancient Near East.* Ed. J. G. Gammie and L. G. Perdue. Winona Lake, Ind.: Eisenbrauns, 1990. Pp. 263–71.

———. "Qoheleth and Theology?" *BTB* 21 (1991) 30–33.

———. "On Translating Ecclesiastes," *CBQ* 53 (1991) 571–79.

Neher, A. *Notes sur Qohélét (L'Ecclésiaste).* Paris: Minuit, 1951.

Nishimura, T. "Quelques réflexions sémiologues à propos de la crainte de dieu' de Qohelet," *Annual of the Japanese Biblical Institute* 5 (1979) 67–87.

———. "Un mashal de Qohelet 1,2–11," *RHPR* 59 (1979) 605–15.

Nötscher, F. "Schicksal und Freiheit," *Bib* 40 (1959) 460–62.

Ogden, G. S. *The Ṭôb-spruch in Qoheleth: Its Function and Significance as a Criterion for Isolating and Identifying Aspects of Qoheleth's Thought.* Unpublished dissertation, Princeton Theological Seminary, 1975.

———. "The 'Better'-Proverb (Ṭôb-Spruch), Rhetorical Criticism, and Qoheleth," *JBL* 96 (1977) 489–505.

———. "Qoheleth's Use of the 'Nothing is Better' Form," *JBL* 98 (1979) 339–50.

———. "Historical Allusions in Qoheleth iv 13–16?" *VT* 30 (1980) 309–15.

————. "Qoheleth ix 17–x 20: Variations on the Theme of Wisdom's Strength and Vulnerability," *VT* 30 (1980) 27–37.

————. "Qoheleth ix 1–16," *VT* 32 (1982) 158–69.

————. "Qoheleth xi 1–6," *VT* 33 (1983) 222–30.

————. "Qoheleth xi 7–xii 8: Qoheleth's Summons to Enjoyment and Reflection," *VT* 34 (1984) 27–38.

————. "The Mathematics of Wisdom: Qoheleth iv 1–12," *VT* 34 (1984) 446–53.

————. "The Interpretation of דור in Ecclesiastes 1.4," *JSOT* 34 (1986) 91–92.

————. "'Vanity' It Certainly Is Not," *BT* 38 (1987) 301–7.

————. "Translation Problems in Ecclesiastes 5.13–17," *BT* 39 (1989) 423–28.

Pautrel, R. "Data sunt a pastore uno (Eccl 12,11)," *RSR* 41 (1953) 406–10.

Pennacchini, B. "Qohelet ovvero il libro degli assurdi," *EuntDoc* 30 (1977) 491–510.

Perry, T. A. *Dialogues with Kohelet*. University Park, Pa.: Pennsylvania State University, 1993.

Pfeiffer, E. "Die Gottesfurcht im Buche Kohelet." In *Gottes Wort und Gottes Land* (*Fs. H. W. Hertzberg*). Ed. H. Reventlow. Göttingen: Vandenhoeck & Ruprecht, 1965. Pp. 133–58.

Pfeiffer, R. H. "The Peculiar Skepticism of Ecclesiastes," *JBL* 53 (1934) 100–9.

Piotti, F. "La lingua dell'Ecclesiaste e lo sviluppo storico dell'Ebraico," *BeO* 15 (1973) 185–96.

————. "Il rapporto tra ricchi, stolti e principi in Qoh. 10,6–7 alla luce della letteratura sapienziale," *Scuola Cattolica* 102 (1974) 328–33.

————. "Osservazioni su alcuni paralleli extrabiblici nell' 'allegoria della vecchiaia' (Qohelet 12,1–7)," *BeO* 21 (1977) 119–28.

————. "Osservazioni su alcuni problemi esegetici nel libro dell'Ecclesiastes (studio I)," *BeO* 20 (1978) 169–81.

————. "Osservazioni su alcuni problemi esegetici nel libro dell'Ecclesiastes (studio II): il canto degli stolti (Qoh. 7,5)," *BeO* 21 (1979) 129–40.

————. "Osservazioni su alcuni problemi esegetici nel libro dell'Ecclesiastes (studio III)," *BeO* 22 (1980) 243–53.

Plessis, S. J. du. "Aspects of the Morphological Peculiarities of the Language of Qohelet," in *De fructu oris sui* (*Fs. A. van Selms*). Ed. I. H. Eybers and F. C. Fensham. Leiden: Brill, 1971. Pp. 164–80.

Podechard, E. "La composition du livre de l'Ecclésiaste," *RB* 21 (1912) 161–91.

Polk, T. "The Wisdom of Irony: A Study of *Hebel* and Its Relation to Joy and the Fear of God in Ecclesiastes," *Studia Biblica et Theologica* 6 (1976) 3–17.

Priest, J. "Humanism, Skepticism, and Pessimism in Israel," *JAAR* 36 (1968) 311–26.

Qimron, E. "שהתקיף (Qoh. 6:10)—An Unnoticed Aramaism," *Leš* 56 (1991) 117 [Hebrew].

Rainey, A. F. "A Study of Ecclesiastes," *CTM* (1964) 148–57.

————. "A Second Look at Amal in Qoheleth," *CTM* 36 (1965) 805.

Ranston, H. *Ecclesiastes and the Early Greek Wisdom Literature*. London: Epworth Press, 1925.

Reines, C. W. "Koheleth on Wisdom and Wealth," *JJS* 5 (1954) 80–84.

———. "Koheleth VIII,10," *JJS* (1954) 86–87.

Renan, E. *L'Ecclésiaste traduit de l'Hébreu avec une étude sur l'age et le caractère du livre*. Paris: Levy, 1882.

Rofé, A. "'The Angel' in Qoh 5:5 in the Light of a Wisdom Dialogue Formula," *EI* 14 (1978) 105–9 [Hebrew].

Rousseau, F. "Structure de Qohélet I 4–11 et plan du livre," *VT* 31 (1981) 200–17.

Rowley, H. H. "The Problem of Ecclesiastes," *JQR* (1951/52) 87–90.

Rudolph, W. *Vom Buch Kohelet*. Munster: Aschendorf, 1959.

Salters, R. B. "The Word for 'God' in the Peshitta of Koheleth," *VT* 21 (1971) 251–54.

———. *The Book of Ecclesiastes: Studies in the Versions and the History of Exegesis*. Unpublished dissertation, University of St. Andrews, 1972.

———. "Qoheleth and Canon," *ExpTim* 86 (1975) 339–42.

———. "A Note on the Exegesis of Ecclesiastes 3,15b," *ZAW* 88 (1976) 419–22.

———. "Text and Exegesis in Koh 10,19," *ZAW* 89 (1977) 423–26.

———. "Notes on the History of the Interpretation of Koh 5,5," *ZAW* 90 (1978) 95–101.

———. "Notes on the Interpretation of Qoh 6,2," *ZAW* 91 (1979) 282–89.

———. "Exegetical Problems in Qoheleth," *IBS* 10 (1988) 44–59.

Savignac, J. de. "La sagesse du Qôhéléth et l'épopée de Gilgamesh," *VT* 28 (1978) 318–23.

Sawyer, J. F. A. "The Ruined House in Ecclesiastes 12: A Reconstruction of the Original Parable," *JBL* 94 (1976) 519–31.

Schmidt, J. "Koh 4,17," *ZAW* 58 (1940/41) 279–80.

Schmitt, A. "Zwischen Anfechtung. Kritik und Lebensbewältigung. Zur theologischen Thematik des Buches Kohelet," *TTZ* 88 (1977) 114–31.

Schoors, A. "The Particle *kî*," *OTS* 21 (1981) 240–76.

———. "Kethib-Qere in Ecclesiastes," in *Studie Paulo Naster Oblata*. OLA 13. Leuven: Peeters, 1982. Pp. 215–22.

———. "La structure littéraire de Qoheleth," *OLP* 13 (1982) 91–116.

———. "The Peshitta of Koheleth and Its Relation to the Septuagint," in *After Chalcedon: Studies in Theology and Church History* (Fs. A. van Roey). OLA 18. Leuven: Peeters, 1985. Pp. 345–57.

———. "Koheleth: A Perspective of Life after Death," *ETL* 61 (1985) 295–303.

———. "The Use of Vowel Letters in Qoheleth," *UF* 20 (1988) 277–86.

———. "The Pronouns in Qoheleth," *HS* 30 (1989) 71–87.

———. *The Preacher Sought to Find Pleasing Words: A Study of the Language of Qoheleth*. OLA 41. Leuven: Peeters, 1992.

———. "Bitterder dan de Dood is de Vrouw (Koh 7,26)," *Bij* 54 (1993) 121–40.

Schubert, M. *Schöpfungstheologie bei Kohelet*. Beiträge zur Erforschung des Alten Testaments und des antiken Judentums 15. Frankfurt am Main/New York: Lang, 1989.

Schulte, A. "Zu Koh 5,7 u. 8," *BZ* 8 (1910) 4.

Schunck, K. D. "Drei Seleukiden im Buche Kohelet?" *VT* 9 (1959) 192–201.

Sekine, S. "Qohelet als Nihilist," *Annual of the Japanese Biblical Institute* 17 (1991) 3–54.

Seow, C. L. "Qohelet's Autobiography," in *Fortunate the Eyes that See* (Fs. D. N. *Freedman*). Ed. A. Beck et al. Grand Rapids, Mich.: Eerdman, 1995. Pp. 257–82.

Serrano, J. J. "I Saw the Wicked Buried (Eccl 8,10)," *CBQ* 16 (1954) 168–70.

Shaffer, A. "The Mesopotamian Background of Qohelet 4:9–12," *EI* 8 (1967) 246–50 [Hebrew].

———. "New Information on the Origin of the 'Three-fold Cord,'" *EI* 9 (1969) 159–60 [Hebrew].

Shank, H. C. "Qohelet's World and Lifeview as Seen in His Recurring Phrases," *WTJ* 37 (1974) 57–73.

Shefi, E. "Ecclesiastes' Treatment of the Concept of Time," *Beth Mikra* 36 (1990–91) 144–51 [Hebrew].

Sheppard, G. T. "The Epilogue to Qoheleth as Theological Commentary," *CBQ* 39 (1977) 182–89.

———. "Canonization: Hearing the Voice of the Same God Through Historically Dissimilar Traditions," *Ex Auditu* 1 (1985) 106–14.

Skehan, P. W. "Wisdom and Ecclesiastes," in *Studies in Israelite Poetry and Wisdom*. CBQMS 1. Washington, D.C.: Catholic Biblical Association, 1971. Pp. 213–36.

Smith, L. L. "Critical Evaluation of the Book of Ecclesiastes," *JBR* 21 (1953) 100–5.

Spangenberg, I. J. J. "Die Struktuur en stekkening van Prediker 4:17–5:6," *Nederduits Gereformeerde Teologiese Tydskrif* 30 (1989) 260–69.

Spina, F. A. "Qoheleth and the Formation of Wisdom," in *The Quest for the Kingdom of God* (Fs. G. E. *Mendenhall*). Ed. H. B. Huffmon et al. Winona Lake, Ind.: Eisenbrauns, 1983. Pp. 267–79.

Staerk, W. "Zur Exegese von Koh 10,20 und 11,1," *ZAW* 59 (1942/43) 216–18.

Staples, W. E. "The 'Vanity' of Ecclesiastes," *JNES* 4 (1943) 95–104.

———. "'Profit' in Ecclesiastes," *JNES* 4 (1945) 87–96.

———. "Vanity of Vanities," *CJT* 1 (1955) 141–56.

———. "The Meaning of *ḥepeṣ* in Ecclesiastes," *JNES* 24 (1965) 110–12.

Steinmann, J. *Ainsi parlait Qohèlèt*. Livre la Bible 38. Paris: Cerf, 1973.

Stern, E. *Material Culture of the Land of the Bible in the Persian Period, 538–332 B.C.* Jerusalem: Israel Exploration Society, 1982 [1973].

Stiglmair, A. "Weisheit und Jahweglaube im Buche Kohelet," *TLZ* 83 (1974) 257–83.

Strange, M. R. *The Questions of Moderation in Eccl. 7:15–18*. Unpublished dissertation, Catholic University of America, 1969.

Strauss, H. "Erwägungen zur seelsorgerlichen Dimension von Kohelet 12,1–7," *ZTK* 78 (1981) 267–75.

Szubin, H. Z. and B. Porten, "Royal Grants in Egypt: A New Interpretation of Driver 2," *JNES* 46 (1987) 39–48.

Taylor, C. *The Dirge of Coheleth in Ecclesiastes XII.* London: Williams and Norgate, 1874.

Thomas, D. W. "A Note on בְּמַדָּֽךְ in Ecclesiastes X.20," *JTS* 50 (1949) 177.

Torrey, C. C. "The Question of the Original Language of Qohelet," *JQR* 39 (1948–49) 151–60.

———. "The Problem of Ecclesiastes IV,13–16," *VT* 2 (1952) 175–77.

Trible, P. "Ecclesiastes," in *The Books of the Bible: The Old Testament.* Vol. 1. Ed. B. W. Anderson. New York: Scribner's, 1989. Pp. 231–39.

Tyler, T. *Ecclesiastes.* London: Williams & Norgate, 1874.

Ullendorff, E. "The Meaning of קהלת," *VT* 12 (1962) 215.

Umbreit, F. W. C. "Die Einheit des Buches Koheleth," *ThStK* 30 (1857) 7–56.

van Hoomisen, G. "'Et je fais l'éloge de la joie?' (Qoh 8,15)," *Lumen Vitae* 43 (1988) 37–46.

Varela, A. "A New Approach to Eccl 5:8–9," *BT* 27 (1976) 240–41.

Vattioni, F. "Niente di novo sotto il sole," *RevistB* 21 (1959) 64–67.

Verheij, A. "Paradise Retried: On Qohelet 2:4–6," *JSOT* 50 (1991) 113–15.

Waard, J. de. "The Translator and Textual Criticism (with Particular Reference to Eccl 2,25)," *Bib* 60 (1979) 509–29.

———. "The Structure of Qoheleth," in *Proceedings of the 8th World Congress of Jewish Studies.* Jerusalem, 1982. Pp. 57–64.

Wagner, M. *Die lexicalischen und grammitikalischen Aramäismen im alttestamentlichen Hebräisch.* BZAW 96. Berlin/New York: de Gruyter, 1966.

Waldman, N. M. "The DĀBĀR RAʻ of Eccl 8:3," *JBL* 98 (1979) 407–8.

Whitley, C. F. *Koheleth: His Language and Thought.* BZAW 148. Berlin/New York: de Gruyter, 1979.

———. "Koheleth and Ugaritic Parallels," *UF* 11 (1979) 811–24.

Whybray, R. N. "Qohelet the Immoralist? (Qoh 7:16–17)," in *Israelite Wisdom* (*Fs. S. Terrien*). Ed. by J. G. Gammie et al. Missoula, Mont.: Scholars, 1978. Pp. 191–204.

———. "Conservatisme et radicalisme dans Qohelet," in *Sagesse et Religion, Colloque de Strasbourg, 1976.* Ed. E. Jacob. Paris: Presses Universitaires, 1979. Pp. 65–81.

———. "The Identification and Use of Quotations in Ecclesiastes," in *Congress Volume, Vienna, 1980.* VTSup 32. Ed. J. A. Emerton. Leiden: Brill, 1981. Pp. 435–51.

———. "Qoheleth, Preacher of Joy," *JSOT* 23 (1982) 87–98.

———. "Ecclesiastes 1.4–7 and the Wonders of Nature," *JSOT* 41 (1988) 105–12.

———. "'A Time to Be Born and a Time to Die,' Some Observations on Ecclesiastes 3:2–8," in *Near Eastern Studies.* Ed. M. Mori et al. Wiesbaden: Harrassowitz, 1991. Pp. 469–83.

Wilson, G. H. "'The Words of the Wise': The Intent and Significance of Qohelet 12:9–14," *JBL* 103 (1984) 175–92.

Wise, M. O. "A Calque from Aramaic in Qoheleth 6:12; 7:12; and 8:13," *JBL* 109 (1990) 249–57.

Witzenrath, H. H. *Süß ist das Licht . . . Eine literaturwissenschaftliche Untersuchung zu Koh 11,7–12,7.* Arbeiten zu Text und Sprache im Alten Testament 11. St. Ottilien: EOS, 1979.

Wright, A. G. "The Riddle of the Sphinx: The Structure of the Book of Qoheleth," *CBQ* 30 (1968) 313–34.

———. "The Riddle of the Sphinx Revisited: Numerical Patterns in the Book of Qoheleth," *CBQ* 42 (1980) 38–51.

———. "'For Everything There Is a Season': The Structure and Meaning of the Fourteen Opposites (Ecclesiastes 3,2–8)," in *De la Tôrah au Messie: Mélanges Henri Cazelles.* Ed. J. Dore et al. Paris: Desclée, 1981. Pp. 321–28.

———. "Additional Numerical Patterns in Qoheleth," *CBQ* 45 (1983) 32–43.

Youngblood, R. "Qoheleth's 'Dark House' (Eccl 12.5)," *JETS* 29 (1986) 397–410.

Zimmerli, W. "Das Buch Kohelet — Traktat oder Sentenzensammlung?" *VT* 24 (1974) 221–30.

———. "'Unveränderbare Welt' oder 'Gott ist Gott': Ein Plädoyer für die Unaufgebbarkeit des Predigerbuches in der Bibel," in *Wenn nicht jetzt, wann dann?* (*Fs. H.-J. Kraus*). Ed. H. G. Geyer, et al. Neukirchen-Vluyn: Neukirchener, 1983. Pp. 165–78.

Zimmermann, F. "The Root *KAHAL* in Some Scriptural Passages," *JBL* 50 (1931) 311–12.

———. "The Aramaic Provenance of Qohelet," *JQR* 36 (1945–46) 17–45.

———. "The Question of Hebrew in Qohelet," *JQR* 40 (1949–50) 79–102.

———. *The Inner World of Qohelet.* New York: KTAV, 1973.

IV. ANCIENT NEAR EASTERN SOURCES

Cardascia, G. *Les archives des Murašû, une famille d'hommes d'affaires babyloniens à l'époque perse (455–403 av. J.-C.).* Paris: Imprimerie Nationale, 1951.

Charles, R. H., ed. *Apocrypha and Pseudepigrapha of the Old Testament.* 2 vols. Oxford: Clarendon, 1913.

Cowley, A., ed. *Aramaic Papyri of the Fifth Century* B.C. Osnabrück: Zeller, 1923. Reprint. 1967.

Davies, G. I. *Ancient Hebrew Inscriptions.* Cambridge, N.Y.: Cambridge University, 1991.

Degan, R., et al. *Neue Ephemeris für semitische Epigraphik* III. Wiesbaden: Harrassowitz, 1978.

Dietrich, M., O. Loretz, and J. Sanmartín, eds. *The Cuneiform Alphabetic Texts from Ugarit, Ras Ibn Hani and Other Places* (*KTU*: 2d, enlarged ed.). ALASP 8. Münster: Ugarit-Verlag, 1995.

Donner, H. and W. Röllig, eds. *Kanaanäische und aramäische Inschriften.* 3 vols. Wiesbaden: Harrassowitz, 1962.

Dossin, G. "L'Inscription de fondation de Iaḫdun-Lim roi de Mari," *Syria* 32 (1952) 1–28.

Faulkner, R. O. "The Bremner-Rhind Papyrus — IV," *JEA* 24 (1930) 41–53.

Fitzmyer, J. *The Aramaic Inscriptions of Sefîre.* BibOr 19. Rome: Pontifical Biblical Institute, 1967.

Gardiner, A. H. *The Admonitions of an Egyptian Sage.* Leipzig: Hinrich's, 1909.

Gibson, J. C. L. *Canaanite Myths and Legends.* Edinburgh: T. & T. Clark, 1977.

Götze, A. *Die Annalen des Muršiliš.* MVAG 38; Leipzig: Hinrich's, 1933.

Gordon, E. I. *Sumerian Proverbs.* Philadelphia: University of Pennsylvania, 1959.

Hackett, J. *The Balaam Text from Deir 'Allā.* HSM 31. Chico, Calif.: Scholars, 1984.

Harper, R. F., ed. *Assyrian and Babylonian Letters.* 14 vols. Chicago: University of Chicago, 1892–1914.

Held, M. "A Faithful Lover in an Old Babylonian Dialogue," *JCS* 15 (1961) 1–26.

Hoftijzer, J. and G. van der Kooij. *Aramaic Texts from Deir 'Alla. Oriens antiquus* 19. Leiden: Brill, 1976.

Knudtzon, J. A., ed. *Die El-Amarna Tafeln.* 2 vols. VAB 2. Leipzig: Hinrich's, 1915.

Kraeling, E. G. *The Brooklyn Museum Aramaic Papyri.* New Haven: Yale University, 1953.

Lambert, W. G. *Babylonian Wisdom Literature.* Oxford: Clarendon, 1960.

Lichtheim, M. *Ancient Egyptian Literature.* 3 vols. Berkeley: University of California, 1971–80.

Lindenberger, J. M. *The Aramaic Papyri of Ahiqar.* Baltimore: Johns Hopkins University, 1983.

Luckenbill, D. D., ed. *The Annals of Sennacherib.* OIP 2. Chicago: University of Chicago, 1924.

———. *Ancient Records of Assyria and Babylonia.* 2 vols. Chicago: University of Chicago, 1926–27. Reprinted 1989.

Meissner, B. *Babylonian und Assyrien* II. Heidelberg: Winters, 1925.

Moran, W. L., ed. *The Amarna Letters.* Baltimore: Johns Hopkins, 1987.

Oppenheim, A. L. *The Interpretation of Dreams in the Ancient Near East. TAPA* 46. Philadelphia: American Philological Society, 1956.

Porten, B. and A. Yardeni. *Textbook of Aramaic Documents from Egypt.* 3 vols. Jerusalem: Hebrew University, 1986–93.

Qimron, E. and J. Strugnell. "An Unpublished Halakhic Letter from Qumran," in *Biblical Archaeology Today: Proceedings of the International Congress on Biblical Archaeology, Jerusalem, April, 1984.* Jerusalem: Israel Exploration Society, 1985. Pp. 400–407.

Segal, J. B. *Aramaic Texts from North Saqqâra.* London: Egypt Exploration Society, 1983.

Strassmaier, J. N. *Inschriften von Cyrus.* Leipzig: Hinrich's, 1890.

Streck, M. *Assurbanipal und die letzen assyrischen Könige bis zum Untergang Ninevehs* II. *VAB* 7. Leipzig: Hinrich's, 1916.

Tigay, J. H. *The Evolution of the Gilgamesh Epic*. Philadelphia: University of Pennsylvania, 1982.

Volten, A. *Studien zum Weisheitsbuch des Anii*. Danske videnskabernes selskab, historik-filologiske meddelelser, xxiii, 3. Copenhagen: Levin & Munksgaard, 1937.

TRANSLATION,
NOTES,
AND COMMENTS

◆

SUPERSCRIPTION (1:1)

1   ¹The words of Qohelet, the Davidide, a king in Jerusalem.

NOTES

1 1. *The words of.* The expression *dibrê PN* frequently introduces anthologies of various sorts. In sapiential and hymnic texts, such superscriptions always indicate origination and/or authorship. Thus, the superscription of Qohelet may be compared with those in other wisdom texts that use more specific terms than the ambiguous *dibrê*: e.g., "the proverbs of Solomon" (Prov 1:1; 10:1; 25:1); "Solomon's song of songs" (Song 1:1). The Egyptian wisdom instructional texts typically begin with the introduction of the text as "instruction(s) of PN" (*AEL* I, p. 62) or "the instruction(s) made by PN" (*AEL* I, pp. 58, 135; II, p. 136). In short, a typical superscription in wisdom literature identifies either the composer or compiler of the work or the person in whose name the teachings of the text are issued.

Qohelet. This name or appellative occurs seven times in the book: three times in the beginning (1:1, 2, 12), thrice in the end (12:8, 9, 10), and once in the middle (7:27). The fact that we find the form appearing with the definite article in 12:8 and 7:27 (emended text) suggests the word was originally an appellative (so Ginsburg), although that does not preclude the possibility that it was used as a proper name (LXX also has the definite article in 1:2). The traditional English translation "the Preacher" (so KJV, RSV) goes back to Luther's rendering, *der Prediger.* That interpretation of the word, however, is already evident in the work of Gregory Thaumaturgos in the third century C.E. The name *Ecclesiastes* is simply the Latin transliteration of the Greek, *ekklēsiastēs,* a word attested in the classical period for a member of the citizens' assembly (*ekklēsia*). Thus, Greek *ekklēsiastēs* means lit. "citizen," not "preacher." Already in the Greek translation we see the interpretation of the name or appellative as related to Hebrew *qāhāl* "assembly." So *Qoh. Rabb.* explains that Qohelet was so called because his words were uttered in public: "Solomon assembled (*yaqhēl*) the elders of Israel" (1 Kgs 8:1) and he addressed the *qāhāl* "assembly" (1 Kgs 8:22). In addition to the allusion to Solomon, the medieval commentators Rashbam and Rashi associated the name with the biblical skeptic mentioned in Prov 30:1, Agur, which is interpreted to mean "Gatherer" in Aramaic.

The apparent feminine form of the word *qōhelet* has prompted a few interpreters to think that it refers to the *collection*, which is personified as the author in a manner analogous to the personification of *ḥokmâ* "Wisdom" (so already Rashi and Ibn Ezra). But whereas *ḥokmâ* is treated as a feminine noun, the form *qōhelet* is not. Besides being identified as king (1:1), the masculine verb is used with the name in 1:2 and 12:9, and the author is identified as a *ḥākām*, lit. "wise man" (12:9). E. Renan took the consonants *qhlt* to be some sort of cryptogram concealing the name of Solomon — like *RMBM* ("Rambam"), which stood for Rabbi Moshe Ben Maimon (= Maimonides) and *RŠY* ("Rashi"), which referred to Rabbi Shelomo Yiṣḥaqi (*L'Ecclésiaste*, pp. 13–15). Renan did not, however, venture to decipher the putative cryptogram and, indeed, any proposal would be purely speculative. F. Zimmermann ("Aramaic Provenance of Qohelet," pp. 43–44) supposed that Hebrew *qhlt* is a mistranslation of Aramaic *knš* ("Gatherer"), the numerical value of which is 375, thus corresponding to the value of Hebrew *šlmh* "Solomon." According to Zimmermann, the translator misunderstood the Aramaic indicator of the emphatic state to be the feminine marker.

The feminine ending for a masculine name or appellative is not without parallel in Hebrew (see GKC §122.r; Joüon-Muraoka §89.b). Analogy may be made with the names *sōperet* and *pōkeret-haṣṣĕbāyîm*, which are listed among the *bĕnê ʿabdê šĕlōmōh* "the sons of Solomon's servants" (Ezra 2:55, 57; Neh 7:57, 59; 1 Esdr 5:33–34). The *qōtelet* form apparently was used to designate various functionaries: thus *sōperet* (originally "scribe"), *pōkeret-haṣṣĕbāyîm* ("the binder of gazelles"?); cf. also *peḥâ* "governor," a word related to Akkadian *pīḥātu/pāḥātu* "governor," originally *bēl pīḥāti/pāḥāti*, lit. "lord of the province." One may also compare Arabic *ḥalîfat* "successor," a substantive that came to be understood as an epithet. Moreover, even as we have both the forms *qōhelet* and *haqqōhelet* (lit. "the Qohelet"), we get *sōperet* and *hassōperet* (Ezra 2:55; Neh 7:57; 1 Esdr 5:33). These may all originally have been epithets that became personal names (cf. English "smith"/"the smith" > "Smith"). There are other masculine personal names in the Bible that are marked with apparent feminine endings: e.g., *misperet* (Neh 7:7); *gĕnūbat* (1 Kgs 11:20); *bĕkôrat* (1 Sam 9:1); *ʿaśwāt* (1 Chron 7:33); *šimrāt* (1 Chron 8:21). In addition, there are numerous examples of Palmyrene masculine names with apparent feminine endings: e.g., *zrzyrt*, *ghynt*, *ʿmrt*.

Some commentators turn to Arabic and Syriac cognates to argue that the word really means "penitent one," "old man," "arguer," "skeptic," and so forth. These cognates are, however, imprecise at best. In support of the meaning "arguer" or "skeptic" the word *qĕhillâ* (Neh 5:7; Deut 33:4; Sir 7:7) is sometimes cited and interpreted to mean "rebuke" (so Zimmermann, "The Root *KAHAL*," pp. 311–12). But the meaning of *qĕhillâ* is secured by its parallelism with *ʿēdâ* "congregation" in Sir 7:7. In any case, it is unlikely that the ancient reader would have connected the name or appellative with anything else other than the common understanding of *qhl*.

Qohelet probably does mean "Gatherer" or "Collector" — whether of wisdom, wealth, or people. One may note that the verb *qhl* in Syriac may mean not only "to assemble (people)" but also "to compile" (Payne Smith, *A Compendious Syriac Dictionary*, p. 491). Indeed, whatever its etymological origin, the name or appellative surely would have been associated with the most obvious meaning of the root *qhl* "gather." This is the meaning of the root assumed by all the ancient versions and other early interpreters. For the use of the Qal participle instead of the expected Hiphil, one may compare *dōbēr* instead of *mĕdabbēr*, *nōgēn* instead of *mĕnaggēn*, *šōhēr* instead of *mĕšahēr*, and so forth.

Whatever the background of the word, it seems likely that one is supposed to think of Solomon here. Perhaps one is supposed to recall Solomon as a gatherer of wisdom and wealth (1 Kings 3–11).

the Davidide. Hebrew *ben-dāwīd*, lit. "the son of David." Hebrew *bēn* does not necessarily mean a literal son. It may refer to a son, grandson, or simply anyone from a particular lineage (cf. "son of David" in Matt 21:9; Mark 10:47; 12:35). Within the Hebrew Bible itself, however, *ben-dāwīd* always refers to a literal son of David, especially Solomon. Only three times does the expression refer to some other son than Solomon (2 Sam 13:1 [2x]; 2 Chron 11:18). While it is true that Solomon is never mentioned explicitly in the book, there can be no doubt that the text intends to evoke the memory of the king in a manner reminiscent of other superscriptions in the wisdom literature of Israel (Prov 1:1; 10:1; 25:1).

a king in Jerusalem. Hebrew *melek bîrûšālayim*. LXX (*basileōs israēl en ierousalēm*) reflects Hebrew *mlk yśr'l byrwšlm* "the king of Israel in Jerusalem," which is certainly expansionistic (so also OL, SyrH, and Copt). The addition of the name "Israel" anticipates the reference to the author as *melek 'al-yiśrā'ēl bîrûšālayim* "a king over Israel in Jerusalem" in 1:12 and may be due to the influence of the superscription of the book of Proverbs, where we have *melek yiśrā'ēl* "the king of Israel" (Prov 1:1). The shorter reading of MT is to be preferred. Vulg and Syr have "a king of Jerusalem," perhaps reflecting Hebrew *mlk yrwšlm* in the *Vorlage(n)*. This is a smoother reading, but MT is acceptable (cf. *melek yiśrā'ēl bĕšōmĕrōn* in 2 Kgs 14:23). Grammatically, *melek bîrûšālayim* can refer to either Qohelet or David, but in light of 1:12 it is virtually certain that the former is meant. The allusion to the kingship of the author is deliberate, as is often the case in sapiential texts of the Bible (Prov 1:1; 10:1; 25:1; Song 1:1) and Egyptian didactic literature. We should not, therefore, repoint *mlk* to derive the meaning "property-holder" or "counselor," as is sometimes done.

COMMENT

The book is introduced as "the words of Qohelet." The expression "the words of So-and-So" occurs most frequently in the Hebrew Bible in reference to anthologies of various sorts, notably (1) prophetic (Jer 1:1; Amos 1:1), (2) historical (1 Chron 29:29; 2 Chron 9:29; 12:15; 20:34; 33:18–19; 1 Kgs 11:41; 15:31; Neh 1:1), (3) hymnic (Ps 7:1; 2 Chron 29:30), and (4) sapiential (Prov 30:1; 31:1; cf. 1:6; 22:17 [according to the Greek]). The title here introduces the work as an anthology, a collection of the teachings of Qohelet, whose name probably means "Gatherer" or "Collector."

The superscription may be compared with the typical introductions of Egyptian didactic literature: "the instruction of So-and-So" or "the instruction made by So-and-So" (see references in Notes above). Such superscriptions lend authenticity and authority to the text, since they are usually issued in the name of someone well-known to the reader. Typically they are written in the third person (the author is talked about), whereas the teachings themselves are in the first person (the author speaks). The superscription often includes some biographical information that may be supplemented at the end of the text in an epilogue.

The superscription of Ecclesiastes attributes the content of the book to Qohelet, who is called "the Davidide, a king in Jerusalem." Since we do not know of a Davidide (literally "the son of David") named Qohelet, especially not one who ruled in Jerusalem, it is reasonable to assume that the author of this superscription means Solomon. If one takes into consideration the phrase "a king over Israel" in 1:12, there can be no doubt that Solomon is meant. Saul, David, and Solomon all are called "king over Israel" (1 Sam 23:17; 2 Sam 5:2–5, 12, 17; 1 Kgs 1:34; 3:28), but only David and Solomon can be said to have ruled "in Jerusalem"; others who are said to be "king over Israel" are from the Northern Kingdom (1 Kgs 14:13–14; 15:25; 16:29; 22:52; 2 Kgs 2:25) and would not have ruled in Jerusalem, while the Judean kings — those who ruled "in Jerusalem" — are never called "king over Israel." It is clear, too, from Qohelet's self-portrait in 1:12–2:11 that he had Solomon in mind: the unmatched wealth and wisdom of the king, the mention of landmarks around Jerusalem that traditionally have been associated with Solomon, and allusions to Solomon's experience at Gibeon in 1 Kgs 3:3–15 all point to the king who was Israel's patron of wisdom *par excellence*. The language of kingship in 1:12–2:11, however, may be part of a fictional royal autobiography employed to show that even kings can have no real control over matters that are beyond human grasp, and, in some ways, even the wisest of kings is no better off than the ordinary fool. Beyond that fictional royal autobiography in 1:12–2:11, there is no hint that the text stems from the royal court. Indeed, in passages where the author comments on governance or on one's attitude toward rulers, one gets the sense that he writes as an outsider to the court. The author is critical of the absence of justice where one might expect it (3:16; 4:1–2; 5:8 [Heb v 7]). That is the kind of social commentary one expects from critics of the royal court, outsiders, not from kings themselves. Moreover, Qohelet's perception of kingship seems to be distant, as if coming from one who only imagines what it is like to be facing a despot (8:2–4; 10:4, 16–17, 20). Some scholars think, therefore, that the superscription originally said only, "the words of Qohelet." The rest of the verse, it is argued, was added by a later editor, probably inspired by the Solomonic fiction in 1:12–2:11 (Galling, Ellermeier, Lauha). That is, however, merely conjectural.

Although Solomon could not have been the author of the book (see Introduction, pp. 36–38), it is likely that the superscription intends to evoke such a belief in the reader. Egyptian wisdom texts were often written in the name of kings

(*AEL* I, p. 136), famous court officials (*AEL* I, pp. 58, 69), or scribes (*AEL* II, p. 136). A great number of these, if not the majority, are pseudonymous — that is, they were composed in later periods but in the name of renowned figures from the past. A few that are associated with kings (e.g., *The Instruction of Merikare* and *The Instruction of Amenemhet*) are classified as "royal testaments," legacies of departing kings to their successors. Some scholars, therefore, identify "the words of Qohelet" with such a genre. But the comparison is not appropriate, for Ecclesiastes is not a political treatise, as the Egyptian royal testaments always are. The content of the book has little to do with governance. Wisdom texts, however, frequently are associated with royalty because kings were supposed to be responsible for preserving the social order that wisdom was supposed to achieve. So, too, within the book of Proverbs, several collections are attributed to King Solomon (Prov 1:1; cf. 10:1; 25:1), as are the Song of Songs (Song 1:1) and the Wisdom of Solomon. This common association of sapiential anthologies with Solomon no doubt arose from the tradition about his divinely endowed wisdom and his patronage of sapiential activities (1 Kings 3–11). Solomon was reputed to have "uttered three thousand proverbs; and his songs were a thousand and five," not to mention his interest in and encyclopedic knowledge of nature (1 Kgs 5:12–13 [Eng 4:33–34]). Although Hezekiah is also known to have been responsible for preserving wisdom collections (Prov 25:1), it was Solomon of all the Israelite kings who was most readily identified as a collector of wisdom — a "gatherer," as it were. Solomon was the archetypical person who had *gathered* everything for himself, and yet, he was subjected to life's vicissitudes as any human being, whether foolish or wise (see 1:12–2:11). Solomon was Qohelet, the Gatherer.

PART I.A. REFLECTION: EVERYTHING IS EPHEMERAL AND UNRELIABLE

I.A.1. PREFACE (1:2–11)

1 ²Vanity of vanities, says Qohelet, vanity of vanities! All is vanity!
  ³What advantage does one have in all the toil,
    at which one toils under the sun?
  ⁴A generation goes and a generation comes,
    yet the earth remains as ever.
  ⁵The sun rises and the sun sets,
    and to its place it presses on,
      there it rises.
  ⁶It goes south and it turns around to the north,
    Around and around goes the wind;
    And on account of its rounds, the wind returns.
  ⁷All the streams flow to the sea,
    but the sea is not full;
    To the place from which the streams flow,
    There they flow again.
  ⁸All words are wearying,
    No one is able to speak.
    An eye is not sated with seeing;
    An ear is not filled from hearing.

  ⁹Whatever has happened—that is what will happen; what has been done—that is what will be done. There is nothing new under the sun. ¹⁰If there is a thing of which one might say, "See this one, it is new!"—already it existed long ago, the ages that were before us had it. ¹¹There is no remembrance of those who

came before, nor of those who will come after. There will be no remembrance of them among those who will come afterwards.

NOTES

1   2. *Vanity of vanities.* Hebrew *hăbēl hăbālîm.* The construct form *hăbēl* (also in 12:8) is unique in Hebrew; one expects *hebel* for the construct. There are some examples of Hebrew construct forms with the *qĕṭal* pattern, even for segolate nouns (see BL §72.x), but the *qĕṭēl* form is another matter. The form is an "aramaized" variant (cf. *ʿăbēd* in Dan 6:21; *ṣĕlēm* in Dan 2:31; 3:1; etc.); Jerome notes in his commentary that the Hebrew has *Abal Abalim,* that is, *hăbal hăbālîm,* the vocalization that one expects. The juxtaposition of the singular and the plural of the same noun is the standard way in Hebrew to express the superlative: e.g., "king of kings" = "supreme king" (Dan 2:37; Ezra 7:12), "servant of servants" = "abject servant" (Gen 9:25), and "god of gods" = "highest god" (Deut 10:17). Thus, *hăbēl hăbālîm* refers to absolute or the ultimate *hebel,* a word that traditionally has been translated as "vanity."

The word *hebel* occurs 73 times in the Hebrew Bible, 38 times in Ecclesiastes alone. The literal meaning of *hebel* is "air" or "vapor" (Ps 62:10 [Eng 9]; Isa 57:13 [// *rûaḥ* "wind"]). This is the understanding of the word in Aq, Symm, and Theod, where it is translated as *atmos/atmis* (so also LXX[B] has *atmos* in 9:9). So, too, in Mishnaic Hebrew the word may refer to breath, air, steam, vapor, gas, and the like (*b. Šabb.* 88b, 119b; *Yebam.* 80b; cf. *Lev. Rabb.* section 29; see Jastrow, *Dictionary,* pp. 329–30). Accordingly, *Qoh. Rabb.* takes the word to be "like the steam from the oven" and the superlative is taken to mean that humanity is even less substantial than steam. Similar meanings are attested in various other Semitic languages (see K. Seybold, *TDOT* III, pp. 313–14). In the Mishnah, the Hiphil participle *mhbyl* means "making steam" (*m. Šabb.* 1:6).

In the Bible, *hebel* is used very often as a metaphor for something that is ephemeral or insubstantial. Thus, the human life span and, by extension, human beings themselves are said to be *hebel* (Pss 39:5–12 [Eng vv 4–11]; 62:10 [Eng v 9]; 78:33; Job 7:16). Human words, too, may be regarded as *hebel* (Job 21:34), as is physical beauty (Prov 31:30). In this sense, *hebel* is that which is of no lasting consequence (cf. *hebel niddāp* "fleeting vapor" in Prov 21:6). The word also may have the connotation of something that is unreliable. Foreign military help is said to be *hebel* (Isa 30:7; Lam 4:17), as are idols (Deut 32:21; 1 Kgs 16:13, 26; 2 Kgs 17:15; Jer 2:5; 8:19; 10:15; 14:22; 51:18; Zech 10:2; Jon 2:9 [Eng v 8]; Ps 31:7 [Eng v 6]). These are variously described as empty or ineffective (Isa 30:7; Job 9:29; 35:16; Jer 16:19; Ps 94:11; Isa 49:4) and delusive (Jer 16:19; Zech 10:2; Jer 10:15; 51:18; Ps 62:10 [Eng v 9]). The point is that these things give the impression of substantiality, but they are only illusory. It is not surprising, therefore, that *hebel* is associated with terms like *ṣelem* "a reflection" (Ps 39:7 [Eng v 6]), *hălômôt šāwʾ* "vacuous dreams" (Zech 10:2), and *ṣēl ʿôbēr* "a passing shadow" (Ps 144:4).

In Ecclesiastes itself, the meaning of *hebel* is difficult to determine. A number of important studies have appeared in this century, variously arguing that the word means "incomprehensible," "unknowable," "mysterious," "ironic," "enigmatic," and "absurd" (see Staples, "'Vanity' of Ecclesiastes," pp. 95–104; id. "Vanity of Vanities," pp. 141–56; Fox, "The Meaning of *Hebel*," pp. 409–27; Good, *Irony in the Old Testament*, pp. 176–83; Ogden, "'Vanity' It Certainly Is Not," pp. 301–7; Pennacchini, "Qohelet ovvero il libro degli assurdi," pp. 491–510; Michel, *Eigenart*, pp. 40–51). No single definition, however, works in every case. As elsewhere in the Bible, Qohelet uses *hebel* to speak of the ephemerality of life (6:12; 7:15; 9:9), and he speaks of *hebel* as something of little consequence, even empty (5:6 [Eng v 7]; 6:4, 11). So, too, he speaks of joy (2:1) and human accomplishments as *hebel* (2:11; 4:4). Youth and the prime of life also are said to be *hebel* (11:10). All these things are fleeting; they cannot be held on to forever. In a similar vein, the author associates *hebel* with *rĕʿût rûaḥ/raʿyôn rûaḥ* "pursuit of wind" (1:14; 2:11, 17, 26; 4:4, 16; 6:9), an idiom for activity that has no chance of success (see Notes at 1:14). Perhaps it was this imagery of a futile pursuit that led the author to use the word *hebel* for matters that are beyond the grasp of mortals—both physically (for the literal meaning of *hebel*) and intellectually (for the figurative use of the word). So the activities in the world and their unpredictable consequences are said to be *hebel* (1:2, 14; 2:17, 19, 21, 26; 4:4, 7–8, 16; 5:9 [Eng v 10]; 6:2, 9). They are unpredictable, arbitrary, and incomprehensible. They cannot be grasped. Hence Qohelet speaks of the common fate of death for the wise and the foolish, humans and animals, and the righteous and the wicked as *hebel* (2:15; 3:19; 8:10, 14). This common fate is *hebel* in the sense that it is confoundingly unpredictable and unknowable. It is beyond human ability to grasp.

The word clearly has negative connotations in the book, for *hebel* is associated with *rāʿâ rabbâ* "a great evil" (2:21), *ʿinyan rāʿ* "a terrible business" (4:8), and *ḥŏlî rāʿ* "a terrible sickness" (6:2). It is important to note, therefore, that *hebel* in Ecclesiastes is used specifically of human existence and human experiences of earthly realities, and not of God or of the cosmos in general (see Lohfink, "'Alles ist Windhauch,'" pp. 201–16). The view that "everything" is *hebel*, then, reflects not so much Qohelet's cosmology as it does his anthropology. What is *hebel* cannot be grasped—neither physically nor intellectually. It cannot be controlled.

In any case, it is clear that no single English word is adequate to convey the nuances of the Hebrew; the nuances of the word vary from text to text. For want of an adequate alternative, we will follow the traditional translations (LXX *mataiotēs*; Vulg *vanitas*) and use the term "vanity" to represent all that *hebel* may mean.

says Qohelet. LXX has *ho ekklēsiastēs* here, reflecting Hebrew *hqhlt*, which may be due to the influence of 7:27 (see Notes ad loc.) and 12:8. All extant Hebrew MSS, however, read the form without the definite article. The presence of the third-person verb has led commentators from Rashbam on to conclude that this verse is editorial, or at least that the words "Qohelet says" are editorial.

Fox has argued, however, that Egyptian wisdom texts frequently were framed by a third-person introduction and/or conclusion ("Frame-Narrative," pp. 83–106). The phrase 'āmar qōhelet "Qohelet says" is, according to Fox, the words not of an editor but the "teller of tales" who is responsible for the entire book, including the words attributed to Qohelet, the author's persona. For the use of a third-person narrative framing first-person materials, Fox cites the Egyptian *The Instruction of Kagemni* (AEL I, pp. 59–60), *The Prophecy of Neferti* (AEL I, pp. 140–44), *The Admonitions of Ipuwer* (AEL I, pp. 150–61), *The Instruction of Dua-khety* (AEL I, pp. 185–91), and *The Instruction of Ankhsheshonq* (AEL III, pp. 116–81).

A similar third-person introduction is found in the Sumerian text known as the *Instructions of Shuruppak* (see BWL, pp. 92–93). These texts demonstrate well the fact of third-person frameworks, although of these, only *The Prophecy of Neferti* and *The Instruction of Dua-khety* introduce the text specifically with "he says." There are other examples, however, that do introduce the teachings of the sage in this way. In *The Complaints of Khakheperre-Sonb*, just after the superscription introducing the author, the text begins with *ḏd.f* "he says" (Gardiner, *The Admonitions of an Egyptian Sage*, p. 97; see also *The Instruction of Hardjedef* [AEL I, p. 38], *The Instruction of Amenemhet* [AEL I, p. 136]). In *The Instruction of Ptahhotep*, one reads after the introduction, where the author is already named: *imy-r niwt ṱ3ty ptḥ ḥtp ḏd.f* "the mayor of the city, the vizier Ptahhotep, (he) says" (Papyrus Prisse, line 2). Thus, the introduction of the teachings of the sage with a third-person "he says" is proper form.

all. In this passage, "all" anticipates *bĕkol-'ămālô* "in all his toil." So it is not that everything that is known to humanity is *hebel*, but that toil and other human activities and earthly experiences are. In the concluding passage of the book, one finds again the judgment that "everything is *hebel*," referring in that case to human existence and earthly experiences.

3. *advantage.* The noun *yitrôn* occurs only in Ecclesiastes (10 times), along with the related words *yôtēr* (7 times) and *môtār* (once). The root is *ytr* "to surpass, exceed, be additional." Thus, the noun means "surplus" or "advantage." Dahood includes the word in a list of commercial terms found in Ecclesiastes ("Canaanite-Phoenician Influence," p. 221). If so, *yitrôn* "profit" is the opposite of another possible economic term, *ḥesrôn* "deficit" (1:15). There is some evidence for this usage in an Aramaic papyrus from North Saqqara in Egypt, where we read: *hyh ytrn ksp' zy qym bšnt 6* "(this) was the surplus of silver that stands in year six" (TAD III, 2.11.6). Plumptre suggested long ago that the word here refers to "the surplus, if any, of the balance-sheet of life" (*Ecclesiastes*, p. 104). The usage of these terms in Ecclesiastes, however, is certainly not limited to economics. While the usage of *yitrôn* in 1:3; 3:9; 5:8, 15 [Eng vv 9, 16]); and 7:12 may have economic overtones, that is not the case in 2:11, 13; 10:10, 11. It is important to observe that *yitrôn* here means "profit" in the sense of something additional, and not "profit" merely as "benefit." In other words, *yitrôn* in this case is not just "a plus" (something positive) but "a surplus" (an advantage). It is not that toil has no benefit whatsoever, but that toil does not give one any additional

"edge." The point is not that "*yitrôn* is not located in this world" (so Ogden, *Qoheleth*, pp. 28–29). Qohelet does not deny that *yitrôn* is possible in this world because he thought that it might be possible in another realm. Indeed, the author says the wise have *yitrôn* (a plus) over fools (2:11), and there is *yitrôn* (a plus) in the application of wisdom (10:10). The problem for Qohelet in this passage is not this world, but toil. When similar rhetorical questions about "advantage" are posed elsewhere in the book, the issue is always toil (2:22; 3:9; 5:15 [Eng v 16]; 6:11).

does one have. The noun *'ādām* occurs forty-nine times in the book, almost always in reference to humanity in general or to any person, regardless of gender. The only exception to this is in 7:28, where *'ādām* refers to a man. Murphy rightly notes that Qohelet's observations "are essentially universal in thrust" (*Ecclesiastes*, p. 5).

in all the toil. Hebrew *bĕ'ămālô*. It is possible to take the preposition here as the *bet pretii* (GKC §119.p) and so translate *bĕ'ămālô* "*for* all the toil." There is no reason, however, to follow Dahood in interpreting the preposition *bĕ-* as "from," in accordance with the usage in Ugaritic ("Phoenician Background," p. 265). The noun *'āmāl* "toil" occurs 22 times in the book; the verb appears 13 times. Perhaps the most startling fact about the occurrences of the noun *'āmāl* "toil" in the Bible is its close association with extremely negative terms: *'āwen* "trouble" (Num 23:21; Job 4:8; 15:35; Pss 7:15 [Eng v 14]; 10:7; 55:11 [Eng v 10]; 90:10; Isa 10:1; 59:4; Hab 1:3), *yāgôn* "grief" (Jer 20:18), *rā'* "evil" (Hab 1:13), *šeqer* "falsehood" (Ps 7:15 [Eng v 14]), *ka'as* "vexation" (Ps 10:14), *šāw'* "lie" (Job 7:3), *sôd* "destruction" (Prov 24:2), *ḥāmās* "violence" (Ps 7:17 [Eng v 16]), *'ŏnî* "affliction" (Deut 26:7; Ps 25:18), *rîš* "poverty" (Prov 31:7), and *mirmâ* "deceit" (Job 15:35; Ps 55:12 [Eng v 11]). Elsewhere, too, the word means pain, misery, or mischief (Gen 41:51; Judg 10:16; Job 3:10; 5:7; 11:16; Pss 73:5, 16; 94:20; 107:12; Isa 53:11). The noun *'āmāl* has strongly negative connotations. Thus, "toil" is not just "work" (*'ăbôdâ*) or "activity" (*ma'ăšeh*); it is not just "effort." In Ecclesiastes, the verb *'ml* is used of a person's physical or intellectual struggle to achieve some end or other (2:11, 18, 19, 20, 21, 22; 3:9; 4:9; 5:15, 17 [Eng vv 16, 18]; 8:17; 9:9). The noun *'āmāl* refers to one's struggle or the outcome of one's struggle (2:10, 18, 19, 21, 22, 24; 3:13; 4:4, 6, 8, 9; 5:14, 17 [Eng vv 15, 18]; 6:7; 8:15; 9:9; 10:15). For Qohelet this struggle is an inevitable inconvenience of life. Indeed, as Fox notes, life itself is *'āmāl*, and Qohelet occasionally uses *ḥayyāyw* "one's life" in place of *'ămālô* "one's toil" (*Contradictions*, p. 54).

under the sun. The expression *taḥat haššemeš* "under the sun" (v 3) is a favorite one for Qohelet (occurring twenty-nine times) and is unique to him among the biblical writers. It is preferred over the phrase *taḥat haššāmayim* "under the heavens," which occurs much less frequently in the book (1:13; 2:3; 3:1) but is very common elsewhere in the Bible. The two expressions are synonymous to the extent that they both refer to the universality of human experience. Most scholars assume that there is no difference at all between the two. But there is perhaps more to the expression "under the sun" that is worth exploring.

The idiom occurs in two fifth-century (B.C.E.) Phoenician inscriptions on the sarcophagi of King Tabnit and his son Eshmunazor (*KAI* 13.7–8; 14.12). Both inscriptions wish that the tomb-robbers would have no progeny "among the living under the sun" (*bḥym tḥt šmš*). In both texts, the expression "under the sun" is associated with the realm of the living and contrasted with "a resting place with the shades." The expression is found even farther afield and earlier. An inscription of the Elamite king Untashgal written in the twelfth century (B.C.E.) concludes likewise with an imprecation against anyone who would destroy the monument: "May his seed not prosper under the sun" (see I. Levy, "Rien de nouveau sous le soleil," *Nouvelle Clio* 5 [1953] 326–27). A similar imprecation is found at the end of the inscription of Yaḫdun-Lim of Mari: "May Bunene the grand vizier of Shamash cut off his life and gather up his descendants so that neither his progeny nor his name will walk about before the sun" (Dossin, "Iaḫdun-Lim," p. 17, lines 29–31). One is reminded, too, of Gilgamesh's reflection on the transitory nature of human life: "only the gods l[ive] forever with the sun; as for human beings their days are numbered; whatever they achieve is but wind" (Gilg Y iv 5–8; cf. Hebrew *wy'ryk* (!) *'m šmš* "may he live long with the sun" in Ps 72:5). The expression may also be attested in an eighth-century B.C.E. Aramaic inscription from Sefire in northern Syria, again in the context of an imprecation (*KAI* 222.C.5; see Fitzmyer, *The Aramaic Inscriptions of Sefire*, pp. 73–74).

The idiom is well attested in Semitic texts, so there is no need to explain this expression as a grecism—supposedly derived from Greek *hyph hēliǭ* (so Wildeboer, Graetz, Plumptre, and others). In the ancient Near East, the light of the sun is equated with life and its blessings, while the deprivation of its rays means death. To be under the sun (or "before the sun" or "with the sun," as some Akkadian inscriptions have it) is the same thing as "to see the sun," a metaphor for living (see Notes at 7:11; 11:7). Thus, "under the sun" is simply the realm of the living—"this world" as opposed to the netherworld (which is without the sun). Qohelet clearly knows the more common expression "under the heavens" and he uses it, but his preference is for "under the sun." This distinction is perhaps not without nuances. Whereas "under the heavens" refers to the universality of human experiences everywhere in the world (i.e., it is a spatial designation), "under the sun" refers to the temporal universe of the living (cf. 8:9, where "under the sun" is defined temporally: "a time when . . ."). In other words, "under the heavens" simply means the cosmos (a term of universality), whereas "under the sun" is a term for "this world" as opposed to the netherworld (see 9:6). The this-worldliness of the expression "under the sun" explains its recurrence in Ecclesiastes (1:3, 9, 14; 2:11, 17, 18, 19, 20, 22; 3:16; 4:1, 3, 7, 15; 5:12, 17 [Eng vv 13, 18]; 6:1, 12; 8:9, 15 [2x], 17; 9:3, 6, 9 [2x], 11, 13; 10:5): Qohelet is concerned with being in this world, where there is light. The expression simply means the realm of the living. Thus, 4:15 speaks of "all the living who walk about under the sun" (*kol-haḥayyîm hamhallĕkîm taḥat haššāmeš*), a phrase reminiscent of the conclusion of the Yaḫdun-Lim inscription, where we have *ina maḥar Šamaš ayyittalak* "may they not walk about before the sun" (see Dossin, "Iaḫdun-Lim," p. 17, line 31). In 5:17 (Eng v 18), "under the sun" is immediately clarified by *mispar yĕmê ḥayyāyw* "their days are numbered" (cf. Gilg Y iv 6–7; also the inscription of Eshmunazor, *KAI* 14.9–13). In 9:9, the phrase "under the sun" occurs with *kol-yĕmê ḥayyê heblekā* "all the days of your ephemeral life" and *baḥayyîm* "in life" (cf. also Notes at 6:11). Interestingly, Targ interprets 1:3 as saying that there is no advantage to human beings *after death*, and "under the sun" is taken as the experiences of this world, and a passage in the Talmud (*b. Šabb.* 30b) also takes the reference to be temporal. The point is that there is no advantage to be gained through struggling in the realm of the living (cf. 2:11).

4. *a generation goes and a generation comes.* Hebrew *dôr hôlēk wĕdôr bā'*. The repetition of *dôr* "generation" and its use together with *'ôlām* ordinarily suggest continuity and permanence. The expressions *dôr wādôr* "generation and generation" and *dôr lĕdôr* "generation to generation" are frequently associated with *'ôlām* "eternity" or *lĕ'ôlām* "forever" (Exod 3:15; Deut 32:7; Pss 33:11; 145:13; Isa 34:10, 17; 51:8; 60:15; etc.). But Qohelet is, in fact, not emphasizing the continuity of generations. As he does often in the book, he uses the root *hlk* "to go" to speak of death (3:20; 5:14–15 [Eng vv 15–16]; 6:6, 9; 7:2; 9:10; 12:5). This is particularly true when *hlk* "to go" is coordinated with *bw'* "to come," which signifies birth (5:14–15 [Eng vv 15–16]; 6:4). The author gives the impression of much activity in speaking of "going" and "coming." The language suggests that he means to speak of a continuation of the generation, but the point is that the going and coming of the generations amount to nothing. In an Egyptian tomb inscription, one reads: "A generation passes on, another remains, since the time of the ancestors" (see Fox, "A Study of Antef," p. 404, v, lines 3–4).

the earth remains as ever. Most interpreters take this phrase to refer to the permanence of the earth, which is contrasted with the passing of the generations. But Fox points out that "the permanence of the physical earth has no relevance to the individual" ("Qoheleth 1.4," p. 109). The point, rather, is the unchanging nature of the world even as generations come and go (so NJPS: "the earth remains the same forever"). Hebrew *'md* may mean "to remain (unchanged)" (e.g., Lev 13:5; Jer 32:14; 48:11 [// *lō' nāmār* "not changed"]; Pss 33:11, 102:27 [Eng v 26]). In Ps 102:26–28 (Eng vv 25–27), even earth and heaven are impermanent.

5. *the sun rises and the sun sets.* Hebrew *wĕzāraḥ haššemeš ûbā' haššāmeš*. The Hebrew MSS overwhelmingly attest to the correctness of *wzrḥ*, despite the dominance of participles in this passage. Hence, we should not follow the commentators who, assuming a metathesis of letters, read *zwrḥ* (so Lauha and many others); nor should one delete the *waw* and read *zrḥ* (so Hertzberg). We are to take *wĕzārah* and *ûbā'* as perfect consecutive forms (see GKC §112.c), an interpretation confirmed by the word order (see Aalders, *Prediker*, p. 33). Some of the ancient versions translate the verb with the present tense (so LXX *kai anatellei*, Vulg *oritur*), but that does not mean they were reading something different from MT; in all likelihood they, too, interpreted the form as consecutive perfect (so Aq has *kai aneteile*; cf. SyrH *wdnḥ*, although the reading is corrected in the margins, which apparently reads *kai anatellei* in Greek). The presence of the *waw* may be a deliberate link of the activities of humanity with the movements of the natural ele-

ments. To secure this linkage, the author purposely switched from the usage of participles to the converted perfects.

and to its place it presses on. MT has a *zāqēp qāṭōn* on *'el-měqômô*, which makes no sense. Perhaps we are to read, "the sun rises and the sun sets, even to its place." This, however, makes the next line exceedingly awkward: "(It) presses on, it rises there." It is better to shift the disjunctive accent to the next word, following the ancient versions and as most commentators have done.

Hebrew *š'p* may mean either "to pant" or "to stomp." The latter meaning is attested in Amos 2:7; 8:4; Ezek 36:3; Pss 56:2, 3 (Eng vv 1, 2); 57:4 (Eng v 3) and in Postbiblical Hebrew. The idea is that the sun is struggling as it presses on to its place; both meanings of *š'p* — puffing and stomping — are relevant (see *HALAT*, p. 1280). The word conveys vigorous activity, but also tiredness.

MT has the support of LXX, which translates with the verb *helkein/helkyein*, the same verb used for Hebrew *š'p* in Ps 119:131 and Jer 14:6 (cf. also Aq in Jer 2:24). Aq has *eispnei* "he inhales," clearly also reading the same Hebrew verb. Both the Sperber and Levy editions of Targ also have *š'yp*, while some MSS read *šhp* "to move," perhaps reflecting *šwp* in Hebrew. Jerome tells us in his commentary that the Hebrew text reads "*soeph*," yet he takes the verb to mean *ducit* "draws," and Vulg has *revertitur* "returns." The latter reading ("returns") is supported by Symm and Theod (*epanastrephei*) and Syr (*t'b*). On the basis of this, therefore, Graetz emends the text to read *šb 'p* (so also Hertzberg, Galling, and many others). But it is difficult to explain how *š'p* in MT could have come from original *šb 'p*; the forms are graphically too dissimilar. One may speculate that an early confusion of *šw'p* "panting" or "stomping" with *š'b* "drawing out" led to a further confusion of the roots *š'b* with *šwb* (probably an aural confusion), an error prompted perhaps by the presence of *šb* in v 6 and *šbym* in v 7 (for examples of the confusion between *bet* and *peh*, see E. Tov, *Textual Criticism of the Hebrew Bible* [Minneapolis: Fortress, 1992], pp. 251–52). MT is superior and should not be emended.

The imagery may be compared with that found in Ps 19:6 (Eng v 5), where the sun is portrayed as a valiant person running a course across the sky. In Babylonian mythology, Shamash the sun-god daily emerges from the horizon and sets out on a journey from morning till night (see Meissner, *Babylonien und Assyrien* II, pp. 20, 166). In a hymn to the sun-god one reads:

> To unknown distant regions and for uncounted leagues
> You press on, Šamaš, going by day and returning by night.
> Among the Igigi there is none who toils but you. . . .

(BWL, pp. 128–29, lines 43–45)

Qohelet, too, portrays the sun as one struggling to reach its destination, only to have to recommence.

there it rises. Here the word *šām* "there" refers to *měqômô* "its place." It is where the sun rises again — presumably the east. In Egyptian and Mesopotamian texts, the sun goes through the darkness of the netherworld in order to reach the east from the west, the earth being stationary in ancient Near Eastern cosmology. Nothing is said in Ecclesiastes of how the sun arrives at the same spot where it rises each day, however.

6. *it goes.* The real subject of *hôlēk* "goes," the wind (*hārûaḥ*), is not expressed till the second *hôlēk* appears several words later. Attention is placed, rather, on the rapid and repeated movements: *hôlēk . . . wĕsôbēb . . . sôbēb sôbēb hôlēk*, lit. "going . . . turning around . . . turning around, turning around, going." This cumbersome construction caused LXX to assume incorrectly that the subject of the first *hôlēk* is still the sun: "arising there it proceeds toward the south, and then turns around toward the north" (cf. Syr and Vulg). So, too, Targ interprets the movement as a reference to the position of the sun at different times of the year: "Round and round it goes to the wind of the southern side in the period of Nisan and Tammuz, and it turns around on its rounds to the wind of the northern side in the period of Tishri and Tebet." As many scholars have noted, however, the references to the Nisan and Tammuz (i.e., vernal equinox and summer solstice) and Tishri and Tebet (i.e., autumnal equinox and winter solstice) have been incorrectly transposed (cf. *b. ʿErub.* 56a; *y. ʿErub.* 5.1).

to the south . . . to the north. Elsewhere in the Bible the winds are called "north wind" and "south wind" (Song 4:16) — that is, winds blowing from the north (properly the northwest) and from the south (properly the southeast). The north wind, coming from the Mediterranean (that is, northwest to southeast) is cold and brings rain (Sir 43:20; Prov 25:23; Job 37:9). This wind is typical of the winter season. The south wind, blowing from the desert (that is, from the southeast to the northwest), is dry and hot (Job 37:17; Luke 12:55). In addition, the wind in Palestine may blow from west to east (e.g., the summer day breezes) and from east to west (see E. Orni and E. Efrat, *Geography of Israel* [Jerusalem: Israel Program for Scientific Translations, 1964], pp. 101–4). Thus, there are literally several rounds (*sĕbîbôt*) for the wind, and not just a single "circuit" or "course" (so NIV "its course"). But only the north-south and south-north movements are mentioned here, probably to complement the east-west movement of the sun.

on account of its rounds. Most translators take ʿ*al* to be used like ʾ*el* or *lĕ-*, thus "*to* its rounds." It is better here to follow Ellermeier, who argues that ʿ*al* indicates purpose, thus meaning "on account of" or "for the sake of" (*Qohelet* I/1, pp. 200–1). The phrase explains why the wind keeps on blowing from north to south and south to north: it returns again and again *because* it has its rounds.

7. *There they flow again.* Hebrew *šām hēm šābîm lālāket* means either "there they flow again" or "they return to flow (again)." The question here is the proper translation of *šābîm*: does it literally mean "return" or does it mean "again"? (see Joüon-Muraoka §102.g). Symm has "into the place from which the rivers flow, there they return" (cf. Vulg). So, too, Targ interprets the text to mean that the streams return to their source: "to the place where the streams flow continually, there they flow again through the channels of the sea" (cf. *b. ʿErub.* 22b: "the whole world is in fact surrounded by the ocean"). This interpretation is consonant with the worldview of the ancient Near East, but the point of the text is

simply that the channels keep flowing. The source of the water is quite beside the point. See Euringer, *Masorahtext*, pp. 33–34; Ellermeier, *Qohelet* I/1, pp. 197–99; Salters, *Ecclesiastes*, pp. 97–100.

8. *all words*. Hebrew *kol-haddĕbārîm* may mean "all the things" (Vulg: *cuntae res*), as it is commonly assumed in this case. That is the meaning one first assumes, since this verse comes immediately after all the activities of vv 4–6. Yet, in every instance through the rest of Ecclesiastes, *dĕbārîm* (5:2; 6:11; 7:21; 10:14) and *dibrê* (1:1; 9:17; 10:12, 13; 12:10 [2x], 11; cf. 5:1; 9:16) always mean "words." The meaning "words" is confirmed by the parallel line that has *lĕdabbēr* "to speak" (v 8b) and the association with the activities of the eye and the ear (v 8c). One may also point to the allusions in the epilogue, which speaks of the abundance of "books" and much talking as a wearying of the body (see Notes at 12:12).

wearying. Hebrew *yĕgē'îm*. The form is either an adjective or a participle that is stative in form (see GKC §136.d). The adjective is attested in Deut 25:18 and 2 Sam 17:2. If *dĕbārîm* refers to "things," then the meaning is that all things are weary (i.e., worn out from all the activities). The verb *yg'* in Hebrew means either "to toil, labor" or "to be weary" (it is associated with *'āmāl* "toil" and *hebel* in Job 9:29; Isa 49:4). The verb *tĕyaggĕ'ennû* occurs in 10:15, where the subject is *'āmāl* "toil"—the toil referring probably to excessive talking. Certainly words can be wearying; cf. "you have wearied YHWH with your words" (Mal 2:17). We should, therefore, probably take the form to be a participle, like *mĕlē'îm* "fill" (cf. Isa 6:1) and *yĕrē'îm* "fear" (2 Kgs 17:32). It should be noted that the distinction "weary" (being worn out) and "wearisome" is one made in English, not Hebrew. Thus, too, Hebrew *mālē'* may mean both "being full" or "filling" and *yārē'* may mean either "being afraid" or "fearing." To preserve this ambiguity, therefore, we translate the participle as "wearying." Like *haddĕbārîm* "the things/words," the participle may be ambivalent: the things/words are wearying—i.e., they are both worn out and wearisome. And like *šô'ēp* in v 5, routine activity and tiredness are both implied. Finally, one may note that the root *yg'* occurs at the end of the book, also in reference to words *wĕlahag harbēh yĕgî'at bāsār* "excessive talking is a wearying of the flesh" (see Notes at 12:12). In *The Complaint of Khakheperre-Sonb*, the wearisome nature of words is described thus:

> That which has been said is repeated;
> When what was said is said (again),
>   there is no boasting.
> As for the words of those who are before,
> Indeed, those who come after shall discover them.

(my translation; text in Gardiner, *Admonitions*, p. 97, lines 3–4)

The text then judges this endeavor to be "searching for what fades away" (*ḥḥy pw r 3qt*, line 6).

no one is able to speak. MT, which is supported by all the ancient witnesses, has *lō'-yûkal 'îš lĕdabbēr*. The point is surely not that one cannot speak at all, for in v 10 there is the possibility of speech. Indeed, elsewhere in the book, it is excessive and useless speech that is the problem (6:10–12; 10:13–15; 12:12), not one's inability to speak. Hence, Galling prefers to emend the text to read *lō' yĕkal-leh* "no one can complete speaking (i.e., speak adequately)." There is no evidence for this reading, however, and it is difficult to explain how a supposed original *yklh* might have been corrupted to *ywkl*. No emendation is necessary.

The phrase, in fact, is elliptical and its meaning becomes clear only as one reads on. In vv 9–10, it becomes clear that "one cannot speak" about anything new or tell what will happen in the future (so Targ). Words are worn out or they wear one out because they cannot provide one with anything new or enlightening. In 6:10–12, Qohelet says that it is impossible for human beings to contend with an all-powerful deity and many words only increase *hebel*, since no one knows what is good and no one can tell what will happen in the future (cf. also 10:13–15). In *The Complaints of Khakheperre-Sonb*, the sage says he searched for the right words, "sayings that are novel, a new word that has never occurred before, free of repetitions" (see Gardiner, *Admonitions*, p. 96, line 2; cf. also line 7: "would that I know what others do not"). New sayings are hard to come by, it seems, even though others are quick to offer their thoughts as new. In truth, the sage maintains, "it is a searching for what fades; it is deceit." It is in this specific sense that Qohelet says "no one can speak."

9. *whatever has happened.* The expression *mah ššehāyâ* occurs also in 3:15; 6:10; 7:24. In each case, the issue is what is or has been happening in the world. It is contrasted with *meh/mah-ššeyihyeh*, which refers to what will happen in the future (3:22; 8:7; 10:14). In the Bible, the construction *mah šše-* is confined to Ecclesiastes, but it is well attested in Mishnaic Hebrew (e.g., *m. 'Abot* 5:7; *B. Bat.* 6:7). See Segal, *A Grammar of Mishnaic Hebrew*, §436. The construction is the same as Aramaic *mh dy* (e.g., Dan 2:28–29) and *mh z* in Egyptian Aramaic (see Whitley, *Koheleth*, pp. 10–11).

under the sun. See Notes at 1:3.

10. *if there is a thing.* Hebrew *yēš dābār*, lit. "there (may be) a thing." LXX *hos lalēsei* and Syr *kl dnmll* probably reflect Hebrew *šydbr*—that is, with metathesis of *yod* and *šin*.

which one might say. The 3 ms verb is used impersonally here (see Joüon-Muraoka §155.b.Note 2), as it often is in the book. There is no need, therefore, to repoint to read the Niphal imperfect (so Ehrlich).

already. The word *kĕbār* occurs in the Bible only in Ecclesiastes (see also 2:12, 16; 3:15; 4:2; 6:10; 9:6, 7), but it is attested in Mishnaic Hebrew with this meaning (*m. 'Erub.* 4:2). The *qĕtāl* pattern may indicate that it is an Aramaism (see Schoors, *Pleasing Words*, pp. 116–17).

which were. Since *'ōlāmîm* is plural in form, a few Hebrew MSS read *hyw* (a reading reflected in LXX, Vulg, Targ), instead of *hyh*, but the latter is the *lectio difficilior*. The former (*hyw*) is probably harmonistic and, therefore, secondary. There appears to be no consistency in the agreement of gender and number with the verb *hyh* (cf. GKC §145.u and Notes at 2:7), and *'ōlāmîm* is, in any case, sometimes treated as singular in Late Biblical Hebrew (cf. Isa 26:4; 45:17; Dan 9:24).

11. *there is no remembrance of.* Hebrew *zikrôn* is sometimes taken as a late form of the noun in the absolute state, comparable with *yitrôn* and *kišrôn* (Delitzsch, Hertzberg). But since in v 11b we have the absolute form, *zikkārôn*, we may assume that *zikrôn* is the construct form. On the construct form before the preposition *lĕ-*, cf. *'ên zikrôn lehăkām* "there is no remembrance of the wise" (2:16), but also *hămat-lāmô* "their venom" (Ps 58:5 [Eng v 4]); *tô'ăbat lĕ'ādām* "the abomination of people" (Prov 24:9); *qinṣê lĕmillîn* "end of talk" (Job 18:2). See GKC §130.a; Joüon-Muraoka §129.n. Similar constructions are found in Mishnaic Hebrew (e.g., *m. 'Abot* 5:14).

those who came before . . . those who came after. LXX and Vulg take the nouns to refer to first and last things (so RSV: "former things . . . things yet to happen." Elsewhere in the Bible, however, *ri'šōnîm* refers to the previous generations (Lev 26:45; Deut 19:14; Ps 79:8; cf. *'ăbôtām hāri'šōnîm* "their ancestors" in Jer 11:10). This word does not occur again in Ecclesiastes, but *hā'ahărōnîm* is attested in 4:16, where it clearly refers to people who come in the future (cf. Job 18:20). Moreover, "former things" is expressed elsewhere by *ri'šōnôt* not *ri'šōnîm* (see Isa 41:22; 42:9; 43:9, 18; 46:9, etc.). Cf. Egyptian "those who come before . . . those who come after" in *The Complaints of Khakheperre-Sonb* (Gardiner, *Admonitions*, p. 97, lines 3–4). If the former and future generations are meant, this verse forms an inclusio with v 4 (cf. NRSV: "the people of long ago . . . people yet to come").

among. The preposition *'im* here means "among" (cf. Gen 23:4; Lev 25:6). See Lys, *L'Ecclésiaste*, pp. 137–38.

COMMENT

The opening chapter contains prefatory remarks that will set the tone for all of Ecclesiastes. A thematic statement appears in v 2, which is repeated in virtually the same form at the end of the book (12:8). The appearance of the thematic statement at the beginning (immediately after the superscription and before the opening poem) and at the end (after the concluding poem and before the epilogue) suggests that these two verses are intended as the framework of the book. As it stands, this thematic statement also serves as the introduction to the preface (1:2–11).

A rhetorical question in v 3 serves as a thesis statement of the preface: human beings have no advantage in all their toil "under the sun." This is followed by a poem in vv 4–8 that demonstrates the thesis, a poem that makes the point that there is a lot of activity in the universe but no advantage is gained and nothing new really happens. The skill of the poet is evident in the construction of the poem (see G. Fecht, *Metrik des Hebräischen und Phönizischen* [ÄAT 19. Wiesbaden: Harrassowitz, 1991], pp. 162–69; L. Alonso-Schökel, *A Manual of Hebrew Poetics* [Subsidia Biblica 11; Rome: Pontificio Istituto Biblico, 1988], pp. 71, 198).

The monotonous nature of the activities is conveyed by the repetition of words. Instead of using a pronoun after a subject has been named, each subject is repeated: generation . . . generation (v 4), the sun . . . the sun (v 5), the wind . . . the winds (v 6), the streams . . . the streams (v 7), the sea . . . the sea (v 7). Verbs, too, are repeated: *hlk* "to go" appears 6 times in vv 4–7, *sbb* "to go around" appears 3 times in v 3, and several other verbs appear twice each (*zrḥ* "to rise," *šwb* "to return," *mlʾ* "to be full"). Thus the language subtly conveys the point about the repetitive character of everything. Moreover, the poem creates an impression of busy-ness through its abundant use of participles; no fewer than fifteen of them are found in vv 4–7. This poem on the monotonous activities is then followed by a commentary in prose in vv 9–11, which makes the point that despite the active routines, nothing new really happens (see Good, "The Unfilled Sea," pp. 59–73). It is clear that the passage ends in v 11, for the verses that follow are written in an autobiographical style.

Thematic Statement (1:2)

There is perhaps no verse in all of Ecclesiastes that is more well known and more often cited than the thematic statement. It is understood by all scholars to be representative of the author's views of life. The Hebrew word *hebel*, which is translated here as "vanity," has no single English equivalent. The literal meaning of the word is "vapor," "breath," "air," "steam," or the like. The word is most commonly used metaphorically for things that are ephemeral, insubstantial, delusive, or unreliable. Qohelet uses the word to speak of the fleeting nature of life (6:12; 7:15; 9:9). This is consonant with the usage of the word elsewhere in the Bible (Pss 39:6–7, 12 [Eng vv 5–6, 11]; 62:10 [Eng v 9]; 94:11; 144:4; Job 7:16; 9:29). That does not mean that human life is "vain" in the sense of being meaningless or worthless, but that it is ephemeral and unreliable.

Psalm 39 is most instructive in this regard. It is the lament of a frustrated individual trying to understand the vicissitudes of life, which every human must endure. The psalmist prays to the deity for the ability to understand the meaning of life and laments the transitory nature of human existence. The entire human life span is as nothing before God, the psalmist observes — like a vapor and a mere reflection. Everyone is *hebel* "vapor" (v 6 [Eng v 5]), and yet people toil without ever knowing who will eventually reap the benefits after they die.

Similar sentiments are found in Psalm 62, against the backdrop of difficult times, where human beings again are said to be *hebel* and a delusion. All humanity together, it is said, is lighter than *hebel* "vapor" on the scales (vv 10–11 [Eng vv 9–10]). Therefore, it is useless to try to count on riches or rely on plunder, for power belongs to God. That which is *hebel* is unpredictable and beyond human ability to control.

So, too, Qohelet speaks of joy, success, and youth as *hebel* (2:1, 11; 4:4; 11:10). These things are "vain" in the sense that they do not last; people cannot hold on to them forever. The word is also used of things that cannot be grasped intellectually — they may be enigmatic, confusing, contradictory, or plain mysterious (1:2, 14; 2:15, 17, 19, 21, 26; 3:19; 4:4, 7–8, 16; 5:9 [Eng v 10]; 6:2, 9; 8:10, 14).

Human attempts to grasp them are said to be "vanity" and a "pursuit of wind" (1:14; 2:11, 17, 26; 4:4, 16; 6:9). For Qohelet, human existence and human experiences of earthly realities are all "vanity" in the sense that they are transitory and beyond human ability to grasp. The word "all" here is not a universal category, but refers specifically to human experiences of reality on earth (so Lohfink). It is not that everything is meaningless or futile, but that people cannot hold on to what they have (life, joy, success, wealth), control their own destiny by sheer effort and will, predict what will happen in the future, or comprehend all the happening. All that humanity is, does, and experiences on earth is *hebel*.

It should be emphasized that the *hebel*-judgment here is matched by the virtually identical words of 12:8. Thus, apart from the superscription (1:1) and the epilogue (12:9–14), Qohelet's sayings are enveloped by these thematic proclamations. This thematic statement is the first verse of the preface (1:2–11) and the last verse of the conclusion (11:7–12:8). In addition, many observations and arguments of the author end with the judgment "all is *hebel*" (1:14; 2:11, 17; 3:19), "this is *hebel*" (6:2), "that, too, is *hebel*" (2:1), or "this, too, is *hebel*" (2:15, 19, 22, 23, 26; 4:4, 8, 16; 7:16; 8:10, 14). It may be observed that 1:2 (and to a lesser extent 12:8) is a spectacle of alliteration in Hebrew, with the repetition of *h* and *l*: *hăbēl hăbālîm 'āmar qōhelet hăbēl hăbālîm hakkōl hābel.*

Routines in the Universe (1:3–8)

Although the thematic statement (v 2) was intended as part of a framework for the book, it also is appropriate as the introduction to the preface. The "all" mentioned in 1:2 is now illustrated in the activities mentioned in the verses that follow, beginning with "all" toil in v 3 and culminating in the two occurrences of "all" at the end of the poem, in v 7 ("all streams") and v 8 ("all things/words"). This is only the first of many illustrations in the book of the point that "all is vanity."

Qohelet asks what advantage humanity has in all the toil (v 3). This is clearly a rhetorical question. A negative answer is implied: there is no advantage in toil. The Hebrew root for "toil" (*'ml*) recurs in the book — thirty-five times in various forms. The term has generally negative connotations. It refers to the routine struggle of humanity to achieve some end or other. Toil is the tiresome effort expended over an enterprise of dubious result. Qohelet does not mean, then, that there is no good that comes from work or effort, but that there is no additional "edge" that one can gain from "toil."

It is important to observe that Qohelet speaks of toiling "under the sun," a favorite phrase of his that appears twenty-nine times in the book. The phrase occurs elsewhere in the ancient Near East, always in the context of life and death (see Notes above). Although the common biblical idiom "under the heavens" is also used (1:13; 2:3; 3:1), it appears that there are some differences in the two expressions. Whereas "under the heavens" is a spatial designation (referring to what is happening in the world), the expression "under the sun" is temporal, referring to the experiences in the realm of the living — this world of light and life, as opposed to the world of darkness in the netherworld (see especially 4:15;

9:6, 9). So the point of our verse seems to be that toil gives one no advantage in the realm of the living, perhaps over life itself.

In v 4 the author speaks of human succession, but the topic is not unrelated to the previous verse. He still has in mind the issue of advantage for humanity under the sun. Significantly, some of the parallel texts that use the phrase "under the sun" or its equivalent are also concerned with the continuity of human existence. In each case, progeny figures prominently. The inscriptions often invoke a curse against would-be grave robbers and vandals—that they would have no descendants among the living "under the sun" (so the inscriptions of Tabnit and Eshmunazor) or that their seed would not prosper "under the sun" or "before the sun" (so the inscriptions of Untashgal and Yaḥdun-Lim). Progeny was one way people tried to ensure some continuity under the sun; it was a way of overcoming the fate of mortality. In the *Gilgamesh Epic*, the protagonist recognized that immortality was beyond human grasp, and so he consoled himself that if he took some heroic actions while he was alive, his name might be remembered forever (see *ANET*³, p. 79). People sought continuity of their existence on earth—if not actual immortality, as Gilgamesh desired, at least the perpetuation of their names through their descendants (the succeeding generations) or through their great accomplishments. In the face of mortality, progeny was a possible advantage that people still coveted. But Qohelet makes the point that the succession of the generations really makes no difference in the larger scheme of things: generations come and go, but nothing really changes on earth. The vitality of the language in v 4 is deceptive. The going and coming of the generations give the impression of much movement, but they only show the transient nature of human existence. Despite the flurry of activities that coming and going suggest, nothing radically new really happens and no advantage is gained. The world remains the same as always.

From the activities of humanity (vv 3–4), Qohelet moves on to speak of the activities of nature: the sun, the wind, and the streams (v 5–7). The sun rises and the sun sets over and over again (v 3). The linkage between the anthropological (v 3) and the cosmological (v 4), a linkage evident in the Hebrew text in the conjunction *wĕ-* ("and"), is made here and also in the final poem of the book (see Comment at 12:3–8). Humanity's busy-ness is mirrored by the activities of the forces of nature. The cosmological activities are illustrative, for the interest of the author is ultimately the human being, as is evident in the thesis statement (v 3), in the denouement of the poem (v 8), and in the prose commentary that follows (vv 10–11). Thus, this is not just a "nature poem" (so Whybray, "Ecclesiastes 1,4–7 and the Wonders of Nature," pp. 105–12). The Hebrew word for the setting of the sun is *bāʾ*, which is literally "comes" or "enters." It is the same form used in v 4. But whereas the word in v 4 refers to people coming into existence, in v 5 it refers to the setting of the sun, the end of a day. Perhaps one is to conclude that there is not much difference between the coming of each generation and the daily setting of the sun: each is part of a routine. Toward its destination the sun struggles—the participle here implies that the sun is both stomping onwards and panting—only to start all over again. The sun participates vigorously in the daily routine, but it seems to have gained no advantage from its tedious work.

The flurry of repetitive activities continues in v 6. And the language conveys at once both vigor and monotony. There is movement this way and that, to the south and to the north, around and around. But the subject is not revealed for awhile, as if the poet wants the reader to ponder about the activities first: going south, turning to the north, around and around. The delaying of the subject prompted the translators of the ancient versions (the Septuagint, Vulgate, Syriac and Targum) to think that it is the sun that moves to the south, then to the north. But it becomes clear that it is the wind that moves. The poem picks up on the other participle used of the generations, *hōlēk* "goes" (here meaning "blows"). One is prompted to make the connection right away with the activities of human beings suggested in v 4: as each generation goes (*hōlēk*) and comes (*bā'*), so, too, the sun sets (*bā'*) and the wind blows (*hôlēk*). Like the generations of human beings, the sun and the wind come and go. The wind moves about a lot, but even the unpredictable wind returns because of its rounds. There is a lot of movement, but ultimately nothing new happens. No advantage is gained, despite all the busy-ness.

By the same token, all the channels of water flow eventually to the sea (v 7). But the expected does not happen. The continuous pouring of water into the sea never causes it to overflow. The Dead Sea would be a particularly poignant example of this phenomenon: it receives water constantly flowing from the Jordan and other sources, but nothing about it seems to change.

The author began with human activities in vv 3–4 and moved on to speak of elements of nature in vv 5–7. Then in v 8, he returns to people. The reference to "all" words in v 8 recalls the activities of "all" streams in v 7, "all" toil in v 3, and ultimately Qohelet's judgment that "all is vanity" in v 2. The emphasis shifts from humanity in general in v 3 to the generations in v 4, and now to individuals in v 8. Initially the expression *kol-haddĕbārîm yĕgē'îm* at the beginning of v 8 may be interpreted to mean "all things are wearying" — the routines are wearisome and the subjects are being worn out. Coming after vv 3–5, with the tedious activities of several subjects, it seems that v 8 is reiterating the tedium of "all things." And this interpretation is prompted by the fact that the preceding verse begins with "all streams" and their routine. But the poet is, in fact, turning his attention now to human speech. As in v 6, where the real subject is held in abeyance, so here in v 8, the meaning of *kol-dĕbārîm yĕgē'îm* is not fully evident till one reads about human inability to speak (*lĕdabbēr*). Now it appears that one is to take *kol-dĕbārîm yĕgē'îm* to mean "all words are wearying" — they wear one out and they are getting old. Qohelet's words are elliptical. The author does not mean that no one is able to speak at all. That obviously would be untrue. Rather, the point is that no one has anything novel to say, and no one can say anything about what will happen. There are words aplenty; the words are, in fact, wearying. Yet, no one is able to say anything new or anything enlightening about the future. The same sentiments are found in the text called *The Complaints of Khakheperre-Sonb* (see *AEL* I, 146–8 and Notes above). The sage in that text wishes that he had a new word to offer and that he knew what others did not know. At the same time, he speaks of those who talk a lot and give the impression that they are offering new solutions — "words never before uttered." But, says the sage, "this is a searching for what fades; it is deceit." All words are wearying; they are wearisome when they offer nothing new or enlightening. As Qohelet himself puts it, "indeed, there are many words that (only) increase vanity" (6:11). There are plenty of words, wearisome words, yet no one is able to say anything new or enlightening. As all streams flow into the sea and the sea is not full (v 7), so all words are wearying, but no one is able to speak (v 8). The eye sees a lot and the ear hears a lot, but no advantage is gained in all that seeing and hearing.

Prose Commentary (1:9–11)
If the meaning of the poem (vv 3–8) is unclear, it is clarified in prose in vv 9–11. This prose commentary generally is seen as an attack on the wisdom tradition, with its emphasis on speech (cf. Prov 15:1, 2, 4, 23; 16:24; 25:11). But the polemic seems to be not so much on speech as it is on the claim of novelty and the ability to tell what will happen in the future. Qohelet says that "what has happened — that is what will happen, and what is being done — that is what will be done. There is nothing new under the sun" (v 9). This is essentially the point made by the poem: human beings and the forces of nature all participate in routines, and there seem to be no breakthroughs despite all the toil.

Qohelet appears to be talking about the predictability of events, even as he had been speaking of the predictability of nature's routines in vv 4–7. But he is, in fact, speaking of the impossibility of knowing what will happen despite all the appearance of routine. This is a theme to which he returns again and again in the book (3:15, 22; 6:10; 7:24; 8:7; 10:14). He insists in 6:10–12 that no one knows what is universally good for humanity and no one can tell what will happen in the future.

The first denial (that no one knows what is good) appears to be a polemic against the purveyors of aphorisms, who believe that they can prescribe behavior that will help people control their destinies. Some traditional wisdom teachers presumed that one can learn from nature and human experiences how one ought to behave in every situation (this is an attitude evident in the teachings in the book of Proverbs). Their assumptions about order and justice also led some to call the deity into question (as in the book of Job). But Qohelet insists that no one is able (*lō' yûkal*) to do such a thing (6:10). In 1:8, he says elliptically that no one is able (*lō' yûkal*) to speak.

The second denial (that no one can tell what will happen) may be a polemic against apocalypticists — those who are constantly pointing to what might happen in the future. Indeed, the words of Qohelet in 1:9–11 echo the protoapocalyptic proclamations of Deutero-Isaiah that new things were about to happen, which would be unlike the former things (Isa 42:9). The exiles were urged not to remember the former things because God was about to do "a new thing" (Isa 43:18–19). According to the poet of the exile, it was God who was "declaring the end from the beginning and from ancient times things not yet done" (Isa 46:10).

God will bring from nowhere a new thing, previously unheard of and unknown (Isa 48:7). Deutero-Isaiah was not alone; other visionaries in the exilic period spoke of the possibility of newness: a new heart and a new spirit (Ezek 18:31; 36:26), a new thing on earth (Jer 31:22), a new covenant (Jer 31:31). In the face of despair over the silence of God, Israel's visionaries in the exilic period pointed to the possibility of radical newness. This expectation of newness was developed into the full-blown eschatology of Trito-Isaiah, who predicted a new heaven and the new earth that will remain forever, as will Israel's descendants and fame (Isa 66:22). Hope was pinned on the possibility of newness in the future, when "the former things shall not be remembered or come to mind" (Isa 65:17). Whereas there will be no remembrance of the former things, Trito-Isaiah spoke of future generations of Israel who will come, and their fame will remain forever.

There is nothing new under the sun, however. There is no remembrance for those who came before, nor for those who will come in the future. Here Qohelet alludes to past and future generations and, in doing so, returns to the point made at the beginning of the passage: generations come and go, but everything remains the same as ever. The additional observation here at the end of the passage is that memory makes no difference in that coming and going. Qohelet observes in 9:5 that when people die, "their memory is forgotten" (9:5). It makes no difference what one has accomplished or who one may be (see 2:16). When death comes, all hopes perish, and no one is better off than others. Qohelet is perhaps speaking against the idea that one can extend one's presence "under the sun," through one's progeny, tangible memorials, or fame. For him, death dashes all hopes of immortality, including the "immortality" of being remembered forever.

I.A.2. NOTHING IS ULTIMATELY RELIABLE (1:12–2:26)

1   ^{12}I am Qohelet. I have been a king over Israel in Jerusalem. ^{13}I set my heart to inquire and to explore by wisdom everything that has been done under the heavens. It is a terrible preoccupation that God has given to humanity with which to be preoccupied. ^{14}I observed all the deeds that have been done under the sun, and lo, all is vanity and a pursuit of wind.

> ^{15}What is made crooked cannot be straightened;
>   what is lacking cannot be counted.

^{16}I spoke with my heart: "I, yes, I have shown greatness and increased wisdom, surpassing all who were before me over Jerusalem." And my heart observed much wisdom and knowledge. ^{17}But when I set my heart to know wisdom and knowledge of < > prudence, I knew that even this is a pursuit of wind, ^{18}for,

> in the abundance of wisdom is much vexation;
>   when one increases knowledge one increases pain.

2 ¹I spoke with my heart: "Come now, let me make you experience pleasure. And enjoy good!" But that, too, is vanity. ²Regarding merriment, I said: "<What> does it boast?" And regarding pleasure: "What does it really accomplish?" ³I went about with my heart to induce my body with wine — and my heart conducted by wisdom and <did not> lead by folly — until I saw what indeed is the good for humans, which they should do under the heavens during the few days of their life.

⁴I achieved great deeds. I built myself houses. I planted myself vineyards. ⁵I made myself gardens and parks and I planted therein all kinds of fruit trees. ⁶I made myself pools of water from which to irrigate a forest sprouting with trees. ⁷I acquired male servants and female servants, and I had home-born slaves. I also had a great possession of cattle and sheep, surpassing all who were before me in Jerusalem. ⁸I accumulated for myself also silver and gold, a private hoard fit for kings, along with the provinces. I acquired for myself male singers and female singers, along with humanity's treasures in chests. ⁹So I became great and surpassed all who were before me in Jerusalem. Yea, my wisdom aided me. ¹⁰Whatever my eyes desired, I did not deprive them. I did not withhold my heart from any pleasure, for my heart had pleasure from all my toil. And this had been my portion for all my toil. ¹¹So I turned to all my works that my hands had done, and my toil that I toiled to accomplish, and, lo, all is vanity and a pursuit of wind, and there is no advantage under the sun.

¹²I turned to observe wisdom and irrationality and folly, for who is the person who will come after <me? Shall he control> what has already been achieved? ¹³I have observed that wisdom has advantage over folly, as light has advantage over darkness: ¹⁴the wise have their eyes in their heads, but fools walk in darkness. But I also know that one fate befalls them all. ¹⁵So I said in my heart: "If the fate of the fool befalls even me, why then have I been acting excessively wise?" I said in my heart that this, too, is vanity, ¹⁶for there is no remembrance of the wise forever — as is the case with the fool — because all too soon everything is forgotten. O how the wise dies just like the fool! ¹⁷So I hated life, for what has been done under the sun is terrible to me. Indeed, all is vanity and a pursuit of wind.

¹⁸I hated all my toil for which I am toiling under the sun, which I will leave to the people who will come after me. ¹⁹But who knows whether they will be wise or fools? They will exercise proprietorship over all the fruit of my toil for which I have toiled and acted wisely under the sun. This, too, is vanity.

²⁰I turned to let my heart despair about all the toil that I toiled under the sun, ²¹for there are people whose toil is for wisdom, knowledge, and achievement, but to those who did not toil for it they give it as their portion. This also is vanity and a great tragedy.

²²Indeed, what is there for humans in all their toil and in the pursuit of their hearts at which they toil under the sun? ²³For all their days are pains, and vexation is their preoccupation; even at night their hearts do not rest. This, too, is vanity.

²⁴There is no good among humans (except) that they should eat and drink, and make themselves see good in their toil. Also this I have observed is from the hand of God; ²⁵for who will eat and who will glean without <him>? ²⁶For to the

one who is favored, he has given wisdom, knowledge, and pleasure; but to the offender he has given a preoccupation of gathering and collecting to give to the one who is good before God. This, too, is vanity and a pursuit of wind.

NOTES

1 **12.** *I am Qohelet. I have been a king.* It is also possible to take the independent personal pronoun as standing in apposition to the personal name, as is the case in various West Semitic and Akkadian inscriptions. Thus, one may translate: "I, Qohelet, have been a king." The style here imitates the self-presentation formula of kings in the royal inscriptions of the ancient Near East. In the West Semitic examples, the *'nk/'nh* RN formula is a typical way of introducing the king in whose name the inscription is issued (e.g., *KAI* 10.1; 13.1; 24.1; 26.I.1; 181.1; 214.1; 216.1; 217.1).

The verb *hāyîtî* is commonly taken to indicate a past fact and, thus, frequently translated as "I was" (KJV, ASV, NIV). LXX translates it with the aorist *egenomēn* "I was" (cf. also Vulg; Targ). In the same vein, a Jewish tradition took the verb to mean that Solomon was no longer king, having been deposed on account of his sins, his throne having been usurped by Ashmedai (Asmodeus), king of the demons (*y. Sanh.* 20c; *b. Git.* 68a–b). But the Hebrew perfect, particularly of stative verbs, need not indicate past realities. The perfect of *hyh* may also indicate an existing state, a reality that began in the past but continues into the present.

Indeed, the use of the perfect is in keeping with the narrative style of the West Semitic royal inscriptions: e.g., *'nk klmw . . . yšbt 'l ks' 'by* "I am Kilamuwa . . . I have sat on the throne of my father" (*KAI* 24.9); *gm yšbt 'l mšb 'by* "I, too, have sat on the throne of my father" (*KAI* 214.8); *'nk mš' . . . w'nk mlkty 'hr 'by* "I am Mesha . . . and I have reigned after my father" (*KAI* 181.1–3). There is no semantic difference between the idiom *hyyty mlk* "I have been king" in Ecclesiastes and *mlkty* "I have reigned" or *yšbt(y) 'l ks'/mšb* "I have sat on the throne/seat" in the West Semitic royal inscriptions. It is important to observe that there are other similarities with the royal inscriptions in the passage (see Seow, "Qohelet's Autobiography"). Specifically, much of 1:12–2:11 resembles the Akkadian fictional autobiographies, on which see Longman, *Fictional Akkadian Autobiography*. Indeed, Longman (pp. 120–23) argues that all of Ecclesiastes belongs to this genre.

a king over Israel in Jerusalem. The combination of "over Israel" (not "over Judah") and "in Jerusalem" makes it virtually certain that the author means a king in the united monarchy. Saul, David, and Solomon are all called *melek 'al yiśrā'ēl* "king over Israel" in the Bible (1 Sam 23:17; 2 Sam 5:2–5, 11, 17; 1 Kgs 1:34; 3:28), but only David and Solomon may be said to have ruled "in Jerusalem." Others who are called "king over Israel" are from the northern kingdom of the divided monarchy (1 Kgs 14:13–14; 15:25; 16:29; 22:52; 2 Kgs 2:25) and could not have ruled "in Jerusalem," while those who ruled in the south (who ruled "in Jerusalem") never are called "king over Israel." Clearly, the author intends to equate himself with Solomon.

13. *I set my heart.* The idiom *nātan lēb* means to set one's mind, that is, to pay attention or be determined (see 1:17; 7:21; 8:9, 16; Ezra 7:27; Neh 2:12; 1 Chron 22:19; 2 Chron 11:16; Dan 10:12). More specifically, one notes the idioms *nātan lēb lidrôš* "to set the mind to seek" (1 Chron 22:19 [Eng v 18]) and *hēkîn lēb lidrôš* "to prepare the mind to seek" (2 Chron 12:14; 19:3; 30:19). The heart is the decision-making organ in ancient Near Eastern anthropology. It should be noted that *nātan lēb* is an idiom of Late Biblical Hebrew. Indeed, all the attestations are in texts dated no earlier than the fifth century B.C.E. In earlier Hebrew, *śām lēb* (1 Sam 25:25; 28:5; 2 Sam 13:13; 18:3; Isa 41:22; Ezek 40:4; 44:5; Zech 7:12) and *šāt lēb* (1 Sam 4:20; Pss 48:14; 62:11; Jer 31:21) are used instead.

by wisdom. Some commentators (e.g., Hertzberg, Ellermeier) take *baḥokmâ* to be the object of the two infinitives (thus, "to seek and to explore wisdom") or of *drš*, thus, "to seek wisdom" (so Lauha, Lohfink). In this context, however, the object of the investigation is not wisdom itself, but "everything under the heavens" (cf. 8:9). Moreover, in the other instances in Ecclesiastes where one finds *baḥokmâ*, the preposition *bĕ-* always indicates agent or instrument, thus "through wisdom" or "by wisdom" (2:3; 7:23; 9:15), and not the object of any verb. Indeed, nowhere in the Hebrew Bible does the preposition *bĕ-* ever mark *ḥokmâ* as an object (cf. Prov 3:19; 24:3; Isa 10:13; Ezek 28:4). The point is not that the king looked for wisdom, but that he *applied* wisdom. The king already has wisdom and uses it (cf. 2:9, "my wisdom aided me"). The motif of royal wisdom is standard fare in the royal inscriptions. The Phoenician inscription from Karatepe mentions the wisdom of Azitawadda as a mark of his legitimacy: "every king made me a father because of my legitimacy, my wisdom, and the goodness of my heart" (*KAI* 26.I.12–13). Akkadian inscriptions are replete with references to the king as "wise," "intelligent," and "knowing." The kings typically claimed to have acquired comprehensive knowledge, and some claimed to have understood everything and experienced everything (see the references in Seow, "Qohelet's Autobiography," pp. 280–81). In short, the claim to use wisdom in this manner is part and parcel of royal propaganda. Qohelet, however, makes the point that such quests do not amount to much. He uses the genre of the royal inscription only to make a point contrary to the intention of such propaganda.

everything that has been done. Hebrew *ʿal kol-ʾăšer naʿăśâ*, lit. "regarding everything that has been done." The preposition *ʿal* here indicates the areas covered by the inquiry; it does not give the reason for the investigation, as Ellermeier claims (*Qohelet* I/1, p. 179). In other words, the inquiry by wisdom was comprehensive (see the preceding Note). The phrase "all that has been done" refers to all that is happening in the world and not just to what people do (cf. 1:9, 14; 4:3; 8:9, 17; 9:3, 6).

under the heavens. Many Hebrew MSS and some of the ancient versions (Syr, Vulg, Targ) read *taḥat haššemeš* "under the sun" instead of *taḥat haššāmāyim* "under the heavens," which occurs also in 2:3; 3:1. But the former clearly is an attempt to make the idiom consistent with the more dominant expression in the book (see Notes at 1:3). The fact that *taḥat haššemeš* "under the sun" does occur in v 14 argues for the probable correctness of *taḥat haššāmāyim* "under the heavens" in v 13 — i.e., the variant that reads *taḥat haššemeš* is trying to harmonize with v 14. "Under the heavens" simply means everywhere in the world, a spatial description. Qohelet's claim of comprehensive search is not nearly as bold as Asshurbanipal's boast that he ventured even into the esoterica of "heaven and earth, the wisdom of Shamash and Adad" (Streck, *Assurbanipal* II, p. 362, line 3).

It is a terrible preoccupation. The "it" refers to the task that Qohelet set for himself (the search by wisdom), not to "all that has been done under the heavens." The noun *'inyān* occurs only in Ecclesiastes (1:13; 2:23, 26; 3:10; 4:8; 5:2, 13 [Eng vv 3, 14]; 8:16), but nowhere else in the Bible. The word is attested in Postbiblical Hebrew in the sense of "subject, business, case" (see Jastrow, *Dictionary*, p. 1095). Sometimes the word has the nuance of something that causes anxiety. In Ecclesiastes, *'inyān* is associated with restlessness, obsession, worry, and human inability to find enjoyment. Here it has to do with efforts to grasp by wisdom all that is happening in the world.

with which to be preoccupied. The root *'nh* "to be busy, preoccupied," to which the infinitive *la'ănôt* is related, occurs in the Hebrew Bible only here and in 3:10. The verb is related to Arabic *'anā* "to disquiet, occupy, make uneasy" and *'aniya* "to be anxious, preoccupied" (see Lane, *Arabic-English Lexicon*, Part 5, p. 2180). One cannot rule out the possibility of wordplay, however. Perhaps one is supposed to think also of *'nh* "to be humble" (Piel, "to afflict") or even "to answer."

14. *I have observed.* The verb *r'h* "to see, observe" (meaning also "to experience") appears 47 times in the book, with Qohelet himself or his heart being the subject no fewer than 26 times. The author uses the verb here, as he often does elsewhere, for purposeful and reflective observation. In the light of the many similarities between Ecclesiastes and the *Gilgamesh Epic*, it is worth noting that the prologue of the latter (in the late version) asserts that Gilgamesh had seen it all, experienced everything, and received wisdom. Indeed, the epic was known in Mesopotamia by its incipit, *ša nagba īmuru* "he who saw it all."

that have been done. Instead of *šn'św*, a few Hebrew MSS and 4QQoh[b] read *'šr n'św* (see Ulrich, "Qoheleth Manuscripts," p. 148). There appears to be no significance in the choice of variants.

under the sun. See Notes at 1:3.

all is vanity. See Notes at 1:2. In this case, the "all" refers to the search for wisdom and the attempt to grasp all that is happening. "Vanity" here refers to something that cannot be grasped.

a pursuit of wind. Or "a desire of wind." The expression *rĕ'ût rûaḥ* (also in 2:11, 17, 26; 4:4, 6; 6:9) is certainly synonymous with *ra'yôn rûaḥ* (1:17; 2:22; 4:16); no distinction between the two can be discerned. Postbiblical Hebrew has *r'ywn* meaning "desire, greed, ambition" (Jastrow, *Dictionary*, pp. 1486–87). Both words correspond to Aramaic *r'wt* and *r'yn* "pleasure, will, ambition, desire" (see Ezra 5:17; 7:18; Dan 2:30; 7:28) and Phoenician *r't* "desire, intention" (*KAI* 60.4), but this is probably an Aramaic loanword. So LXX renders the phrase by *proairesis pneumatos* "choosing of wind/spirit" (but Aq and Theod *nomē* "pasturing"; Symm *boskēsis* "feeding"). The basic meaning here is "pursuit" or "striving" (i.e., a striving after something that one desires). In Hos 12:2, there is a related expression *rō'eh rûaḥ* "pursuing of wind," which is parallel to *rōdēp qādîm* "chasing the eastwind." In that passage both *rōdēp qādîm* and *rō'eh rûaḥ* are activities of Ephraim as the fool who desires things that are ephemeral and unreliable (see C. L. Seow, "Hos 14:10 and the Foolish People Motif," *CBQ* 44 [1982], pp. 221–22). We may also compare Prov 15:14, where we have *yĕbaqqeš-da'at* "seeks knowledge" contrasted with *yir'eh 'iwwelet* "pursues folly." The word is related to Hebrew *rō'eh* "shepherd" — that is, one who runs after and minds sheep (cf. Arabic *ri'âyat* "keeping, minding"). The imagery of a fool pursuing wind is found also in Sir 34:1–2 (Greek, Syriac, and Latin versions only):

> Empty and false are the hope of the senseless,
>   and fools are carried on wings by dreams.
> Like one who grasps at shadows or *pursues wind*,
>   is one who puts trust in dreams.

Indeed, throughout the wisdom literature of the Bible, *rûaḥ* "wind" is frequently a metaphor for things that have no abiding value or are insubstantial. Thus, the sages spoke of inheriting wind (Prov 11:29), restraining wind (Prov 27:16), gathering wind (Prov 30:4), windy knowledge (Job 15:2), and windy words (Job 16:3; cf. 6:26; 8:2). In every case "wind" indicates futility or meaninglessness (see Isa 41:29). In Akkadian, too, *šāru* "wind" may have this connotation. So in a wisdom text, one who does foolish things is characterized as *sākil šārim* "one who acquires wind" (see Held, "A Faithful Lover in an Old Babylonian Dialogue," p. 6, line 7). In the *Gilgamesh Epic*, life is seen as transitory and all that humans do is but *šāru* "wind" (Gilg Y iv 8).

15. *be straightened.* Reading *lĕtuqqan* "be straightened" with Driver ("Problems and Solutions," p. 225), for MT's *litqōn* "is straight." LXX (followed by SyrH and Copt), Vulg, and Targ translate with passive verbs. The Qal stem of this verb is unattested in Hebrew; the verb is always in Piel in the Bible (see also 7:13; 12:9; Sir 47:9), so the corresponding passive ought to be Pual. In Postbiblical Hebrew, too, the verb occurs only in Piel, Hiphil, and Niphal, but never in Qal. Thus, *lō' yûkal lĕtuqqan* "cannot be straightened" may be compared with the rhetorical question *mî yûkal lĕtaqqēn* "who can straighten?" (7:13). Others emend to read *lĕhittāqēn* (the Niphal infinitive construct), citing the parallelism with *lĕhimmānôt* (Lauha). But it is unnecessary to change the consonantal text. If the Niphal is to be read, we should assume syncope of the *he'*: *lĕhittāqēn* > *littāqēn* (see GKC §51.1; so Graetz). In any case, one is reminded of a saying in an Egyptian text, *The Instruction of Anii*, that even a crooked stick can be straightened, while a straight stick can be bent (see Volten, *Studien zum Weisheitsbuch des Anii*, pp. 170–71, lines 13–14). The Egyptian proverb stresses the effectiveness of instructions: even the crooked can be straightened out and the straight can be made to bend. The proverb in Ecclesiastes, however, seems to say the opposite: what is crooked *cannot* be straightened.

what is lacking. The noun *ḥesrôn* occurs only here in Hebrew. The noun *ḥissārôn* is, however, attested in Postbiblical Hebrew, where it means "loss, deficiency, deficit." The word is also related to Aramaic *ḥsrn/ḥwsrn* and Arabic *ḥus-*

rān "deficit, lack." This is an economic term, opposite in meaning to *yutrān* (Hebrew *yitrôn*) "surplus, gain." Thus, one reads in a late fifth-century (B.C.E.) document from Egypt: "You, lavish from our houses goods (*nksn*). Give him as much as you can. It is not a loss (*ḥsrn*) for you" (*TAD* I, 4.3.8–9).

be counted. There is no warrant for emending *lĕhimmānôt* "to be counted" to *lĕhimmālôt* "to be filled," presumably a late variant of the Niphal inf. cs. of *mlʾ* (so Levy, Galling, and many others). As Fox points out (*Contradictions*, p. 176 n. 16), Symm does not have *anaplērōsai* alone, but *anaplērōsai arithmon*, which is the contextual translation of MT. It is puzzling, however, that Fox should nevertheless read *lĕhimmālôt*. LXX, Vulg, Syr, and Targ all support MT. There is no need to emend the text. The point is that one cannot count what is not there, or that the deficiency is so great that one cannot compute it.

16. *I spoke with my heart.* The appearance of the independent personal pronoun after the verb is a peculiar feature of Qohelet's style (1:16; 2:11, 12, 13, 14, 15, 18, 20, 24; 3:17, 18; 4:1, 4, 7; 5:17 [Eng v 18]; 7:25; 8:15; 9:15, 16). In a thorough analysis of this phenomenon, Isaksson has concluded that the pronoun in such constructions is not intended to emphasize the subject but the thought: "the pronoun is added in instances of greater importance, where the narrative halts for a moment to make a conclusion or introduce a new thought" (*Studies in the Language of Qoheleth*, pp. 163–71, quotation from p. 171).

There are analogous expressions elsewhere in the Bible: *ʾāmar ʾel libbô* "speak to one's heart" (Gen 8:21; 1 Sam 27:1) and *ʾāmar bĕlibbô* "speak with one's heart" (Gen 27:41; 1 Kgs 12:26, Obadiah 3; Pss 10:6, 11, 13; 14:1; 53:2 [Eng v 1]; 74:8, Esth 6:6; Zech 12:5). In no other instance, however, is the thing said introduced by a quotation marker (*lēʾmōr* or *kî*), as is the case here. Nor is the heart ever addressed directly in the second person, as it is in 2:1. Moreover, one may note that the heart is very active in Qohelet, often functioning as an independent entity: the heart sees the abundance of wisdom and knowledge (1:16), the heart rests (2:23), the heart finds pleasure (2:10), the heart leads (2:3), the heart rushes (5:1 [Eng v 2]), the heart is in the house of mourning (7:4), the heart knows (7:21; 8:5), and the heart delights a person (11:9). It is likely, therefore, that the heart is personified here. This is a literary device used in Egyptian pessimistic literature. So one reads in *The Complaints of Khakheperre-Sonb*: "He said to his heart: "'Come, my heart, that I may speak to you, and that you may answer me . . . I speak to you, my heart, answer me! A heart that is approached must not be silent'" (see Gardiner, *Admonitions*, p. 105, line 1; p. 108, lines 5–6). A similar device is found in *The Dispute Between a Man and His Ba* (*AEL* I, pp. 163–69). Such texts typically present conflicting positions assumed, respectively, by the physical self and the heart or the soul. So, too, Qohelet speaks "with" (*ʿim*) his heart. Certainly the heart is personified in 2:1–3. One may also compare the NT "Parable of the Rich Fool," where the soul is personified: "I will say to my soul, Soul, you have many good things laid up for many years; take it easy, eat, drink, be merry" (Luke 12:19).

I, yes, I have shown greatness. Instead of the redundant independent personal pronoun, Dahood vocalizes *ʾny* as *ʾōnî* "my wealth": thus, "I increased my wealth" // "I added to my wisdom" ("Phoenician Background," pp. 266–67). This has no textual support whatsoever. The independent pronoun is attested in LXX (*egō*) and Syr (*'n'*), although Targ and Vulg do not translate it. In any case, LXX, Vulg, and Syr all take the verb to be intransitive. This does not necessarily mean that they were reading a Qal form, however. The Hiphil of *gdl* has an intransitive meaning in 1 Chron 22:5; Dan 8:4, 8, 11, 25. What we may have here is an instance of an "inwardly transitive" or "intensive" Hiphil (see GKC §53.d). Examples of this usage of the Hiphil verb abound: *hiqrîb* "to draw near," *hiqšîb* "to listen," *hēšîb* "to reply" (see Joüon-Muraoka §54.e). Other commentators assume a dittography of *he'* and read *hinnēh* < > *gādaltî* with 2:9 (so Zimmerli). This move is both unnecessary and without warrant.

all who were before me. Cf. also 2:7, 9. This is a stock phrase in royal boasts, corresponding to Akkadian *mamman maḥrīya* "any before me," *ša ellamūa* "those who were before me," *mamman ina šarrāni ālikūt maḥrīya* "any among kings who went before me," or *šarrāni maḥrūt* "former kings" in Assyrian royal inscriptions (see Seow, "Qohelet's Autobiography," p. 281, n. 35). The idiom is formulaic. Hence, even though Qohelet is assuming the role of Solomon, there is no need to ask if he had slipped in the plural reference to his predecessors in Jerusalem (since there had been only one Israelite king who ruled over Jerusalem) or if he was referring to pre-Israelite kings. Qohelet is adopting the language and style of royal propagandistic literature. The historicity of the Jerusalemite kings before Solomon is not at issue for him.

over Jerusalem. Well over a hundred Hebrew MSS have *byrwšlm* and the ancient versions reflect the same, but that is the easier reading and it anticipates *byrwšlm* in 2:7, 9. Some scribe wrote *byrwšlm* instead of *'l yrwšlm* because the former is what he expected.

17. *Hence I set my heart*. As it is commonly noted, *wā'ettĕnâ* is one of only three *waw*-consecutive forms in the book; the other occurrences are in 4:1, 7. A possible explanation for the rare use of the *waw*-consecutive in this instance is given by Isaksson (*Studies in the Language of Qoheleth*, pp. 58–63). As Fox has it, vv 16–18 are "a narration and evaluation" of the inquiry described in vv 12–15 (*Contradictions*, p. 174). So the narrative sequence is appropriate.

to know wisdom and knowledge of < > prudence. MT takes *wd't* as an infinitive (i.e., "and to know"), but the ancient versions (LXX, Syr, Vulg, Targ) all understand four nouns to be the object of the infinitive *lāda'at* "to know": thus, "to know wisdom and knowledge, irrationality and *śiklût*." If these versions are correct, *wĕda'at* "and to know" in MT should simply be repointed as *wāda'at* "and knowledge." But the difficulty with the verse is not solved even with this change, for the phrase *hôlēlôt wĕśiklût* seems intrusive. We note that v 18 identifies only "wisdom" and "knowledge" as the issues at hand, and nothing is said about *hôlēlôt wĕśiklût*. Moreover, v 16 has only "wisdom and knowledge." Some have argued, therefore, that the phrase *hôlēlôt wĕśiklût* is secondary and anticipates a virtually identical expression in 2:12 (Ginsburg, Lauha, Fox). Others prefer to omit *ḥokmâ wĕda'at* as a vertical dittography, suggesting that the phrase is repetitive after v 16 (so Jastrow). Rejecting these moves, Gordis takes v 17a to mean "to know that wisdom and knowledge *are* madness and folly."

The assumption of virtually all commentators is that *śiklût* here is a mere variation of *siklût* "folly" attested elsewhere in the book (2:3, 12, 13; 7:25; 10:1, 13). This is reasonable, inasmuch as *hôlēlôt* and *siklût* are juxtaposed three times (2:12, 7:25, and 10:13). Vulg assumes that *śiklût* and *siklût* are synonymous, and numerous Hebrew MSS read *siklût* instead of *śiklût*. Yet, it must be noted that LXX, Syr, and Targ apparently take *śiklût* to be from *śkl* "to be prudent" and, thus, not identical with *siklût* "folly." The interchangeability of *samek* and *sin* is, indeed, well-documented for Late Biblical Hebrew, as many scholars have pointed out (see Whitley, *Koheleth*, p. 16). But Qohelet himself manifests no such tendency; the only instance in the book of a confusion is in the noun *maśmĕrôt* in the epilogue (12:11). The spelling of *śiklût* is still odd, when compared with *siklût* everywhere else in the book. It is possible that the original text had *wĕdaʿat śiklût* "knowledge of prudence," but a later scribe, incorrectly interpreting *śiklût* "prudence" as a variant spelling of *siklût* "folly," read *daʿat <hôlēlôt wĕ> śiklût* under the influence of 2:12, 7:25; 10:13. Thus, the original objects of *lādaʿat* are *hokmâ* "wisdom" and *daʿat* "knowledge," precisely the two items observed by Qohelet (v 16) and commented on in the aphorism of v 18. One might add that both *hokmâ* and *daʿat* are found as objects of *ydʿ* elsewhere in the Bible (cf. Prov 24:14; 17:27; Num 24:16; Dan 1:4), and *ydʿ* is used with *śēkel* "prudence" (2 Chron 2:11 [Eng v 12]). The likeness of *śiklût* "prudence" and *siklût* "folly" is not accidental, however, since Qohelet could have used the more common noun *śēkel/sekel* instead. Qohelet probably intends the ambiguity, and not a little irony, in his choice of *śiklût*, a homonym for *siklût* "folly."

pursuit of wind. See Notes at 1:14.

18. *vexation.* LXX *gnōseōs* (followed by SyrH and Copt) reflects Hebrew *dāʿat* "knowledge" instead of *kāʿas* "vexation." This reading anticipates *daʿat* in the parallel line. MT is undoubtedly correct; it is supported by Aq and Theod (*thymou*), Symm (*orgē*), Vulg (*indignatio*), Syr (*rwgzʾ*), Targ (*rgz*). The noun *kaʿas* "vexation, anger, grief, trouble" occurs five times in the book (1:18; 2:23; 7:3, 9; 11:10); the verb appears twice (5:16 [Eng v 17]; 7:9).

when one increases . . . one increases. The Hiphil imperfect 3 ms is used impersonally here. There is no need of an emendation to read the Qal participle (so Galling, Lauha, and others). The reading *yôsîp* (with a second *mater lectionis*, i.e., *yod*) is supported by most Hebrew MSS. The Hiphil of *ysp* also occurs in 1:16; 2:9; 3:14.

2 1. *I spoke with my heart.* Hebrew *ʾāmartî ʾănî bĕlibbî* may mean "I thought to myself," but, in light of the expression *dibbartî ʾănî ʿim-libbî* "I spoke with my heart" in 1:16 and the personification of the heart as a conversation partner in this passage, a more literal rendering is preferred.

let me make you experience. The form *ʾănassĕkâ* cannot be derived from *nsk* "pour out" (so Vulg, followed by Ibn Ezra), but *nsh* "test, try" with a 2 ms suffix (so LXX and Syr). The full spelling of the 2 ms suffix (with the *mater lectionis*) in *lĕkâ-nāʾ* and *ʾănassĕkâ* is found elsewhere in the Bible, although with other verbs (Joüon-Muraoka §94.h); this *plene* spelling is widely attested at Qumran. The verb *nsh* is normally "to test, try," but when it is coordinated with verbs of seeing, hearing, knowing, and learning, the meaning is "to experience," the object of the experience being indicated by the preposition *bĕ-*. See Greenberg, "נסה in Exodus 20:20," pp. 273–76.

enjoy good. Lit. "see good" or "look into good," but *rʾh* is regularly used to mean "to experience," as in *rĕʾēh ḥayyîm* "experience life" (9:9), which may be contrasted with the idiom *yirʾeh-māwet* "experience death" (Ps 89:49 [Eng v 48]). We may also compare *rāʾâ bĕṭôb* (Pss 27:13; 128:5), *rāʾâ ṭôb* (Ps 34:13 [Eng v 12]; Job 7:7), or *rāʾâ ṭôbâ* (Eccl 5:17 [Eng v 18]; 6:6; Job 9:25) — all meaning "to experience good" = "to live." Conversely, one finds the idiom *rāʾâ bĕrāʾâ* (Num 11:15; 2 Kgs 22:20) and *rāʾâ rāʿ* (Hab 1:13), both meaning "to experience evil" = "to suffer."

that, too, is vanity. The word *hebel* here is used in the sense of something that is fleeting and insubstantial (see Notes at 1:2).

2. *Regarding merriment . . . and regarding pleasure.* The preposition is to be taken as the *lamed of specification* (cf. Gen 17:20, *ûlĕyišmāʿ[ʾ]ēl šĕmaʿtîkā* "regarding Ishmael, I have heard you"; see Waltke-O'Connor §11.2.10.d, g).

<what> *does it boast.* Reading *me<h> hôlēl* (cf. Isa 3:15; Mal 1:13; 1 Chron 15:13; 2 Chron 30:3) instead of *mĕhôlāl* in MT. The latter is usually assumed to be a Poal participle and supposed to be used as a synonym of *hôlēlôt* "irrationality" and thus is translated "[it is] mad" (so KJV, ASV, RSV) or the like. But apart from the syntactical and poetic inelegance, the form *mĕhôlāl*, which occurs elsewhere only in Ps 102:9 (Eng v 8), does not have this meaning (in Ps 102:9, LXX and Syr take the form to be active, and most scholars emend accordingly). Thus, both the form of the word and its translation are dubious. Syr has *mnʾ hnyn* ("what use is it?"), which is not from *mâ yôʿîl* "what does it profit?" — as is sometimes supposed (so Euringer), but merely a free rendering of original *meh hôlēl* "what does it boast?" The original text may have had either *m<h> hwll* or *m hwll* (cf. *ma-* "what?" in Exod 4:2; Isa 3:15; Mal 1:13; 1 Chron 15:13; 2 Chron 30:3). Thus, we have *mh hwll* "what does it boast?" // *mh-zh ʿśh* "what does it really accomplish?" A similar pairing of *mh . . . mh* is found in Gen 31:36; 44:16; Exod 17:2; Ps 120:3; Isa 21:11; Jer 16:10; Mic 6:3, 5, 8.

what . . . really. Hebrew *mah-zzōh* is probably emphatic, not interrogative (see Waltke-O'Connor §17.4.3.c). In Ecclesiastes, the form *zōh* is used in place of the more common form *zōʾt* (2:24; 5:15, 18 [Eng vv 16, 19]; 7:23; 9:13). Cf. *lōʾ zeh hadderek . . . lōʾ zōh hāʿîr* (2 Kgs 6:19); *kāzōh wĕkāzeh* (Judg 18:4). In our passage, seven Hebrew MSS read *zʾt* while seven others have *zw* instead of *zh*, but these are merely attempts to conform to the "standards" in Biblical and Mishnaic Hebrew, respectively (see Schoors, *Pleasing Words*, pp. 52–53).

3. *I went about with my heart.* The verb *twr* occurs two other times in Ecclesiastes, both times meaning "to explore, search" (1:13; 7:25). But "explore" or "search" makes no sense here. All the ancient versions have trouble with the expression; most of them interpret the verb figuratively to mean some sort of

mental activity (LXX *kateskeupsamēn* "I examined"; Aq and Symm *enoēthēn* "I considered"; Theod *dienoēthēn* "I purposed"; Vulg *cogitavi* "I thought"). It is possible to take *twr* here to mean "to go about" (cf. *tārîm* "travelers" in 1 Kgs 10:15 and 2 Chron 9:14). The root in Arabic may mean "to turn, return," but also "to flow, run, go about" (see Lane, *Arabic-English Lexicon*, Part 1, pp. 322–23). Thus the Hebrew expression *twr blb* "to go about with the heart" means roughly the same thing as *twr 'ḥry blbb* "to follow the heart" in Num 15:39 and *hlk bdrky lb* "to walk in the ways of the heart" in Eccl 11:9, where the issue is also enjoyment. In the latter passage, the youth is called upon to let the heart bring enjoyment (11:9a), to follow the heart (11:9b), and to remove trouble from the body (11:10). Here in 2:3 the body is carried away.

to induce. The reading and meaning of *limšôk* are debated. Scholars sometimes conjecture from the context that it means "to refresh" (Delitszch, Gordis, Lauha), or they emend to read *lśmwk* "to support" (Kroeber) or *lśmḥ* "to rejoice" (see Joüon, "Notes philologiques," p. 419). But all witnesses confirm that *lmšwk* is correct; we ought not emend the consonantal text. The question is what the verb *mšk* means. The closest parallel to what we have is in Ps 28:3, where the verb *mšk* also takes a personal object, as it does in our passage: *'al timšĕkēnî 'imrĕšā'îm* "Do not lead me (away) with the wicked." Here LXX reads, *mē synelkysēs meta hamartōlōn tēn psychēn mou* "do not lead my soul (away) with sinners," reflecting Hebrew *'al timšōk 'et-napšî 'im rĕšā'îm*, where the expression *māšak 'et-napšî* corresponds to *māšak 'et-bĕśārî* in Eccl 2:3. The basic meaning of *mšk* is "to lead along, carry along, take away, pull (up, along, away)," whether literally or figuratively. This is also the range of meaning of the verb in Postbiblical Hebrew. So one reads in the Talmud: *b'ly 'gdh šmwškym lbw šl 'dm kmym* "the experts of the Aggadah draw the hearts of people like water" (*b. Ḥag.* 14a). It is primarily on the basis of this text that scholars interpret *mšk* to mean "refresh." The point of the comparison with water is not its refreshing quality, however, but its pull as it flows downstream (cf. *m. Mo'ed Qat.* 1:3; *y. 'Abod. Zar.* III.42c). One may relate the verb to Ugaritic *mtk* "to grasp, lead": *rģb yd mtkt // mzma yd mtkt* "the hungry she leads by the hand // the thirsty she leads by the hand" (*KTU* 1.15.I.1–2). So the infinitive *limšôk* in our passage should mean "to induce" (cf. Latin *inducere* "to lead"). Aq and Theod accurately translate the Hebrew: *helkysai* "to induce" (so also SyrH). In any case, the point is the bravado of youth. So one reads in a fragment of the *Gilgamesh Epic*: "You are young, O Gilgamesh, and your heart carries you away. You do not know what you continually do" (Gilg III v 10).

and <did not> take hold. Reading *wĕlō' <'ō>ḥēz* instead of *wĕle'ĕḥōz* in MT (so Horst in BHS; Fox). With this minor emendation, it is no longer necessary to regard *wĕlibbî nōhēg baḥokmâ* "and my heart leads by wisdom" as an awkward parenthetical comment or a gloss, as many commentators do. Since *'ōḥēz bĕsiklût* is parallel to *nōhēg baḥokmâ*, one should perhaps take *'ōḥēz* to mean "hold (the hand)," that is, "lead." See Ps 139:10, where *'ḥz* is in parallelism with *nḥh* "lead." Thus, *mšk, nhg, 'ḥz* are all synonyms.

what really is good. Hebrew *'ê-zeh*, lit. "where indeed" (but see the discussion in Schoors, *Pleasing Words*, pp. 57–58). It is possible that *ʾê-zeh ṭôb* may be harking back to the imperative *rĕʾēh ṭôb* "enjoy good" in v 1. In that case, *zeh* would be emphatic, even as *zōh* is emphatic in v 2. Thus, vv 2 and 3 together call into question both the experience of *śimḥâ* and *ṭôb* commanded in v 1: *lĕśimḥâ mahzzōh* in v 2 corresponds with *ʾê-zeh ṭôb* in v 3; v 1 is subverted by vv 2–3.

under the heavens. LXX, Vulg, and Syr have "under the sun," another attempt to conform the text to the standard idiom in Ecclesiastes. See Notes at 1:13.

during the few days of their life. The phrase *mispar yĕmê ḥayyêhem* may be interpreted as the accusative of time, as in 6:12. Qohelet speaks of the transitory nature of human life in terms of their numbered days (so also 5:17 [Eng v 18]). One may also compare the saying in the *Gilgamesh Epic:* "As for humanity, their days are numbered" (Gilg Y iv 142).

4. *I accomplished great works.* This section (vv 4–11) is about the works of the king; the root *ʿśh* occurs seven times. This listing of the king's accomplishments corresponds to similar lists in the royal inscriptions elsewhere in the ancient Near East. Here Qohelet describes his achievements in "resumé style," using verbs in the perfect (see Isaksson, *Studies in the Language of Qoheleth*, pp. 47–56): *hgdlty* "I accomplished greatly" (v 4), *bnyty* "I built" (v 4), *nṭʿty* "I planted" (vv 4, 5), *ʿśyty* "I made/gained" (vv 5, 6, 8), *qnyty* "I acquired" (v 7), *knsty* "I accumulated" (v 8). The same "resumé style" is evident in the West Semitic royal inscriptions. Many of the items listed in these inscriptions are also found in Qohelet's boast. Also relevant is the Tell Siran Bottle, which speaks of "works of Amminadab," including a vineyard (*hkrm*), a garden (*hgnt*), an enclosed park (*hʾšhr?*), and a pool (*ʾšht*). See H. O. Thompson and F. Zayadine, "The Tell Siran inscription," *BASOR* 212 (1973), pp. 5–11; E. J. Smit, "The Tell Siran Inscription. Linguistic and Historical Implications," *Journal of Semitics* 1 (1989) 108–17. One might also observe that the inscription ties the works of the king with pleasure for him: *ygl wyšmḥ* "may he rejoice and be happy" (cf. *śmḥ* in Qoh 2:10).

vineyards. This is, perhaps, an allusion to Solomon's vineyards, one of which was reputed to have been in Baal Hamon (Song 8:11).

5. *gardens.* Several texts in the Bible speak of "the King's Garden" (Jer 39:4; 52:7; 2 Kgs 25:4; Neh 3:15) located near the Pool of Shelah (Neh 3:15) in the Kidron Valley. The brook of Kidron apparently irrigated the various gardens and orchards that were regarded as royal property.

parks. Hebrew *pardēs* is a loanword from Old Persian **paridaida*, a word that is first attested in an Elamite document from Persepolis (see W. Hinz, *Altiranisches Sprachgut der Nebenüberlieferungen* [Wiesbaden: Harrassowitz, 1975], p. 179). This Elamite text dates to around 500 B.C.E. Akkadian has the cognate *pardēsu*, attested in texts from the reigns of Cyrus and Cambysus in the second half of the sixth century B.C.E. It is probably by way of Akkadian that the Persian word came into Hebrew in the fifth century. The Persian word is also attested later in other languages: Greek (*paradeisos*), Aramaic and Syriac (*pardēs*), Armenian (*pardez*), and so forth. The term is used of an enclosed park or grove and is attested elsewhere only in Late Biblical Hebrew (Neh 2:8; Song 4:13) and Postbiblical Hebrew.

6. *pools of water.* Several pools (*bĕrēkôt*) are mentioned in the Hebrew Bible, including one at Gibeon (2 Sam 2:13), one at Hebron (2 Sam 4:12), one at Samaria (1 Kgs 22:38), and several in the vicinity of Jerusalem (2 Kgs 18:17 [= Isa 36:2]; 20:20; Isa 7:3; 22:9, 11; Neh 3:10). The Siloam tunnel inscription, too, mentions a pool (*brkh*) fed by the waters from a spring nearby (*KAI* 189.5). This is to be connected with the tunnel constructed by Hezekiah (2 Kgs 20:20; 2 Chron 32:30; Isa 22:11; Sir 48:17). Josephus knew of "Solomon's Pool" between the Pool of Siloam (*Birket es-Silwan*) and a place called Ophlas (*War* V.145). This may refer to "the King's Pool" mentioned in Neh 2:14 or "the Pool of Shelah" (perhaps "Pool of Shiloah" = "Pool of Siloam" in John 9:7) near "the King's Garden" (Neh 3:15). Remnants of a plastered pool recently have been uncovered in precisely this vicinity, a pool that may have been identified with an earlier one at the same site attributed by tradition to Solomon. See D. Adan, "The 'Fountain of Siloam' and 'Solomon's Pool' in First-Century C.E. Jerusalem," *IEJ* 29 (1979), pp. 92–100.

from which. Lit. "from them." Here, as elsewhere in Ecclesiastes (2:10; 10:9; 11:8; 12:1), the 3 mp suffix is used in place of the 3 fp suffix, which is unattested at all.

to irrigate. One thinks here of the Siloam canal, a partially covered aqueduct that carried water from the Spring of Gihon along the Kidron Valley into a large pool at the lowest part of the Tyropoeon Valley. The canal has several openings along one wall, which allowed irrigation of the gardens and orchards along the Kidron (see A. Mazar, *Archaeology of the Land of the Bible* [ABRL; New York: Doubleday, 1990], p. 483). Perhaps Qohelet had something like this water project in mind.

a forest sprouting with trees. LXX[BP] (supported by Copt) do not mention "trees," but they are probably translating somewhat freely. "Trees" is the accusative of specification. Cf. Isa 1:30, *kĕʾēlâ nōbelet ʿālehā* "like an oak, withering with respect to its leaves"; see Joüon-Muraoka §126.e.

7. *I acquired.* Some Hebrew MSS and Syr add *ly* "for myself," probably under the influence of the other verses. The verb *qnh* is used for the buying of slaves (Gen 39:1; 47:23; Amos 8:6; Neh 5:8). The practice of buying slaves is well attested in the Persian period, as we know from the Wadi Daliyeh papyri, a number of which record such transactions.

I had home-born slaves. Instead of *hyh ly*, a few MSS have *hyw ly*, but the former is the more difficult and, therefore, the preferred reading. The reading *hyw ly* was produced by some scribe who was, whether intentionally or unintentionally, "correcting" the grammar of the text. One may take *hāyâ lî* to be an impersonal expression (lit. "there was to me") and note the nonagreement of number and gender in the use of *hyh* in 1:10 and elsewhere in the Bible (cf. Gen 47:24; Exod 28:7; see Joüon-Muraoka §150.1; GKC §145.u). The term "home-born slaves" (lit. "children of the household" — so LXX *oikogeneis*) refers to children of slaves who were born while their parents, or perhaps only their mothers, "belonged to the household." Thus, the king had slaves that he bought and those that were born into his household.

a great possession of large cattle and small cattle. It is possible to take *miqneh* as a noun in construct, since III-Weak nouns are not vocalized consistently in Ecclesiastes (see Notes at 3:19). But one may also take *bāqār wāṣō'n* as the accusative of specification: thus, "a possession, namely, (both) large cattle and small cattle." The noun *ṣō'n* may denote either a flock of sheep only or a flock of sheep and goats. For a description of the animals among Solomon's provisions, see 1 Kgs 5:3 (Eng 4:23).

all who were before me. See Notes at 1:16. Five Hebrew MSS read *'šr hyh*, while 27 have *šhyh*, thus harmonizing the text with 1:16 and 2:9, respectively. There is no need to emend; *kl* may take either the singular or plural verb.

8. *a private hoard fit for kings.* Hebrew *sĕgullat mĕlākîm*, lit. "a private hoard of kings." The noun *sĕgullâ* may refer to one's private collection. It is cognate to Ugaritic *sglt* (*KTU* 2.39.7, 12) and Akkadian *sikiltu*. One may compare the expression *kesep wĕzāhāb ûsĕgullat mĕlākîm* with David's reference to his own treasury: *yēš lî sĕgullâ zāhāb wĕkesep* "I have a private hoard of gold and silver" (1 Chron 29:3). Elsewhere in the Bible, Israel is seen as YHWH's *sĕgullâ* "private possession" (Exod 19:5; Deut 7:6; 14:2; 26:18; Mal 3:17; Ps 135:4).

along with the provinces. Some commentators want to emend *whmdynwt* to *whmdwt* "and precious things" (Ehrlich, Delitzsch), or read <hmwn> mdynwt "riches of the provinces" (Galling, Lauha). These are, however, without warrant and unnecessary. The problem for most interpreters is the absence of the definite article in *mĕlākîm* and the presence of the article in *hammĕdînôt*. Dahood ("Phoenician Background," p. 268) takes the word to be related to Ugaritic *mdnt* (*KTU* 1.3.II.16), which he translates as "prefects" — thus "possessions of kings and prefects." But Dahood's interpretation of *mdnt* in Ugaritic is questionable; "province" is a perfectly good translation of the Ugaritic word in question. In our passage, the provinces are regarded as belonging to the king's private domain. The conjunction in this case is an example of the *waw-concomitaniae* (see GKC §154.a, Note 1).

I appointed for myself male singers and female singers. The mention of singers (*šārîm wĕšārôt*) here seems out of place; one expects them to be mentioned in the preceding verses with the acquisition of personnel, rather than with the accumulation of treasures here. It is possible to read *'āsîtî lî šērîm wĕšērôt* "I made for myself chains and necklaces." In Isa 3:19, *haššērôt* is mentioned in a list of women's jewelry, and the masculine plural form is attested in Postbiblical Hebrew (*Gen. Rabb.* section 98; see Jastrow, *Dictionary*, p. 1568). Yet, the royal inscriptions from the ancient Near East frequently mention the presence of "male singers and female singers" in the courts as an accomplishment of the king (see Seow, "Qohelet's Autobiography," pp. 282–83). In light of this fact, we should retain the reading of MT and take *'śh* to mean "appoint" (so 1 Kgs 12:31; 13:35; 2 Chron 2:17).

humanity's treasures. Hebrew *ta'ănûgōt bĕnê hā'ādām*, lit. "delights of humanity." The noun *ta'ănûgōt* does not necessarily have sexual connotations, as many commentators have insisted, who take *ta'ănûgōt bĕnê hā'ādām* to refer to a harem (i.e., "the delights of men"). Comparison is usually made with Song 7:7, but there the term is *battaʿănûgîm* = *bat taʿănûgîm* "daughter of delights." Erotic connotation in the usage of the word in that passage is undeniable, but elsewhere the term simply means delightful or fine things (Prov 19:10; Mic 1:16; 2:9; Sir 11:27; 14:16; 31:3; 37:29; 41:1). In Mic 1:16, the children of nobility are called *běnê taʿănûg* "precious children" and their home is called *bêt taʿănûg* "luxurious home" (Mic 2:9). Targ and *Qoh. Rabb.* took the expression to refer to public baths (cf. also the Talmud, *b. Sanh.* 68a). It should be noted that *taʿănûg* by itself never refers to people, so it seems improbable that *taʿănûgōt* by itself refers to women. Those who want to interpret the word as referring to women take *běnê hā'ādām* to mean "men." But *běnê hā'ādām* recurs in the book (1:13, 14; 2:3; 3:10, 11, 17, 18, 19, 20, 21; 8:11; 9:3, 12), always meaning human beings in general and never just "men." Thus, *taʿănûgōt* does not refer to women, but to the finest possessions of humanity — i.e., luxuries (so NJPS).

in chests. The meaning of *šiddâ wěšiddôt* is disputed (see Bons, "*šiddā-w-šiddōt*," pp. 12–16). The words occur only here in the Hebrew Bible, and the syntax (singular noun + conjunction + plural of the same noun) is without precise parallel anywhere. LXX[BS] and Syr translate the expression as "male-cupbearer and female-cupbearers," reflecting Hebrew *šōdeh wěšōdôt*, with only minor variations in LXX[AV], Aq, Symm, and Theod. Vulg has *scyphos et urceos* "cups and pots," probably a paraphrase. All in all, the ancient versions attest to the essential correctness of the consonantal text of MT (see Euringer, *Masorahtext*, pp. 44–47), and together they argue against any attempt to emend to *śārâ wěśārôt* "princess and princesses," *śārîm wěśārôt* "princes and princesses," or the like.

As for the etymology, the words have been conjectured as deriving from *šdd* "seize," from which one gets the meaning "ones seized in war" and hence, "concubine and concubines" (so Ibn Ezra; Ginsburg). Some scholars suggest that the nouns are related to *šad* "breast," thus taking *šiddâ wěšiddôt* as a synecdoche for "concubines" (so Gordis). Others cite the appearance of an Akkadian gloss in one of the Amarna letters (EA 369.8), read by G. Dossin as *ša-di-tum* ("Une Nouvelle Lettre d'el-Amarna," *RA* 31 [1934], p. 127, line 8) and interpreted by some to mean "concubine." The word does not exist in Akkadian, however. The Amarna gloss should, in fact, be read as *ša-qí-tu* and interpreted as "cupbearer" (so W. L. Moran, "Amarna Glosses," *RA* 69 [1975], p. 151 n. 4). Others cite Ugaritic *št* "lady" and *sitt* "concubine" in vulgar Arabic, presuming PS *šidt* (cf. also Arabic *sayyidat* "mistress"). But the root of *šiddâ* appears to be geminate. At all events, the general tendency to think of *šiddâ wěšiddôt* as "concubines" comes from the dubious interpretation of *taʿănûgōt běnê hā'ādām* as referring to women. If *taʿănûgōt* refers to treasures, then *šiddâ wěšiddôt* may be related to Postbiblical Hebrew *šiddâ* "chest, box" (see Jastrow, *Dictionary*, p. 1558). The noun is attested in Akkadian as *šaddu*, a term referring to chests for silver, gold, jewelry, and other precious things (see CAD XVII/1, pp. 42–43; cf. Jerome: *sadda et saddoth*).

The syntax of *šiddâ wěšiddôt* is also bothersome, but this is not nearly as formidable a problem as the etymology of the nouns. Scholars usually cite examples of idioms with either (1) a singular noun + a plural of the same noun (e.g., *dôr dôrîm* "generation [and] generations," Pss 72:5; 102:25 [Eng v 24]; Isa 51:8) or (2) a singular noun + conjunction + another singular noun (e.g., *'eben wā'eben* "all kinds of stones," Prov 20:10; *lēb wālēb* "two kinds of hearts," Ps 12:3 [Eng v 2]; *'ăbôdâ wa'ăbôdâ* "every service," 1 Chron 28:14). The first type (singular + plural without conjunction) denotes plurality. The second (singular + conjunction + singular) denotes variety. Although *šiddâ wěšiddôt* is distinguished from the examples in the first type by its use of the conjunction, the usage is probably similar. Here *šiddâ wěšiddôt* may be interpreted as accusatives of measure, thus, "by chests" or "in chests" (cf. Joüon-Muraoka §126.j). Cf. NJPS: "coffers and coffers of them."

9. *all who were before me.* See Notes at 1:16.

aided me. Hebrew *'āmědâ lî*, lit. "stood by me," but the idiom *'āmad lě-* means "to attend to" or "to serve" (1 Sam 16:22; 1 Kgs 1:2; Ezek 44:11, 24; Ezra 2:63; Neh 7:65). Targ explicates: "my wisdom attended to me, that is, it helped me." The idiom is similar to *'āmad 'al*, as in *hā'ōmědîm 'ālāyw* "the ones who stood by him" = "his attendants" (Judg 3:19); *wěkol-sěbā' haššāmayim 'ōmēd 'ālāyw* "the entire host of heaven was attending to him" (1 Kgs 22:19); *hā'ōmědîm 'al-'ădôn kol-hā'āreṣ* "the ones attending to the lord of all the earth" (Zech 4:14). In Ugaritic, the corresponding idioms, *qm l* and *qm 'l*, both mean "to attend to" (*KTU* 1.10.II.17; 2.I.21). The point, then, is not that wisdom remained with him, but that it served him well.

10. *Whatever my eyes desired.* The language is reminiscent of the account of Solomon's dream at Gibeon: all that Solomon desired (*š'l*) was given to him (cf. 1 Kgs 3:5, 10, 11, 13; 2 Chron 1:7, 11).

I did not deprive them. Lit. "I did not take away from them" (cf. Gen 27:36; Num 11:17, 25; Sir 42:21). For the 3 mp suffix used for the feminine noun (*'ênāyw*), see Notes at 2:6.

my heart had pleasure from all my toil. Although three MSS (Kennicott Nos. 225, 226, 384) read *bkl-'mly* instead of *mkl 'mly*, and some of the ancient versions translate the preposition as "in" (so LXX), there is no need to emend. The idiom *śmḥ mn* is attested in Prov 5:18 (*ûśěmaḥ mē'ēšet ně'ûrekā* "have pleasure from the wife of your youth") and 2 Chron 20:27 (*śimměḥām yhwh mē'ôyěbêhem* "YHWH made them take pleasure from their enemies"). Interestingly, this very idiom is attested in Ugaritic, despite the rarity of the preposition *mn* in that language: *wum tšmḥ mab* "and may my mother have pleasure from my father" (*KTU* 2.16.10–11).

my portion. The noun *ḥēleq* "portion, lot" in Ecclesiastes indicates what humans can do with all that they have (2:10, 21; 3:22; 5:17, 18 [Eng vv 18, 19]; 9:6, 9). It is, as Galling says, a technical term for "the space allotted for human existence" ("Prediger," p. 89). Elsewhere in the Bible, the term is often associated with *naḥălâ* "inheritance" (Deut 10:9; 12:12; 14:27, 29; 2 Sam 20:1; 1 Kgs 12:16; etc.). The portion may refer concretely to a given plot of land, an assigned share (Josh 19:9; 18:5), or simply a field (Hos 5:7; Mic 2:4). In various Aramaic documents from the Persian period, it is used of a share of property, including land, slaves, and other assets. For Qohelet, this lot is something that one has only in life. After that, one never again will have a portion (9:6). The imagery of an assigned lot conveys both the possibilities and the limitations that one has in life. This is the way Qohelet uses the noun; only in 11:2, in the context of a proverb, is *ḥēleq* used differently.

11. *turned to.* The idiom *pānâ bĕ-* means to "to turn to look at" or "to turn to consider" (see Job 6:28). It is semantically no different from the more common idiom *pānâ 'el* (see Num 12:10; 2 Sam 9:8; Ezek 36:9; Hag 1:9; Mal 2:13; etc.). One may compare English "to face," as in "to face facts" or "to face the problems."

all my toil which I toiled. The toil of the king is reminiscent of the prologue of the *Gilgamesh Epic* in the Middle-Babylonian version, which refers to the king's *mānaḫtu* "toil" (Gilg I i 8) and all his *marṣātu* "troubles" (Gilg I i 26). The reference there is to the achievements of Gilgamesh.

to accomplish. The presence of *la'ăśôt* at the end of the listing of the king's accomplishments is reminiscent of *la'ăśôt* Gen 2:3. Here it indicates the purpose of the toiling (cf. GKC §114.o).

all is vanity and a pursuit of wind. See Notes at 1:2 and 1:14.

there is no advantage. See Notes at 1:3.

under the sun. See Notes at 1:3.

12. *irrationality and folly.* The words *hôlēlôt* and *siklût* usually occur together (see also 7:25; 10:13, where we have *hôlēlût* instead of *hôlēlôt*). They refer essentially to the same thing. Gordis omits the *waw* before *hôlēlôt* and reads, "I saw that wisdom is *both* madness and folly," contending that only wisdom is observed in this passage, not wisdom and folly (*Koheleth*, pp. 219–20; cf. Hertzberg). The problem for Qohelet is not wisdom *per se*, however, but the fact that wisdom ultimately has no advantage over folly. One notes the mention of "folly" in vv 12–13 and "the fool" in vv 14, 15, and 16 (2x). Fox takes the pair here to be a hendiadys meaning "inane folly" (*Contradictions*, p. 183). He is certainly right that the pair indicates one and the same thing, since the contrast is really between wisdom and folly. Perhaps we should take the *waw* to be explicative, so that *hôlēlôt wĕsiklût* may be interpreted as "irrationality, that is, folly" (see GKC §154.Note 1b; cf. also the expression *'l w'lyn* "El, that is the Most High" in *KAI* 222.A.11 and the Ugaritic divine name *ktr-wḫss*).

The noun *hôlēlôt* appears several times in Ecclesiastes, along with one occurrence of *hôlēlût* (10:13), but it is attested nowhere else in the Bible. The verb form appears in 7:7 — *hā'ōšeq yĕhôlēl ḥākām* "oppression turns the wise into fools (i.e., oppression makes the wise irrational)" (cf. Isa 44:25; Job 12:17). Elsewhere in the Bible, *hll* may indicate behavior that is totally irrational, senseless, or wild (1 Sam 21:14 [Eng v 13]; Jer 25:16; 46:9; 50:38; 51:7; Nah 2:5 [Eng v 4]). As for the alternate vocalizations of *hôlēlôt* and *hôlēlût*, one may conclude that both forms are singular, the former being like *hokmôt* "wisdom" in Prov 1:20; 9:1; 14:1 (reading *hokmôt*, instead of *hakmôt*; see GKC §68.1). There is no need, therefore, to repoint the word to read *hôlēlût* everywhere (so Barton). There is a singular form *hôlēlâ*, attested in *Qoh. Rabb.* (at this verse). As far as I know, that is the only occurrence of the form; it may, in fact, have been secondarily generated from a misunderstanding of *hôlēlôt* as a plural form.

who is the person. Hebrew *meh hā'ādām*, lit. "what is the person" (but LXX *tis anthrōpos* correctly renders the Hebrew). Cf. *mah-šadday* "who is Shaddai?" in Job 21:15. The interrogative *meh hā'ādām* is reminiscent of other rhetorical questions involving *mh/my* (2 Kgs 8:13; Pss 8:5 [Eng v 4]; 144:3; Job 7:17; 15:14). These typically are used in self-deprecation and insults. See G. Coats, "Self-Abasement and Insult Formulas," *JBL* 89 (1970), pp. 17–19. Such an interpretation is preferred to the common practice of arbitrarily adding *ya'āśeh* after *hā'ādām* (thus, "what will the person <do>?"), the word being presumed lost by homoioteleuton (so Whitley).

after me. MT has *'aḥărê hammelek* "after the king." There are two problems with this reading: (1) the sudden shift in style — the author, who has been using an autobiographical style, suddenly refers to himself objectively as "the king," and (2) the relation of this phrase to the next. It is easier to repoint *'ḥry* to read *'aḥărāy* (so Graetz, Galling, Ehrlich). Thus, this line is similar to v 18: *lā'ādām šeyyihyeh 'aḥărāy* "to the one who will come after me."

shall he control. Reading *hămōlēk* instead of *hammelek* in Codex Leningrad. Already in LXX, *hmlk* is taken as something other than "king": *tēs boulēs* "the counsel" (Symm has *boulē*, but Aq and Theod have *tou basileōs*). Ginsberg, who reads *hammōlēk*, notes that the force of the word is clarified later by *šlṭ* "to control" in v 19 (*Studies in Koheleth*, pp. 9–10). Indeed, vv 18–19 show that the issue is the control of property after one dies (cf. *'aḥăray* in v 18). The normal idiom is *mlk 'l* or *mlk b*, but here we have *mlk 't*, indicating that in this case *mlk* means not just "to be king, reign" (intransitive) but "to control" (transitive). Cf. Arabic and Ethiopic *malaka* "to take possession, take over, own, dominate" and Syriac *mlk* "to rule, reign," but also "to take possession." The verb is a synonym of *šlṭ* "to control, rule, have right over." Perhaps the verb *mlk* is used here instead of *šlṭ* because royal power is at issue. In any case, the pointing of Codex Leningrad was prompted by the kingship fiction in 1:12–2:11 and by the reference to Qohelet as king in 1:1.

what has already been achieved. Hebrew *'ēt 'ăšer-kăbār 'ăśûhû*, lit. "that which they have already achieved it." The 3 mp verb is used impersonally, as is often the case in Ecclesiastes, and the suffix *-hû* is resumptive. Numerous Hebrew MSS have *'śhw* "he has achieved it" (cf. LXX^B, Syr, Vulg) and many commentators accept this reading. But *'śwhw* is the *lectio difficilior*, and undoubtedly correct. The variant with the singular verb (*'śhw*) is an attempt to harmonize with the singular verb *yābô'*. On the problems in this verse and various solutions, see the discussion in Lys, *L'Ecclésiaste*, pp. 230–37. The plural form is supported by LXX^A and Theod, which read *epoēsan*.

13. *like the advantage of light.* Hebrew *kîtĕrôn hā'ôr*. Instead of *kîtĕrôn* in Codex Leningrad, many MSS read *kĕyitrôn* (see Baer, *Quinqua Volumina*, p. 61). For the former vocalization, cf. *wîlĕlat* instead of *wĕyilĕlat* in Jer 25:36 (see GKC §24.e).

14. *But I also know.* The *waw* here is adversative, as is the particle *gam*, both

indicating Qohelet's view that the axiom stated in v 13 is contradicted by reality. It is not that he is quoting a tradition with which he disagrees (so Gordis), or that he is taking exception to the traditional saying (so Hertzberg). Rather, he is insisting that there are contradictory truths in life. On the one hand, it is true that the wise do have advantage over fools, even dramatic advantage (like light over darkness!). On the other hand, the reality is that death sets a limit to the advantage. The wise have no advantage over fools as far as death is concerned.

15. *if the fate of the fool*. Codex Leningrad has *kĕmiqrēh hakkĕsîl*. Baer (*Quinqua Volumina*, p. 61), however, claims that *miqreh* is the correct reading (instead of *miqrēh*). If so, see Notes at 3:19. In any case, the Hebrew is elliptical: "like the fate of the fool" means "a fate like the fate of a fool." The noun *miqreh* occurs seven times in the book, always referring to death (2:14, 15; 3:19 [3 times]; 9:2, 3), along with three occurrences of the verb (2:14, 15; 9:11). All living things suffer the same fate, namely, death. Fate is something that just happens, apparently without rhyme or reason that humanity could discern (see Machinist, "Fate, *miqreh*, and Reason," pp. 165–75). This fate is related to *ḥēleq* "lot" only insofar as both are arbitrarily assigned. Both are divinely given. But whereas *ḥēleq* refers to something one has only in life and may be different for individuals, *miqreh* refers to the common lot of all mortals, namely, death. It is not amiss to observe that the Greek translators did not relate either *ḥēleq* or *miqreh* to Greek *tychē* "fate"; the former is translated by *meris* "portion, part, lot," the latter by *syntantēma* "accident." Qohelet's notion of "fate" is not to be identified with the Greek notion of fate. His conception of fate is Semitic.

befalls even me. The independent pronoun in *gam 'ānî yiqrēnî* is emphatic (see GKC §135.b–f). Cf. Gen 27:34; 1 Kgs 21:19; Zech 7:5. See also Ugaritic *šmk* at "your very own name" (*KTU* 1.2.4.11, 19); *p'ny ank* "my very own feet" (*KTU* 1.17.6.45). In the Phoenician inscription from Karatepe one reads: *wbymty 'nk* "but in my very own day" (*KAI* 26.II.5).

why then have I been acting excessively wise. Hebrew *yôtēr* is used adverbially here. See 7:16, where it is parallel to *harbēh* "much," and probably also 12:9 (but not 12:12, see Notes there). Cf. *bywtr* in Mishnaic Hebrew (Sipre Deut. 31). The particle *'āz* is not represented in LXX[BS] (along with some cursives), Syr, Vulg, and Jerome, but these need not indicate an absence of *'z* in their *Vorlagen*; these versions merely translate as the context requires (see Schoors, *Pleasing Words*, pp. 28–29). In any case, the reading in MT (supported by LXX[AV]) is not inappropriate. It indicates the logical conclusion of the matter (e.g., Ps 119:92; Job 3:13; see Waltke-O'Connor §39.3.4f). There is no need to delete it (so *BHS*), or emend it to *'āk* "indeed" (Knobel), *'ê* "where?" (Whitley), or *'ēn* "there is not" (Galling).

this, too, is vanity. See Notes at 1:2.

16. *there is no remembrance of the wise*. See the Notes on 1:11.

as is the case with the fool. Hebrew *'im-hakkĕsîl*, lit. "with the fool" or "like the fool." The preposition *'im* indicates sameness here, as it does in 7:11. It is parallel to the preposition *kĕ-* in Job 9:26; 1 Chron 25:8 (cf. also Pss 72:5; 73:5). The preposition also has this meaning in Ugaritic: e.g., *dq anm lyrẓ 'm b'l ly'db mrḥ 'm bn dgn* "one weak of strength cannot run like Ba'l, cannot release the spear like the son of Dagan" (*KTU* 1.6.I.51–52); *ašsprk 'm b'l šnt 'm bn il tspr yrḥm* "I will make you count years like Baal, like the sons of El you will count months" (*KTU* 1.17.VI.28–29).

for all too soon. The expression *běšekkěbār hayyāmîm habbā'îm* is peculiar. The first word in the phrase is analyzed as *běše-*, which is synonymous with *ba'ăšer* "because, inasmuch as, since" (cf. 7:2; 8:4; Gen 39:9, 23) + *kěbār* "already" (see Notes at 1:10). Thus, *běšekkěbār* by itself would refer to something that has already happened or is already happening. Yet the expression *hayyāmîm habbā'îm* usually refers to the future ("days to come," lit. "the coming days"). The tension between what already is and what is to come is probably deliberate. The point is that the days to come are already here. The translation "all too soon" is only an approximation of the meaning. In any case, the expression is to be interpreted as an adverbial accusative.

O how. The particle *'êk* is used in elegies (2 Sam 1:19, 25, 27; Hos 11:8; Isa 14:12; Jer 49:25; 50:23; Ezek 26:17). Occurring here with the verb *yāmût* there can be no doubt about its function: Qohelet is lamenting the death of the wise and the fools alike. Thus, *'êk* is used here to introduce an exclamatory question.

17. *under the sun.* See Notes at 1:3.

terrible to me. Hebrew *ra' 'ālay.* The expression may be contrasted with its opposite *ṭôb 'al* in 1 Chron 13:2; Esth 1:19; 3:9. The use of *'al* in the datival sense is a mark of Late Biblical Hebrew (see Joüon-Muraoka §133.f). So, too, we get *'al kol-hamma'ăśeh* instead of *lěkol-hamma'ăśeh* in 3:17, and *šûb 'al* instead of *šûb 'el* in 12:7. See also the related idioms in 6:1 (*rabbâ hî' 'al-hā'ādām* "it is great upon humanity") and 8:6 (*rā'at hā'ādām rabbâ 'ālāyw* "humanity's evil is great upon them").

for all is vanity and a pursuit of wind. See Notes at 1:2 and 1:14.

18. *my toil.* Hebrew *'āmāl* may refer to the activity of toiling, or it may be a metonym for the benefit of toil, whether it be wealth or other tangibles. Here it is clearly a metonym, since it could be left to others (v 18), who would then have control over it (v 19). This usage of the noun is also found in 2:22; 3:13; 9:9, and Ps 105:44.

under the sun. See Notes at 1: 3.

which I will leave. Hebrew *še'annîḥennû*, lit. "which I will leave it." The function of *še-* is unclear: it is either relative, as in *še'ănî 'āmēl* "for which I am toiling" (earlier in the verse), or causal (i.e., I hated my toil for which I am toiling "because I will leave it . . ."). See Ellermeier, *Qohelet* I/1, pp. 277–78.

to the one who will come after me. Cf. *hā'ādām šeyyābô' 'aḥărāy* (emended text) "the one who will come after me" in v 12.

19. *they will exercise proprietorship.* In the Bible, the verb *šlṭ* occurs only in late texts (see also 5:18 [Eng v 19]; 6:2; 8:9; Neh 5:15; Esth 9:1; Ps 119:133; also Biblical Aramaic, Dan 2:39; 3:27; 5:16; 6:25). In the Persian period, the verb is used in legal expressions to refer to the right of disposal of property, a transferable right. The root appears in various Aramaic legal documents from Elephantine in the fifth century B.C.E. and from Wadi Daliyeh in the fourth century: e.g., loan

contracts, marriage contracts, grant of building rights, real estate contracts, slave contracts (see Gropp, "The Origin and Development of the Aramaic *šallīṭ* Clause," pp. 31–35). See also Notes at 5:18 (Eng v 19); 6:2; 7:19; 8:9.

I have toiled and acted wisely. It is not necessary to take *še'āmaltî wĕšehākamtî* as a hendiadys (so Delitzsch, Gordis).

under the sun. See Notes at 1:3.

this is also vanity. See Notes at 1:2.

20. *I turned.* The idiom *sbb* + an infinitive means "turn to (do something)," and can refer to doing something new or doing something again (see 1 Chron 16:43; 1 Sam 15:27; 1 Sam 14:21). Qohelet also uses other words to convey the same idea, *pnh* (2:11, 12) and *šwb* (4:1, 7; 9:11). All three are synonyms and no special nuances of meaning can be discerned for each.

to let my heart despair. Codex Leningrad has *lĕya'ēš* (so also Baer in his *Quinqua Volumina*) — that is, with virtual doubling of the *'alep* instead of compensatory lengthening of the *pataḥ*. This is often corrected (so GKC §64.e and many commentators), but one may compare *la'ênayim* instead of expected *lā'ênayim* in 11:7 and *ba'ēr* instead of *bā'ēr* in Deut 27:8.

which I toiled. Hebrew *še'āmaltî*. Many Hebrew MSS and Targ add *wšhkmty* "and for which I acted wisely" under the influence of v 19 (*še'āmaltî wĕšehākamtî*). The shorter text is to be preferred.

under the sun. See Notes at 1:3.

21. *there are people who.* Hebrew *yēš 'ādām še-*, lit. "there is a person who." The expression corresponds to Egyptian *wn p3 nty* "there is the one who . . . ," which in Papyrus Insinger is used for introducing paradoxes in life (see M. Lichtheim, *Late Egyptian Wisdom in the International Context* [OBO 52, Göttingen: Vandenhoeck & Ruprecht, 1983], p. 139). As the Egyptian text shows, such a formulation is not casuistic; it does not refer to a specific historical case, and it does not concern hypothetical situations. Rather, it is meant to introduce comments on the general human condition. This formulation makes it improbable that Qohelet was referring to very specific historical situations, as Lohfink has it (*Kohelet*, pp. 29–30).

for wisdom, knowledge, and achievement. Or "for wisdom, knowledge, and success." The preposition before all three nouns should be taken as the *bet pretii* (see GKC §119.p). The word *kišrôn* occurs in the Bible only in Ecclesiastes: in 4:4, the noun is associated with toil and probably means "achievement"; in 5:10 (Eng v 11) it refers to something that one achieves that one can enjoy. Thus, "achievement" or "success" is a suitable meaning. The verb *kšr* occurs twice in the book, both times having to do with achievement or success (10:10; 11:6). Cf. Akkadian *kašāru* "to achieve" and *kušīru* "success, profit"; Arabic *katara* "to surpass, be(come) abundant" and *kutr/kîtr* "abundance" (used of money, property, etc.); and the Ugaritic divine name *ktr* ("skillful one" or "abundant one"?) and the epithet *ktrt* "the Kotharātu."

but to those who did not toil for it. The phrase anticipates *yittĕnennû ḥelqô* "they give it as a portion." This anticipatory style is typical in Ecclesiastes.

they give it. Hebrew *yittĕnennû* is ambiguous. Dahood has argued persuasively that the 3 ms suffix with the verb is datival — that is, "give to him" ("Northwest Semitic Philology," pp. 352–53). The datival suffix is well attested in Biblical Hebrew (GKC §117.x; Joüon-Muraoka §125.ba.Note 1). In Ugaritic, likewise, the verb *ytn* may take a datival suffix: *irš ḥym watnk* "Ask for life and I will give it to you" (*KTU* 1.17.VI.27). Dahood also cites *ltty* in the Phoenician inscription from Karatepe (*KAI* 26.A.III.4), interpreting the 3 ms suffix as datival and noting that the suffix is redundant in this inscription, as it is in Ecclesiastes. This interpretation has the support of LXX[BS] and Vulg, although LXX[A] and Targ take the suffix as accusative. However, since Qohelet elsewhere uses the idiom *ntn l-* for "to give to" (1:13; 2:26; 3:10; 5:17, 18 [Eng v 18, 19]; 6:2; 8:17), and since the indirect object has already been mentioned (*lā'ādām*), it is better to take the suffix as accusative (cf. *nĕtānāh* in 12:7, where the suffix is accusative). In this case, the verb *ntn* takes the double accusative and the object is anticipated by the pronominal suffix. The anticipation of the object by a pronominal suffix is possibly a feature of northern Hebrew, or it is a colloquialism, with the object provided as an afterthought. See also *yitqĕpô* in 4:12.

as a portion. See Notes on "portion" at 2:11.

this, too, is vanity. See Notes at 1:2.

22. *what is there.* The root *hwh* is normal for the verb "to be" in Aramaic, being attested in the earliest inscriptions from Zinčirli, Carpentras, Sefire, Tell Fekhiriyeh, and, indeed, in Aramaic texts from all periods. In Hebrew, the root is usually *hyh*, but *hwh* is attested in Gen 27:29; Isa 16:4; Neh 6:6 (*hōweh*) — and twice in Qohelet (here and in 11:3); it is also well attested at Qumran and in Postbiblical Hebrew.

in all their toil and the pursuit of their hearts. Or "for all their toil and the pursuit of their hearts" (that is, interpreting the preposition *bĕ-* as *bet pretii*, as in v 21). The meaning of *'ămālô ûbĕra'yôn* is the same as *'āmāl ûrĕ'ût rûaḥ* "toil and a pursuit of wind" in 4:6. See also Notes at 1:14.

under the sun. See Notes at 1:3.

23. *in all their days.* Hebrew *kol-yāmāyw* may be the subject of a nominal sentence: "all their days are pain, and vexation is their preoccupation." It is better, however, to interpret the phrase as the accusative of time (cf. 2:3; 6:12): thus, "in all their days is pain, and vexation is their preoccupation" // "also at night (*ballaylāh*) their minds do not rest." The accusative of time ("in all their days") is paralleled by the temporal expression *ballaylāh* "at night." On the meaning of *'inyān*, see Notes at 1:14.

their hearts do not rest. Hebrew *lō' šākab libbô*, lit. "his heart does not lie down." The heart is again personified: it does not rest (or sleep). On the motif of restlessness, see Notes at 8:16–17.

This, too, is vanity. See Notes at 1:2.

24. *There is no good among humans (except) that they should eat.* Hebrew *'ên ṭôb bā'ādām šeyyō'kal.* The intent here seems clear enough: it is calling for enjoyment. But what do we make of the Hebrew in MT? It is possible to assume that an interrogative was intended but indicated only by intonation, thus, "Is it not good for humanity that they should eat and drink?" This is how Rashi took it

(cf. also Vulg). Yet, Qohelet always marks questions either with an interrogative pronoun (*mî, mâ/meh*) or an interrogative particle *hă-/ha-/he-*. There are no other instances of an unmarked interrogative sentence. Moreover, other *'ên ṭôb* expressions in Ecclesiastes do not appear as questions, but as statements of what humans can do: *'ên ṭôb bām kî 'im-liśmôaḥ* "there is no good among them except to enjoy" (3:12); *'ên ṭôb mē'ăšer yiśmaḥ hā'ādām* "there is no good except that humanity should enjoy" (3:22); *'ên-ṭôb lā'ādām taḥat haššemeš kî 'im-le'ĕkôl* "there is no good for humanity under the sun, but to eat" (8:15).

In the light of these parallels, some scholars assume that a *mem* marking the comparative has dropped out (haplography) — that is, *bā'ādām miššeyō'kal* was inadvertently copied as *bā'ādām < > šeyō'kal* (so Ginsburg and many others). Such an emendation is unnecessary. The parallel statements in the book show that Qohelet expresses the same sentiment in a variety of ways: *bām* (3:12) vs. *lā'ādām* (8:15), *kî 'im* (3:12; 8:15) vs. *mē'ăšer* (3:21), the infinitive (3:12; 8:15) vs. the imperfect (3:21). In 2:24, *še-* functions like *kî* "that" — perhaps it stands for *kî 'im* "except that." Thus, "there is no good among humanity that they should eat and drink . . ." is simply elliptical for "there is no good among humanity (except) that they should eat and drink." The ancient versions probably do not reflect a different reading in the *Vorlage(n)* — i.e., they probably translated the sense of the Hebrew.

and enjoy themselves. Hebrew *wĕher'â 'et-napšô ṭôb*, lit. "and make themselves see (experience) good." We should probably take the phrase as elaborating on *šeyō'kal wĕšātâ* "that one should eat and drink." There is a wordplay here: there is no good (*ṭôb*) among humanity, except that they should make themselves see good (*ṭôb*). This wordplay is not incidental, since *ṭôb* appears again two other times in the next two verses.

that. Many MSS read *hw'* instead of *hy'*, but there is no need to emend. Those who read *hw'* instead of *hy'* probably were interpreting *zh* incorrectly as a masculine form (i.e., vocalizing as *zeh* instead of *zōh*).

25. *and who will glean.* The interpretation of *ûmî yāḥûš* is controversial. We may begin by rejecting the reading presupposed by LXX, Theod, and Syr, all of which apparently reflect Hebrew *yšth* "will drink." LXX (*pietai*), on which Syr seems to have depended at this point, is too literalistic to have been interpretive, and so the reading is likely to have been simply a mistake. If so, that mistake probably arose under the influence of v 24, which juxtaposes *'kl* and *šth*. MT is the more difficult and undoubtedly correct reading. The more difficult question is the meaning of *yāḥûš*. Should one take it as positive or negative? Is *yāḥûš* a synthetical or antithetical parallel to *yō'kal*? In Biblical Hebrew, *ḥwš* usually means "to hasten" (so KJV: "who can hasten *hereunto*"), but this does not seem appropriate in the context. Aq and Symm (*pheisetai*), SyrH (*yḥws*), and Jerome (*parcet*) all take the verb to mean "to spare," reflecting Hebrew *yḥwś* (presumably for *yḥws*). This assumes that the verb is antithetical to *y'kl*. But *ḥws* is nowhere else spelled with a *śin*.

There is, in fact, no need to emend; *yḥwš* is most likely the original reading. If the verb is a synonym of *y'kl*, it must mean something like "enjoy" (so Vulg *deli-*

ciis affluet "abound in pleasure"). Modern commentators sometimes cite *ḥwš* "to feel, experience" in Job 20:2 and in Postbiblical Hebrew and Aramaic. But the argument of scholars that *ḥwš* here means "to feel (*good*)," from which they secondarily derive the meaning "to enjoy," is unconvincing. The root attested in the documents always refers to the feeling of pain and agony (so, too, in Job 20:2; also in *b. ʿErub.* 54a). The meaning is always negative; it never means "to feel good" or "to enjoy." Levy points to Akkadian *ḥašāšu* "to rejoice" (*Qoheleth*, pp. 77–78) and Dahood cites Ugaritic *ḫšt*, which he takes to mean "joy" ("Recent Discoveries," pp. 307–8). In a careful study of this verse, de Waard judges Levy's case to be "not too strong" ("The Translator and Textual Criticism," p. 526). Nevertheless, de Waard chooses to interpret *yāḥûš* as "enjoy," largely on the basis of Dahood's analysis of *ḫšt*. But Ugaritic *ḫšt*, which occurs several times (see *KTU* 1.16.I.3, 4, 17, 18; I.2.39, 41), is of uncertain meaning. The parallelism with *bt* "house" would make the translation "joy" improbable. Ugaritic *ḫšt* probably refers to a chamber, perhaps a burial chamber (cf. Akkadian *ḥaštu* "hole, pit"), not "joy."

It is easiest to take *mî yāḥûš* as antithetical to *mî yōʾkal*, as the contrast in v 26 between the two types of people would suggest. There are several options here: (1) interpret the verb to mean "suffer" or "be troubled," as in Postbiblical Hebrew and Aramaic, (2) relate the verb to Akkadian *ḥâšu* "worry, fret" (see the extensive study in Ellermeier, "Das Verbum חוש in Koh. 2,25," pp. 197–217), or (3) relate the verb to Arabic *ḥâsa* "gather," a verb used for rounding up game, collecting food, and hoarding various things (see Lane, *Arabic-English Lexicon*, Part 2, pp. 668–69). If (1) or (2) is correct, *ʾkl* must be interpreted to mean "to enjoy" or "to have pleasure." This interpretation is forced. The last option is the most suitable in this context, since the next verse contrasts those who are favored with the gifts of wisdom, knowledge, and joy and those who are given the task of collecting and gathering. In v 25, the contrast is between those who are able to eat heartily and those who either must sweep up the crumbs or those who hoard: hence "who will eat" // "who will glean." The following contrasts are made in vv 25–26:

whoever eats	whoever gleans
the one who is favored	the offender
wisdom-knowledge-pleasure	gathering-accumulating-giving

without <him>. Codex Leningrad and the majority of MSS (supported by Targ and Vulg) have *mmny*, but eight Hebrew MSS, LXX (followed by SyrH, Copt, and Syr), and Jerome read *mmnw*. If *mmny* is correct, the suffix would refer either to God or to Solomon. The first solution assumes a quote of God's words: "who eats or who gleans except by me?" But this is without parallel in Ecclesiastes, where God never speaks. Moreover, God is clearly referred to in the third person: *ʾĕlōhîm* "God" (v 24), *lĕpānāyw* "before him" (v 26), *nātan* "he gave" (v 26), *lipnê hāʾĕlōhîm* "before God" (v 26). The first-person voice in the book always indicates the author. Euringer thinks that the *mmny* reading was secondarily introduced because of the tendency to attribute everything to Solomon (*Masorahtext*, pp. 54–55). Euringer is probably correct in arguing for the priority of *mmnw* over *mmny*, but the change is perhaps not deliberate. Since *waw* and *yod* were very similar in several scripts, it is easy to see how a scribe (who had Solomon or God in mind) might have inadvertently read *mmny* for *mmnw*. This error was further prompted by the proximity of the word to others in the vicinity that end in *-y*: *rʾyty . . . ʾny . . . ky . . . ky . . . my . . . wmy . . . ky*. If the suffix indeed refers to Solomon, the whole line is intrusive, for the 3 ms suffix clearly refers to God, who is also the subject of the verb *nātan* "he gave," which occurs twice in v 26.

With the slight emendation, the problem is removed: v 24 leads naturally to v 25, and v 25 leads naturally into v 26. Indeed, vv 25–26 are intended as an explication of the expression "from the hand of God" (v 24). Dahood recognizes that the suffix must refer to God in the third person, but he wants to keep *mmny* and take the *yod* as a 3 ms suffix akin to Phoenician **-yu* ("Phoenician Background," p. 269; see also Whitley, *Koheleth*, p. 29). It is doubtful, however, if *-y* is attested as a 3 ms suffix in Hebrew (see Z. Zevit, "The Linguistic and Contextual Arguments in Support of a 3 m.s. Suffix *-y*," *UF* 9 [1977], pp. 315–28). In any case, the 3 ms suffix in Ecclesiastes is always *-w*, *-hw*, or *-nw*, but never *-y*. Indeed, *mimmennû* is attested several times (3:14; 5:18 [Eng v 19]; 6:2, 3, 10), while *mimmenî* occurs just once, with the suffix clearly being 1 cs (7:23). It makes the most sense to read with the tradition that has *mmnw*. The idiom *ḥûṣ min* "without, except" is well attested in Postbiblical Hebrew (*m. Ber.* 6:1; *b. Ber.* 33b; *Nid.* 16b; see Qimron, *Hebrew of the Dead Sea Scrolls*, p. 90).

26. *to the one who is favored.* Hebrew *lĕʾādām šeṭṭôb lĕpānāyw*, lit. "to the person who is good before him [i.e., God]." A similar expression is found in 7:26 (*ṭôb lipnê hāʾĕlōhîm*), where it also is contrasted with *ḥôṭeʾ* "offender." The one who is *ṭôb lipnê hāʾĕlōhîm* is pleasing before God (cf. Lev 10:19; Mal 2:17), whereas the *ḥôṭeʾ* — is displeasing. Here the author may be thinking analogically of the Persian court, where there were favorites of the king — those who were pleasing to the king — who received royal grants, while others were left out (see Introduction, pp. 23–33).

the offender. The noun *ḥôṭeʾ* is vocalized as if it were from a III-Weak root. This phenomenon is evident elsewhere in Ecclesiastes: *ḥôṭeʾ* in 8:12; 9:2, 18 (but *ḥōṭēʾ* in 7:26), *môṣeʾ* in 7:26, *yōṣāʾ* in 10:5, and *yĕšanne[ʾ]nnû* (emended) in 8:1 (see GKC §75nn–rr). It is evident especially in Late Biblical Hebrew (e.g., *ḥôṭeʾ* in Isa 65:20, a text from the Persian period), in Qumran, and Mishnaic Hebrew (see Schoors, *Pleasing Words*, pp. 98–99). It is important to observe that *ḥōṭeʾ* is not a religious category in the wisdom tradition. The word *ḥôṭeʾ*, etymologically meaning "one who misses, lacks," refers to one who makes mistakes and bungles all the time, who cannot do anything right (Prov 8:36; 13:22; 14:21; 19:2; 20:2; Eccl. 7:26; 9:2, 18; cf. Job 5:24). The *ḥōṭēʾ* is what one may call "a bungler" or "a loser" in contemporary parlance. The *ḥôṭeʾ* is displeasing. In contrast to the *ḥôṭeʾ*, the one who is *ṭôb* is the smart one, the one who does everything right. The same pair, *ṭôb* // *ḥôṭeʾ*, occurs two other times in Ecclesiastes. In 7:26, the one who is "favored by God" (*ṭôb lipnê hāʾĕlōhîm*) will escape the snares of Folly (see Comment at 7:26), while the *ḥôṭeʾ* "offender" is captured by her. The different destinies of "the one who is favored" and "the offender" in that context are reminiscent, respectively, of the wise and the fool in Proverbs 1–9, where the smart ones escape the dangerous seductress (personified Folly), but the fools are caught in her traps (see Comment at 7:26). In 7:20 one reads: "there is no one so righteous (*ṣaddîq*) on earth, who does only good (*ṭôb*) and does not err (*yeḥĕṭāʾ*)" (7:20). In this context, *ṣaddîq* also is not a religious term; it refers to one who is always correct — the opposite of the fool (see Notes at 7:16). The one who "does only good" is one who is always correct and does not make mistakes. The contrasting pair of *ṭôb* and *ḥôṭeʾ* also occurs in 9:2, with other pairs that typically portray positive and negative characters. In 9:18, the *ḥôṭeʾ* is contrasted with the sage; a single *ḥôṭeʾ* destroys much "good." See also 10:4, where the term *ḥăṭāʾîm* "offenses" is used in a secular, rather than religious, sense.

preoccupation. See Notes at 1:14.

this, too, is vanity and a pursuit of wind. See Notes at 1:2 and 1:14.

COMMENT

It is clear that 1:12 begins a new literary unit; the impersonal style of the introductory poem (1:3–11) gives way to the autobiographical account, and this break is indicated in the Leningrad Codex with the strongest marker of a division, the *Pĕtûḥāʾ*. The question of the unit's ending is, however, disputed. Scholars have variously posited 1:18, 2:11, 2:26, or 3:15 as the end.

One may begin by observing that a certain symmetry is evident in 1:13–18, with two roughly equal parts (1:13–15, 16–18), each concluding with the judgment that the author's inquiry is a "pursuit of wind" (1:14, 17), and each supported by a proverb (1:15, 18). But the apparent symmetry is somewhat flawed. Whereas the first part (1:13–15) contains the judgment "all is vanity and a pursuit of wind" in 1:14 (a judgment that is repeated strategically in 2:11, 17, 26), the second part (1:16–18) has only "this is a pursuit of wind" in 1:17, but not "all is vanity." The full formulaic judgment may be completed if one includes the phrase "that, too, is vanity" in 2:1.

There are, in fact, many continuities between 1:13–18 and 2:1–3. In the first place, the heart is mentioned repeatedly in 1:13–2:3: "I set my heart" (1:13), "I spoke with my heart" (1:16), "my heart observed" (1:16), "I set my heart" (1:17), "I spoke with my heart" (2:1), "I went about with my heart" (2:3), and "my heart conducted" (2:3). Indeed, "heart" occurs repeatedly from 1:13 through 2:3 — seven times in all, a significant figure. Furthermore, in these verses the heart is closely associated with observation: "I set my heart . . . I observed (*rāʾîtî*)" (1:13–14); "I spoke with my heart . . . my heart observed (*rāʾâ*)" (1:16); "I spoke with my heart . . . 'enjoy good (*rĕʾēh*)!'" (2:1); "I went about with my heart . . . my heart conducted . . . until I saw (*rāʾîtî*)" (2:3). Clearly, the heart is personified from 1:13–2:3. In 1:13 the heart investigates "by wisdom" (*baḥokmâ*); in 2:3 the heart conducts "by wisdom" (*baḥokmâ*).

There are sufficient grounds, therefore, to think that 1:13–2:3 forms a distinctive section marked by the phrase "under the heavens" at the beginning (1:13) and the end (2:3): that is, the expression "under the heavens" forms an *inclusio* for the first section. These verses constitute an extended introduction to the entire unit, identifying the problem of the terrible preoccupation (*'inyān*) that God has given to humanity, the place of wisdom (*ḥokmâ*), knowledge (*da'at*), and joy (*śimḥâ*) in seeing what is good (*ṭôb*).

Curiously, God is not mentioned again until 2:24–26. There God is portrayed again as one giving a preoccupation (*'inyān*) to some, but to others are given wisdom (*ḥokmâ*), knowledge (*da'at*), and joy (*śimḥâ*). The idea of seeing good (*ṭôb*) also reappears in these verses. In short, the author returns to the themes raised in the introductory section (1:13–2:3): God, the giving of a preoccupation, the place of wisdom, knowledge, joy, and seeing good. One may argue, then, that 2:24–26 constitutes the concluding section of the entire literary unit, forming with the introduction in 1:13–2:3 a theological framework within which to interpret the whole. A similar theological framing is evident in 6:10–7:14, where the concluding section (7:13–14) repeats the vocabulary and theological emphasis of the introduction in 6:10–12. Again, God is mentioned only in the introduction and the conclusion.

The other divisions in the passage are easily identified: there are three sub-units. The first (2:4–11), emphasizing the author's achievements, is marked by the mention of "my works" (*ma'ăśāy*) at the beginning and the end (2:4, 11), as well as the repetition of the root *'śh* "do, work" (2:4, 5, 6, 8, 11 [three times]). The end of this section is marked by the formulaic judgment that "everything is vanity and a pursuit of wind" (2:11).

Skipping 2:12–17 for the moment, we note that the third section (2:18–23) is marked by the threefold "vanity"-judgments occurring at regular intervals (2:19, 21, 23). The focus of this section is made obvious by the recurrence of the root *'ml* "toil" — 10 times in 6 verses! But toil is not introduced for the first time in this subunit; it is already anticipated in 2:10–11. The issue in this section is, in fact, no different from that of 2:4–11. One section focuses on "work" (*'śh* occurs 7 times), the other on "toil" (*'ml* occurs 10 times), but the problem is the same: human efforts. The sections concerning work (2:4–11) and toil (2:18–23) correspond to one another. Each ends with the judgment that "all is vanity."

This leaves 2:12–17 as the hinge of the entire literary unit. And that pivotal text is carefully linked to the preceding and following sections by the repetition of certain catchwords: *pānîtî* "I turned" in 2:11 is repeated in 2:12, and *śānē'tî* "I hated" in 2:17 is repeated in 2:18. In other words, *pānîtî* "I turned" links the central section to the preceding subunit, and *śānē'tî* "I hated" links it to the following. The basic argument of this pivotal section is that death is a great leveler and so the wise has no advantage over the fool in that regard. This is, indeed, the point of the entire unit: the wise king (Qohelet-Solomon) has no real advantage over the ordinary fool; the wise and the fool are alike, as far as mortality is concerned.

Thus, apart from 1:12, which must be taken as the introduction of the whole unit, the following structure is discernible:

A   Introduction (1:13–2:3)
  B   Accomplishments of the Wise King (2:4–11)
    C   Death the Leveler (2:12–17)
  B'   Toil of the Wise (2:18–23)
A'   Conclusion (2:24–26)

There are several features in the passage that are similar to royal inscriptions from the ancient Near East: (1) the text begins with a self-presentation formula similar to those found in the royal inscriptions, (2) using a "resumé style," the text itemizes the king's many exploits and accomplishments, (3) several of the items mentioned are typical of those in royal boasts, and (4) the text repeatedly compares the author with his predecessors, a prominent feature in the royal inscriptions.

Thus, in terms of style, vocabulary, and content, the passage resembles the typical royal inscription, specifically the genre known as "fictional royal autobiography" (see Longman, *Fictional Akkadian Autobiography*). Yet, the intent of the passage is decisively different from the royal texts found elsewhere in the ancient Near East. The inscriptions of kings are typically propagandistic. They were written to show that the king was extraordinary, indeed, better than anyone else; they were supposed to enhance respect for the king and memorialize his achievements forever. Against such a background, Qohelet's imitation of the genre is all the more poignant in its irony. In the end the passage makes the point that none of the accomplishments — even the royal accomplishments that are so assiduously recorded and preserved in lasting monuments — really matters. For human beings, even kings, there is no immortality of any sort. At first blush, Qohelet's "fictional royal autobiography" paints a picture of enormous success. But the mention of the king's deeds, and especially the superiority of his deeds over those of his predecessors, leads to the surprising conclusion, one that is quite contrary to the purpose of royal propaganda. The legendary acts, wealth, and wisdom of Solomon turned out not to have abiding significance after all. The genre of "fictional royal autobiography" is used to make the point about the ephemerality of wisdom and human accomplishments. Qohelet itemizes his many deeds and possessions to show ironically that kings are no better off than ordinary people. In the face of death's leveling effect, neither wisdom, nor toil, nor success makes any difference (2:12–17), for "everything is vanity and a pursuit of wind" (1:14; 2:11, 17, 26).

The Royal Self-Presentation (1:12)

Qohelet's self-presentation is reminiscent of the introduction of kings in royal inscriptions throughout the ancient Near East: e.g., "I am Mesha son of Chemosh-[Yat], king of Moab" (see *ANET*³, p. 320); "I am Yehawmilk, king of Byblos" (*ANET*³, p. 656); "I am Bir-Rakib, the son of Panammu, the king of Sam'al" (*ANET*³, p. 655), "I am Sennacherib, king of Assyria" (*ARAB*, II, p. 193), "I am Esarhaddon, king of the universe, king of Assyria" (*ARAB*, II, p. 203). It is important to recognize the literary form that this self-presentation formula presupposes: royal propaganda. One expects, then, the text to tell of the king's extraordinary achievements and how the king is better off than other people.

There can be little doubt that the author intends to evoke the memory of Solomon here. Only David and Solomon may be called "king over Israel in Jerusalem" (see Notes at 1:12), but the latter's legendary wisdom and wealth make him the most likely referent.

Introduction (1:13–2:3)
The king set his heart "to inquire" (*lidrôš*) and "to explore" (*lātûr*) all that is in the universe. It is difficult to discern any nuance between the two infinitives, *lidrôš* "to inquire" and *lātûr* "to explore." Crenshaw suggests that the former "refers to the length and breadth of the search," while the latter "adds the inner depth dimension, the penetration beyond the surface of reality" (*Ecclesiastes*, p. 72). But Gordis arrives at the opposite conclusion regarding the same two words: the first infinitive refers to "searching the depths" and the second to "the breadth of the matter" (*Koheleth*, p. 209). The distinction between the two infinitives may not, in fact, be a matter of extent or depth. No spatial dimension is discernible in the usage of those verbs, whether literal or figurative. The verb *drš* "to inquire" is not limited to any specific kind of search, but it is very frequently used in Biblical Hebrew of a search for something authoritative or normative: God (1 Chron 10:14; 22:19; 2 Chron 12:14; 14:3; Job 5:8; Isa 9:12; Hos 10:12; Ezra 6:21), oracles (Gen 25:22; Exod 18:15; 1 Sam 9:9; 1 Kgs 14:5; 22:8; 2 Kgs 1:2–3, 16; 22:18; 1 Chron 21:30; Ezek 20:1), or the Torah (Ezra 7:10). As for *twr* "to explore," it is always associated with new or alien terrain (Num 10:33; 13:16–17, 32; 14:7, 36, 38; Deut 1:33; Judg 1:23); it is the verb used of the reconnaissance of the spies prior to Israel's entry into the land. Perhaps the point is that the search included both the normative (*drš*) and the novel (*twr*), the well-defined paths and the untried avenues.

The king was determined to examine by wisdom everything that happens under the heavens. The emphasis on the search of the heart by wisdom calls to mind Solomon's "wise heart" (*lēb ḥākām*), and the universal scope of the exploration recalls the king's legendary sapiential activities (1 Kgs 3:4–15; 5:9–14 [Eng 4:29–34]). Here, as elsewhere in the ancient Near East, wisdom is held as a royal ideal. Kings in the ancient Near East typically highlighted their wisdom in their public "autobiographies" (see Notes above). Often they boasted of their intellectual pursuits, their attempts to learn what no one else had been able to discover before, and the comprehensiveness of their knowledge. Thus Asshurbanipal of Assyria spoke of how the gods had given him wisdom so that he was able to explore even "the secret of heaven and earth, the wisdom of Shamash and Adad" (see Notes at 1:13; also *ARAB* II, pp. 291–92, 323–24, 2361–62, 2378–79). Reference to the king's extraordinary wisdom is part and parcel of royal propaganda. The version of the *Gilgamesh Epic* found in the library of Asshurbanipal begins with a prologue that refers to Gilgamesh, the renowned king from the city of Uruk (biblical Erech), as "the one who has seen it all." Gilgamesh is supposed to have explored the mysteries of the universe fully. He had received wisdom and experienced everything (*ANET³*, p. 73). Yet he had to come to terms with his limitations. Qohelet, too, says he employed wisdom in exploring all that happened under the heavens (1:13) and he observed (*r'h*) everything that happened (1:14).

In 1:13c, God is mentioned for the very first time in Ecclesiastes. Here, as in thirty-nine other instances in the book, God is called by the generic name, *'ĕlōhîm*, the name preferred in the wisdom tradition over YHWH. The preference may have to do with wisdom tradition's interest in universal truths, rather than the relation of a particular deity to a particular people. YHWH is the name for the God of the covenant, the God of Israel, whereas *'ĕlōhîm* is the universal term for the deity, the God of the universe and of every person. This God described by Qohelet is very present and very active in the cosmos, always giving (1:13; 2:26; 3:10, 11; 5:17–18 [Eng vv 18–19]; 6:2; 8:15; 9:9; 12:7) and doing/making (3:11, 14; 7:14, 29; 8:17; 11:5). But the deity never speaks and never deals directly with individuals or with nations (unlike YHWH). It is a transcendent and inscrutable God of whom Qohelet speaks. This God has given humans a "terrible preoccupation" (v 13). The text does not say here what that "preoccupation" is, but elsewhere in the book the same Hebrew word is associated with restlessness, obsession, and people's inability to find enjoyment (2:23, 26; 3:10; 4:8; 5:13 [Eng v 14]; 8:16). He is thinking here of the efforts of people to grasp — by wisdom — all that is happening in the world. He concludes, however, that "all is vanity and pursuit of wind" (v 14). Here, again, one is reminded of the words of Gilgamesh that "only the gods live forever with the sun," but mortals are fated to live only a few days and "whatever they achieve is but wind" (see *ANET³*, p. 79).

One must not miss the irony of Qohelet's summary judgment that "everything is vanity and a pursuit of wind." In the wisdom tradition it is axiomatic that "the mind (literally 'the heart') of the intelligent one seeks knowledge, but the face of the fool *pursues* folly" (Prov 15:14; Sir 34:1–2). The sages of the ancient Near East assumed a marked difference between the activities of the wise and those of fools. But the irony of the matter here is that the text is referring precisely to the activities of the wise king, not the ordinary fool. This king had set his mind to seek knowledge and understanding, but the result of his search was no better than the venture of fools. The consummate wise king (Solomon) is engaged in such windy pursuits!

A proverb is introduced in 1:15 to reinforce what has been said: "what is crooked cannot be straightened; what is lacking cannot be counted." In the history of interpretation "what is crooked" (*mĕ'uwwāt*) and "what is lacking" (*ḥes-rôn*) have often been taken to refer to people who are perverse and shallow (so the Vulgate, Targum, Rashi, Rashbam). Some modern commentators imagine that the saying originated with the wisdom teachers about their unteachable students (Zimmerli, Michel). The saying was uttered by the teachers of wisdom, according to this view, in disdain of those who would not or could not learn: the students were permanently "crooked" and "lacking" — that is, they were recalcitrant and stupid. It is possible, perhaps even probable, that such was the background of the saying. The Egyptian wisdom text known as *The Instruction of Anii* includes a proverb suggesting that even a crooked stick may be straightened, while a straight stick may be bent by a skilled artisan (*AEL* II, p. 145). The saying occurs in the epilogue of the text, in the context of a debate between a father (the sage) and a son. The son is apparently resisting the instructions because they are too difficult to understand and to follow. The father points out that it is important to heed instructions, for through the teachings of the wise even the crooked can be straightened and the straight can be bent. In other words, miracles can happen through wisdom.

It is possible that a saying such as the one cited by Qohelet may have existed alongside one like Anii's. One may compare, for instance, two contradictory sayings in Proverbs 26: "Do not answer fools according to their folly, or you will be a fool yourself" (v 4) and "Answer fools according to their folly, or they will be wise in their own eyes" (v 5). One proverb balances the other; each is pertinent in certain situations. Possibly, then, the proverb cited in our passage was meant to balance one like the saying in *The Instruction of Anii*. While it is true that instructions may straighten the crooked and bend the straight (so the proverb in *The Instruction of Anii*), there are situations when the crooked simply cannot be straightened (so the proverb in Ecclesiastes). The latter makes the point that sometimes effort is not enough. Qohelet is not referring to recalcitrant students, however. If the proverb was used originally by wise teachers against their students, Qohelet is using it subversively. He means that even the wise cannot straighten out the world in all its perversity and disorder.

The focus has not shifted in 1:15; the proverb continues and reinforces the thought of the preceding verses. The passive participle *mĕ'uwwāt* "what is made crooked" echoes the passive forms in 1:13 (*na'ăśâ*) and 1:14 (*na'ăśû*), which refer to what has been happening in the world, presumably with the tacit approval of God. When the active form of the verb *'wt* "to make crooked" is used later in the book, it is God who appears as the subject, even as God is the implied subject in 1:13–14: "See what God has done, for who is able to straighten that which he has made crooked (*'iwwĕtô*)" (7:13). In that passage, the problem is the apparent disorder in the universe: the world is crooked, as if by divine design. Elsewhere in the Bible, too, one finds God as the subject of the same verb. In the book of Job, Bildad asks what was intended as a rhetorical question: "Does God distort (*yĕ'awwēt*) justice? Does Shaddai distort (*yĕ'awwēt*) righteousness?" (Job 8:3). The expected answer is negative. Elihu, the young sage representing traditional wisdom, states so: "Truly, God does not act wickedly, Shaddai does not distort (*lō'-yĕ'awwēt*) justice" (Job 34:12). That is the conservative view. Job would demur, however, charging that the absence of justice is surely God's distortion: "God has done me injustice (*'iwwĕtanî*)" (Job 19:6). And so Job demanded an accounting from on high and yearned for injustice to be corrected. Like Job, Qohelet accepts that there are distortions in the world for which God must ultimately be responsible. But unlike Job, Qohelet does not insist that these distortions must be straightened out. In fact, what has been made crooked — presumably by God — cannot be made straight by anyone.

The second part of the proverb has no parallel anywhere: "what is lacking cannot be counted." The noun *ḥesrôn* "what is lacking" occurs only here in Hebrew. The root *ḥsr* "to lack, be deficient" is widely attested in the wisdom literature of the Bible, however, most frequently pertaining to the fool's deficiency in understanding: the fool is *ḥăsar-lēb* "deficient of mind" (Prov 6:32; 7:7; 9:4, 16; 10:13; 11:12; 15:21; 17:18; 24:30) and *ḥăsar-tĕbûnôt* "deficient in understanding" (Prov 28:16). Qohelet, too, speaks of the fool whose mind is mentally deficient (10:3). In its context, however, the proverb in 1:15 no longer is about fools in general. Rather, the point is probably that people cannot hope to find order and meaning where none is discernible: what is not there cannot be counted. All people, even the wise, will have to be content with this unavoidable deficiency. In the face of the world's mysteries, the wise will be no different from fools, after all. Here one sees, again, Qohelet's use of irony. He uses what may have been a wisdom saying to undermine excessive confidence in wisdom. As it turns out, the wise are not really better off than fools.

Qohelet says in 1:16 that he surpassed his predecessors, presumably other kings who had ruled before him. The idiom "all who were before me over Jerusalem" is repeated in slightly different forms in 2:7, 9. Interpreters, both ancient and modern, have been troubled by the allusion to a plurality of kings "over Jerusalem" or "in Jerusalem" (1:12; 2:7, 9). Some have assumed that this is a slip in historical detail on the part of the author, since strictly speaking only one Israelite king (David) ruled over Jerusalem before Solomon. The author is anachronistic here, it is said. His Solomonic mask has slipped (Barton). Others argue that Qohelet is thinking of the pre-Israelite rulers of the city. But the historicity of the Jerusalemite kings before Solomon is not really at issue here. Rather, Qohelet is adopting the language and style of royal propagandistic literature to demonstrate, ironically, the impotence even of kings. The comparison with the predecessors is a prominent motif in West Semitic and Mesopotamian royal inscriptions. Kings typically boasted in sweeping terms that they were better than their predecessors. This is evident, for instance, in the Phoenician inscription of Kilamuwa, where the king puts forth his own accomplishments over those of his predecessors, each of whom is judged to have been ineffective (*ANET*[3], pp. 654–55). The comparison is formulaic in such royal texts. The Akkadian royal inscriptions, too, are replete with phrases like "any before me," "those who were before me," "any among kings who went before me," or "former kings." Each time the comparison is made with the predecessors, the point is to highlight the extraordinary accomplishments of the king in whose name the inscription is made. The purpose of the comparison is to portray the hero of the inscription as unique in history—someone who has gained a real advantage over others.

Qohelet alludes to the legendary greatness of Solomon's wisdom and knowledge. The language in 1:16 echoes the legends of Solomon's prowess. The expression "I increased wisdom (*wĕhôsaptî ḥokmâ*)" recalls the Queen of Sheba's comment to Solomon, "you increased wisdom (*hôsaptā ḥokmâ*)" in 1 Kgs 10:7, and "I showed greatness" (*higdaltî*) is similar to the assessment in 1 Kgs 10:23 that "King Solomon became greater (*wayyigdal*) than all the kings of the earth in wealth and wisdom." Any advantage that Qohelet claims, however, quickly fades away like mist. His superiority over his predecessors turns out to be a farce. He set his heart to know wisdom and knowledge, a task that the wisdom tradition urged (Prov 1:2; see also 4:1), but what he knew was that even this was "a pursuit of wind" (v 17).

Another proverb is introduced in 1:18, which summarizes and reiterates what has been said. The particle *kî* "for" at once introduces the quote and links the saying to the preceding remarks. Some commentators argue that this was a proverb quoted by wisdom teachers to warn their students that intellectual discovery always came with a price and that punishment might be necessary in the process (Galling, Crenshaw, Whybray). The proverb also may have been quoted to parents and teachers to warn them against withholding punishment if they intended to teach the young wisdom (Prov 3:11; 6:23; 13:24; 22:15). Ben Sira later would say that while there are wrong times to do some things, "punishment and discipline are wisdom at all times" (Sir 22:6; see also 6:8). This was an ancient "no pain, no gain" adage.

It was, indeed, a common pedagogical assumption in the wisdom literature of the ancient Near East that pain and trouble would lead to wisdom. Indeed, in hieroglyphic Egyptian, the verb *sb3* "to instruct, teach" is regularly written with a determinative of a man striking with a stick. The wisdom tradition was adamant that one must not "spare the rod and spoil the child" (so already in the Aramaic *Proverbs of Ahiqar*). Qohelet, however, does not use the saying in the expected way. Pain commonly was advocated by wisdom teachers as a necessary means to an end. In Qohelet's usage of the proverb, however, pain and vexation are the very *results* of wisdom, not just means to an end. They are precisely what one gets when one has too much wisdom. The more one knows, the more painful life can be.

As in 1:16, Qohelet uses the literary device of a conversation with his heart in 2:1–3 (see Notes at 1:16). The heart is called upon, as if it were an independent entity, to experience pleasure and enjoy good (literally "see good"). One is reminded of the Parable of the Rich Fool in the NT: "And I will say to my soul, 'Soul, you have ample goods laid up for many years; relax, eat, drink, be merry'" (Luke 12:19). The fool in that parable was indulging himself and trying to accumulate more and more. But the parable warns that death would render all efforts futile, and the fool would not even know who would inherit his possessions: "the things you have prepared, whose will they be?" (Luke 12:20). Indeed, the similarities in language, style, and content between this parable (Luke 12:13–21) and Ecclesiastes are such that one must wonder if the teachings of Qohelet somehow lie in the background of the parable. At all events, Qohelet uses this device of a conversation with his inner-self to explore contradictory positions. And the discovery of the author is that even this quest for pleasure is "vanity" (see Notes at 1:2). By saying that this is "vanity," however, he does not mean to say that it is something to be avoided altogether. His point is simply that such things are ephemeral. They do not last.

In 2:3 we find a *crux interpretum*. The place of the verse in the overall argument is uncertain. The meaning seems to be that the author indulged himself with wine (see Notes at 2:3). The comment about the heart leading by wisdom has sometimes been taken as a parenthetical comment or a gloss intended to absolve Qohelet from the charge of debauchery and foolishness: that is, the heart only *intended* to indulge, but it actually did not. Instead, the heart conducted itself wisely. But no sudden contrast is intended by the text. In fact, *wělibbî* "and my heart" (not "*but* my heart," as many translations have it) deliberately picks up on *bělibbî* "in my heart" in the preceding bicolon. Thus, the author followed his heart *and* the heart led wisely, as expected. In this context, *mšk* "induce" (literally "carry away"), *nhg* "conduct," and *'ḥz* "take hold" are all synonyms. The point of the verse is probably to assert the rationality of the action (so Barucq). The indulgence in pleasure did not stem from an inexplicable impulse, nor did it originate from wisdom. The action of the heart was deliberate and thoughtful. Indeed, 2:3 corresponds to 1:13, inasmuch as the heart acts "by wisdom" in both cases. As Qohelet set his heart to inquire and explore by wisdom, so he set about to follow his heart's guidance by wisdom.

The end of this willful leading by wisdom is that he saw what was really "good" for humanity (2:3). The words "until I saw what indeed is good" echo the imperative in 2:1 that calls on the heart to enjoy life. The heart was told to enjoy, literally to "see good." And it did so deliberately. The author's heart led him by wisdom and not by folly until he really saw what is good. It is important to observe here that the author does not deny the validity of pleasure, as if it were a youthful mistake. Indeed, in 11:9–10, he calls on the young to let their hearts please them while there is still time. For him, pleasure is what is indeed good in one's transitory life. He does make clear that it is possible only within one's "few days" on earth. For Qohelet, enjoyment is good, but it is always only a fleeting possibility (see also Comment at 11:9–10).

Accomplishments of the Wise King (2:4–11)

Beginning in 2:4, Qohelet itemizes his accomplishments and wealth. These verses read like a resumé of the king. He speaks of his building projects (2:4), the creation of gardens and parks (2:4–5), the construction of reservoirs (2:6), an irrigation system (2:6), his acquisition of slaves (2:7), his appointment of male and female singers (2:8), his acquisition of herds of large and small cattle (2:7), and his private hoards of treasures (2:7–8). These verses paint a picture of legendary success. In particular, they call to mind the activities and fabulous wealth of Solomon in 1 Kings 3–11. Indeed, it is difficult not to think of Solomon when the author concludes in 2:9 that he "became great and surpassed" all who preceded him in Jerusalem. Tradition has it that "Solomon became greater (*wayyigdal*) than all the kings of the earth in riches and in wisdom" (1 Kgs 10:23). Even the Queen of Sheba remarked to the king: "you have increased in wisdom and prosperity" (1 Kgs 10:7; cf. 2 Chron 9:6).

Qohelet says that his wisdom attended to him (2:9) and he did not deprive himself of anything that his eyes desired (*šā'ălû*, v 10). One is instantly reminded of God's gift of wisdom to Solomon and how the king could ask (*š'l*) for anything that he desired (1 Kgs 3:5, 10, 11, 13). Moreover, the text as a whole is reminiscent of similar royal resumés in inscriptions from Egypt, Anatolia, Mesopotamia, and Syria-Palestine. A small bronze bottle from Tell Siran in Jordan contains a list of "the works of Amminadab, king of the Ammonites," including a vineyard, a garden, and pools (see Thompson and Zayadine, "Tell Siran Inscription," pp. 5–11). The Moabite Stone includes a resumé of King Mesha's accomplishments, including his many building projects, reservoirs, and wells (*ANET*[3], pp. 320–21). The royal inscriptions from Mesopotamia, too, are replete with such resumés. Several Neo-Assyrian inscriptions mention the royal treasures and the acquisition of slaves, harems, as well as "male and female singers" (see Luckenbill, *Annals of Sennacherib*, pp. 24, 34, 52; *ARAB* II, p. 334). Others listed the planting of gardens, orchards, and parks, as well as irrigation projects. In his various inscriptions, Sargon II wrote of his incomparable wisdom, boasted of his building projects that surpassed all that his predecessors had done, and told of how he had created a pleasure garden wherein he planted every kind of tree, set out orchards, and dug irrigation canals (*ARAB* II, pp. 42, 45). Sargon's successor, Sennacherib, likewise spoke of his own achievements in a similar way, claiming that he had surpassed all his predecessors in his building activities, the cultivation of gardens and orchards, and the irrigation of the land by means of reservoirs and canals (Luckenbill, *Annals of Sennacherib*, pp. 79–85).

The listing of Qohelet-Solomon's deeds, however, leads to a surprising conclusion, one that is quite contrary to the purpose of royal inscriptions. The legendary acts and wealth and wisdom do not make the king an extraordinary hero after all. Such listings are supposed to show the king to be more successful than the ordinary person and more accomplished than all other kings who preceded him. But Qohelet itemizes the king's many accomplishments only to show that even Solomon, Israel's most glamorous king, is no better off than ordinary people in some ways. Nevertheless, Qohelet is clear that he did have pleasure (2:10). Pleasure was his "portion" (*ḥēleq*) from all his toil, he says.

It is important to pay attention to the word "portion," since it occurs several times in the book (2:10, 21; 3:22; 5:17, 18 [Eng vv 18, 19]; 9:6, 9). The word may be used concretely in the sense of an assigned plot of land or an inheritance. But Qohelet uses it figuratively for "the space allotted for human existence" (Galling). He seems to think of life as an inherited lot that one works and from which one reaps whatever benefits that may be derived when one is alive. In this lot one finds *both* the inevitable reality of toil and the possibility of enjoyment. But only in life does one have this possibility of enjoyment, for after death there will never again be a "portion" (9:6). The word "portion," then, conveys a sense of limitation both in space and in time. Yet, there are distinct possibilities for enjoyment within this admittedly restricted and impermanent lot. It is in this sense that Qohelet says he was able to have pleasure from his toil. Joy in the midst of toil was his portion, his lot. Even kings are subject to the limitations of such a portion. So Qohelet concludes that "everything is vanity and a pursuit of wind, and there is no advantage under the sun." This conclusion does not mean that everything is meaningless, or that all human efforts are to be abandoned. It means, rather, that there are limitations and no one can have more than is assigned.

The imitation of the royal inscriptions genre in this passage is deliberate. By appealing to the successes of the king, indeed, the wise king *par excellence*, the author shows the limitations of human successes. The effect of the genre, then, is to make the reader aware of human frailty, for all that is accomplished by humanity is but "a pursuit of wind." In other words, "all is vanity." This is the same point made in the prologue to the standard version of the *Gilgamesh Epic*. As the story develops, it becomes clear that it was the reality of death — the death of Gilgamesh's friend Enkidu — that brought home the ephemerality of human accomplishments. Gilgamesh, the illustrious and wise king, who succeeded in so many kingly deeds and surpassed his predecessors, is in the end just like any mortal. That same movement from the accomplishments of the king to the stark reality of death is evident in Ecclesiastes, which now turns to reflect on death as the great leveler.

The Leveling Effect of Death (2:12–17)

This is the pivotal section of the whole unit, so it is important to note that it is stylistically linked to the preceding and following subunits by the repetition of the catchwords: "I turned" in 2:11 and 12, and "I hated" in 2:17 and 18. Qohelet says in 2:11 that when he turned to consider his deeds, he came to the conclusion that "all is vanity and a pursuit of wind" and that "there is no advantage under the sun."

The issue in this section appears to be the relationship between wisdom and folly. The words "wisdom," "wise," and "be wise" together occur six times in 2:12–17. This is matched by six occurrences of the words "folly" and "fool." Qohelet says at the outset that he observed wisdom and folly (2:12a), but he proceeds immediately to speak of succession. Indeed, he introduces his observation about succession with the causal conjunction "for," as if the issue of succession is what made him reflect on wisdom and folly. The text is difficult, however. The Hebrew text as we have it reads, literally, "what is the person who comes after the king, that which already they have done it?" Not a few scholars have concluded, therefore, that the text is hopelessly corrupt and its meaning cannot be retrieved (so Ehrlich, Podechard). It has also been suggested that 2:12b is intrusive, having been transposed erroneously from the next unit where it may have belonged, in 2:18 or 2:19 (e.g., Lauha). Omitting the second part of 2:12, it is argued, one finds the transition from the first part of 2:12 to 2:13 to be smooth and easy (see NEB). But there is no textual evidence to support such a theory, and the supposed transposition cannot readily be explained. Why would anyone transpose this odd phrase from its supposedly comfortable place in 2:19 to its awkward new position in 2:12? There are no literary clues that can account for such an error, nor is there any obvious logical connection that explains why someone might have thought it belonged here. Others try to rearrange the text (see NAB; NJPS). These moves are without warrant, however, and they do not significantly ease the interpretive problems. It is better to repoint the Hebrew and read, instead, "who is the person who will come after <me? Shall he control> what has been achieved?" (see Notes above).

Qohelet is apparently thinking about his own death and the matter of succession. Whenever he speaks of what comes "after" someone, he means not a future point in the life of that person, but the unpredictability of what happens when one dies (2:18; 3:22; 6:12; 7:14; 9:3; 10:14). Therefore, when he says "after me" (*'aḥărāy* [emended text]) in 2:12b, he really means "when I die." He seems to be addressing or anticipating the argument that, even if one cannot take one's possession along when one dies, there is the possibility that one could leave what one has to posterity. Succession, then, would be a possible advantage over death. There is always the next generation. Then again, Qohelet points out, people cannot dictate the result of the turnover. One may not know what kind of person will end up controlling what one has built up. That successor could well be an undeserving fool (see 2:19). So succession is not an advantage over death. Certainly in this case it is not an advantage to the one who has toiled.

Qohelet considers the assumption that wisdom must have advantage over folly (2:13). Some commentators think that he was answering his opponents (either real or imaginary), while others argue that he was merely anticipating the suggestion that surely wisdom has advantage over folly. In any case, he does concede that wisdom has an advantage over folly. The concession is surprising to the reader, for one has just been told in 2:11 that there is no advantage under the sun. Now the author appears to contradict himself: *yēš yitrôn* "there is advantage" in 2:13 stands in stark contrast to *'ēn yitrôn* "there is no advantage" in 2:11. Is there advantage, or is there not? Commentators often gloss over the problem by calling the advantage over folly "relative." But the contradiction between 2:11 and 2:13 is far too glaring to be dismissed so. Indeed, the advantage of wisdom over folly is stated in no uncertain terms: "like the advantage of light over darkness." Frequently in the Bible, when light is compared with darkness, light is life and darkness is death (Isa 9:1; Ezek 32:8; Amos 5:18–20; Job 17:12–13; 18:18; Lam 3:2). Darkness belongs to the realm of the dead; when one dies one does not see light (Ps 49:20 [Eng v 19]; Job 3:16; 33:28). Light is synonymous with life (Job 3:20, 23; 33:28; Ps 36:10 [Eng v 9]), as the idiom *'ôr ḥayyîm* "light of life" confirms (Ps 56:14 [Eng v 13]; Job 33:30). The contrast between wisdom and folly is supposed to be that stark — like light over darkness!

Qohelet cites a proverb in 2:14: "the wise have their eyes in their heads, but fools walk in darkness." As in 1:15 and 1:18, this saying must be seen as substantiating what is said. It must be illustrating the supposedly clear advantage of wisdom over folly. In the wisdom literature of the Bible, darkness is often a metaphor for the lack of knowledge or sheer stupidity (Job 12:24–25; 37:19; 38:2), and that lack of knowledge may have ethical connotations (cf. Prov 2:13; Ps 82:5). The wise, then, are able to see their way around in life, while fools grope about in the darkness of ignorance. Elsewhere in the book, Qohelet uses "darkness" to refer to death or absolute human misery (5:16 [Eng v 17]; 6:4 [twice]; 11:8). Indeed, the precise idiom "walk in darkness" (or "go into darkness") occurs in reference to the stillborn child (6:4). It seems that Qohelet is deliberately using extreme terms of light and darkness to speak of wisdom's advantage over folly. He exaggerates the advantage of wisdom, only to undermine it immediately by pointing to the reality of death. It is death, again, that serves as the great leveler, proving in the end that wisdom has no advantage over folly.

Qohelet does admit that wisdom has advantage. The wise do have an advantage over fools. Yet, it is also a fact that the wise and the foolish are subjected to the same "fate," namely, death (2:15). There are contradictions in life: reality contradicts the axioms that mortals hold dear. In this case, death is the reality that contradicts the axiom. For Qohelet, the fate of death comes to all mortals: the wise and the foolish alike (2:15), animals and humans alike (3:19), the wicked and the righteous alike (9:2–3). Death does not discriminate among mortals. It is the fate of one and all.

Death is the fate of the wise as much as it is of fools. This observation is especially poignant in the light of traditional wisdom's rhetoric about the advantage of wisdom over folly. The sages maintained that it is the destiny of fools to die young (see Prov 2:21; 3:2, 16; 4:10; 10:27; 11:19), whereas wisdom adds years of life (Prov 3:2; 4:10; 9:11). Indeed, it is said: "the instruction of the wise is a spring of life, so that one may escape the snares of death" (Prov 13:14; 14:27) and "for the wise, the path of life leads upwards, in order that one may avoid Sheol beneath" (Prov 15:24). Those who find wisdom find life (Prov 8:35), and wisdom is a "tree of life" to those who take a hold of it (Prov 3:18). To be sure, the sages spoke of life and death only metaphorically. Certainly they did not mean that the wise will literally escape death. Yet, it is the case that traditional wisdom used the rhetoric of extremes to portray wisdom's advantage over folly: one is light, the other darkness; one leads to life, the other death (so especially Proverbs 1–9). Qohelet stands in the wisdom tradition, but he chooses to call attention to the *physical* reality of death in his own rhetoric of extremes. He carries the exaggeration of traditional wisdom's rhetoric to its logical conclusion in order to deny that such is wisdom's advantage. On the matter of death, the wise have no advantage whatsoever. The wise die just like fools!

That being the case, Qohelet wonders to what end anyone, and he in particular, should be excessively wise (2:15). The phrase "even me" refers to Qohelet as the consummate wise man, the sage as king, indeed, Solomon himself. If *even* he is subject to the same fate as the fool, *then* there is no sense in anyone being wise to such an extent. The occurrence of "even" in the protasis and "then" in the apodosis together identifies the heart of the problem for Qohelet. The fact that even the archetypical wise person is subject to the same fate as the ordinary fool makes mockery of any oversimplification about different destinies for the wise and the foolish. The issue is, however, not just having wisdom, which is a "plus," but desiring a "surplus" (*yôtēr*) of it. As Fox has noted, Qohelet always speaks of *much* wisdom as the problem (1:18; 7:16), not just having wisdom (*Contradictions*, p. 184). The problem with having too much wisdom is that it produces much trouble (see 1:18), as one becomes alert to "all that is done under the sun" — the good and the bad. There is a point of diminishing returns where wisdom is concerned, and more is not better, it seems.

Moreover, wisdom does not carry one over into the future. It is no way to "beat the system" of life and death. Neither the wise nor the foolish will be remembered forever; both will be forgotten (2:16). Qohelet affirms elsewhere that when people die their reputation is forgotten (*niškaḥ zikrām,* 9:5). He is thinking perhaps of the sapiential adage that a good reputation will outlast the individual, and that the wise can outlast fools by their wisdom: "the reputation (*zēker*) of the righteous becomes a blessing, but the fame of the wicked will rot" (Prov 10:7). In truth, Qohelet insists, there is no difference because fame will not give one true immortality. In the face of death, which is the inevitable fate of all, the wise and the foolish are equals.

This lack of distinction leads Qohelet to despair: "so I hated life" (v 17). The conjunctive *waw* (here translated as "so") links the statement with what precedes (vv 12–16). His conclusion is not at all surprising, given his observation that wisdom ultimately has no advantage over folly in the face of death. In traditional sapiential rhetoric, the alternatives of wisdom and folly are clearly distinguished. Conservative wisdom assumes discernible order in the cosmos. But when one expects order and there is none discernible, even the wise will speak and act as fools (cf. Job 3; Jer 20:14–18). So even Qohelet, in his masquerade as Solomon the consummate sage, was led to the conclusion that only a fool would make: "I hated life!"

The rationale for this conclusion is restated in a summary form, which is introduced by the causal conjunction *kî* ("for, because"): "*for* what has been done under the sun is terrible to me." Qohelet's assessment of what is terrible harks back to 1:13, where he speaks of the "terrible preoccupation" (*'inyan rā'*) that God has given to humanity. The summary-judgment here clarifies to some extent what is so terrible about the preoccupation that God has given: "the deed" itself, that which is being done, seems terrible. What Qohelet means by "terrible" here and in 1:13 is simply that which cannot be distinguished from "good." The problem for Qohelet is that everything has gone topsy-turvy in life and no order can be discerned by anyone. Wisdom cannot be distinguished from folly when it comes to the issue of death. So Qohelet concludes with his usual refrain: "all is vanity and a pursuit of wind" (2:17).

Toil of the Wise (2:18–23)
This next subunit (2:18–23) is linked to the preceding one in the same manner that the preceding subunit is linked to the one before it. "I hated" in 2:18 picks up on "I hated" in 2:17, even as "I turned" in 2:12 repeats "I turned" in 2:11. It is as if the pivot section (2:12–17) is linked to the other sections by means of these "hinges." The object of the hatred in 2:17 is life, but in 2:18 it is "toil" (see the Comment on 1:3). Toil is the focus of these verses; the verb and noun together occur 11 times in these 9 verses. These references are not new in the passage. They are already anticipated in 2:11, as the author reflected on his "por-

tion." Here, again, the specter of death looms large, for Qohelet speaks of those who will come after him (2:18), that is, when he dies (see 2:12). The problem is that when people die, they have to leave behind whatever they have accumulated. If wisdom will not allow one to bypass the fate that all mortals face, neither will toil. Death will put an end to every aspiration for which one has striven. Qohelet is not just saying that "you can't take it with you," however. Rather, he is also pointing out that one cannot beat the system by passing on one's accumulation to posterity either. This point was anticipated already in 2:12. People are always trying to gain immortality, if not in reality, at least somehow through one's posterity. So people toil and suffer in the present in order to pass on the fruits of their labor when they die. But it is preposterous that one should toil while another who has not labored at all reaps the rewards.

Qohelet speaks of the toil (meaning the fruits of the toil) for which he labored "and acted wisely" (2:19). The introduction of wisdom here seems intrusive, inasmuch as toil seems to be the focus of this subunit (2:18–23), not wisdom. Even so, one notes that "I acted wisely" picks up on "I acted wisely" in 2:15. In both instances (2:15, 19) the verb denotes conduct according to the precepts of the wisdom tradition. Ironically, Qohelet "acted wisely" only to discover that the formulas of wisdom did not always come out right. The wise and the foolish have the same fate, and those who toil "for wisdom and knowledge and success" (2:21) do not reap the rewards — not even the reward of knowing if their labor will benefit the right people. According to Prov 17:2, even "a slave who acts wisely will have control over a child who acts shamefully" and that one who acts wisely will have a portion (*yaḥălōq*) of the family wealth. But Qohelet laments that even those who toiled and acted wisely cannot know who will finally have control over their property (2:19), and it could well be the undeserving one who will get the "portion" (2:21). In traditional wisdom's rhetoric, it is the right and worthy people who will get the inheritance:

> Tragedy pursues the sinners,
>   but good will reward the righteous.
> A good person gives an inheritance to the children's children,
>   but the wealth of the sinner is hoarded for the righteous.
>
> (Prov 13:21–22)

Qohelet notices, however, that in reality one cannot predict the true character of those who will inherit. They are just as likely to be fools as wise. It is not always true that tragedy (literally "bad") is the lot of the undeserving, and good is what the worthy will receive. It is utterly unpredictable what will happen to anyone. In fact, it is this lack of distinction between the deserving and the undeserving that is the "great sadness" (2:21). Reality contradicts the rules by which mortals conduct themselves.

In view of such disorder, Qohelet asks the logical question in 2:22: "what is there for humans in all their toil and in all the pursuit of their heart at which they toil under the sun?" With only minor variations, the first part of this question repeats the rhetorical one broached in 1:3. The question "what is there for mortals in all their toil" (2:22) means the same thing as "what advantage is there for mortals in all their toil" (1:3). So, too, "pursuit of their heart" probably means the heart's "pursuit of wind" (see 1:14; 2:11, 17, 22, 26; 4:4, 6; 6:9), that is, it is foolish empty endeavor (see the Comment on 1:14). In particular, the reference to the heart's pursuits recalls 1:13–18, where the heart is set on tasks that are deemed to be "a pursuit of wind." The link is also secured by the assessment of the human life span as "pain" and human preoccupation with matters beyond their control as "trouble," thus recalling the proverb that the author cited in 1:18 to suggest that wisdom brings much "trouble" and knowledge increases "pain."

Conclusion (2:24–26)
Qohelet decides that there is no good for people but to "eat and drink and enjoy (literally 'see good')" in their toil (2:24). He is not referring here to specific activities of eating and drinking, but to a general attitude toward life. In the light of what he perceives to be bad, namely, what God has given (1:13) and the way the world is (1:17, 21), Qohelet reckons that the only good is to partake of life in the present. Enjoyment is the antidote to people's experience of all that is bad. And one can enjoy ("see good") despite the reality of toil. God makes a reentrance here, having been mentioned only once at the beginning of the entire unit (1:13): "this, too, I perceive is from the hand of God (2:24b)." The antecedent of the demonstrative pronoun "this" is unclear. Probably it refers to the entire statement in 2:24a, namely, the fact that people have no alternative but to partake of good in the moment. In 5:17–18 (Eng vv 18–19), 8:15, and 9:9 Qohelet speaks of enjoyment as something that God has given (*ntn*), although Qohelet also uses the same verb to speak of God's giving of the preoccupation (1:13; 2:26; 3:10, 11). God gives both the pleasant and the unpleasant, joy as well as trouble. Here Qohelet uses the expression "from the hand of God" to mean the same thing, namely, that enjoyment comes from the decision of a sovereign deity. In 9:1 the fate of the righteous and the wise and all their works are said to be "in the hand of God" — that is, subject to God's free will. This results in either positive or negative experiences for humanity: either enjoyment, or preoccupation. Indeed, whether one eats or gathers for others to eat depends entirely on the will of God (2:25).

This point is elaborated on in 2:26. To the one who is favored or pleasing (*ṭôb*), God gives all the good things in life, symbolized by wisdom, knowledge, and pleasure. In contrast to the one who is *ṭôb*, there is the *ḥôṭeʾ* "an offender" (literally "one who misses the mark"). In the vocabulary of the wisdom tradition, the *ḥôṭeʾ* is the bungler, the loser, the one who is always making mistakes. The *ḥôṭeʾ* is the fool. To such a one, God gives the unpleasant task of gathering and accumulating only to give to the one who is favored. The one who is already in a good position gets all the good things, but the loser loses. The pairing of *ṭôb* (the one who does well) and *ḥôṭeʾ* (the loser) is reminiscent of Prov 13:22, where the one who is *ṭôb* acts wisely (leaves something for posterity), while the *ḥōṭēʾ* (the loser) hoards possessions only to give them to others. For Qohelet, however, it is not up to mortals to choose between being *ṭôb* and *ḥôṭe'*. Everything comes from the hand of God; no one eats and no one gathers apart from God. Conventional wisdom asserts that it is the fool who hoards to give to others, but even the consummate wise person that Qohelet presents himself to be has accumulated wealth only to benefit others. The wise have toiled only to give to others who come after them, who may well be fools (see 2:12, 18–21). The fool accumulates and gathers to give to the favored, and yet the author of this entire unit introduces himself at the start as Qohelet, literally a "Gatherer" (see Notes at 1:1). The wise king seems to be no different from the ordinary fool!

I.A.3. Everything Is in the Hand of God (3:1–22)

3 ¹For everything there is a season,
 and a time for every matter under the heavens.
²A time for birthing and a time for dying;
 a time for planting, and a time for uprooting what is planted;
³A time for killing, and a time for healing;
 a time for breaking, and a time for building;
⁴A time for crying, and a time for laughing;
 a time of mourning, and a time of dancing;
⁵A time for throwing stones, and a time of gathering stones;
 a time for embracing, and a time for shunning embrace;
⁶A time for seeking, and a time for losing;
 a time for keeping, and a time for throwing out;
⁷A time for tearing, and a time for sewing up;
 a time for being silent, and a time for speaking;
⁸A time for loving, and a time for hating;
 a time of war, and a time of peace.

⁹What advantage does the worker have in all the toiling? ¹⁰I have seen the preoccupation that God has given to people with which to be preoccupied. ¹¹He has made everything right in its time, yet he has also put eternity in their hearts, so that people will not discover what it is that God has done from the beginning to the end. ¹²I know that there is nothing good among them, except to rejoice and to do well as long as they live. ¹³Moreover, all people should eat and drink and enjoy the fruit of their toil. That is the gift of God. ¹⁴I know that whatever God does is eternal; one cannot add to it and one cannot take away from it, and God has acted so that they may be reverent before him. ¹⁵Whatever happens has already happened, and what will happen has already happened. God will seek that which is pursued.

¹⁶Furthermore, I have seen under the sun that in the place of justice there was wickedness, and in the place of righteousness there was wickedness. ¹⁷I said in

my heart, "God will judge the righteous and the wicked, for there is a time for every matter, and over every activity there is a destiny." [18]I said in my heart, "As regards human beings, surely God has chosen them < > to show that they are animals < > themselves." [19]For the fate of humans and the fate of animals are one and the same. As one dies, so the other dies. They all have one breath. As for the advantage of the human over the animal, there is none, for everything is vanity. [20]All go to one place; all came from dust and all will return to dust. [21]Who knows the life-breath of human beings, whether it goes upward on high; or the life-breath of animals, whether it goes downward below to the netherworld? [22]I saw that there is nothing better than that people should take pleasure in their activities, for that is their portion. Indeed, who will lead them to see how it will be after them?

NOTES

3 1. *For everything.* The parallelism of *lakkōl* with *lĕkol-ḥēpeṣ* suggests that *lak-kōl* means "for everything," not "for everyone (person)," as Targ has it (*lkl gbr*).

season. The word *zĕmān* occurs only late in the biblical period (Neh 2:6; Esth 9:27, 31; cf. Sir 43:7), and it is attested with the same meaning in Postbiblical Hebrew and in Biblical Aramaic (Dan 2:16; 3:8; 4:33; 7:12). It is also well attested in Imperial Aramaic (see *DNWSI*, p. 332). Like other nouns of the *qĕṭāl* pattern (cf. *ʿăbādêhem* in 9:1; *qĕrāb* in 9:18), it is to be regarded as an Aramaism (see Schoors, *Pleasing Words*, pp. 60–61). It is always used of predetermined or appointed time. Not surprisingly, therefore, one finds in Late Biblical Hebrew the denominative verb meaning "to set, appoint, designate" (Ezra 10:14; Neh 10:35; 13:31). Akkadian *simanu*, a virtually certain cognate of Hebrew *zĕmān*, refers to agricultural seasons, the timing of cosmological phenomena, as well as to periods in human life (*CAD* XV, pp. 268–71). These are appropriate meanings of *zĕmān* in this context.

matter. The root *ḥpṣ* appears 8 times in Ecclesiastes, 7 times in the form of the noun *ḥēpeṣ* (3:1, 17; 5:3, 7 [Eng vv 4, 8]; 8:6; 12:1, 10), and once in a verb form (8:3). The verb occurs in a stereotypical expression of God's authority and power: *kol-ʾăšer yaḥpōṣ yaʿăśeh* "he will do whatever he pleases" (see Notes at 8:3). This is consonant with the range of meaning of the root: "to want, will, be delighted, have pleasure." So the noun *ḥēpeṣ* means "delight" or "pleasure" in 5:3 (Eng v 4) and 12:1, and LXX accordingly translates the noun in those passages as *thelēma* "pleasure." In 3:1, however, the word seems to mean "matter" or "activity," as also in 3:17, 5:7 (Eng v 8), and 8:6. In these passages, LXX translates with *pragma* "matter, occurrence." The meaning is suggested by the parallelism of *kol-ḥēpeṣ* "every matter" and *kol-hammaʿăśeh* "every activity" in 3:17. The semantic overlap between "delight, will" and "matter, affair" is evident in Isa 58:13, where we have *ʿăśôt ḥăpāṣêkā* "to do your own pleasures" or "to accomplish your own matters." At Qumran, the word refers to specific assignments or tasks of individuals (1QS 3.17; CD 14.12). In Sir 10:26, Hebrew *ḥpṣk* is translated in Greek *to ergon sou* "your work." This is a meaning attested in Postbiblical Hebrew. Cf. also *ḥpṣ* "business" in one of the Aramaic inscriptions from Sefîre (see Fitzmyer, *The Aramaic Inscriptions of Sefîre*, pp. 97, 112). The occurrence of *ḥēpeṣ* in 12:10 is ambiguous (LXX has *thelēma*); probably both meanings of the noun are meant there (see Notes at 12:10).

under the heavens. See also 1:13 and 2:3. A few MSS read *tḥt hšmš* "under the sun," but this is harmonistic.

2. *for birthing.* Infinitival forms appear consistently in vv 2–8a, but in v 8b the nouns *milḥāmâ* and *šālôm* are used instead. This substitution of nouns for infinitives in the poem suggests that the forms should be taken as gerunds. Thus, we should translate "birthing" rather than "to bear," "dying" rather than "to die," and so forth. In fact, the preposition *lĕ-* in these verses does not function differently than the preposition in v 1: *lakkōl zĕmān . . . lĕkol-ḥēpeṣ* "for every season . . . for every matter," so "*for* birthing . . . *for* dying." Contrary to many commentators and translators, *lāledet* cannot be taken as intransitive and corresponding in meaning to the passive forms *hiwwālēd* or *hulledet/hûledet* "being born." The passive form *hiwwālĕdô* is, in fact, found in 7:2. The argument that an antonym of *lāmût* is required is not persuasive, since not all the pairs furnish strict antonyms (e.g., *lahărōg* "for killing" // *lirpô'* "for healing" in v 3a; *sĕpôd* "mourning" // *rĕqôd* "dancing"). Nor do we need to assume that the birth and death here must pertain to the same person. The poet is speaking of the events of birth and death in general, not of a particular individual's birth and death. LXX quite readily translates *lāledet* as transitive: *tou tekein.* Moreover, the precise expression *'ēt ledet* "a time of birthing" is attested in Job 39:1, where *'ēt ledet ya'ălê-sāla'* "a time of the ibexes' birthing" is paralleled by *ḥōlēl 'ayyālôt* "the writhing of hinds (in labor)." It is clear that *'ēt ledet* in the Job passage refers not to the animals being born, but to their giving birth, a fact confirmed by the next verse, which refers to *'ēt lidtanâ* "a time of their birthing." Cf. also *'ēt lidtāh* "the time of her birthing" (Gen 38:27). There is a "time for birthing" but the precise time is unknown. Nevertheless, when the time comes, people must respond accordingly. Even the infant must know to respond at the appropriate time (see Hos 13:13).

planting . . . uprooting. The literal meaning is adequate, although it is also possible that this line continues the subject matter of v 2a, as many scholars suggest. That is, "planting" may be a metaphor for coming to life and "uprooting" may be a metaphor for death. Agricultural activities are frequently used metaphorically in the Bible, with God as the subject and people as the object (2 Sam 7:10; Jer 1:10; 2:21; 11:17; 12:2; 18:9; 24:6; 31:28; 32:41; 42:10; 45:4; Ezek 36:36; Amos 9:15; Ps 80:9, 16 [Eng vv 8, 15]). As for the root *'qr*, we note its use in connection with the destruction of animals (Gen 49:6; Josh 11:9; 2 Sam 8:4) and people (Zeph 2:4, in a wordplay with the name *'eqrôn*). In Postbiblical Hebrew and Aramaic the verb means "to uproot, eradicate, bring to an end," or the like. This meaning is intended in our passage. Dahood, however, cites *'qrt* "granaries" in the Phoenician inscription from Karatepe to argue for the translation of *la'ăqôr* as "to harvest" ("Phoenician Background," p. 270). The association of *'qr* with "root" is, however, incontrovertible in the Karatepe inscription and elsewhere.

Biblical Aramaic has the noun *'iqqar* "root" (Dan 4:12, 20, 23), while Biblical Hebrew has *'ēqer* "offspring" (Lev 25:47). In one of the Sefîre inscriptions, *'qr* apparently means "offspring" (*KAI* 222.A.2–3). The basic meaning of the verb is probably "to be at the root" or "to be at an end" — hence the probable association of Phoenician *'qrt* with harvest in the Karatepe inscription (the harvest is an event that takes place at the end of the agricultural cycle).

3. *killing*. In the light of v 3b ("a time for breaking" // "a time for building"), one is tempted to emend *lahărôg* "for killing" to *lahărôs* "for demolishing," per- haps a better parallel for *lirpô'*, if we take it to mean "for repairing," as in 1 Kgs 18:30: *wayyarpē' 'ēt mizbēaḥ YHWH hehārûs* "and he repaired the altar of YHWH, which had been demolished." All textual witnesses attest to the correct- ness of MT, however.

breaking . . . building. This is perhaps a reference to the dismantling and (re)- building of stone fences. See Notes at 10:8.

of mourning . . . of dancing. Here and in v 5a (*wĕ'ēt kĕnôs*) and v 8b the preposi- tion *lĕ-* is omitted before the gerunds, thus breaking the pattern in the poem. I discern no significance for this variation. In search of a better parallel for *sĕpôd*, Levy suggested that *rĕqôd* may mean "singing" (*Qoheleth*, pp. 80–81). But one must note a similar juxtaposition of mourning and dancing in Ps 30:12 (Eng v 11): *hāpaktā mispĕdî lĕmāḥôl lî* "You have turned my mourning to dancing for me." The contrast is between mourning and celebration.

5. *throwing stones . . . gathering stones*. Targ interprets this verse as referring to the demolishing of a building and preparation for rebuilding (so also Ibn Ezra and some modern interpreters). In contrast, *Qoh. Rabb.* takes the gathering of stones as sexual intercourse and the casting of stones as continence, thus con- necting this pair with embracing and shunning embrace in v 5b. Thus, throwing stones is a positive thing and gathering stones is negative. Levy has argued for the sexual connotations of throwing and gathering stones in the Levant (*Qoheleth*, p. 81). Supporting this view, Gordis (*Koheleth*, p. 230) cites Exod 1:16, Jer 2:27, and Matt 3:9. The "stones" (*'obnayim*, not *'ăbānîm*) in Exod 1:16 have been interpreted variously to mean birthstools, vulva, or testicles. It is doubtful, how- ever, if the "stones" in Jer 2:27 and Matt 3:9 are associated with sexuality. Galling ("Das Rätsel der Zeit," pp. 1–15) thinks of the practice of keeping stones in a bag for counting (cf. Deut 25:13–15). Others note that the expression *hašlîk 'eben* is used in 2 Kgs 3:19, 25 of people casting stones onto an enemy's field to destroy it. It is a military action. Conversely, it is argued, the gathering of stones would refer to the preparation of a field for use (cf. Isa 5:2). In any case, the throwing of stones appears to be destructive, while the gathering of stones is constructive. The former is negative, whereas the latter is positive. In some versions of the *Proverbs of Ahiqar* one finds the following saying: "Better to remove stones with a wise man than to drink wine with a fool" (see *APOT* II, pp. 730–31). Unfortu- nately, it is unclear what action is meant by "to remove stones." We know only that it is contrasted with drinking wine. In that context, "to remove stones" ap- pears to be negative, as "to drink wine" is positive. Beyond this distinction, one cannot be more specific. Should we interpret *hišlîk 'ăbānîm* to mean "throwing

out stones" (cf. *hišlîk* in v 6), thus corresponding to "removing stones" in the *Proverbs of Ahiqar?*

6. *losing.* Or "giving up (the search)" as the verb may mean in Postbiblical Hebrew (see *y. Ketub.* 4.7; 16.6). The verb is used in Jer 23:1 of shepherds who give up on their sheep—let them perish. One notes that *'bd* is used of lost sheep in 1 Sam 9:3, and the root is used with *mṣ'* "to find" in 1 Sam 9:20. Importantly, *'bd* is often juxtaposed with *bqš: wĕ'et-hā'ōbedet lō' biqqaštem* "and the stray you did not retrieve" (Ezek 34:5); *'et-hā'ōbedet 'ăbaqqēš* "I will retrieve the stray" (Ezek 34:16). See also Levine, "The Semantics of Loss," pp. 149–54.

7. *tearing . . . sewing up.* This pair has been taken to refer to the practice of tearing the garments during a period of mourning and the sewing together of the garments when the time of mourning is over (cf. *b. Moʿed Qat.* 22b). In a similar vein, *Qoh. Rabb.* takes the time of silence as a reference to a period of mourning, and the time of speaking as the period after the mourning. This is a view that some modern commentators accept (so Gordis). But it is doubtful if one should confine the meaning of this pair in this manner.

8. *loving . . . hating . . . war . . . peace.* These four items are listed chiastically. None of the other sets manifest this structure.

9. *what advantage.* See Notes at 1:3.

the worker. Hebrew *hā'ôśeh,* lit. "the doer." The rhetorical question in this verse is essentially the same as *mah-yyitrôn lā'ādām bĕkol-'ămālô* (1:3), *meh-hōweh lā'ādām bĕkol-'ămālô* (2:22), *ûmah-yyitrôn lô šeyya'ămōl lārûaḥ* (5:15 [Eng v 16]), and *mah-yyôtēr lā'ādām* (6:11). Thus *hā'ôśeh* corresponds to *hā'ādām.* The reference is to human efforts in general. The choice of this word was probably made for rhetorical reasons—to set up the emphasis on what God has done. The presence of *h'wśh* anticipates the recurrence of *'śh* in vv 10–15, 6 times out of 7 referring to God.

10. *preoccupation.* See Notes at 1:13.

with which to be preoccupied. See Notes at 1:13.

11 *right.* Hebrew *yāpeh* here means "right, proper, appropriate, good." It is not an aesthetic judgment, as the common translation "beautiful" may suggest (so KJV, RSV). The same usage of *yāpeh* is found in 5:17 (Eng v 18): "it is right (*yāpeh*) to eat and to drink." We may compare the usage of the word in the Talmud: *yph llb wṭwb* "appropriate for the heart and good" (*b. Ber.* 39a). Ben Sira seems to have been familiar with this saying, but in his version of it *ṭôb* is used in place of *yāpeh:* "All the works of God are good (*ṭôb*); for he provides every need in its time" (Sir 39:16, 33).

in its time. Hebrew *'ittô* is ordinarily used of things that happen as part of natural order—rain, the fruition of trees, seasons, birth, death, etc. (Lev 26:4; Deut 11:14; 28:12; Isa 60:22; Jer 5:24; Ezek 34:26; Hos 2:11; Pss 1:3; 104:27; 145:15; Prov 15:23; Job 5:26; 38:32; Eccl 9:12). The antecedent of the suffixed pronoun is *hakkōl* "everything" (i.e., "its time"), not God (i.e., "his time").

yet he has put. It is likely that *gam* is used adversatively here, as it is in 4:8 (the second *gam*) and 6:7. It is the same God who is responsible for what is timely ("everything in its time") and eternal ("eternity in their hearts").

eternity. The word *hā'ôlām* is a well-known crux. Scholars who reject the most obvious meaning of *hā'ôlām* propose various alternatives: (1) emend *hā'ôlām* to *he'āmāl* "toil" (so Ginsberg, Fox), (2) relate the word to postbiblical *'ôlām* "world" (cf. so LXX *aiōna*; Vulg *mundum*), (3) take it as a *hapax legomenon* in Hebrew related to the Arabic noun *'ilm* "knowledge" and the verb *'alima* "know, learn," thus "knowledge" (so Hitzig), (4) assume a noun meaning "darkness," "obfuscation," "enigma," "ignorance," or the like, from the verb *'lm* "hide" (so Targ, Rashi, and numerous recent commentators). The first solution is purely conjectural; there is no textual support for it whatsoever. The second and third solutions assume meanings not found elsewhere in the Bible. More seriously, they do not improve the meaning of the text. In support of the last interpretation, scholars have called attention to Qohelet's reference to *ne'lām* in 12:14 and to wisdom literature's concern with God's hiding of knowledge (Job 28:21; 42:3; Sir 11:4). The noun form is unattested anywhere, however, unless one takes *'ălū-mēnû* in Ps 90:8 as a substantive + suffix, "our hidden (sin)," an unsatisfactory solution. Ugaritic *ǵlm* "darkness" is cited often as a cognate for this meaning of *'ôlām*. Whitley (*Koheleth*, p. 33 n. 28) and Crenshaw (*Ecclesiastes*, pp. 97–98) also refer to *'lm* in the Phoenician inscription on the sarcophagus of Ahiram (*KAI* 1.1), but the parallel is hardly appropriate; *'lm* in the Phoenician inscription does not mean "darkness" but "eternity," a metonym for "grave" analogous to Egyptian *nḥḥ* "eternity" = "necropolis" or "grave." Qohelet himself, in fact, uses *'ôlām* "eternity" in this sense (12:5).

In the end, it appears that *hā'ôlām* in 3:11 must mean the same thing as *'ôlām* only three verses later (v 14) and elsewhere in the book (1:4, 10; 2:16; 9:6; 12:5). It is difficult to imagine that the ancient reader would not associate *'ôlām* in v 11 with *lě'ôlām* only three verses later, in v 14. The noun does not refer to what one would call "timing," "a sense of time," or the like (so NRSV: "a sense of past and future"). It means simply "eternity" — that which transcends time. It refers to a sense of that which is timeless and, as such, stands in contrast to *'ittô* "its time." Qohelet's point is ironic: God who has made everything right in its time has also put a sense of timelessness in human hearts. The same God who has given (*nātan*) humanity a preoccupation (v 10), has given (*nātan*) humanity this "eternity."

in their hearts. Hebrew *bĕlibbām.* That is, in the hearts of *bĕnê 'ādām* "human beings" (v 10). Some scholars prefer to read *bĕlibbô* (so one Hebrew MS and LXX^A), or even *bô* or *lô* (so Horst in *BHS*, Galling), but the reading with the singular suffix is the *lectio facilior*; it may be due to the influence of *bô* at the end of the preceding verse and anticipates the singular verb *yimṣā'* in the next line. MT, supported by most ancient versions, has the superior reading.

so that. The phrase *mibbĕlî 'ăšer lō'* is without parallel. The phrase probably introduces a result or final clause (so LXX, Vulg, Targ, and Syr).

end. Hebrew *sôp* "end" is a term of Late Biblical Hebrew (see also 7:2; 12:13; 2 Chron 20:16; Joel 2:20). It occurs also in Biblical Aramaic (see Dan 4:8, 19; 6:27; 7:26, 28).

12. *among them.* Codex Leningrad has *bām* (cf. LXX *en autois*; Syr *bhwn*).

Two MSS, however, read *b'dm*, the easier reading, which conforms to the for-mula found elsewhere in the book. The idiom in 2:24 is *'ên-ṭôb bā'ādām* and in 8:15 it is *'ên-ṭôb lā'ādām*. In any case, *bām* "among them" probably refers back to *hā'ādam* in v 11. It refers to people in general, not to the times and moments of vv 2–8 (so Rashbam), and not to *ḥayyîm* "life." Gordis eliminates the word altogether, the *bet* as a dittography and the *mem* as a "virtual dittography" (*Kohe-leth*, p. 232). But this is without textual support. The problem with *bām* is the tension between its plural suffix and the singular suffix in *ḥayyāyw*. Hence many emend *bām* to *bā'ādām*, but the tension is precisely why someone who has the idiom in 2:24 and 8:15 in mind might have read *bā'ādām* instead of *bām*. It is clear that *bām* is the more difficult and probably correct reading, whereas *bā'ā-dām* is harmonistic. G. R. Driver ("Once Again Abbreviations," *Textus* 4 [1964], p. 80) has proposed that *bm* is an early abbreviation for *bā'ādām*, but this has failed to convince. There is no need to take *bām* as anything other than what it is. The reference to humanity in the plural is already anticipated by *bĕlibbām* "their (people's) heart" in v 11, and the shift between singular and plural suffixes can be seen in *bô* (v 10) and *bĕlibbām* (v 11), and again in *šeyyō'kal wĕšātâ wĕrā'â ṭôb bĕkol-'ămālô* (v 13) and *šeyyîrĕ'û* (v 14). Human beings are referred to by the singular *hā'ôśeh* (v 9) and *hā'ādām* (vv 11, 13), but also by the plural *bĕnê hā'ā-dām* (v 10).

do well. The parallelism with *lismôaḥ* "to enjoy" suggests that *la'ăśôt ṭôb* does not have the moral connotations it has elsewhere in the Bible. Here it must mean something like *lir'ôt ṭôb* "to see good" = "to enjoy," as the next verse makes clear.

13. *all people should eat.* Hebrew *kol-hā'ādām šeyyō'kal*, lit. "every person, that one should eat. . . ." There can be little doubt that *kol-hā'ādām* is the subject of the verbs to follow. This is another example of Qohelet's tendency to anticipate what is to come (see Schoors, *Pleasing Words*, pp. 213–16). It is also certain that the relative particle *še-* is introducing the fact of human enjoyment (cf. Whitley, *Koheleth*, p. 34), which is then picked up by the feminine demonstrative pro-noun *hî'*.

enjoy the fruit of their toil. Hebrew *wĕrā'â ṭôb bĕkol-'ămālô*, lit. "see the good in all their toil." Here "toil" refers to the fruit of their toil (see Notes at 2:18).

14. *eternal.* That is, not bound by time and invariably coming to pass (cf. *lĕ'ô-lām* in 1:4). The meaning of *'ôlām* is clarified by the next line: one can neither add nor take away from all that God will do.

one cannot add . . . one cannot take away. The construction *'ên + lĕ- + Infini-tive Construct*—meaning "cannot, must not, may not"—occurs exclusively in Late Biblical Hebrew (e.g., Esth 4:2; 8:8; Ezra 9:15; 1 Chron 23:26; 2 Chron 5:11; 14:10; 20:6; 22:9; 35:15; cf. Sir 10:23 [twice]; 39:21; 40:26) and in the Qumran texts (1QS 3.16; 1QH 7.28; etc.; see Qimron, *Hebrew of the Dead Sea Scrolls*, pp. 78–79). Alongside this construction, Late Biblical Hebrew and the Qumran scrolls and fragments also use the related construction *lō' + lĕ- + Infin-itive Construct*. By contrast, earlier Biblical Hebrew typically uses *lĕbiltî* to negate the infinitive construct. The difference between the idiom in Late Biblical He-brew and older Hebrew is evident when one compares the similar formula in the book of Deuteronomy, where we get *lōʾ* + *Imperfect*, instead of *ʾēn/lōʾ* + *Infinitive Construct*: *lōʾ tōsīpû . . . lōʾ tigrĕʿû* (Deut 4:2); *lōʾ tōsēp . . . lōʾ tigraʿ* (Deut 13:1). It is true that there is an isolated instance of *ʾēn* + *lĕ-* + *Infinitive Construct* in 1 Sam 9:7, but the construction there has nothing to do with prohibition: *ʾēn-lĕhābîʾ lĕʾîš hāʾĕlōhîm* means "there is nothing for the man of God to bring."

so that they may be reverent before him. Hebrew *šeyyīrĕʾû millĕpānāyw.* The relative article *še-* may introduce a result or purpose clause, as *ʾăšer* frequently does in the Bible (Gen 11:7; 13:16; 22:14; Deut 4:10). See GKC §165.b.

15. *and what will happen.* Hebrew *waʾăšer lihyôt,* lit. "and what is to happen." The infinitive is in this case a periphrasis for the imperfect. This usage of the infinitive is known in Hebrew and Phoenician. So in the Bible: *YHWH ʾĕlōhênû lĕhôšîʿēnî* "YHWH *will* save me" (Isa 38:20); *bābel linpōl* "Babylon *will* fall" (Jer 51:49); *šōmēr tĕbûnâ limṣōʾ-ṭôb* "whoever keeps understanding *will* find good" (Prov 19:8). See GKC §114.i and C. R. Krahmalkov, "The Periphrastic Future Tense [*l* + infinitive construct] in Hebrew and Phoenician," *Rivista degli Studi Orientali* 61 (1987), pp. 73–80.

that which is pursued. Hebrew *ʾet-nirdāp* is an ancient crux. In the first place, one expects a definite article with *nirdāp* after the *nota accusativi.* A few Hebrew MSS omit *ʾt* or add the article, but these are obviously intended to "correct" the problem. There are other examples, however, of free-standing nouns that are marked by the *nota accusativi* but without the definite article, including *ʾet-kol-ʿāmāl* in Eccl 4:4 and *ʾet-lēb* in Eccl 7:7 (see Schoors, *Pleasing Words,* pp. 164–69). Cf. also Lev 26:5; Num 21:9; Isa 41:7; 50:4; Ezek 43:10; Prov 13:21; Job 13:25. In Late Biblical Hebrew, the *nota accusativi* may have simply marked the accusative, whether or not the article was present (see GKC §117.c; Joüon-Muraoka §125.h). The noun *nirdāp* may, therefore, be definite or indefinite. The same phenomenon is evident in the Yabneh Yam Ostracon: *kl [ʿ]bdk ʾt qṣr* "your servant measured the harvest" (text in *KAI* 200.6). In any case, the definite article is not used with consistency in Ecclesiastes. The more serious problem is with the meaning of *nirdāp*: does the noun refer collectively to things that are pursued or to people who are pursued or persecuted? LXX is ambiguous, but Symm and Syr take *nirdāp* as "the persecuted," while Vulg takes it as a reference to *quod abiit* "what has passed away" (see Salters, "A Note on the Exegesis of Ecclesiastes 3, 15b," pp. 419–22).

The ancient versions attest to the correctness of MT, and Sir 5:3, which is widely recognized as an allusion to Eccl 3:15, has *yy mbqš nrdpym* "God seeks *nrdpym.*" Since *rdp* is a synonym of *bqš,* some have suggested that this line means something like "God seeks what has been sought" and take the phrase to mean that God does what has been done before (so Fox, *Contradictions,* pp. 194–95). But if that were the meaning, one would expect Qohelet to use *mĕbuqqāš* instead of *nirdāp.* We should note that *rdp* is also a synonym of *rʿh* "pursue" (see Notes at 1:14), as is evident in the parallelism of *rōʿeh rûaḥ* "pursuing the wind" and *rōdēp qādîm* "chasing the east wind" (Hos 12:2). Thus, *nirdāp* may be an allusion to the *rĕʿût rûaḥ* (1:14; 2:11, 17, 26; 4:4, 6; 6:9) and *raʿyôn rûaḥ* (1:17; 4:16). As Blenkinsopp observes, "every other occurrence of the verbal stem in Niphal has to do with *the action of wind driving something before it*" ("Ecclesiastes 3.1–15: Another Interpretation," p. 63). It refers to that which people seek in vain (cf. Sir 34:2) — in this case, trying to make sense of all God's activity "from the beginning to the end." But God will look after what people have pursued in vain.

16. *Furthermore, I have seen under the sun that.* The introduction *wĕ'ôd* both signals a new section and links the new section to the preceding unit: the author observes again (cf. *rā'îtî* in v 10), but he sees a new thing. Cf. *šabtî wĕrā'ōh taḥat-haššemeš kî* "I turned and saw under the sun that" (9:11). In 3:16, however, the objects of the observation are introduced without *kî*.

in the place of. LXX and Vulg take the "place of justice" (v 16b) as the direct object of the verb *rā'îtî* in v 16a (i.e., "I have seen the place of justice under the sun"). But the Masoretic accents are to be taken seriously; *mĕqôm* begins a new clause and is to be taken as an adverbial accusative (cf. *mĕqôm* in 11:3), which is strongly reinforced by the adverb, *šāmmâ*.

wickedness. The form *hrš'* occurs twice in v 16, both times taken as the noun "wickedness" in MT (*hārešaʿ* in v 16b and the pausal form *hārāšaʿ* in v 16c), Vulg, and Syr. LXX, however, translates the first *hrš'* as *ho asebēs* "the wicked" (reflecting Hebrew *hārāšaʿ*) and the second as *ho eusebēs* "the pious," which is probably an inner Greek error for *ho asebēs* (so Euringer). An earlier Greek translator apparently interpreted *hrš'* both times to mean "the wicked" (rather than "wickedness"). Targ reads the second *hrš'* the same way: *ḥyyb'* "the guilty." Along with these readings, one notes that instead of *haṣṣedeq* "righteousness" in v 16c, two MSS read *ḥṣdyq* "the righteous" (Kennicott nos. 30, 244). The latter is reflected in LXX[B] (*tou dikaiou*, but LXX[A] has the plural *tōn dikaiōn*) and Targ (*gbr zk'y*). In short, LXX and Targ both read "the righteous" // "the wicked" in v 16c. This anticipates the pairing of "the righteous" and "the wicked" in v 17. Moreover, the reading of *ḥṣdq* as "the righteous" (presuming defective spelling, *haṣṣaddîq*) is belied by its parallelism with *mišpāṭ*: *mĕqôm hammišpāṭ* (v 16b) // *mĕqôm haṣṣedeq* (v 16c). MT is superior.

17. *God will judge.* This expression need not refer to eschatological judgment. It simply means that judgment is in the hand of God: God will judge in God's own time. Similarly, *yaʿăśeh hā'ĕlōhîm* in v 14 does not imply God's future action, nor does *wĕhā'ĕlōhîm yĕbaqqēš* imply that God will seek in the future. The point is that judgment belongs to God (cf. 11:9). The imperfect *yišpōṭ* does not presume certain future occurrence any more than *yĕbaqqēš* "God will seek" (3:15) and *yiqṣōp* "God will be angry" (5:5 [Eng v 6]). The imperfect merely indicates *potential* here.

there is a time for every matter. See Notes at 3:1.

there is a destiny. The last word in v 17 is an ancient *crux interpretum*. MT, LXX, and Syr all read *šām* "there" and Vulg has "then." But it is unclear what "there" or "then" would refer to. Many commentators follow Targ in assuming that "there" or "then" is an allusion to the future. In a variation of this view, Gordis argues that *šām* is a veiled reference to Sheol. Thus, Qohelet is supposed to have said ("sarcastically," according to Gordis) that there is a time for every matter and every deed "over yonder" — in the future, or in Sheol. But this position is difficult to sustain, since Qohelet repeatedly insists that people cannot know what will happen in the future. Indeed, he states explicitly that there will be no *maʿăśeh* "activity" in Sheol to which (*šammâ*) all people will surely go (9:10). Others take *šām* concretely to mean "place" (Dahood, "Phoenician Background," p. 271). But *šām* never has this meaning anywhere. Whitley takes *šām* as an asseverative particle with the nuance "too, also" (*Koheleth*, pp. 34–36). The particle probably does not have this nuance, however, and even if it did, it would not come at the end of a sentence in Hebrew. Still others prefer to read *śām* "he appointed," instead of *šām* (Barton, Scott). But the position of the finite verb at the end of the sentence is awkward, and the idiom is problematic with the preposition *ʿal*. Other emendations — to *zĕmān* (Hertzberg), *šōmēr* (BHK), *mēśîm* (BHS), or *mišpāṭ* (Podechard) — are too farfetched to be persuasive. The ancient versions (LXX, Vulg, and Syr) all attest to the correctness of the consonantal reading of MT. The word probably should be repointed either as a noun or gerund from *śym/śwm* (cf. Dahood, "Northwest Semitic Philology," pp. 354–55). In this connection, one notes that Hebrew *śym/śwm* could refer to the determination of events (2 Sam 13:32), or the setting of a date (Exod 9:5; Job 34:23 [reading *mwʿd* for *ʿwd*]). The word thus corresponds to Akkadian *šiāmu/šâmu* "to determine" and *šīmtu* "fate, destiny" (*AHW* III, pp. 1225, 1238–39). Alternatively, one may read *šēm* "name, designation" and note that the idiom *niqrāʾ šēm* "called by name" in 6:10 refers to the predetermination of events.

18. *as regards.* The expression *ʿal-dibrat*, lit. "concerning the matter of," occurs also in 7:14 (*ʿal-dibrat še-*) and 8:2. Cf. Biblical Aramaic *ʿal-dibrat dî* in Dan 2:30. The expression corresponds to the more common and older *ʿal-dĕbar* "concerning the matter of" or "as regards" (see Exod 8:8 [Eng v 12]; Num 17:14 [Eng 6:49]; 25:18 [3 times]; 2 Sam 18:5; Prov 29:12).

surely God has chosen them. The form *lĕbārām* is difficult. It is possible to take the form to be the infinitive construct of *brr* + 3 mp suffix (cf. Joüon-Muraoka §821), thus "to choose them" or "to test them" (so most commentators): *lĕbārām hāʾĕlōhîm wĕlirʾôt*, lit. "to choose them — God — and to see." Even the normally literalistic ASV is free in its translation: "that God may prove them, and that they may see" (cf. NEB: "it is God's purpose to test them and to see"; NIV: "God tests them so that they may see"). This analysis is problematic, for there is no finite verb in the sentence and it is difficult to account for the word order. Why is the subject, God, placed after the infinitive + object? It is easier to take the form to be the asseverative *lamed* + 3 ms Perfect of *brr* "choose, select." There is a clear example of the asseverative *lamed* in 9:4.

< > *to show.* The reading of MT (*wĕlirʾôt*) makes no sense. It is better to follow most of the ancient versions (LXX, Syr, and Vulg) in taking the infinitive to be Hiphil, with the syncope of *h*: *larʾôt* from *lĕharʾôt* (cf. *larʾōtĕkem* in Deut 1:33; see GKC §53.q). A similar syncope is attested in Eccl 5:5 (Eng v 6), where we find the Hiphil infinitive form *laḥăṭîʾ* for *lĕhaḥăṭîʾ*. Obviously in the case of Eccl 3:18 the loss of the causative marker, *h*-, caused the misinterpretation of the form as Qal instead of Hiphil. The syncope of the causative marker (*h*-) is common in Mishnaic Hebrew (see Segal, *A Grammar of Mishnaic Hebrew*, §143).

The conjunctive *waw* in MT should also be deleted. It was probably added secondarily when *lĕbārām* was incorrectly analyzed as an infinitive + object.

that they are animals < > themselves. Reading *šehem-bĕhēmâ < > lāhem.* The addition of *hemmâ* after *šehem-bĕhēmâ* in MT is redundant and should be deleted as a dittography. The final *lāhem* is also difficult. Whitley and Crenshaw take it to be emphatic: "they are *really* beasts." But all the examples cited are the so-called "ethical dative," which should follow an imperative or, in any case, a verb (see GKC §119.t). One should probably take *lāhem* to mean something like "of themselves."

19. *the fate of . . . the fate of.* Taking *miqreh* as a construct noun, following LXX, Syr, Vulg, and Targ. The vocalizations of III-Weak nouns in absolute and construct are not consistent in Ecclesiastes (cf. GKC §93.rr).

are one and the same. Lit. "and one fate is to/for them." LXX (supported by SyrH and Copt), Syr, and Targ do not reflect the conjunction and many Hebrew MSS omit it. But the form with the conjunction is the *lectio difficilior*; it is also supported by Vulg. What we have here is an example of the *waw apodoseos*, where the *waw* introduces the predicate of the *casus pendens* (see GKC §143.d). Cf. *tiqwātĕkā wĕtōm dĕrākêkā* "your hope, *it is* the integrity of your ways" (Job 4:6); *mispar šānāyw wĕlō'-ḥēqer* "the number of his years, *it is* unsearchable" (Job 36:26).

advantage. Hebrew *môtār* occurs elsewhere only in Prov 14:23; 21:5. The first of these parallel passages asserts that there is "advantage" in toil; the second claims that there is advantage in thinking ahead. Qohelet's point, made emphatic by the word order, is that there is no advantage of people over animals: lit. "as for advantage of humanity over animals — None!" In context one understands the point to be that human beings have no advantage as far as death is concerned.

vanity. See Notes at 1:2.

21. *whether it is goes upward on high . . . whether it goes downward below.* MT has *hāʿōlâ . . . hayyōredet.* The interrogative is certainly meant, however. The ancient versions so interpret the verse. Hence most commentators repoint to read *haʿōlâ . . . hăyōredet.* It is possible that an orthodox scribe was pointing the forms as indicative, in answer to the doubt that was perceived in the question. Yet, the forms are not impossible as interrogatives. Cf. *hayyîṭab* instead of *hăyîṭab* (Lev 10:19), *hāʾîš* instead of *hăʾîš* (Num 16:22). See GKC §100.m.

netherworld. For this meaning of Hebrew *ʾereṣ*, see Exod 15:12; Num 16:32; Ps 18:8; Isa 14:12; 26:19; etc., and N. J. Tromp, *Primitive Conceptions of Death and the Netherworld in the Old Testament* (BibOr 21, Rome: Pontifical Biblical Institute, 1969), pp. 23–46. Prov 15:24 suggests that for the wise, the path of life leads upward, so that they may avoid Sheol below.

22. *portion.* See Notes and Comment at 2:10.

after them. Hebrew *ʾaḥărāyw* must mean "when they die," like Akkadian *arkīšu* "after him" = "after his departure (from life)" (see *CAD* I/2, p. 280). Cf. Eccl 2:12; 7:14, 10:14, and esp. 9:3 which has *wĕʾaḥărāyw ʾel-hammētîm* "and after them, to the dead." This is how Targ interprets it. The idiom does not mean a future point in a person's life (so Podechard).

COMMENT

Next to the thematic statement of the book in 1:2 and 12:8, the poem on times and seasons in 3:1–8 is probably the most well-known and oft-quoted of the words of Qohelet. The poem is popularly understood to mean that there are appropriate moments for people to act and, at the proper moment, even an ordinarily objectionable situation can be "beautiful in its own way." There is an appropriate time for everything. Placed properly in its present context, however, it becomes clear that the poem is not about human determination of events or even human discernment of times and seasons. It is about God's activity and the appropriate human response to it. Although the text refers to the human "worker" (v 9), the principal actor/doer turns out to be God (vv 10–15). Indeed, the activity of God overwhelms and overshadows the activities of humanity in this chapter.

Qohelet concludes the poem in Chapter 3 with a rhetorical question in 3:9: "what advantage does the worker have in all the toiling?" The "what advantage" question here recalls 1:3. But whereas the question in 1:3 introduces a poem (1:3–9), the rhetorical question here concludes the poem on times and seasons (3:1–9). The poem in Chapter 1 concerns nature's routines, representing everything that is "vanity"; the poem in Chapter 3 concerns times and seasons for "everything" and "every matter." As a prose commentary follows the poem in the introductory chapter (1:10–11), so a prose commentary follows the poem on times and seasons (3:10–15). The conclusions are similar in both cases, as well: whatever happened happens again. In other words, what goes around comes around (1:9; 3:15).

It is clear that 3:1–15 constitutes a coherent passage, but the central issue raised in that passage is continued into the next (3:16–22). The link is evident from the introduction in v 16: *wĕʿôd rāʾîtî* "furthermore, I have seen." While *wĕʿôd* "furthermore" signals a shift in focus, it also links the passage with what precedes it, specifically with *rāʾîtî* "I have seen" in v 10. The author's observation in vv 16–22 somehow adds to, or elaborates on, the observation in vv 10–15. It should occasion no surprise, therefore, when one encounters the conviction in v 17 that "there is a time for every matter and a destiny over every activity." Thus, the two sections in the chapter (vv 1–15, 16–22) are closely related; they are two parts of a whole. Qohelet is apparently not quite through with the subject raised in 3:1–15, namely, the sovereignty of God in the determination of events. The author raises the question of *miqreh* "fate" in 3:16–22, thus resuming the issue discussed in 2:12–17, although now the problem is not the common fate of wise and foolish people, but of human beings and animals. In the face of mortality, Qohelet observes that there is nothing better for people than to take pleasure in their present activities (3:22). This is his conclusion also in 3:13 and, even earlier, in 2:24–26.

In many ways, then, Chapter 3 elaborates and expands on previous issues: the activities of humanity, toil, the lack of advantage. Nevertheless, there is an unmistakable focus in the chapter on the activity of God and the appropriate human response to whatever God does. The dominant motif throughout the chapter is

God's sovereign activity, illustrated in the determination of events (3:1–15) and the determination of the lot of humanity (3:16–22).

The Determination of Events (3:1–15)

Qohelet begins with a thesis statement that encompasses "everything" (*lakkōl*) and "every matter" (*lĕkol-ḥēpeṣ*). From the start one gets a hint that the issue is not the human decision to choose the opportune moment to act. The noun *zĕmān* "season" is ordinarily used of predetermined or appointed time. Elsewhere Qohelet speaks of every matter (*ḥēpeṣ*) having "a time and judgment" (*'ēt ûmišpāṭ*) that, the truly wise will recognize, human beings cannot control (see Notes and Comment at 8:5–6). So the issue in our passage is not human intention or timing, but human activities in predetermined times and seasons.

Following the thesis statement (v 1), there is a rhythmic series of twenty-eight items occurring in broadly antithetical pairs (vv 2–8). These may be grouped into seven sets, each with two pairs of opposites (see Sir 33:15). The form of the list may be likened to the various "onomastica" (noun-lists) that the people of antiquity collected, among other reasons, to study and to instruct about the way things in nature work (see Whybray, "'A Time to be Born and a Time to Die,'" pp. 469–82). There are catalogs of every sort in Egypt and Mesopotamia (compare Prov 30:19). Here we have a Catalog of Occasions, of times and situations that human beings encounter. It is possible that this catalog was composed earlier and was adopted by Qohelet, who then gave it his own application by introducing the thesis statement (v 1) and concluding with the rhetorical question about the advantage of toil (v 9), before providing the prose commentary of vv 10–15a (see Wright, "'For Everything There Is a Season,'" pp. 321–28).

It appears that in vv 4, 6, and 8, we have a particular tension expressed by two antithetical pairs in each verse, thus:

crying // laughing (v 4a) :: mourning // dancing (v 4b)
seeking // losing (v 6a) :: keeping // throwing out (v 6b)
loving // hating (v 8a) :: war // peace (v 8b).

This pattern has prompted scholars to propose that other verses in the poem also deal with a common tension in each case, expressed by two antithetical pairs in each verse. Thus, if one takes planting and uprooting in v 2 as metaphors for life and death, then the two antithetical pairs in the verse are concerned with the same issues (birthing // dying :: "planting" // "uprooting"). By the same token, it has been argued that "tearing" in v 7a refers to the ritual rending of garments during mourning and "being silent" in v 7b refers to acceptable behavior during mourning, while "sewing up" in v 7a refers to the ritual mending of garments when the mourning period is over and "speaking" in v 7b is what one does when mourning is over (so Gordis). If each verse can be explained in this manner, then one may identify a heptad of polarities (7 x 2), representing the totality of life's tensions. J. A. Loader has also proffered a detailed analysis of the activities as either desirable (D) or undesirable (U), and discerned a deliberate and intricate structure in the poem ("A 'Sonnet' in the Old Testament," pp. 240–42; *Polar*

Structures in the Book of Qohelet, pp. 1–13, 29–33). The persuasiveness of such structural analyses, however, depends on one's acceptance of the labels that are put on each item. In fact, the activities cannot be categorized easily. So v 2a is about life and death, but v 2b is apparently about agricultural activities (planting // uprooting); v 3a is about killing and healing, but v 3b about architectural or agricultural activities (breaking up // building). The nature of some of the activities is also unclear, such as "throwing stones" and "gathering stones" in v 5 (see Notes). For his thesis to work, Loader has to interpret casting stones as desirable, whereas gathering stones is regarded as undesirable. In some versions of the *Proverbs of Ahiqar*, "removing stones" (= "throwing out stones"?) seems to be a negative experience (*APOT* II, pp. 730–31).

Despite the impression of a deliberate structure, no clear pattern is discernible. The Catalog of Occasions begins with birth and death, and it ends with war and peace, but from the beginning to the end one can detect no progression or structure of any sort. All that is evident is that there are opposite activities and opposite situations, but there is no pattern. In any case, the specific activities and events in the catalog do not appear to be of particular concern to Qohelet himself. No specific item in the poem is repeated anywhere else in the book, although the noun *ʿēt* "time" appears another eleven times (3:11, 17; 7:17; 8:5, 6, 9; 9:8, 11, 12 [twice]; 10:17). The list is not exhaustive, but it is meant to be representative of every occasion and situation in which human beings find themselves. The introductory thesis statement in v 1 suggests that these events and activities represent "everything" and "every matter." The occasions are not those that human beings plan, nor are they contingent upon human decisions. People cannot actually choose a time of birthing or dying, nor do they really determine the seasons for specific agricultural activities. Indeed, people do not decide when to heal, weep, laugh, mourn, lose, love, hate, or be in war or peace. These are occasions in which people find themselves, and they can only respond to them. All that mortals can do in the face of these times is to be open to them.

It is sometimes supposed that the passage is affirming that there is a pattern for times and seasons, that events do not happen in a haphazard manner, and so it is incumbent on humans to discern the appropriate moment for any activity. Perhaps that was the original purpose of such a Catalog of Occasions. Conventional wisdom assumed that there are felicitous moments for any human deed, and that the wise ought to know what they are, so that they might maximize their chances of success. According to some wisdom teachings, the wise know the right time to do everything (Prov 15:23; 25:11; Sir 1:23–24; 4:20, 23), and even a child yet unborn ought to be wise enough to know the right time to present itself for birth (Hos 13:13).

Such a Catalog of Occasions, then, may at one time have identified the situations of which people ought to be aware in order to act responsibly (see Lang, "Ist der Mensch hilflos?" pp. 109–24). This is not how Qohelet uses the catalog, however. He does not say that there is any kind of order in these occasions. One can, indeed, find no order in the presentation of the list, despite the temptations to find a deliberate structure. This is the way the world is. People are tempted to discern an order so that they can predict the changes and not have to face surprises. Yet the occasions simply present themselves, and people simply have to respond appropriately in each situation. The mortal is not in control.

Qohelet concludes with his rhetorical question in v 9: "what advantage does the worker have in the toiling?" The question is the same as that raised in 1:3, 2:22, and 6:11, except that Qohelet here uses *hāʿôśeh* "the worker" (literally "the one who does" or "the one who acts"), instead of *hāʾādām* "the human," as we have it everywhere else the question appears. Here it is clear that *hāʿôśeh* "the worker" refers to the human, the one who is supposedly "the worker" in the world. But this "worker" gains no advantage despite all the toil. The substitution of *hāʿôśeh* "the worker" for *hāʾādām* "the human" in the typical formulation of the question is deliberately ironic. The human is identified as the doer (*hāʿôśeh*), but what does this doer do that really makes a difference? What advantage does toiling yield for this doer, after all? The rhetorical question is Qohelet's conclusion to the Catalog of Occasions, but it is really a setup for the point that he wants to make in the prose commentary that is to follow.

Qohelet's understanding of the issue is clarified in the prose commentary (vv 10–15). It turns out that God is the principal *doer* of activities. The root *ʿśh* "to do, work, make, act" is used repeatedly of God, who is also mentioned several times in vv 10–15: it is God who has made (*ʿāśâ*) everything (v 11); people cannot discover the deed (*hammaʿăśeh*) that God has done (*ʿāśâ*) from the beginning to the end (v 11); what God does (*yaʿăśeh*) is "eternal" (v 14); and God has acted (*ʿāśâ*) that people might be reverent before God (v 14). The only thing that the human is able to do (*laʿăśôt*) is to find pleasure in life (v 12), but even that is a gift of God (v 13).

In the prose commentary, Qohelet reiterates what is said in 1:13. God has given people "a preoccupation," to put them in their place, as it were (v 10). The author also speaks of God's giving of this preoccupation in 2:24–26. Qohelet stresses the futility of wisdom and toil in discerning God's intentions in 1:13 and 2:23, and the apparent arbitrariness of God's decisions in 2:26. Now he intimates that the situations in which people find themselves are determined by God and beyond human ability to control. People do not determine the timing of those occasions, nor can they even anticipate them. Even though the human is called *hāʿôśeh* "the worker" at the conclusion of the Catalog of Occasions (v 9), it becomes clear in v 11 that it is God who is the real doer: "he made everything right in its time" (*ʾet-hakkōl ʿāśâ yāpeh bĕʿittô*). If there has been any doubt as to the real "doer" of everything mentioned in vv 1–9, it is clarified in v 11: God has done "everything." The reference to "everything" in v 11 recalls "everything" in v 1, and the mention of "time" alludes to the entire catalog. God is the one responsible for bringing about everything in its time.

What Qohelet says immediately after this is not easy to comprehend. The problem hinges on the meaning of the word *hāʿōlām*, which refers to something that God has also put in human hearts. Commentators, if they do not emend the text, will sometimes repoint or otherwise interpret the word to mean "the world," "knowledge," "ignorance," or the like (see Notes above). But these do not improve the meaning of the verse. The word cannot be separated from the occurrence of ʿōlām elsewhere in the book (1:4, 10; 2:16; 3:14; 9:6; 12:5). It is difficult to believe that hāʿōlām in v 11 could be radically different in meaning from lĕʿô-lam "eternal" only three verses later in v 14. Nor can one avoid the immediate contrast between hāʿōlām "eternity" and bĕʿittô "in its time" in v 11. The adverb gam "yet" or "also" highlights the contrast and brings out the irony: the same God who has made everything right "in its time," *also* put "eternity" in human hearts. The word hāʿōlām "eternity" refers probably to a consciousness of and yearning for that which transcends the present—it includes everything "from the beginning to the end." God is responsible for giving both time and eternity, and the human being is caught in the tension between the two. The God who makes everything appropriate only "in its time," also puts eternity in human hearts. Thus, v 11 expands on v 10 and clarifies the statement that God has given a preoccupation to people. The Hebrew verb for God's giving in v 10 and putting in v 11 is one and the same: nātan "he gave" (v 10) or "he put" (v 11). The preoccupation that God has given to people to keep them in their place is this "eternity" in their hearts that inevitably confronts the reality of each moment. That is the irony of the human's situation. Humanity can expect to know the appropriateness of what God has done only in its moment, in its time, but one cannot hope to discover what God has done "from the beginning to the end" (v 11). Qohelet is thinking here of the effort of people to bypass the moment in order to grasp the totality of existence. Mortals cannot discover that sort of thing, however. Humanity knows of eternity, but can only cope with activities in their time. The eternity in human hearts only serves to underscore the ephemerality of the moment that each person experiences.

Qohelet's observation leads him to two certainties; rāʾîtî "I have seen" in v 10, gives way to two comments introduced by yādaʿtî "I know" in vv 12 and 14. The first "I know" refers to what humans are supposed to do (v 12); the second "I know" is what God does (v 14). In the first place, Qohelet says he knows that there is nothing better for people than to have pleasure and do well in their lives (v 12). Here he returns to the theme already broached in 2:24–26, that all people can do in the face of the inscrutability of the universe is to live life fully in the present. One must enjoy the fruit of one's toil. The mention of God's "gift" (*mat-tat*) echoes the verb nātan used of God's *giving* a preoccupation to people (v 10) and God's *putting* eternity in human hearts (v 11). Qohelet also restates what is said in 2:24, that living fully in the present is something that God wills. The expression *mattat ʾĕlōhîm hîʾ* "that is the gift of God" in 3:13 corresponds to *miyyad hāʾĕlōhîm hîʾ* "that is from the hand of God" in 2:24. In both cases, the feminine demonstrative pronoun hîʾ "that" refers not to toil, which is masculine in gender, but to all that precedes it, namely, the fact that people should live as fully as possible in the present despite the inevitable toil that life entails. Here in 3:13, the demonstrative hîʾ "that" (as in "*that* is a gift of God") resumes the relative "that" (še-, as in "*that* one should eat and drink"), which refers to the fact of human enjoyment.

The second thing that Qohelet knows is that all that God does will be lĕʿôlām "eternal." By this the author does not mean that everything that God does will *last* forever. The duration of divine deeds is irrelevant to Qohelet's point in this context. It is also not true that everything God does is everlasting. Rather, Qo-helet reckons that whatever God does will not be confined by time. That is what *'ōlām* means: it is that which transcends time. Everything will invariably come to pass and at any moment that God decides. Although God has made (*'āśâ*) everything appropriate "in its time" (v 11a), everything that God does (*ya'áśeh*) is, nevertheless, "eternal" (v 14) — not bound by time. God's activity, it appears, is at once temporal (*bĕ'ittô* "in its time") and eternal (*lĕ'ôlām* "forever"). The timeless, eternal character of God's activity (v 14) stands in contrast to the "eter-nity" that exists only in human hearts that are limited by their inability to discover the activity of God "from the beginning to the end" (v 11). In contrast to God, human beings can only "do well in their lifetime" (v 12). Their activities are only transient, whereas God's are eternal.

The meaning of *lĕ'ôlām* "eternal" is clarified by the statement that no one can add to, or subtract from, all which God will do. The language of adding and subtracting is used elsewhere in the Bible for something that is decisive, authori-tative, and invariable (Deut 4:2; 13:1 [Eng 12:32]; cf. Jer 26:2; Prov 30:6; Rev 22:18–19). Ben Sira may have been thinking of Qohelet's words when he con-fessed that "one cannot subtract from, or add to, or penetrate" the wonders of God (Sir 18:6; cf. 42:21). Qohelet's point is that what God wants to do will invari-ably be done, and no human being can hope to alter the course of things by sheer effort. He suggests, too, that God has acted (*hā'ĕlōhîm 'āśâ*) in order that people might be in awe before the divine presence.

The notion of the "fear of God," which appears elsewhere in the book (5:6 [Eng v 7]; 7:18; 8:12–13), does not connote absolute terror. Rather, the concept of the fear of God here, as elsewhere in Israelite wisdom literature, stresses the distance between divinity and humanity. It is the recognition that God is God and people are human. Qohelet stands in the wisdom tradition in its acknowledg-ment of wisdom's limits. Human knowledge can only take people so far. Eventu-ally people must accept that they are dealing with a sovereign and inscrutable deity.

Qohelet reinforces this by affirming a certain amount of determinism in events: "whatever has happened has already happened, and whatever will hap-pen has already happened, and God will take care of the pursued" (v 15). The first part of the verse has been anticipated by the prose commentary in the pref-ace, which emphasizes the cyclical nature of events (1:9–11). Here, however, the routine of occurrences is placed in a theological context. Things happen because of God's activities, which human beings may not understand. The final phrase in the verse is difficult (see Notes above), but it seems to suggest that it is God who will take care of what is pursued, namely, all those matters that are beyond human grasp. The noun *nirdāp* "what is pursued" approximates what Qohelet elsewhere calls "pursuit of wind" (*rĕ'ût rûaḥ/ra'yôn rûaḥ*). These are not matters about which people should concern themselves (see Sir 34:1–2), for God will look after those things.

174

The Determination of the Lot of Humanity (3:16–22)

The introduction of v 16 with *wĕ'ôd rā'îtî* "furthermore I saw" suggests a connection with the preceding unit of thought, specifically harking back to *rā'îtî* "I saw" in v 10. It also signals a shift in emphasis. Qohelet had considered the absolute sovereignty of God in the determination of times and seasons (vv 1–15), now he turns to the specific problem of injustice. The problem is that wickedness is rife precisely where justice is expected — presumably in the law-courts and temples (cf. 5:7 [Eng v 8]).

Qohelet's response to this inexplicable situation is essentially the same as before (3:10–15). In the face of the seeming arbitrariness of God's activity Qohelet concludes that "*God will seek* that which is pursued" (v 15). Now confronting the prevalence of injustice, he suggests that "*God will judge* the righteous and the wicked" (v 17). A few scholars, finding here a reference to the notion of eschatological judgment, have rejected the statement as the work of a pious glossator in answer to Qohelet's despair (so Podechard, Lauha). Others think that it is an orthodox sentiment quoted by Qohelet and adapted for his own purposes (so Zimmerli). But the verb *yišpōṭ* "(God) will judge" need not suggest a time of judgment in the future, as in a final judgment day, or the like. Qohelet is not asserting the certainty of eschatological judgment. Indeed, he denies that one can look into the future (3:22). Rather the statement is merely an acknowledgment that whatever will be done is entirely in the hand of God. The message of the imperfect verb *yišpōṭ* "(God) will judge" is probably the same as the imperfect verb *yĕbaqqēš* "(God) will seek" in v 15b: God will take care of it all. And what God will do (*ya'ăśeh*) is not bound by time (v 13). Or, as Murphy puts it, "[j]udgment belongs to God's time" (*Ecclesiastes*, p. 36). The link to the preceding unit of thought is evident in Qohelet's rationale for this judgment: "for there is a time for everything and over every matter is a destiny" (v 17). There is a time for everything, but it is not for mortals to decide.

If the affirmation of God's judgment causes one to be complacent about its outcome, one is sobered by Qohelet's next observation. He turns to the ultimate evidence of God's inexplicable judgment, the common fate of all living creatures. He returns to the issue that he first broached in 2:12–17. But whereas in Chapter 2 he equates the fate of the wise with that of fools, here he compares the fate of humanity with that of animals. Qohelet uses irony again when he says in no uncertain terms that God chose them (human beings), but only to show that they are no better than animals because they are mortal. The leveling effect of death is thus made more poignant than before. Human beings have one breath, just like animals, and they die just like animals. As the wise die like fools, so people die like animals. As far as mortality is concerned, there is no difference between the wise and the foolish, or people and animals. Qohelet is not saying that the quality of human life is no different from that of animals, but that the quality of human life does not include immortality. The same sentiment is expressed elsewhere, in a wisdom psalm lamenting the transient nature of life: the wise and the foolish alike die, leaving their wealth to others, and human beings perish along with animals (Ps 49:11–13, 21 [Eng vv 10–12, 20]). In the face of this common fate, then, Qohelet concludes that people have no advantage over animals because everything is "vanity" — ephemeral and unreliable (v 19). The syntax here places the issue of advantage at the fore, making the denial of it even more poignant: "as for the advantage of humans over animals — none!" The emphatic denial is perhaps in reaction to the wisdom teachings about the advantage of human efforts (compare Prov 14:22–23).

Traditional wisdom teachers often affirmed that the plans of the diligent will certainly lead to "advantage" (Prov 21:5). But for Qohelet, people do not even have advantage over animals because all living creatures "go to one place" and return to the dust from whence they came (v 20). Elsewhere he speaks of what happens when a person dies: "the dust returns to the earth as it was, but the life-breath (*rûaḥ*) returns to God" (12:7). This is a view found elsewhere in the Bible. When mortals die, God takes the life-breath back, but the body returns to dust (see, e.g., Job 34:14–15; Ps 104:29–30). But here in 3:20–21, perhaps in reaction to the speculations of others in his generation, Qohelet refuses to entertain any notion of separate destinies for the life-breaths of people and animals. The issue is not whether the human spirit itself will ascend or descend, but whether the destiny of the human spirit is distinctly different from that of animals. Indeed, only two verses earlier, in v 19, he claims that there is only one life-breath for all, animals and human beings alike. So he suggests that no one knows if the life-breath of human beings leads upward, while the life-breath of animals goes downward to the netherworld. People and animals have the same fate.

Qohelet is led to the conclusion he reached earlier in the book (2:24–26; 3:12–13), that people ought to find enjoyment in all their "activities." That is all that the human "worker" can really do in the light of God's unpredictable activity. Here he speaks of the possibility of enjoyment in terms of the "portion" that humanity has. The "portion" conveys both the sense of the limitations and the possibilities of life (see Notes at 2:10). The portion is like an inherited plot that one has to work. Toil is an inevitable part of that heritage, but from that very same lot one may also find enjoyment. The lot is limited and it involves work. But it is also possible for one to find enjoyment in that limited portion that is life. There is no possibility of a portion when one dies. The conclusion he draws from his observation of the lot of humanity is the same as the conclusion from his observation of God's activity in general (3:12–13). The present is what really matters because people will not be led to see what will happen in the future, that is, when they die (v 22).

I.A.4. RELATIVE GOOD IS NOT GOOD ENOUGH (4:1–16)

4 ¹Further, I saw all the oppressions that are being done under the sun: lo, the tears of the oppressed, but there is none to comfort them; power comes from the hand of their oppressors, but there is none to comfort them. ²So I extolled

the dead, who have already died, more than the living who are still alive; [3]but better than both of them is the one who has never existed, who has not seen the terrible activity that has been done under the sun.

[4]I saw that every toil and every achievement come from one's envy of another. This, too, is vanity and a pursuit of wind. [5]Fools fold their hands and they eat their flesh. [6]Better is a handful with repose, than two fistfuls with toil and pursuit of wind.

[7]Further, I saw a vanity under the sun: [8]there are those who are alone and without anyone else — they do not even have children or siblings. But there is no limit to all their toil. Yet, their eyes are dissatisfied with wealth. So for whom am I toiling and depriving myself of good? This, too, is vanity and it is a terrible business.

[9]Better are two than one because they have a good benefit for their toil. [10]For if either of them should fall, one will lift up the other; but alas for those who are alone when they fall and there is no one else to lift them up. [11]Moreover, if two lie together they will be warm; but as for those who are alone, how shall they be warm? [12]Though the one may be overpowered, two together may resist. The three-ply cord will not readily snap.

[13]Better is a youngster who is a commoner but wise, than a king who is old and foolish, who can no longer be admonished: [14]for (one) went forth from the prison to reign, while (another), though born into his kingship, is impoverished. [15]I saw that all the living who walk about under the sun are with the next youngster who arises in his stead. [16]There is no limit to all the multitude, to all before whom he comes, although those who come later would not rejoice in him. Indeed, this is vanity and a pursuit of wind.

NOTES

4:1. Further, I saw. The auxiliary use of *šwb* is well attested in the Hebrew Bible (cf. BDB, p. 998). The phrase *wěšabtî 'ănî wā'er'eh* is, thus, equivalent to *wě'ôd rā'îtî* in 3:16. However, whereas *wě'ôd rā'îtî* seems to stress continuity with the preceding materials, *wěšabtî* appears to stress the discontinuity. Cf. also a similar usage of *šwb* in 4:7; 9:11. The form *wā'er'eh* is only one of three *waw*-consecutive imperfect forms in the book (also 1:17; 4:7).

oppressions. Although *hā'ăšūqîm* may also mean "the oppressed," as it does in the same verse, that meaning is unlikely in the first instance. Rather, it is here an abstract noun understood in terms of concrete acts, since they are observed being done. The noun is used the same way in Job 35:9 and Amos 3:9 (also with *r'h* "see").

under the sun. See Notes at 1:3.

the tears of the oppressed. The singular noun *dim'at* is collective here, as it is in Isa 25:8; Pss 39:13 [Eng v 12]; 42:4 [Eng v 3]). The noun *'ăšūqîm* "(the) oppressed" is identical to *'ăšūqîm* "(acts of) oppression" in the first instance, but the next line suggests that oppressed people are meant here.

power comes from the hand of their oppressors. There is no need to emend *miyyad* "from (the) hand" to *bĕyad* "in (the) hand," as is sometimes suggested. Jerome has *in manibus* "in the hands," but that may be a paraphrase. All other witnesses support MT.

but there is none to comfort them. Some commentators either excise the final *wĕʾên lāhem mĕnaḥēm* as a dittography (Siegfried) or emend *mĕnaḥēm* to read *mĕnaqqēm* "avenger" (Galling, Scott), *minnaḥēm* "avenging oneself" (G. R. Driver, "Problems and Solutions," pp. 227–28), *manḥēm* "one leading them" (Dahood, "Phoenician Background," p. 272), *môšîaʿ* "savior" (Graetz), or the like. But the repetition is reinforcing here (cf. the repetition of "wickedness" in 3:16).

2. I extolled the dead. Hebrew *wĕšabbēaḥ ʾănî ʾet-hammētîm*. There is no evidence for assuming that the text originally had *wĕšibbaḥtî* (cf. 8:15), as is sometimes suggested (S. R. Driver in *BHK²*). The Piel infinitive absolute is used here in place of a finite verb (GKC § 113.gg), a usage that is well attested in the Northwest Semitic languages, corresponding to the *qatāli anāku* construction in the Amarna letters (cf. Joüon-Muraoka §123.x.Note 1). Here the infinitive absolute is followed by an independent personal pronoun, as in *wĕnahăpôk hûʾ* "it has been changed" in Esth 9:1. The same construction is found in the Phoenician inscription from Karatepe (*mlʾ ʾnk* "I filled," *pʿl ʾnk* "I acquired," *trq ʾnk* "I eradicated," etc.; see *KAI* 26.A.I.6, 6–7, 9) and in the Kilamuwa inscription (*wškr ʾnk* "and I hired," see *KAI* 24.7–8). Cf. also Ugaritic *ngš ank* "I encountered" (*KTU* 1.6.II.21). In any case, the sentiment expressed here may be compared with what we find in other texts (Jer 20:14–15; Job 3:1–26; Sir 30:17; 40:28). In *The Admonitions of Ipuwer* from Egypt one reads:

Lo, great and small <say>, "I wish I were dead,"
Little children say, "He should not have made me live!"

(*AEL* I, p. 153).

still. The form *ʿădenâ* (perhaps to be pointed *ʿădennâ*) and the related form *ʿāden* in 4:3 may be contracted from *ʿad-hēnnâ* (1 Chron 9:18; 12:30) and *ʿad-hēn*, respectively (*HALAT*, p. 749). This remains the simplest explanation. Both forms appear only in Ecclesiastes and nowhere else in Hebrew.

3. one who has never existed. The phrase *ʾēt ʾăšer-ʿăden lōʾ hāyâ* "the one who has never existed" cannot be the accusative of *wĕšabbēaḥ ʾănî* "I extolled" in v 2, as it is sometimes argued (Barton, Lauha, Whybray). LXX and Syr take the phrase to be nominative in spite of the presence of the *nota accusativi*. Ketib of Jer 38:16 has *ʾēt ʾăšer* as nominative, and the Mishnah has the related *ʾt š-* in the nominative in *Ber.* 3:1; *Dem.* 2:5; *Šeqal.* 8:7; *Giṭ.* 9:7. This usage of *ʾēt* is not limited to late texts (*contra* Schoors, *Pleasing Words*, p. 191; see BDB, p. 85), but it is certainly more frequent in exilic and postexilic Hebrew.

has been done. MT has the perfect (*naʿăśâ*), which is supported by Syr and Targ.

under the sun. See Notes at 1:3.

4. I saw that every toil and every achievement. Lit. "I saw every toil and every achievement of work, that. . . ." The objects of what is observed, *'et-kol-'āmāl wĕ'ēt kol-kišrôn*, anticipate the assessment introduced by *kî*, as in 2:24; 8:17, and Gen 1:4; 6:2; 12:14; Exod 2:2; Ps 25:19; Prov 23:21; etc. (GKC §117.h). The singular demonstrative *hî'* refers collectively to the things observed, namely, toil and accomplishment. For the meaning of *kišrôn*, see Notes at 2:21. On the use of *'ēt* with an indefinite noun, see Notes at 3:15.

come from one's envy of another. The phrase *qin'at-'îš mērē'ēhû*, lit. "envy of a person from another," refers to human competitiveness. The noun *qin'â* means "rivalry" in Isa 11:13, a meaning attested also in the Talmud (*b. B. Bat.* 21a). The precise relation of this envy with the preceding "toil and achievement" is, however, ambiguous. Grammatically one cannot ascertain if *qin'at-'îš* is the cause or the result of human strivings. One could reasonably say that toil and success cause envy, so that "envy" is the result. Yet, it is clear in the wisdom tradition that *qin'â* is always the cause of self-destructive behavior (Prov 6:34; 14:30; 27:4; Job 5:2). The relation between human striving and envy is clarified to some extent by Prov 14:30, which also manifests the same syntactical ambiguity: *ḥayyê bĕśārîm lēb marpē' ûrĕqab 'ăṣāmôt qin'â* "a sound physique (comes from) a serene mind, but rottenness of body (comes from) envy."

this, too, is vanity and a pursuit of wind. See Notes at 1:2 and 1:14.

5. *Fools fold their hands.* This is a metaphor for relaxation or inactivity. One may compare the expression with *ḥibbūq yādayim liškab* "a folding of hands to rest" (Prov 6:10; 24:33), which is synonymous with the "sleep" and "slumber" of the lazy fool.

and eat their flesh. The meaning of *wĕ'ōkēl bĕśārô* is disputed. It has been proposed that *bĕśārô* means "his meat" and the aphorism in v 5 means that the fool does nothing and still is able to eat well (Ginsburg, *Coheleth*, pp. 324–25; Lohfink, *Kohelet*, pp. 36–37). Accordingly, v 5 supports what is said in v 4: that effort causes nothing but envy and even fools who are lazy do not become destitute. On the contrary, even fools may eat well. It is doubtful, however, if *bĕśārô* means "his meat." The noun *bāśār* occurs four other times in the book, always referring to the human body, not to food (2:3; 5:5 [Eng v 6]; 11:10; 12:12). Indeed, the noun *bāśār* with the pronominal suffix occurs ninety-seven other times in the Hebrew Bible, always referring to the body or part of the body, thus flesh. It never refers to one's own portion of food. In Exod 21:28 and 29:31 *bĕśārô* means "its flesh," referring to the flesh of an animal. If the eating of meat is meant, one would expect the noun without the suffix—"they eat flesh/meat," not "they eat their flesh." The suffixal form is confirmed by all textual witnesses. Qohelet is using the grotesque imagery of self-cannibalism to speak of self-destruction. Fools who are so lazy will end up devouring themselves. Apart from the obvious references to cannibalism (Lev 26:29; Deut 28:53; Jer 19:9; Ezek 39:18; Mic 3:3), the idiom *'ākal bāśār* is also used figuratively of the destruction of persons (Ps 27:2; Prov 30:14; and Isa 49:26).

6. *Better is a handful with repose.* One should assume the adverbial accusative with *nāḥat* "(with) rest" or "restfully" (see GKC §118.q), as Symm and Targ do, rather than take *kap nahat* as a construct chain meaning "a handful *of rest*" (so

LXX). One does not measure rest by handfuls. The noun *naḥat* does not refer to the folding of hands in v 5. It does not mean inactivity, but rather, quietness or peace (Eccl 6:5; 9:17; Prov 29:9; Isa 30:15). The Akkadian cognate *nēḫtu* refers to situations of peace and security, with absence of worry or trouble (*CAD* XI/2, pp. 150–51). Hebrew *mĕlō'-kap* refers to a very small amount (cf. 1 Kgs 17:12). The emphasis is on the limited nature of a handful, not on the fullness. In Egyptian Aramaic, *kp* "hand" is used for an extremely small measure, a third in length or in volume. The latter is the equivalent of a ladle or a small bowl (see *TAD* III, p. 295; B. Porten, *Archives from Elephantine* [Berkeley/Los Angeles: University of California, 1968], p. 93). Cf. Akkadian *kappu* "bowl" (*CAD* VIII, p. 188).

fistfuls with toil. Cf. Exod 9:8; Lev 16:12. It is, again, preferable to assume the adverbial accusative for *'āmāl*, rather than posit the presence of an enclitic *mem* (thus "fistfuls *of* toil"), as Dahood has suggested ("Northwest Semitic Philology," pp. 355–56). It is doubtful if repose could be measured by handfuls or toil by fistfuls. Nor would anyone, whether foolish or wise, require the instruction of a *ṭôb-saying* ("better than"-saying) to know that any amount of rest is preferable to twice the amount of toil. Thus, the comparison is not between an amount of rest and twice the amount of toil, but an amount of anything with peace *vs.* anything with toil. We may also compare similar sayings found elsewhere in wisdom literature (Prov 15:16; 16:8; 17:1). It is interesting to observe that the word *ḥōpen* "fist" is the Hebrew equivalent of Aramaic *ḥpn* "handful," a term used in the Persian period for the smallest measure of ration, either of grain or legumes (see Porten, *Archives from Elephantine*, pp. 70–72). We know from official records of distribution of ration to workers at Persepolis in the fifth century B.C.E. that 30 handfuls (*ḥpnn*) made 1 *griw*, and 3 *griws* made 1 *ardab*. These were the measures used throughout the empire in the fifth and fourth centuries B.C.E.

a pursuit of wind. See Notes at 1:14.

7. *Further, I saw.* See Notes on 4:1.

vanity. See Notes at 1:2. In this case *hebel* indicates something that is enigmatic.

under the sun. See Notes at 1:3.

8. *there are those who are alone.* The meaning of *'eḥād* is "a loner" or "a solitary one" (Isa 51:2; Ezek 33:24; Job 23:13). In Ugaritic, *aḥd* can mean "solitary one" or "a loner" (*KTU* 1.14.IV.21; cf. the parallel passage, *KTU* 1.14.II.43, where we have *yḥd* "single person" instead of *aḥd*). The *waw* in *wĕ'ên šēnî* is to be taken as the *waw explicativum*; it clarifies what *'eḥād* means (GKC §154.a.Note1b). The word *šēnî* is also a substantive, meaning "another, someone else," as in Akkadian *šanû* (see *CAD* XVII/1, pp. 395–96) and Ugaritic *tn* (see *KTU* 1.14.II.48–49, where *tn* "another" is parallel to *nkr* "stranger"). Thus, *yēš 'eḥād wĕ'ên šēnî* means, lit., "there is a single person, that is, without another" (NAB: "a solitary man with no companion"). Rashbam interprets the "other" as another person who would share the wealth: the miser is alone but refuses to take a partner who would share the earnings.

they do not even have children or siblings. In this case, *gam* is emphatic (see Schoors, *Pleasing Words*, pp. 132–33).

yet their eyes are dissatisfied with wealth. Here *gam* is adversative, as it is in 3:11 and 6:7. The verb *tiśbaʿ* is singular, hence numerous Hebrew MSS and some of the ancient versions (LXX, Syr, Targ) reflect the singular noun *ʿênô*, as *Qere* has it. But the plural reading of *Ketib* (supported by Vulg) is the *lectio difficilior* and probably correct; the singular form of the noun attempts to correct what is perceived to be a discrepancy. Objects grouped under a single conception, however, will frequently be treated as collective in Hebrew (GKC §145.k)—a few examples involve parts of the body: "eyes" (1 Sam 4:15; Mic 4:11), "hands" (Deut 21:7); "feet" (1 Kgs 14:6, 12; Ps 73:2). For the singular noun with *śbʿ*, see 1:8; for the dual noun with the same verb, see Prov 27:20. In Semitic psychology it is the eye that is the seat of desire; the eye desires what it sees (cf. 1:8; 2:10; 5:10 [Eng v 11]). In the *Proverbs of Ahiqar,* preserved in the Syriac version, one reads:

> My son, the eye of man is like a fountain of water,
> and it is not satisfied with riches until filled with dust.
>
> (APOT II, p. 737)

but for whom am I toiling. The switch from the third person to the first poses a difficult problem for the interpreter. The identity of the speaker is unknown: it is either Qohelet himself or the miser. Not surprisingly, therefore, interpreters sometimes add words to clarify the issue. So NEB: "'For whom,' he asks, 'am I toiling and denying myself the good things of life?'"

this, too, is vanity. See Notes at 1:2. "Vanity" here means an enigma, something that makes no sense.

terrible business. See Notes at 1:13.

9. *Better are two than one.* Lit. "Better are *the* two than *the* one." The definite articles on the numerals probably refer to those who are not solitary (that is, those with companions, partners, or family) and those who are solitary, respectively. Ogden finds it significant that in this probable adaptation of a numerical saying the greater number appears before the lesser ("two . . . one"), instead of the usual numerical saying, where we have a number (N) followed by higher number (N + 1). He surmises, therefore, that the author reversed the order "to insist that there are advantages to accrue at times from 'more' rather than 'less'" ("'Better'-Proverb," p. 499; see also "The Mathematics of Wisdom," pp. 452–53). Ogden may well be correct about the significance of this irregularity, but the reversal took place much earlier than Qohelet. There is an Akkadian fragment of the *Gilgamesh Epic* that may have contained teachings very similar to what we have in our passage (see Shaffer, "New Light on the 'Three-Ply Cord,'" pp. 159–60; B. Landsberger, "Zur vierten und siebenten Tafel des Gilgamesh-Epos," *RA* 62 [1968], pp. 108–9). Placed in its proper context in the *Gilgamesh Epic,* the text shows the same numerical sequence that we find in our passage, with the progress from one to three:

> One alone c[annot. . . .]
> Strangers [. . . .]

Slippery ground can[not. . . .]
Two . . . triplets[. . . .]
A three-stranded rope [. . . .]
. . . strong . . . two . . . [. . . .]

(Gilg V ii 20–25; CT 46, 21, rev.)

Shaffer has contended that this entire passage in Ecclesiastes has been influenced by the account in the Gilgamesh story (cf. also de Savignac, "La sagesse du Qôhéléth et l'épopée de Gilgamesh," pp. 321–22). In any case, the durability of this proverb is evident in its survival as a Malay folk saying, probably brought to the Malay Archipelago by Middle-Eastern traders: *tali yang tiga lembar itu ta'* *suang suang putus* "A three-ply cord is not readily snapped" (see R. Winstedt, *Malay Proverbs* [London: John Murray, 1950], p. 26).

because. The particle *'ăšer* is causal here (see Gen 30:18; 31:49; 34:13, 27; 42:21; Num 20:13; Deut 3:24). See also 8:11, 15; 10:15.

10. *if either of them should fall.* There is no need to emend *yippōlû* to the singular (S. R. Driver in *BHK*²), or to supply *haššěnayim* "the two" as the subject (Galling). The latter has no textual evidence; the former has the support of a few Hebrew MSS, but it is the *lectio facilior*, probably harmonistic and anticipates *yippōl* in the next line. Syr, Vulg, and Targ translate the verb as a singular, but this does not mean that their *Vorlage(n)* had the singular form. Rather, they probably assumed, as we should also do, that the plural verb is used distributively: "if they fall" = "if either of them falls" (cf. Gen 11:3; Judg 6:29). LXX also reflects a plural form.

alas for them. Instead of *wě'îlô*, twenty-three Hebrew MSS read *wě'î lô* "and alas for him," an attractive alternative in the light of *'î-lāk* in 10:16. The meaning corresponds to *'ôy-lô* in earlier Hebrew. We note 1QIsa^a 6:5 has *'y* for *'wy* in MT. So also LXX, Vulg, and Syr. One may compare Mishnaic Hebrew *'y*, as in *'y ly* "alas for me!" (*m. Yebam.* 13:7); *'y lhn* "alas for them!" (*Exod. Rabb.* §46), and so forth (cf. *b. Ta'an.* 7a; *Roš. Haš.* 19a; *Sanh.* 11a). The use of *'y* instead of *'wy* is a late innovation (see Schoors, *Pleasing Words*, p. 149). Here *lô* anticipates the subject, *hā'eḥād* (see GKC §131.n).

when they fall. Hebrew *šeyyippôl*, lit. "when he (that is, the solitary one) falls." It is likely that *še-* is temporal in this case, but one may also take the relative particle personally and translate: "(woe to the solitary one) *who* falls."

11. *they will be warm.* Hebrew *wěham lāhem*, lit. "it (will be) warm for them." The *waw* here is the *waw apodosis* (see Notes at 3:19 and GKC §143.d).

12. *though the one may be overpowered.* Hebrew *wě'im-yitqěpô hā'eḥād*, lit. "and though one may overpower him, the one who is alone." For *yitqěpô* instead of *yitqěpēhû* (so *titqěpēhû* in Job 14:20), cf. *yirděpô* instead of *yirděpēhû* in Hos 8:3 (see GKC §60.d). The 3 ms object suffix is proleptic; it anticipates *hā'eḥād*, in the same way that *'î-lô* in v 10 anticipates *hā'eḥād* (see also Exod 2:6; Lev 13:57). The anticipatory object suffix is a feature of Northern Hebrew (see Notes on *ytnnw* at 2:21). The redundant use of the suffix is due probably to the ambiguity attendant upon the noun *hā'eḥād*. The subject of the verb is an impersonal

"one" who is made explicit in the 3 ms suffix of *negdô*. If not for this explicit reference, one might be tempted to read *yitqĕpû hā'eḥād*, "they may overpower the solitary one," an impersonal expression meaning the same thing as "the one who is alone may be overpowered." LXX (*epikrataiōthē*) and Syr (*n's̆n*) do not reflect the suffix, but this may simply mean that the translators did not think it necessary to reproduce the redundancy of the Hebrew. There is no need to emend MT, as some commentators do. It may be observed that all occurrences of *tqp* in the Hebrew Bible are late (Job 14:20; 15:24; Eccl 4:12; 6:10; Esth 9:29; 10:2; Dan 11:17).

the two together may resist. Hebrew *haššĕnayim ya'amdû negdô*, lit. "the two will stand before him." The antecedent of the 3 ms suffix in *negdô*, lit. "before him," is the impersonal subject of the verb *yitqĕpô* "one may overpower him." Although someone may overpower the solitary person, people in partnership with one another may be able to stand up to that someone.

13. *a youngster who is a commoner but wise.* Hebrew *yeled* usually means a child or a boy — that is, someone who has not reached full maturity. The companions of Rehoboam, who were about forty years old (assuming they were roughly as old as he) were, nevertheless, called *yĕlādîm*, perhaps derogatorily (1 Kgs 12:8, 10, 14; cf. Gen 4:23). The word *miskēn* occurs in Biblical Hebrew only here and in 9:15–16 (cf. also the related noun *miskēnût* in Deut 8:9), but it is well attested in Postbiblical Hebrew and cognates are found in Targumic Aramaic (Jastrow, *Dictionary*, pp. 807–8) and elsewhere. The word is usually translated "poor," but the word does not necessarily imply poverty. It is a loanword from Akkadian *muškēnu/maškēnu*, which was used already in Old Akkadian and Old Babylonian for people of ordinary status. The term indicates a less-than-noble social status, someone of the dependent class, as it were. It is frequently contrasted with royalty and nobility, but a *muškēnu* may also own slaves, land, and other property (see E. A. Speiser, "The Muškênum," in *Oriental and Biblical Studies* [eds. J. J. Finkelstein and M. Greenberg; Philadelphia: University of Pennsylvania, 1967], pp. 332–43; G. Buccellati, "A Note on the *muškēnum* as 'Homesteader,'" *Maarav* 7 [1991], pp. 91–99). So the issue in our passage is not economics but social status. Rashbam is correct, therefore, that *miskēn* "commoner" relates to *melek* "king," while *yeled* "youngster" relates to *zāqēn* "old" and *ḥākām* "wise" to *kĕsîl* "fool."

can no longer be admonished. Lit. "no longer knows to be admonished." This is a reference to the king's senility (cf. 6:8; 10:15). The point is that he disregards advice. The Hebrew verb *yd'* may mean "to care for, have regard" (Gen 39:6; Deut 33:9; Job 9:21). One may compare the usage of *idû* "to know" in Akkadian: *zēr ḫalgatî šunu [mā]mēti ša ili u adê ul idû* "they are an accursed people, they do not have regard for (lit. "know") any oath sworn by a god or any oath of allegiance (to the king)" (*ABL* 1237:16).

14. *for (one) . . . for (another).* C. C. Torrey perceives that a lacuna exists between vv 13 and 14, and proceeds to fill it with 10:1–17 ("The Problem of Ecclesiastes IV 13–16," pp. 175–77). The problems are exaggerated, however, and there is no textual evidence whatsoever for the proposed insertion. In fact, the

two *kî*-clauses give the rationale for the *ṭôb*-saying in v 13, with the first *kî*-clause referring to the destiny of the youngster, and the second to the fate of the old king.

prison. The form *hāsûrîm* (with long *ā*) is from *hāʾăsûrîm*, with the elision of *alep*. Cf. *hārammîm* "the Aramaeans" (2 Chron 22:5) with *hāʾărammîm* (2 Kgs 8:28), *hāšăpôt* "the Dung Gate" (Neh 3:13), and *hāʾašpôt* (Neh 3:14); also *māsōret* < *maʾăsōret* "bond" (Ezek 20:37). See GKC §68.i; BL §31.f. So some Hebrew MSS have *hʾsrym* instead of *hswrym*, supplying the "correct" reading. LXX, Symm, and Vulg also rightly understood the term to mean "prison" (cf. *bêt hāʾăsûrîm* in the Qere of Judg 16:21, 25; *bêt hāʾēsûr* in Jer 37:15). It should be noted, however, that the ancient Levantine prison was not a penitentiary. People were not thrown in prison for punishment or to be reformed. Rather, they were placed there usually for economic or political reasons (see K. van der Toorn, *ABD* V, pp. 468–69). In the Bible we read of people who were imprisoned because they were unable to pay their debts (Matt 18:28–30; Luke 12:58–59). Sometimes the members of a debtor's family, including children, were imprisoned (2 Kgs 4:1; Isa 50:1; Neh 5:5). We learn from the Aramaic papyri from North Saqqara that in Persian-period Egypt debtors were seized as prisoners, branded as slaves, their lands and other property confiscated (see Segal, *Aramaic Texts*, Nos. 3, 4). The prisoners were beaten and put to work until their debts were paid off (Segal, *Aramaic Texts*, No. 8.10; 28b.3–4; 30.5). One may note, too, that such debtors' prisons in North Saqqara were called *bt ʾsrn* (Segal, *Aramaic Texts*, No. 30.5; 50.9). From some Aramaic letters discovered at Hermopolis, one learns that a man and his son were imprisoned but released after a friend paid 6½ shekels (*TAD* I, 2.2; 2.6). Such debtors' prisons were also found in Mesopotamia during the Achaemenid period, as we know from the Murashu archives (see Cardascia, *Les archives des Murašû*, pp. 160–65). In any case, our passage is about the poor person who has made good. This unnamed person may be the wise *miskēn* mentioned in v 13.

went forth to reign. The subject of the verb is unclear, although the undistinguished youngster in v 13a is probably meant. There is no need to read the imperfect with LXX (*exeleusetai*).

though. The particle *gam* is concessive here, as it is in 6:7 (cf. BDB, p. 169).

born into his kingship. We should disregard the Masoretic accents and take *bĕmalkûtô nôlad* as corresponding in grammatical structure to *mibbêt hāsûrîm yāṣāʾ* "from the prison he went forth" in the parallel line. The stories of two persons are contrasted, each one's case being introduced by *kî*: one went forth from prison to be king, the other was born into kingship but became poor. The first person is the wise and young commoner; the second person is the old and foolish king. According to the Masoretic punctuation, the sentence reads: "though in his kingdom he was born poor."

is impoverished. The form *rāš* corresponds to *limlōk* in the parallel line; it is to be taken as the perfect (3 ms), not the participle or adjective. The perfect is attested in Ps 34:11 [Eng v 10], *kĕpîrîm rāšû wĕrāʿēbû* "young lions are deprived and starved." One may compare the reversal of fortune of this king to the fate of the king in the Ugaritic Legend of Kirta: *krt ḥtkn rš // krt grdš mknt* "Kirta our ruler is impoverished; Kirta is deprived of his dynasty" (*KTU* 1.14.I.1–11).

15. *I saw that all the living.* Lit. "I saw the living." The verse is elliptical.

those who walk about under the sun. This phrase is in apposition to *haḥayyîm* "the living." Thus, "those who walk about under the sun" simply means those who are alive. Cf. the Yaḥdun-Lim inscription from Mari: *ina maḥar Šamaš ayyittalak* "may (his descendants) not walk about before the sun" (see Dossin, "Iaḫdun-Lim," p. 17, line 31). See Notes at 1:3.

the next youngster. Some have proposed to delete *haššēnî* here as a meaningless addition or a gloss (Ehrlich), but it is difficult to see why anyone would add the word that has caused so much anguish for interpreters. All textual witnesses support its authenticity. The question really is what *haššēnî* means. Gordis takes *hay-yeled haššēnî* to be in apposition, thus, "the youngster, the second one (i.e., the successor)." Others suggest that the word means "the second" in rank or authority in the kingdom, thus someone who has risen to position of vizier, deputy, or the like (Hertzberg). It is most likely, however, that *haššēnî* simply means "the next," as in *bayyôm haššēnî* "the next day" (so Ellermeier, Fox). The point is that someone else will come along to take the throne. Cf. Akkadian *ina kussīšu šanûm uššab* "someone else will sit on his throne" (YOS 10 56 i 35).

who arises in his stead. In Late Biblical Hebrew, *'md* is frequently used in place of *qwm* (Ps 106:30; 1 Chron 20:4; 21:1; Dan 8:22–23, 25). Specifically, the verb may be used of people taking office (Ezra 2:63; 10:14). In contrast to the verbs in vv 13–15, the author uses the imperfect, *ya'ămōd*, which we should probably take as frequentative or habitual (see GKC §107.g). There is no tension between the perfect verb *rā'îtî* and the imperfect *ya'ămōd*, nor can *rā'îtî* strictly mean "foresee," as Fox surmises (*Contradictions*, pp. 207–8).

16. *there is no limit to all the multitude.* Cf. *'ên qēṣ lĕkol-'ămālô* (v 8).

to all before whom he comes. Hebrew *lĕkōl 'ăšer-hāyâ lipnêhem.* It is tempting to read *yihyeh* with a single Hebrew MS (Kennicott no. 107), but this is unnecessary (cf. the Notes on 1:12). Syr, Vulg, and Targ apparently reflect Hebrew *hyw lpnyw*, assuming that the people came "before him (the king)." This is a misunderstanding of the text. Kings are typically described as going before their subjects (1 Sam 18:16; 2 Chron 1:10). The author has in mind the king going before the vast multitudes to acknowledge their allegiance.

Indeed. The *kî* here must be emphatic.

although. Here *gam* is concessive (see v 14).

this, too, is vanity and a pursuit of wind. See Notes at 1:2 and 1:14.

COMMENT

In 4:1–16 we get the first series of *ṭôb-sayings* ("better than"-sayings). Another series is found in 7:1–12 (compare Sir 30:14–17; 40:18–27). There are many examples of this type of sayings in Israelite wisdom literature (Prov 15:16–17; 16:8; 28:6; Sir 29:22; 30:14). There are also numerous examples of this type of sayings in the Egyptian instructional literature which may, in fact, have provided the models for the Israelite proverbs (*Amenemope* VIII.19–20; IX.5–8; *Ankhsheshonq* XVIII.5; XXI.20–22). The sages of the ancient Near East were always ready to proffer such sayings about relative good, it seems. Now, even Qohelet, who has so assiduously asserted that there is no advantage under the sun, gives a series of *ṭôb-sayings*.

We must note, however, that this series immediately follows the conclusion in Chapter 3 that there is "nothing better" (*'ên ṭôb*) than to enjoy oneself (3:12, 22). First the author states baldly that there is "nothing better," and then he proceeds to give a series of *ṭôb-sayings*. A similar contradiction is evident in 6:10–7:14. There the text begins with the claim that no one knows what is good (*ṭôb*) for humanity (6:11), and then it proceeds to give a series of proverbs about what is better (*ṭôb*) in 7:1–12. The introductory claim that no one knows what is good thus relativizes the claim of the sages to know what is good or better. So, too, the assertion that there is "nothing better" but to enjoy oneself must be kept in mind as one reads the *ṭôb-sayings*.

The new literary unit (4:1–16) consists of five sections pertaining to human responses to life-situations. Each of the first two sections (vv 1–3, 4–6) *concludes* with a *ṭôb-saying*; each of the last two sections (vv 9–12, 13–16) is *introduced* by a *ṭôb-saying*. In the middle section (vv 7–8), however, there is no *ṭôb-saying*. There is only the observation of a terrible situation of people who are single, who apparently have no kinship, friendship, or partnership with anyone else, but who, nevertheless, cannot enjoy themselves. One who toils in this way deprives oneself of the only good one can have, namely, the possibility of enjoyment. This seems to be the pivotal section of the entire unit.

Better Not to Have Lived (4:1–3)
Qohelet says he saw "*all* the oppressions" that occur in life (v 1). This is a hyperbole that must not be taken literally. The author intends to convey the sense that he saw the pervasiveness of oppression. Perhaps he means that he has seen all kinds of oppressions. This prevalence is further indicated by the repetition of the root '*šq* "oppress": "oppressions," "the oppressed," "their oppressors" all occur in one verse. The text does not say who the oppressors are, nor what their outrages entail, however. It states only that in the face of this pervasive oppression, "there is none to comfort" the oppressed. This repeated complaint (twice in v 1) echoes the refrain "none to comfort" in the opening chapter of the book of Lamentations (Lam 1:2, 9, 16, 17, 21), which climaxes with the charge that tragedy was effected (*'āśâ*) by none other than God (Lam 1:21). In the book of Job, too, culpability for the existence of oppression in the world is traced to God. Job complains that it seems good to the deity to oppress (*'āšaq*) the innocent and to endorse the plans of the wicked (Job 10:3). In such a situation, Job finds life to be despicable and death the better alternative (Job 10:1, 18–22; cf. 3:1–21). Even though Job is innocent, "there is none to deliver" him from God's hand (Job 10:7). In contrast to such texts, one finds no explicit tracing of culpability to God in Ecclesiastes (see Bianchi, "'Essi non hanno chi li consoli,'" pp. 299–307). Rather, in-

justice is simply laid out as a fact of life, something that everyone who is alive sees.

The author goes on to say that he extolled those who have already died more than those who are still living (v 2). That does not mean that death is a happy prospect to be eagerly anticipated. He does not speak positively of death in the future, but of those who have already passed away. The point is that the living still have to witness the injustices of life, whereas the dead have already done that and no longer have to do so. This point is underscored in the *ṭôb-saying* in v 3, which concludes that what is better than being alive or dead is not to have come into existence at all and not to have seen the injustices of the world. But that is, in fact, not an option for the humans, inasmuch as they already are living and have already been witnessing life's inevitable tragedies. The alternative of not having lived is not an option that people can choose. The *ṭôb-saying* thus points to the irony of human existence: what is really "better" in this regard is not within the grasp of mortals. People, by their very existence, have already been assigned their lot. Life is just so to Qohelet. For him, to be is to see these tragic things that happen in life. What is better, then, is not to somehow be shielded from life's painful realities but, as he intimates in 3:22, to enjoy oneself whenever it is possible to do so.

Better to Have a Little (4:4–6)

Qohelet begins to comment on his observation of "every toil and every achievement of work." As in v 1, he uses hyperbole to indicate the severity and prevalence of the problem in his generation. It appears to him that *every* human striving is the result of envy. Competition drives people to excessive efforts. This assessment is in accord with the wisdom tradition. According to Prov 14:30, a serene mind results in a sound body, but envy is destructive to the physical self. Moreover, it is acknowledged in the wisdom tradition that envy causes one to engage in destructive behavior (Prov 6:34; 27:4), so that it may even be said that envy destroys the fool (Job 5:2). According to Qohelet, it is this destructive element that drives people to toil and to bring even more pressure on themselves. This, he says, is also "vanity and a pursuit of wind." Toil and success driven by competition are ephemeral and utterly unreliable.

Given what Qohelet says in v 4 (that competition drives one to self-destruction), one may perhaps conclude that inactivity is advocated. That is not his point, however. The author calls to mind traditional teachings against laziness ("fools fold their hands"). The idiom "to fold the hands" is found elsewhere in the wisdom literature of the Bible to be synonymous with "rest" or "sleep"; it refers to idleness (Prov 6:10; 24:33). It is what the lazy fool prefers, and the result of this inactivity is poverty and want (see 10:18; also Prov 10:4–5; 19:15; 20:13). Qohelet's version of the proverb is more poignant: the fools who do nothing will not only be poor and hungry; they will end up eating their own flesh! Qohelet is using the grotesque imagery of self-cannibalism to speak of self-destruction. Apart from the obvious references to cannibalism (Lev 26:29; Deut 28:53; Jer 19:9;

Ezek 39:18; Mic 3:3), the idiom "eat the flesh" is also used figuratively of the destruction of persons (Ps 27:2; Isa 49:26). Thus, vv 4 and 5 present paradoxical realities: human effort (manifested in competition) is unreliable (v 4), but the lack of effort (the folding of hands) brings destruction (v 5).

The resolution of the dilemma is stated in the *ṭôb-saying* in v 6. The word translated "repose" does not mean inactivity; it does not refer to the "folding of hands" in v 5. Rather, it refers to a situation of peace and security, one that is free of worry and trouble. We may also compare similar sayings (Prov 15:16; 16:8; 17:1). The point is that the smallest amount of anything (a handful, a fistful) is better than twice as much in toil and futile pursuits. It is true that one cannot have it all (v 4) and one cannot do nothing (v 5), but there is the possibility of having only a little. One may not be able to control life and dictate what one should have, but one can navigate through it as best one can, taking advantage of whatever is available at the moment.

Depriving Oneself of Good (4:7–8)

Unlike the other sections in this chapter, this one does not contain a *ṭôb-saying*. The opening words in v 7 seem to signal a new turn, and the mention of the single person (*'eḥād*) seems to lead to the "one" (*hā'eḥād*) in v 9. Yet, the reference to the futility of toil and the dissatisfaction with wealth link these verses to the preceding section.

Qohelet calls attention to a "vanity," a ridiculous and enigmatic situation. He refers to the case of people who are solitary and "without anyone else" (see the Notes). These are loners, people who are unrelated to and unconnected with other people. The medieval commentator, Rashbam, speculates that this verse refers to misers who refuse to accept anyone as a partner because they do not want to share their wealth. They have neither friends nor kin and, yet, there is no limit to their toil. They cannot resist toiling, it seems. Qohelet may be thinking of the fool who does not cease to labor for the future, even though there is no one to whom the fruit of toil can be passed on (2:18–23), or to the obsessive individual who must have more and more, even though there is none with whom to share whatever benefits there are (5:9–6:12 [Eng 5:10–6:12]). In both instances, the problem is that people are somehow unable to enjoy the present.

The ridiculousness of the situation is highlighted by an abrupt rhetorical question in the first person: "but for whom do I toil and deprive myself of good?" The identity of the speaker is unclear. Either Qohelet is so incensed by the ridiculous situation in which he thinks every mortal is somehow caught, and so interrupts his own thoughts, or he imagines the miser asking that question. The latter is more likely. The point of the question is clear, in any case: there is no use toiling and depriving oneself of pleasure if one has no one with whom to share the benefits either in the present or the future. Thus Qohelet concludes that this, too, is vanity, a ridiculous situation and a terrible preoccupation for mortals.

Better Not to Be Alone (4:9–12)

The mention of the solitary one (*'eḥād*) in vv 7–8 probably prompted these comments on the benefits of being with others. In contrast to the solitary person who toils for nothing and enjoys no good (v 8), those who are partnered (literally "the two") have a benefit in their toil that is called "good" (v 9). And this good benefit is evident in three instances (vv 10–12).

In the first place, people who are together can help one another when either of them gets into trouble (v 10). The author is probably thinking here of the perils of traveling alone through the wilderness. The loner who falls into a pit (cf. Prov 26:27; 28:10, 14; 28:18), presumably a camouflaged trap set for animals (see Comment at 10:8), is doomed. It is safer to travel with others: when either one falls into such a pit, the other will be able to lend a helping hand.

Moreover, people who are together can keep one another warm at night, whereas the loner will have difficulty keeping warm (v 11). Again, the author is probably referring here to people who are traveling through the wilderness. Under normal circumstances, people kept themselves warm by building a fire or burning coals (Isa 44:15–16; 57:14; Ezek 24:11), but when it was impossible or inadequate to have the warmth of fire, people often relied on the warmth of the human body by lying together under the same cover. The human body has this potential. Thus, David was warmed in his old age by the body of a Shunammite woman (1 Kgs 1:1–2) and the prophet Elisha saved the child of a woman by lying upon him until the body of the child became warm (2 Kgs 4:32–34). So people who are cold can keep one another warm with their bodies. The loner cannot have this benefit of having another.

Finally, there is strength in numbers when one is attacked. A loner is an easy prey to robbers, but people can stand up to the attackers together (v 12). Qohelet cites a proverb that illustrates the advantage of having associates: "the three-ply cord will not readily snap." Interpreters are sometimes troubled by the apparent introduction of another numerical element beyond "the one" and "the two," and they wonder about the felicity of the *three*-ply cord imagery in Qohelet's argument about the advantages of "the two." One should not be literalistic in interpreting the numerical values, however. The author is simply contending that there is safety and strength in numbers. To illustrate his point, Qohelet probably reworked an old numerical saying (see Prov 30:15, 18), adding his own interpretation and illustrations (see Comment on 3:1–15). A small Akkadian fragment of the *Gilgamesh Epic* apparently cites a similar saying, referring to a "three-ply cord." The context and meaning of this Mesopotamian numerical saying are clarified by a fuller account in Sumerian, where Gilgamesh is reminding his friend Enkidu that there is safety and strength in numbers:

Two men will not die; the towed boat will not sink.
A three-ply cord cannot be cut.

The point of the proverb in the context of the *Gilgamesh Epic* is that people are better able to cope with crises if there is solidarity and if they help one another. The loner loses out on this score. It is probable that Qohelet adapted such a numerical proverb for his own purpose. The point of the whole passage is not, as commentators sometimes suppose, that "two is better but three is best." Rather,

Qohelet intimates that because life's journey is difficult and perilous, it is better that one not face it alone. It is not that there is absolute certainty in numbers. The benefit is, rather, only relative. All advantages are only relative to Qohelet. One may note that the noun *ḥûṭ* "cord" is elsewhere not something of exceptional strength. This is evident in the story of Samson, where Delilah is said to have brought new ropes to bind Samson because he easily "snapped" the old ones "like a cord" (see Judg 16:12). The three-strand cord may indeed snap, but such a reinforced cord will not snap as readily as the single-strand one. The strength is only relative. So, too, Qohelet means that it is "better" to have others around than to be a loner.

Better to Start Out Poorly (4:13–16)

In 4:13–16 we find a tantalizing text. The opening *ṭôb-saying* seems clear enough, but the details which illustrate the saying are rather obscure and confusing. The entire passage has a historical ring to it, tempting scholars to identify the figures in the account. Those who find historical allusions in the passage are divided, however, about the nature of the allusions. On the one hand, there are those who take the persons mentioned to be figures from the distant past. Thus, the youngster of humble origins and the senile old king are, respectively, interpreted as Abraham and Nimrod, Joseph and Pharaoh, David and Saul, Jeroboam and Solomon, Rehoboam and Solomon, Joash and Amaziah. The narrative traditions of the Bible do not provide a perfect fit for any of the theories, however. Nor need one assume that the principle figures in the passage are all Israelites; they could just as well be legendary figures in Canaanite, Mesopotamian, Egyptian, or even Persian lore. On the other hand, there are those who find in the passage references to contemporaneous persons. Thus, depending on one's dating of the book, the young upstart and the old king are thought to refer respectively to Cyrus and Astyges, the High Priest Onias and Joseph the Tobiad, Antiochus III and Ptolemy Philopater, Ptolemy Philopater and Antiochus Epiphanes, Antiochus Epiphanes and Alexander Balas, Antiochus Epiphanes and Demetrius I, Ptolemy IV and Ptolemy V, Herod and his son Alexander, and so forth (see Schunck, "Drei Seleukiden im Buche Kohelet?" pp. 192–201).

It is tempting to place the figures in Qohelet's time, for in 10:16–17, another passage that has a historical ring, we also have allusions to a *na'ar*, either a youngster or a parvenu, who has become king. There is also the tantalizing account of the wise commoner (*miskēn ḥākām*) pitted against a certain "great king" (9:13–15). Each of these passages may easily be explained as a story invented by the author to make a point. They may all be *Beispielerzählungen* (Example Stories). Together, however, these three passages create a historical feeling. They seem to point to a historical situation known to Qohelet's audience. Unfortunately, scholars know very little of the political history of the period when the book was probably composed. So one cannot be certain.

The *ṭôb-saying* in v 13 compares two alternatives and it judges one to be better than the other. On the one hand, there is the one called *yeled* "a youngster," a word that was traditionally associated with immaturity. This youngster is said to be *miskēn* "a commoner," a term that indicates undistinguished sociopolitical status, usually with its economic implications (see Notes). But this person, although undistinguished and ordinary, is also wise. On the other hand, there is a king who, in contrast to the wise but young commoner, is "old." Traditionally such a one should have earned the respect of others and be in a position to give advice (Job 32:4–7; Prov 16:10, 13). But this old king is a fool who no longer heeds admonition. Those are the realities: an undistinguished but wise youngster, or an experienced but foolish king. And in the face of those imperfect alternatives, the one is said to be better than the other.

Qohelet then goes on to support and illustrate his *ṭôb-saying* by two clauses introduced by *kî* "for" (v 14). On the one hand, there is one who went from prison to become king. Although it is possible that this clause tells how the old king got to be in his position, it is more likely, in the light of the next line, that it refers to a reversal of fortune for the undistinguished youngster. The background of this person's initial imprisonment is obscure to the modern reader, but Qohelet's audience was probably acquainted with the situation, whether it was contemporaneous, legendary, or historical. It must be remembered that the prison in antiquity was not a penitentiary, a place in which criminals are locked up for punishment and in hope of reform. Rather, people were thrown in it largely for economic and political reasons. The prison was a source of cheap labor. It was a place where one may be forced to pay off a debt. Thus people who were unable to pay off their debts on their own may be forced to go to prison. Sometimes even the debtor's family, including children, were imprisoned. So our text is not referring to a criminal, but probably to a poor person. The *miskēn* "commoner" in this case is a poor person. This is the story of a pauper who left poverty behind to become king. In context, it seems likely that Qohelet still has in mind the commoner who was young but wise.

In contrast to the pauper who rose to become king is another reversal. The text speaks of one who was born into kingship but became impoverished. We think of the old king who was too foolish or senile to accept advice. Taking vv 13 and 14 together, we gather that there were two reversals. The young commoner (apparently a poor person) was in prison but went on to become king. By contrast, the king was born into the royal family but became impoverished. And the former situation is judged to be "better" — that is, it is better to start poor but end up well, than to start well and end up poor.

In v 15, the author seems to shift his focus (note also "I saw" in vv 1, 4, 7). He speaks of "the next youngster" (or "another youngster"). This is apparently not the same youngster of vv 13–14. As in vv 1 and 4, Qohelet uses hyperbole to stress his point: *all* living persons are, or will be, with this "next youngster," who arises to take the place of the one before (v 15), and there will be no limit to the crowds (v 16). Qohelet is observing a reality of life: people will always gravitate toward the new underdog-turned-hero. Every generation will have its new hero. The new youngster will, as always, have seemingly limitless support when he comes to power: "there will be no limit to the multitude." According to the wisdom tradition, it was the glory of the king to have a multitude of people with him, whereas "the ruler without people is ruined" (Prov 14:28). It follows, then, that this "next youngster" is eminently better than the senile old king—perhaps he who had once been the young upstart himself. The glory of the king is only ephemeral.

Qohelet goes on to warn that the next generation will not "rejoice in him" (*yiśmĕḥû-bô*). The idiom he uses here may indicate acceptance of the king's rule. In the story of Abimelech's claim of kingship, those who wish to go with him are told to "rejoice in Abimelech" (*śimḥû ba'ăbîmelek*) so that he will also rejoice in them (Judg 9:19). A psalm celebrating deity's kingship ends with the imperative: "rejoice in YHWH" (Ps 97:12; cf. Ps 32:11). History repeats itself. Like nature's routines, historical events occur in cycles (1:3–11). What goes around comes around. The reversal of fortune for the young upstart in vv 13–14 is said to be "better" but that advantage does not last; he himself gets caught in the cycle of history and he ends up as the old king, being replaced by "the next youngster." In the end, then, Qohelet casts doubt on the durability of the things that are better. Even those that are "better" are not ultimately enduring or reliable. Even the wise, who gain success through tremendous disadvantage, must nevertheless face the same fate as the foolish old king. Relative good is not good enough. So Qohelet concludes that "this, too, is vanity and a pursuit of wind." That which is better proves eventually to be unreliable.

PART I.B. ETHICS:
COPING WITH UNCERTAINTY

I.B.1. ATTITUDE BEFORE GOD (5:1–7 [HEB 4:17–5:6])

5 ¹Watch your steps when you go to the house of God: it is more acceptable to give heed than for the fools to give a sacrifice, for they do not recognize that they are doing evil.

²Do not be hasty with your mouth, nor let your heart rush to bring forth a matter before God, for God is in heaven but you are on earth. Therefore let your words be few, ³for dreams come with much preoccupation and the voice of the fool with many words.

⁴When you make a vow to God, do not be slack to fulfill it, for there is no pleasure in fools; fulfill what you vow! ⁵Better that you not vow than that you should vow and not fulfill.

⁶Do not permit your mouth to bring condemnation to your body, and do not say before the messenger that it is an error — lest God be angry at your voice and take away the work of your hands. ⁷For vacuous dreams are in abundance, and there are words aplenty. But as for you, fear God!

NOTES

5 1 [Heb 4:17]. *Watch your steps.* This translation assumes the dual noun, *rglyk*, with *Ketib. Qere* has the singular, as do numerous Hebrew MSS, LXX, Syr, Vulg, and Targ. There are many analogies for the singular (Pss 26:12; 119:105; Job 23:11; Prov 1:15; 3:26; 4:26–27), but the dual is also well attested (Pss 31:9 [Eng v 8]; 40:3 [Eng v 2]; 56:14 [Eng v 13]; 119:59). The meaning of the text is not affected whether one reads the singular or plural.

when. Since LXX usually renders *ka'ăšer* with *kathōs* (cf. 5:3, 14 [Eng vv 4, 15]; 8:7; 9:2), the translation *en hǭ ean* may reflect Hebrew *ba'ăšer*, a reading also attested in a few Hebrew MSS (Kennicott nos. 30, 99, 180, 693). This is probably a simple case of graphic confusion of *bet* and *kap*. The reading in MT should be retained.

the house of God. It is probable that *bêt hā'ĕlōhîm* refers to the temple, not the synagogue, since sacrifice is mentioned. The expression *bêt hā'ĕlōhîm* is used of the second temple in Jerusalem (Ezra 3:8; 6:22; 8:36; 10:1, 6, 9; etc.).

it is more acceptable. The form *qārôb* may be analyzed as an adjective or an infinitive absolute. In light of the frequent juxtaposition of the imperative of *qrb* with the imperative or infinitive of *šm'* (Deut 5:24; Isa 34:1; 48:16), it is reasonable to posit that *qārôb* here is the infinitive absolute substituting for the imperative (GKC §113.bb; the normal imperative is *qĕrab*), thus meaning "draw near (to listen)." Thus, Aq, Syr, and Vulg render *qārôb* with an imperative force (so also KJV: "be more ready to hear"; NIV: "Go near to listen"). The infinitive absolute of *qrb* is not attested anywhere, however, and the comparative *min* in *mittēt* makes this reading problematic. In light of the comparative *min*, the presence of which is confirmed by the ancient versions, some commentators have assumed an ellipsis, with *ṭôb* as the unexpressed element in the thought of the writer (cf. 9:17; cf. GKC §133.e), thus, "(it is better) to draw near than to obey" (so ASV; RSV). But apart from the need to assume an ellipsis, the syntax of the verse is awkward, with the juxtaposition of an infinitive absolute and a prefixed infinitive construct. It is easier to take *qārôb* as an adjective meaning "presentable" or "acceptable" (so NJPS). This meaning of the adjective is attested in 1 Kgs 8:59, "let these my words, with which I pleaded before YHWH, be acceptable (*qĕrōbîm*) to YHWH."

to give heed. Comparison of this verse with 1 Sam 15:22 has prompted translators to interpret *lišmōa'* here as referring to obedience. Qohelet's emphasis is not on obedience, however, but on attention and caution before God. Moreover, in the verses that follow, Qohelet warns against hasty promises and excessive speech. In contrast to the approach of noisy fools, it is better that one should listen, rather than speak. This understanding of *lišmōa'* is consistent with the usage of *šm'* elsewhere in the book, where the verb always means "to listen" or "to give heed," and never "to obey" (1:8; 7:5 [twice], 21; 9:16, 17; 12:13).

than for the fools to give a sacrifice. Lit. "than the fools' giving a sacrifice." LXX (supported by SyrH, but not Aq and Theod) reflects *zbḥk* "your sacrifice," with the dittography of *kap*.

for they do not recognize that they are doing evil. Hebrew *kî-'ênām yôdě'îm la'ăśôt rā'*, lit. "they do not know of doing evil." Since the obvious subject is *hak-kĕsîlîm* "the fools," *kî-'ênām yôdě'îm la'ăśôt rā'* can hardly mean "they do not know how to do evil." Fools certainly know how to do evil; the problem is that they do not know how to do good. Although the ancient versions generally support MT, commentators usually emend by (1) substituting *ṭôb* "good" for *rā'* "evil" (thus, "they do not know how to do *good*"), (2) inserting *ṭôb* in the text to yield *ṭôb 'ô rā'* or *ṭôb wārā'* (i.e. "fools do not know how to do *good or* evil"), (3) reading *kî 'im* "except" at the beginning ("fools do not know anything *except* to do evil"), and (4) assuming haplography of *mem* and reading *kî-'ênām yôdě'îm*

<mi>lla‘ăśôt rā‘ "they do not know *except* to do evil." The first three options must be rejected for want of evidence; they are also graphically too distant from the text attested in MT. The last emendation is the most plausible of the proposals, but it requires that *min* has the meaning "except" or "but," a meaning it does not have. There is, in fact, no need to emend the text. The idiom *yāda‘ lě-* here means "to know of," thus, "to recognize, acknowledge." We may compare the idiom with *yāda‘tā lě’iwwaltî* "you know of my folly" = "you recognize my folly," Ps 69:6 (Eng v 5). In Deut 33:9, *yāda‘* "acknowledge" is parallel to *hikkîr* "to recognize": "he did not recognize his kin; he did not acknowledge his children" (see also 2 Sam 7:20; Jer 3:13; 14:20; Isa 59:12). Thus, *yāda‘ la‘ăśôt rā‘* means "to know of doing evil," that is, "to recognize doing evil." It does not mean "to know *how to do* evil." One may compare Akkadian *la mudû arna* "one who knows no wrongdoing," an expression meaning "one who does not recognize wrongdoing," not "one who is without wrongdoing" (see *BWL*, p. 116). The expression occurs in the Akkadian version of a bilingual inscription found at Ugarit, a text that parallels our passage in more ways than one:

> One who acknowledges no guilt rushes to his god,
> Without thinking he quickly raises his hands (in prayer) to the god.
> . . . his guilt. . . .
> A man in ignorance rushes to his god.

> (*BWL*, p. 116, lines 10–13)

The text is concerned with proper attitude before a god. It warns against haste in taking oaths and uttering prayers. Some people are so arrogant, it seems, they do not even recognize that their hasty words and actions before a god are wrong. Qohelet, similarly, speaks of fools who are so stupid that they do not even recognize that they are doing wrong.

2 [Heb 5:1]. *Do not be hasty with your mouth.* Lit. "Do not be hasty in regard to your mouth." The parallelism of *bhl* with *mhr* suggests that the former does not mean "be dismayed," as in earlier Hebrew, but "be in haste," as in Late Biblical Hebrew (7:9; 2 Chron 35:21; Esth 2:9; 8:14; cf. *Qere* of Prov 20:21) and in Postbiblical Hebrew (Jastrow, *Dictionary*, p. 142). For the meaning of *‘al pîkā* "with your mouth," one may compare the expressions *qwr’ ‘l-ph* "reads with (the) mouth" = "reads out loud" in the Mishnah (*m. Yoma* 7:1; *Sota* 7:7) and *‘al-lěšōnô* "with his tongue" in Ps 15:3. The problem here is with overzealousness in prayers and oaths.

3 [Heb 2]. *dreams come with much preoccupation.* Lit. "the dream comes in the abundance of preoccupation." On the meaning of *‘inyān* "preoccupation," see Notes at 1:13.

5 [Heb 4]. *It is better that.* Here, as often in Ecclesiastes, *’ăšer* means "that" (see 7:18, 22, 29; 8:12, 14; 9:1). This usage of *’ăšer* is especially common in Late Biblical Hebrew (e.g., Neh 2:5, 10; 7:65; 8:14, 15; 10:31; 13:1, 19, 22; Esth 1:19; 2:10; 3:4; 4:11; 6:2; 8:11; Dan 1:8). See Joüon-Muraoka §157.a. The related par-

ticle *še-* also functions the same way, as evident in the parallel line: *miššettiddôr* "than *that* you should vow."

6 [Heb 5]. *to bring condemnation.* The form *laḥăṭî'* is syncopated from *lĕha-ḥăṭî'* (cf. Notes at 3:18). For the meaning of *laḥăṭî'*, cf. Isa 29:21; Deut 24:4. In the warning against the non-fulfillment of vows, Deuteronomy states baldly: *wĕ-hāyâ bĕkā ḥēṭ'* "this will be a sin to you" (Deut 23:22 [Eng v 23]). Qohelet, however, speaks not of sin (*ḥēṭ'*) but of the condemnation that one may bring to oneself (*laḥăṭî'*).

do not say. A. Rofé ("'The Angel' in Qohelet 5:5," *EI* 14 [1978], pp. 105–9) calls attention to similar "do not say" type of admonitions in the wisdom literature of the ancient Near East, in which a sage quotes the opponent in order to refute certain erroneous views (cf. Prov 3:28; 20:22; 24:29; Eccl 7:10; Sir 5:6; 15:11). Rofé cites examples from the Aramaic *Proverbs of Ahiqar* and various Egyptian instructional texts.

messenger. LXX (supported by SyrH) and Syr have "God," but that reading is probably interpretive — it assumes that *hammaľʾāk* meant "God," especially since in the same verse it is God who will be angry if one behaves inappropriately. MT is supported by Aq, Symm, Theod, Vulg, and Targ. It is sometimes argued that *hammaľʾāk* is secondary, being an attempt to "soften the anthropomorphism" (see Whitley, *Koheleth*, pp. 48–49). It must be observed, however, that no such attempt to soften the language is evident in 5:1 (Eng v 2), which speaks of people bringing forth a matter "before God" (*lipnê hā'ĕlōhîm*), or in 5:3 (Eng v 4), which refers to people making vows *lē'lōhîm* "to God." MT is probably correct. The problem is with the identification of the *maľʾāk* — whether it refers to a celestial or human representative of the deity (see Salters, "Notes on the History of the Interpretation of Koh 5,5," pp. 95–101). Targ takes the *maľʾāk* to be an avenging angel who will carry out the punishment on Judgment Day. *Qoh. Rabb.*, on the other hand, takes the *maľʾāk* to be a human messenger, an official of the temple or synagogue who has been sent to collect the promised dues. Other scholars, however, note that the priest is called *maľak YHWH-ṣĕbā'ôt* in Mal 2:7 (Barucq, Podechard, Salters). The reference is probably to the priest who presides at the ceremony when the offender goes to confess a *šĕgāgâ* "error." One may also point to a tantalizing inscription from the fifth century B.C.E., a votive inscription on an incense altar found at Lachish: *lbnt 'yš bn m[ḥ]ly hmľ'[k]* "The incense (altar) of 'Iyyōš son of Maḥlī, the messeng[er]" (see F. M. Cross, "Two Notes on Palestinian Inscriptions of the Persian Age," *BASOR* 193 [1969], pp. 19–24]).

an error. There is no claim that the one who committed the *šĕgāgâ* is ignorant of the law, although it is quite clear that the consequences of the acts are unexpected.

lest God be angry. Lit. "why should God be angry?" — a rhetorical question used to introduce undesirable alternatives (cf. 7:16, 17; 1 Sam 19:5, 17; 20:8, 32). So the ancient versions correctly understand the force of *lammâ* (cf. LXX *hina mē*).

take away. Reading *wĕḥābal*, instead of *wĕḥibbēl*. In Postbiblical Hebrew, *ḥbl* in Qal may mean "to destroy" or "to take away" (see Jastrow, *Dictionary*, p. 419).

In Akkadian, *ḫabālu* in the G-stem also means "take away" (*CAD* VI, pp. 4–5). The Akkadian verb is frequently used of the seizing of another's property. There is no need, therefore, to relate this verb to *ḥebel* "pledge" (see Kugel, "Qohelet and Money," pp. 33–35).

7 [Heb 6]. *for vacuous dreams.* This line has been difficult for commentators largely because of a literalistic understanding of "dreams." Thus, Lauha re-arranges the words to read *běrōb děbārîm ḥălōmôt wahăbālîm harbēh* "when words increase, dreams and vanities are plenty" (*Kohelet*, p. 97), Gordis posits a dubious translation for *běrōb* as "in spite of" (*Koheleth*, pp. 249–50), Whitley argues for an equally unconvincing instance of the asseverative *waw* in *ûděbārîm harbēh*, which he takes to mean "there are indeed many words" (*Koheleth*, pp. 49–50), and others emend in various ways. MT is supported by LXX and substantially by Syr and Vulg. Since *ḥālôm* may be a figure for anything that is illusory and ephemeral and, thus, synonymous with *hebel*, one may take the expression *ḥălōmôt wahăbālîm* as a hendiadys. The two words mean the same thing and only reinforce the idea of emptiness.

But as for you, fear God. Reading *ky 'th 'lhym yr'* (cf. LXX, SyrH, Syr, and Jerome) instead of *ky 't h'lhym yr'* in Codex Leningrad. There are other instances in the book of the misdivision of words (see Notes at 7:19, 27; 8:1; 10:1). Other scholars, who also prefer to follow LXX and other ancient versions, assume a defective spelling *'attā* "you": thus *kî 'attā hā'ělōhîm yěrā'* (see Lauha, *Kohelet*, p. 97). For the adversative use of *kî* (cf. Symm *alla*; Vulg *vero*), see Gen 18:15; 19:2; Isa 8:23.

COMMENT

A new literary unit is signaled by the change in tone. The language of reflection in 4:1–16 gives way to the language of instruction in 5:1–7 (Heb 4:17–5:6). Qohelet moves now from the first block of materials (1:2–4:16), to the second block (5:1–6:9 [Heb 4:17–6:9]) — from reflection to ethics. Indeed, this literary unit opens and closes with imperative forms: *šěmōr* "watch" (5:1 [Heb 4:17]) and *yěrā'* "fear" (5:7 [Heb 5:6]). Sandwiched between these is a series of warnings: "do not be hasty with your mouth" (v 2 [Heb v 1]), "do not let your heart rush" (v 2 [Heb v 1]), "do not be slack to fulfill" (v 4 [Heb v 3]), "do not permit your mouth" (v 6 [Heb v 5]), "do not say" (v 6 [Heb v 5]). The style adopted here is reminiscent of the admonitions of the wisdom teachers throughout the ancient Near East and is best exemplified in the Bible in the book of Proverbs. The common issue in these verses is one's attitude before God, with Qohelet counseling caution, reverence, restraint, moderation, and sincerity. The emphasis throughout the passage is on the necessity of respecting the distance between humanity and God, an emphasis that is encapsulated by the admonitions "watch your steps" (5:1 [Heb 4:17]) and "fear God" (5:7 [Heb 5:6]).

Qohelet begins by warning that one should watch one's steps, literally one's "feet," whenever one goes to temple. In poetic biblical texts, the feet are used as a figure for human conduct. One's feet could lead one astray (Prov 1:15–16; 4:27;

5:5; 6:18; 19:2; Job 31:5; Ps 119:101; Isa 59:7) or lead one aright (Job 23:11; Pss 26:12; 119:59). People must be careful, therefore, to hold back their feet from the wrong way (Prov 1:15; Ps 119:101), turn their feet away from evil (Prov 4:27), and hold fast their feet in the right way (Job 23:11). It appears that going to the temple is, for Qohelet, not synonymous with being on the right track. Those who are going to the temple must still watch their feet. Moreover, in contrast to a few other texts in the Bible, here it is not God who will watch one's feet (1 Sam 2:9; Prov 3:26; compare Ps 121:3), but people must look out for themselves as they approach the sacred precinct, as if there is some danger in their going there.

Qohelet elaborates that it is more acceptable to listen than to show off religiosity, as fools are wont to do. Israel's prophets and sages alike taught that proper conduct is more appropriate than sacrifices (Prov 21:3; 1 Sam 15:22; Amos 5:22–24; Hos 6:6). In the Egyptian wisdom text known as *The Instruction for Meri-ka-re* one finds a similar attitude about the ostentatious display of piety: "More acceptable is the character of one upright of heart than the ox of the evildoer" (*ANET*³, p. 417). It is not amiss to observe that this Egyptian text is also concerned that people should "revere the god" because the deity, though hidden and mysterious, knows the character of all people (see *ANET*³, p. 417).

Qohelet counsels caution in one's approach to God and urges quiet attention over the loud religiosity of fools, "for they (the fools) do not recognize that they are doing evil." The fools are so ready and eager to approach the deity that they do not even recognize that they are acting inappropriately. A bilingual inscription discovered at Ras Shamra (ancient Ugarit), written in Akkadian and Hurrian, comments similarly on the careless impulsiveness of the fool:

One who acknowledges no guilt rushes to his god,
Without thinking he raises his hands (in prayer) to the god.

(BWL, p. 116, lines 10–11)

The text speaks of people who are quick to swear oaths to the gods, to show off their piety and utter prayers without thought. They rush to their gods without even knowing that they are doing wrong.

Qohelet may also be thinking of such fools when he warns against people who are too ready to come before God with any matter (v 2 [Heb v 1]). The problem is not with the fact of their approach — he does not counsel against coming before God — but with their carelessness and haste: they are hasty with their mouth and their hearts rush to bring every matter before God.

Qohelet then gives the rationale for the warning with a motive clause: "for God is in heaven but you are on earth." In Deuteronomy it is said that there is no god "in heaven or on earth" who is like YHWH (Deut 3:24) and that YHWH "is in heaven above and on earth beneath" (Deut 4:39). The point in such expressions is the uniqueness and omnipresence of God: there is none like YHWH in heaven or on earth (see 2 Chron 6:14). Qohelet, however, does not speak of God on earth. He distinguishes between God who is in heaven and humans who are on earth, thus emphasizing God as Wholly Other, the transcendent One. This is an attempt to correct any misunderstanding about God's immanence and to emphasize the distance between God and humanity. God and mortals do not belong in the same realms, and so one ought not rush to bring forth every inane matter, as if the deity is an earthly agent available to respond to every human whim and fancy. As it is said in Ps 115:3, "Our God is in the heavens, he does whatever he pleases" (see also v 16). It is not that God is oblivious to prayer, but that God is transcendent, the Wholly Other, and should not be treated otherwise.

Qohelet, therefore, urges quiet restraint: "let your words be few." In the Egyptian text called *The Instruction of Anii*, one finds a similar preference for moderation in words spoken before the deity, inasmuch as the deity already knows even the words that are hidden (*AEL* II, p. 137). Jesus apparently knew such a tradition, for he taught in the Sermon on the Mount: "when you are praying, do not babble like the gentiles do; for they think that they will be heard for their many words. Do not be like them, for your father knows what you need before you ask him" (Matt 6:7–8).

Qohelet introduces another motive clause in v 3 (Heb v 2): "for dreams come with much preoccupation and the voice of the fool with many words." Interpreters are often puzzled about the relation of this saying to what precedes it. Some perceive that it is a gloss that should be excised, a misplaced verse, or a parenthetical remark. Most recognize the second part of the aphorism as pertinent to the point made in the preceding verse but think the mention of dreams is completely out of place. Gordis contends that Qohelet quoted a proverb in full, even though only the second half of it was really germane to his point (*Koheleth*, p. 248). Yet there is nothing in the aphorism that suggests that it is a quote. Indeed, its vocabulary and style are consistent with Qohelet's own. Certainly *bĕrōb ʿinyān* "with much preoccupation" in the first half of the proverb bears his imprint. In any case, most commentators take the first half of the saying to mean that *bad* dreams occur when one becomes overly preoccupied with certain issues. This is not an uncommon view of dreams in many cultures. A. L. Oppenheim cites an Akkadian wisdom text that reflects this perspective: "Remove [wo]e and anxiety from your heart, [wo]e and anxiety create dreams!" (*The Interpretation of Dreams*, p. 227). Among the Greeks, too, there was a view that dreams were derived for the most part from the anxieties of the day (*Herodotus* VII.16.2). This is similar to a Chinese proverb: "What one thinks about during the day, one dreams about at night." But if this is the message of the first half of the proverb, then it is indeed not apt in its context, as scholars often concede. It is also difficult to see how it is related to the second half of the saying. How does the effect of anxieties on dreams correspond to the relation between the voice of the fool and many words?

The text in fact says nothing about the causes or results of *bad* dreams. It may not even be referring literally to dreams. In the literature of the ancient Near East a dream is often a figure for anything that is an illusion and not a reality — something that is "unreal." So things that seem to transcend earthly realities are often likened to dreams (see Oppenheim, *The Interpretation of Dreams in the Ancient Near East*, pp. 228, 234). In Egyptian literature dreams are a figure for things that are fleeting, illusory, or even deceptive (see H. Grapow, *Die bildlichen*

Ausdrücke des Ägyptischen [Leipzig: Hinrich's, 1924], p. 140). Thus, in *The Instruction of Ptahhotep* a brief moment of pleasure is said to be "like a dream" (*AEL* I, p. 68), and in a so-called "Harper's Song" life is compared to a dream: "a short moment like a dream" (*AEL* II, p. 116). A dream is transient, a fleeting thing. So it is used as a figure for things that last only a short while: "he goes quickly like a dream" (*AEL* III, p. 51). In the wisdom literature of the Bible, the pleasures of the wicked are likened to a dream: "like a dream he flies away and one cannot find him, he is dispelled like a vision of the night" (Job 20:8). As elsewhere in the ancient Near East, dreams are a figure for things that are illusory (Isa 29:7–8).

So this is how one ought to take the mention of dream in our verse: it is that which is unreal and ephemeral. The significance of "dream" here approximates *hebel*—it is something ephemeral and unreliable. Indeed in v 7, the two terms occur together in a hendiadys, *ḥălōmôt wahăbālîm* "vacuous dreams." The point of the aphorism, then, is that much preoccupation amounts to nothing more than a dream, and many words produce nothing more than the hollow sound of the loquacious fool. The entire proverb is coherent and pertinent. Qohelet coins an aphorism to support the point that he just made in v 2 (Heb v 1): it is futile and foolish to multiply words (see also 6:11; 10:14). This thought is continued in his admonition to be cautious with oaths.

Qohelet speaks of the seriousness of vows made to God: "when you make a vow to God, do not be slack to fulfill it, for there is no pleasure in fools" (v 4 [Eng v 3]). The admonition nearly duplicates the wording of Deut 23:22 (Eng v 21). Unlike the parallel text in Deuteronomy, however, the deity is not called by the name YHWH. Qohelet prefers the more universal name of God (see the Comment at 1:13). Moreover, the motive clause in Deuteronomy invokes the retribution of God: "for God will surely require it of you, and it would be sin to you." Qohelet's motive clause is, by contrast, typical of the wisdom tradition's tendency to avoid any language of divine causality. He does not say that God will intervene in history to hold human beings accountable. Rather, he resorts to circumlocution: "there is no delight in fools." Anyone familiar with the passage in Deuteronomy would, however, have understood that to mean "God has no delight in fools." Moreover, whereas Deuteronomy states plainly that there is nothing wrong with not vowing (Deut 23:23 [Eng v 22]), Qohelet presents the option of not vowing in the form of a *ṭôb-saying* ("better than"-saying): "Better that you not vow than that you should vow and not fulfill it" (v 5 [Heb v 4]). In the Akkado-Hurrian inscription found at Ugarit cited above, one finds a similar warning to take oaths seriously (*BWL*, p. 116, lines 1–4). One must "respect the oath" and personally fulfill it (*pagarka šullim*).

The admonition to be quick in fulfilling vows is also echoed in Sir 18:22, within a context that stresses the greatness of God and the relative insignificance of mortals. The text counsels restraint in speech and caution in judgment. Both Qohelet and Ben Sira may have been responding to a problem among people in their respective generations who were quick to make vows, only to retract them later when they realized the implication of their words (see Prov 20:25). The

Mishnah in fact tells of a series of excuses that people gave when they failed to fulfill their vows (*Ned.* 9).

Qohelet warns against the lack of restraint in speech, for the mouth may bring condemnation to the entire person (see also Jas 3:1–12). The problem is that people utter words thoughtlessly and then try to exonerate themselves by claiming that they did not mean what they said. Such situations are anticipated in the levitical laws: "if anyone utters aloud a rash oath whether for a bad or good purpose, any sort of rash oath at all that people swear but are unaware of it, when they come to know it, they shall be guilty of these things" (Lev 5:4). For these people, confession of inadvertent error appears to be a convenient way out of the trouble that they bring upon themselves.

It is not clear who the "messenger" is in this context (see Notes), but one may conjecture that it is the priest who officiates at the temple to which people come to confess that they have erred (Num 15:22–31; Lev 4:2, 22, 27–30). The confession before the intermediary (*hammaľ āk*) is useless in any case, because God will still be angry at the voice of the fool and punish the fool accordingly. The motive clause in v 7 (Heb v 6) is a version of the saying in v 3 (Heb v 2), and it conveys the idea that God will not tolerate the foolish utterances despite the confession because there is an overabundance of futile words.

Qohelet then concludes with an admonition to fear God, that is, respect the distance between the divine and the human. This conclusion in fact summarizes the content of the entire passage (vv 1–7 [Heb 4:17–5:6]).

I.B.2. ENJOYMENT, NOT GREED (5:8–6:9 [HEB 5:7–6:9])

5   ⁸If you see the oppression of the poor and the violation of justice and righteousness in the province, do not be surprised over the matter — for an arrogant one is above an arrogant one, (and) arrogant ones have watched over them all. ⁹But the advantage of the land is in its provision, that is, if the field is cultivated for provision. ¹⁰One who loves money will not be satisfied with money, nor whoever loves abundance with yield. This, too, is vanity. ¹¹When bounty increases, those who consume it increase. But what accomplishment do those who possess it have, except what their eyes see? ¹²The sleep of the worker is pleasant, whether that one consumes little or much; but as for the surfeit of the rich, it does not allow them to sleep.

¹³There is a sickening tragedy that I have observed under the sun: wealth was hoarded by one who possessed it, to his own hurt. ¹⁴That is, that wealth disappeared in a terrible venture. Then he sired a son, but there was nothing in his possession. ¹⁵Just as he came forth from the womb of his mother, so he will return naked, going as he came. And he will carry away nothing for his toil that he may bring in his hand. ¹⁶Yes, this is a sickening tragedy: exactly as he came, so he will go. But what advantage is there for him that he should toil for wind? ¹⁷Indeed, all his days he consumes in darkness and much vexation, sickness, and rage.

¹⁸Here is what I have observed is good: that it is appropriate (for people) to eat, drink, and enjoy good in all their toil which they toil under the sun, during the few days of their lives, which God has given them, for this is their portion. ¹⁹Indeed, to all people God has given wealth and assets, and he has authorized them to partake of them, to take up their portion, and to have pleasure in their toil. This is the gift of God.

²⁰Indeed, they should not much call to mind the days of their lives, for God gives a preoccupation through the joy of their hearts!

6 ¹There is an evil that I have observed under the sun — and it is great upon humanity — ²that there is a person to whom God gives wealth, assets, and plenty, so that there is nothing lacking of all that is desired. Yet God does not authorize that one to partake of them, but rather, a stranger consumes it. This is vanity, and it is a terrible sickness.

³If a man sires a hundred and lives many years, but he complains that the days of his years will come to pass and his appetite is not satisfied with bounty and, also, (that) he has no burial site, I say the stillborn child is better than he. ⁴For it came in vanity and in darkness it goes, and in darkness its name will be covered. ⁵Even though it has not seen the sun, and has no awareness, it has more rest than he. ⁶If he had lived a thousand years twice over, but good he does not see — does not everyone go to one place?

⁷All the toil of people is for their mouths, and yet the gullet is not filled. ⁸Indeed, what advantage does the wise have over the fool? What is there for the afflicted that they should know to go along with life? ⁹What the eyes see is better than the passing of life. This, too, is vanity and a pursuit of wind.

NOTES

5   8 [Heb v 7]. *and the violation of justice and righteousness.* The precise expression is not found anywhere else, but the meaning is the same as *ligzōl mišpāṭ* "to violate justice" (lit. "to take away justice") in Isa 10:2, where the expression is parallel to *lĕhaṭṭôt middîn dallîm* "to turn away the poor from justice." In Ezek 18:18, *gēzel* "violation" (lit. "taking away") is likewise associated with *ʿōšeq* "oppression." Cf. also *gĕzēlat heʿānî* "the spoil of the afflicted (i.e., the poor)" in Isa 3:14. The noun *gēzel* implies violence (J. Schüpphaus, *TDOT* II, pp. 456–58; so RSV: "right violently taken away").

in the province. Hebrew *bammĕdînâ.* In light of Isa 10:2, which juxtaposes *ligzōl mišpāṭ* "to violate justice" and *lĕhaṭṭôt middîn* "to turn away from justice" (cf. also *mišpāṭ // dîn* in Job 36:17; Ps 9:5 [Eng v 4]), it seems likely that there is also a wordplay here in the word *mĕdînâ* "province," there being an allusion to its etymological meaning, "a place of jurisdiction" (see *HALAT*, p. 521). In 3:16, Qohelet speaks of wickedness in "the place of justice" // "the place of righteousness." The problem is not that oppression occurs within any geographical or administrative district, but that there is injustice precisely where justice should be found. From the Jewish colony at Elephantine comes a petition dated to the second half of the fifth century B.C.E., wherein appeal is made to rectify an injustice (*ṣq*). Apparently the plaintiff had worked on a field leased to the local military detachment, but he was not paid for his work. He brought the case to court—before three judges of the province (*dyn' mdnt'*)—but those judges found against him. So the plaintiff made an appeal to a higher court, hoping to overturn the earlier decision (*TAD* I, 5.2).

the matter. See Notes at 3:1.

an arrogant one . . . arrogant ones have watched over them all. This entire line is exceedingly difficult to interpret. The ancient versions attest to the accuracy of the consonants in MT. Most modern exegetes have assumed that the author is commenting on governmental bureaucracy, where the officials either "watched over" (spied on) or "looked out for" (protected) one another. The text is supposed to indicate the extent of governmental corruption. In this view, the Hebrew word *gābōah* is taken to mean "a high one" in the sense of "a high official" (so NRSV). Kugel objects, however, that *gābōah* does not have this meaning in Hebrew ("Qohelet and Money," pp. 35–38). He argues that the word in the Hebrew Bible, when used as a substantive, always means "an arrogant one" or "a haughty one" (cf. Job 41:26 [Eng v 34]; Ps 138:6; Isa 10:33; Ezek 21:31 [Eng v 26]). The word never means "high official" anywhere. Kugel notes further that there is "an assymetry between the two prepositions"—between *mē'al* and *'ălêhem*—and observes that the idiom should be *šāmar 'al* not *šāmar mē'al*, which is not found anywhere else. Hence, he proposes to read *gōbeh* < > *'al-gōbeh šōmēr wĕgōbîm*(!) *'ălêhem* "one payment-taker upon another is at watch, and other payment-takers are upon them." Instead of *gābōah*, Kugel assumes the III-Weak root *gbh/y* "to collect [a bill, taxes, mortgage]," a root that is well attested in Mishnaic Hebrew. One might add that the root *gby* is attested in Aramaic papyri from the Persian period, where it refers to the collection of taxes and debts (see Segal, *Aramaic Texts*, No. 22.4; 35.4; 38.6; 43a.6). So it is tempting to follow Kugel in this interpretation. To arrive at this reading, however, Kugel has to omit the *mem* on *mē'al* without evidence and assume an original reading *gōbîm* that was corrupted to *gĕbōhîm* by virtue of a supposed misunderstanding of *gōbeh* as *gābōah*. This is difficult to prove.

Kugel's objections to the interpretation of the majority are valid, but there is no need to alter the consonantal text. The ancient versions do not contradict the reading of MT. It is easier to disregard the Masoretic accents, redivide the consonants, and read: *gābōah mē'al gābōah šāmĕrû gĕbōhîm 'ălêhem*, lit. "an arrogant one is above an arrogant one, (and) arrogant ones have watched over them all." That is, we read *šmrw* instead of *šmr w-*. There are several other instances of misdivision of words in Ecclesiastes (see Notes at 5:7 [Eng v 6]; 7:19, 27; 8:1; 10:1). The disjunctive accent should be placed on the second *gābōah*.

For the meaning of *mē'al* "above," one may compare 2 Kgs 25:28; Pss 108:5 (Eng v 4); 148:4; Esth 3:1; Neh 8:5. Alderini's proposal to read *gbh-m 'l* (with an enclitic-*mem*) is unconvincing, for he depends on Dahood's claim that there are several other instances of the enclitic-*mem* in Ecclesiastes (4:6; 9:4; 10:15; 10:18a). But none of the examples is compelling ("Qohelet 5,7–8," pp. 14–17).

As for the meaning of *gābōah*, it probably refers to anyone who is of higher socioeconomic or political status than the ordinary person, but not necessarily a bureaucrat. They are arrogant in their wealth or power. The *gābōah* "arrogant one" or "lofty one" is opposite of "the lowly one." The word is used thus in the Talmud: *gbwh rw'h 't hgbwh w'yn gbwh rw'h 't hšpl* "a lofty one looks up to the lofty one, but no lofty one looks at the lowly one" (*b. Soṭa.* 5ᵃ). The word may also be used of people who are ambitious (see Jastrow, *Dictionary*, p. 204).

9 [Heb v 8]. *But the advantage of the land is in its provision.* The whole verse as it stands is problematic because of the awkwardness of its syntax, its apparent lack of internal coherence, and the difficulty of relating it to the preceding and following units of thought. Perhaps it is hopelessly corrupt. MT, although substantially supported by the ancient versions, makes no sense. It reads, lit. "but the advantage of land is in everything, a king for a cultivated field." In the first place, it is unclear what the demonstrative pronoun at the end of the first half refers to. *Ketib* has *hy'*, but *Qere*, supported by numerous MSS and Syr, has *hû'*. Moreover, *bakkōl* is usually taken to mean "in all respects" or "on the whole," a meaning that is dubious in classical Hebrew. Furthermore, the sudden mention of a king is odd, if not altogether meaningless. A. T. Varela ("A New Approach to Eccles 5,8–9," pp. 240–41) suggests that these are slogans that, by their nature, need not be related to one another. But to make sense of these "slogans," Varela has to supply additional words of clarification.

Without changing the consonants of the Hebrew text and assuming the reading *hw'* with *Qere*, many Hebrew MSS, and Syr, one may read *wĕyitrôn 'ereṣ bĕkīlāh wĕ'im lĕkīl śādeh ne'ĕbad* "the advantage of land is in its yield, that is, if the field is cultivated for [its] yield." Thus, original *wytrwn 'rṣ bklh w'm lkl śdh n'bd* is misdivided as *wytrwn 'rṣ bkl hw' mlk lśdh n'bd*. The vocalization of *kl* in *bklh* and *lkl* is uncertain. It may be analyzed either as an infinitive construct (in which case it should be *kīl*) or a noun from the root *kyl/kwl* "to measure, measure out" (cf. *kāl* "he measured" in Isa 40:12), which is related to the harvest in the Gezer Calendar (*KAI* 182.5) and in an ostracon from Yabneh Yam (*KAI* 200.5–6). If the word is a noun, it is related to the Aramaic *kaylā'* and Arabic *kayl* "measure, apportionment," and we should then vocalize it as *kēl* (for *kêl*). Cf. Hebrew *kilkēl* "to support, nourish"; Akkadian *kullu* "to provide" (see *CAD* VIII, p. 517); Arabic *kâla* "to apportion, mete out." In either case, the *he'* at the end may be interpreted as a 3 fs suffix, referring to *'ereṣ*, thus "its (the land's) measure/provision." The *waw* on *wĕ'im* is epexegetical (cf. Gen 4:4; Exod 24:7; 2 Sam 14:5; Deut 32:28; Isa 40:10). The verse thus makes the point that land ought not to be accumulated for its own sake but is to be cultivated for what it produces — its yield.

The Niphal of *'bd* occurs only in Deut 21:4; Ezek 36:9, 34; in every case the verb has to do with cultivated land — the form *ne'ĕbād* is to be taken with "field" (so also LXX, Theod, and Syr) rather than "king."

10 [Heb v 9]. *loves abundance.* MT has *'ōhēb behāmôn*, but since the verb *'āhab* never takes the preposition *bĕ-* (cf. *'ōhēb kesep* in the parallel line, not *'ōhēb bĕkesep*), most commentators think there is a dittography of *bet* here. Yet, *behāmôn* has the support of all Hebrew MSS. We may compare *'ōhēb bĕ-* here

with analogous expressions: *he'ĕmîn bĕ-, bāṭaḥ bĕ-, śāmaḥ bĕ-, ḥāpeṣ bĕ-*, and so forth (see GKC §119.1). There is no need to eliminate the preposition.

nor . . . with yield. The expression *lō' tĕbû'â* is elliptical, with the force of the verb *yiśba'* in the preceding line still being felt but not explicitly stated (so Fox). Instead of the negative particle, LXX and Targ apparently read *lô* "to/for him." Whitley posits that the original text had *lô lō' tĕbû'â* "he has no gain," arguing that *lô* was omitted in the *Vorlage* of MT through homonymy. With the possible exception of Targ, however, all the ancient versions reflect either *lō'* or *lô*, but not both.

This, too, is vanity. See Notes 1:2.

11 [Heb v 10]. *those who consume it increase.* Hebrew *rabbû 'ôkĕlêhā*. The meaning of *rbb* may be "to multiply" or "to become great, become large." In light of the economic subject matter of the passage, it is appropriate to call attention to the nouns *marbît* and *tarbît*, both of which may refer to monetary profit or interest. Qohelet, however, may be thinking that the consumers "increased" or "expanded" in more than one sense of the word — perhaps financially, socially, and physically. One may note that *'kl* is also used for the consumption of goods in Persian period Aramaic (see, for example, *TAD* II, 2.7.4).

accomplishment. See Notes at 2:21. Here *kišrôn* "accomplishment" is virtually synonymous with *yitrôn* "advantage."

those who possess it. Hebrew *lib'ālêhā*, lit. "its possessor." For *ba'al* with the "plural of majesty," see Exod 21:29, 34; 22:10 [Eng v 11]; Isa 1:3; Eccl 7:12; 8:8 (see GKC §124.i; Joüon-Muraoka §136.d). The singular meaning of the noun is confirmed by the 3 ms suffix in *'ênāyw*.

what their eyes see. Qere has *rĕ'ût* (a noun) or *rĕ'ôt* (infinitive construct of *r'h*). The former is unattested in Biblical or Mishnaic Hebrew, however. Ketib has *r'yt*, which perhaps suggests *rĕ'iyyat*. This is probably the correct reading. The word is well attested in Postbiblical Hebrew, meaning "seeing, sight" (see Jastrow, *Dictionary*, p. 1436). The structure of the literary unit here suggests that this line mirrors 6:9, and so we should take the reference here to approximate *mar'ēh 'ênayim* "what the eyes see" (cf. *r'yyt h'yyn* "the faculty of sight" in *m. Nid.* 31:2). See also Notes at 6:9.

12 [Heb v 11]. *the worker.* LXX, Symm, and Theod all have "the slave" (*doulos*) — either interpreting *hā'ōbēd* to mean "the slave" and not just "the worker" (cf. LXX's rendering of *'ōbēd* with *doulos* in IV Reigns 10:19–23), or reflecting Hebrew *hā'ebed*. Ibn Ezra conjectured that *hā'ōbēd* may be a short-hand reference to the *'ōbēd 'ădāmâ* "tiller of the ground" (cf. Gen 4:2; Prov 12:11; 28:19; Isa 30:24; Zech 13:5). A saying in the book of Proverbs states that the *'ōbēd 'ădāmâ* "tiller of the ground" will be satiated (*yiśba'*) with food, whereas the one who pursues meaningless activities will be satiated (*yiśba'*) with poverty (Prov 12:11 // 28:19). The contrast there is between one who works hard, namely, the tiller of the ground, and one who does not work (the lazy one). But Qohelet is not making that distinction here. The point is not that the rich are lazy. In fact, the problem is precisely that the rich toil to acquire more and more, and they do not know when to stop. The issue, rather, is whether one has the accumulation

and protection of wealth about which to worry. The worker does not have to worry about all the "increase," as the rich do. The contrast is simply between the wealthy and the not-wealthy. Thus, we should take *hāʿōbēd* to refer to "the worker" or "the employee." Besides *ʿōbēd ʾădāmâ* "tiller of ground," the Hebrew Bible also mentions *mas-ʿōbēd* "corvée laborer" (Gen 49:15; Josh 16:10; 1 Kgs 9:21) and *ʿōbēd hāʿîr* "the city worker" (Ezek 48:18–19]). Thus, *hāʿōbēd* refers to one from ancient Palestine's equivalent of someone from "the working classes." A similar social stratification may be evident in Egypt of the Persian period, for one reads in an Aramaic papyrus from North Saqqara of *ʿbd mšḥ* "oil worker," along with other employees who were paid monetary wages (see Segal, *Aramaic Texts*, Nos. 19, 20). Qohelet here pits the working classes against the rich. Furthermore, if the reading and interpretation proffered for v 9 (Heb v 8) are correct, the "worker" here may be an allusion to those who worked the "cultivated field" (cf. *śādeh neʿĕbād* "the field is cultivated") — that is, land that is abandoned or misused by the rich (see Notes and Comment at 5:9 [Heb v 8]).

pleasant. See Notes at 11:7.

the surfeit. Interpreters are divided over the meaning of *haśśābāʿ* "the surfeit." Some take it to mean surfeit of food (satiety), while others interpret it to refer to the surfeit of wealth (abundance). Both meanings are possible and, indeed, probably intended by the author. The rich have consumed so much food that they are not able to sleep, presumably because of their physical discomfort: that is, their fullness will not permit them to sleep. At the same time, they have so much wealth invested that they cannot sleep because they worry too much. Their material abundance will not permit them to sleep.

it does not allow them to sleep. Hebrew *ʾênennû mannîaḥ lô*. For the Hiphil of *nwḥ* meaning "allow," see Ps 105:14 (// 1 Chron 16:21); Judg 16:26. This is a meaning known also in Postbiblical Hebrew (see Jastrow, *Dictionary*, pp. 885–86).

13 [Heb v 12]. *under the sun.* See Notes at 1:3.

wealth is hoarded by. The preposition *lĕ-* in *šāmûr libʿālāyw* indicates agent (Joüon-Muraoka §132.f). Cf. *dĕrûšîm lĕkol-ḥepṣêhem* "sought by all who delight in them" (Ps 111:2); *ʾāhûb lēʾlōhāyw* "loved by his God" (Neh 13:26).

one who possessed it. See Notes at v 11 (Heb v 10).

to his own hurt. In vv 13–17 (Heb vv 12–16), Qohelet is referring to a specific case of a man who sired a son. The subject is not intended to be generic, as in the previous section.

14 [Heb v 13]. *That is, that wealth disappeared.* The *waw* in *wĕʾābad* may be interpreted as a *waw explicativum* (see GKC §154.a.Note 1b). It introduces the clarification of the preceding verse.

but there was nothing in his possession. Hebrew *wĕʾên bĕyādô mĕʾûmâ*. Building on an earlier proposal that *byd* in a Qumran document (1QS VI.20) and in a papyrus from Elephantine may refer to a deposit in a commercial account, Lohfink has argued that *bĕyādô* here should also be interpreted in that specific sense ("Kohelet und die Banken," pp. 488–95). He conjectures that *ʿōšer šāmûr libʿā-lāyw* refers to a deposit "kept *by a bank* for its owner." That deposit, according to Lohfink's reconstruction, was lost in an economic disaster (i.e., the terrible venture). But *byd* in the two texts cited from Elephantine and Qumran does not necessarily have the technical meaning that Lohfink presupposes; they have nothing to do with banks (cf. *bydy* "in my possession," *bydk* "in my possession," *bydkm* "in your possession," and the like, in *TAD* I, 2.2.5; A3.8.13; A3.10.2). More importantly, the idiom *mě'ûmâ běyad*, as attested in the Bible, always means "anything in the possession of" (cf. Gen 39:23; Deut 13:18 [Eng v 17]; 1 Sam 12:5), even as *mě'ûmâ 'ên běyad* means "nothing in the possession of," hence, "empty-handed" (Judg 14:6). Akkadian attests a similar idiom in *mimma ina qāti* "anything in possession" (see *CAD* XIII, p. 189). The suffix in *běyādô* is somewhat ambiguous: it may refer either to the father or the son.

15 [Heb v 14]. *Just as.* Instead of *ka'ăšer*, 4QQoh^a has *ky'*, a genuine variant. LXX has *kathōs*, reflecting Hebrew *k'šr* (per MT).

for his toil. The preposition is the *bet pretii* (GKC §119.p).

that he may bring. Hebrew *šeyyōlēk*. LXX, Symm, and Syr reflect Hebrew *šey-yēlēk* "that it may go," but the presence of *běyādô* makes that reading unlikely. This reading (*šeyyēlēk*) anticipates *yēlēk* in the next verse. We should retain the Hiphil, a reading supported by a number of MSS that have *ywlk*.

16 [Heb v 15]. *Yes, this is a sickening tragedy.* The initial conjunction should be omitted with 4QQoh^a and a few Hebrew MSS (Kennicott MSS 80, 147, 180, 188; so, too, in the Bomberg edition). The reading with *waw* reflects a simple dittography. Here *gam* is rhetorical and is intended to reiterate a point.

exactly. Reading *kil'ummat* (i.e., *kě-* + *lě'ummat*) instead of *kol-'ummat* in MT; *'ummat* is always preceded by the preposition *lě-* (Exod 25:27; 37:14; 2 Sam 16:13; 1 Chron 25:8; also *m. Ketub.* 5:8; *Šeqal.* 6:3; *Mid.* 2:6).

17 [Heb v 16]. *Indeed.* Following the rhetorical question in the preceding line, *gam* is emphatic and intensive.

he will eat in darkness. Hebrew *baḥōšek yō'kēl*. LXX has *en skotei kai en pen-thei*, reflecting Hebrew *bḥšk wb'bl* "in darkness and in mourning." LXX^V alone of the Greek MSS reads *en skotei kai penthei*, reflecting Hebrew *bḥšk w'bl* (cf. SyrH; Copt). Yet it may be the more original reading in the Greek tradition (so Rahlf chooses it in his eclectic edition). This reading may be explained as a simple graphic confusion of *yod/waw* and *kap/bet*: thus original *bḥšk y'kl* was misread as *bḥšk w'bl*, a mistake caused in part by the difficult idiom of eating in darkness and the mention of vexation later in the verse; and *bḥšk w'bl* was then expanded to *bḥšk wb'bl*. In any case, LXX has the easier reading; it is unlikely that anyone would correct *bḥšk w'bl* or *bḥšk wb'bl* to *bḥšk y'kl*. So MT is superior. Ehrlich, and recently Kugel ("Qohelet and Money," pp. 38–40), suggest reading *běḥāsāk* "in want" instead of *baḥōšek* "in darkness." Within the structure of the whole literary unit (see Comment below), however, this verse mirrors 6:4, which speaks of the stillborn child going *baḥōšek* "in darkness." The meaning of that verse is clarified by the next (6:5), which says that the stillborn has not seen the sun and has no consciousness. Moreover, the expression "go in darkness" here cannot be separated from the mention of the fool's walking in darkness (*wěhakkěsîl baḥōšek hôlēk*) in 2:14 and with Qohelet's use of "coming" and "going" to speak of birth and death, respectively (see Comment at 1:4). The verb *'ākal* "to eat, consume" is probably figurative, and refers to one's attempt to survive or make a living. One may compare Akkadian *akālu* "to eat," which may also have the meaning "to sustain oneself." See *BWL*, p. 242, line 7, and R. F. Harper, *Assyrian and Babylonian Letters* (London: University of Chicago, 1909), Part IX, p. 999, text 925, line 7. The latter text has *alik . . . ina ṣillīya akul* "Go! . . . make a living in my protection" (cf. the translation in *CAD* I/1, p. 248), which is reminiscent of Hebrew *lēk . . . 'el-'ereṣ yĕhûdâ we'ĕkōl-šām leḥem* "Go! . . . to the land of Judah and make a living there" (Amos 7:12).

vexation. Reading *wĕka'as* (*wĕ-* + noun) with the ancient versions against *wĕkā'as* "and he is vexed" in Codex Leningrad. The preposition *bĕ-* in *baḥōšek* also governs the three nouns in v 17 (Heb v 16). This is an instance where one preposition does duty for more than one noun (Waltke-O'Connor §11.4.2; see *UT* §10.10 n 2, for the phenomenon in Ugaritic). See further, the discussion of Whitley (*Koheleth*, pp. 54–55).

and sickness. Reading *woḥŏlî* with the ancient versions, instead of MT's *wḥlyw*, which shows a dittography of *waw*.

18 [Heb v 17]. *Here is what I have observed is good.* Hebrew *hinnēh 'ăšer rā'îtî 'ānî ṭôb*. The Masoretes placed the pause on *'ānî*. This leaves one with the problem of having to explain the syntactically awkward and redundant phrase *ṭôb 'ăšer yāpeh*. It is easier to disregard the accents and read: *hinneh 'ăšer-rā'îtî 'ănî ṭôb*.

that it is appropriate (for people). The particle *'ăšer* introduces the object of the seeing, substituting for *kî* (see Notes at 5:4; GKC §157.c). For the meaning of *yāpeh*, see Notes at 3:11. The subject in these verses is not the man of vv 13–17 (Heb vv 12–16), but *kol-hā'ādām* "all people," a subject that is held in abeyance until v 19 (Heb v 18). A similar phenomenon is evident in 1:6, where the introduction of the subject is delayed, only to be revealed later on in the text.

to enjoy good. Lit. "to see good." See Notes at 2:1.

under the sun. See Notes at 1:3.

during the few days. MT shows a haplography of *yod*. This phrase assumes the accusative of time (GKC §118.k). See Notes at 2:3.

their portion. See Notes at 2:10.

19 [Heb v 18]. *Indeed to all people God has given.* Hebrew *gam kol-hā'ādām 'ăšer nātan-lô hā'ĕlōhîm*, lit. "indeed all people: that God has given to them. . . ." The *gam* here is rhetorical (cf. *gam* in v 17 [Heb v 16]) and echoes *hinnēh* in v 18 (Heb v 17). The objects of the verb are marked by *'ăšer* both times:

hinnēh 'ăšer-rā'îtî ṭôb
    (a) *'ăšer-yāpeh le'ĕkôl-wĕlištôt wĕlir'ôt ṭôbâ*
    (b) *'ăšer nātan-lô hā'ĕlōhîm*
Here is what I have observed is good:
    (a) that it is appropriate to eat, drink, and enjoy good,
    (b) that God has given to them (wealth and assets).

The *'ăšer* in v 19 (Heb v 18) functions the same way as it does in v 18 (Heb v 17) and 6:2. Thus, one should not take *'ăšer* as the relative pronoun referring specifically to *kol-hā'ādām*, for that interpretation leaves the main clause without a verb and its thought incomplete, being interrupted by the syntactically unrelated phrase *zōh mattat 'ĕlōhîm hî'* "this is the gift of God." It is typical of Qohelet's style to isolate the most important element first in the sentence.

assets. Hebrew *nĕkāsîm.* This is a loanword that first appears in Late Biblical Hebrew, in Josh 22:8, a text belonging to the exilic redaction of "the Deuteronomistic Historian." Other occurrences are also clearly late: Eccl 6:2; 2 Chron 1:11–12; Sir 5:8. It is interesting to observe that *nĕkāsîm* occurs in the Chronicler's version of Solomon's dream, but not in the earlier version in 1 Kgs 3:11, 13. The word came into Hebrew either directly from Akkadian, where *nikkassu* meant "property" or "asset" from the Neo-Assyrian period on (see *CAD* XI/2, p. 229), or, as it seems more likely, indirectly by way of Aramaic. The word is well attested in Aramaic documents from the Persian period.

and he has authorized them. Hebrew *wĕhišlîṭô.* That is, God has given them the right of disposal. This is legal terminology (see Notes at 2:19).

their portion. See Notes at 2:10.

20 [Heb v 19]. *they should not much call to mind.* Hebrew *lō' harbēh yizkōr.* The Masoretic disjunctive accent on *harbēh* is peculiar, perhaps reflecting the view that *harbēh* is adjectival and is referring awkwardly to *'et-yĕmê-ḥayyāyw* (cf. 11:8). It is better to ignore the accents and take *lō' harbēh* as an adverbial phrase (so LXX^B, Syr, Vulg). The meaning of *zākar* here is to "call to mind" (see Fox). The object of the verb need not be the past, but may be the present, or even the future. So *lō' zākĕrâ 'aḥărîtāh* "she did not call to mind her future" (Lam 1:9). Qohelet himself uses the verb in this way in 11:8, which refers to the days to come.

The consensus among translators is that *yizkōr* in 5:20 (Heb v 19) is indicative. They assume Qohelet to be saying that human beings "do not" or "will not" brood much over their miserable lives. Yet, people do brood much over their lives. Indeed, Qohelet's problem is precisely that people do brood about their days — too often and too much — although he thinks that they will not discover anything in all their brooding (3:11). Hence, we should take *yizkōr* as injunctive rather than as indicative: one must not call to mind the days of misery (see Joüon-Muraoka §113.m). Thus, *yizkōr* here means the same thing as *yizkōr* in 11:8, except that in this case (5:20 [Heb v 19]), the injunction is negative (see Notes at 11:8). In both cases, the emphasis is not on the future, but on the possibility of enjoyment in the present. Qohelet means that one should not bring to mind the days of one's life, if doing so takes away the possibility of joy.

God gives a preoccupation. Hebrew *hā'ĕlōhîm ma'ăneh.* Most commentators emend *ma'ăneh* to *ma'ănēhū*, citing LXX (*perispą auton*) and Syr (*m'n' lyh*). But the ancient translators, who seemed to have assumed that the word is to be derived from *'nh* "to occupy, preoccupy," simply may have been supplying the object for clarification. Their translations do not necessarily reflect a different reading in their *Vorlage(n)*. MT is quite satisfactory. The meaning of the word is, however, more difficult. Interpreters have traditionally chosen from one of the meanings of the root: "to occupy" (so the ancient versions), "to answer" (so Ibn Ezra), "to sing" (so Rashbam). Most modern scholars are divided between the first two possibilities, usually excluding the other options. It is likely, however, that Qohelet is ambiguous on this score, intending more than one meaning: *maʿăneh* as "preoccupation" and as "answer." This is a view that has been argued well by Lohfink in "Revelation by Joy," pp. 625–35. It is perhaps to preserve the ambiguity that Qohelet does not give the direct object here. We miss the point if we emend the text!

6 1.*There is a tragedy.* Hebrew *yēš rāʿâ*. A number of MSS read *yš rʿh ḥwlh* or *rʿh ḥlh* "there is a terrible sickness" (see Kennicott and de Rossi) but this is expansive and may be attributed to the influence of 5:13 (Heb v 12). The ancient versions support the shorter reading.

under the sun. See Notes at 1:3.

2. *that there is a person to whom God gives.* Hebrew *ʾîš ʾăšer yitten-lô hāʾĕlōhîm*, lit. "a man, that God should give to him." Here the subject is anticipated (see Ellermeier, *Qohelet* I/1, pp. 292–95). The subject, *ʾîš* "a person," is not intended to be gender-specific here; it refers to *any* person, not to a particular man. Here *ʾîš* corresponds to *kol-hāʾādām* "all people" in 5:19 (Heb v 18), except that *kol-hāʾādām* refers to what is universally true, whereas *ʾîš* refers to what may be true in some instances. Hence, *ʾîš* here means a certain person — anyone. The particle *ʾăšer* does not refer to the person, but to the situation that the author observed (cf. NJPS: "that God sometimes grants"). Note the syntactical similarities between 5:18–19 (Heb vv 17–18) and 6:1–2: *hinnēh ʾăšer-rāʾîtî ʾānî ṭôb* "here is what I have observed is good" (5:18 [Heb v 17]) // *yēš raʿâ ʾăšer rāʾîtî* "there is a tragedy that I have observed" (6:1); *kol-hāʾādām ʾăšer nātan-lô hăʾĕlōhîm* "all people — that God has given them" (5:19 [Heb v 18]) // *ʾîš ʾăšer yitten-lô hāʾĕlōhîm* "a person — that God gives to him" (6:2).

wealth, assets, and plenty. Hebrew *ʿōšer ûnĕkāsîm wĕkābôd*. Inasmuch as one can partake of these things (*leʾĕkōl, yōʾkălennû*), *kābôd* must mean not "honor" but "abundance" or "plenty." See Salters, "Notes on the Interpretation of Qoh 6:2," pp. 283–84. This meaning of *kābôd* is evident in Gen 31:1; Isa 10:3; 61:6; Nah 2:10 (Eng v 9). Isa 61:6 is particularly suggestive since we have "you shall partake (*tōʾkĕlû*) of the wealth of nations" // "in their riches (*bikbôdām*) you shall glory" (cf. LXX, *en tǭ plytǭ autōn*). The same three nouns — *ʿōšer ûnĕkāsîm wĕkābôd* — appear in 2 Chron 1:12 in reference to Solomon's gifts from God.

God does not authorize. That is, God does not give the right of disposal in this case. See Notes at 5:19 (Heb v 18).

stranger. Given the stress on succession and inheritance in the passage, one should take the *ʾîš nokrî* to refer not to an ethnic "foreigner," as the term is often used in the Bible, but simply to an outsider — i.e., one who is not from the family. There was a particular concern in the Persian period that the patrimonial estate should not fall into the hands of those outside the extended family, the *bêt ʾābôt*.

this is vanity. See Notes at 1:2.

3. *If a man.* Since 6:3–6 mirrors 5:13–17 (Heb vv 12–16), we may take the

subject here to be gender-specific. That is, it refers or alludes to the man in the mirror section.

yet he complains that the days of his years will come to pass. Reading *wĕrāb*, the consecutive perfect 3 ms from *ryb*, instead of *wĕrab* in Codex Leningrad. As it stands, *wĕrab šeyyihyû yĕmê-šānāyw*, lit. "and/but it is numerous, that the days of his years will come to pass" is exceedingly awkward: the singular *rab* ("it is numerous") with the plural *šeyyihyû yĕmê-šānāyw* ("that the days of his years will come to pass") is most odd. One may note that the plural noun *šānîm* in the preceding line has the plural adjective *rabbôt*, not the singular *rab*. Moreover, the function of *še-* in the phrase has never been satisfactorily explained. Zapletal emends *rab* to *rabbîm* out of necessity (*Kohelet*, p. 166). Ginsburg cites Deut 33:7 and Ps 18:15 (Eng v 14) to show that *rab* may take the plural, but both texts are corrupt and the reading of *rab* is questionable in each case (*Coheleth*, p. 359). Still others read *wĕrob* (so Ehrlich), but the syntactical problem created by the presence of the relative particle *še-* remains unresolved. Furthermore, most interpreters are forced to regard the clause as a parenthetical comment, if not an altogether redundant remark. But when we repoint the first form to read *wĕrāb* "but he complains" (assuming the root *ryb*), the line is not out of place. It indicates the sheer ridiculousness of the fool's endless quarrels and complaints (cf. Prov 3:30; 15:18; 18:6; 20:3; 25:8): when he seems to have everything, including abundant wealth and progeny, as well as longevity, he complains about the days to come, he is not satisfied with all the good that he has, and he is already worried about a proper burial.

also he has no burial site. Hebrew *qĕbûrâ* in this instance does not refer to the act of burial, as many translations imply (so NIV: "proper burial"), but to the *place* of burial (Deut 34:6; Gen 35:20; 1 Sam 10:2; 2 Kgs 9:28; 23:30; 2 Chron 26:23; Ezek 32:23–24). The word is attested in various West Semitic inscriptions, always referring to the place of burial, not the funeral rite (see *DNWSI*, p. 986). The allusion here is to the practice among the rich of securing their burial sites to ensure proper interment (cf. Gen 23:3–9; Isa 22:16). The rich man in this case is already worried about his days to come and complaining about not having secured a burial site. Commentators, who generally fail to see this clause as one of the fool's many ridiculous complaints, are hard pressed to relate this clause to what precedes it. Hence, the clause is often excised as a marginal gloss, transposed to another place (usually v 5), or emended in some way (see Michel, *Eigenart*, pp. 144–47). There is no need for any of these moves, however. The consonantal reading of MT is completely supported by the ancient versions. Those who see the clause as reflecting Qohelet's own view must account for the author's putative concern with proper funeral rites here, when he is so consistently focused on the enjoyment of life and so assiduously evasive about what happens in the future.

stillborn child. Hebrew *hannāpel*. Cf. Ps 58:9 [Eng v 8]; Job 3:16. The latter example is especially suggestive, since *nēpel* occurs with *ṭāmûn* "one who is hidden" and *kĕ'ōlĕlîm lō'-rā'û 'ôr* "like infants who had not seen light." Horst in *BHS* notes that *mmnw hnpl* is inverted in LXX. This is incorrect; Greek *hyper auton to ektrōma* reflects the word order in MT. It is in 4QQoh^a that we have the words inverted: *hnpl mmnw* instead of *mmnw hnpl*.

4. *it came in vanity.* Hebrew *bahebel bā'*. M. Dahood ("Northwest Semitic Philology and Three Biblical Texts," *JNSL* 2 [1972], p. 20) interprets *bā' bahōšek* as "came *from* darkness," citing Isa 27:13 (*ûbā'û hā'ōbĕdîm bĕ'ereṣ 'aššûr*) and the inscription of Abibaal of Byblos (*KAI* 5.1), which is, however, reconstructed. Qohelet could hardly have meant that people "came from void," as Dahood insists. The author probably means that the stillborn comes into the world in vain or that it comes only for a moment (cf. *kol-šebbā' hābel* "all that comes is vanity" in 11:8).

and goes in darkness. Hebrew *ûbahōšek yēlēk*. LXX has *en skotei poreuetai*, exactly as in 2:14, where the Hebrew has *bahōšek hôlēk*. Instead of *ylk* in MT, 4QQoh^a has *hlk*. But *hlk* in 4QQoh^a is probably to be interpreted as a perfect instead of a participle, since the participle would probably be written in the Qumran fragments as *hwlk*, as it is in 6:6. MT has the more difficult reading; the participle and perfect both represent attempts to conform to *b'*.

and in darkness its name will be covered. Hebrew *ûbahōšek šĕmô yĕkusseh*. The memory of the stillborn child will be buried with it. Pertaining to people who have lived, the biblical writers used the idioms *'ābad šĕmô* "one's name is ruined" (Ps 41:6 [Eng v 5]), *hišmîd šĕmô* "destroy one's name" (1 Sam 24:21), and *māhâ šĕmô* "wipe out one's name" (Deut 9:14; 29:19 [Eng v 20]; Ps 109:13). One may also consider the verb here to mean "disregard" or "ignore," a meaning we find in Persian period Aramaic: *'l tksh mlt mlk* "do not disregard the command of the king" (see *TAD* III, 1.1.84).

5. *Even though it has not seen the sun.* Hebrew *gam-šemeš lō'-rā'â*. As in 4:14, *gam* is concessive. To see the sun is to be alive. Those who are alive are called *rō'ê haššemeš* "those who see the sun" (7:11). Cf. *lir'ôt 'et-haššemeš* "to see the sun" = "to be alive" (11:7); *nēpel 'ēšet bal-ḥāzû šāmeš* "the stillborn child who never sees the sun" (Ps 58:9 [Eng v 8]); *kĕnēpel // kĕ'olĕlîm lō'-rā'û 'ôr* "like a stillborn // like infants who have not seen light" (Job 3:16). A similar expression occurs in an Egyptian imprecation: "their names shall not be remembered in the entire earth, and they shall not see the rays of the sun" (see R. O. Faulkner, "The Bremner-Rhind Papyrus—II," *JEA* 24 [1930], p. 11, lines 37–38).

and has no awareness. Hebrew *lō' yāda'*. There is no object indicated, so some have assumed that the object is *šemeš* "sun," since *rā'â* "see" and *yāda'* "know" are commonly paired for emphasis (so Ginsburg). But Qohelet speaks of seeing the sun in two other places (7:11; 11:7) without reference to knowing the sun. Indeed, the expression "know the sun" is not attested anywhere in the Bible. There is, in fact, no need to supply an object for *yāda'*; the verb may be used intransitively with the meaning "be aware, conscious" or "have knowledge" (Isa 44:9, 18; 45:20). Thus *lō' yāda'* means "[the stillborn] has no awareness/consciousness." In the Amarna letters *idû* (a cognate of Hebrew *yd'*) is used in a similar way. Thus Biridiya of Megiddo concludes his report to Akhenaton: *u lu idīmi šarru bēlīya* "and let my lord the king be aware!" (*EA* 245.6; cf. 147.70; 170.18). LXX^{BSA}, Vulg, and Targ take *yāda'* with what follows (i.e., "he does not know rest"), but the syntax is exceedingly awkward in that case and the resulting translation makes little sense.

it has more rest than he. Hebrew *naḥat lāzeh mizzeh*, lit. "the one has more rest than the other." Regarding the syntax, Ehrlich correctly calls attention to Prov 26:12, *tiqwâ liksîl mimmennû* "a fool has more hope than he" (*Randglossen*, p. 79). Many interpreters take *naḥat* (*nwḥt* in 4QQoh^a) to be related to Postbiblical Hebrew *nwḥ* "satisfaction," which may be used in comparison to mean "better than" (so Symm, Vulg, and Targ). But in all the examples cited, the form is *nwḥ*, not *nḥt*. The word here cannot, in fact, be separated from the use of *naḥat* elsewhere in the book (4:6; 9:17) and in the rest of the Bible (Prov 29:9; Isa 30:15). It must mean "rest" or "repose." Here it picks up on the theme of the person who cannot have rest (5:12 [Heb v 11], especially note *'ênennû mannîaḥ*). The noun is also attested in some West Semitic inscriptions with the same basic meaning and, occasionally, in reference to the eternal rest, i.e., the tomb. Inscribed on a jar found in a tomb, for instance, are the letters *bnḥt* "in repose" (*RES* 1975). In the Phoenician inscription on the Ahiram Sarcophagus, *nḥt* may have a double reference, to the royal rest and to the eternal repose of the king (*KAI* 1.2).

6. *If he had lived a thousand years twice over, but good he does not see.* Hebrew *wě'illû hāyâ 'elep šānîm pa'ămîm wěṭôbâ lō' rā'â.* Elsewhere in the Bible, *'illû* ("if . . . not") occurs only in Esth 7:4. But the form is well attested in Jewish Aramaic (usually as *'ylw*), Syriac (*'ellū*), and Mishnaic Hebrew (*'ylw*). The form is probably an Aramaism, derived from **'in* + *lû*, the Aramaic equivalent of Hebrew *'im lû*. Indeed, 4QQoh^a has *w'm lw'*, reflecting a correction of the form to the older Hebrew idiom (cf. *'im . . . lû* in Gen 23:13), although *'lw* is not unattested in the Qumran scrolls and fragments. In any case, Qohelet's sentence here is incomplete. We expect him to say, "if he had lived a thousand years twice over, but good he does not see, *then*. . . . " There is no *then*-clause, however. Instead, there appears to be an ellipsis. In any case, the meaning of the sentence is clear: if one does not enjoy good when one is able, then there is no difference between the living and the dead.

one place. There can be little doubt that the "one place" of which Qohelet speaks is the netherworld, the place of darkness (vv 4–5) to which all living creatures are destined to go. Cf. *hakkōl hôlēk 'el-māqôm 'eḥād* "all go to one place" (3:20; see also 9:10).

7. *and yet.* Here *gam* is adversative, as in 3:11 and 4:8.

the gullet. Hebrew *hannepeš.* The reference is to people who cannot seem to consume enough and are never satisfied. The structure of the whole passage suggests it, for this verse echoes 5:10 (Heb v 9) and 6:3. P. R. Ackroyd thinks that there is an allusion to Sheol, the "one place" in the preceding verse ("Two Hebrew Notes," pp. 84–85). This would be a tantalizing possibility had Sheol been explicitly mentioned. It is difficult to imagine that *māqôm 'eḥād* would have been personified so, however. The recurrence of *nepeš* in the whole passage must first be considered, for it always refers to the insatiable people (6:2, 3, 9; cf. Prov 16:26). So the *nepeš* probably refers to the insatiable appetite of greedy people.

Cf. *napšô lōʾ tiśbaʿ* "his appetite is not satisfied" in 6:3. The mythological imagery of Death's appetite is, however, often used in the Bible to speak of the seeming insatiability of the arrogant rich (see Comment below).

8. *what is there for the afflicted that they should know.* Hebrew *mah-lleʿānî yô-dēaʿ.* This line has troubled interpreters through the centuries in large measure because the function and meaning of *yôdēaʿ* are unclear. Various emendations have been proposed (see Whitley, *Koheleth,* p. 59). All the ancient versions attest to the substantial accuracy of the consonantal text in MT, however. A number of scholars seek to solve the problem by taking *ʿānî* variously to mean "ascetic" (Graetz), "intelligent man" (Whitley), and so on. It is possible that *ywdʿ* has been metathesized from original *wydʿ* (*wĕyēdaʿ*) "so that he may know" (cf. GKC §166.a). The change is slight. Nevertheless, in the absence of compelling evidence, it is better to take the clause as elliptical for *mah-lleʿānî šeyyôdēaʿ* or *mah-leʿānî kî yôdēaʿ.* A similar ellipsis is evident in Isa 3:15, where *mallākem tĕdakkĕʾû ʿammî* means "what's with you *that* you crush my people?" We may compare this to similar constructions in the Mishnah: *mh-lk mqyp lśmʾl* "what's with you *that* you should go to the left?" (*m. Mid.* 2:2); *mh-lzh mbyʾ* "what's with this one *that* he should bring . . . ?" (*m. Ker.* 5:2). The Hebrew idiom *mah-llĕ-*X may mean "what does X have?" (cf. 1 Kgs 12:16 // 2 Chron 10:16, and *Qere* of Isa 52:5). The verse is not referring to the ordinary conduct of the afflicted, but to the general assumption of the wisdom tradition that all people should become skilled in the art of living. For *yôdēaʿ* meaning "skilled," we may compare *yôdēaʿ likrot* "skilled in cutting" (cf. 1 Kgs 5:20 [Eng v 6]), *yôdēaʿ lĕpattēaḥ pittūḥîm* "skilled in engraving" (2 Chron 2:6 [Eng v 7]), *yôdēaʿ laʿăśôt bazzāhāb ûbakkesep* "skilled to work in gold and silver" (2 Chron 2:13 [Eng v 14]). The point is that if there is no advantage even for the wise (so v 8a), then there is no use for the poor to be skilled in the art of living (so 8b).

to go along with life. It is possible that *haḥayyîm* refers more concretely to "the living" (cf. 4:15, where *haḥayyîm* is in parallelism with *hamhallĕkîm taḥat haššāmeš* "those who walk about under the sun"). The point of the whole passage (5:10–6:9 [Heb 5:9–6:9]) is not that the afflicted should "get along" with the living, however. Rather, all people should cope with life appropriately — "go along with life." Moreover, *hălōk neged haḥayyîm* can hardly be separated from *hălōk-nepeš* in the next verse, which refers to the passing of life.

9. *what the eyes see.* Hebrew *marʾēh ʿênayim* normally refers to vision, the ability to see (Lev 13:12; Isa 11:3). But here it refers to the experiencing of what the eyes see — what one has. So Targ correctly interprets the idiom as *mh dʾyt lyh* "what he has." The expression recalls *rĕʾiyyat ʿênāyw* "what their eyes see" in 5:11 (Heb v 10), which suggests that one must live with what is present — before the eyes. In 11:9 one is exhorted to "walk in the ways of your heart and in the seeing of your eyes (*marʾê ʿênêkā*)." That is to say, one must deal with reality as one *thinks* and *observes.* The idiom is related to *rāʾâ ṭôb* "see good" = "enjoy" (see Notes on 2:1). In the Talmud, *mrʾh-ʿynym bʾš* refers to the pleasure of looking at a woman (*b. Yoma* 74b).

than the passing of life. Hebrew *mēhălok-nāpeš* probably has more than one meaning. On the one hand, *hălok-nepeš* (NRSV: "the wandering of desire") alludes to the voracious appetite of those who are discontented with their lives (cf. *wĕnapšô lō’-tiśbaʿ* "he is not satisfied" in v 3 and *wĕgam-hannepeš lō’ timmālē’* "and yet the gullet is not filled" in v 7). The reference to *mar’ēh ʿênayim* "the seeing of the eyes" certainly points back to *rĕ’iyyat ʿênayim* "what their eyes see" in 5:11 (Heb v 10), which has to do with enjoyment of one's bounty. On the other hand, the use of the verb *hālak*, recalls remarks about the destiny of mortals: they "go" in darkness (v 4) and all "go" to one place (v 6). Indeed, Qohelet regularly uses the verb *hālak* to speak of death (1:4; 2:14; 3:20; 6:4, 6; 9:10; 12:5). Elsewhere in the Bible, too, *hālak* may be so used. This is evident in Ps 39:14 (Heb v 13), where *’ēlēk* "I depart" is parallel to *’ênennî* "I exist not." See also the use of *hālak* in Gen 15:2; Ps 109:23; Job 10:21; 14:20; 19:10; 2 Sam 12:23; Hos 6:4; 13:3. The departure of the *nepeš* is synonymous with the passing of life (see Gen 35:18). One may note that *alāku* "to go" in Akkadian may have similar nuances.

this, too, is vanity and a pursuit of wind. See Notes at 1:2 and 1:14.

COMMENT

There is no agreement among scholars on the boundaries of the passage. One difficult issue is its beginning, specifically the place of 5:8–9 (Heb vv 7–8). Some commentators are of the view that these two verses belong with the preceding unit, continuing the admonitions on proper attitude before God (Loader, Barucq). The link is not strong enough to suggest literary unity, however, for the subject matter in the two verses appears to be socioeconomic, whereas in 5:1–7 (Heb 4:17–5:6) the focus is on quiet reverence before God. Yet, even those who do not see 5:8–9 (Heb vv 7–8) as belonging to the preceding unit often hesitate to link them with what follows, preferring to isolate them as an independent unit unrelated to what goes before or after it (Lauha, Whybray, Zimmerli). Only a few have attempted to link 5:8–9 (Heb vv 7–8) with the verses after them (so Beek, Ravasi), while others merely admit to a loose connection (Fox), or that these verses are somehow transitional (Murphy). The difficulty is compounded by the obscurity of the text: apart from the first line, the meaning of v 8 (Heb v 7) is unclear, and v 9 (Heb v 8) is unquestionably disturbed (see Notes above).

One may begin by observing that the subject of injustice and oppression has already been broached in 3:16 and 4:1. In the first instance, the prevalence of injustice prompted Qohelet's immediate remark that God is in control, for there is a time "for every matter" (*lĕkol-hēpeṣ*) and a destiny for every activity (3:17). Qohelet contends that one should not be overly worked up over things that one cannot change. God has given humans and animals a common fate inasmuch as "everyone goes to one place" (*hakkōl hôlēk ’el-māqôm ’eḥād*), returning to the dust whence they came (3:20). Since humans have no advantage over animals, they should take pleasure in all their activities, for that is their "portion" (3:22). Now in 5:8–9 (Heb vv 7–8), Qohelet speaks of oppression and the obliteration of justice, even in places where one might expect it, and he counsels one to take things in stride: "Do not be astonished over the matter (*ʿal-haḥēpeṣ*)." Indeed, throughout 5:10–6:9 (Heb 5:9–6:9) he makes the point that people must be content with what they have because it is their "portion" (5:19 [Heb v 18]). People ought to enjoy themselves whenever they are able because "everyone goes to one place" (*māqôm 'eḥād hakkōl hôlēk*, 6:6). In short, the movement from the observation of oppression and injustice to the admonition to be content and to enjoy, evident in 3:16–22, is also noticeable in 5:8–6:9 (Heb 5:7–6:9). Qohelet's remarks on injustice and oppression in 5:8–9 (Heb vv 7–8) are not out of place in his overall presentation in 5:8–6:9 (Heb 5:7–6:9).

Following his observation of oppression in 4:1, Qohelet goes on to say that those who have already passed on in life are better off than those who are alive, and that those who have never existed are better off than both the dead and the living (4:2–3). Then he observes that it is envy that impels people to seek accomplishment (*kišrôn*), and he suggests that a little with "rest" (*naḥat*) is better than twice as much with toil (4:6). There are people who toil without end, he observes, because "their eyes are not satisfied with wealth" (*'ênāyw lō'-tiśba' 'ōšer*) and one's being is deprived of "bounty" (*ûmĕḥassēr 'et-napšî miṭṭôbâ*), making it all "a terrible venture" (*'inyan rā'*, 4:8). The same issues are evident in 5:8–6:9 (Heb 5:7–6:9). Oppression, the lack of contentment, people's inability to rest and enjoy are all addressed. The idioms are the same as those in 4:1–8, as well: *'ōšeq* "oppression" (5:8 [Heb v 7]), *kišrôn* "accomplishment" (5:11 [Heb v 10]), *'inyan rā'* "terrible venture" (5:14 [Heb v 13]), *napšô lō'-tiśba' min-haṭṭôbâ* "his appetite is not satisfied with bounty" (6:3), and so forth. It can hardly be a coincidence, then, that Qohelet moves from oppression to speak of the lack of contentment in 5:8–6:9 (Heb 5:7–6:9). It appears that 5:8–9 (Heb vv 7–8) is the beginning of the larger literary unit.

Indeed, a comparison with 3:16–22 and 4:1–7 suggests not only that 5:8–9 (Heb vv 7–8) belongs with the verses that follow, it indicates that there is substantial coherence within 5:8–6:9 (Heb 5:7–6:9). This is borne out by a structural analysis of the entire passage. In such a study, Fredericks recently has shown that this portion of the book manifests a "chiastic structure" ("Chiasm and Parallel Structure in Qoheleth 5:6–6:9," pp. 17–35). Fredericks, however, omits 5:8–9 (vv 7–8) from his definition of the larger literary unit. This is odd, since the mention of the "afflicted" (*'ānî*) at the end of the unit (6:8) recalls the situation identified in 5:8 (Heb v 7). Elsewhere in the Bible, *'ānî* "afflicted" is associated with the poor and the oppressed — people who have been deprived of justice (Deut 24:14; Ps 82:3; Prov 22:22; Isa 3:14; 10:2; Ezek 18:12; 22:29; Zech 7:10), as opposed to those who have a surfeit of food (Ezek 16:49). As will become evident below, there are other allusions in 6:7–9 to oppression, as well. Thus, oppression is mentioned at 5:8–9 (Heb vv 7–8), and it is again in focus in 6:7–9: the poor (5:8 [Heb v 7]) and the afflicted (6:9) form an *inclusio*. In light of this framing, and on the basis of a comparison with 3:16–22 and 4:1–7, it is appropriate to include 5:8–9 (Heb vv 7–8) within the first section of the larger literary unit, namely, 5:8–12 (Heb vv 7–11). Moreover, Fredericks does not include 5:20 (Heb v 19) in his analysis. There is no discussion at all of its content or its place in the whole passage. In fact, 5:20 (Heb v 19) stands in isolation, sandwiched between the innermost sections (5:13–19 [Heb vv 12–18] and 6:1–2).

With these observations, we are ready to present schematically the overall structure of the unit, thanks in large measure to the perceptive analysis of Fredericks:

A *5:8–12 (Heb 5:7–11)*   A' *6:7–9*

the poor (v 8 [7])   the afflicted (v 8)
not satisfied (v 10 [9])   not satisfied (v 7)
what accomplishment (v 11 [10])   what advantage (v 8)
seeing of their eyes (v 11 [10])   seeing of eyes (v 9)

B *5:13–17 (Heb 5:12–16)*   B' *6:3–6*

he sired a son (v 14 [13])   he sires a hundred (v 3)
going as he came (v 15 [14])   he came . . . he went (v 4)
he eats in darkness (v 17 [16])   he goes in darkness (v 4)

C *5:18–19 (Heb 5:17–18)*   C' *6:1–2*
good (v 18 [17])   evil (v 1)
God has given (v 19 [18])   God gives (v 2)
this is a gift (v 19 [20])   this is a sickness (v 2)

D *5:20 (Heb 5:19)*
must not remember much
God preoccupies/responds with joy in their heart

The pattern that emerges is similar to that which we have already encountered in 1:12–2:26. The sections correspond to one another in such a way that one small unit, 5:20 (Heb v 19), is left as the pivot on which the two halves of the larger literary unit turn. Thus 5:20 (Heb v 19) is the center of the entire passage. The outermost sections deal with the insatiability of certain people (5:8–12 [Heb vv 7–11] // 6:7–9), the two middle passages concern people who cannot enjoy the present (5:13–17 [Heb vv 12–16] // 6:3–6), the innermost sections pertain to the good and bad of divine arbitration (5:18–19 [Heb vv 17–18] // 6:1–2), and the central verse (5:20 [Heb v 19]) provides the resolution to the problem posed in the entire passage. Thus, the following sections are discernible:

A People Who Cannot Be Satisfied (5:8–12 [Heb vv 7–11])
  B People Who Cannot Enjoy (5:13–17 [Heb vv 12–16])
    C What Is Good (5:18–19 [Heb vv 17–18])
      D Enjoy the Moment (5:20 [Heb v 19])
    C' What Is Bad (6:1–2)
  B' People Who Cannot Enjoy (6:3–6)
A' People Who Cannot Be Satisfied (6:7–9)

There are good reasons, then, to assume that the literary unit is 5:8–6:9 (Heb 5:7–6:9). It is also evident that the entire passage is concerned with the problem of human insatiability and lack of contentment. Qohelet's purpose is to address this problem by calling for enjoyment in the present. This is made clear at the heart of the passage, in 5:20 (Heb v 19), through an admonition for people not to call to mind the days of their lives too often. Insofar as this passage is focused on the appropriate response to God and the right attitude to life's bounty, this passage properly follows 5:1–7 (Heb 4:17–5:6), which is concerned with one's attitude before God. There are also several thematic and vocabulary links between this passage and the reflections in 1:11–4:16. Indeed, it appears that this literary unit is the denouement of the first half of the book. It is the author's instruction to the reader in the light of the fact that everything is ephemeral and ultimately unreliable.

People Who Cannot Be Satisfied (5:8–11 [Heb vv 7–10])

Qohelet begins by calling attention to the oppression of the poor and the obliteration of justice. Whereas he speaks only generally of injustice and oppression in 3:16 and 4:1, now he seems to emphasize *economic* inequities. The oppressed are called "poor" and he speaks of "the violation of justice and righteousness." The Hebrew word for "violation" normally has to do with robbery, extortion, and usury (Lev 5:20–21 [Eng 6:1–2]; Pss 35:10; 62:11 [Eng v 10]; Prov 22:22; Isa 3:14; 61:8; Ezek 18:16–18; 22:29; 33:15; Sir 16:13). In Isa 10:2, the expression "to violate justice of the afflicted of my people" is juxtaposed with other expressions of economic oppression. This situation of oppression, says Qohelet, is what one may see "in the province" (*bammĕdînâ*).

Qohelet elaborates on the matter, but it is not entirely clear what he says or means. The text is exceedingly difficult. The dominant view among commentators is that he is referring to the bureaucratic satrapial system of his time in which different levels of lofty officials either spied on or looked out for one another as they perpetrated their crimes. The government was corrupt. But it is doubtful whether the Hebrew will sustain this view (see Notes at 5:8 [Heb v 7]). The arrogant ones are ambitious people who think that they can achieve anything they want at anybody's expense. They are haughty and ambitious. This view is more consonant with the usage of the Hebrew word for "arrogant" or "lofty" (cf. Isa 10:33; Ezek 21:31 [Eng v 26]). The point is that there are such haughty people everywhere trying to climb the socioeconomic ladder, who have no regard for the poor and lowly. No matter how high they get, however, there are always people who are higher than they, looking down at them. And so they cannot be content till they get to the next rung of the ladder.

Qohelet may have been thinking of the upper and middle classes in his generation, who were increasingly attracted by the opportunities of the urban centers and by new means of acquiring wealth. They were the ones driven by envy to do whatever they had to in order to get ahead (4:4–6). If this is the background, then the very problematic words of v 9 (Heb v 8) may make some sense. Perhaps Qohelet was urging the ambitious not to abandon the agrarian way of life too readily in their quest for success, for land has its advantage in its yield and must be cultivated for what it provides. Or, as a proverb has it, "the tillage of the poor yields much food, but substance is swept away for lack of moderation" (Prov 13:23 in NJPS). Land is good for its measure and the field is cultivated for its yield.

Alternatively, Qohelet may have been addressing those who were accumulating property, "adding land to land and field to field" (compare Isa 5:18), as it were. They were trying to buy up more and more land for investment only, but the text makes the point that land is cultivated for its yield. It is meant to produce food. It is not meant for economic speculation. Ambition and greed are at issue. In any case, the gist of 5:9 (Heb v 8) is that land is intended only for the sustenance it provides: it should neither be abandoned nor misappropriated.

Qohelet appears to be linking ambition with the presence of oppression and injustice. The problem is with greed, the insatiability of the haughty rich. He goes on then to say that people who love money will not be satisfied with money (5:10 [Heb v 9]). Wealth itself is not the problem here, but the insatiability of those who love money. There is always more that they want, always something else. They will not be satisfied with *tĕbûʾâ* "yield," a word which may refer both to the yield of the land (Ps 107:37; 2 Chron 31:5; Isa 30:23) or just income in general (see Prov 3:14; 10:16; 15:6; 16:8). The writer of the first Epistle to Timothy in the NT may have been thinking of Qohelet's words when he speaks of the "love of money" being the root of all evil (1 Tim 6:10). The same writer also urges Timothy to charge the rich "not to be haughty" but to set their aspirations on God who has richly provided people "with everything to enjoy" (1 Tim 6:17). The author urges contentment, "for we brought nothing into the world and we cannot take anything out of the world" (1 Tim 6:7, compare Eccl 5:15 [Heb v 14]). For Qohelet, the insatiability of the rich is "vanity," something that is unreliable, ephemeral, and deceitful (see Notes at 1:2).

As he often does, Qohelet supports his contention with a proverb: "when bounty increases, those who consume it increase" (5:11 [Heb v 10]). It is clear that the bounty here refers to wealth and its benefits (4:8; 5:18 [Heb v 17]; 6:3; 6:6; 7:14), but interpreters do not agree on the identity of those who "consume" or "eat" this bounty. The majority of scholars contend that Qohelet is referring to the self-seeking relatives or friends of those who have become rich; the sycophants are ever ready to claim their share of the bounty. The richer one becomes, the more these greedy relatives and friends demand. Others think that Qohelet is referring to the expenses that the rich have to incur for the management of their estates and taxes. It is costly to be rich, as it were: the greater the wealth the greater the expenses. If either of these views is correct, this verse may tell us something of Qohelet's economic background, for it takes a very rich person to bemoan the cost of wealth. Certainly the middle classes and the poor would not mind the opportunity to incur such expenses. It must be noted, however, that this verse is only one of numerous references in the larger literary unit to consumption and satisfaction, whether literal or figurative (5:10, 11, 12, 17, 18 [Heb vv 9, 10, 11, 16, 17]; 6:2, 3, 7). Indeed, in the very next verse (5:12 [Heb v 11]), one notes the mention of consumption and satiation. It is more likely, therefore, that the consumers of the bounty (literally "those who eat it") are the greedy ones themselves: the more the wealth, the more its consumers "increase" — in every sense of the word!

The rhetorical question in 5:11 (Heb v 10) presupposes a negative answer. There is, in fact, no benefit to those who possess the wealth, "except what their eyes see." This does not mean that the rich can only see the accumulation of their wealth, before it disappears (Whybray). Rather, "what the eyes see" refers to what is present and enjoyable (see Notes above). What Qohelet means is that wealth is good only when it is enjoyed in the present, and that satisfaction should not be postponed in anticipation of some greater benefit in the future.

The point is substantiated by another proverb, this one contrasting the pleasant sleep of "the worker" with the lack of rest for the rich person (5:12 [Heb v 11]). At first blush, the language here reminds one of the proverb about the "worker of the ground" (*ʿōbēd ʾădāmâ*) being satiated with food, while the lazy are being satiated with poverty (Prov 12:11 // 28:19). But that is not the point of the saying here. The contrast is not between one who works and one who is a sluggard, but between the poor "worker" and the rich one who toils. It is more appropriate to compare this verse with Qohelet's own saying that it is better to have "a handful with rest" than twice as much with toil (4:6), for the rich one here is granted no rest, whereas "the worker" ironically has pleasant sleep. Not impossibly, "the worker" (*hāʿōbēd*) here alludes to the poor and economically exploited people who are responsible for the "cultivated land" (*śādeh neʿĕbād*) in 5:8–9 (Heb vv 7–8). They are the ones who are pitted against the arrogant rich, the "lofty." Their means are few, but they sleep well whether they consume little or much. The rich, by contrast, cannot sleep because of their surfeit (they have more than "much"!).

The mention of the surfeit of the rich immediately after the amount that the worker consumes, leads one to think that the author means that the rich are sated with food and, therefore, are unable to sleep because of indigestion, or the like. This is a possible interpretation of the saying. Indeed, there is a Sumerian proverb that is reminiscent of this: "He who eats too much will not (be able) to sleep" (see Gordon, *Sumerian Proverbs*, p. 97). One must not miss Qohelet's humor, however. The surfeit here in fact refers to overindulgence *both* in food and in economic enterprises. The rich have a tendency to "over-consume," so to speak, and so they are unable to sleep either because of indigestion or worry — or both! Greed is, again, the issue. The rich cannot seem to get enough. From beginning to end the problem in this section is with the insatiability of the rich who will do anything to consume more and more. But the more they consume, the more they "increase" (both physically and economically) and their "surfeit" (both physical and economic) allows them no rest.

People Who Cannot Enjoy (5:13–17 [Heb vv 12–16])

Qohelet turns next to speak of a "sickening tragedy" that he has observed. He has spoken of the accumulation of wealth by those who never seemed to be satisfied with what they have. He has intimated that there is no accomplishment for those who possess bounty, except what they are able to enjoy at the moment. Now he speaks of wealth that is hoarded to the point where it hurts the one who possesses it. Perhaps he is thinking of people who think it is good to store up an inheritance and to save for posterity (see also Prov 13:21–22 and Comment at 2:20–21). The result is not good but harm, however, and the wealth that is hoarded brings only pain—perhaps the pain of its loss.

Qohelet's "rich fool" is a parabolic figure, a man who stored up his possessions, only to lose them all (compare Luke 12:13–20). One scholar has hypothesized that the man was the victim of a bank failure who lost everything that was kept for him in his account (Lohfink). But the text says nothing about the circumstances surrounding the failure, only that it was "a terrible venture." There is no attempt to blame anyone or any event for the tragedy. We are only told the cold fact— that it happened. Life is unpredictable, and the hoarding of wealth guarantees one nothing. On the contrary, the loss of that great hoarded wealth brings one only pain.

The parsimonious man sired a son, "but he has nothing in his possession." Elsewhere Qohelet speaks of people who toil without having anyone to inherit or share their wealth (2:18; 4:8). Now he presents the ironic situation of a man who lost his hoarded wealth and then sired a son. The birth of the son is ironic, for now the man has someone to whom to bequeath his possessions, only now "he has nothing in his possession." Perhaps this parsimonious man had reasoned that it was for his heirs that he had to defer his own enjoyment of the wealth, but now "there is nothing in his possession" (5:14 [Heb v 13]).

Here we note that the phrase "he has nothing in *his* possession" is somewhat ambiguous, for "his" may refer to either the father or the son. While the phrase points backward to the father's loss of wealth (he leaves this world with nothing in his possession), it also may point forward to the son's plight—the son comes into the world with nothing in his possession. In fact, it is this ambiguity that allows Qohelet to move from the specific instance of the rich fool to the general moral of the story. He cites a popular saying similar to one cited by Job when he lost everything he had: "just as he came from the womb of his mother, so he will return, going as he came" (5:15 [Heb v 14]; see also Job 1:21; Sir 40:1; 1 Tim 6:7).

The language of going and coming is used of birth and death (see Comment at 1:4). The point of the aphorism is that material goods can only be enjoyed as long as one lives. You cannot take it with you when you die. Or, as the Egyptian *Song of Antef* puts it: "No one can bring his property with him. No one who goes will come back again" (Papyrus Harris 500, lines 40–41; cf. Fox, "A Study of Antef," p. 407). It is "a sickening tragedy" that people come and go, that the human life span is limited. People do not bring anything with them when they enter the world, nor can they take anything with them when they leave. What is gained in a lifetime matters only in the lifetime. So there is no advantage in trying to hold on to what one has, for the gain is as elusive and unpredictable as wind (5:16 [Heb v 15]).

The meaning of 5:17 (Heb v 16) is disputed. The difficulty lies in the interpretation of the reference to the person consuming in darkness (*baḥōšek yōʾkēl*). It has been suggested that the rich miser had been so devastated by his loss that he was forced to work long hours in the day and had to eat his meals when it was dark, or that he had become so poor he could not not even afford light by which to have his meal, or that he was too parsimonious to spend money on oil for his lamps (see Ginsburg, *Coheleth*, pp. 353–55). Others take the language to be figurative, assuming that darkness is a metaphor for loneliness or misery. This is how the Targum interprets it.

To understand the imagery, one must first note that the author has already used the verb "to eat, consume" to speak of the lifestyles of the rich and the poor (5:11, 12 [Heb vv 10, 11]). Hence, one may take the verb here to be a figurative expression for living or even making a living, a usage attested in Akkadian and in Amos 7:12 (see Notes at 5:17 [Heb v 16]). Moreover, "darkness" occurs twice in 6:4, referring to the lifeless state of the stillborn child (see also 2:14). In 11:8 the author refers to the days of pain and misery as "the days of darkness." Thus, consuming in darkness means roughly the same thing as going in darkness, being dead. C. Barth's comment about people in misery is appropriate here as well: "The life of a sick person has become so weak that it no longer deserves the name, and can now only be termed darkness. The power of death has already gained the upper hand over him" (*Die Errettung vom Tode in den individuellen Klage- and Dankliedern des Alten Testamentes* [2d. ed; Zurich: Theologischer Verlag, 1987], p. 101). The gist of the idea is that these people, though they are alive, go through life as if they were already dead. Despite all their wealth and other possessions, they live life in utter darkness. Unable to enjoy life in the present, they make themselves exceedingly miserable all their lives.

What Is Good (5:18–19 [Heb vv 17–18])

In the preceding verses Qohelet speaks of two ways by which people show that they are not able to accept what they have in the present: (1) there are those who are never satisfied with what they have and keep trying to acquire more (5:8–12 [Heb vv 7–11]), and (2) there are those who hoard what they have acquired and cannot enjoy themselves (5:13–17 [Heb vv 12–16]).

Now in 5:17–19 (Heb vv 16–18) Qohelet states the issue positively, articulating what he sees as "good." It is apparent that he intends for the attitude advocated in these verses to be a counterpoint to what has been discussed in the preceding section. This is evident in the similar manner in which 5:13–17 (Heb vv 12–16) and 5:18–19 (Heb vv 17–18) are introduced. The clause "here is what I have observed is good" in 5:18 (Heb v 17) stands in stark contrast to "there is a sickening tragedy that I have observed" in 5:13 (Heb v 12). In 5:13–17 the author speaks repeatedly of what is bad, terrible, tragic, and hurtful (see *rāʿâ* in vv 13, 16 [Heb vv 12, 15], *rāʿ* in v 14 [Heb v 13]). Now in 5:18–19 the text lifts up what is "good" and "appropriate" (see *ṭôb* in v 18 [Heb v 17], *ṭôbâ* in v 18 [Heb v 17], *yāpeh* in v 18 [Heb v 17]). What is sad for him is that human life span is limited: generations "come" and "go." Yet there is also that which is "good." What Qohelet perceives to be good is that it is appropriate "to eat, and drink, and enjoy good" despite all the toil.

This section is related by vocabulary and content with 3:10–15, which also pertains to what is *yāpeh* "appropriate" (3:11), the enjoyment of life (3:12–13), and the gift of God (3:10, 11, 13). Qohelet speaks of toil and the possibility of joy in one breath, for he thinks of life as a "portion" (5:18–19 [Heb vv 17–18]), perhaps like an inherited lot that has spatial and temporal limitations but also the possibility of joy (see Notes and Comment at 2:10). Toil is inevitable in this lot of life that each mortal has, but there can also be pleasure in that lot. As in 2:24–26 and 3:10–22, he makes his point theologically: "God gave them" (5:18 [Heb v 17]), "God gave them" (5:19 [Heb v 18]), "it is the gift of God" (5:20 [Heb v 19]). It is God who has bequeathed to humanity their portion and granted them the right—the authority—to enjoy their gifts.

Enjoy the Moment (5:20 [Heb v 19])
In the overall structure of the larger literary unit, this verse is the midpoint and the focus. The three preceding sections lead to it, and it anticipates the three sections that follow it. Here we have the message of the entire passage in a nutshell.

The first half of the verse is usually interpreted as a statement of fact, that people "will scarcely brood over the days of their lives" (NRSV). One may, however, take the verb as a negative injunction, thus, "they should not much call to mind the days of their lives." Qohelet's point can hardly be that people will not brood over their lives, for they certainly do. Indeed, the problem throughout the book is that people do so excessively, paying so much attention to their misery and their uncertain future that they cannot enjoy what they have. In another passage, the author suggests that people should remember that the days of darkness will be many, and so they should take pleasure in all their days while they still can (11:7–10). There the Hebrew verb is exactly the same as in 5:20 (Heb v 19), only without the negative particle before it (see Comment at 11:8). People do think about their days, and will continue to do so, but there is an appropriate calling to mind and an inappropriate, harmful one, it seems. In 11:7–9, the purpose of the consideration of the days ahead is to call one to consider the possibilities and pleasures of the present, while it is still possible to enjoy. Qohelet's call in 5:20 (Heb v 19) for people *not* to bring their days to mind ironically achieves the same end. It is addressed to people who already think too much of their lives and of their future, and hence, cannot accept the pleasures of the moment.

The basis for this admonition is theological. It has to do with God's activity. The nature of that activity is ambiguous, however. The meaning of Hebrew *ma'ăneh* is debated (see Notes at 5:20 [Heb v 19]). It has traditionally been associated with the root from which one derives *'inyān* "preoccupation," and so it is assumed that God keeps humanity preoccupied with the joy that is in their hearts. So NRSV translates, "God keeps them occupied with the joy of their hearts." But, as with the use of *la'ănôt* "to be preoccupied" in 1:13 and 3:10, the word here may be multivalent. Perhaps Qohelet means to say that one ought not think about the days of one's life because God is giving one a preoccupation through the pleasures of the heart. That is, God has made it possible to forget about one's ephemeral life (see also 6:12; 9:9) through the enjoyment of life. This idea is not without precedent in the ancient Near East, as a few scholars have noted (Galling, Lauha, Fox). In the Egyptian *Song of Antef,* one finds the following injunction: "May you be whole, as your heart makes itself forget" (Papyrus Harris 500, lines 23–24; cf. Fox, "Song of Antef," p. 410). As Fox points out, the Egyptians called entertainment "distracting the heart," an expression that appears in the captions of various scenes of merrymaking (*Contradictions,* p. 217).

Qohelet apparently also thinks of pleasure in this way. So he urges people not to think of "the days of their lives," presumably their days of misery, because God has made the pleasures of the heart a possible diversion. It appears that the same God who gives mortals *'inyan rā'* "a terrible preoccupation" (see also 1:13; 3:10) is the one who gives the possibility of joy. This is how the oppressed (5:8–9 [Heb vv 7–8]) and the afflicted (*'ānî*) can cope with life: they can have what their eyes see (6:8–9).

Yet, there may be more to the word *ma'ǎneh* than meets the eye. Indeed, the Hebrew word, if it means "one who gives preoccupation," is not found anywhere else. At the same time, the form *ma'ǎneh,* meaning "answer," is found several times in the wisdom literature of the Bible (Prov 15:1, 23; 16:1; 29:19; Job 32:3, 5). Prov 15:23 is particularly intriguing since it says that an apt *ma'ǎneh* "answer" is a joy to people. Inasmuch as the form in our passage (5:20 [Heb v 19]) is precisely *ma'ǎneh* (without the object indicated!), it is difficult not to associate the word with the other occurrences of *ma'ǎneh* in the Bible. It does not make much sense to suggest that God is the "answer in joy," but one must nevertheless consider it likely that Qohelet uses the word to evoke the idea that it is God who *answers* humans through the joy of their hearts. Lohfink takes such a position, arguing that Qohelet intends to convey the idea that God "reveals" through joy ("Revelation by Joy," pp. 625–35). God is the one who gives a preoccupation through joy, but God also gives a response to humanity through joy in their hearts. It is the same God who makes possible this positive preoccupation, perhaps as a resolution to the *'inyan rā'* "terrible preoccupation" that humanity must face in life.

What Is Bad (6:1–2)

These verses are problematic for the interpreter because they seem to negate what has been said in 5:18–20 (Heb vv 17–19). This appears all the more so because the vocabulary and style in 6:1–2 suggest that this section is intended to mirror 5:18–19 (Heb vv 17–18) in some way, as if the two were together a paradox, the one as true as the other.

Despite the similarities, however, there are significant differences. Indeed, the lexical and stylistic similarities only serve to highlight the real differences between the two situations. The following divergences are evident:

5:18–19 (Heb vv 17–18)	6:1–2
all people	a person
God has given	God gives
God has authorized	God does not authorize
this is the gift of God	this is vanity

The details are important. In the first place, 5:18–19 (Heb vv 17–18) speaks of "all people" (*kol-hā'ādām*), whereas 6:1–2 pertains to "a person" (*'îš*). The first concerns the universal, the second the particular. Or, as Isaksson puts it, 5:18–19 (Heb vv 17–18) states the general rule, while 6:1–2 indicates "the possibility of exceptions to the rule" (see *Studies in the Language of Qoheleth*, p. 122). To be sure, 6:1 speaks of the evil being great over humanity (*hā'ādām*), but that means only that humanity as a whole is subject to the possibility of such instances as described in 6:2. Moreover, in regard to God's role, 5:19 (Heb v 18) uses Hebrew verbs in the perfect ("God gave," "he has authorized"), whereas 6:2 uses the imperfect ("God gives," "God does not authorize"). The former describes what is, the latter what could be. In sum, there are three fundamental differences between 5:18–19 (Heb vv 17–18) and 6:1–2: (1) one is positive, the other negative; (2) one is universal, the other particular; (3) one indicates the rule, the other the exception. As a general rule, God already has permitted humans (*kol-hā'ādām*) to enjoy what they have, given them material possessions, and authorized them to partake of what they have as their portion. This is the manifestation of God's gift to humanity. Yet there are instances when that gift is not evident, when the same God who gives material possessions may not give certain individuals the ability to enjoy them.

We do not know what kind of person Qohelet has in mind, or what circumstances may cause one not to enjoy material possessions. One can only guess whether the author is thinking of economic, physical, or psychological handicaps. In 2:24–26, he speaks of an arbitrary deity who allows some to enjoy good but not others. Now he says only that a "stranger" — someone who is not expected to partake in that person's place — will, in fact, reap the benefits. Qohelet speaks readily of God's gift to humanity, but he is also realistic in admitting that there are painful, inexplicable exceptions. Such a situation he calls *hebel* "vanity" — an enigmatic situation — and a "terrible sickness."

People Who Cannot Enjoy (6:3–6)
As 6:1–2 corresponds to 5:18–19 (Heb vv 17–18), so 6:3–6 matches 5:13–17 (Heb vv 12–16). There are echoes in 6:3–6 of the section it mirrors in Chapter 5: "he sires" (6:3), "he came in darkness and he walks in darkness" (6:4). To be sure, the illustration in Chapter 5 calls attention to wealth that is hoarded, whereas 6:3–6 speaks of other matters of importance to people, namely, fecundity and longevity. Yet, the fundamental problem is the same in both sections: there are people who simply cannot enjoy what they have. In the ancient Near East, wealth, progeny, and longevity are the items that humans, even kings, most commonly requested from the deity (*KTU* 1.14.1.52–2.5; 1.17.6.17–18; see *ANET*[3],

pp. 143, 151). These are the gifts that wisdom bestows on the wise (Prov 3:16; 8:18). Yet, even these gifts will not make some people happy. They are always troubled and angry (5:17 [Heb v 16]), and they complain about every ridiculous matter, even about both life and death — that their days are still to come and that they have no grave site (6:3). If they have everything in life — wealth, progeny, and longevity — they will complain about the days that are still to come and about death. Such people think too much about the days of their lives (see also 5:20 [Heb v 19]).

In such a case, Qohelet says, the stillborn child is better off, echoing Job's complaint when he lost both his wealth and children (Job 3:16). The saying in 6:4 is also reminiscent of the aphorism in 5:15 (Heb v 14) about birth and death, except that in this instance there is no life span to speak of: the stillborn child enters the transient world already devoid of life and goes in darkness, its memory hidden in darkness forever. It neither has seen the sun (see Job 3:16; Ps 58:9 [Eng v 8]), nor did it have consciousness. Those who are alive are in a different situation — for better or for worse: the living "see" and "know." Inasmuch as they inevitably see evil, they are worse off than the stillborn child (4:3). At the same time, however, the living are also capable of "seeing good," enjoying what is present. The living know to have rest (see 4:6). Thus, the living may be better off, but they may also be worse off, depending on how they see and know. It's a matter of perspective, as it were. Thus, even if one lives a thousand years twice over — more than twice the nine-hundred-and-sixty-nine-year life span of Methuselah (Gen 5:27) — but cannot enjoy good, then the stillborn child is indeed better off. For Qohelet, life consists of both the good and the bad. It is inevitable that one will observe the evil that exists (4:1–3), but one can also "see good," that is, enjoy what one has in the present.

People Who Cannot Be Satisfied (6:7–9)
In this final section of the literary unit, Qohelet returns to the issue broached in the first section, namely, the problem of human insatiability. As in the first section, the language of consumption and satiation is metaphorical for human greed. Hence he speaks of human "toil" for their mouths. It has been observed that the language here is reminiscent of idioms pertaining to the insatiability of Sheol, or, in Canaanite mythology, Death. This is probably correct, but that does not mean that Qohelet is thinking that human toil only leads to Sheol, the "one place" to which he alludes in the preceding verse, as Ackroyd contends ("Two Hebrew Notes," pp. 82–86).

We note first that Hebrew *nepeš*, the word for "gullet," is used in 6:2 and 6:3 for human appetite, as also in 4:8. The word appears again in 6:9, where the proper translation is debatable, but the possibility of allusion to Sheol is certainly precluded. Moreover, the corresponding section (5:8–12 [Heb vv 7–11]) is concerned with the insatiability of the arrogant rich. The larger literary context demands, therefore, that one interpret 6:7 as referring to the insatiability of people, specifically the rich. The "gullet" of these people is at issue. Nevertheless, it would be erroneous to ignore the mythological background of the text. In Canaanite mythology, deified Death is portrayed as an insatiable monster with an opened mouth, one lip reaching the netherworld, the other reaching the sky, and its tongue reaching the stars (*KTU* 1.5.2.2–4; 1.23.61–62; cf. *ANET*³, p. 138). Death waits impatiently to take its victims into its gullet (Ugaritic *npš*). The Biblical writers applied this imagery to speak of Sheol (Isa 5:14; Prov 27:20; 30:16), as Ackroyd has correctly observed. But what is more important for our interpretation, though not noted by commentators, is that the same idioms have also been applied to the rich and oppressive people who seem as insatiable as mythological Death. Thus a psalmist speaks of the haughty rich who threaten oppression from on high: "they set their mouth in the heavens and the tongue goes to the netherworld" (Ps 73:9). The rich oppressors are ever ready to consume the rest of humanity like mythological Death. The prophet Habakkuk describes an arrogant oppressor in a similar way: "[he] widens his gullet like Sheol, like Death he is never satisfied" (Hab 2:5). Habakkuk also alludes to the myth of Baal's defeat by Death when he speaks of the wicked swallowing up the righteous (1:13; compare Isa 57:4). In short, the language of Death's insatiability is not infrequently appropriated to describe the insatiability of human oppressors. This is surely the background of Qohelet's words. The insatiable rich are that monstrous and deadly!

The implication of what Qohelet is saying is that the insatiability of the rich is not only self-destructive, it poses dangers to others who fall prey to their greed. Here, as in the mirror section (5:8–12 [Heb vv 7–11]), personal greed has social consequences. The author is thinking of the oppressive rich, who will gobble up anything and anyone. Qohelet elevates the issue to a higher plain so that discontentment is seen to have consequences not only for individuals, but also for society at large, even for the cosmos. Greed endangers the world. It endangers life itself.

It is in the face of such monstrosity that Qohelet asks what advantage the wise have over the fool. Here, as elsewhere, the question is rhetorical. He means that the wise are no less vulnerable than the fool before the gaping gullet of the insatiable oppressors. Everyone is endangered by the greedy!

The next line is difficult (see Notes at 6:8). Scholars are often troubled by the mention of "the afflicted" and they wonder about its relevance here. Some emend the text, while others seek recourse in alternative explanations of the Hebrew word. But the reference to the afflicted properly ties the passage to its beginning in 5:8–9 (Heb vv 7–8). The Hebrew word for "afflicted" is a synonym for "poor" and "oppressed" (see Notes and Comment at 5:8 [Heb v 7]). Thus, Isaiah speaks of what is taken away from "the afflicted" (*gĕzēlat heʿānî*; compare *gēzel* in 5:8 [Heb v 7]) in a passage that speaks of the rich gobbling up the vineyards and crushing the poor (Isa 3:13–15; see also *ligzōl mišpaṭ ʿăniyyê ʿammî* "to violate the justice of the afflicted of my people" in Isa 10:2). It is appropriate, therefore, that Qohelet mentions the afflicted in this context about the insatiability of the oppressive rich. Qohelet's dilemma here is ostensibly with the conduct of those who are oppressed: if the wise has no advantage over fools, why should the afflicted learn how to cope with life?

The answer is given the form of another *ṭôb-saying*, a "better than"-saying (see

Comment on Chapter 4): "what the eyes see is better than the passing of life." The meaning of the first half of the saying is clear enough from the usage of the idiom elsewhere; it has to do with enjoying the pleasures of the moment. Ironically, Qohelet's response to the poor here is the same as what he said to the rich in 5:11 (Heb v 10). To the rich he intimates that there is no accomplishment, except in what is present and enjoyable. To the poor he suggests that there is no advantage for anyone, although what is present and enjoyable is relatively good.

The meaning of the second half of the *tôb-saying* is more difficult. The idiom *hălok-nepeš* has often been translated as "the roving of the appetite" (NIV), "the wandering of desire" (RSV), or the like. This meaning is not impossible, particularly in light of the association of the *nepeš* with satiation in 6:2, 3, 6. But the metaphor of a wandering appetite is somewhat forced. It is more probable that the idiom means "the passing of life," thus referring to death. At the same time, the mention of *nepeš* does recall the insatiability of mortals. Thus the whole verse suggests that it is better to have what is before the eyes, what is present, rather than to die on account of one's insatiability. This saying is directed at all people, the rich and the poor alike.

PART II.A. REFLECTION:
EVERYTHING IS ELUSIVE

II.A.1. NO ONE KNOWS WHAT IS GOOD (6:10–7:14)

6   [10]Whatever happens has already been designated; the course of human beings is known, and they cannot dispute with the one who is stronger than they. [11]Indeed, there are many words that increase vanity. What advantage do human beings have? [12]For who knows what is good for human beings in life, in the few days of their fleeting life? They will spend them as in a shadow, for who can tell people what will happen afterwards under the sun?

7   [1]Fame is better than fine ointment,
   and the day of death than the day of birth.
  [2]It is better to go to a house of mourning
   than to go to a house of feasting.
   Since that is the end of all humanity,
   let the one who is alive lay (it) to heart.
  [3]Vexation is better than merriment,
   for in the sadness of the countenance the heart will be glad.
  [4]The heart of the wise is in the house of mourning,
   but the heart of the foolish is in the house of pleasure.
  [5]It is better to hear the rebuke of the wise,
   than for one to hear the ode of fools.
  [6]For like the crackling of thorns under a pot,
   so is the mirth of the fool.
   But this, too, is vanity;
  [7]for oppression turns the wise into fools,
   And a payment perverts the mind.
  [8]The end of a matter is better than its beginning;

It is better to be patient than arrogant.
⁹Do not be quick to anger,
for anger stays in the bosom of fools.
¹⁰Do not say, "How is it that the former days
were better than these?"
Indeed, it is not out of wisdom that you ask so.
¹¹Wisdom is as good as inheritance,
and an advantage to those who see the sun.
¹²For wisdom is as a shadow, money is as a shadow;
knowledge is an advantage, wisdom lets its possessor live.

¹³See the activity of God, for who is able to straighten what he has made crooked?
¹⁴When times are good, enjoy; when times are bad, see — yes, God has made the one just like the other so that people will not discover anything after them.

NOTES

6   10. *Whatever happens.* The expression *mah-ššehāyâ* refers to current events or state of affairs, as it does also in 1:9, 3:15, and 7:24. Always when the expression is used in Ecclesiastes, the issue is what is happening or what has been happening in the world, rather than just "what exists" (so NIV, REB, NAB) or "what has already existed" (NEB). It means essentially the same thing as *kol-ʾăšer naʿăśâ taḥat haššāmayim* "all that has been done under the heavens" (1:13) and *kol-hammaʿăśîm šennaʿăśû taḥat haššāmeš* "all the deeds that have been done under the sun" (1:14). Note the parallelism of *mah-ššehāyâ* "whatever has happened" with *mah-ššennaʿăśâ* "what has been done" in 1:9. In short, "whatever happens" is what has been done in the universe.

has already been designated. Hebrew *kĕbār niqrāʾ šĕmô*, lit. "already its name has been called." The idiom *qārāʾ (bĕ)šēm* "call (by) name" often means "to designate, appoint, destine." In Ps 147:4, for example, *qārāʾ šēmôt* "call the names" occurs in parallelism with *mānâ mispār* "assign the number" = "appoint" (see also the use of *mānâ* in Isa 65:12; Jon 2:1; 3:6, 7). In this Psalm and in Isa 40:26, the luminaries are assigned by the Creator to their specific stations in the cosmos (compare *Enuma Eliš*, Tablet V; ANET³, pp. 67–68). The idiom is used frequently in Deutero-Isaiah in a manner that echoes the Akkadian royal inscriptions, with their idioms of royal election (see Isa 41:25; 43:1; 45:4). That is, *qārāʾ (bĕ)šēm* "call (by) name" means roughly the same thing as Akkadian *šumam nabû* "to call the name" = "to appoint, designate, choose" (see references in CAD XI/1, pp. 34–39). The idiom in this context simply refers to the divine predetermination. One may compare the following saying in the Aramaic *Proverbs of Ahiqar*: "Many are [the s]tar[s of heaven who]se names one does not know. Behold, thus the individual human does not know" (see TAD III, 1.1.164).

the course of human beings is known. Assuming Hebrew *wĕnôdaʿ ʾăśūrēhû < > ʾādām*, with one *alep* deleted as dittography, and taking the verb to be the Niphal perfect 3 ms (rather than the Niphal participle). MT's *wĕnôdāʿ ʾăšer-hûʾ ʾādām* (lit. "and it is known that he is human") is very awkward in this context. LXX takes the text to mean "it is known what the human is," and this is the way many translators understand it (see NIV: "what man is has been known"; JB: "we know what people are"). But the Hebrew can hardly mean that. As Gordis has noted, one should expect Hebrew *mah* instead of *'ăšer* for the indirect question (*Koheleth*, p. 263); *'ăšer* can mean "what" as a relative pronoun (= "that which") but not "what" as an answer to an implicit or explicit question. After verbs of perception the particle *'ăšer* should mean "that," not "what." Thus, *'ăšer-hû' 'ādām* ought to mean *"that* he is a human," not *"what* the human is." Cf. *šehem-běhēmâ* "that they are beasts" in 3:18. So Vulg, correctly, reads *et scitur quod homo sit* "it is known *that* he is human."

Some translators try to circumvent the syntactical problems by disregarding the Masoretic accents and separating *wěnôdā' 'ăšer hû'* and *'ādām*. In that case, the former is read with the preceding line (so NJPS: "and it was known that it would happen"), while the latter is taken as a *casus pendens* introducing the next line. The conjunction on *wělō'* is also deleted (see Ehrlich, *Randglossen*, p. 80). So, for instance, NJPS reads: "as for man, he cannot contend. . . ." Fox even transposes *'ādām* and *wělō' yûkal* to yield *wělō'-yûkal 'ādām* "and humanity is not able . . ." (*Contradictions*, pp. 223–24).

Clearly the text is difficult as it stands in MT. The phrase appears to be disruptive and meaningless in the context, if MT is correct. Instead of *'ăšer-hû' 'ādām*, M. Dahood ("Canaanite-Phoenician Influence," p. 208) has proposed to read *'ašrēhû < >'ādām*. He cites Ugaritic *atryt*, which, following many scholars, he takes to mean "destiny" or "fortune." The Ugaritic cognate is most suggestive because of its usage in tandem with *uḥryt* "the hereafter" or "the end" (see *'ḥryw* in Eccl 6:12), and because it occurs in *The Legend of Aqhat*, in a context concerning human mortality, as our text does also:

As for the human, what *uḥryt* will that one obtain?
What *atryt* will the human obtain?

(KTU 1.17.6.35–36)

The parallelism in *The Legend of Aqhat* is compelling. There is no doubt as to the meaning of *uḥryt* in the Ugaritic parallel: it refers to the future, specifically, "the end." As for the word *atryt*, one may note that Arabic has a verb *'aṯara* that may mean "to follow, determine, decide, choose," as well as "to take sole possession, appropriate," and so, perhaps, a related noun might signify something like "destiny" or "future." Such a specific meaning is not found in classical Arabic, however (see Lane, *Arabic-English Lexicon* Part I, pp. 18–20). The Arabic noun *'aṯar* means "footprint, impression, trace," but it may also refer to a "track" or "course." It may refer to one's origin, as in the expressions *mā yudrā lahu 'ayna 'aṯarun* "it is not known where was his origin" and *mā yudrā lahu mā 'aṯarun* "it is not known what was his origin" (cited by Lane, *loc. cit.*). In this usage, the noun points back to the beginning of the course — the path from which one comes. But the word is often used, too, in the sense of a path that one follows (so frequently in the Qur'an, V.46; LVII.27; XLIII.22). In this sense, Ugaritic *atryt* is an appropriate parallel term for the noun *uḥryt* ("the end, the future"), for it implies a course that obviously leads to some destination. So the parallel in the Aqhat text is as follows: *mt uḥryt mh yqḥ // mh yqḥ mt atryt.* Only by implication can Ugaritic *atryt* be taken to mean "destiny." As in Arabic *'aṯar*, the Hebrew word *'āšūr* may refer to one's footstep, or it may be a metonym for the course one takes. The latter usage is found in Prov 14:15, where the gullible simpleton is contrasted with the shrewd one who carefully considers the course (*la'ăšūrô*; RSV: "the prudent looks where he is going"). For Job, however, it is the deity who knows the way that one takes, although the mortal can choose to follow a course (*ba'ăšūrô,* Job 23:11).

Qohelet's contention is that the course has already been set and it is known (to God). As in the Ugaritic *Legend of Aqhat*, the mortal does not know what the end of the course might be, or even what the course is that one will take. Divine (fore)knowledge is contrasted with human ignorance. Compare *wĕnôda'* "it is known" in v 10 and *mî yôdēa'* "who knows?" in v 12. The former refers to God's (fore)knowledge, the latter to the fact that no human can know.

In his emendation of the text, Dahood takes *'ādām* with the next line and deletes the conjunctive *waw* in *wĕlō'-yûkal lādîn*, so that *'ādām* becomes the subject of the clause. There is no evidence for the deletion of the conjunction, however. There is, in fact, no need for the excision, and the traditional accentuation of the sentence is accurate. We should take the suffix on *'ăšūrēhû 'ādām* as proleptic. This is an instance of the so-called "*bêtô mōšeh* construction," where "his house, Moses" means "the house of Moses." Thus, the suffix anticipates the noun to which it refers (see BL §65.i; Brockelmann, §68.b). Examples are found in Phoenician and Punic (*KAI* 14.1; 26 I.17; III.4; Plautus, *Poenulus,* V.933). There are also many examples in Hebrew (Num 23:18; Ezek 42:14; Prov 13:4). So, too, *'ăšūrēhû 'ādām*, lit. "his course, the human," means "the course of human beings."

Thus in Eccl 6:10, *mah-ššehāyâ kĕbār niqrā' šĕmô* "whatever happens is already designated" is parallel in meaning to *wĕnôda' 'ăšūrēhû 'ādām* "the course of human beings is known." Any difference there is between the two is very subtle: the former refers generally to events, the latter refers to the course of humanity in particular. Here, as so often in Ecclesiastes, passive verbs are used to refer obliquely to what the deity does (see Comment at 1:13). The deity is not mentioned explicitly, and remains unnamed till the conclusion (7:13–14).

and they cannot dispute. With the preposition *'im* ("with") the verb *dyn* certainly means "to argue with, quarrel, dispute," a meaning that is well attested in Postbiblical Hebrew (cf. *m. 'Ed.* 1:10; *b. Sanh.* 17b). But the verb probably still retains its legal connotations and may suggest a legal dispute. Curiously, in the Aramaic *Proverbs of Ahiqar*, the root *špṭ* is used, whereas the Aramaic verb expected is *dyn*: [*m*]*h yšpṭwn 'qn 'm 'š* "[H]ow can wood contest with fire . . . ," a proverb about the futility of challenging awesome power (*TAD* III, 1.1.88).

one who is stronger. Reading *šettaqqîp* with *Qere*, many Hebrew MSS, Syr, and Targ. *Ketib* reflects a conflation of two readings: *šetaqqîp* and *hattaqqîp.* A similar conflation is found in 10:3, where *Ketib* has *kĕšehassākāl* (a conflate reading), but *Qere* has *kĕšessākāl*. The form *taqqîp* itself is found only here in Biblical Hebrew (although the verb is found in 4:12), but it is found in Biblical Aramaic (Dan 2:40, 42; 3:33; 7:7; Ezra 4:20) and Postbiblical Hebrew. The "one who is stronger" is an oblique reference to the deity. One is reminded of Job's admission that no one can contend with the deity because "he (the deity) is wise of heart and mighty in power" (Job 9:4–5). Cf. Job 14:20, where God is said to overpower (*tqp*) people (see also Jer 20:7, although the verb is different there). It is common advice in the wisdom texts of the ancient Near East that it is unwise to contend with one who is more powerful, whether that one is divine or human. So in the Aramaic *Proverbs of Ahiqar* one reads: "With one who is more exalted than yourself, do not pick a quar[rel]" (Lindenberger, *Aramaic Proverbs of Ahiqar*, pp. 142, 262). Lindenberger cites various other examples and surmises that the saying in Ahiqar "may refer to things that are too exalted to understand." See also Sir 8:1; 3:21–23. The same sentiment is found in Isa 45:9 and Rom 9:20–21.

11. *Indeed there are many words that increase vanity.* Hebrew *kî yēš-dĕbārîm harbēh marbîm hābel*, lit. "indeed, there are words aplenty that increase vanity" (see also LXX). The Hebrew does not mean "the more the words, the less the meaning" (NIV, cf. NRSV; REB). As Fox has noted, only some types of wordiness increase *hebel*, not all (*Contradictions*, pp. 225–26). The literal meaning of the Hebrew suffices. The author uses alliteration, perhaps to imitate the bombast of the sages: *dĕbārîm harbēh marbîm hābel*. In English one might say "wordiness is not worthiness."

vanity. See Notes and Comment at 1:2.

12. *in the few days of their fleeting life.* The phrase *mispar yĕmê-ḥayyê heblô* reflects the accusative of time (see Notes at 2:3). The word *hebel* here clearly refers to the brevity of life (cf. *kol-yĕmê ḥayyê heblekā* "all the days of his fleeting lifetime" in 9:9). See Notes and Comment at 1:2. The idiom *mispar yĕmê ḥayyîm* (lit. "the numerability of the days of life") occurs also in 2:3 and 5:17 (Eng v 18). In the *Gilgamesh Epic* one reads: *awīlūtumma manû ūmūša* "as for humanity, their days are numbered" (Gilg Y iv 142).

and they will spend them. The antecedent of the object pronoun "them" is "days." The Hebrew idiom *ʿāśâ yāmîm* means "to spend days." This usage of *ʿāśâ* is attested in Mishnaic Hebrew: *lʿśwt šm* "to live there" (*Gen. Rabb.*, section 91; *šʿśh bmʿrh* "who lives in a cave" (*Midrash Tillim* on Ps 17:4). It is often suggested that the idiom is a result of Hellenistic influence, since in Hellenistic Greek there is a similar usage for the verb *poiein* when it is used with words of time (see Whitley, *Koheleth*, p. 61). Similar idioms are found in Egyptian, however, where the verb *iri* (lit. "to do, make") may mean "to spend (time)": e.g. *iri.n.i hrw 3* "I spent 3 days" (*Shipwrecked Sailor* [Pap. Leningrad 1115, 1. 41]); *iri.n.i rnpt gs im* "I spent a year-and-a-half there" (*Story of Sinuhe* [Pap. Berlin, lines 29–30]). The Akkadian equivalent of this idiom, *epēšu ūma* "spend the day," is attested in a letter discovered at Boghazkoi (*KUB* 3, text 34, rev., 1. 5), but there it is almost certainly a translation of the Egyptian idiom. In any case, there is nothing distinctly Hellenistic about the expression. No Hellenistic influence can be established on the basis of this idiom.

as in a shadow. Hebrew *kaṣṣēl*, lit. "like the shadow." Hebrew does not require a second preposition to say "as in": e.g., *kammilḥāmâ hāri'šōnâ* "as in the first battle" (Judg 20:39); *kĕdobrām* "as in their pasture" (Isa 5:17); *kîmê qedem* "as in days of old" (Isa 51:9). See GKC §118.t, u. The point is clear: human life is ephemeral. So one reads in Job 8:9, "we are of yesterday and we are ignorant; indeed, our days upon the earth are a shadow" (note Syr and Targ have "like a shadow"—i.e., reflecting Hebrew *ksl*). Elsewhere in the Bible mortals are said to "flee like a shadow" and not abide (Job 14:2; 1 Chron 29:15). Cf. also Pss 102:12 (Eng v 11); 109:23; 144:4; Eccl 8:13; Job 17:7. LXX (followed by SyrH and Copt) and Targ have "in a shadow"—either freely interpreting Hebrew *ksl* or reflecting *bṣl*, in anticipation of *bṣl . . . bṣl* in 7:12. LXX^V and three cursives, however, read *hōs skian*, reflecting Hebrew *ksl*. MT is sound and need not be emended. Vulg has *velut umbra* "like a shadow," supporting the reading in MT.

for who can tell. The function of *'ăšer* is unclear here (see Ellermeier, *Qohelet* I/1, pp. 171–72; Lauha, *Kohelet* p. 120). It probably functions the same way as *kî* at the beginning of v 12: *kî mî-yôdēa'* "for who knows" // *'ăšer mî-yaggîd* "for who can tell."

afterwards under the sun. The suffix on *'aḥărāyw* (lit. "after him") obviously refers to *'ādām*, but what does the expression mean? If *taḥat haššemeš* ("under the sun") refers to being alive or being on earth (see Notes at 1:3), *'aḥărāyw* cannot refer to the afterlife: "after them under the sun" would be an oxymoron. Given the fact that this line probably forms an *inclusio* with v 10, and given the parallelism of *'uḥryt* ("end") and *'atryt* ("course") in Ugaritic (*KTU* 1.17.6.35–36), one may interpret *'aḥărāyw* not as a preposition with a suffix ("after them"), but as a substantive, meaning literally "their end" (cf. *bĕ'aḥărê hahănît* "at the end of the spear" in 2 Sam 2:23) or figuratively "their future" or "their destiny." This word would then be the subject of the sentence. The word is a cognate of Ugaritic *uḥry* and Arabic *'uḥrāy*, both meaning "destiny" or "end." Thus, one may better translate *mî-yaggîd lā'ādām mah-yyihyeh 'aḥărāyw taḥat haššāmeš* as "who can tell human beings what their future (or "their destiny") will be under the sun." This line is to be contrasted with v 10: no one knows what the course of humanity is (v 10) // no one can tell mortals what their future will be (v 12). Note also that *nôda'* "it is known" (v 10) // *mî yôdea'* "who knows" (v 12); *mah-ššehāyâ* "whatever happens" (v 10) // *mah-yyihyeh* "what will be" (v 12). Thus in vv 10–12 we have a tightly woven subunit.

7 1. *Fame is better than fine ointment.* Hebrew *ṭôb šēm miššemen ṭôb* contains a chiastically arranged wordplay that is very difficult to reproduce in English. A similar wordplay between *šēm* "name" and *šemen* "oil" is found in Song 1:3. The word *šēm* "name" by itself (without any adjective) may mean a *good* reputation, as it does in Prov 22:1 and Zeph 3:19. The Proverbs passage is especially suggestive, since it compares a good name favorably to other desirable things in life (see also *The Instruction of Amenemope*, XVI.11–14; *AEL* II, p. 156). This is how *šēm* is generally understood: thus, a good reputation is better than the finest luxuries. This is probably the original meaning of the proverb. But *šēm* may mean more than current reputation. It may be used in the sense of a lasting name, the name

of someone who has died. It may refer to a memorial, as in Ps 9:6; Isa 55:13 and 56:5. In the last instance (Isa 56:5), a lasting reputation is said to be *ṭôb mibbānîm ûmibbānôt* "better than sons and daughters." In light of Qohelet's concern with death in 7:1–4, it seems appropriate to take *šēm* here as referring to lasting fame — a good name that outlasts life itself. In Ezek 39:13, *šēm* is associated with burial and clearly refers to one's posthumous name. If so, the author could be alluding to the view that a good reputation is one way to achieve immortality. As Ben Sira puts it: "Take care of your name, for it will remain for you longer than a thousand stores of gold. The goodness of life lasts only for a few days, but the goodness of a name lasts forever" (Sir 41:12–13). This is a view that Qohelet is subtly challenging.

As for *šemen ṭôb* "fine ointment," it is mentioned among the treasures of the king, along with gold, silver, armaments, and spices (2 Kgs 20:13 // Isa 39:2). Whereas in Isa 39:2 the expression is *haššemen haṭṭôb* (where *haṭṭôb* is an adjective), in the parallel text in 2 Kgs 20:13 it is *šemen haṭṭôb* (where *šemen* is in construct to *haṭṭôb*). In any case, *šemen ṭôb* is associated with great pleasures (see Song 1:3); it is an item of luxury and represents the good life (Ps 133:2–3). Cf. also *šemen hammōr* "oil of myrrh" (Esth 2:12) and *šemen rôqēaḥ* "perfumer's oil" (Eccl 10:1). The expression *šemen ṭôb* is similar to Akkadian *šamnu ṭābu* (or *šamnu ša ṭābi*) "fine ointment/perfume," which is frequently listed with various items of great value sent as tribute in international diplomacy (see citations in *CAD* XVII/1, pp. 321, 328).

birth. Hebrew *hiwwālĕdô*, lit. "his being born." The antecedent of the pronominal suffix is unexpressed in this case, so the suffix is used impersonally: "his being born" = "one's being born." The presence of the suffix is attested by LXX[AC], SyrH, and Aq, but the suffix is omitted in LXX[BS] and Syr. The omission of the suffix in translation, however, does not indicate a different reading in the Hebrew *Vorlage*. LXX[BS] and Syr merely reflect translations according to the sense of the text. As for the idiom *ywm hwldw*, one may compare it with Aramaic *ywm yldʾ* "birthday," attested on an Aramaic papyrus from North Saqqara (Segal, *Aramaic Texts*, No. 41.8).

2. *a house of mourning.* Hebrew *bêt-ʾēbel* is without precise parallel in the Bible, but it appears many times in the Mishnah and Talmud, not infrequently in contrast to *bêt mišteh* "house of feasting," as is the case here (e.g., *m. Ter.* 11:10; ʿ*Erub.* 8:1; *Ketub.* 7:5; *b. Šabb.* 50a; *Ketub.* 71b). The former refers to the home of mourners, the latter to a place for the wedding feast. Significantly, eating and drinking took place not only at the *bêt mišteh* "house of feasting," but also at the *bêt ʾēbel* "house of mourning." The mourners' feast took place both in the mourners' homes and outside the homes (see *b. Šabb.* 105b), usually sponsored by the permanent clubs called *ḥăbārôt*, the equivalent of the Greek funerary societies. In Jer 16:5 one reads of a *bêt marzēaḥ*, apparently a club house for funerary purposes (see *b. Ketub.* 69b). Jeremiah was forbidden to go to this "house of mourning" (*bêt marzēaḥ*), as well as "the house of feasting" (*bêt-mišteh*, Jer 16:5, 8). From several West Semitic inscriptions one gathers that the *marzēaḥ* was an institution associated with funerary rituals and is most often marked by

excessive drinking and revelry (see the survey in T. J. Lewis, *Cults of the Dead in Ancient Israel and Ugarit* [HSM 39; Atlanta: Scholars, 1989], pp. 80–94).

house of feasting. Instead of *mšth* "feasting," one MS (Kennicott no. 107) has *śmḥh* "joy, pleasure," a reading supported by 4QQoh[a] ([*ś*]*mḥh*). This is a variant reading that anticipates *byt śmḥh* in v 4. MT, supported by the ancient versions (LXX *eis oikon potou*), is to be preferred. Hebrew *bêt mišteh* "house of feasting," an expression occurring in the Bible only from the exilic period on, probably refers to a banquet hall of some sort (Esth 7:8; Jer 16:8; *m. Ber.* 1:1; Soṭa 9:11; Neg. 3.2). Cf. also Biblical Aramaic *bêt mištěyā* in Dan 5:10.

that is the end of all humanity. Hebrew *hû' sôp kol-hā'ādām.* It is not clear what *hû'* refers to; its antecedent may be *lāleket 'el-bêt-'ēbel* "to go to the house of mourning," or the fact that it is better to go to the house of mourning than to the wedding banquet. The "end" (*sôp*) refers to the end of a human life span in 3:11. This is a term of Late Biblical Hebrew (see Notes at 3:11).

lay (it) to heart. Hebrew *yittēn 'el libbô.* Cf. the same expression in 9:1 (also Isa 42:25; 57:11), but also the idiom *śām 'el-libbô* in 2 Sam 13:33; 19:20.

3. *in the sadness of the countenance.* Hebrew *běrōa' pānîm* may mean either a sad or angry face (Fox: "a scowl"). A similar idiom is attested in Gen 40:7 and Neh 2:2–3.

the heart will be glad. Hebrew *yîtab lēb.* Cf. Judg 18:20; 19:6, 9; 1 Kgs 21:7; Ruth 3:7. Cf. the Aramaic expression *lbby l' ṭyb* "my heart was not glad" in a letter from the fifth century B.C.E. (*TAD* I, 3.3.2).

4. *in a house of mourning.* Hebrew *běbêt 'ēbel.* Instead of *bbyt 'bl* and *bbyt śmḥh*, 4QQoh[a] omits the preposition in both cases. This is perhaps simply a case of haplography. We should retain the preposition (so LXX).

in a house of pleasure. Hebrew *běbêt śimḥâ.* Two Hebrew MSS read *byt mśth* instead of *byt śmḥh*, but *byt mśth* is clearly secondary, being an attempt to make the text conform to v 2. There is, however, no semantic difference between the two expressions.

5. *rebuke.* Hebrew *ga'ārat.* 4QQoh[a] has the plural *g'rwt* which, if correct, would be unique in the Bible. This noun is not attested in the plural anywhere else. Both variants are possible.

than for one to hear the ode of fools. Given the contrast with "rebuke," the word *šîr* here probably refers to a song of praise and adoration (Judg 5:12; 2 Chron 5:13; Pss 33:3; 45:1; 149:1; Song 1:1; Isa 26:1; 42:10; Jer 20:13). Instead of *m'yš šm'* in MT, 4QQoh[a] has [*m*]*lm'*, which is then corrected to [*m*]*lšm'* "than to hear" (see Ulrich, "Ezra and Qoheleth Manuscripts from Qumran," pp. 145–46). MT has the *lectio difficilior*, which is probably more original than the syntactically smoother reading of 4QQoh[a].

6. *like the crackling of thorns under a pot.* Hebrew *kěqôl hassîrîm taḥat hassîr.* There is an obvious wordplay between *hassîrîm* "thorns" and *hassîr* "the pot," but also between *hassîr* "the pot" and *šîr* "ode" in the preceding line. Again, it is difficult to reproduce the wordplay in English, although "nettle" // "kettle" has been suggested. The repetition of sibilants (*š, s, ś*) and palatals (*k, q*) is probably

intended to imitate the crackling of thorns and cackling of fools, as well: *šîr kĕsîlîm kî kĕqôl haššîrîm taḥat hassîr kēn śĕḥôq hakkĕsîl*. The sibilants reflect the hissing sound of the fire, while the palatals reflect the crackling of the wood. In Nah 1:10, *sîr* refers to entangled thorns that are easily consumed.

vanity. see Notes at 1:2.

7. *for.* The *kî* here is causal, giving the rationale for the conclusion in v 6. Since the *hebel*-judgment in the preceding verse is seen as conclusive, the introduction of this verse with *kî* is troubling for many commentators. It is sometimes supposed that something has fallen out (so Barton, McNeile, Lauha). Delitzsch proposed years ago that something like Prov 16:8 may have been present originally: *ṭwb m'ṭ bṣdqh mrb tbw'wt bl' mšpṭ* "Better is a little with righteousness than great revenues without justice" or *ṭwb ml' kp bṣdqh mml' ḥpnym b'šq* "Better is a handful with righteousness than two fistfuls with oppression" (cf. Eccl 4:6). The discovery of 4QQoh[a] has given new impetus to the old lacuna theory, inasmuch as the fragment has space for 15 to 20 letters between verses 6 and 7. Some scholars think that there is enough room for something like Prov 16:8, or a shorter version of it (see Fox, *Contradictions*, p. 229). But there is no evidence for a missing link, only this blank in the Qumran text that may simply have been an erasure, as Muilenburg concluded ("Qoheleth Scroll," p. 26).

turns the wise into fools. Hebrew *yĕhôlēl ḥākām*, lit. "makes the wise irrational." Since the noun *hôlēlût* is associated with *siklût* "folly" and apparently means something like "silliness" or "stupidity" (see Notes at 2:12), the verb must mean something like "make fools" or "turn into fools."

a payment. Hebrew *mattānâ* does not refer to just any gift, but a "gift" that is exacted by oppressors, namely, a bribe. It is used in roughly the same sense as the *mattān bassēter*, lit. "a payment in secret," that is demanded of the poor (Prov 21:14). In Prov 15:27, *śônē' mattānôt* "one who hates payments is contrasted with *bôṣēa' bāṣa'* "one who takes a bribe" (cf. also *śônē' beṣa'* "one who hates a bribe" in Prov 28:16). So one should understand *mattānâ* to be a synonym of *beṣa'*. The word may be related to Aramaic *mndt'*, a term used in Persian period texts for taxes, payment for slaves, rental payments, and so forth (see *TAD* III, 3.7.1.11, 19; II, 3.6.7). In any case, the Greek traditions and Vulg in our text assume that *lēb* is in the construct state, contrary to the Masoretic accents. Moreover, in those traditions the absolute is not read as *mattānâ* ("exaction"), but some other noun *mtn* (Aq and Theod have *eutonia* "strength"; Vulg: *robur* "vigor") + the 3 ms suffix (*-ōh* instead of *-ô*). It is commonly assumed that there is such a noun, which is related to the Postbiblical Hebrew verb *mātan* "to be long, to wait" and the adjective *mātûn* "patient" (see Driver, "Problems and Solutions," pp. 229–30). Whitley proposes to read *motnōh* (lit. "his loin"?) and translates the verse thus: "for oppression stupefies the wise man, and destroys his strong heart" (*Koheleth*, p. 63). The noun is, however, attested in Hebrew only in the dual form *motnayim* ("loins"). It never occurs in the singular form. Scott, therefore, emends slightly to read *motnāw*, lit. "his loins" and takes the term to be figurative for "his courage." But the noun in Hebrew and its cognates in other Semitic languages always refer to loins, hips, sinew, tendon, or nerve. They are never used figuratively for "strength" or "courage." To read "strength" one would have to posit an otherwise unattested Hebrew word corresponding to Arabic *matānat* ("strength, firmness").

The proposed emendations are both unconvincing and unnecessary. The reading in MT is the *lectio difficilior*, inasmuch as it takes the feminine noun *mattānâ* to be the subject of the masculine verb and leaves an indefinite object marked by the *nota accusativi*. The use of masculine verbs with feminine subjects is, in fact, not unparalleled in Biblical Hebrew (cf. Deut 32:32; Isa 2:17; 9:18; 14:11; 1 Kgs 22:36; Jer 13:16; see GKC §145.o) and the *nota accusativi* is in Ecclesiastes sometimes used with nouns without the definite article (3:15; 4:4; 7:7; see GKC §117.d). The Hebrew of MT is difficult but possible. Symm transliterates the form (*matthana*), thus supporting the reading in MT. In any case, the parallelism of *'ōseq* "oppression/bribe" and *mattānâ* "bribe" is appropriate. In Prov 22:16 one finds *'ōšēq* "oppressor" juxtaposed with *nōtēn lĕ'āšîr* "one who gives to the rich." A similar sentiment is found in Deut 16:19, although the vocabulary is a little different: "You shall not take a bribe, for the bribe blinds the eyes of the wise" (cf. Sir 20:29; Exod 23:6–8).

perverts. Reading *wî'awweh* instead of *wî'abbed* in MT. The former is the reading in 4QQohᵃ, although MT is supported by LXX and OL. We cannot account for one reading or the other in terms of orthographic confusion, and both meanings are appropriate in this context. Perhaps the confusion arose as a consequence of oral dictation. The verb *'bd* occurs five other times in Ecclesiastes (3:6; 5:13 [Eng v 14]; 7:15; 9:6, 18), but the root *'wh* is unique. Possibly *wy'bd* is an attempt to substitute a rare verb with one that is more at home in the book. Hence *wî'awweh* is preferred. As for the idiom *wî'awweh 'et-lēb*, one notes the comparable expression *na'ăwēh-lēb* "perverted of mind" in Prov 12:8, where it is contrasted with *śēkel* "intelligence."

8. *a matter.* Hebrew has *dābār*, but LXX has *logōn* "words," which probably reflects Hebrew *dbrm* (*dĕbārîm*). The latter reading is possible, if one assumes a haplography of *mem*, since there was no distinction between medial and final forms until the third century B.C.E.: thus, original *dbrm mr'štw* was misread as *dbr mr'šytw*. Yet, the 3 ms suffix in *mērē'šîtô* "its beginning" suggests a singular noun, the antecedent of the pronominal suffix being *dābār*. So the noun should be singular. Even the Greek translation retains the 3 ms suffix: *hyper archēn autou*. The additional *mem* reflected in the reading of LXX is probably a dittography, prompted in part by the interpretation of the verse as a critique of the many words of the wise (cf. 6:11).

to be patient. Hebrew *'erek-rûaḥ*, lit. "[being] long of spirit." A few Hebrew MSS read *'rk 'pym*, substituting the unusual expression *'rk-rwḥ* with a more common idiom in the Bible (cf. Exod 34:6; Num 14:18; Joel 2:13; Jon 4:2; Nah 1:3; etc.). At Qumran we have the expression *'rwky rwḥ* used of horses (1QM vi.12). In that context, the expression probably means "having stamina," or the like. It is clear, however, that *rûaḥ* in our passage means temperament. The idiom may be compared with Syriac *dngr rwḥ'* "long of breadth" = "patient" (Brockelmann, *Lexicon Syriacum²*, pp. 414–15) and late Akkadian *ikki arāku* "to be long of temper" = "to be patient" (see *CAD* I/2, p. 224). One should also contrast the expression with Hebrew *qōṣer rûaḥ* "shortness of spirit" = "impatience" (Exod 6:9); *qĕṣar rûaḥ* "short of spirit" = "impatient" (Prov 14:29 // *'erek 'appayim*). Dahood cites Phoenician/Punic *'rkrḥ*, attested in *CIS* 97.2, 2434.3 ("Canaanite-Phoenician Influence," pp. 208–9). The form is a personal name, however, whose etymology is uncertain; one cannot be sure to interpret the compound as *'rk rḥ* or *'r krḥ* (see F. L. Benz, *Personal Names in the Phoenician and Punic Inscriptions* [Studia Pohl 8; Rome: Biblical Institute, 1972], pp. 63, 335).

than arrogant. Hebrew *miggĕbah-rûaḥ*, lit. "than [being] lofty of spirit." Cf. *gōbah rûaḥ* "arrogance" (Prov 16:18) and Postbiblical Hebrew *rûaḥ gĕbôhâ* "arrogance" (*m. 'Abot* 5:19). Contrast, too, *šĕpal-rûaḥ* "low in spirit" = "humble" (Isa 57:15; Prov 16:19; 29:23).

9. *do not be quick to anger.* Hebrew *'al-tĕbahēl bĕrûḥăkā lik'ôs*, lit. "do not hasten in your spirit to be vexed." Contrast Greek *bradys eis orgēs* "slow to anger" in Jas 1:19.

10. *Do not say.* See Notes at 5:6 (Heb v 5).

out of wisdom. With verbs of speaking and looking, *min* often means "out of" (Deut 4:36; Amos 1:2; Ps 14:2). There is no need, therefore, to emend *mem* to *bet* (to read *baḥokmâ* "in wisdom"), as is sometimes done. LXX, SyrH, and Syr have "in" (or "with") and Targ has "over," but these are probably contextual translations and do not reflect different readings. MT has the superior reading.

11. *Wisdom is as good as inheritance.* Hebrew *ṭôbâ ḥokmâ 'im-naḥălâ*. The preposition *'im* poses a problem for many exegetes, who expect Qohelet to say that wisdom is *better than* inheritance. Hence some commentators emend *'im* to *min* (Zapletal) or *mē'im* (Galling, Hertzberg), usually citing Syr, *mn m'ny zyn'* "than weapons." Others, who accept the correctness of the preposition, think of it as indicating accompaniment—that is, wisdom is only good "together with" inheritance (cf. LXX *meta*, Vulg *cum*, and the commentaries of Ibn Ezra and Rashbam). The preposition *'im*, in fact, indicates sameness, as it does in 2:16. In the Bible, *'im* occurs in parallelism with *kĕ-* "like" (Job 9:26; 1 Chron 25:8) and in Ugaritic it may mean "like" or "the same as" (see the examples cited in Notes at 2:16). The point is not that wisdom is "better than" inheritance, but that it is only *as good as* inheritance. But Qohelet would go on to imply that both are (equally) fleeting (see Comment at 7:12).

those who see the sun. That is, those who are alive (see Notes at 1:3 and 6:5). Conversely, those who do not or have not seen the sun are those who are not alive. See Pss 49:20 (Eng v 19); 58:9 (Eng v 8); Job 3:16.

12. *as a shadow . . . as a shadow.* Hebrew *bĕṣēl . . . bĕṣēl*. One should assume the *bet essentiae*: e.g., *bĕ'ēl šadday* "as El Shadday" (Exod 6:3); *'ĕlōhê 'ābî bĕ'ezrî* "the God of my ancestor is my help" (Exod 18:4; cf. Ps 146:5). See GKC §119.i; Joüon-Muraoka §133.c. One may note that Symm, Vulg, and Syr seem to reflect Hebrew *kĕṣēl . . . kĕṣēl*, but that is the *lectio facilior*. LXX (supported by SyrH and Copt) reflects Hebrew *bĕṣēl . . . kĕṣēl*. For various proposed emendations, see Kugel, "Qohelet and Money," pp. 40–44.

knowledge is an advantage. Hebrew *wĕyitrôn da'at*. LXX, Syr, and Vulg take *da'at* with what follows, that is, as a construct noun: *da'at haḥokmâ* "the knowledge of wisdom." The Masoretic accents, however, suggest that one ought to see knowledge and wisdom as parallel terms, as they are often in Ecclesiastes (see 1:16, 17; 2:21, 26; 9:10). To be sure, there is the definite article with *ḥokmâ* but not with *da'at.* Yet, the article is not used consistently in this book. We have a very similar situation in 7:25, where there are four nouns, but only one has the definite article (see Notes at 3:15).

13. *See.* The imperative *rě'ēh* occurs also in 2:1 and 9:9. In both those instances, *rě'ēh* means more than "observe" or "consider." Rather, the imperative is a call to experience the goodness of life. To "see" is not just to "look at," but to recognize as reality. So in Deut 33:9, *rā'â* occurs in parallelism with *hikkîr* "recognize" and *yāda'* "know." In Deut 11:2, we find the expression *rā'â 'et-mûsar YHWH* "see the discipline of YHWH" (// *yāda'* "know"), whereas the more common idiom is *lāqaḥ mûsār* "accept discipline" (Jer 2:30; 5:3; 7:28; etc.). It is for good reason, therefore, that Kimḥi interprets the imperative here as "accept lovingly."

who is able to straighten what he has made crooked. In 1:15 we have *mě'uwwāt lō'-yûkal lětuqqan* (emended text) "what is crooked cannot be made straight" (see Notes and Comment there). Whereas God is not named as the agent of the action in 1:15, it is clear in 7:13 that it is God who has made things crooked.

14. *when times are good . . . when times are bad.* Hebrew *běyôm ṭôbâ . . . běyôm rā'â,* lit. "in the day of good . . . in the day of bad."

enjoy. Hebrew *hěyēh běṭôb,* lit. "be in good." The expression probably means the same thing as *rě'ēh ṭôb* in 2:1 (see Notes and Comment there).

see. The imperative *rě'ēh* appears to end abruptly. The reader expects an object of seeing, but there is none. One is only led to the emphatic *gam,* the particle that emphasizes the dialectical nature of God's activity.

yes. The particle *gam* is emphatic here. See, e.g., Gen 27:33; 46:4; Isa 14:10.

the one just like the other. Hebrew *'et-zeh lě'ummat-zeh,* lit. "this one corresponding to this one." Cf. *lě'ummat* in 1 Chron 24:31.

that. Hebrew *'al-dibrat še* occurs only here. It corresponds to Aramaic *'al dibrat dî* (Dan 2:30; 4:14 [Eng v 17]).

anything. Hebrew *mě'ûmâ.* Vulg (*querimonia* "complaint") and Symm (*mempsis* "blame") both assume Hebrew *mûm* "blemish," which is spelled with an *'alep* (i.e. *mě'ūm*) in Job 31:7 and Dan 1:4.

after them. That is, they can know nothing of the future in one's lifetime (cf. 3:22; 9:3; 10:14). See Notes at 6:12.

COMMENT

A marginal note by the Jewish tradents who copied and otherwise preserved the Hebrew text observes that 6:10 is the midpoint of the book. The preceding literary unit ends with a familiar refrain that recurs in the first half of the book: "this, too, is vanity and a pursuit of wind" (1:14; 2:11, 17, 25; 4:4, 16; 6:9). Now begins the second half of the book, which is marked by a repeated emphasis on what people cannot know, cannot tell, and cannot discover. The first literary unit of this half of the book extends from 6:10 to 7:14. It includes a theological introduction (6:10–12) and a theological conclusion (7:13–14), which together frame a series of proverbial sounding instructions, mostly about what is "good" or "better" (7:1–12). A similar theological framing is found in 1:12–2:26. The introduction and conclusion emphasize human ignorance and impotence, over against divine determination and the deity's incomprehensible activity. The sayings in 7:1–12, then, are not meant to be read in isolation. Rather, they are to be interpreted within the theological framework of the passage.

The author asserts in 6:10–12 that humans are not able to take issue with what is happening in the universe (v 10); they have no advantage (v 11), and no one knows what is good (*ṭôb*) for humanity (v 12). Yet, seemingly in contradiction to that claim, one finds in 7:1–12 a whole series of *ṭôb-sayings* ("better-than" sayings), most of which are in the style of traditional Israelite and Egyptian didactic (proverbial) literature. In the first eight verses, the word *ṭôb* occurs seven times, all in the form of *ṭôb-sayings*. Read in the context of Qohelet's denial that anyone can really know what is good (*ṭôb*) or has advantage, these *ṭôb-sayings* must be seen as proving precisely the point made in the introduction (6:10–12). Then, in 7:9–12 one finds further advice, together with a reflection on wisdom's advantage. Again, these verses must be interpreted in the light of the insistence at the beginning of the passage (6:10–12) that no one can predict what is going to happen and that human beings have no advantage.

All in all, we must see 7:1–12 as a parody of the verbosity of all those who readily dish out advice of what is good and tell other people what they should do in every situation. But all these "many words" will prove to be as ephemeral as life itself (6:11). They give humanity no real advantage.

The unity of the whole passage is suggested by the repetition of key expressions, particularly at the beginning and the end of the unit. We may note especially the following:

6:10–12	*7:10–14*
whatever happens (*mah-ššehāyâ*, v 10)	how is it? (*meh hāyâ*, v 10)
they cannot (*lō'-yûkal*, v 10)	who can? (*mî yûkal*, v 13)
advantage (*yōtēr*, v 11)	advantage (*yōtēr*, v 11)
like a shadow (*kaṣṣēl*, v 12)	as a shadow (*bĕṣēl*, v 12)
afterwards (*'aḥărāyw*, v 12)	after them (*'aḥărāyw*, v 14)

Theological Introduction (6:10–12)

The passage begins by affirming that everything that comes to pass has already been designated and that the course of humanity is already known (v 10). As elsewhere in the book, passive verbs are used to refer obliquely to what the deity does: "has already been designated" // "is known" (v 10). What is meant is that God has designated and God has known, although the deity is not explicitly named. Humans cannot control what happens on earth, for everything has been and is being predetermined and foreknown by an inscrutable power. Indeed, people are in no position to contend (*lādîn*) with "one who is stronger" than they. And many words—perhaps here referring to the verbosity of those who bring disputations (like Job), as well as those who formulate proverbs—may amount to empty talk, *hebel* "vanity." In contrast to what is known to the deity (v 10) is the fact that nobody, no human being, knows what is good (*ṭôb*, v 12).

It is possible that the author is alluding to Job in these verses. Although Job admitted at one point that people cannot contend with a deity who is "mighty in power" (Job 9:1–4), he nevertheless brought his dispute (*dîn*) before God, engaged in empty talk (*hebel*), and "multiplied words without knowledge" (Job 35:14–16; see also 13:22–28). Qohelet uses alliteration to illustrate such prolixity: *děbārîm harbēh marbîm hābel* "wordiness is not worthiness" (v 11). He would say later that it is the fool who "multiplies words" (10:14). Indeed, there are "many words" that only increase *hebel*, literally a breath or a whiff, something that is fleeting and quite unreliable (see Notes at 1:2). They may give an impression of effectiveness, but they soon dissipate.

By using a rhetorical question (v 11), the author suggests that humans have no advantage, because no one knows what is "good" for people in life (v 12). In context we understand the point to be that no one, neither the foolish nor the wise, can give others advice on what is universally "good"—at least not in the sense of some formula that would give one an edge in life. Human life is as ephemeral as a shadow (Job 14:2; 1 Chron 29:15; Pss 102:12 [Eng v 11]; 109:23; 144:4; Eccl 8:13; Job 17:7). A shadow provides shade only for a while, but it soon disappears. Humanity stands in this shadow, as it were, as history runs its course. The mortal may be a mere bystander or, at best, a participant in the course, but it is not the mortal who determines what will happen. One does not even know what will happen. Destiny lies not within human grasp, but in the power of a mysterious Other. As all that happens in the present has already been determined (v 10), so all that will happen in the future is beyond the knowledge of humanity (v 11). Neither the present nor the future is within human control.

What Is Good (7:1–12)?

Commentators frequently isolate the sayings in 7:1–12 from the preceding introduction, but such a move leads to a serious misunderstanding of the author's intention. In 6:10–12, Qohelet concludes that no one knows what is *ṭôb* "good." Yet in 7:1–12, the word *ṭôb* (usually translated as "better") is repeated nine times. Given the placement of these sayings immediately after the comments in 6:10–12, one should consider these *ṭôb-sayings* to be something of an illustration of the "many words" of the wise. They are supposed to instruct one on what is *ṭôb* "good" for humanity, but how reliable are they in reality? The sayings all sound like traditional wisdom teachings composed in proverbial style, with their tendency to present issues in convenient dialectical pairs. So we find the contrast between fame and luxury (v 1a), birth and death (v 1b), funeral and wedding (v 2), merriment and sadness (v 3), mourning and pleasure (v 4), rebuke and praise (v 5), the wise and the fool (vv 6–7), beginning and end (v 8), patience and arrogance (v 8). The effect of the overall presentation is to show that it is indeed true that no one — not even the sages, the teachers who propounded the *ṭôb-sayings* — knows what is really *ṭôb* "good" or "better" for humanity in general. Each saying may contain an element of truth, but the sum total of these many words is "vanity" — just so much empty talk (v 6, compare 6:11).

The series of *ṭôb-sayings* begins with a popular adage that a name is better (*ṭôb šēm*) than "fine ointment" (*šemen ṭôb*), the latter representing exceptional wealth and pleasure. Most commentators cite a traditional proverb extolling the advantage of a good reputation over great fortune: "A name is preferable to great wealth, and favor to silver and gold" (Prov 22:1). Qohelet's words certainly recall such proverbs. Yet he is not simply praising the advantage of a good name in one's lifetime, for he goes on to contrast birth and death. In fact, the *ṭôb-saying* here is reminiscent of traditional teachings about protecting one's reputation because reputation is supposed to outlast material possessions and even life itself. A good name was one way to achieve an immortality of sorts. Thus Job 18:17 speaks of the fate of the wicked: "their reputation perishes from the earth, and they have no name in the street." The name of the wicked dies with them. By contrast, it is assumed, the righteous will have the immortality of an everlasting name. In like manner, Prov 10:7 praises the abiding reputation of the righteous and asserts that "the name of the wicked will rot." In Isa 56:5, an enduring name (a lasting memory) is said to be "better than sons and daughters." Having a good reputation was one way of achieving immortality — a better way than having progeny, it seems. A similar attitude is reflected in the teachings of Ben Sira, who may well have had Qohelet's passage in mind:

A human body is a fleeting thing (*hebel*),
   but a reliable name will never be cut off.
Take care of your name, for it will remain for you
   better than precious treasures by the thousands;
The goodness of life lasts but for a few days,
   but the goodness of a name lasts forever.

(Sir 41:11–13)

Death is an undeniable reality, but the sages taught that there is a way to beat the system, so to speak: have a good name, a name that will be remembered forever. So came the proverb that a good name is better than material possessions; a good name is better than life itself. Here is one way, it seems, to have an advantage over others, even over death!

The same concern with a good name as a substitute for bodily immortality is evident in the *Gilgamesh Epic*, as well. In the Sumerian version, the protagonist says to his friend Enkidu in regard to the "Land of the Living":

"I would enter the 'land,' I would set up my name,
   in its places where the names have not been raised up,
   I would raise up the names of the gods."

(ANET[3], p. 48)

In the Old Babylonian version of the epic, Gilgamesh acknowledges that only divine beings live forever "with the sun," whereas mortals have their days numbered and their achievements are but "wind" (see Comment at 1:3). Hence Gilgamesh reckons that one should be willing to take some risks in life: "Should I fall, I shall have made me a name" (*ANET*³, p. 79). In the face of the impossibility of true immortality, fame was a desirable way of having an advantage in life. So a good name was often regarded as better than tangible benefits in the present, indeed, better than life itself. Or, as an Egyptian pessimistic text has it, "though you are dead, your name lives on" (*The Dispute Between a Man and His Ba*, 1.35, AEL I, p. 165; see also *The Eloquent Peasant*, AEL I, p. 181). In another Egyptian text, a satirical work extolling the immortality of writers, it is argued that scribes are better off than people of other trades because their names will be remembered, whereas the name of others will be forgotten as soon as they die (AEL II, pp. 175–77).

Thus, Qohelet alludes to the adage in the wisdom tradition that an enduring reputation is preferred over material possessions, even over life. But he quickly challenges the seriousness of the proverb. He does so by carrying the assumption of the saying to its absurd conclusion: if one's name (memory) is better than the present possession of good, then the day of death is better than the day of birth (v 1). Do sayings like this actually mean that a name can be *that* good, or are they just "many words" that prove to be "vanity" (6:11)?

The undermining of one statement by another is a typical method employed in ancient Near Eastern pessimistic literature to show that there is no real solution to life's contradictions. This is a technique used in the Egyptian text known as *The Dispute Between the Man and His Ba* (AEL I, pp. 163–69) and, especially, in the satirical Akkadian *Dialogue of Pessimism* (BWL, pp. 139–49). Something like that seems to be going on in our passage, although it is difficult to show that there are several dialogical voices within the passage (so Perry, *Dialogues with Koheleth*, pp. 118–26). The author employs a rhetoric of subversion. He deliberately presents each proposition in aphoristic style, and then carries the argument to its logical conclusion in order to show that the proposition is of dubious value. In this way, he undermines any confidence in the reliability of the "good advice," such as the advice that one typically gets in the didactic wisdom tradition. It is in only this limited sense that he is engaging in a "dialogue." Otherwise, the only hint we have of a real or imaginary conversational partner in this passage is in v 10.

At all events, unlike the first *ṭôb-saying* about one's name (v 1a), the second saying is without parallel anywhere in the wisdom literature of the ancient Near East: the day of death is better than the day of birth (v 1b). The second seems to be Qohelet's rejoinder to the popular adage. Taken at face value and out of context, the conclusion is troubling. Although there is no evidence anywhere that birthdays were widely celebrated among the Jews, the day of birth was always regarded as a time of rejoicing (see Notes above). It was eagerly anticipated in the community as a day of blessing (see Ruth 4:13–17).

This attitude is reflected in Jeremiah's regret of his own birth (Jer 20:14–15).

Although negatively stated, this passage suggests that the day of birth was generally expected to be a day of rejoicing (see also Job 3:3–26). But Qohelet puts forth
the shocking assertion that the day of death is better than the day of birth. Failing
to recognize the rhetoric of subversion at play, one may try too hard to put the
best face on this saying, and explain how it is possible that the day of death is
better than the day of birth. Perhaps Ben Sira had Qohelet's literal statement in
mind when he concluded that we should "call no one happy" before his or her
death, inasmuch as the goodness of one's life is known only at the end (Sir 11:28).
But one who takes Qohelet's *ṭôb-sayings* all too seriously misses the point. The
author is not saying that the day of death is literally better than the day of birth.
Rather, he is merely taking the first *ṭôb-saying* ("fame is better than fine ointment") to its logical, if absurd, conclusion: if a name is really better than material
possessions, then the day of death is better than the day of birth.

The argument is continued in v 2: "it is better (*ṭôb*) to go to the house of
mourning than to the house of feasting." If the day of death is better than the day
of birth, then one ought to prefer going to a place where there is mourning than
to a place where there is celebration. The "house of mourning" and "house of
feasting" occur together often in later Jewish writings. They appear to be general
references to funerals and weddings — the mourners' house and the house of the
wedding banquet. Qohelet is claiming, then, that it is better to go to a wake than
to a wedding. One must recognize, however, that the wakes of antiquity were not
necessarily somber occasions. On the contrary, there is a lot of evidence to suggest that they often became gala events, with feasting and excessive drinking.
One tradition has it that Moses himself instituted seven days of feasting for the
"house of mourning" and seven days of feasting for "the house of feasting"
(*y. Ketub.* 1.1; 25a; *Moʻed Qaṭ.* 28b; compare also Gen 50:10; Sir 22:12). At the
wakes, however, the drinking sometimes got so out of hand that the rabbis later
on had to institute a rule allowing only ten cups of wine to be imbibed at "the
house of mourning." And the rule had to be reaffirmed after people began adding
three or four more cups in honor of this or that person or institution (*Sem.* 14;
b. Ketub. 8b). In short, the wake often became an occasion for much eating and
drinking — as at a wedding.

Despite the impression conveyed in the English translation, the contrast is not
between "mourning" and "feasting," for there is feasting in both "houses." In fact,
often the feasting at the "house of mourning" can be as much revelry as that at
the "house of feasting," if not more so. One can, therefore, imagine someone
admitting that the party was at times "better" at a wake than at a wedding. Is an
insensitive joke like that behind this *ṭôb-saying*? Obviously one expects most
people to say that it is better to go to a wedding than a wake. If so, Qohelet is
turning a cliche on its head by saying out loud and in the form of a *ṭôb-saying*
what many would only say privately. That is one way to read the proverb.

In context, however, the point seems to be that it is better to face the reality of
death than to be caught up in the euphoria of a wedding celebration. Confronting the reality of death would prompt one to live in recognition of life's ephemerality, whereas one may be deceived by the gaiety of a wedding into thinking that

the joy of the moment will last forever. That is another way of reading the proverb.

In either case, one is left a little uncomfortable and unsure as to what really is *ṭôb* "good." One is made to ponder if one can really know what is *ṭôb* "good," after all. That is precisely the point that the text is making: no one really knows what is *ṭôb* for humanity in general and at all times. One can accept what is true and good at any given moment and in a given situation. The cliches about what is "good" or "better" for humanity are just so many words that dissipate as quickly as mist before life's inconsistencies. Even the cleverly constructed and memorable sayings that humans are wont to repeat are, like human beings themselves, all "vanity." They usually come up empty. They are unreliable.

In v 3 we get another *ṭôb-saying*: "vexation (*kaʿas*) is better than merriment." The saying is patently strange. Elsewhere in the Bible, the word *kaʿas* may refer to a woman's vexation over her barrenness (1 Sam 1:6, 16), a parent's anguish over a foolish child (Prov 17:25), or a person's distress over a contentious spouse (Prov 21:19). The word is used of the experience of pain and misery in general, whether provoked by human beings or perceived to be from God (Deut 32:27; Pss 6:8; 31:10; 85:5; 1 Kgs 15:30; 2 Kgs 23:26). In the wisdom tradition, vexation is associated with fools (Prov 12:16), although Qohelet himself sees it as the unpleasant result of having too much wisdom (1:18). If taken seriously, the proverb here contradicts Qohelet's own teachings elsewhere in the book (1:18; 7:9; 11:10).

He explains the proverb in paradoxical terms: "for it is in the sadness of countenance that the heart is glad" (v 3). Although without precise parallel, this saying echoes a traditional proverb that is equally paradoxical: "even in merriment the heart suffers, and the outcome of joy is grief" (Prov 14:13). The point of this traditional saying is that life is full of contradictions. It is a "mixed bag": it is neither all good, nor all bad. Even in times of general happiness the human mind is constantly cognizant of the limitations of joy and the fact that grief is always a threat to human happiness. So the wise live in awareness of the reality of death and other tragedies, whereas fools are aware only of mirth. Is this what Qohelet means? He is certainly aware that life consists of both good and bad times. Indeed, the conclusion of this whole literary unit (7:13–14) proves that he is keenly aware that life is like that. Here in vv 3–4 he caricatures the teachings of the traditional sages, and exaggerates their general advice in extreme terms: vexation is better than merriment, sadness of the face equals happiness of the heart, the heart of the wise is in the house of mourning. The sayings are perhaps deliberately ludicrous. By their sheer absurdity, Qohelet challenges the audacity of anyone to tell others what is good and how to have an advantage in life. No one can reduce the realities of life and death, or happiness and sadness, to a set of propositions. The realities of life are simply too contradictory for one to be governed by axioms.

Through vv 1–4 Qohelet parodies the teachings of those who would give advice about what is good or what is better. Then in v 5, he appears to give credit to the wise. He lays out another *ṭôb-saying*: "it is better (*ṭôb*) to hear the rebuke of the wise than the ode of the fool." This saying echoes traditional teachings that there were clear benefits to discipline, despite the pain of it (Prov 1:23; 3:11; 6:23; 13:24; 22:15; Job 5:17–18; Sir 22:6). The wise know this, but fools deceive others with empty praise (Prov 26:28; 29:5). So it is said among the sages, "one who rebukes a person will find more favor afterwards than one who flatters" (Prov 28:23; see also Prov 27:14). To illustrate the emptiness of the fool's words, Qohelet uses the simile of thorns crackling in the fire under a cooking-pot, reinforcing the point through wordplay: "like the crackling of nettles (*hassîrîm*) under the kettle (*hassîr*), so is the cackling of the fool" (v 6). Thorns are used as fuel throughout the Middle East because they are dry and readily combustible (see Nah 1:10; Ps 58:9). But they also generate a lot of disconcerting noises that are entirely inconsequential to their function and they do not last very long as fuel. Perhaps the author has in mind the contrast between noisy fire fueled by thorns, and fire that is produced by more substantial wood or coals, that are quieter, more enduring, and give out much more heat. The mirth of fools is like the fire of thorns: it is irritating and inconsequential; there is a lot less substance than there seems.

So the point is made that the wise can be trusted more than fools, even if what one hears from the wise is hurtful (v 5). Unlike the other *tôb-sayings* presented so far, this one does not appear to be a parody. The author appears to be arguing with tradition that wisdom is indeed superior and preferable to folly. But he does not allow that impression to remain for long. He immediately subverts the claim of wisdom's superiority: "but this, too, is vanity!" The antecedent of "this" is not just the cacophony of the fool, but the whole argument that immediately precedes this judgment, namely, that those who propound the *tôb-saying* — the wise who know "better" — can really be relied on more than fools. Any impression of the utter reliability of the wise quickly dissipates in the face of reality. The reason is that the wise are also susceptible to corruption and they could become fools: "for oppression turns the wise into fools, and a bribe perverts the mind" (v 7).

Since the "vanity"-judgment in v 6 is often taken to conclude the preceding verses, the introduction of v 7 with *kî* ("for" or "indeed") is troubling for many commentators. It is often supposed that something has fallen out (see Notes above). There is no evidence of anything missing, however. One must, indeed, not isolate v 7 from v 6. On the contrary, v 7 seems to be supporting the judgment in v 6 that wisdom is "vanity." Even if the wise are relatively superior to fools, they are still susceptible to corruption. The wise could be fooled, so to speak. We should take the beginning particle in v 7 as causal ("for" or "because"): "but this, too, is vanity" (v 6), *for* oppression makes the wise foolish, and exaction perverts the mind" (v 7). Ben Sira, too, knew of the vulnerability of the wise: "gifts and presents can blind the eyes of the wise and avert reproofs like a muzzle on the mouth" (Sir 20:29). Wisdom, like all other things in life, is a fleeting thing. It is only relative. The wise can be fooled just like the rest of humanity! So one cannot count on what they teach to be "good."

The series climaxes with two more *tôb-sayings* in v 8. The first suggests that the end of a matter is better than its beginning. The second says that patience is better than arrogance. The Hebrew words for "end" and "beginning" occur together several times in the Bible, and in each case a contrast is being made between a former situation and an eventual one (Deut 11:12; Isa 46:10; Job 8:7; 42:12).

If all the *ṭôb-sayings* in this series are thematically linked, and v 8 is the climax, then one may see the saying as confirming the assumption in vv 5–6 that the result of rebuke (its "end") is more important than one's initial feeling of hurt from the rebuke (its "beginning"). So one must be patient and humble, and wait for the "end" to judge any matter. Yet, if one considers Qohelet's caveat that even the wisdom of the wise is unreliable and that the wise themselves are susceptible to becoming fools (v 6–7), then the point here must be that the final outcome of anything is more important than its initial stage. So it is less important who is wise or foolish to begin with, since it is more important to see the result of one's action.

The negative command in v 9 is deliberately linked to the *ṭôb-sayings* in v 8. The two verses are linked in the Hebrew by the presence of the word *rûaḥ*: *'erek rûaḥ* ("patience") and *gĕbah-rûaḥ* ("arrogance") in v 8 and *rûḥăkā* ("your spirit") in v 9. The theme of patience in v 8 is also continued in v 9. The Hebrew verb for "be quick" occurs two other times in Ecclesiastes, both times referring to haste in human speech (5:1 [Eng v 2]; 8:2–3). The problem in each case is the presumptuousness of human beings who act as if they know the outcome of what they say. Here in 7:9, the issue is *ka'as* "anger" or "vexation" (see Comment at 1:18). Perhaps, the author has in mind the warning in traditional wisdom against an excessive show of passion, since "vexation kills the fool and passion destroys the simpleton" (Job 5:2). In any case, the saying here seems to contradict the *ṭôb-saying* in v 3, if one were to take that saying at face value: "vexation is better than merriment." Normative wisdom suggests that fools are quick to show their displeasure: "the vexation of a fool is known at once, but a shrewd person conceals shame" (Prov 12:16). So patience is better. But in speaking of patience, Qohelet does not mean that one should nurture resentment inwardly, for he adds that "anger stays (*yānûaḥ*) in the bosom of the fool." The verb *yānûaḥ* here is part of a wordplay with *rûaḥ* "spirit." It is fools who are "patient" (literally "long of *rûaḥ*") in this sense: they nurture their seething anger in secret. Qohelet thus undermines in v 9 what is said about patience in v 8. Is patience always better? Is it really better in the case of the fool? The universal applicability of the *ṭôb-sayings* in v 8 is thus called into question, at least where anger is concerned: the "end" of anger is not so desirable that one should be patient about getting it. It does not pay to be patient till the end in this instance.

In v 10 the author warns against idealizing the past (v 10). We get a rare opportunity here to hear the voice of Qohelet's audience through his direct quote of them: "How is it that the former days were better than these?" It is not the point of view of a disinterested third party that the author criticizes, but the view brought forth by the audience. Says he: "It is not out of wisdom that you ask so" (v 10). One is let in on a dialogue here between the wisdom teacher (see 12:9) and an audience that seems to belong to the wisdom tradition. And one hears the voice of the teacher chiding his listeners for missing the point that the sages of old were making.

The conversation is all too faint and elliptical, however, and one is left wondering what the teacher really means. The problem, one can only surmise, is that the rules of days gone by do not seem to work anymore; the sayings that once were axiomatic no longer appear so. The reliability of wisdom, as reflected in the proverbs, is shattered on the rocks of life's contradictions. In the best of times, the experiences and observations of the wise may have provided ordinary people with generally reliable guidelines on what is good and what is bad. But at other times, particularly in periods of great social, economic, and political turmoil, the reliability of wisdom is sorely tested. So people asked in exasperation, as we often do even now: "Why can't things be as they used to be, when we knew better than we know now?" This was the problem that Qohelet's audience faced: the contradictions of life had made it impossible for people to take control of it, and the guidelines they had received from tradition did not seem to hold anymore.

In v 11 Qohelet says wisdom is as good as wealth and, as such, is an advantage to "those who see the sun," namely, those who are alive (v 11). This sudden praise of wisdom seems out of character for the author and it is especially out of place in this literary unit. He has already asserted in the introduction (6:10–12) that humans have no advantage, and the reliability of wisdom has been relativized in various ways in the verses immediately preceding (7:1–10). One must look carefully at the text, therefore, and not be tricked by one's initial impression.

Even though wisdom is called *ṭôb* in this verse, what we have here is not at all like the other *ṭôb-sayings* in the passage. In fact, we do *not* have the same type of *ṭôb-saying* here. The Hebrew is quite clear, even though many commentators try to emend it: "Wisdom is *as good as* inheritance." The shift in form from the *ṭôb-sayings* that so dominate the passage to a different kind of *ṭôb-saying* is not accidental. The difference between this *ṭôb-saying* and the others in this unit is especially stark, when one considers the fact that elsewhere wisdom is said to be *better than* material possessions (Prov 3:14; 8:11, 19; 16:16). So it is striking that Qohelet does not say that wisdom is "better than" material possessions. Having encountered the "better than"-proverbs in vv 1–10, one certainly expects him to use a "better than" form. But he does not. He says, instead, that wisdom is "as good as inheritance." When we remember, too, that Qohelet does not consider material possessions to be very reliable (see especially 5:12–16 [Eng vv 13–17]), we understand that he is, in fact, undermining any confidence in the utter reliability of wisdom when he compares it to possessions. The slight shift in form is part of Qohelet's subversive strategy. We realize that he is saying, after all, that wisdom is *only* as good as inheritance — and both are in the end unreliable. This is finally how we are to understand the *ṭôb-sayings*: what is *ṭôb* is still ephemeral and unreliable.

Any overconfidence that one may still have in wisdom is certainly tempered by the judgment that "wisdom is as a shadow and money is as a shadow" (v 12). It is true that the word translated as "shadow" may also mean "shade" or "protection," so the text could have been alluding to the power of wisdom and wealth, as some commentators insist (see NAB: "the protection of wisdom is as the protection of money"; KJV: "wisdom is a defence and money is a defence"). It has also been suggested that the author was quoting the arrogant rich who believed that "money makes everything possible" (Whybray). That may, indeed, be the original meaning of the saying. It may have been the popular understanding of the proverb. Yet Qohelet does not always use a proverb according to its original intent. He often turns the proverb on its head to say the very opposite of its original meaning, as if to show by this technique that many words are elusive, like wind (*hebel*). In this case, given all that he has said in this passage, particularly the fact that the word "shadow" has already appeared in the introduction to the passage (6:12), one should understand him to emphasize not the protective power of wisdom and money, but their unreliability. If anyone should think of these things as a permanent shelter, then they must learn that wisdom and wealth can only provide a shade — like a shadow. They are not a lasting shelter (compare 6:12). They provide no permanent protection.

Among the texts that use the Hebrew word for "shadow" or "shade," Job 7:2 is particularly suggestive: "As a slave pants for the shade, and as a hireling waits for remuneration." The context in that passage is a reflection about the misery of human existence, and the poet specifically laments that life is a "breath" (*rûah*) and "vapor" (*hebel*), and that one cannot "see good" forever (Job 7:1–21). In the face of this reality, the human being can only accept whatever gains there are, if only for momentary relief. Like a slave, the human being longs for the shade and whatever rewards there are, even though the relief and advantages are only for a moment and do not make much of a difference in the overall scheme of things. So, too, we should understand Qohelet's analogy of wisdom and wealth with "shade/shadow." Wisdom is only as good as material possessions. They may give one temporary relief, but they are ultimately unreliable. They are only as good as the shade that a shadow may give, but they provide no permanent protection.

In light of this, we must understand the comment about the advantage of knowledge and wisdom only in this limited and relative sense: "knowledge is an advantage, and wisdom lets its possessor stay alive" (v 12b). The point is not that wisdom assures life, or is life-giving. That is what many people understood the purpose of wisdom to be (see Prov 3:13–18). But Qohelet does not mean that wisdom's advantage is its life-generating power. He means that wisdom allows one to live — just like the relief that a shadow may provide. It allows one the possibility of survival. It helps one cope. Wisdom, for Qohelet, affords one no permanence, it gives one no control over life itself. It is, like all possessions, but a shadow. It provides one only momentary relief.

Theological Conclusion (7:13–14)
At the beginning of the passage, in 6:10–12, the author speaks of human inability to dispute what is happening in the world. Although not explicitly mentioned, the deity stands in the background. The deity is obviously the stronger one with whom humans cannot contend, the one who has determined all events that come to pass and knows the course of humanity. But this mysterious Other is

not named. Now, in the conclusion to the passage (7:13–14), God is explicitly mentioned, and it is an active God of whom the text speaks. Before the activity of this mysterious God the human being is impotent. Even as human beings are unable to contend with God (so 6:10), so they are unable to straighten what God has made crooked (see Comment at 1:15). Here again, as in 6:10–12, the author seems to have Job in mind. Conservative wisdom apparently denied that the deity ever made anything crooked, that God has perverted (*'wt*) justice (Job 8:3; 34:12). But Job maintained that it was God who perverted justice in his case: "God has done me injustice" (*'iwwĕtanî*, Job 19:6). Job insisted that there were things in the world that were crooked because of God, and he insisted that what was crooked be straightened out by God. Qohelet acknowledges that the world is not perfect, but he does not think that anyone can straighten what God has made "crooked" (*'iwwĕtô*). It is this mysterious "activity of God" that the reader is called to "see," to recognize for what it is (v 13). The conclusion, then, is that people can only take things as they come, accepting good when it is accessible and facing adversity when that is the reality (v 14). Even as one is called to accept what God has done (v 13), one is called to see that the good and the bad are the result of God's doing (v 14). In fact, v 14 elaborates on what the "activity of God" in v 13 entails, namely, both the good and the bad (see Notes above).

In the Akkadian text known as the *Dialogue of Pessimism* the point is also made that human beings do not know how to give any advice that is universally applicable (*BWL*, pp. 139–49). And the solution to the impasse, according to that text, is death:

What, then, is good?
To have my neck broken
and to be thrown into the river is good.

(BWL, p. 149, lines 80–82)

Qohelet, too, raises the question of "what is good." He insists that no human can tell "what is good" (6:12). But his exploration of the issue leads neither to death, nor to utter despair. In the end he does affirm that there is good along with the bad. Indeed, God "has made" what is good, only it is beyond human ability to know when that will come. The human can only "see" and "be in good" when there is good, and "see" that both the good and the bad come from God. This is Qohelet's theological conclusion to the realities of life's contradictions.

II.A.2. RIGHTEOUSNESS AND WISDOM ARE ELUSIVE (7:15–29)

7 [15]Both (of them) I have seen in my fleeting lifetime: there are righteous ones who perish in their righteousness, and there are wicked ones who live long in

their badness. ¹⁶Do not be exceedingly righteous and do not show yourself excessively wise, lest you be confounded. ¹⁷Do not be exceedingly wicked and do not be a fool, lest you die before your time. ¹⁸It is good that you grasp the one but also not let go of the other, for the one who fears God goes forth with both of them.

> ¹⁹Wisdom is dearer to the wise
>> than the \<wealth\> of the proprietors who are in the city;
> ²⁰But there is no one on earth so righteous,
>> who does only good and does not err.
> ²¹Yes, do not take to heart the things that people say,
>> lest you hear your servant disparaging you;
> ²²For, very often too, your heart knows
>> that you yourself have disparaged others.

²³All this I have tested by wisdom. I said, "I would be wise," but that is beyond me. ²⁴All that happens is inaccessible and utterly unfathomable; who can discover it? ²⁵I, that is, my heart, turned to know and to explore, and seek wisdom and accounting, to know wickedness to be foolishness and folly to be irrationality. ²⁶And I find the woman more bitter than death, inasmuch as she is a trap, her heart is a net, her hands are fetters. One who is favored by God will escape from her; but the offender will be captured by her.

²⁷See what I have found, says Qohelet, one by one to find an accounting. ²⁸The one whom I have sought continually, but have not found. {One man in a thousand I have found, but I have not found a woman among all these.} ²⁹Only, see what I have found: that God has made humanity just right, but they have sought many inventions.

NOTES

15. *Both (of them) I have seen.* Hebrew *kōl*, when referring to just two items, may be translated as "both" rather than "all." See, especially v 18, but also 2:14; 3:19–20.

in my fleeting lifetime. Hebrew *bîmê heblî*, lit. "in the days of my *hebel*," is elliptical for *bîmê ḥayyê-heblî* (cf. 6:12; 9:9). See Notes at 6:12. There can be little doubt that *hebel* "vanity" (see Notes at 1:2) here refers to the ephemerality of human life (cf. 11:10; Ps 39:5–7 [Eng vv 4–6]; 78:33; 144:4; Job 7:16).

in their righteousness . . . in their badness. The preposition *bĕ-* in *bĕṣidqô* and *bĕrā'ātô* may indicate condition — that is, "they perish in (their condition of) righteousness" or "they perish with their righteousness" (see Exod 5:19; 32:12; Lev 19:15; Deut 28:62; Pss 17:15; 25:5; 81:8 [Eng v 7]; 91:15; Prov 19:1). It is also possible, however, to take the preposition to mean "in spite of" or "despite" (Lev 26:27; Num 14:11; Deut 1:32; Isa 47:9). In either case, the meaning is clear.

who live long. Hebrew *ma'ărîk* is probably elliptical for *ma'ărîk yāmîm*, lit. "prolong days" (cf. Exod 20:12). See also *ma'ărîk* in 8:12 and *ya'ărîk* in Prov 28:2.

16. *do not be exceedingly righteous.* Whybray is probably correct to stress that the adverb *harbēh* "exceedingly" qualifies the verb *tĕhî* "be" rather than the ad-

jective *ṣaddîq* "righteous" ("Qoheleth the Immoralist?," pp. 191–204). That is, the extreme is in the verbal idea; the emphasis is on the verb "to be." It is difficult, however, to accept Whybray's arguments that the problem in v 16 is hypocrisy, that is, self-righteousness. According to Whybray, if the author had intended to say "do not be righteous," he would have used *'al tiṣdaq* rather than *'al-těhî ṣaddîq*. It is further argued that the Hithpael form *hithakkam* in the second half of the verse should, on analogy with the Hithpael of some other roots, be interpreted to indicate pretense. Thus, *'al-tithakkam* means "do not pretend to be wise" or "do not act like a sage." But the Hithpael of *ḥkm* never indicates pretense anywhere. Moreover, as Whybray himself admits, the parallel admonition in v 17 cannot indicate pretense: *'al-těhî sākāl* "do not be a fool" and *'al-tirša'* "do not be wicked" must be taken literally. Thus, the expression *'al-těhî ṣaddîq* "do not be righteous" in v 16 does not indicate pretense any more than *'al-těhî sākāl* "do not be a fool" in v 17. The usage of *ṣaddîq* in the immediate context, too, militates against Whybray's hypothesis, for neither in v 16 nor in v 20 can the word indicate one who is only pretending to be righteous. It is unlikely that in vv 16 and 20 the word indicates genuine righteousness, while in v 19 it implies only pretense.

In the chiastic structure of vv 16–17, *'al-těhî ṣaddîq* "do not be righteous" is contrasted with *'al-těhî sākāl* "do not be a fool," whereas *'al-tithakkam* "do not show yourself wise" is contrasted with *'al-tirša'* "do not be wicked." This suggests that the terms used here are not intended as moralistic categories (see Loader, *Polar Structures*, pp. 47–48). That is, the righteous is the opposite of the fool; "to be wise" is the opposite of "to be wicked." Righteousness is wisdom, wickedness is folly. It seems clear, therefore, that the author chose the expression *'al-těhî ṣaddîq* for poetic reasons — to balance *'al-těhî sākāl*. The expression means the same thing as *'al-tiṣtaddîq* "do not show yourself to be righteous." Compare Sir 7:5, where *'l tṣṭdyq* means "do not show yourself righteous" = "do not flaunt your righteousness."

show yourself excessively wise. Hebrew *hithakkam* means either "behave wisely" (Exod 1:10) or "become wise" (Sir 6:32; 38:24; *b. Ber.* 63b; *B. Bat.* 25b). The problem here appears to be extreme wisdom, as in 2:15. The verb does not indicate pretense. The Hithpael form of *ḥkm* in classical Hebrew never means "to pretend to be wise" or "to imagine oneself wise." In Sir 10:26, the verb means "to show oneself wise" not in the sense of pretense but pretentiousness (so NAB: "flaunt not your wisdom"). The issue there is not hypocrisy but boasting (the verb is parallel to *ttkbd* "glorify yourself"). The same is true with the use of the verb in Sir 32:4, where one is urged not to show off one's wisdom. Such overconfidence can be very dangerous. See Sir 7:5 (MS A).

A suggestive parallel may be found in a fragmentary text from the Aramaic *Proverbs of Ahiqar*, circulating among the Jews of Elephantine in Egypt in the Persian period: *'l tstkl kbyr [w']l yd'k ḥ[. . .]* "do not be overly clever, lest . . . be extinguished" (see *TAD* III, 1.147). This Aramaic proverb has been related to our text in Ecclesiastes. The meaning of *tstkl* in that context is ambiguous, however. It is also possible to translate it as "do not be overly foolish. . . ." If so, one should relate the Aramaic text to v 17 (*wĕ'al tĕhî sākāl* "do not be a fool") rather than v 16 (so, Lindenberger, *The Aramaic Proverbs of Ahiqar*, pp. 147–48). As Lindenberger has noted, the proverb is too fragmentary for one to choose one reading over the other. It may also be that we have an instance here of *double entendre*. Perhaps the proverb is capable of double meaning, illustrating the fact that wisdom cannot be easily distinguished from folly, a point also made by Qohelet. Although the text is fragmentary, it is clear that this Aramaic proverb advocates moderation in one's behavior. The next saying in this text, likewise, advocates avoidance of extremes: "Do not be too sweet lest you be . . . ; do not be too bitter. . . ." The text then goes on to urge humility and restraint. It is important to highlight this parallel because of a tendency among commentators to associate Qohelet's thought here with notions of moderation in Greek philosophy, notably Theognis' *mēden agan* "nothing very much" and Aristotle's *mesotēs* "median." Certainly Qohelet's admonition to avoid extremes cannot be termed a mere Hellenistic by-product or a reproduction of Greek thought (so Plumptre).

lest you be confounded. Hebrew *lāmmâ tiššômēm*, lit. "why should you be confounded." The use of *lāmmâ* (lit. "why?") does not mean that the author is thinking of the outcome only as a probability (so Zimmerli). Rather, *lāmmâ* here means "lest" or "otherwise" (see Notes at 5:5 [Eng v 6]). The form *tiššômēm* (from **titšômēm*) shows the assimilation of *t* instead of the expected metathesis of *š* and *t* (see Joüon-Muraoka §53.e). The unassimilated and metathesized form is attested, however, in two Hebrew MSS. The Hithpolel form of the verb in the Bible usually means "be shocked" or "be dumbfounded" (Ps 143:4; Isa 59:16; 63:5; Dan 8:27). The verb may, however, mean more than being amazed or being in a state of shock. It may also connote emotional or psychological devastation. Ps 143:3–4 describes someone who is completely devastated and appears to be, as one might say today, "deeply depressed":

> My foe has pursued me,
> He has crushed my being to the ground;
> He has caused me to sit in darkness,
> Like those long dead.
> Therefore my spirit has collapsed;
> My mind (lit. "heart") within me is confounded (*yištômēm*).

This usage of the verb is attested in the Talmud, as well: "the world was devastated (*mištômēm*) until Simon ben Shetah came and restored the Torah" (*b. Qidd.* 66a). Although the words are different, the mention of self-destruction here recalls the demise of the righteous in v 15b.

17. *lest you die.* Lit. "why should you die." See Notes at 5:5 (Eng v 6) and v 16 above.

before your time. Hebrew *bĕlō' 'ittekā*, lit. "when (it is) not your time." The point is premature death, the fate of the wicked (see Job 22:16). Similar idioms are found in the Phoenician inscription of Eshmunazor (*KAI* 14.3, 12) and in the Aramaic *Proverbs of Ahiqar* (see Lindenberger, *The Aramaic Proverbs of Ahiqar*, p.

81). Cf. similar uses of *bĕlô* in Job 15:32 (*bĕlô-yômô* "before his time"); Sir 30:24 (*bl̄ 't* "before [due] time"; Greek *pro kairou*). One may also compare Akkadian *ina la ūmēšu* "before his time," which also refers to a premature death. Indeed, in at least one instance, the Akkadian idiom is used in a manner very similar to our text: *ina la ūmēšu imât* "he will die before his time" (*CT* 38 28:29; also *CT* 39 42 K.2238+ ii 4). The reference to premature death here recalls the mention of the longevity of the wicked in v 15b (cf. Piotti, "Osservazioni," pp. 252–53). While it is true that there are wicked people who live long, extreme wickedness may lead literally to premature death.

18. *grasp.* The verb *'āḥaz* may have the same connotations as Akkadian *aḥāzu*, which may mean "to understand, to learn, to be aware," with the causative meaning "to teach," or the like (see *CAD* I/1, pp. 177, 180–1). Thus, the verb "to grasp" in Hebrew, as in English, may refer to physical or intellectual grasping.

let go. Hebrew *'al-tannaḥ 'et-yādekā*, lit. "do not relax your hand," as in 11:6. LXX[BSA] has *mē mianēs* "do not defile (your hand)," an inner Greek error for *mē anēs* (i.e., *mē anēs > mē mēanēs > mē mianēs*), as Theod has it. The latter correctly understands the meaning of the verb. Aq and Symm, however, are more literal in their rendering (*aphēs*).

one who fears God. See Notes and Comment at 3:14 and 5:7 (Eng v 8). The fearer of God is one who knows the place of humanity, both human potential and human limitations. For Qohelet in this passage, the fear of God is the recognition of human limitations and the acceptance of divine will. See Lux, "'Lebenskompromiß,'" pp. 276–78.

goes forth. The verb *yēṣē* is often taken to mean "escape from" or "avoid" (Hertzberg, Zimmerli, Barucq; NIV: "will avoid all extremes"). This translation is grammatically possible (Gen 44:4; Exod 9:29, 33; Deut 14:22; Jer 10:20; see Joüon-Muraoka §125.n). Such an interpretation, however, flies in the face of the admonition in the preceding line, namely, that one must hold on to the one and not let go of the other. The most natural reference of *kullām* "all/both of them" is to *zeh . . . zeh* "the one . . . the other" in v 18a. In terms of the structure of vv 15–18, this line corresponds to the reference to the fate of the righteous and the wicked in v 15b, and "both of them" (*'et-kullām*) recalls "both" (*'et-hakkōl*) in v 15a. The point is that one can *not* escape the two, namely, righteousness-wisdom and wickedness-folly! Other scholars have suggested that the verb *yāṣā* is used here for the idiom *yāṣā yĕdê ḥôbâ* "to fulfill obligation," as in Postbiblical Hebrew (see *b. Ber.* 8b, 20b; so already in Targ, but also Rashi, Rashbam; cf. NJPS: "will do his duty"). This reading finds plausible support in Vulg, which reads *nihil negligit* "neglects nothing." It is true that the verb *yāṣā* is used in this pregnant sense in Postbiblical Hebrew (so *m. Ber.* 2:1; *b. Pesaḥ.* 86b), but there is no need to assume such an ellipsis here. Nor should one posit that the verb means "succeed" (so NEB) or "win through" (NAB). The literal meaning of the verb is adequate, if one takes *'et* as the preposition "with," rather than the sign of the direct object. Qohelet is simply stating a reality: the "fearer of God" will venture forth in life *with* both righteousness-wisdom and wickedness-folly. Syr has *nqp* "adhere," which is a mistake for *npq* "go forth."

both of them. Hebrew *kullām* (lit. "all of them") refers to both — i.e., *bāzeh . . . mizzeh* (as in 2:14; 3:19–20; 7:15). Note that *'et-kullām* here forms an *inclusio* with *'et-hakkōl* in v 15.

19. *is dearer.* The verb is *tā'ōz*. The normal meaning of *'zz* "be strong" does not seem to fit. Why would wisdom be stronger *for the wise* than for anyone else? Hence, many scholars prefer to take the verb to have a transitive meaning, for which they cite Ps 68:29 and Prov 8:28. Thus, the phrase is taken to mean "wisdom gives strength to the wise," or the like. Psalm 68, however, is notoriously difficult and the text of v 29 is corrupt; certainly *'ûzzâ* (if MT is correct) is both morphologically and semantically difficult. As for Prov 8:28, the form in question is repointed by most scholars to a Piel form. In any case, neither example is followed by the preposition *lĕ-*. The translation of *tā'ōz* as "give strength to" seems forced.

It may be noted that the noun *'ōz* (usually "strength") is used frequently with words like "majesty," "honor," and "glory" (Jer 48:17; Pss 29:1; 63:3 [Eng v 2]; 68:35; 78:61; 89:18 [Eng v 17]; 93:1; 96:6–7 [Eng vv 5–6]; Prov 31:25; 1 Chron 16:27–28). The adjective *'izzûz* (usually "strong") may, similarly, mean "majestic" or "glorious" (Ps 24:8; *b. Ber.* 33b). Thus, the verb may mean not just "be strong," but also "be honored, be cherished," or the like. This very root in Arabic may mean "be strong" or "strengthen," but also "be elevated, be esteemed, be greatly valued" (Lane, *Arabic-English Lexicon*, Part V, pp. 2030–32). It is also suggestive that in Ps 52:9 (Eng v 7) *'zz* occurs in parallelism with *bṭḥ*: "he trusted (*wayyibṭaḥ*) in the abundance of his riches" // "he is esteemed (*yā'ōz*) in his wealth" (reading *bĕhônô* with Syr). So *tā'ōz* may mean "be esteemed, be dear, be cherished," or the like. 4QQoh[a] has *t'zr* "helps," a reading apparently supported by LXX (*boēthēsei* "helps"). But this is the easier reading that attempts to clarify the meaning of the verse. MT has the more difficult, and probably more original, reading. In any case, the verb *'zz* may, in a few instances, be taken as a near synonym of *'zr*, perhaps *'zr* II "be strong" (see *HALAT*, p. 767). For this reason, the Greek translators of the Hebrew Bible sometimes rendered Hebrew *'ōz* "strength" as *boēthos* "help," which normally translates *'ēzer* or *'ezrâ* "help" (Exod 15:2; Pss 27:2; 59:17; 62:8; 81:2 [Eng v 1]). So the *Vorlage* of LXX may not be reading Hebrew *t'zr*, after all. It should be mentioned that *'zr* II "be strong" is related to Arabic *ġazura* "be abundant, copious" and *ġazīr* "copious, rich" (Wehr-Cowan, *Arabic-English Dictionary*, p. 672). There is no clear instance of such a usage of *'zr* in Hebrew, however. For the possible synonymity between *'zr* and *'zz*, see G. Brin "The Roots 'ZR-'ZZ in the Bible [in Hebrew]," *Leš* 24 (1960), pp. 8–14.

than the <wealth> of the proprietors. Reading *mē'ōšer haššallîṭîm* "than the wealth of the proprietors" (so F. Perles, *Analekten zur Textkritik* I [Leipzig: Engel, 1922], p. 42; Fox, *Contradictions*, p. 232), rather than MT's *mē'ăśārâ šallîṭîm* "ten proprietors." If MT were correct, we must wonder how wisdom is supposed to be stronger to the wise "than the ten proprietors ones who are in the city." Is wisdom being compared to the "ten proprietors"? The phrase *'ăšer hāyû bā'îr* "who are in the city" gives the reference a certain historical ring, indicating that the audience probably knew who these "proprietors" were. So this is not a timeless aphorism. Nor can "ten" be taken as figurative (so Rashbam).

Most scholars identify the "ten *šallîṭîm*" with the *deka prōtoi* "ten first (citizens)" who, according to Josephus, had administrative duties in cities like Tiberius (Josephus, *Life*, 13, 57). The *deka prōtoi* were not mentioned before 66 C.E., however; this council of ten appears to have been a Roman institution well attested in a variety of sources from the end of the first to the beginning of the fourth century in this era, but not earlier (see A. H. M. Jones, *The Greek City from Alexander to Justinian* [Oxford: Clarendon, 1940], p. 139).

In any case, the sudden mention of "ten *šallîṭîm*" is problematic. A copyist probably misdivided the words (taking the definite article on *hšlyṭym* with the preceding word) and misinterpreted the *š* in ʿ*šr* as *ś* (cf. 8:1, where MT has *yšnʾ*, but LXX and Syr interpret the word as *yśnʾ*; also 1 Kgs 8:31 and 2 Chron 6:22, where *nšʾ* is read as *nśʾ* in some MSS and LXX; Ps 68:26, where MT has *šārîm*, but some MSS, LXX, and Syr read *śārîm*). We may note that a similar misplacing of the definite article is evident in v 27, where MT reads *ʾmrh qhlt* for *ʾmr hqhlt* (for other examples, see Perles, *Analekten zur Textkritik* I, p. 42). There are also other examples of misdivision of words in Ecclesiastes (see Notes at 8:1; 10:1). The comparison of wisdom with wealth makes more sense. Certainly in the instructional literature, wisdom is more valued than wealth (Prov 3:14; 8:19; 16:16). Specifically, it is said that those who rely on their wealth will fall, whereas those who are "righteous" will flourish (Prov 11:28, see also v 4).

As for the *šallîṭîm*, we note that the singular form occurs in 8:8 and 10:5, although one learns nothing about them in those passages except that they are powerful. In any case, the Hebrew word does not refer to local rulers or governors (so Lohfink, "Melek, *šallîṭ* und *mōšēl*," pp. 541–43). In Gen 42:6, Joseph is said to have been the *šallîṭ* over the land (of Egypt), and he had authority over the rations. The word is used there in the sense of one who has the authority to dispose of goods (cf. Akkadian *šalāṭu*; *CAD* XVII/1, p. 239). The feminine form occurs in Ezek 16:30, where Zion is called *ʾiššâ-zônâ šallāṭet* (NJPS: "self-willed whore"). In this imagery, the woman in question is clearly not an ordinary prostitute; instead of receiving payments, she gives gifts to her paramours and seduces them with her bribes (see J. C. Greenfield, "Two Biblical Passages in the Light of Their Near Eastern Background—Ezekiel 16:30 and Malachi 3:17," *Eretz-Israel* 16 [1982], pp. 56–61; Y. Muffs, *Studies in the Aramaic Legal Papyri from Elephantine* [Studia et Documenta ad Iura Orientis Antiqui Pertinentia 8; Leiden: Brill, 1969], pp. 24, 177–78). Indeed, it seems clear from the Aramaic documents from the fifth and fourth centuries B.C.E. that the term always refers to authority over property, including the right of acquisition and disposition of the property (see Notes at 2:19). A *šallîṭ* is someone who has power or right over property, thus a "proprietor."

The term *šallîṭîm* in Ecclesiastes is not a political one. It does not appear to designate an official status in the government. Indeed, we would not expect a plurality of governors or high government representatives "who are in the city." Rather, the *šallîṭîm* indicates the socioeconomic positions of these people.

Translation, Notes, and Comments

20. *but.* Hebrew *kî* is used in the adversative sense normally after a negative clause, but context occasionally requires that *kî* be interpreted as adversative, even if there is no explicitly negative clause preceding it. If a negative sense is discernible, or if the author intends the preceding to be negative, then the adversative *kî* may follow. Cf. Ps 130:4; Gen 31:14–16; Isa 28:28; Schoors, "The Particle כי," pp. 252–53.

there is no one on earth so righteous. Hebrew *'ādām 'ên ṣaddîq bā'āreṣ*, lit. "as for humanity, there is none righteous." The point is not that no righteous person exists, for that would contradict the observation in v 16 that some righteous people perish in their righteousness. Rather, *'ên ṣaddîq* in v 20 stands in stark contrast with *yēš ṣaddîq* in v 15. The point is that no one is so righteous as to avert destruction simply on the basis of one's righteousness. For the syntax, cf. Gen 7:8; Exod 5:16; and see Joüon-Muraoka §160.i. Rashbam understood this verse as clarifying v 19, and he identified the "righteous" with the "wise" in vv 17, 19.

does not err. Or "does not sin." On Qohelet's use of *ḥṭ'* see Notes at 2:26. See, also, the pairing of *ṭôb* and *ḥōṭē'* in 7:26.

21. *Yes.* The function of *gam* here is unclear. Perhaps it is rhetorical, as in v 14. See Michel, *Eigenart*, p. 240.

people say. Lit. "they say." The indefinite subject is often indicated by the third-person masculine forms in Hebrew (Gen 29:2; 26:18; 41:14, etc. GKC §144.f.). LXX^BS (*asebeis*), Syr (*ršy'*), and Targ (*ršy'y'*) apparently add *ršym*, clearly an "explicatory plus." As in MT, LXX^AC and SyrH do not have the addition. The shorter text is to be preferred.

take to heart. Lit. "take to your heart." See Notes at 7:2.

lest. Hebrew *'ăšer lō'*, lit. "so that not" (see GKC §165.b). Cf. Gen 11:7; 2 Kgs 9:37. Compare the Aramaic idiom *dî lā'* in Dan 2:18.

your servant. Taken at face value, the text suggests that the intended audience had or knew what it was like to have an *'ebed*. Yet, it must be said that Hebrew *'ebed* need not mean "slave" or "bond-servant"; the word may simply refer to a subordinate (1 Sam 29:3; 1 Kgs 11:26; 2 Kgs 22:12; 25:8; 2 Chron 24:20). Even a high official may be called an *'ebed*, as long as that high official is a subordinate to someone else. This was certainly the case with several owners of personal stamp seals, who bore the title *'bd hmlk* "servant of the king" or "servant of So-and-So," where the superior is a king (see Davies, *Ancient Hebrew Inscriptions*, 100.065.1, 100.067.4, 100.068.2, 100.069.2, 100.070.2, 100.071.1, 100.125.1, 100.141.1, 100.504.2, 100.205.2, 100.759.2). One of these seals (100.069.2) belongs to a certain "Ashanyahu the servant of the king," apparently a high official in Persian-period Palestine. The *'ebed* is simply a subordinate.

It is possible, then, for one who has an *'ebed* to be an *'ebed* himself. This was true, too, in Mesopotamia of the Persian period, where the *ardu* "slave" may own other slaves and may represent an employer in significant business transactions, as we know from the Murashu documents. Thus, the fact that someone may own "slaves" says nothing about that one's social status. Significantly, the issue of disparaging others appears again in 10:20, where the author urges the reader not to disparage the king or the rich (are these the *šallîṭîm* "proprietors"?), for fear that even those words uttered in private may reach those powerful people who are criticized. It seems clear that Qohelet's audience belonged neither to the powerful and rich upper classes (10:20), nor to the lowest class of people. Most likely they belonged to the dependent classes. They are people with subordinates, but who are themselves subordinate to others.

disparaging you. Hebrew *qll* usually means "to curse," but here it has the more general meaning "to slight, discredit, disparage, ridicule." The verb is used the same way in 10:20, where the reader is asked not to bad-mouth the rich. This usage of the verb is attested in Lev. 19:14; Judg 9:27. By the same token, the noun *qĕlālâ* may mean "slight" or "defamation" (so in Jer 24:9; 25:18; 42:18; 44:8, 12, 22; 49:13). The middle-class status of the audience is, again, evident. They are paranoid about what their subordinates might say about them, but they themselves are disparaging their superiors (10:20).

22. *your heart knows.* Hebrew *yāda' libbekā*. One Hebrew MS, LXX, and Symm suggest *yāra'* "acted injuriously," indicating a confusion of *reš* and *dalet*.

23. *all this.* Commentators are divided in taking *kol-zōh* "all this" to refer to what precedes or what follows. Both are possible and may, indeed, be intended (cf. *'et-hakkōl* in v 15, and see Notes at 8:9).

by wisdom. See Notes at 1:13.

I said, "I would be wise." Or, "I thought, 'I want to be wise.'" Commentators are sometimes troubled by the apparent contradiction between Qohelet's claim of wisdom's elusiveness and his claim to have tested "by wisdom." The contradiction is no more poignant, however, than the observation that there are righteous people who perish in their righteousness (v 15) and the claim that there is no one righteous (v 20). Even as no one is so righteous as to make no mistakes in life, and hence avoid destruction altogether, so there is no one wise enough to understand the world thoroughly. The wisdom that allows one to know the mysteries of the universe, to explain all the discrepancies that exist therein, is simply beyond humanity. Some scholars (Ginsberg, *Kohelet*, p. 101; Fox, *Contradictions*, pp. 239–41) repoint *'ehkāmâ* to read *'ehkāmehā* "I will understand it," assuming that the object "it" refers to "all that occurs" (v 24). There is no need for this emendation, however. More importantly, *hkm* in Qal does not have a transitive meaning anywhere in Hebrew (see Notes at 1:13). Certainly the verb is always intransitive elsewhere in Ecclesiastes (cf. 2:15, 19). In any case, the putative object suffix would not refer explicitly to *mah-ššehāyâ* "all that happens," which is interpreted as masculine at the end of v 24: *mî yimṣā'ennû* "who can find *it*." There is nothing wrong with the cohortative form; it is the form that one expects after *'āmartî*, as in 2:1, *'āmartî . . . 'ănassĕkâ*.

24. *all that happens.* See Notes at 6:10. Instead of *mh-šhyh* "all that happens" or "all that has happened," LXX, Syr, SyrH, Copt, and Vulg all reflect Hebrew *mšhyh* "beyond what is," apparently interpreting the *mēm* as the comparative *min*. This is probably due to the influence of the common idiom *rāḥôq min* "far from" or "too far" (so the preceding line, *rĕhôqâ mimmennî*, but also Ps 22:2 [Eng v 1]; 119:155; Prov 15:29; 27:10; 31:10). MT is preferable.

inaccessible. Hebrew *rāḥôq*, lit. "remote, distant." The language of wisdom's inaccessibility is reminiscent of Prov 31:10: "the woman of quality, who can find (*mî yimṣā'*)? Her worth is beyond (*rāḥôq*) that of jewels." The extraordinary wife and mother (*'ēšet ḥayil* "woman of quality") is described in terms used of wisdom, for it is said in Prov 3:13–18 that the one who finds Wisdom (*māṣā' ḥokmâ*) will find her more precious than jewels. This wise woman embodies the traits of wisdom. She is Wisdom personified (compare Prov 9:1–6).

utterly unfathomable. The repetition of *'āmōq* in MT is probably correct. This repetition is a periphrasis for the superlative (see GKC §133.k-l). LXX has *bathy bathos* "the deep is deep," an interpretation corroborated by SyrH, Copt, and Syr, and other ancient witnesses. MT is supported by Targ. The ancient versions do not necessarily reflect a different reading from MT, such as *'ōmeq 'āmōq* (see Hertzberg). Rather, the Greek translators may simply have interpreted the first *'āmōq* as a substantive. This is, in fact, a possible interpretation of the Hebrew. What is deep is simply what is unfathomable — mysterious (Ps 64:7 [Eng v 6]; Job 11:8; 12:22; cf. Prov 25:3). Note that wisdom is both distant (*rāḥôq*) and deep (*'āmōq*).

who can discover it. The root *mṣ'* recurs in this section (7:23–29), with emphasis sometimes on the process, and sometimes on the end result. Here the rhetorical question "who can discover" probably means that no one can *grasp* it. See Ceresko, "Function of Antanaclasis," pp. 565–69.

25. *I, that is, my heart, turned.* Hebrew *sabbôtî 'ănî wĕlibbî*, lit. "I turned, I and my heart." The *waw* here is explicative (cf. GKC §154.a.Note 1). As Schoors observes, "sometimes the main subject can be specified by a more particular subject, mostly an organ or a capacity (e.g., Ps 3:5; 44:3; Isa 26:9)" (*Pleasing Words*, p. 154; cf. Joüon-Muraoka §151.c). Compare 1:17, where it is the heart that is given the task of knowing wisdom and knowledge. MT *'ănî wĕlibbî* is supported by LXX and Syr. A few Hebrew MS omit *wlby*, yielding an easier reading. Many more Hebrew MSS read *blby*, supported by Targ and Vulg, but that reading is probably secondary, resulting from an attempt to ease the admittedly awkward reading of *sabbôtî 'ănî wĕlibbî*.

to explore. See Notes and Comment at 1:13.

wisdom and accounting. Hebrew *ḥokmâ wĕḥešbôn*, lit. "wisdom and accounting." The words *ḥokmâ* and *ḥešbôn* do not refer to separate ideas, however. Rather, *ḥešbôn* defines wisdom more precisely (cf. Michel, *Eigenart*, pp. 235–36); it is, in fact, a synonym of *ḥokmâ* (cf. 9:10, where *ḥešbôn* is associated with wisdom and knowledge). Schoors regards the expression here as a hendiadys ("Bitterder dan de Dood," p. 132). The word *ḥešbôn* literally means "accounting" or "calculation." It is used here in the sense of a meticulous accounting of matters, such as one would find in a ledger or an inventory. Its Aramaic equivalent is found in a document clearly dated to the end of the fifth century B.C.E. (see *TAD* I, 6.2.4, 23). In three Ugaritic economic texts, we find the cognate *ḥtbn* "account" (*KTU* 4.158.2; 4.337.1, 4.771.7). The Ugaritic word means something like a summary (account), which may be distinguished from the "total" or "the sum" (see esp. *KTU* 4.337.28). In Egyptian Aramaic *ḥšbn* is used in the sense of an account (see *DNWSI* I, p. 411). This meaning is also preserved in later Aramaic and Syriac and is found in Arabic as well. The term is clearly at home in the commercial world of the ancient Levant. But it is also used in a more general sense for all sorts of detailed accountings. In both the economic and general usages, the word may refer not just to the sum of matters, as many commentators suggest, but also to a summary of details, as well as to the process of accounting. In this passage it is used in the sense of an intellectual accounting, that is, an explication (so Barucq; cf. Sir 9:15) of the events in the universe. In the Talmud, the word is used of an accounting of the world on the day of judgment (*b. B. Bat.* 78b) — that is, a reckoning of the fate of the good and the wicked. Although the word probably includes activities that approximate what we call "philosophy," it is unlikely that the word refers specifically to Greek philosophy (so Loretz, "'Frau' und griechisch-jüdische Philosophie," pp. 258–60).

to know wickedness to be foolishness. Lit. "to know wickedness is foolishness" (so Delitzsch, Gordis, and others). See GKC §117.ii.

folly. Four nouns are mentioned here, but only folly has the definite article. The definite article is not used with consistency in the book, however. See Notes at 3:5 and 7:12. LXX has *kai sklērian,* which may reflect the omission of the article in its *Vorlage.*

irrationality. See Notes at 2:12. Many Hebrew MSS, LXX, and Syr add a conjunction before the noun, thus *whsklwt <w> hllwt,* a reading that may have been influenced by *hwllwt wsklwt* in 2:12. Alternatively, *hwllwt* was misread as *whllwt,* that is, with a metathesis of *he'* and *waw* (so Euringer).

26. *I find.* The form *môṣē'* is simply the Qal active participle, written with a *mater* for long ō, as is usually the case in the Qumran documents. Here the form is vocalized as if it were a III-Weak root (cf. *ḥōṭē'* instead of *ḥōṭē'* in 2:26; 8:12; 9:2, 18; see GKC §75.oo). LXX (including LXX[P]), SyrH, and Copt all reflect Hebrew *wmwṣ' 'ny 'th* "I find her." The introduction of the direct object may be an explicatory addition, although its presence is very surprising in LXX of Ecclesiastes, which tends to be quite literalistic. Apparently this tradition interpreted the object of the search as personified folly (so Hertzberg). The use of the participle instead of the perfect suggests that this "woman" continues to be a problem in the author's judgment (so Galling, Hertzberg). Thus, we may translate: "and I find/am finding the woman to be more bitter than death."

more bitter than death. Since the "woman" is in view, we expect *mārâ* instead of *mar,* but see Exod 17:12 where we have a rare instance of a predicate adjective not agreeing with the noun. The word order is also reversed for emphasis; we expect *ûmôṣē' 'ănî 'et-hā'iššâ mārâ! mimmāwet* (cf. Neh 9:8). Dahood proposes to relate *mar* to another meaning of *mrr,* namely, "be strong" ("Recent Discoveries," pp. 308–10; "Phoenician Background," pp. 275–76). This meaning is attested in Aramaic, Ugaritic, and Arabic. Despite the challenge posed by D. Pardee ("The Semitic Root *mrr* and the Etymology of Ugaritic *mr(r) // brk,*" *UF* 10 [1978], pp. 249–88), there is good evidence that the root can mean "strong" in Hebrew, as in other Semitic languages (see especially L. Kutler, "A 'Strong' Case for Hebrew MRR" *UF* 16 [1984], pp. 111–18; W. A. Ward, "Egypto-Semitic MR," *UF* 12 [1980], pp. 357–60). The question is whether the word in this context means "bitter" or "strong," or if both meanings are intended. Certainly, Hebrew *mar* "bitter" is associated with death in 1 Sam 15:32, where the expression *mar-hammāwet* means "bitterness of death," and in Sir 41:1, where we have *lmwt [m]r zkrk* "O Death, how bitter is the remembrance of you." Job 21:25 is also suggestive: *wĕzeh yāmût bĕnepeš mārâ* "and this one dies in the bitterness of being." A similar expression is found in the Aramaic of Sefire: *mr ḥy'* "the bitterness of life," perhaps a euphemism for "the bitterness of death" (see E. Lipiński, *Studies in Aramaic Inscriptions and Onomastics* I [OLA 1; Leuven: Leuven University, 1975], p. 38). Most importantly, in Prov 5:1–6, the dangerous seductress is said to be bitter (*mārâ*) as wormwood, and her feet descend to Death (*māwet*). This parallel is most compelling since the description of the woman in our passage is reminiscent of the dangerous seductress in other ways, as well.

the woman. Commentators do not agree on the identity of "the woman" (*hā'iššâ*) in v 26. Some see here a generally negative attitude toward women in general, while others believe that the author is thinking of a particular woman (perhaps his own wife) or a certain type of women (adulteresses and harlots). Occasionally it is speculated that Qohelet's attitude was formed by his bitter experiences with a woman, either his wife or his mother. So Zimmermann imagines that Qohelet had become impotent and harbored deep resentment toward his wife and mother and, consequently, toward women in general (*The Inner World of Qohelet*, pp. 29–30, 152). Recently Lohfink has proffered a different approach to the problem ("War Kohelet ein Frauenfeind?" pp. 259–87). Following Dahood's suggestion that *mar* may mean strong in Hebrew, he takes *mar mimmāwet 'et-hā'iššâ* "Woman is stronger than death" to have been a positive judgment at one time, related to the saying that "love is strong (*'azzâ*) as death" (Song 8:6). According to Lohfink, the saying "Woman is stronger than death" was originally an expression of admiration, but it was naively interpreted to mean that Woman would literally overcome death. So Qohelet tested the veracity of the saying (v 28) and found it to be untrue, since in his investigation no woman is found to be immortal. One can understand, particularly in the context of a love song, how someone might claim that love is "as strong as death." It is difficult to imagine, however, that anyone would believe that any human being can literally be stronger than death.

Given the context, with its focus on wisdom and folly, it seems unlikely that Qohelet is suddenly introducing the topic of women in general, or even of a particular type of women. The use of the definite article (*hā'iššâ* "the woman") does suggest that the audience is expected to know who this feminine figure is. If one looks for an antecedent referent, the most obvious would be *hassiklût* "folly" in the preceding verse. This was apparently the understanding of the tradition best represented by the Greek witnesses. But the recognition of this feminine figure comes not only from the reference to folly in v 25, but also from the depiction of this *femme fatale* in language reminiscent of the personification of folly in conventional wisdom (see especially Proverbs 1–9): she is deadly, she lays a deadly trap, one must escape from her. These are not, however, just cliches about women (so Lohfink, "War Kohelet ein Frauenfeind?" p. 263 n. 21). Rather they are images used to describe anyone who represents folly, anyone who seduces people away from wisdom. In Prov 1:10–19, for instance, wicked men are described in terms reminiscent of personified Death in Canaanite mythology: "let us swallow them alive" (see Notes and Comment at 6:7). These men, too, set a trap for their victims and wait to pounce on them (cf. 2:12–19, which is parallel in structure to 2:16–19; Ps 140:1–5). The *femme fatale* is the principal figure representing the deadly seductive power of evil, but she is, by no means, the only one.

inasmuch as. Depending on one's interpretation of the preceding words, 'ăšer is variously taken to be causal ("because, for, since") or relative ("who"). The options are not mutually exclusive, however. Both meanings of 'ăšer are pertinent: the "woman" (folly) is more dangerous than death *because* she entraps; the woman *who* entraps is dangerous. There is no need to emend 'ăšer hî' to 'ăšū-rêhā with F. Perles ("A Miscellany of Lexical and Textual Notes on the Bible," *JQR* 2 [1911–12], p. 131) or to 'ăšūrê-hî' with Dahood ("Phoenician Background," pp. 275–76).

a trap. The Masoretic punctuation suggests "her heart is a trap and a net" (so KJV: "whose heart is snares and nets"), but the ancient versions separate the noun *mĕṣôdîm* from *wahărāmîm*. Hebrew *mĕṣôdîm* (here with plural of complexity, as in *miškānôt* = *miškān*, *miškābîm* = *miškāb*) is a hunter's or fowler's trap (see Ezek 12:13 and 17:20). The trap consists of a net spread out on the ground or over a concealed pit (Prov 29:5; Ps 9:16 [Eng v 15]; 31:5 [Eng v 4]; 35:7; 57:7 [Eng v 6]; 140:6 [Eng v 5]), hence the frequent reference to one's feet being caught in a net-trap. In Ben Sira, the dangerous woman is described in a similar way: "Do not approach a strange woman, lest you fall into her trap (*mṣwdtyh*) // Do not associate with a harlot, lest you be caught (*tlkd*) in her snares" (Sir 9:3 [MS A; cf. *b. Sanh.* 100b]); "A harlot is regarded as spittle // A married woman is a deadly trap (Gk *pyrgos thanatou* = Heb *mĕṣûdat māwet*) to those who embrace her" (Sir 26:22). See P. Skehan, "Tower of Death or Deadly Snare? (Sir 26,22)," *CBQ* 16 (1954), p. 154.

a net. The noun *ḥērem* (here *ḥărāmîm*, with plural of complexity) usually refers to a fishing net, but it is a hunters' net in Mic 7:2. The extreme danger that this "woman" poses may also be suggested by the association of this word with the *ḥērem* ("ban"), something to be utterly destroyed!

fetters. The fetters do not refer to the woman's "voluptuous embrace" (so Delitzsch). Rather, the hunting imagery is continued. What is alluded to is probably the fettering of animals and birds after they are caught. E. Otto describes a hunting ritual in Egypt, where the animals are caught, fettered, and then slaughtered ("An Ancient Egyptian Hunting Ritual," *JNES* 9 [1950], pp. 164–77).

One who is favored . . . but the offender. Hebrew *ṭôb lipnê hā'ĕlōhîm . . . wĕ-ḥôṭē'*. A similar usage of *ṭôb* // *ḥōṭē'* occurs in 2:26. See Notes and Comment there. The one who is *ṭôb* is synonymous with the one who is "righteous" or "wise," whereas the one who is *ḥōṭē'* is the one who is "wicked" or a "fool." We must read this verse in light of v 20, where Qohelet says that there is no one who does only good (*ṭôb*) and does not err (*lō' yeḥĕṭā'*).

27. *what.* Here *zeh* functions like *ʾăšer* (Exod 15:13; Isa 25:9; 42:24; 43:21; Ps 9:16; 10:2; 17:9; 31:5; 32:8; 62:12; 74:2; Prov 23:22 (GKC §138.g, h).

says Qohelet. Reading *ʾāmar haqqōhelet* with LXX (supported by Copt) and 12:8, rather than *ʾāmĕrâ qōhelet* in MT. The latter may have been influenced by the apparent feminine form of *qōhelet*, but see 1:2 and 12:8, where the name is clearly understood as masculine. The words have simply been misdivided here, as elsewhere in the book (see Notes at 5:6 [Eng v 7]; 7:19; 8:1; 10:1). Apart from the superscription (1:1) and the epilogue (12:9–14), the three verses that have "Qohelet says" (1:2; 7:27; 12:8) are the only places where the editor's voice is heard (see Fox, "Frame Narrative," pp. 83–106).

one by one. We should take *ʾaḥat lĕʾaḥat* as the accusative of manner (cf. Exod 24:3; Zeph 3:9; Joüon-Muraoka §126.d), with the *lāmed* indicating continuous sequence (so NJPS: "item by item"). The image is that of someone checking the *ḥešbôn* (ledger or inventory) item by item.

accounting. See Notes on *ḥešbôn* at 7:25.

28. *the one whom I have sought continually, but have not found.* Some scholars think that *ʾăšer* "that/whom" anticipates the negative judgment in v 28b, namely, that there is no (good/capable?) woman to be found. But surely one must not divorce the usage of *mṣʾ* ("to find") here from its use elsewhere in the passage (vv 24, 26, 27, 29), nor can *bqš* ("to seek") be understood apart from its usage in vv 25 and 29. Indeed, the presence of the adverb *ʿôd* "still, continually" before the verb *biqšâ* ("sought") prompts one to consider the earlier mention of *bqš* ("to seek") in v 25, where the object is "wisdom and accounting." We should not be surprised, too, that the object of *mṣʾ* in v 27b is *ḥešbôn* ("accounting"), which in this context is more or less synonymous with *ḥokmâ* ("wisdom"). The verb *mṣʾ* in v 24, likewise, refers to the search for elusive wisdom, understood as the ability to comprehend what goes on in the universe. The language used to describe wisdom's inaccessibility in v 24 (*rāḥôq, yimṣāʾennû*) is, in fact, reminiscent of the elusiveness of the ideal woman — the very embodiment of Wisdom herself — in Prov 31:10 (*mî yimṣāʾ, rāḥôq*). But such wisdom is not attainable. Wisdom is elusive. Indeed, the motif of seeking and not finding belongs to the language of a lover's pursuit (see especially Song 3:1–6; 5:6; 6:1; Hos 2:9 [Eng v 7]; Prov 1:28; 18:22). The elusive lover in this case, it appears, is Wisdom herself. Qohelet has continually sought, but has not found her.

{*One man in a thousand . . .* }. Hebrew *ʾādām* here clearly means a man, a male. Otherwise, "one person in a thousand" would make no sense in light of the contrast with "woman." It is possible for *ʾādām* to be used as the opposite of *ʾiššâ* "woman" (so in Gen 2:22, 23, 25; 3:8; etc.). In the Phoenician inscription of Azitawadda, *ʾdm* "man" is juxtaposed with *ʾšt* "woman" (see *KAI* 26.b.4–5). Inasmuch as *ʾādām* is juxtaposed with *ʾiššâ* in v 28b, it must mean "man." The problem, however, is that the word occurs forty-eight other times in Ecclesiastes, always with the meaning "humanity" or "a person," and never referring to males in general or to a specific man. Indeed, the use of *ʾādām* as "a man" in v 28b contradicts the usage of the noun in the very next verse (v 29), where all humanity is meant. The vocabulary in v 28b is uncharacteristic of Qohelet. In this sense, the scholars who attribute the thought here to someone other than Qohelet are right (so Murphy, Lohfink, Zimmerli). Yet, it must not be supposed that Qohelet was quoting someone else, for the line is intrusive. After *lō' māṣā'tî* "I have not found" (v 28a) we certainly do not expect *māṣā'tî* "I have found" (v 28b). Minimally, one expects the positive claim in v 28b (*māṣā'tî* "I have found") to be qualified by "only," "except," or the like.

There is, in fact, a marker of exception (*lĕbad* "only"), but it comes in the next verse (v 29). This makes the intrusion all the more apparent, for "only" in v 29 makes little sense, if v 28b already identifies what has been found. Indeed, if one omits v 28b altogether, one can read the passage without skipping a beat. For all these reasons, one must conclude that v 28b has been secondarily inserted. It comes probably from the hand of a copyist who missed the point about the dangerous "woman" in v 26. Thinking that the passage was meant to be an indictment of women in general (and not of personified Folly), the copyist added what may have been intended as an illustration of the point of the passage. This marginal comment, unfortunately, found its way into the body of the text, thereby skewing the meaning of the passage. Schoors ("Bitterder dan de Dood is de Vrouw," p. 135) also recognizes the cue from the presence of *lĕbad* "only" at the beginning of v 29, but he regards all of v 28 as a parenthetical comment.

29. *only.* For the meaning of *lĕbad* "only" (Isa 26:13; Esth 4:11; Exod 26:9; 36:16; Judg 7:5; Zech 12:12, 13, 14).

that. The particle *'ăšer* here functions the same way it does in 5:17 (Eng v 18); 9:1. It substitutes for the nominalising *kî* (GKC §157.c).

just right. The word *yāšār* here means "right" or "correct." That which is *yāšār* is straight and direct (Gk *euthēs*), not crooked and perverted (see in Prov 8:6–9; Job 33:27; cf. Mic 3:9). If so, this conclusion harks back to v 13 (so Alonso-Schökel).

inventions. The word *ḥiššĕbōnôt* is used only one other time in the Hebrew Bible, in 2 Chron 26:15, where the term is clarified as *maḥăšebet ḥôšēb*, lit. "invention of an inventor." The word there refers to a war machine. It does not mean "war machine," however (so Baltzer). A war machine may be called an "invention," but the word "invention" does not mean "war machine." We do not know if the word is correctly vocalized in this passage in Ecclesiastes. The Greek translators render the word here as *logismous* "accountings" (i.e., assuming the plural of *ḥešbôn*), whereas *ḥiššĕbōnôt* in 2 Chron 26:15 is translated as *mēchanas* "devices." The saying in Ecclesiastes may be a modification of a proverb: "Many are the machinations (*maḥăšābôt*) in the mind of a person, but it is the counsel of YHWH that will be established" (Prov 19:21). Yet it must be observed that the word for human ingenuity in our passage is not *maḥăšābôt* "machinations," as in Prov 19:21. The author here uses *ḥiššĕbōnôt* instead, probably intending a wordplay with *ḥešbôn* "accounting": humans seek not only an accounting of what is in the ledger or inventory, but they also let their imaginations run wild with theoretical matters (see Michel, *Eigenart*, pp. 238–39). Thus, one might say: they seek not only the *inventory* (*ḥešbôn*, vv 25, 27), but also many inventions (*ḥiššĕbō-nôt*). Following Targ and *Qoh. Rabb* 7 §50, M. V. Fox and B. Porten see an allusion here to the story of the Fall in Genesis 3, arguing that the story prompted the polemic against "the Woman" ("Unsought Discoveries," pp. 26–38).

COMMENT

Verse 15 provides a transition from the previous literary unit (6:10–7:14) to the new one (7:15–29). The former ends with a call to "see" what God has done, both the good and the bad (7:13, 14). Now in v 15 the author says that he himself has *seen* "both." The "both" in v 15a may refer backwards to the good and the bad that God has done (7:13–14). The placement of the "both" at the beginning of the Hebrew sentence makes it inevitable that the reader connects the "both" with the two occurrences of "see" in vv 13, 14. But one realizes as one reads on, that the "both" refers also to the fate of the righteous and the wicked (v 15b). The tension between the good and the bad that God has made (vv 13–14) is matched by the tension between the realities of righteousness-wisdom on the one hand and wickedness-folly on the other (vv 15–18).

We may divide the larger literary unit into two parts: the first part concerns the impossibility of extreme righteousness and wisdom (vv 15–22); the second concerns the threat of folly and the elusiveness of wisdom (vv 23–29). The literary unit ends, as in the previous passage (7:13–14), with a reference to what God has done (7:29).

The Impossibility of Righteousness-Wisdom (vv 15–22)

Qohelet observes that sometimes things do not work out according to human expectations. On the one hand, there are righteous people who perish despite their righteousness; on the other hand, there are wicked people who enjoy longevity despite their wickedness (v 15). In traditional wisdom it is taught that the righteous will be delivered from trouble or even from death (Prov 10:2; 11:4, 8, 21; 12:21; 18:10), whereas the wicked will perish with their hopes (Prov 11:5–8; 12:12; 14:32). In the book of Deuteronomy, longevity in the land is frequently said to be the lot of all who act aright, that is, all who obey the legal stipulations (Deut 4:26, 40; 5:16; 6:2; 11:9; 22:7; 25:15; 32:47; 30:18). According to the teachings of the wise, the prolongation of life is one of the benefits of wisdom, which implies right conduct (see Prov 3:2, 16; 28:2, 16). The sages taught that the righteous will live long, whereas "the years of the wicked will be short" (Prov 10:27). But in reality, Qohelet observes, the rule is contradicted. There are all kinds of exceptions.

In addressing this contradiction, Qohelet does not stand alone. Indeed, in the prophetic, hymnic, and wisdom traditions of Israel one finds occasional challenges to the doctrine that the righteous and the wicked will receive their appropriate recompense in this life. Sometimes people receive the opposite of what they deserve (see Jer 12:1; Hab 1:4, 13; Job 21:7–26; Pss 10:1–3; 73:2–14). Typically in these challenges the contradiction is left unresolved. Qohelet, however, goes a step further in offering an admonition in the face of that contradiction: do not be exceedingly righteous and do not be excessively wise (v 16), but do not be exceedingly wicked and do not be a fool (v 17). Unique in the Bible, this admonition poses a problem for the interpreter. In what sense is it bad to be too righteous or too wise? Is Qohelet teaching that a moderate amount of wickedness or folly is a necessary thing? Is he amoral? Or is he merely being sarcastic, as some commentators have suggested (so Lauha, Beek)?

Scholars differ on the interpretation of the admonition. Some are of the view that in v 16 Qohelet is speaking against self-righteousness and pretense of wisdom, rather than against genuine righteousness and wisdom, and so the issue is hypocrisy (Whybray). This view, however, hinges on a questionable interpretation of the verb "show yourself excessively wise" as indicative of pretense. But in classical Hebrew, the verb in this particular pattern (the Hithpael) is never used of pretense. To "show oneself wise" may mean either to prove oneself wise or to flaunt one's wisdom, but it never means to pretend to be wise. The danger lies in overconfidence, rather than in a lack of sincerity. This is the problem, too, with righteousness in the extreme. As Ben Sira puts it: "Do not show yourself righteous before the king; do not show yourself clever before the king" (Sir 7:5). Here Ben Sira is warning people not to be overly ambitious or overly confident (see v 4, 6).

Likewise, what is rejected by Qohelet is overconfidence in righteousness and wisdom. He has in mind specifically the notion that it is possible for one to be so righteous that one could always avert destruction and extend life (v 15b). In the vocabulary of the wisdom tradition, "the righteous" is one who simply does the right things (Prov 10:1–4; 12:10; 28:1; 29:7), says the right things (Prov 10:11–21, 30–31), and has the right thoughts and attitudes (Prov 12:5; 13:5; 15:28). The one who is righteous is wise and the one who is wise is righteous. The terms are virtually synonymous (see Prov 10:3–32). By the same token, the one who is wicked is a fool and the one who is a fool is wicked. What is righteous in wisdom's ethic is right attitudes and right conduct, according to the norms of nature and society. This comes close to the original meaning of the Semitic root ($ṣdq$), for righteousness is also rightness, legitimacy, and legality. So one may understand the author to mean "do not be overly correct" or "do not be overly proper."

If there is any doubt as to the meaning of righteousness in this context, it is clarified in v 20: "there is no human so righteous, who does only good and does not err." This is what it means to be exceedingly righteous. It is to aspire to a righteousness that admits only of good but allows no mistakes at all. The text does not specify the realms of righteousness, but to judge from the range of meanings associated with the root, one may surmise that it means rightness in the legal, social, and cultic realms.

No one can attain that level of righteousness-wisdom, and one who aspires to that may, indeed, "be confounded." Perhaps what is meant here by "confounded" is a state of emotional or psychological torpidity akin to what is identified today as depression (see Notes above). One will end up harming oneself when one strives to attain that level of righteousness-wisdom.

Contrary to conventional wisdom, the righteous and the wise are not shielded from destruction (v 15b), and any attempt to be overly right and wise could, in fact, be destructive (v 16). Nevertheless, one must not go to the other extreme in being wicked and foolish, for one may die prematurely (v 17). Even though it is true that there are wicked people who live long despite their wicked conduct (v 15b), it does not follow that one should risk the dangerous consequences of wickedness-folly. What the author advises, rather, is a realistic approach to life (v 18b): it is good to grasp the one (righteousness-wisdom) but also not to let go of the other (wickedness-folly).

In contrast to the approach in the practical and prescriptive wisdom tradition (like Proverbs), Qohelet does not present one with two radically different alternatives with radically different consequences, as if life's choices can be so simplified (compare Prov 4:10–27). The advice to "grasp" even the negative side of human conduct is a concession to the reality of human imperfection. It is impossible for anyone to be always right and without fault, but it is possible to avoid the extreme of wickedness. Perfection is beyond the grasp of humanity, and neither righteousness nor wisdom offers a fail-safe way to cope with life and avert death. Hence, even as one must recognize the realities of both good and evil in the world (so vv 13–14), so one must grasp the realities of both righteousness-wisdom (v 16) and wickedness-folly (v 17). The mortal at best is, as it were, *simul iustus et peccator* — at once a just one and a sinner (see v 20).

It is remarkable that Qohelet not only acknowledges both the realities of righteousness-wisdom and wickedness-folly in human conduct as necessities, he even puts the whole issue in theological terms. He gives a theological reason for his admonition. For him, one who fears God goes forth with "both of them" (v 18b). Here the "both" harks back to the "both" at the beginning of v 15, and even to the good and the bad that God has done (vv 13–14); "both" refers to the good and the bad, the righteous and the wicked, the wise and the foolish. The "one who fears God" is the one who recognizes the chasm between the divine and the human, the one who knows the proper place of humanity in relation to the deity. The fear of God entails a recognition that one is human, and so one can be no less but also no more. For Qohelet, it is the place of humanity simply to accept life with its contradictory realities. One cannot be too ambitious about righteousness or wisdom. As Hertzberg observes, this notion of the fear of God is the very opposite of the hubris evident in the attempt to be exceedingly righteous or excessively wise (*Der Prediger*, p. 154). For the mortal there can be no alternative but to recognize the reality of human shortcomings and not act as if one can be above the grasp of wickedness-folly.

The argument that extreme righteousness and wisdom are beyond humanity's reach is continued in vv 19–22. In contrast to v 16, wisdom is dealt with first (v 19), before righteousness (v 20). No distinction between the two is intended, however. Wisdom and righteousness are two sides of the same coin in the wisdom tradition and certainly in Qohelet's arguments.

One hears echoes of traditional wisdom in v 19 inasmuch as wisdom is favorably compared to wealth and power — not just to wealth in general, but to the wealth of the powerful. Yet, Qohelet's purpose is not to praise wisdom. Qohelet is not extolling the virtue of wisdom himself. Rather, he is illustrating the kind of overconfidence against which he warns in v 16 (compare 7:7, where even the wise may become fools). The sages value wisdom over wealth and the rich value power, but neither wisdom nor power will avert death. Indeed, Qohelet says in 8:8 that "no human is a proprietor" (*'ên 'ādām šallîṭ*; compare *'ādām 'ên ṣaddîq* "no human is righteous" in 7:20) that he or she can detain the life-spirit and somehow overcome death.

Even as he illustrates overconfidence in wisdom's strength in v 19, so he speaks of overconfidence in righteousness in v 20: no one on earth is so righteous, who does only good and does not err (or "does not sin"). That is surely what he means when he says that no one can be "exceedingly righteous" or "exceedingly wise" (v 16). People make mistakes. They miss the mark.

This recognition of human frailty did not originate with Qohelet, and it is not unique to him. Already in a Sumerian pessimistic wisdom text, one finds an admission that there is no human being who is without fault (*ANET*[3], p. 590, lines 102–3). Elsewhere in the Bible, too, we find a similar recognition of human imperfection (1 Kgs 8:46; 2 Chron 6:26; Pss 14:1–3; 53:1–2 [Eng v 1–3]; 143:2; Prov 20:9; Job 4:17; Rom 3:10, 23; 1 John 1:8). In the NT, the Apostle Paul argues in Romans 3 that among humans "there is none righteous" (*ouk estin dikaios* in Rom 3:10, as in the Greek of Eccl 7:20), "no one (who) does good" (v 12), "their mouth is full of curses and bitterness" (v 14), "there is no fear of God before their eyes" (v 18), and "all have sinned" (v 23). For the apostle, it is the impossibility of human righteousness in this sense that necessitates the righteousness of God by grace alone, and he makes his case with distinct echoes of our passage in Ecclesiastes.

The impossibility of super-righteousness among mortals is precisely what Qohelet is addressing. The issue is not hypocrisy, but presumptuousness. The problem is overconfidence in human ability to attain extreme righteousness and wisdom, the ability to achieve perfection on one's efforts and natural ability. One notes that *'ên ṣaddîq* "there are no righteous ones" in v 20 stands in stark contrast to *yēš ṣaddîq* "there are righteous one" in v 15. Clearly the problem is with the idea that one can be so righteous and so wise that death can be averted and one can extend one's life. The delusion is that human beings can escape the reality of wickedness and folly simply by being smart and doing all the right things. That is the hubris that one must avoid (vv 16–17). That attitude is the very opposite of the fear of God.

Having admitted, then, that no human can be that righteous or that wise, the author goes on to advise against taking what people say too seriously. This is a very practical example of human imperfection. When one tries so desperately to be correct on every score, one will inevitably hear every word as a criticism of oneself. The point is that one may become so sensitive to what others say that even the words of one's subordinates are heard as disparagement. But, says the author, "very often too, your heart knows that you yourself have disparaged others" (v 22). This tendency for people to utter negative words is identified in the NT as one of the signs that there is no one on earth who is righteous (Rom 3:14, "their mouth is full of curses and bitterness"). Qohelet's advice is not to take the negative words of others to "your heart" (*libbekā*, v 21), because "your heart" (*libbekā*, v 22) knows that you have done the same to others. Perhaps the lesson is that one should not take the negative words of others too seriously because one ought to know that one's own negative words are not meant to be destructive. In any case, the admonition reaches beyond the external acts to one's inner being, to the "heart" (the mind). Even if no one else knows your deeds, your own heart often knows. The author is making the point in v 20, that "no one is so righteous, who does only good and does not err." One knows in one's own heart that one, too, is not perfectly righteous, so one ought not to take the words of others to heart. In 10:20 we see the relevance of Qohelet's advice for his audience, for they were furtively disparaging the rich and powerful others (see Comment at 10:16–20). But they were warned that even their secret and subtle criticisms will become known. Qohelet's audience appears to have belonged to the middle strata of society. They were insecure about their subordinates disparaging them, but they themselves were engaged in subversive activities against their superiors.

The Dangers of Folly and the Elusiveness of Wisdom (vv 23–29)

Qohelet says he tested "by wisdom" (*baḥokmâ*) and aspired to be wise, but he found it impossible (v 23). This verse recalls 1:13, where the author says he decided to explore by wisdom (*baḥokmâ*) "all that has been done under the heavens." The expression "all that happens" in v 24 means the same thing as "all that has been done under the heavens" in 1:13.

The author claims to have the ability to test by wisdom, yet he admits that wisdom is beyond him. There is no real contradiction, however. What he means is that he applied reason (as traditional wisdom does), but found that it did not make him as wise as he had wished. No one is so wise as to be able to understand the universe and control life. There is a difference between the practical wisdom — what we may call "common sense" — and the ideal wisdom that gives one control over life.

All that is happening in the world is distant and unfathomable (literally "deep, deep"), and no one can comprehend it (v 24). Here the link with the preceding literary unit (6:10–7:14) is evident, for the text reiterates that the realities of life ("whatever happens") are beyond control (compare 6:10; 7:24), and human beings cannot grasp them (compare 7:14, 24). Within the wisdom tradition itself there is an awareness of wisdom's limitations, for many things remain a mystery even to the wise (Job 28:23–28; Prov 30:1–4; Sir 24:28–29). Mortals aspire to attain perfect wisdom, to grasp that ideal. Wisdom is elusive.

It is important to note that here in 7:24 the language of wisdom's elusiveness is in part reminiscent of the elusiveness of the ideal woman of Proverbs 31, who is the embodiment of Woman Wisdom herself. According to Prov 31:10, that "woman of quality" is elusive (*mî yimṣā'* "who can find?") and her worth is far beyond (*rāḥōq*) jewels. So, too, ideal wisdom is for Qohelet unattainable (*rāḥôq*) and far beyond discovery (*mî yimṣā'ennû* "who can find it?").

Qohelet says he turned "to know and to explore, and seek wisdom and accounting" (v 25). The word "accounting" (*ḥešbôn*) is a commercial term widely found in the Near East, often in reference to economic documents like a ledger or an inventory. But, as in English, the word may be used figuratively for a detailed accounting of any issue, an accounting of discrepancies. The image conjured up for us is that of a merchant or an accountant poring over the documents, trying to give an account of every item, perhaps to assign everything to one side or the other of the ledger and then to tally it all up in order to arrive at the balance. Along with his search for "wisdom and accounting" (v 25a), Qohelet says he tried to know wickedness-folly (v 25b). Again, one imagines the merchant or accountant going over the documents, trying to decide where each item belongs. Specifically, in v 25b the merchant seems concerned to place wickedness and folly: "to know wickedness to be foolishness and folly to be stupidity." The implication is that it is not an easy task to sort out such details. Perhaps he means that it is difficult to find a clear distinction between righteousness-wisdom as opposed to wickedness-folly (compare vv 15–22). In the didactic wisdom tradition, the sages speak of wisdom and folly as clear categories that everyone can discern. But in truth, Qohelet seems to imply, they are not so easily distinguished. It is not as if one can assign them to the appropriate portions in an economic document, a ledger, or an invoice.

Then the author says in v 26, "and I find more bitter than death is the woman, inasmuch as she is a snare, her heart is a net, her hands are fetters." This is not a polemic against womankind in general (contrast JB: "I find woman more bitter than Death"; NEB: "The wiles of a woman I find mightier than death"). Nor is it a barb directed at a specific woman or a particular type of woman. The text speaks in definite terms of "*the* woman" (with the definite article in Hebrew), as if the reader ought to know who that "woman" is. In the immediate context, the most likely referent is folly (*hassiklût*), a feminine noun in Hebrew, the only noun in the preceding verse marked by the definite article. This is the interpretation of the Greek translators, the earliest interpreters of the text on record. This conclusion is all the more likely when one realizes that the language in v 26 echoes the teachings in conventional wisdom about the dangerous woman, a seductress who lures one away from wisdom's embrace. The deadly seductress is the "other woman" — the opposite of Wisdom. In the Egyptian wisdom text called *The Instruction of Anii*, this dangerous one is seen as a foreign woman, a wanton adulteress who is ready to pounce on the innocent youngster: "She waits to ensnare you, a great deadly wrongdoing when one hears of it" (see *AEL* II, p. 137; *ANET*[3], p. 420). Sir 9:3, too, portrays the *femme fatale* as one waiting to ensnare those unaware (compare 25:21), and in Sir 26:22 she is called a "deadly snare." In Proverbs, the dangerous seductress is described thus:

In the end, she is bitter as wormwood,
Sharp as a two-edged sword.

Her feet go down to Death,
Her steps follow the path to Sheol.

(Prov 5:4–5)

Similar images of the *femme fatale* are found in Prov 2:16–19; 5:20; 6:24–35; 7:5–27, 23:27–28. This "woman" is relentless in her pursuit and deadly in her seduction. These are not merely clichés about women in a patriarchal society (Lohfink), though they do reflect a generally negative attitude toward women. Rather, they are idioms pertaining to the deadly seductive power of wickedness and folly in general. Dangerous men also entice, trap, and otherwise lead one away from the influence of wisdom (see Prov 1:10–19; 2:12–15; 6:1–5; compare Ps 140:1–5) and one's own wickedness and folly are described in similar ways (5:22–23; 12:13). Nevertheless, it is true that the deadly seducer representing Folly is most frequently portrayed as a woman: the "other" woman. She is set over against another female figure, Woman Wisdom, the one who protects and watches and gives life (Prov 1:20–33; 3:13–18; 4:5–13; 8:1–31). These two women are illustrative of the tension between Wisdom and Folly, both personified in Proverbs 9. One represents life, the other death; one represents right, the other wrong. The *femme fatale* is not, therefore, an individual woman. She is not necessarily a specific type of woman or women in general. Rather, she is a composite image of Folly herself (Prov 9:13–18). Folly is out on a hunt, as it were, trying to lure and trap people and lead them down the deadly path. She is as pernicious as the wicked men who threaten to swallow up the innocent like Sheol and who spread a net to trap their victims (Prov 1:10–19; compare Ps 140:1–5). This is the "woman" of whom Qohelet speaks in 7:26. The one who is favored by God (*tôb lipnê hā'ĕlōhîm*) will be able to escape her, but the one who slips (*ḥōṭē'*), the bungler, will be captured (see Prov 5:22–23). Apparently in the author's judgment, no one escapes from Folly-Wickedness, for he says in v 20 that there is no one who does good (*tôb*) and does not err (*lō' yeḥĕṭā'*). Everyone is vulnerable in the face of Folly's deadly snares!

The hand of an editor is evident in v 27. This is indicated by the third-person reference to the author: "Qohelet says." It has been suggested that the editor is telling the reader that the comment to follow represents Qohelet's private opinion (Galling). We have no way to tell if that is the intent of the editor, however, and we are not sure how much more should be considered a quotation. One notes that apart from the superscription (1:1) and the epilogue (12:9–14), there are only three instances where the text refers to Qohelet in the third person: in this verse and at the beginning (1:2) and the end (12:8) of the book. Neither in 1:2 nor 12:8 can the words attributed to Qohelet be taken lightly, for they are clearly central for the book. We must not, therefore, regard the viewpoint expressed in this passage as incidental, as Galling implies. On the contrary, it may be that the editor is deliberately invoking the authority of the author, calling attention to this passage as the main point of his message. At the beginning and the end of the book the editor tells us that Qohelet's message is that everything is absolute "vanity" (see Notes and Comment at 1:2). Now he tells us that Qohelet is saying that what he seeks is elusive. What Qohelet says here is just as important as the thematic statements. Indeed, the point he is making is no different from the rest of the book.

The text in 7:27 continues the idea of the quest for an accounting (*ḥešbôn*), an idea first broached in v 25. Like a merchant or an accountant, the author runs down the imaginary inventory item by item — "one by one" — hoping to find an accounting. Apparently something is eluding him. Something requires an explanation.

Suddenly, in v 28b, we find an odd remark: "one man in a thousand I have found, but a woman among all these I have not found." Most commentators presume the text to be saying that there is one reliable or capable man in a thousand (see Prov 20:6; 31:10), but there is no equivalent woman among all these. In other words, a good man is extremely rare (0.1 percent of those searched!), but a good woman is nonexistent. The statement is a notorious crux for the interpreter. It is difficult to explain it as anything other than a misogynistic remark, although some scholars have proffered nonderogatory interpretations or insisted that Qohelet is quoting a well-known attitude only to reject it.

From a sociohistorical standpoint, the probability of such a sexist statement in Israel during the postexilic period does not come as a surprise. The Israelites who returned to their homeland after years in exile found themselves a minority in an alien environment, surrounded by people who had already staked their claims in the land, people of various ethnic, cultural, and religious backgrounds. Nothing less than the survival of their community was at stake, as the former exiles faced the temptation of assimilation into their new environment and, through exogamy, faced the loss of their legal claim to property (see H. C. Washington, "The Strange Woman (אשה זרה/נכריה) of Proverbs 1–9 and Post-Exilic Judaean Society," in *Second Temple Studies 2: Temple and Community in the Persian Period*, ed. T. C. Eskenazi and K. H. Richards [JSOTSup 175; Sheffield: JSOT, 1994], pp. 207–32). Consequently, marriages to men or women outside the community were forbidden, but as usual, it was the women who bore most of the blame and the brunt of the polemics. Some, like Ezra, Nehemiah, and Malachi, called for the banishment of foreign wives or otherwise warned against foreign women (Ezra 9:10; Neh 13:23–27; Mal 2:10–16). At the same time, there were stories told in that period of heroic women like Ruth and Esther, the former a foreigner. In the androcentric culture that was ancient Israel, women became metaphors for negative or positive influences in society. They represented either what was unsavory or what was safe. In such a world, women were either aggressive deadly seductresses or elusive virtuous brides.

That same tension between the two types of women, representing Wisdom and Folly, is found in the book of Proverbs, which was probably collocated during the Persian period also. In the rhetoric of Proverbs 1–9, Folly is depicted in terms of the dangerous "other" woman, the outsider, while Wisdom is portrayed as the good wife on whom one can always rely (see C. A. Newsom, "Woman and the Discourse of Patriarchal Wisdom: A Study of Proverbs 1–9," in *Gender and Difference in Ancient Israel*, ed. P. L. Day [Minneapolis: Augsburg Fortress, 1989], pp. 142–60). In antiquity, as in modern times, men are wont to view women in terms of caricatures of virtue or vice. Such is the case, for instance, in the Akkadian wisdom text called *The Dialogue of Pessimism*:

"Slave, listen to me." "Here I am, sir, Here I am."
"I am going to love a woman." "So love, sir, love.
The man who loves a woman forgets sorrow and fear."
"No, slave, I will by no means love a woman."
["Do not] love, sir, do not love.
Woman is a pitfall—a pitfall, a hole, a ditch,
Woman is a sharp iron dagger that cuts a man's throat."

(BWL, p. 147, lines 46–52)

Given the androcentric perspective of the wisdom literature, as well as the sociohistorical circumstances of the postexilic period, a misogynistic remark in Ecclesiastes would not have been uncharacteristic. Exegetically, however, the remark in v 28b is acutely problematic because it seems intrusive in this passage. In the first place, the passage is not about women in general. Neither is it about certain types of women, nor a particular woman. The sudden polemic is out of place, for the passage is concerned with the dangers of Folly and the elusiveness of Wisdom.

Moreover, the use of the Hebrew word *'ādām* for "man" as opposed to "woman" is out of character for Ecclesiastes. In forty-eight other instances in the book, *'ādām* refers to a human (as opposed to animals or the deity) or to any person ("anyone, someone"). When a specific person is meant, the author uses *'îš* (see Notes at 6:2; 9:14–15). Certainly in contrast to "woman" one expects the word *'îš* "man" instead of *'ādām*. The uncharacteristic usage of *'ādām* in v 28b is all the more striking when one notes that *'ādām* is used in the very next verse, and there it clearly refers to all humanity, since the pronoun that follows is the plural "they" (*hēmmâ*).

In short, the usage of *'ādām* in v 28b contradicts the meaning of the word in the immediate context, as well as elsewhere in the book. In terms of logic, too, v 28b contradicts v 29: the "only" at the beginning of v 29 makes sense only when it follows v 28a directly—without the intrusive comment in v 28b on what is found (see Notes above). Omitting v 28b, the reader would not miss a beat. We conclude, therefore, that v 28b was a marginal gloss that had been inadvertently incorporated into the body of the text.

Furthermore, the adverb "continually" or "still" (*'ôd*) in v 28a suggests that the search is not new. One is prompted to ask what it is that the author still "seeks" (*bqš*), and one is led back to the same verb "seek" (*bqš*) in v 25: "to seek wisdom and accounting." It is not amiss to observe that the motif of seeking and not finding is at home in the language of courtship (see especially Song 3:1–6; 5:6; 6:1; Hos 2:9 [Eng v 7]). In the wisdom tradition, the elusive lover may be Woman Wisdom herself. According to the sages, the one who is able to find Wisdom finds life and obtains divine favor (Prov 8:35; compare also Prov 18:22), but the one who misses the mark in the search (*ḥōṭĕ᾿î*; compare *ḥōṭĕ᾿* "the offender" in Eccl 7:26) will be in mortal danger (Prov 8:36; see also Sir 6:27). For those who so err, Wisdom is particularly inaccessible: "they will call upon me, but I will not answer; they will *seek* me diligently, but they will not *find* me" (Prov 1:28). One who is able to "find Wisdom" is said to be fortunate, for Wisdom is more unattainable than jewels (3:13–15).

The language is reminiscent of the description of the consummate wise woman, perhaps representing Woman Wisdom herself, who is said to be difficult to find (*mî yimṣā᾿* "who can find?") and more inaccessible (*rāḥôq*) than jewels (Prov 31:10). That is the same language that we find in 7:24 of Qohelet's quest to understand all that is going on in the world: all that happens is inaccessible (*rāḥôq*) and cannot be found (*mî yimṣā᾿ennû* "who can find it?"). In short, it is likely, too, that wisdom, specified as the quest for explanation, is the intended object in v 28.

Thus vv 25b–26 are balanced by vv 27–28a. The former concern Folly; the latter concern Wisdom. It appears, however, that in the end neither Folly nor Wisdom is a real option for the mortal: the one is deadly, but the other is elusive. It is in such a crazy game of hide-and-seek that humans find themselves. They are pursued by Folly, a pernicious hunter from whom they must try to escape but cannot, even as they try desperately to find the one who will keep them safe, namely Wisdom. But Wisdom eludes them.

The author concludes, as at the end of the preceding literary unit (7:12–14), by calling attention to what God has done. One is asked to see (*rĕ᾿ēh*) what the author has discovered (7:29), namely, what God has done (*᾿āśâ hā᾿ĕlōhîm*), even as one is asked in 7:13–14 to see (*rĕ᾿ēh . . . rĕ᾿ēh*) what God has done (*ma᾿ăśēh hā᾿ĕlōhîm, ᾿āśâ hā᾿ĕlōhîm*). God has made humans just right, literally, "balanced" or "straight." If *yāšār* means "balanced" this verse harks back to v 18, where the one who fears God is said to proceed in life with both wisdom-righteousness and folly-wickedness. If *yāšār* means "straight" (see Prov 8:8–9; Job 33:27), one must not miss the irony in the references to God's work here and in 7:13–14. In the latter passage, the author says that God has made some things "crooked" which no human can straighten (7:13). People are always trying to straighten out what cannot be straightened (see also the proverb in 1:15). Yet, though God has made humankind just right (*yāšār*), literally "straight," people do not seem able to live with that "straightness." Rather, "they have sought many inventions" (v 29).

The Hebrew translated here as "inventions" may also, with slight repointing of the vowels, be read as "accountings" (compare vv 25, 26). If "inventions" is meant, the author must be referring to the many devices of the human imagination (compare Prov 19:21). Perhaps a wordplay is intended. People seek detailed accountings of all that goes on in the world, poring over an imaginary ledger or inventory, as it were, as they try to achieve a balance (see v 27). But they are not merely trying to go over the inventory; they are also being very ingenious in their "inventions." There is more than meets the eye in humanity's quest for explanations. Through wordplay the author hints at the crookedness of the merchant or accountant. They give the impression of trying to straighten out a messy account, but they are also doing some "imaginative accounting," as it were. Humans want to straighten out what God has made crooked (so 7:13), but they also try to make crooked what God has made straight (so 7:29)!

II.A.3. It's an Arbitrary World (8:1–17)

8 ¹Who is <so> wise? And who knows the solution of anything?
   One's wisdom brightens one's countenance,
   so that one changes one's impudent look.
²<   > Keep the king's command,
   yea, according to the manner of a sacred oath.
³Do not be stupefied at his presence, leave!
   Do not persist in a harmful thing,
   for he will do whatever he pleases.
⁴Inasmuch as a king's word is authoritative,
   who can say to him, "What are you doing?"
⁵Whoever keeps the commandment will not experience a harmful thing. As for time and judgment, a wise heart knows: ⁶that for every matter there is time and judgment; that the evil of humanity is heavy upon them; ⁷that no one knows what is going to happen; and that no one can tell them when it will happen. ⁸There is no one who is a proprietor over the life-breath, to detain the life-breath, and there is no proprietorship over the day of death. There is no substitution in the battle, and wickedness will not deliver those who practice it.

⁹All this I have seen when I set my heart on all that has been done under the sun, a time when people exercise proprietorship over one another to their detriment. ¹⁰Thereupon I saw the wicked <brought> to burial, and they proceeded from a holy place; but those who have acted justly were discarded in the city. This, too, is vanity.

¹¹Since sentence for evil work is not executed quickly, people dare to do evil; ¹²an offender does the evil of hundreds but lives long. Even though I know that good will come to those who fear God, who are fearful in his presence, ¹³and good will not come to the wicked and they will not prolong their shadowy days because they are not fearful before God, ¹⁴there is a vanity that is done on earth inasmuch as there are righteous ones who are treated as if they have acted wickedly, and there are wicked ones who are treated as if they have acted righteously. I said that this, too, is vanity.

¹⁵So I have commended joy because there is nothing better for people under the sun, but to eat, drink, and enjoy. And that may accompany them in their toil during the days of their life that God has given them under the sun.

¹⁶When I determined to know wisdom and to observe the business that has been done on earth, {   } ¹⁷I saw all the work of God, that people are not able

to discover the work that is done under the sun, {even though neither by day nor by night do they sleep}. Therefore, people toil to seek and to discover, but even if the wise desire to know, they cannot discover.

NOTES

8   1. *who is so wise*. Reading *my kh ḥkm* (following the Greek traditions), instead of *my khḥkm* "who is like the wise" in MT (supported by Syr, Targ, and Vulg). Here — as in 5:6 (Eng v 7), 8 (Eng v 9); 7:19, 27; 10:1 — the words are incorrectly divided. The unsyncopated definite article is not uncommon in the later books of the Hebrew Bible (GKC §35.n). Yet, the article is always syncopated after the preposition in Ecclesiastes (see *lehākām* in 6:8; 7:19). To be sure, the definite article after *še-* is unassimilated in *šehannĕḥālîm* (1:7), *šhtqyp* (*Ketib* in 6:10), and *kšhskl* (*ketib* in 10:3), but the nonsyncopation of the article in these cases may be specific to the particle *še-* (cf. *šehammelek* in Song 1:12). As Euringer has argued, *tis oiden sophous* "who knows the wise" in LXX may be the result of an inner Greek corruption from *tis hōde sophos* "who is so wise" (as in Aq; cf. *tis houtōs sophos* in Symm; also SyrH, OL), an error prompted in part by the next rhetorical question: *kai tis oiden lysin rhēmatos* "who knows the solution of a saying" (see Euringer, *Masorahtext*, pp. 93–94). Apparently the *Vorlage* of the Greek traditions read *my kh ḥkm* instead of *my khḥkm*.

solution. The precise meaning of the Hebrew word *pēšer* is uncertain. It occurs only here in Biblical Hebrew, although the feminine form *pšrh* is attested in Sir 38:14, where it may mean either "diagnosis" or "cure." The noun is a cognate of Akkadian *pišru* "interpretation, solution," a word used for the unraveling of mysteries and secrets and for solutions of difficult problems (see Oppenheim, *Interpretation of Dreams*, pp. 217–20), and occurs in the phrase *iṣ pišri*, which refers to a magic wand (see *AHW* II, p. 868). The noun *pišrā* in Syriac is used for the interpretation of dreams or the solution of riddles (Payne Smith, *A Compendious Syriac Dictionary*, p. 469). In Biblical and Targumic Aramaic, the same noun occurs most often in conjunction with the interpretation of dreams (see Dan 2:45; 4:3; 5:15). In this usage, the word refers to the unraveling of the mysteries of dreams. The word occurs frequently in the Qumran texts, where it refers to the clarification of biblical texts, and it is related to Biblical Hebrew *pātar* "interpret" and *pitrôn* "interpretation" (in the sense of solving mysteries), all occurring in Genesis 40–41. The meaning "solution" fits most contexts.

anything. Lit. "a thing," or "a matter" or "a word." The root *dbr* occurs five times in vv 1–5, linking the verses.

One's wisdom brightens one's countenance. Hebrew *ḥokmat 'ādām tā'îr pānāyw*, lit. "the wisdom of a person brightens his countenance." Here, in contrast to 7:29b, the noun *'ādām* refers not to all humanity, but to any individual. In the Bible, it is always God who "causes the countenance/face to shine" (see Num 6:25; Pss 31:17 [Eng v 16]; 67:2 [Eng v 1]; 80:4, 8, 20 [Eng vv 3, 7, 19]; 119:135; Dan 9:17). The idiom "to cause the face to shine" means "to be gracious" or "to be pleasant." One may also note the references to the "light of the countenance"

(Pss 4:7 [Eng v 6]; 89:16 [Eng v 15]; Job 29:24; Prov 16:15). In Job 29:24, the expression occurs in parallelism with *śḥq ʾl* "to smile at." In Prov 16:15, "the light of the king's face" is parallel to "his favor." A comparable idiom is found in Ugaritic: *pn špš nr by* "the countenance of the sun shines upon me," referring to the favor of the (Hittite) king (*KTU* 2.16.9–10). In Akkadian, the causative of *namāru* "to shine" is used with *panū* "face" and *zīmu* "countenance" in a similar manner to Hebrew *hēʾîr pānîm: kayānamma panūka lišnammir* "May (Aya) always cause your face to shine" (*VAB* 4, p. 258, ii.20]; *panīšu ušnammirma* "she caused his countenance to brighten" (*Enuma Eliš*, Tablet V, line 82); *gattašin lišaqqâ liš-nammir z[īmīšin]* "May she elevate their stature, may she cause their cou[ntenance] to shine" (*BWL*, p. 172, iv.14). The point in this verse in Ecclesiastes is that wisdom causes one to have or to put on a pleasant appearance.

one changes. Reading *yšnʾ < > nw*, lit. "one changes it" (that is, *yĕšan-ne[ʾ]nnû*) instead of *yĕšunneʾ ʾǎnî* in MT: thus, lit. "(ʾādām) changes it" (so Galling). Vulg also takes the verb to be active, rather than passive. The verb *šnh* "to change" is sometimes spelled with the *ʾalep* in Late Biblical Hebrew (cf. *šinnāʾ* in 2 Kgs 25:29; *yišneʾ* in Lam 4:1; see GKC §75.rr). The substitution of *šnʾ* for *šnh* led also to the misreadings in LXX (followed by SyrH and Copt) and Syr, both of which take the verb to be *śnʾ* "to hate" (this is followed by NEB: "grim looks make a man hated"). Many Hebrew MSS, however, have *yśnh*, giving the correct root. The idiom *šinnâ pānîm* "to change (one's) face" = "to change (one's) expression" is attested elsewhere (Job 14:20; Sir 12:18 [*yšnʾ pnym*]; 13:24 [*yšnʾ pnyw*]). Indeed, Sir 13:24–25 is probably an allusion to this passage in Ecclesiastes, although there the subject is *lēb* "mind" instead of *ḥokmâ* "wisdom": "The mind (*lēb*) of a person changes his countenance (*yšnʾ pnyw*) for good or for ill . . . the sign of a good mind (*lēb*) is a bright countenance (*pnym ʾwrym*)." One may also compare Akkadian *pānû šanû* "the face changes" = "the appearance changes." The following sentence, involving the verb *ezēzu* (= Hebrew *ʿzz*) is especially suggestive: *Ṣaltu uzziz išnû panūšma* "Ṣaltu became angry, her face changed" (*VAS* 10, p. 214, viii.26). Thus, the change in expression could be for better or for worse—from an angry look to a pleasant one, or vice versa. People's wisdom will cause them to suppress an angry or defiant look before the king and show, instead, a pleasant countenance. The saying is rather similar to one in the Aramaic *Proverbs of Ahiqar*, although the Aramaic text is unfortunately fragmentary: *kʾšr [y]šlḥ[k]lmh tštnh bpnyw [ ]pnyw ʿl dbr ʾšr* "when [he] sends [you.] Lest you be changed in his presence (?) [ ]his presence on account of which . . ." (see *TAD* III, 1.1.200–1).

one's impudent look. Lit. "the severity of his face." The idiom *ʿōz pānāyw* is unique (supported by a number of Hebrew MSS that have *ʿwz*, with the *mater* clearly indicating a noun), but *ʿaz pānîm* "strong of face" = "impudent" is attested in the Bible (Deut 28:50; Dan 8:23) and in Postbiblical Hebrew (*b. ʾAbot* 5.20; *Ber.* 16b; *Šabb.* 30b.; *Beṣa* 25b). So, too, LXX has *anaidēs* "impudent," probably reading *ʿaz pānîm* (cf. Vulg *potentissimus faciem*), but the unique expression *ʿōz pānîm* is to be preferred, since it is likely that the other reading merely conforms to the more common idiom. One may also note the related idiom *hē'ēz pānîm* "to be impudent" in Prov 7:13, and Postbiblical *'azzût pānîm* "insolence" (*b. Qidd.* 70b; *Ber.* 16b; *Šabb.* 30b). Cf. Akkadian, *[lumnu] ša panī ezzu* "[the evil one] whose face is fierce" (cited in *CAD* IV, p. 428).

2. < > *Keep the command of the king.* MT has *'ănî* at the beginning of v 2, which makes no sense as it stands (see Notes at v 1). Some scholars assume that something like *'āmartî* "I said" or *'ōmēr* "say" has fallen out after *'ănî* (cf. 2:1, 15), or they take *'ănî* to be elliptical for *'ănî 'āmartî* "I said," or the like. In support of the latter view, Gordis cites *b. Qidd.* 44a (*Koheleth*, p. 288). But the "I" in that Talmudic text is necessitated by the contrast with other speakers mentioned in the text, whereas no other speaker is identified in our passage. Many scholars prefer to emend *'ny* to read *'t*, usually citing the ancient versions (so Euringer, Galling, Podechard). The readings in the ancient versions, however, do not prove that the *nota accusativi* was present in their *Vorlage(n)*. Indeed, while the presence of the *nota accusativi* with an indeterminate object is not impossible in Ecclesiastes (see Notes at 3:15), the absence of the definite article does make the emendation far less compelling. Even less likely is the proposal to read *'npy mlk* "before the king" instead of *'ny py mlk* in MT (so Ginsberg, Whitley). To account for the unassimilated *nûn* in *'npy*, one would have to assume an Aramaism here. It is easiest to take *'ny* as a corruption of the object suffix in the preceding form. Thus, *yš'nw yš' <'>ny* (dittography of *'alep* and graphic confusion of *waw* and *yod*). As for the expression *pî melek* "command of the king," one may compare it with *pî YHWH* "YHWH's command" used most frequently to speak of YHWH's word that must not be transgressed (Num 14:41; 22:18; 24:13; Deut 1:26, 43; 9:23; 1 Sam 12:14, 15; 15:24; 1 Kgs 13:21, 26).

yea, according to the manner of. Only one Hebrew MS omits the *waw*; all other witnesses have it. The *waw* should be retained as the more difficult and, thus, probably correct reading, and interpreted as having an explicative or emphatic function (see GKC §154.a, Note 1b). The idiom *'al-dibrat* in this context is probably not causal ("because of, on account of"), as it is commonly assumed, but modal ("in the manner of, according to the order of"). One may compare Ps 110:4, where we have *'al-dibrātî malkî-ṣedeq* "according to the manner of Melkizedeq" (cf. LXX *kata tēn taxin melchisedek* and Vulg *secundum ordinem Melchisedech*). It is not that one must keep the command of the king because God has sworn an oath to the king or because one has sworn an oath of loyalty to the king in the name of God. Rather, one must keep a king's command *in the same manner* that one would keep an oath sworn to God.

a sacred oath. Hebrew *šĕbû'at 'ĕlōhîm* occurs only here in the Bible, but it may be compared with the expression *šĕbû'at YHWH* "an oath by YHWH" (Exod 22:10; 2 Sam 21:7; 1 Kgs 2:43) — that is, an oath sworn in the name of YHWH, the most solemn oath possible in ancient Israel. The substitution of the term *'ĕlōhîm* for the more specific name YHWH is expected for a wisdom text.

3. *do not be stupefied at his presence.* The pointing in MT (*'al-tibbāhēl*) is probably correct; there is no need to repoint to read *'al-tĕbahēl* "do not hasten,"

as in 5:1 (Eng v 2) and 7:9. See the discussion of Aalders (*Prediker*, pp. 177–78). Some translators follow LXX, Symm, and Syr in taking the verb with the preceding line (so REB: "and if you have to swear by God, do not rush into it"; NJPS: "don't rush into uttering an oath by God"). The idiom *nibhal mippānāyw* "be stupefied at his presence" is, however, attested in Gen 45:3 and Job 23:15, precisely in regard to crippling stupor before someone who is powerful — a human in the former case and God in the latter. As elsewhere in Hebrew, the Niphal of *bhl* is to "be dismayed, be terrified, be anxious," not "hasten, or hurry," for which one expects the verb to be Piel (*nibhal lĕ-* in Prov 28:22 means "be anxious about," not "hasten after"; so NAB: "is perturbed about"). Moreover, it is strange if the advice is interpreted as "do not hasten." One should expect the opposite advice — that one should hasten to carry out the instruction or to depart from the king's presence. So in a parallel passage from the Aramaic *Proverbs of Ahiqar,* one reads: "If something is commanded you, it is a burning fire. Hurry, do it" (*TAD* III, 1.1.87). Immediate response to the king's command or quick departure from his presence is expected. Our passage in Ecclesiastes urges a measured response: one must not be so terrified by the king's presence that one cannot react appropriately.

do not persist in a harmful thing. Waldmann has argued that *dābār raʿ* in this context means rebellion ("The *DĀBĀR RAʿ* of Eccl 8:3," pp. 407–8). This phrase is ambiguous. It could refer to a lot of things, including sedition (see esp. Ps 64:6). Certainly, Qohelet's audience is not above subversive activities, as may be evident in 10:16–20. Not impossibly, the *dābār raʿ* here anticipates the *dābār* mentioned in 10:20, which refers to their secret and or subtle talk against the powerful. Sedition may also be at issue in a suggestive parallel from the Aramaic *Proverbs of Ahiqar* (see *TAD* III, 1.1.84–90).

In the face of overwhelming odds, one ought not do anything that is dangerous. One does what one must to survive the difficult situation. Qohelet may well have had some seditious activities of his audience in mind, but he is appropriately ambiguous. He couches the danger only in terms of "a harmful thing." The phrase "harmful thing" appears again in v 5, where he says that one who keeps the command will not experience "a harmful thing." Probably "harmful thing" in v 2 means the same as "harmful thing" in v 5. Both may refer to the threat of death before the awesome power of the king.

he will do whatever he pleases. This expression is used everywhere else in the Bible only of God's supreme power (see Pss 115:3; 135:6; cf. Isa 46:10; Jon 1:14). The Aramaic equivalent of the phrase occurs in Dan 4:14, 22, 29, 32 (Eng vv 17, 25, 32, 35), again, only in reference to God's supreme power. A. Hurvitz has demonstrated that this expression belonged originally to the domain of jurisprudence and is found only after 500 b.c.e. ("The History of a Legal Formula," pp. 257–67).

4. *the command of the king is authoritative.* Hebrew *dĕbar-melek šilṭôn,* lit. "the word of the king is power." For the syntax here, one may compare *mišpĕṭê yhwh ʾĕmet* "the judgments of YHWH are truth" = "the judgments of YHWH are true" (Ps 19:10), *wĕkol-nĕtîbōtĕhā šālôm* "all her paths are peace" = "all her paths are

peaceful" (Prov 3:17). See GKC §141.c; Joüon-Muraoka §154.e. Hebrew *děbar melek* corresponds to Aramaic *mlt mlk* "word of the king," which occurs several times in the parallel passage from Ahiqar (see *TAD* III, 1.1.84, 88). The word *šiltôn* occurs only here, in 8:8, and Sir 4:7.

5. *keeps the commandment.* Here *miṣwâ* refers to the royal command, as in 1 Kgs 2:43; 2 Kgs 18:36; 2 Chron 8:15. It refers to the same thing as *pî-melek* in v 2 and *děbar-melek* in v 3. Yet, the author may be alluding to the absolute nature of divine imperatives.

will not experience. The verb *yādaʿ* is used of the experience of retribution in Hos 9:7; Isa 9:8; Ezek 25:14.

a harmful thing. Here *dābār rāʿ* refers to retribution from the "king" (see also Notes at v 2).

As for time and judgment. Some Hebrew MSS read *wʿt mšpṭ* "a time of judgment" (omitting the *waw* conjunctive), a reading supported by LXX, which has *kairon kriseōs* (but in the next verse, LXX has *kairos kai krisis*, reflecting Hebrew *ʿt wmšpṭ*, as in MT). The word *mišpāṭ* has been taken variously to mean "procedure" (NASB; NIV), "method" (NEB), or "way" (RSV). But apart from this passage, *mišpāṭ* occurs four other times in the book, always meaning judgment or justice (3:16, 5:7 [Eng v 8]; 11:9; 12:14). There is, in fact, nothing wrong with the coordination of "time" and "judgment." In 3:17–18, in the face of injustice and human impotence in dealing with it, Qohelet says that God "will judge (*yiš-pōṭ*), for there is a time for every matter (*kî-ʿēt lěkol-ḥēpeṣ*)." God will render judgment in God's own time. The point made in 8:5b–8 is, indeed, not different from that in 3:16–22. It is not that the wise will know "when and how to act" (Scott) or "the proper time and manner of procedure" (Gordis), for that would contradict Qohelet's repeated insistence that no one knows such things. Rather, the issue of "time and judgment" is introduced and then elaborated on in vv 6–8, the point being that everyone knows that there is "time and judgment" (v 6), but no one knows when and how God will act (v 7). Thus, *wěʿēt ûmišpāṭ* must be treated as nominative absolutes isolated for emphasis (see Joüon-Muraoka §156), but the real objects of *yēdaʿ* are identified in v 6 by the four *kî*'s (see Notes in v 7).

a wise heart. The ancient versions all interpret *lēb ḥākām* as "heart of the wise," but we should probably expect *lēb heḥākām* (see *heḥākām* in v 17). We should take the term *lēb ḥākām* to mean "a wise heart," as it does in 1 Kgs 3:12.

6. *that.* The particle *kî* appears four times in vv 6–7. The significance of each occurrence is debated (see Michel, *Eigenart*, pp. 201–3; Schoors, *Pleasing Words*, pp. 106–7). In most cases, scholars see several different functions of *kî* at work in these two verses. Crenshaw, for instance, takes the first *kî* as asseverative, the second as adversative, the third as resultative, and the fourth as causative (*Ecclesiastes*, pp. 151–52). We may, however, take all four the same way, as indicating the objects of *yēdaʿ*. With verbs of perception, like *yādaʿ*, the subject or object is often anticipated (see Joüon-Muraoka §157.d.Note 2). The four assertions introduced by *kî* (vv 6–7) are matched by four negative statements in v 8, three introduced by *ʾên* and one by *lōʾ*.

the evil of humanity. There is some question whether *rāʿat hāʾādām* should be interpreted as a subjective or objective genitive phrase. Is *'ādām* the subject or object of evil? Those who favor the latter view, take the "evil" to mean "misfortune," probably death (cf. *rā'â rabbâ* in 2:21 and *rabbâ hî' 'al-hā'ādām* in 6:1). But the precise idiom "evil of humanity" occurs in Gen 6:5, together with the adjective *rabbâ*: "the evil of humanity was great on earth" (cf. 1 Sam 12:17; Joel 4:13). We should also take *'ādām* as the source of the evil, that is, wickedness (compare Targ: *ḥwbt 'nšyn 'bdyn byš'* "the sin of the people who do evil"). The point is that the wickedness of mortals is great upon them (cf. Ezek 33:10). Thus, there is certainly a time and a judgment against people because of their terrible evil.

8. *There is no one who is a proprietor over the life-breath, to hold back the life-breath.* The word *rûaḥ* here may be interpreted in two ways. On the one hand, it may refer to the elusive "wind" that human beings try to pursue, but simply cannot catch (1:14; 2:11, 17, 26; 4:4, 16; 6:7; 11:4). In that sense this line continues the thought of the preceding, namely, that no one knows what is going to happen or when it will happen. On the other hand, it may also refer to the human spirit—one's life-breath (so Targ *rwḥ nšmt'*)—which, like wind, is equally unpredictable and incomprehensible (3:19, 21; 11:5; 12:7). This double meaning of *rûaḥ* is also evident in 11:4–5, where the word first refers to wind (11:4) and then to the life-breath (11:5). What is meant in our passage, then, is that even the *šallîṭ* "proprietor" cannot detain the life-breath, as one might detain a debtor. No one is that rich or powerful. No one owns the right of disposal to life-breath. So this comment is appropriately followed by a reference to the day of death.

proprietorship. Hebrew *šilṭôn* may refer to proprietary rights—the authority to dispose of one's property (see Notes on *šlṭ* at 2:19).

over the day of death. The phrase *yôm hammāwet* here is used in the same sense as in 7:1, where the *yôm hammāwet*—opposite of *yôm hiwwālĕdô* "the day of one's birth"—must refer to the day of one's own death. No one has control over the day of death. Death is inevitable and even the powerful cannot have control over it. For the function of *bĕ-* in *šilṭôn bĕyôm* "proprietorship *over* the day of death," compare *šālaṭ hā'ādām bĕ'ādām*, lit. "a person exercising proprietorship *over* (another) person."

no substitution. The phrase *mišlaḥat bammilḥāmâ* is difficult to interpret. Most commentators take it to mean that there is no exemption or discharge from war. Yet, there were legal provisions for exemption from war in Israel (Deut 20:1–8; 24:5), and Judas Maccabaeus is said to have invoked such a law (1 Macc 3:56). The word *mišlaḥat* occurs only one other time in the Hebrew Bible, in Ps 78:49, where it refers to a detachment of celestial emissaries dispatched to carry out a destructive task in God's behalf. *Num. Rabb.* 14.11 also uses the word in the sense of a "mission" or "assignment." The point in our passage is not exemption or discharge from war, but deputation (so LXX *apostolē* "dispatch"). The background of this verse is the common practice in the Persian period of sending substitutes to war on one's behalf. People who received military fiefs as a grant were required to fulfill their military obligations. But the wealthy often paid someone else to do their duty (see Introduction, pp. 28–30). Each person must face the day of death personally.

the battle. LXX *en hēmera̧ polemou* "in the day of battle" (a reading followed by SyrH and Copt) reflects Hebrew *bywm mlḥmh*. But *bywm* may have been secondarily added as a result of the influence of the phrase *bywm hmwt* in the preceding line; *bywm* may have been added for clarification. The shorter text is to be preferred. Yet, it is probably correct to relate the "battle" here to the day of death mentioned in the preceding line. The power of death is still the issue in v 8b.

While there are no explicit references in the Bible to human struggle with death as a battle, the martial language here is reminiscent of Canaanite mythology, where Mot, deified Death, is engaged in battle with Baal, the god of life and nature. Indeed, the primary account of Mot's combat with Baal appears to be a variant of the mythic battle between Baal and Yamm, Sea (see *KTU* 1.5; 1.6). Some of the language pertaining to Death's overwhelming strength in combat is applied also to the human struggle with death. In a Ugaritic letter, a writer reports that "Death is very strong" (*mtm ʿz mid*), presumably because a plague of some sort has struck his city (*KTU* 2.10.12–13). The language in this context is reminiscent of the description of Baal's struggle with Mot elsewhere: "Mot is strong; Baal is strong" (*mt ʿz bʿl ʿz*, *KTU* 1.6.VI.17–20). The language of Death's cosmic power is applied to the encounter of humans with death. It is pertinent to note, too, that in Canaanite mythology Death's entourage includes a certain Šly̧ṭ (Powerful), "the one with seven heads" (*KTU* 1.5.I.3, 29–30). This is apparently an epithet of Lothan, biblical Leviathan. In any case, as Baal's defeat of Death is portrayed as a victory in combat, so, too, the defeat of Death is depicted in the biblical traditions as victory. Thus, recalling Isa 25:8 and Hos 13:14 (cf. Ps 91:5–7), texts that have their background in the mythology of Death's defeat in a decisive combat, the Apostle Paul cites a traditional response to death (1 Cor 15:54–55).

It appears that Qohelet, too, raises the issue of power to control one's final destiny in terms that are reminiscent of the struggle between Baal, the god of nature and life, and Mot, deified Death. This is not to suggest that Qohelet was deliberately using mythology here, or even that he was cognizant of the mythological background. Indeed, myth lies at a distance. Yet, the language of warfare is not out of context in that culture when one speaks of death's power. Against the hope held out in folklore that death might be defeated in decisive combat, Qohelet reaffirms death's might over everyone. The struggle with death is what every individual will have to undergo, it is not a fight that someone else (like Baal?) can assume on one's behalf. For the form *bĕʿālāyw*, lit. "its lord," see 5:12 (Eng v 11); 7:12.

9. *when I set my heart.* For the use of the infinitive absolute in place of the finite verb, see Notes at 4:2 and 9:11.

under the sun. See Notes at 1:3.

a time when. Cf. the use of *ʿēt* in Jer 51:33; *ʿēt ʾăšer* here is the accusative of time (GKC §118.i). LXX, SyrH, and Copt, however, reflect '*t* instead of '*t*. The "time" word here recalls "time" in vv 5–6.

people exercise proprietorship over one another. Hebrew *šālaṭ hā'ādām bĕ'ā-dām*. The verb *šlṭ* is a legal-economic term, referring to the exercise of proprietary rights, including rights of the freedom of another human being (see Notes at 2:19). Clearly the point here is economic oppression, perhaps usury and/or slavery.

to their detriment. It is unclear if the harm is to the one who exercises proprietorship over others ("to their *own* detriment"; so Symm: *eis kakon heautou*) or to the ones ruled (so LXX, Syr, Targ). The former is preferred if one takes v 9 with the preceding verses. The latter is preferred if one takes the verse with what follows. Perhaps the ambiguity is intentional: oppression is harmful to humanity, oppressor and oppressed alike.

10. *Thereupon.* Hebrew *ûbĕkēn* is a late idiom occurring in Esth 4:16 and Sir 13:7 (also a gloss for '*ḥr* "then" in Sir 35:2), as well as in Mishnaic Hebrew and at Qumran. The presence of *ûbĕkēn* here suggests that v 10 and what follows cannot be separated from v 9.

<brought> to the grave. Assuming *qbr* < > *mwb'* <*ym*> with Ehrlich and others, instead of *qbrym wb'w*. This is the reading reflected in LXX, SyrH, and Copt, although in LXX (but not SyrH and Copt) we have a plural, by attraction to *rš'ym: eis taphous eisachthentas* "brought to the graves." The original reading was probably *qbr mwb'ym* "brought to the grave," which, through a dittography of *mem*, yielded *qbr* <*m*> *mwb'ym*. The form *qbrm* was then interpreted (incorrectly) as a plural and "corrected" to *qbr* <*y*> *m*. It was probably an early "correction" of *qbrm* to *qbrym* that prompted the subsequent pointing of the word as a passive participle (*qĕbūrîm*), which then made original *mwb'ym* impossible. Hence, MT (supported by Syr, Vulg, and Targ) reads *wb'w* "and they came," assuming a finite verb to parallel *yhlkw* "they went." But the reading of MT makes no sense as it stands (lit. "the wicked are buried and they came and from the place of the holy one they went"). Many scholars emend the text to yield *qĕrēbîm* "approaching," instead of *qĕbūrîm* "buried" (assuming a metathesis of *reš* and *bet*), so that one might read: *qĕrēbîm ûbā'îm māqôm qādôš* "approaching and entering the holy place" (see Driver, "Problems and Solution," p. 230). It is clear that Qohelet intends to say that the wicked had fared well, whereas they deserved punishment. Qohelet's argument, however, is not that the wicked have died (which he would surely have regarded as a good thing), but that they were accorded proper burial ("brought to the grave") and, indeed, with rites usually reserved for the honored ("they proceeded from the holy place"), whereas the righteous are ignominiously abandoned in the city. The same point is made by Job, who complained that the wicked are not getting what they deserve; instead, when they die they are "brought to the grave, a watch is kept over their tomb," and a long funeral procession accompanies them (Job 21:32–33). Even in death the wicked are honored.

from a holy place. Reading *ûmimmāqôm qādôš* instead of *ûmimmĕqôm qādôš*, which may have been prompted by the interpretation of *qādôš* as an epithet for the deity (Fox, *Contradictions*, p. 250). The *māqôm qādôš* probably does not refer to the temple as a whole, for which one expects *hammāqôm haqqādôš* "the holy place." Numerous times in the Bible, *māqôm qādôš* refers to various areas within the sanctuary compound (see Exod 29:31; Lev 6:9, 16, 20; 7:6; 10:13; 16:24; 24:9). In all these passages, however, *māqôm qādôš* probably designates the religious purpose of a general area rather than a specific place (see D. P. Wright, *The Disposal of Impurity: Elimination Rites in the Bible and in Hittite and Mesopotamian Literature* [SBLDS 101; Atlanta: Scholars, 1987], pp. 232–35). In any case, the term probably refers not to the temple but the synagogue. In this regard, one may note that the synagogue is known in several Aramaic inscriptions as *'trh qdyšh* "a holy place" (see DNWSI, p. 997; M. Dothan, *Hammath Tiberias: Early Synagogues and the Hellenistic and Roman Remains* [Jerusalem: Israel Exploration Society, 1983], p. 54), and in Greek inscriptions it is called *ho hagios topos* "the holy place" (see B. Lifshitz, *Donateurs et Fondateurs dans les Synagogues Juives* [CahRB 7; Paris: Gabalda, 1967], pp. 18, 55, 70; W. Horbury and D. Noy, *Jewish Inscriptions of Graeco-Roman Egypt* [Cambridge: Cambridge University, 1992], nos. 16, 127). It is possible that synagogues existed alongside the temple during the postexilic period, supported by a certain group or groups of those who returned from the diaspora (cf. M. Smith, *Palestinian Parties and Politics that Shaped the Old Testament* [2nd edition; London: SCM, 1987], p. 77). We can only speculate that in the time of Qohelet, some people who were considered important (perhaps including wealthy donors of the synagogues) were publicly eulogized at the synagogues before they were buried. The practice of bringing the bodies to the synagogue was later forbidden, along with private eulogies, but public orations for scholars and particularly pious people continued to be allowed (see *b. Meg.* 28b; cf. *b. Roš. Haš.* 25a; *Mo'ed Qat.* 21b).

proceeded. There is nothing wrong with the form *yĕhallēkû*. It should not, therefore, be repointed (so Whitley) or otherwise emended (so Ginsberg). The verb is used of people walking about in mourning (cf. Pss 38:7 [Eng v 6]; 42:10 [Eng v 9]; Job 30:28). A funeral procession is in view here.

those who acted justly. The phrase *'ăšer kēn-'āśû* may be variously interpreted (NIV: "where they did this"; RSV: "where they did such things"; NJPS: "such as had acted righteously"). We should probably take it as the subject of the sentence. The word *kēn* should be taken as an adverb "justly" or "rightly" (cf. Judg 12:6), or as a substantive "justice" or "right" (see 2 Kgs 7:9; cf. Prov 11:19). So Symm renders *kēn* as a substantive (*dikaia praxantes*), and Vulg has *quasi iustorum operum*. Thus, *'ăšer kēn-'āśû* "those who acted justly" is contrasted with *rĕšā'îm* "the wicked," but also *ma'ăśēh hārā'â* "evil work" (v 11a), *la'ăśôt rā'* "to do evil" (v 11b), *'ōśeh rā'* "one who does evil" (v 12a). The fate of "those who are righteous" is contrasted with the fate of the wicked.

are discarded. Many commentators emend *wĕyištakkĕḥû* to *wĕyištabbĕḥû* "and they boasted" or "they are praised," citing LXX, Aq, Symm, Theod, SyrH, Jerome, and some Hebrew MSS (see de Rossi). This reading, however, anticipates *wešibbaḥtî* in v 15. Fox (*Contradictions*, pp. 250–51) accepts the reading *wěyiš-takkěḥû*, but observes that in 2:16 the point is made that memory will not distinguish one group of people from another, for "all too soon everyone is forgotten." Moreover, Fox observes, it is odd that the author should specify "in the city," whereas one should expect him to say that the just are forgotten everywhere (*Contradictions*, p. 251). Why should they be forgotten only in the city? Hence, Fox argues that *škḥ* in this context means "neglected," as it does in Pss 9:19 [Eng v 18], 102:5 [Eng v 4]; Isa 49:15; Deut 24:19. Indeed, *škḥ* is often taken as a synonym of *'zb* "to abandon" (Jer 30:14; Job 19:14; Isa 49:14; 65:11). Thus, in contrast to the wicked who are accorded a decent burial, those who have acted justly are abandoned in the city — a particularly ignominious fate, since their demise is presumably noticed and ignored by the multitudes. Alternatively, one may connect the verb here with Ugaritic *tkh* "to wither, be wasted," a word used of the disintegration of the heavens (*KTU* 1.5.I.4, 30). This meaning is found in Ps 137:5, in a wordplay, "If I forget you (*'eškāḥēk*), O Jerusalem, let my right hand be wasted (*tiškaḥ*)," and Ps 102:5, "I am too wasted to eat my food (*šākaḥtî mē'ăkōl laḥmî*)." In any case, the point is that the righteous are not given a decent burial: their corpses are abandoned in the city. That is one of the worst curses that one can receive (Deut 28:26; 1 Kgs 14:11; 21:23–24; Jer 7:33; 16:4; 22:19; Ezek 29:5). For this reason, biblical biographies frequently end with some reference to the burial of the principal figures (the ancestors, Moses, Joshua, etc.), lest one should imagine other possibilities.

vanity. See Notes at 1:2.

11. *since sentence for evil work is not carried out quickly.* Lit. "since a sentence for evil work is not being done quickly." If the Masoretic punctuation is correct, one should translate, "since sentence is not carried out, the work of evil is quick." But apart from such a dubious use of *měhērâ*, which is almost always adverbial, this interpretation makes *ma'ăśēh hārā'â měhērâ* the apodosis. This is an unlikely proposition, since that leaves the next line "*therefore* people dare to do evil" without any connection to a protasis. We should ignore the disjunctive accent on *pitgām* "sentence," take the word to be in construct with *ma'ăśēh hārā'â* "evil work," and interpret *měhērâ* as an adverb (its normal usage). The punctuation may have been affected by the vocalization of *pitgām* "sentence," which may have been interpreted incorrectly as an absolute form (one expects *pitgam*, according to the rules for Hebrew nouns), whereas it is actually construct, as in *pitgām hammelek* "the king's decree" in Esth 1:20.

As is widely recognized (see *HALAT*, p. 925), *pitgām* is a Persian loanword both in Hebrew (Esth 1:20; Sir 5:11; 8:9) and Aramaic (Dan 3:16; 4:14 [Eng v 17]; Ezra 4:17; 5:7, 11; 6:11). It is attested in Aramaic documents from Elephantine (see *TAD* II, 8.8.2, 3), as well as from North Saqqara (Segal, *Aramaic Texts*, No. 1.2–3). Basically *pitgām* means "word" or "matter," thus corresponding to Hebrew *dābār*, but it is used here in the specific sense of a word of judgment (elsewhere also "decree"). In any case, we may compare the idiom *na'ăśâ pitgām* with Hebrew *'āśâ dābār* "carry out the word/order" in 2 Sam 17:6; Joel 2:11; Pss 103:20; 148:8; Deut 29:28 [Eng v 29]. One should also probably repoint the participle as *na‘ăśeh* instead of the feminine singular form *na‘ăśâ*, since *pitgām* is masculine (Esth 1:20). The ancient versions interpret the form as a participle. It is possible that *na‘ăśâ* is the perfect 3 ms form, but that is unlikely after the negative particle *’ên*; we expect either *’ên na‘ăśeh* (with the participle) or *lō’ na‘ăśâ* (with the perfect).

people dare to do evil. Hebrew *mālē’ lēb běnê-hā’ādām bāhem la‘ăśôt*, lit. "the heart of human beings is full within them to do evil." The closest parallel within the Bible is in Esth 7:5, *’ăšer mělā’ô libbô la‘ăśôt kēn* "the one who dared to do this." The idiom may be compared with Egyptian *mḥ ib m* "to be full of heart in" = "trust in, have confidence in" (*WbÄS* II, p. 118).

12. *an offender.* Hebrew *’ăšer ḥōṭe’*, lit. "the one who errs." Compare Neh 5:2–4, where we also have *’ăšer* + a participle: *’ăšer ’ōměrîm* "those who say." Alternatively, one may take *’ăšer* to introduce a real condition, as in Lev 4:22, *’ăšer nāśî’ yeḥěṭā’* "if a leader sins . . . (see GKC §159.cc). If this is the function of *’ăšer*, v 12a would be a bitter parody of casuistic law. One expects the apodosis to indicate punishment for the sinner, but what one learns instead is that sinners are blessed with longevity: *if* one is a sinner, then one will live long! For the form and meaning of *ḥōṭe’* "offender," see Notes at 2:26.

the wrong of hundreds. Reading *rā‘ mē’ōt*, instead of *ra‘ mē’at* in Codex Leningrad. The word *m’t* is usually taken to be elliptical for "a hundred years," "a hundred times," or the like, or it is assumed that the absolute has fallen out. LXX has *apo tote* "from then," apparently reflecting Hebrew *m’z* (thus also SyrH and Copt). This has prompted some scholars to emend the text accordingly (so recently Fox). But LXX also has *apo makrotētos autō* "from his length [of time]" for MT's *m’ryk lw*. The *Vorlage* of LXX apparently had *m’rk lw* (i.e., without the internal *mater lectionis*), which is interpreted by LXX as "his length [of time]" — i.e., Hebrew *mē’ōrek lô*. It is possible that the reading *m’z* reflected in the Greek traditions generated the misinterpretation of *m’r(y)k* (so Schoors, *Pleasing Words*, p. 29). Yet, it is also possible that *m’z* was generated by the misinterpretation of *m’r(y)k lw* in the first place. The latter explanation makes more sense. LXX first misinterpreted *m’rk* in its *Vorlage*, then misread *m’t* as *m’z*. In any case, LXX reflects a corruption of some sort. One should not, therefore, simply choose *m’z*. The consonantal reading of MT is to be retained. Since the archaic *-at* ending is unlikely in this late book (see the form *mē’â* in 6:3, not *mē’at*), one should probably assume a defective spelling, *mē’ōt* "hundreds" or "centuries" (so Jerome: *centies*). Hebrew *mē’â* may refer to a group of significant size, "a century" (Amos 5:3; Judg 20:10; plural in Exod 18:21, 25; 2 Kgs 11:4, 9, 10, 15). One may also compare Aramaic *rby m’thm* "their centurions" (lit. "chiefs of their centuries") mentioned in a Persian period text (*TAD* I, 5.5.7). Alternatively, one may take *mē’ōt* "hundreds" to mean "hundreds of times." As an example of such an adverbial use of the noun, Schoors cites *KTU* 2.34.27–29, where Ugaritic *mat* is interpreted as "a hundred times" (*Pleasing Words*, p. 76). The text is, however, fragmentary; one suspects that another numeral precedes *mat*, as is the case in every clear occurrence of the word in Ugaritic. Moreover, *mat* cannot mean "a hundred," for which the alphabetic Ugaritic texts always have *mit*, but "hundreds." Ugaritic *mat* must mean "hundreds" (that is, *mat* = *miʾātu* "hundreds," but *mit* = *miʾtu* "hundred").

lives long. Hebrew *maʾărîk lô* is elliptical for *maʾărîk yāmîm lô* (cf. v 13; 7:15).

Even though. It is certain that *kî gam* is concessive (cf. *kî gam* in v 16): it introduces what Qohelet accepts as truth (v 12b–13). Note that *wĕlōʾ-yaʾărîk* in v 13 contradicts *ûmaʾărîk lô* in v 12a. Most translators and commentators assume that Qohelet is unwilling to give up this knowledge, despite what is said in vv 11–12a. But this concession is merely parenthetical, it seems, and without much conviction, for he quickly returns to note the injustice in the treatment of the just and unjust in v 14. The problem is obviated if we take the concession to precede the reassertion of injustice in v 14. That is, Qohelet accepts the orthodox doctrine of retribution, but he points to a contradiction of it in reality. He does not deny that there are all sorts of contradictions in the world.

I know. In speaking of his own knowledge, Qohelet always uses the perfect form *yādaʿtî* (1:17; 2:14; 3:12, 14). Only in this verse does he use *yôdēaʿ* in reference to himself. Isaksson argues that Qohelet uses the perfect form whenever he refers to what he himself has come to know, but he uses the participle here for what he knows to be traditional and of common sense (see *Language of Qohelet*, p. 67). Thus, Qohelet is agreeing with common knowledge, as it were. We may, perhaps, bring out this nuance better by translating *yôdēaʿ ʾănî* as "I recognize" or "I acknowledge," as opposed to *yādaʿtî* "I know."

13. *shadowy days.* Hebrew *yāmîm kaṣṣēl,* lit. "days like a shadow," meaning "days that are like a shadow." MT is supported by Vulg and Syr, but LXX (*en skią*) reflects Hebrew *baṣṣēl,* a secondary reading that perhaps originated in an attempt to ease the awkward syntax. The shadowy (i.e., transient) nature of human "days" is a persistent lament in the Bible (Pss 102:11 [Eng v 11]; 109:23; 144:4; Job 8:9; 14:2; 17:7; 1 Chron 29:15). See Notes at 6:12.

14. *vanity.* See Notes at 1:2.

who are treated. Hebrew *ʾăšer maggîaʿ ʾălēhem,* lit. "whom (one) treats them." For the idiom *higgîaʿ ʾel-*, one may compare Esth 9:26, *mah higgîaʿ ʾălêhem* "what has befallen them" (i.e., what has brought them that condition). This idiom is also widely attested in Postbiblical Hebrew.

acted wickedly . . . acted righteously. Hebrew *kĕmaʿăśēh hārĕšāʿîm . . . kĕmaʿăśēh haṣṣaddîqîm,* lit. "according to the deeds of the wicked . . . according to the deeds of the righteous." In both cases, *maʿăśeh* is a collective.

vanity. See Notes at 1:2.

15. *under the sun.* See Notes at 1:3.

that. The antecedent is all that precedes, "eating, drinking, and enjoying" treated as one action.

may accompany them. Cf. Sir 41:12. The verb may also be attested in Persian period Aramaic, in the *Proverbs of Ahiqar* (TAD III, 1.1.100).

in their toil. That is, in their trouble. See 2:24; 4:9; 5:18 [Eng v 19]; 9:9 (cf. also Judg 10:16; Pss 73:5; 107:12).

during the days of their life. Hebrew *yĕmê ḥayyāyw* reflects the accusative of time (see Notes at 2:3).

that God has given them. It is unclear what *ʾăšer* "that" refers to. Does the author mean enjoyment, toil, days, or life? Syntactically, the last named noun (life) seems the most likely referent.

under the sun. See Notes at 1:3.

16. *I determined.* Hebrew *nātattî ʾet-libbî*, lit. "I set my mind." See Notes at 1:12.

to know wisdom. Cf. 1:17 and 3:10.

business. See Notes at 1:13.

{   }. Hebrew has *kî gam bayyôm ûballaylâ šēnâ bĕʿênāyw ʾênennû rōʾeh*, lit. "even though neither by day nor by night do they see sleep with their eyes." But the line is disruptive and difficult to interpret in its present position for several reasons: (a) the 3 ms suffixes — in *ʿênāyw* "their eyes," *ʾênennû* "they do not" — have no antecedent, (b) the function and meaning of *kî gam* "even though(?)" are unclear, (c) the vacillation between the first-person and the third-person subjects in vv 16–17 is awkward. Most commentators regard the line as parenthetical and anticipatory of v 17b. Ginsberg (followed by Fox) emends *bĕʿênāyw ʾênennû* to *bĕʿênî ʾênennî* "with my eyes I do not . . . ," eliminating the tension between the first person in vv 16a, 17 and the third person in v 16b. In any case, the whole line has to be seen as parenthetical. The problems are obviated if one assumes that the line has been inadvertently transposed from v 17, after *ʾăšer naʿăśâ taḥat-haššemeš* "that which has been done under the sun," where it originally belonged. The likeness of the phrases *ʾăšer naʿăśâ ʿal hāʾāreṣ* "that which has been done on earth" in v 16 and *ʾăšer naʿăśâ taḥat-haššemeš* "that which has been done under the sun" in v 17 probably prompted the error. The transposition is even more understandable when one considers that at least one Hebrew MS (Kennicott no. 95) adds *taḥat haššemeš* "under the sun" after *naʿăśâ* "that which has been done" in v 16. With the removal of the intrusive line, transition between the protasis in v 16 and the apodosis in v 17 is smooth: *kaʾăšer nātattî ʾet-libbî . . . wĕrāʾîtî* " when I determined . . . (then) I saw."

17. *under the sun.* See Notes at 1:3.

{*although . . . sleep*}. This line has been incorrectly transposed from its original position here to v 16, after *hāʾāreṣ* (see Notes at v 16). Deprivation of sleep is a motif found in the ancient Near East for religious fervor; people who describe their total dedication to certain tasks speak of their efforts day and night and how they deprive themselves of sleep (cf. C. L. Seow, *Myth, Drama, and the Politics of David's Dance* [HSM 44; Atlanta: Scholars, 1989] p. 158). We should probably take *kî gam* in the concessive sense. The expression occurs two other times in Ecclesiastes — 4:14; 8:12 — in both those instances, the concessive sense is intended.

Therefore. Hebrew *bĕšel ʾăšer*, lit. "on account of which" (cf. *bĕšellĕmî* in Jon 1:7 and *bĕšellî* in Jon 1:12). The idiom is similar to *bĕšel še-* attested in 4QMMT B 12, C 32 (see E. Qimron and J. Strugnell, "An Unpublished Halakhic Letter from Qumran," in *Biblical Archaeology Today: Proceedings of the International Congress on Biblical Archaeology, Jerusalem, April 1984* [Jerusalem: Israel Exploration Society, 1985], p. 405) and the Bar Kochba letter (DJD II, pp. 165–66).

The expression corresponds to Targumic Aramaic *bdyl d*, which is used to translate Hebrew *lm'n* "so that" or "in order that," and the negated form is used to translate *lblty* "so that not." As Qimron and Strugnell have noted (p. 405), the Hebrew expressions should not be considered as Aramaisms, since the Aramaic expression appears much later.

desire to know. Lit. "say to know." The verb *'āmar* is frequently elliptical for *'āmar ballēb* "to say in the heart" or "to say to oneself," thus, "to think" (Gen 20:11; 26:9; 44:28, etc.). It is tempting to connect *yō'mar* here with *'āmar ballēb* elsewhere in Ecclesiastes. Yet, *'āmar* + infinitive normally indicates purpose or expectation (Exod 2:14; Josh 22:33; 1 Sam 30:6; 2 Sam 21:16; 1 Kgs 5:19). Thus, "think to know" means "desire to know."

COMMENT

There is little agreement on the beginning of the literary unit. Many commentators are of the view that v 1, or at least v 1a, is the conclusion of the preceding unit. There is merit to the latter view, inasmuch as v 1a does allude to the impossibility of wisdom, which is the point of 7:23–29. The rhetorical questions in v 1a suggest that no one is wise enough to solve the "accounting" problem that is the focus of the preceding passage. At the same time, the word *dābār* "anything" (also meaning "word") serves as a catchword, linking this verse to the mention of *dābār* "thing" (vv 3, 5) or "word" (v 4). Moreover, the rhetorical question "who knows" anticipates the assertion that "no one knows" (v 7) and, eventually, also the admission at the end of the passage that the wise who think they know are not able to discover anything (v 17). In short, the references to the wise and their quest for knowledge frame the literary unit: the passage begins with the rhetorical questions "who is so wise . . . who knows" (v 1); it ends with the conclusion that the really wise do not know (v 17).

Arbitrariness and Power (vv 1–8)
These verses are difficult to interpret. The issue seems to be power, a theme that recurs in vv 1–9: *šilṭôn* "authority, proprietorship" (v 4, 8), *šallîṭ* "proprietorship" (v 8), *šālaṭ* "exercise proprietorship" (v 9). It is possible that the arbitrariness of divine power is in question, as the Targum, Midrash, and various early interpreters have it. In this view, the "king" who is all-powerful, whose command must be obeyed without hesitation, is none other than God. Yet, it seems clear as one reads on in the passage that the author also has in mind the oppressive power of human beings who do not have proprietorship over death (v 8), but exercise proprietorship over other people (v 9).

There is a suggestive parallel in the Aramaic *Proverbs of Ahiqar*, a wisdom text in circulation among the Jews of Elephantine during the Persian period. This text warns that one should take the command of the king seriously, that the king's wrath is extremely dangerous, and that no one can question the king's authority (*TAD* III, 1.1.84–90). The significance of this parallel from Elephantine for the interpretation of our passage lies not only in its similar subject matter, namely, proper conduct in the face of the king's wrath (see also Prov 16:14; 19:12; 20:2; Eccl 10:4), but also in the fact that it compares the supremacy of the king with the supremacy of the gods. Echoing descriptions of the power of the divine warrior in Canaanite mythology, the Aramaic text speaks of the king's tongue breaking the ribs of the dragon: "The language of the k[ing] is tender, but it will break the ribs of a dragon like death, which is [n]ot seen" (*TAD* III, 1.1.89–90). Moreover, the king is compared to the high-god El, called by one of his best-known epithets, "the Merciful" (compare Hebrew *ʾēl raḥûm* in Exod 34:6; Deut 4:31; Ps 86:15; Jon 4:2; Ugaritic *lṭpn il dpid* "the Merciful, El who is Compassionate"). Before him, it is said, no one can stand. Qohelet seems to be making a similar comparison between the supremacy of the king and the supremacy of the deity (compare Ps 89:28 [Eng v 27]). In so doing, he counsels the reader to adopt a proper attitude before one with absolute power, both human and divine.

The author begins with a pair of rhetorical questions (v 1a): "who is so wise? And who knows the solution to anything?" These questions serve to introduce the sayings of the wise in vv 1b–5a, although the instructions that follow really illustrate the fact that no one is that wise or knows the solution to anything. It is likely that Qohelet is either citing or alluding to traditional wisdom sayings, not unlike those found in the Aramaic *Proverbs of Ahiqar*. Such instructions are supposed to teach people how to behave before authoritarian figures. Yet, they do not really provide a solution to the problem of oppressive power. No one is that wise.

Wisdom, it is said, causes one to display a pleasant appearance and to change one's impudent look (v 1b). Before a superior, especially someone whose wrath is swift, it is wise not to display any animosity. Instead, despite one's feelings, it is smart to act pleasantly. The point seems to be that people ought not to incur the king's disfavor, for the king acts with the same arbitrary power as a high-god. One is to keep the king's command, as one would an oath invoked in the name of God (v 2). What Qohelet means is that the king's command (*pî-melek*), like YHWH's command (*pî-YHWH*), is absolute; one must not violate it in any way. The king is like a deity; the deity is like a king. Both are authoritative, perhaps even authoritarian. The sage Ahiqar, too, warns that people should not take the king's command lightly, but be quick and cheerful in their response.

The exhortation in v 3 is very difficult to interpret (see Notes above), but it seems to suggest that people ought not to be so terrified before the king that they cannot react appropriately. In the Egyptian *Instructions of Ptahhotep* one is admonished to respond immediately and precisely to a superior's command, keeping emotions in check (see *ANET*[3], p. 413). So Qohelet advises that one should proceed, presumably to do what is commanded. Defiance, whether evident in one's countenance (v 1b) or in one's reluctant manner (v 3) can be dangerous. So one should proceed and not "persist in a harmful thing."

There is some ambiguity about what is meant by the "harmful thing" here. It is possible that the author is subtly warning against sedition, for the "harmful thing" may refer not only to the harm that one might receive from the king, but also to the dangerous activity in which the audience is involved. Perhaps he is alluding to the audience's subversive talk against the king and the rich and powerful (see Comment at 10:16–20).

The danger lies in the fact that the king will do whatever he wants: "all that he desires he will do" (v 3). The expression here is reminiscent of similar sayings pertaining to the sovereignty of God (see Pss 115:3; 135:6; Jon 1:14; Isa 46:10; 55:11; Dan 4:14, 22, 29, 32 [Eng vv 17, 25, 32, 35]). The power of the king is also indicated by the fact that no one can ask him what he is doing: "who will say to him 'What are you doing?'" (v 4). This question is found almost verbatim in Job 9:12 and Sir 36:8, again, in an affirmation of God's absolute power (see also Dan 4:32 [Eng v 35]). Elsewhere in the Bible, the unquestionable sovereignty of the deity is affirmed in the imagery of the potter and the clay: "Does the clay say to the one who fashions it, 'What are you doing?'" (Isa 45:9; see also Isa 29:16; 64:8; Jer 18:6). A similar analogy is drawn in the Aramaic *Proverbs of Ahiqar*: "[H]ow can wood contest with fire, flesh with knife, or anyone with a king?" (*TAD* III, 1.1.88). Both in Ecclesiastes and Ahiqar, the unquestionable power of the king is likened to that of the deity. Not surprisingly, therefore, Qohelet refers to the king's commandment as *miṣwâ*, a term most often used in the Bible of the divine imperative: those who keep the commandment (*miṣwâ*) will not experience "a harmful matter" (v 5a). It is for good reason, therefore, that many interpreters see an analogy between this passage and the Apostle Paul's view about human "authorities" being an extension of divine authority (Rom 13:1–7).

The instructions given in vv 1b–5a may be practical and necessary. Yet, they do not really solve the problem of arbitrary power — of human beings and of the deity. They only illustrate the claim that no one is that wise and no one knows the solution of anything (v 1b). The author uses wisdom forms — evident in the parallels with the *Proverbs of Ahiqar* — ironically to demonstrate the limits of wisdom. So in vv 5b–8, the author clarifies what it is that people know or, rather, do not know. In 3:16–22, the problem of injustice prompted Qohelet to say *in his heart* that "God will judge" and that there is "a time for every matter" (3:17). His contention in that context is that God will judge whenever God wills, and that there is a time for everything, although human beings do not know what will happen or when anything will happen. Now he says that the wise *heart* knows about time and judgment (v 5). He does not mean that the wise — or anyone else — can know the "whens-and-hows," for that would contradict what he says elsewhere in the book and in the immediate context (see v 7). Rather, he asserts only that there is (*yēš*) a proper time and a proper judgment (v 6a). He admits, too, the extent of humanity's evil, but he neither proffers an answer to the problem, nor does he venture to predict what will happen to human beings (v 6b). And, as he does repeatedly in the book, he insists that no one knows what will happen or when anything will happen (v 7).

Dealing with the problem of timing and judgment in 3:16–22, Qohelet points to death as the great leveler. Death is the common fate of every mortal and no one can control what will happen to the life-breath. Now he makes the same point in 8:7, asserting through four negative statements that death is the great equalizer. No human has the authority (*šallîṭ*) to exercise control over the life-breath, and no one has authority (*šilṭôn*) over the day of death (v 8). It is possible that he has in mind the *šallîṭîm* "the proprietors" mentioned in 7:19 and the king, whose word is said to be *šilṭôn* "authority" (v 4). These people may seem all-powerful, but even they have no power over death. Everyone must die, the weak and the powerful alike (compare 3:18–22).

The language about the powerlessness of humans in the face of death recalls Canaanite mythological accounts of the threat of deified Death (Gibson, *Canaanite Myths and Legends*, pp. 68–81). According to the Ugaritic traditions, Mot (Death) is engaged in combat with Baal (literally "lord"), the god of nature and life. Accompanied by his deadly entourage that included a certain "*Šlyṭ* (Powerful), the one with seven heads," Death scores an initial victory over Baal, swallowing Baal. However, whereas in the mythological account Death is eventually defeated by Baal, in Qohelet's observation there is no human who has power over the *rûaḥ* ("wind" or "life-breath") or has power over the day of Death (compare 1 Cor 15:53–55). There will be no substitution in that battle (v 8b). Here he may be alluding to the common practice among the rich in the Persian period of paying for substitutes to go to war. People who had been given proprietary rights over military fiefs were required to do military service in time of war. Akkadian texts from the Persian period show that these proprietors commonly paid others to go on their behalf (see Introduction, pp. 28–30). The proprietors in that period may be that powerful. Qohelet, however, points out that no one has authority over the life-breath. No one has authority over the day of death. When the time comes for someone to die, no one can send a substitute. And there will be no one who will fight on one's behalf — like Baal in Canaanite mythology — so that death will cease to be a threat. Death is an equalizer that shows no respect for status or wealth. There is no escape even for the powerful lords, the *šallîṭîm* "proprietors." As Qohelet puts it: "wickedness will not deliver one who possesses it" (*bĕ'ālāyw*, literally "its lord" or "its lords").

Responses to the Arbitrariness (vv 9–17)

The function of v 9 is twofold (compare 7:15). On one hand, it recalls what precedes it, namely, the issue of power or authority (*šālaṭ*; see especially vv 4, 8). The word "time" (*'ēt*) also serves as a catchword linking this verse with the preceding (see vv 5–6). Simultaneously, this verse introduces the new section, with its concern about the inequities of this world. In what follows, the writer appears to have in mind the fate of oppressors, in comparison with the fate of the oppressed. Probably the former are those identified as the wicked and the latter are they who have "acted justly" and are righteous. The mention of "all that has been done under the sun" anticipates the many references to the activities of the righteous and the wicked, as well as the activities of God. Indeed, the root *'śh* ("do, act") occurs fourteen times in vv 9–17. The author says he set his heart (*wĕnātôn 'et-libbî*) on all that has been done under the sun. This theme will be picked up again at the conclusion of the unit, in vv 16–17, where he speaks of setting his heart (*nātattî 'et-libbî*) to know wisdom and to see all that has been done on earth. God is not mentioned in v 9, but it becomes clear by the end of the passage that the writer is speaking not only of what is done by humans, but more generally of what has been done by God. Thus, vv 10–17 elaborate on what is meant by "all that is done under the sun" — that is, activities human and divine.

While it is true that death is an equalizer, inasmuch as every person whether powerful or powerless must die (vv 7–8), it is nevertheless true that there are inequities even at death. Qohelet observes that the wicked are brought to burial (v 10a). The point is not that the wicked die, for death is the fate not only of the wicked, but also of the righteous. The problem here, as in 7:15, is that the wicked are not getting what they deserve. They do not have to pay for their wickedness, it seems. In 7:15 Qohelet observes that some of them in fact live long, while there are righteous who die prematurely. Now in 8:10 he notes that the wicked are accorded the right of a decent burial. Not only that, they are even honored with a procession from the synagogue: "from a holy place they proceed" (see Notes above). Like Qohelet, Job was incensed that the wicked were getting away with their wickedness even at their death: they were being brought to their grave, watch was being kept at their tomb, and they were honored by a long procession (Job 21:32–33). Ironically, the leveling effect of death is perceived to be itself an injustice, for those who are wicked and those who are righteous end up exactly the same way. Death provides the sameness of fate for all, but the sameness of fate is not quite fair, because there are inequities in life. The sameness of fate at the end only heightens the injustice. For Qohelet, the injustice is even more intolerable because, in stark contrast to the wicked, those who have acted righteously are not properly interred. Denial of a proper burial is a curse that the worst sinners were supposed to suffer (Deut 28:25–26; 1 Kgs 14:10–11; Jer 16:4). Yet, not only are the righteous left unburied, they are forgotten in the city, a particularly humiliating fate, since their abandonment is public and apparently deliberate. The wicked should be the ones whose "memory perish in the street" and who have "no name in the street" (Job 18:17), but Qohelet observes that it is the righteous who are so forgotten. Such a situation is said to be *hebel* "vanity," something that simply makes no sense and provides no assurance (v 10; compare Job 21:34).

The issue of delayed justice is raised in v 11. Significantly, the author never denies that there will be retribution. He is of the view that there will be "a time and a judgment" for every matter (see 7:6; 3:17), but he insists that no one knows when or how that will be (7:7). The inequities that exist in the world suggest to him that justice has been delayed, and a consequence of that delay is that more injustice is perpetrated because the wicked are emboldened to do even more. Already in vv 11–12a one senses the tension between what Qohelet acknowledges to be true (that there must be just retribution somehow) and what he sees as reality (that there is no retribution that he can perceive). That tension is clarified in a long concession that reflects popular belief, but that the author himself also acknowledges to be true (vv 12a–13; see Notes), and what he recognizes as a contradiction (v 14). He acknowledges with traditional wisdom that it will be well with those who fear God, but not with those who are wicked. Qohelet tries to cope with that tension to some extent. He admits that the wicked may indeed live long (v 12), but he asserts that they will not finally be able to prolong the limited human life span (vv 13–14). They may live longer than they deserve, but they cannot change the ephemeral nature of human life. Nevertheless, something is amiss for him: there is *hebel* "vanity," something that simply makes no sense (v 14). What is done under the sun remains an utter mystery. Even if one rationalizes that death is a great equalizer in the end, the fact remains that there are inequities in the present. The righteous are treated as if they are wicked and the wicked as if they are righteous. This incomprehensible reality he calls *hebel* "vanity" (v 15). It is an enigma.

In the face of this "vanity"—the impossibility of control—the author commends enjoyment (v 15). To be sure, toil is not something that is desired, but it is a reality in life. So Qohelet advises that enjoyment should accompany toil as long as one lives. As elsewhere in the book, the advice is given theological grounding: God has given (v 15).

Qohelet repeats his earlier assertion (in v 7) that one cannot understand the workings of the arbitrary world (vv 16–17). There is a new element here, however. He speaks of the quest for wisdom and knowledge in terms of the deprivation of sleep: "by day and by night they do not sleep." This is the language of religious fervor and complete dedication to a task (see Notes above). Even people who are so completely committed to understanding God's mysterious activity cannot find what they yearn to know. No one is that wise (see v 1). Wisdom is elusive.

PART II.B. ETHICS:
COPING WITH RISKS
AND DEATH

II.B.1. CARPE DIEM (9:1–10)

[1]Indeed, all this I have laid on my heart, even to examine all this: that the righteous and the wise and their works are in the hand of God, (including) both love and hate. People do not know everything that is before them. [2]Everything is as for everyone: there is one fate for the righteous and the wicked, the good <and the bad>, the clean and the unclean, the one who sacrifices and the one who does not sacrifice. The good person and the offender are alike; the one who swears (falsely) is as the one who reveres the oath.

[3]This is the evil in all that is done under the sun: that there is one fate for all. So, too, the mind of human beings is full of evil; irrationality is in their mind when they are alive. {   } [4]Indeed, who is the one who chooses? Unto all the living there is certitude, {and unto the dead is finality}. Yes, a living dog is better than a dead lion, [5]inasmuch as the living know that they will die, but the dead do not know anything, they no longer have recompense; indeed, their reputation is forgotten. [6]Even their love, even their hatred, even their zeal have already perished; they will never again have a portion in all that is done under the sun.

[7]Go, eat your food in pleasure and drink your wine with a merry heart, for God has already favored what you have done. [8]Always let your garments be white, and let not oil be lacking upon your head. [9]Enjoy life with your beloved spouse all the days of your vain life which has been given to you under the sun <   >, for that is your portion in life and in your toil which you are toiling under the sun. [10]Everything which your hand finds to do, do it with your strength, for there is no action, or accounting, or knowledge, or wisdom in Sheol, whither you are going.

NOTES

9   1. *Indeed.* The translation of *kî* depends on how one interprets the relationship of this verse with the preceding. If v 1 continues the preceding thoughts,
then *kî* may be causal (so NASB: "*For* I have taken all this to my heart") or adversative (so RSV: "*But* all this I laid to heart"). If, however, v 1 begins a new unit,
then it should be taken as asseverative (so JB: "*Yes,* I have applied myself"). The
reference in 8:17 to the inability of the wise to know forms an *inclusio* with the
rhetorical question in 8:1, "who is so wise?" Thus, we may take 9:1 as beginning
a new unit and the phrase *'et-kol-zeh* "all this" as anticipatory; the phrase introduces the topic to be discussed in the verses that follow.

laid on my heart. Codex Leningrad has *'l lby,* which has the support of the
ancient versions (so LXX, Vulg, Targ). Many Hebrew MSS, however, read *'t lby,*
thus leveling to match the more common idiom in 1:13, 17; 8:9, 16. The reading
of Codex Leningrad should be retained. For the idiom *ntn 'l lb* "lay to heart/take
to heart," see Notes at 7:2.

even to examine all this. LXX (followed by SyrH and Copt) and Syr apparently
reflect Hebrew *wlby r'h* "and my heart saw," instead of *wlbwr 't* in MT. Many
commentators, therefore, emend MT accordingly (so Galling, Zimmerli). But it
is difficult to imagine why anyone seeing *wlby r'h,* would have read *wlbwr 't* instead, since the form *lbwr* is unique in Hebrew and its syntactical relation with
the preceding words is admittedly awkward. MT is clearly the *lectio difficilior.*
The other reading has probably been derived secondarily through the influence
of 1:16, which has *wlby r'h* "and my heart saw." It is an error prompted in part
by the graphic similarities of *waw* with *yod* on the one hand and *he* with *taw* on
the other. Thus, *wlbwr't — wlbwr 't* when properly divided — was read incorrectly
as *wlbyr'h* and then divided incorrectly as *wlby r'h* (so Delitzsch). The conjunction on *wlbwr* may be taken as the *waw explicativum* (GKC §154.a.Note 1). The
vocalization of MT suggests the root *bwr* (so BDB, p. 101; *HALAT,* p. 111),
which, if correct, occurs only here in the Hebrew Bible. The root is attested in
classical Arabic, however, where it may have the meaning "to examine, try, prove,
experience" (see Lane, *Arabic-English Lexicon,* Part 1, p. 274). Akkadian also
attests a related verb *bâru* "to become certain, proved, certified," which in the
D-stem means "to establish (something as true), to find" (see *CAD* II, pp. 125–
30). Targ correctly interprets the word here as *lmblš* "to examine" (it is not reading Hebrew *ltwr,* as it is sometimes suggested).

their works. Along with other nouns of the *qĕṭāl* pattern (see also *zĕmān* "time"
in 3:1 and *qĕrāb* "war" in 9:18), this word is to be regarded as an Aramaism, as
far as its morphology is concerned (Schoors, *Pleasing Words,* pp. 60–61). Zimmermann goes too far, however, when he contends that this word "was copied
almost directly from the Aramaic Vorlage" (*Inner World,* p. 155). According to
this view, the translator, who typically renders the Aramaic word with Hebrew
ma'ăśeh, simply failed to do so in this instance (so also Fox, *Contradictions,*
p. 256). But Hebrew *ma'ăśeh* in Ecclesiastes is always translated by the Aramaic
noun *'wbd* not *'bd* in Targ (1:14; 2:4, 11, 17; 3:17, 22; 4:3, 4; 5:5; 7:13; 8:9, 11,

14 [2x], 17 [2x]; 9:7, 10; 11:5; 12:14). At the same time, 'ăbādêhem in this passage is rendered in Aramaic as *tlmydyhwn* "their students." The Targumists apparently took the word here to be Hebrew 'abdêhem "their slaves"; they did not seem to have recognized 'ăbād as an Aramaic word. The word is, indeed, not listed in any of the standard lexicons for Jewish Aramaic. One can only speculate, there-fore, as to why the text has 'ăbādêhem instead of the expected form *ma'ăśehem*. Perhaps *ma'ăśeh* means "activity," whereas 'ăbād means "labor" or "effort." It is also possible, however, that no nuance was intended in the choice of the word here. The author simply uses variety for variety's sake. Also, the occasional substi-tution of an Aramaic word for a Hebrew one should occasion no surprise. Thus, too, in 9:18 we find the Aramaic form *qěrāb* "battle," whereas elsewhere in the book the author uses the Hebrew noun *milhāmâ* (3:8; 8:8; 9:11).

in the hand of God. To be "in the hand of God" is to be subject to God's power (see Prov 21:1; Deut 33:3; Wis 3:1). What is in the hand of God or comes from the hand of God is utterly unpredictable (cf. *miyyad hā'ělōhîm* "from the hand of God" in 2:24). In the *Gilgamesh Epic* it is said that the gods have ap-pointed death for all humanity while retaining life "in their hands" (Gilg M iii 3–4). In other words, everything depends on the sovereign power and will of the gods. In this passage from the *Gilgamesh Epic*, immediately following this ref-erence to the arbitrary power and will of the gods, is the exhortation to enjoy life.

both love and hate. Hebrew *gam-'ahăbâ gam-śin'â*. It is debatable whether it is human or divine love and hate that are at issue. Many scholars interpret this line to mean that no one knows *whether* anyone would receive divine favor *or* divine disfavor (so Podechard, Lohfink). Thus, NRSV has "whether it is love or hate one does not know" (cf. also NIV; NAB). But if that were the point, one should expect the Hebrew to have *'im . . . 'im*, instead of *gam . . . gam*. Moreover, in v 6 we have *gam 'ahăbātām gam-śin'ātām* "even their love, even their hatred," where *both* love and hate refer to human attitudes or even activities, rather than to God's favor and disfavor. Certainly in that context, Hebrew *gam . . . gam* does not indicate uncertain alternatives. We should, therefore, take love and hate in 9:1 as related to "their works." The point is that the righteous and the wise are in the hand of God — subject to God's power and will — together with their works, including both their love and their hate. When people die, their passions and their zeal go with them into the unknown (see v 6).

People do not know everything that is before them. The meaning of *lipnêhem* "before them," however, is unclear. It may be taken temporally: "before them" = "in advance" (so Vulg). Or, it may be interpreted spatially: "before them" = "before their eyes" (cf. Lauha, *Kohelet*, p. 166). If the former is correct, the point is that one cannot tell ahead of time what the outcome of anything will be, since everything is subject to the deity's sovereign will (i.e., "in the hand of God"). If the latter is correct, the author means that people do not always recognize all that they see. In other words, the judgment of God may turn out to be radically different from what one perceives in the present. Many commen-tators, however, prefer to read *lipnêhem* with the first word in v 2 (*hkl*), which is commonly emended to *hbl*, in accordance with LXX, Symm, and Syr — *hakkōl lipnêhem <hābel>* "everything before them is <vanity>." This reading may well be correct, but it is also possible that it is influenced by the ubiquitous judgment in the book that "everything is vanity." In cases like this — and there are many in this book — the exegete is compelled to make a choice purely on instincts. It is difficult to argue for one reading or the other. For now I am inclined to try and make sense of the reading in MT and also retain the versification in *BHS*.

2. *Everything is as for everyone.* Or "everything is the just same for everyone." Because of the difficulty in interpreting *hakkōl lipnêhem* in the preceding line, commentators frequently emend *hakkōl* at the beginning of v 2 to read *hābel* with LXX, Symm, and Syr, thus yielding *hakkōl lipnêhem hābel* "everything that is before them is vanity." But there is no need for this. For Hebrew *kᵊ'šr lkl*, LXX has *en tois pasin*, which is apparently an inner-Greek corruption from *en hois tois pasin*. This does not mean, however, that the *Vorlage* of LXX had *b'šr*, instead of *kᵊ'šr* here, for LXX typically renders Hebrew *kᵊ'šr* with the preposition *en* + a relative pronoun (so in 4:17 [Eng 5:1]; 8:16; 11:5). The expression *hkl kᵊ'šr lkl* simply means everything is the same for everyone. In other words, there is one fate for everyone.

<and the bad>. Adding *wlrᶜ* with LXX, which has *kai tǭ kakǭ* (also Syr *wlbyš'*; Vulg *et malo*). LXX of Ecclesiastes is too literalistic to have added a word simply for balance (see Fox, *Contradictions*, p. 257). MT reflects a haplography owing to homoioarcton. There is no evidence for dropping *laṭṭôb*, as has been suggested by Zapletal, Ginsburg, and many others.

the offender. See Notes at 2:26.

the one who swears (falsely). Hebrew *hannišbā'*, lit. "the one who swears." LXX *hōs ho omnyōn* "as the one who swears" is an idiomatic translation of *hnšbᶜ*; there is no need to assume that the *Vorlage(n)* of LXX, Syr, Targ, and Vulg may have been reading *knšbᶜ*. Even if *knšbᶜ* is a genuine variant, it must be regarded as secondary and owing to the influence of the surrounding words prefixed by the preposition *kᵊ-*: *ktwb khṭ'* ... *kᵊ'šr*. The reading in MT is probably original. The one who takes the oath is the one who does not respect the seriousness of the oath, namely, the perjurer. This is evident in the usage of *hnšbᶜ* in Zech 5:3–4. Cf. also Sir 23:9–12; Matt 5:33–37. Conversely, the one who fears the oath is the one who has the proper reverence for the seriousness of oaths (cf. 5:4 [Eng v 5]). Analogously, in Akkadian, the participle *tāmi* "one who swears" is normally used in the sense of one who swears *falsely* (see AHW, p. 1317). As in our passage in Ecclesiastes, so too a bilingual inscription in Akkadian and Hurrian found at Ras Shamra contrasts the reverence for the sacred oath with the readiness to commit perjury (see BWL, p. 116, lines 2–4).

the one who reveres the oath. The Hebrew idiom *yr' šbwᶜh* is semantically equivalent to Akkadian *palāḫu māmīta* "to revere the oath" (see AHW, p. 813), which is used in the Akkado-Hurrian parallel text cited above (BWL, p. 116, lines 2–4), where it is contrasted with "the one who swears (falsely)."

3. *This is the evil in all.* Ehrlich and many other commentators assume a hap-

lography of *he*, thus reading *zh <h> rᶜ bkl* instead of *zh rᶜ bkl*. But this move is unnecessary.

under the sun. See Notes at 1:3.

irrationality. For the meaning of *hôlēlôt*, see Notes at 2:12.

{   }. The last three words in v 3 have been incorrectly transposed from the following verse. MT makes no sense as it stands, despite the enthusiasm of some commentators who think that the verse is deliberately fragmentary and "breaks off like life itself" (Wildeboer; Crenshaw). The 3 ms suffix on *'aḥărāyw* contradicts the 3 mp suffixes in *bilbābām bĕḥayyêhem* "in their mind when they are alive." Even if one emends the suffix to read *'aḥărêhem* "after them" (following LXX, Copt, and Syr), the text makes no sense. Ehrlich takes *'aḥărāyw* to contain a fossilized suffix (like *yaḥdāw*), thus simply meaning "afterwards," while other scholars take the suffix to refer to God (see Schoors, *Pleasing Words*, pp. 118–19). But these explanations are strained.

4. *who is the one who chooses*. The *Ketib* has *ybḥr*, which has been interpreted as *yĕbuḥar* (Pual imperfect 3 ms) "is chosen," *yibbāḥēr* (Niphal imperfect 3 ms), or *yibḥar* (Qal imperfect 3 ms). The Pual form of the verb is unattested, however, and the Niphal does not mean "exempted," as is often suggested. Other commentators follow the *Qere*, some twenty Hebrew MSS, LXX, Symm, and Syr to read *yĕḥubbar* "is associated" or "is joined" (so KJV; RSV; NASB; JB; see also NEB: "counted among the living"; NJPS: "reckoned among the living"). The Targumists seem to have been divided on this problem: Sperber's edition has *ytbḥr* (following the *Ketib*), but Lagarde has *'tḥbr* (following *Qere*). The reading of *Ketib* makes the most sense as the Qal imperfect: *mî 'ăšer yibḥar* "who is the one who chooses?" This is simply another of Qohelet's many rhetorical questions. Note that both LXX, Symm, and Vulg assume an interrogative, and compare the usage of *mî 'ăšer* "who is the one" in Judg 21:5. The implicit answer is that no one — that is, no human being — has a choice in the matter. It is not the mortal who chooses, but the sovereign deity.

certitude. The word *biṭṭāḥôn* does not mean "hope," as most translations have it (RSV; NIV; NASB). It is not "something to look forward to" (NJPS) or something that is a wish. Rather, the word refers to one's confidence or certitude that something will happen (see 2 Kgs 18:19 // Isa 36:4 and, in the Talmud, *y. Ber.* ix, 13; *b. Šabb.* 139a).

{*and unto the dead is finality*}. Or, "unto the dead is the end." Reading *w'ḥry < > 'l-ḥmtym*, instead of MT's *w'ḥryw 'l-ḥmtym* "after it unto the dead," which is incorrectly transposed to the end of v 3. In a tablet from Ugarit, a cemetery is called A.ŠÀᵐᵉˢ *ša uḫ-ra-a-yi* "fields of finality" (*PRU* 3 52f:17–18), and in another Ugaritic text one reads: *wuḥry ykly rsp* "And Resheph will destroy him fatally (lit. 'to the end')" (*KTU* 1.103.39–40). In Arabic, *'al-'uḫrāy* means "the end, the ultimate" (Lane, *Arabic-English Lexicon*, Part 1, p. 32). Thus, we have the appropriate pairing of *biṭṭāḥôn* "certitude" and *'aḥărāy* (?) "finality" (cf. Symm *ta de teleutata autōn* and Targ *wbtr swpyhy*, where a noun is assumed). Qohelet is using bitter irony here, arguing that there is really not much difference between the living and the dead: the living have a certitude — of death; the dead have the finality of the grave. If this reconstruction is correct, we may note the threefold pairing of "the living" and "the dead" in vv 4–5:

v 4a	*'el-kōl haḥayyîm*	// *'el-hammētîm* (v 3 in MT)
v 4b	*ḥay*	// *hammēt*
v 5	*ḥayyîm*	// *hammētîm*

Yes, a living dog is better than a dead lion. The *lāmed* of *lĕkeleb* is emphatic, so the expression *lĕkeleb . . . tôb min* does not mean "it is better *for* a living dog" (see J. Huehnegard, "Asseverative **la* and Hypothetical **lu/law* in Semitic," *JAOS* 103 [1983], p. 591). The use of the dog as a metaphor for the living is ironic. Dogs were among the most despised of creatures in the ancient Near East. Together with the pig, they were not to be offered as sacrifice. Rather, they were regarded as scavengers. In contrast, the lion is regarded as the most admired of creatures. The irony is especially bitter, since dogs may have been associated with death and the underworld (see M. H. Pope, *Song of Songs* [AB 7C; Garden City, New York: Doubleday, 1977], pp. 210–14).

5. *recompense.* Hebrew *śākār* is perhaps to be understood economically here, meaning "wages." Cf. 4:9, where *śākār* may refer to wages for hired labor.

their reputation. Hebrew *zikrām*, lit. "their memory" or "their name," as in Akkadian *zikru* "mention, name, fame" (*CAD* XXI, pp. 112–16). See also Isa 26:14 on the fate of the dead: God will cause their reputation (*zēker*) to perish (cf. Ps 6:6 [Eng v 5]). One may compare the description in Wis 2:4 of what happens when one dies: "Our name will be forgotten in time, and no one will remember our works."

6. *portion.* See also Notes and Comment at 2:10.

under the sun. See Notes at 1:3.

7. *with a merry heart.* See Notes on *wîṭîbĕkā libbĕkā* "let your heart delight you" in 11:9. Cf. also the expression *tôb lēb* "merry of heart" in Esth 5:9.

8. *Always let your garments be white.* That is, let your garments be fresh and bright. Clean garments indicate a good life (so "white/bright garment" symbolizes the good life in the *Tale of Sinuhe* [Text B 153], translated in *AEL* I, p. 228). In a parallel passage from the *Gilgamesh Epic* (cited in full below), one reads: "let your garments be clean, let your hair be washed" (Gilg M iii 10).

9. *Enjoy life.* See Notes at 2:1.

your beloved spouse. Hebrew *'iššâ 'ăšer-'āhabtā*, lit. "a woman/wife whom you love." Some interpreters think that *'iššâ* without the article simply refers to any woman, rather than to one's wife (e.g., Whitley). Yet, *'iššâ* by itself (without the definite article) may refer to one's wife when the context demands it (e.g., Gen 30:4, 9; 1 Sam 25:43; Deut 22:22). It may be pertinent to note, too, that the Akkadian word in the *Gilgamesh Epic* is *marḫitu* "wife," rather than *sinništu* "woman."

vain life. See Notes and Comments at 1.3. The noun *hebel* here no doubt refers to the ephemerality of life.

has been given. We may take *nātan* impersonally to mean "one has given" and, hence, freely translate: "has been given." The subject, however, is no doubt God, who is mentioned in v 7. The object of the verb is the enjoyment of life (see 3:18 [Eng v 19]).

under the sun. See Notes at 1:3.

< >. The Hebrew text has *kōl yĕmê heblekā* "all your vain days," which should probably be deleted as an instance of vertical dittography. Several Hebrew MSS, LXX^A, OL, Targ, and Jerome omit the phrase. LXX^BP read *pasai hēmerai hēmerai (sic) atmou sou.*

your portion. See Notes and Comment at 2:10.

in life. LXX "in your life" does not necessarily reflect a different reading in the *Vorlage*. Rather, the Greek translators may simply be rendering the sense of the idiom.

under the sun. See Notes at 1:3.

10. *Which your hand finds to do.* This saying has to do with ability, rather than the luck of the draw (cf. Lev 12:8; 25:28; 1 Sam 10:7; 25:8; Judg 9:33; Isa 10:10).

do it with your strength. The Masoretic punctuation suggests that *bĕkōḥăkā* is to be read with the infinitive *laʿăśôt:* "Whatever your hand finds to do with strength, do!" We should, however, follow several MSS, Syr, and Vulg in taking *bĕkōḥăkā* with the imperative *ʿăśēh:* "Whatever your hand finds to do, do with strength!" The point is that one should wholeheartedly do whatever one is able to do. LXX has *hōs hē dynamis sou,* which may reflect Hebrew *kkḥk* "according to your strength." This is possibly a genuine variant, but it makes no difference in our interpretation. The point is that one should do whatever one is able to do, nothing more and nothing less.

accounting. See Notes at 7:25.

COMMENT

The passage consists of two sections: the first (vv 1–6) affirms that all mortals face the common fate of death, regardless of their character; the second (vv 7–10) contains a call to enjoy life while one is still able to do so. In terms of linguistic clues, one notes that the three references to life in the first section (vv 4–5) are matched by three in the second (v 9). The first section ends by pointing to what the dead will not have (vv 5–6). The second ends by pointing to what will not be in Sheol, where all mortals must go after life on earth (v 10). The statement that the dead never again will have a portion (v 6), is answered by the affirmation of enjoyment as the portion of the living (v 9). This portion in life, it seems, is the primary difference between the dead and the living.

One Fate for All (9:1–6)

The beginning of the passage is difficult. There are all kinds of textual, syntactical, and interpretive problems. Nevertheless, the issue that these verses raise seems clear enough: it is the fact that there is a common fate for everyone. The text begins by noting the common fate of the righteous and the wise: they and all their works are "in the hand of God, (including) both love and hate" (v 1). This is an admission that human beings do not know the consequences of their actions, for they and their passions and deeds are all "in the hand of God." One does not know that the righteous and the wise will be better off than the wicked and the foolish. What is meant by "love and hate" in this verse is, however, ambiguous. A number of commentators are of the view that love and hate refer to divine favor or disfavor, respectively. That is to say, the righteous and the wise are in the hand of God like everyone else, and no one can predict what God's response will be — it may be love or it may be hate. At the same time the author says in v 6 that when people die, "even their love, even their hate, even their zeal" will perish with them. There it seems clear that human love and hate are meant.

One should not, however, interpret love and hate as purely emotional terms. Rather, love and hate in Hebrew psychology are attitudes that generate certain actions (see Pss 25:19; 109:3–5; 139:21–22; Prov 10:12; 26:26). One may interpret love and hate in v 1, therefore, as further definitions of the works of the righteous and the wise. All these works, both of love and of hate, are perplexingly "in the hand of God." As for mortals, the author says they do not know "everything that is before them."

The meaning of the saying is also obscure. Perhaps what is meant is that people's perceptions of their own works and attitudes may not be the total reality. They do what they do, and they think what they think, but they do not really know the significance or outcome of their deeds and thoughts. In other words, what you see may not be what you get. No one knows the will or the intention of the deity. God may perceive love and hate differently from humans. The issue is stated thus in the pessimistic Babylonian wisdom text known as *Ludlul Bēl Nēmeqi* ("I will Praise the Lord of Wisdom"):

> I wish I knew that these things were pleasing to one's god!
> What is proper to oneself is an offence to one's god,
> What in one's own heart seems despicable is proper to one's god.
> Who knows the will of the gods in heaven?
> Who understands the plans of the underworld gods?
> Where have mortals learnt the way of a god?
> He who is alive yesterday is dead today.
>
> (*BWL*, pp. 40–41, lines 33–39)

As in the Babylonian text, the problem in Ecclesiastes is that there seems to be no formula that allows people to determine the consequences of their works. What seems to be good to humans may be regarded as bad in the eyes of the deity, and what seems bad may turn out to be good in divine judgment. Mortals simply do not know what is before them, for everything seems to depend on the whimsical will of the deity. There are no rules that will guarantee one certain desired results. The righteous and wise cannot know for sure that they will be better off. Indeed, as far as human beings can tell, the end is the same for everyone; there is a common fate for all mortals (v 2).

As elsewhere in the book, the "one fate" here refers to death as the great leveler. In 2:14–15, the fool and the wise are said to have "one fate," inasmuch as they all die. In 3:19, it is said that human beings have the same fate as animals, since they all die. Now the author reiterates that there is one fate for everyone: the righteous as the wicked, the good as the bad, the one who is religiously observant and the one who is not. When it comes to death, nothing that one learns from priests, prophets, or sages really matters. In the end one's cultic, ethical, or practical conduct seems to make no difference, since there is one fate for all.

This commonness of fate is judged by Qohelet to be "the evil in all that is done under the sun" (v 3). What is meant is not that there is something bad in every act, but that the quality of human deeds does not seem to matter in the end. Whatever is done, the end is the same bad fate: death. The evil is in the injustice of this sameness.

Significantly, that injustice is blamed for the presence of human evil: as there is evil in the fact that there is one fate for all (v 3a), "so too" (*wĕgam*) the mind of humanity is full of evil (v 3b). The reference to the evil in the human mind is reminiscent of the reason given for the destruction of the world by the great deluge (Gen 6:5). Destruction would have been total had it not been for the righteousness of one good person, Noah. Because of this person's righteousness, so the story goes, a remnant of earth's creatures was kept alive, including animals both clean and unclean.

Qohelet, however, seems to challenge that tradition. For him, righteousness makes no difference whatsoever in humanity's efforts to avert the fate of death (see also 7:15). The righteous die with the wicked, the clean with the unclean, those who sacrifice with those who do not. Ironically, too, it is not the fullness of evil that leads to death, as is the case in the flood story. Indeed, the opposite is true: it is the common fate of death that leads to the fullness of evil. It is not that evil leads to death, but the inequity of death as a common fate that leads to evil. It is the inequity of death's leveling effect that explains the fullness of evil in the human mind. This is essentially the same sentiment as in 8:11, where the delay of retribution causes the wicked to do even more evil. But whereas in 8:11 the injustice is evident in the treatment of people while they are alive, in 9:3 it is evident in the common experience of death. Injustice prevails up to and including death.

Through the use of a rhetorical question, the author makes plain his conviction that life and death are not a matter of choice for people: "who is the one who chooses?" (see Notes at v 4). This use of the language of choice, particularly as it pertains to life and death, is perhaps intended to recall traditional exhortations to make the right decisions in any moral dilemma: "choose life that you may live!" (Deut 30:19). In Deuteronomic theology, the options are presented as "life and good" or "death and evil" (Deut 30:15), and one is called upon to choose one or the other. But, for Qohelet, the leveling effect of death makes a mockery of such exhortations, if they are taken literally. The choice does not belong to mortals. Our passage deliberately gives the initial impression that life and death are polarities that can be clearly identified (vv 4–5):

to the living there is certitude	to the dead there is finality
a living dog	a dead lion
the living know	the dead do not know

In Deuteronomic theology the contrast between life and death is stark: life means good and blessings, death means evil and curses. The polarities are well defined. Qohelet's perspective, by contrast, is tempered by the realities of life's pain. There is no idealization of life or exaggeration of its blessings or goodness. The author says that the living have something in which they can have confidence, whereas for the dead all is at an end (v 4). The dead do not know anything, but the living know that they will die (v 5). The one thing that mortals trust and know is that they will die! His point seems to be that life and death are not poles apart after all. They only appear that way. It is not that life is blessings and death curses, and that people can choose one or the other. For Qohelet, people have no choice but to live — to live till they die. The contrast between life and death is not between good and evil, or blessings and curses. Rather, it is the difference between possibilities and impossibilities. For the dead, there are only impossibilities. There is no more reward and no more reputation. In death all is gone, "even love, even hate, even zeal" (v 6). The dead will never again have a portion, namely, whatever life has to offer. For the living, however, there are still some possibilities, however uncertain, however elusive, however unsatisfactory. There is still the possibility of enjoyment.

Carpe Diem (9:7–10)

The only appropriate response to the certainty of death is to enjoy life while one is able to do so. The call to enjoy life includes feasting (v 7), fresh clothes (v 8a), oil upon one's head (v 8b), and the love of one's family (v 9). These are precisely the kinds of things enjoined in the *Gilgamesh Epic*, as evident in the speech by Šiduri, the tavern keeper:

As for you, Gilgamesh, let your belly be full,
Enjoy yourself day and night.
Find enjoyment every day,
Dance and play day and night.
Let your garments be clean,
Let your head be washed; bathe in water.
Look upon the little one who holds your hand,
Let your spouse enjoy herself in your embrace!

(Gilg M iii 6–14; see ANET³, p. 90)

It is remarkable that this passage in the *Gilgamesh Epic* contains not only the same items that we find in Qohelet's call for enjoyment, but the items appear in the same order: (1) feasting, (2) fresh clothing, (3) washing one's head, and (4) family. Moreover, the point of the passage in *Gilgamesh,* as also in Ecclesiastes, is that life is something that mortals cannot hold on to forever. Immortality is something that human beings cannot find; people cannot live forever. And so one must make the most of the present. The gods have ordained death for all humanity, retaining life "in their own hands" (see *ANET*³, p. 90). Everything is in the hand of the gods (see 9:1).

Similar attitudes are reflected in the genre of Egyptian texts known as "Harpers' Songs," inscriptions that reflected on death and sometimes on the impossibility of immortality. In the face of the inevitable fate of death, the living are urged to enjoy themselves while they are able (see *AEL* I, pp. 196–97). Likewise, in a late Hellenistic tomb found in Jerusalem, one finds an inscription urging those who are alive to enjoy themselves: "You who are living, Enjoy!" (see P. Benoit, "L'Inscription Greque du Tombeau de Jason," *IEJ* 17 [1967], pp. 112–13).

For Qohelet, too, people ought to enjoy life precisely because life is ephemeral. This, he says, is the *portion* of humanity in life (v 9), a *portion* that the dead no longer have (v 6). That is the difference between the living and the dead: the living still have a portion (the possibility of enjoyment), the dead do not. Therefore, one is urged to do vigorously all that one is able (v 10), for in Sheol there will no longer be the possibilities and opportunities that one may find on earth. However bad things may seem on earth, there is still the possibility of good.

II.B.2. THE WORLD IS FULL OF RISKS (9:11–10:15)

¹¹Further I have observed under the sun that the race does not belong to the swift, nor the battle to the valiant. So, too, bread does not belong to the wise, nor wealth to the intelligent, nor favor to the clever, for a timely incident befalls them all. ¹²For, indeed, people do not know their time; like fish taken in a terrible net, and like birds caught in a snare, so humans are trapped at a time of calamity, when it falls upon them suddenly.

¹³This, too, I have observed about wisdom under the sun, and it seemed great to me. ¹⁴There was a little town with a few persons in it; and a great king came to it and besieged it and built great <siegeworks> against it. ¹⁵And there was a wise commoner therein, and he might have delivered the town through his wisdom; but no one gave thought to that commoner. ¹⁶So I thought, wisdom is better than might, but the wisdom of the commoner is despised and his words are not heeded. ¹⁷The words of the wise in calmness are heeded more than the ranting of a ruler among fools. ¹⁸Wisdom is better than weapons of war, but a single offender destroys much good. 10¹A fly that dies causes <a bowl of> perfumer's oil to turn rancid; a little folly outweighs wisdom and honor. ²The mind of the wise is to their right; the mind of fools is to their left. ³Yea, even on the way, when

fools travel, their minds are deficient and they tell everyone they are fools. ⁴If the ruler's temper is aroused against you, do not leave your place, for calmness allays great offenses.

⁵There is an evil that I have observed under the sun, a veritable mistake stemming from the proprietor. ⁶The simpleton is set in great heights, but the rich abide in low estate. ⁷I have seen slaves on horses, but princes walk on foot like slaves. ⁸One who digs a pit may fall into it, and one who breaks down a wall may be bitten by a snake. ⁹One who quarries stones may be injured by them, one who splits logs may be endangered by them. ¹⁰If an implement is blunt and one does not sharpen it first, then one must exert more force. It is an advantage to appropriate wisdom. ¹¹If a snake that cannot be charmed bites, then there is no advantage for a charmer.

¹²The words from the mouth of the wise bring favor, but the lips of fools consume them. ¹³The words from their mouth begin in folly, their talk ends in terrible irrationality. ¹⁴Yet the fool multiplies words! No one knows what will happen, and who can tell what will happen hereafter? ¹⁵The toil of fools wearies them, for they do not know the way to town.

NOTES

9   11. *Further I have observed.* Hebrew *šabtî wĕrā'ōh*. Here *rā'ōh* is another instance of the infinitive absolute used in place of a finite verb. See Notes at 4:2 and 8:9. Thus, the expression *šabtî wĕrā'ōh* means the same thing as *wĕšabtî 'ănî wā'er'eh* in 4:1, 7, even as *nātôn 'et-libbî* in 8:9 means the same thing as *nātattî 'et-libbî* in 8:16. The use of *šabtî*, lit. "I turned," probably indicates a new section, despite the presence of a *sĕtûmâ* at the end of v 10 in Codex Leningrad (we expect a *pĕtûḥâ*).

under the sun. This is another instance of anticipation of what is to follow (see Gordis, *Koheleth*, p. 308). For the expression "under the sun," see Notes at 1:3.

the race does not belong to the swift. The word *mērôṣ* does not occur anywhere else in classical Hebrew. It is probably to be compared with Ethiopic *mĕrwāṣ* "race, course, contest" (see Leslau, *Comparative Dictionary of Ge'ez*, p. 477). The race in this context is probably not an athletic contest, however, as it is often suggested. There is no allusion here to a Hellenistic athletic event. In the Bible, "the swift" may refer to horses used in battles (Isa 30:16; Jer 46:6), or to people in a deadly pursuit (see 2 Sam 2:18–19; Amos 2:14–16). The point is that there is no guarantee that the fastest persons in a chase will become victorious. In 2 Sam 2:18–23, the swift-footed Asahel turned out to be a loser in his pursuit of Abner: he was killed in the end. The race certainly did not belong to the swift in that case.

battle. Just as "the race" meant victory in the race, here victory in war is meant (cf. Symm: *to kratēsai polemou*). Heroes are not assured of triumphs.

bread does not belong to the wise. In the wisdom literature of the Bible, availability of food is contrasted with poverty (Prov 20:13; 28:19); the fool may become poor and starve, but the wise will not lack sustenance.

favor. Hebrew *ḥēn* is attested in all the ancient versions; emendation to *hōn* "wealth" (to parallel *ʿōšer*) is without textual evidence and unnecessary. Cf. Prov 13:15, "good sense wins favor" (so NJPS). It is also possible that *ḥēn* is understood in the sense of "respect" (see Prov 3:4, 34; 28:23; Lam 4:16).

clever. This meaning of the participle of *ydʿ* is attested in Prov 28:2; Neh 10:29 (Eng v 28); 2 Chron 2:11 (Eng v 12); Sir 40:29. Alternatively, one may read *yĕdūʿîm* "experienced ones" and note the coordination of *ḥăkāmîm* and *nĕbônîm* with *yĕdūʿîm* in Deut 1:13, 15. A significant number of MSS, however, have *ywdʿym*, supporting the reading in Codex Leningrad. Cf. also the combination of *daʿat*, *bînâ*, and *ḥokmâ* in Isa 11:2.

a timely incident. Taking *ʿēt wāpegaʿ* as a hendiadys, lit. "a time and an incident" (so Galling). The word *pegaʿ* occurs only one other time in the Hebrew Bible—in 1 Kgs 5:18 [Eng v 4], where *pegaʿ raʿ* refers to a misfortune. Since the verb *pāgaʿ* means "to meet, encounter," the noun *pegaʿ* by itself simply means "incident," or, better, "accident," in the proper sense of something that happens by chance (Latin *accidens*, cf. *accidere* "to happen" from *ad* + *cadere* "to fall"). Like the English word "accident," however, the word *pegaʿ* tends to have negative connotations in Postbiblical Hebrew, referring to tragic incidents (see Jastrow, *Dictionary*, p. 1135).

12. *terrible net.* Even though *rāʿâ* in *bimṣôdâ rāʿâ* is lacking in Vulg, we cannot delete it, as Galling and Lauha do. Cf. *mĕṣôd rāʿîm* in Prov 12:12. It is true that the adjective is repeated in *lĕʿēt rāʿâ* in the next line, but the repetition is probably deliberate. One may speculate that the omission in Vulg was based on a defective Hebrew MS, in which the word *rʿh* was accidentally left out through haplography—homoioteleuton.

snare. The snare (*paḥ*) refers probably to a self-springing bird trap. Although it is technically possible to escape such traps (see Ps 124:7), the suddenness with which they work make them especially deadly (see Amos 3:5; Prov 7:23). Once the trap springs, there is little chance of escape.

so. Hebrew *kāhēm*, lit. "like them," perhaps meaning "as such" (2 Sam 24:3 = 1 Chron 21:3; 2 Chron 9:11). Syr has *hkn'* "thus, so," a proper interpretation of the word (see Whitley, *Koheleth*, p. 81). Some scholars, however, prefer to read *kōh* (citing Syr) and take the *mēm* with the following word: thus *kh mywqšym* instead of *khm ywqšym* (Podechard, Hertzberg, Gordis).

are trapped. There is no need to emend *yûqāšîm* or to take it as a Pual participle without the *mēm*-prefix, as is usually done. The form is to be analyzed as a participle of the old Qal passive (see BL §38.o–p; Schoors, *Pleasing Words*, p. 78). Cf. *ywld* (Judg 13:8); *mwrṭ* (Isa 18:2, 7).

when it falls. Hebrew *kĕšettippôl* = *kaʾăšer tippôl*. The subject of the verb is probably *mĕṣôdâ rāʿâ* "the terrible net." The author is thinking of a fishing net cast upon the waters (see Matt 13:47), but one may also compare *mĕṣûdô ʿālay* "his net is upon me" in Job 19:6. Cf. also Ezek 12:13; 17:20.

13. *about wisdom.* We cannot delete *ḥokmâ*, as some have suggested (Jastrow). Nor is it grammatically justifiable to translate *zōh . . . ḥokmâ* as "this wisdom" (so Vulg); the word order makes such an interpretation improbable. Rather, *ḥokmâ*

is to be taken as the accusative of specification, thus, "I have seen this, specifically, of wisdom" (see Joüon-Muraoka §126.g). Cf. LXX: *kai ge touto idon sophian* "and this, too, I saw — wisdom."

under the sun. See Notes at 1:3.

great. The word *gĕdôlâ* anticipates *gādôl* and *gĕdōlîm* in v 14 and, indeed, the whole discussion of matters great and small, of insignificant things that have great consequences and of apparently great things that are of little real importance (9:13–10:4). We should not, therefore, emend the word (so Driver, "Problems and Solutions," p. 231). The adjective here means "great" in the sense of being "important" or "significant" (cf. Jon 3:3; Esth 10:3). Cf. Symm: *megalē dokei moi* "it seems great to me."

14. *to it.* Instead of *'ēleyhā* "to it," some Hebrew MSS read *'āleyhā* "against it" or "over it." The latter interpretation prompted Ibn Ezra to conjecture that the city was built on a slope, thus enabling the enemy to build bulwarks overlooking the city. But *'ēleyhā* is the superior reading; *'āleyhā* is interpretive and anticipates *ûbānâ 'āleyhā* in the next line.

<*siegeworks*>. Reading *mĕṣûrîm* with two Hebrew MSS, LXX, Symm, Syr, and Vulg. The form *mĕṣôdîm* — properly "net" (see Job 19:6; Eccl 7:26) — does not make sense here; it is due to the influence of *mĕṣôdîm* "nets" in 7:26 and *mĕṣôdâ* "net" in 9:12. The form *mĕṣôdîm* is sometimes thought to be related to *mĕṣûdâ* or *mĕṣād*, whose plurals are always *mĕṣûdôt* and *mĕṣādôt*, respectively, never with an -*îm* ending. If *mĕṣôdîm* does mean "stronghold," it is unique in classical Hebrew. Moreover, the word *mĕṣûdâ* (like *mĕṣād*) is always associated with defense, security, and inaccessibility. It is never used in the sense of a siege-tower, siege-ramp, or the like. It is inappropriate to speak of an invader building a "stronghold" (i.e., a defensive structure) against a city. Nowhere in Hebrew do we have reference to a *mĕṣād* or *mĕṣûdâ* used against (*'al*) a city. By contrast, both *māṣôr* and *mĕṣûrâ* may be used of offensive machines (see BDB, pp. 848–49). In Deut 20:20 we have the expression *ûbānîtā māṣôr 'al-hā'îr* "you build a siege-work against the city" (cf. *māṣôr 'al* "a siege-work against" in Mic 4:14; Ezek 4:2). These terms probably refer to the movable assault towers, such as those used by the Assyrians (see Y. Yadin, *The Art of Warfare in Biblical Lands* II [New York: McGraw-Hill, 1963], pp. 390–93). In the Aramaic inscription of Zakkur, *mṣr* is also used in the sense of a siege-work (see *KAI* 202.A.9, 15), as it is in the recently discovered inscription from Tell Dan (A. Biran and J. Naveh, "An Aramaic Stele Fragment from Tell Dan," *IEJ* 43 [1993], pp. 81–98 [see *mṣr 'l* in line 13 of the inscription]). The *mṣwr/mṣwrh*, an offensive machine, must be distinguished from the *mṣd/mṣwd/mṣwdh*, a defensive structure.

15. *there was.* Hebrew *māṣā' bāh*, lit. "one found in it." Vulg, Syr, and Targ all translate the verb as passive, but this does not indicate that a Niphal form of the verb was read. We should not emend to read *nimṣā'* (with Galling and Kroeber) or repoint the form as a Pual passive (Driver) or Qal passive (see Whitley, *Koheleth*, pp. 81–82). For the translation of this clause, we may compare the following: *lō'-māṣā' 'ēzer* "one did not find a helper" = "a helper was not found" = "there was no helper" (Gen 2:20). See also Notes on *yō'mar* "one said" at 1:10.

LXX reads the verb as active, although it assumes the subject to be the king. Some commentators follow this interpretation. So, recently, Fox takes the verb to refer to the king, but he interprets *māṣā'* to mean "apprehend": "and in it he (the king) apprehended a man who was poor but wise" (*Contradictions*, pp. 261–62). It is doubtful, however, if *māṣā'* means to physically "apprehend" in Biblical Hebrew.

a wise commoner. The word *miskēn* is a noun referring to someone who is not among the elite of society: the *miskēn* (Akkadian *muškēnu*) is typically contrasted with rulers and nobles (see Notes at 4:13) and, thus, is the ancient Palestinian equivalent of the smallholder, homesteader, or tenant. The word does not strictly mean "poor." The nouns *'îš* and *miskēn* are in apposition (cf. *'îš lēwî* "a man, a Levite," Judg 19:1), and *ḥākām* is simply the adjective qualifying *'îš miskēn*. Likewise, *hā'îš hammiskēn* at the end of v 15 must be interpreted as nouns in apposition. Many Hebrew MSS, LXX^A, Vulg, and Targ read *wĕḥākām*, instead of *ḥākām*, apparently taking *miskēn* also as an adjective (thus "a poor but wise man," or the like), but Syr supports MT.

and he might have delivered. Hebrew *ûmillaṭ-hû'*. On the verb + independent pronoun construction, cf. *'āmartî 'ănî* in the next verse and see Notes on *dibbartî 'ănî* at 1:16. The perfect is used here to indicate a hypothetical situation (what might have happened), as it sometimes does in Biblical and Mishnaic Hebrew (see GKC §106.p). Indeed in Mishnaic Hebrew, such hypothetical sentences are very frequently unmarked, as is the case here (see Segal, *A Grammar of Mishnaic Hebrew*, §310). In part, the translation depends on how one interprets what follows, specifically, how one understands the verb *zākar*. If one takes *wĕ'ādām lō' zākar* to mean "but no one remembered him," then one must assume *ûmillaṭ-hû'* to indicate also a past situation: i.e., "he delivered . . . but no one remembered him" (so RSV; REB; NIV). Yet, *wĕ'ādām lo' zākar* could be taken to mean "no one brought him to mind," that is, "no one thought of him" (so NJPS).

no one gave thought to that commoner. The verb *zākar* is found in parallelism with *śîm 'al lēb* "to take to heart" (cf. Isa 47:7; 57:11), *he'ĕlâ 'al lēb* "to raise to mind" (Isa 65:17; Jer 3:16), *śîaḥ* "to consider" (Ps 77:4, 7 [Eng vv 5, 8]), and *bîn* "to pay attention" (Deut 32:7; Isa 43:18). Indeed, Qohelet himself uses *zākar* in this sense in 5:19 (Eng v 18), 11:8, and 12:1. Here in 9:15 he means that no one thought to consult or to pay attention to the commoner, even though they had known of him as a sage. This meaning of *wĕ'ādām lō' zākar* is confirmed in the next verse (v 16). Fox objects, however, that Qohelet could not have been talking about a hypothetical situation, since "[t]he reader would certainly wonder how Qohelet could know that the wise man *could* have done this" (*Contradictions*, p. 263). And so Fox prefers to interpret the verse to say that no one *remembered* what Qohelet had in fact accomplished. But Fox is unnecessarily second-guessing the ancient readers. If the readers were so literalistic, they would, likewise, have wondered how Qohelet could have remembered the incident, when he himself just said that no one did. The ancient reader, as does the modern, understands Qohelet to be the "omniscient narrator" who knows all the facts of the story and lays them out as he deems appropriate. In this case, one presumes

that Qohelet knew the plan of the sage and he judged that it might have succeeded, if it had been given a chance. D. N. Freedman has reminded me that we
have an analogy to this hypothetical situation in Ahitophel's advice to Absalom in
2 Samuel 16–17. The advice of Ahitophel was ignored, so we do not know how
things would have turned out. Nevertheless, the narrator in that passage is very
confident that Ahitophel's advice was sound, and that if it had been followed,
Absalom would have succeeded and David would have been defeated. Within
the confines of the story, it is important for the narrator to establish that Ahitophel's advice was sound and that it would have succeeded. The author knows
very well what the outcome would have been because he is the "omniscient narrator." Even if the story was based on historical reality, it has been shaped by the
narrator's purpose.

17. *in calmness.* The calmness here probably refers to the delivery of the words
(so NJPS: "words softly spoken"), rather than their reception (so RSV has "heard
in quiet," although NRSV has "quiet words"). The contrast is between the calm
words of the wise and the loud rantings of the ruler among fools. The Masoretic
punctuation supports this interpretation.

a ruler among fools. There is some ambiguity in the expression *môšēl bak-
kĕsîlîm*: it may be taken to mean either "a ruler of fools" (NAB; NIV; JB: "Someone commanding an army of fools") or "a ruler among fools" (RSV; NASB;
NEB) — that is, a chief fool. The ambiguity is perhaps deliberate. If the ruler is
considered a fool, indeed, the chief fool, he is also the offensive one (*ḥôṭe'*) who
singly destroys much good (v 18).

18. *offender.* See Note at 2:26 on the spelling of *ḥôṭe'* and its meaning. Instead
of *ḥôṭe'*, Syr assumes *ḥēṭ'* "sin," a reading favored by many scholars (so NJPS: "a
single error"; NEB: "a single mistake"; JB: "a single sin"). But the best Hebrew
MSS support MT (reading *ḥwṭ'*), as do LXX and Targ. In fact, the "offender"
probably refers to the "ruler among fools" mentioned in the preceding verse.

10 1. *A fly that dies.* Reading *zĕbûb yāmût* as an asyndetic relative clause (so
Delitzsch, Galling, Lauha), like *'ĕnôš yāmût* "a mortal who dies" (Isa 51:12).
MT's *zĕbûbê māwet*, lit. "flies of Death," has usually been taken to mean "dead
flies" (cf. Symm, Vulg, Syr, and Jerome) and is often presumed to be analogous
with *'îš māwet* (1 Kgs 2:26), *'anšê-māwet* (2 Sam 19:29), *ben-māwet* (1 Sam 20:31;
2 Sam 12:5), and *bĕnê-māwet* (1 Sam 26:16). But the analogy is not entirely satisfactory. Without exception, these expressions occur in denigrations and insults.
Moreover, *māwet* in such expressions is an allusion to the god, Mot (Death), the
Canaanite deity of death and the king of the netherworld (cf. 2 Sam 22:5, 6; Job
18:13; Pss 7:14; 18:5; 116:3; Prov 13:14; 14:27). In any case, *zĕbûbê māwet* does
not mean "dead flies," which would have been expressed by Hebrew *zĕbûbîm
mētîm*, as Gordis has observed (*Koheleth*, p. 314).

Furthermore, as Fox notes, "flies are not deadly and in any case their deadli-
ness would not spoil the ointment; nor is it relevant that they are doomed" (*Contradictions*, p. 264). This verse seems to be making the same point as the preceding and following verses: that a single or a little thing that is bad may outweigh a
whole lot of good. It is best, therefore, to assume that the Hebrew text as we have

it reflects a misdivision of the consonants because the asyndeton had not been properly understood. There are other instances in the book of misdivisions of words (see Notes at 5:6 [Eng v 7]; 7:19, 27; 8:1). The singular *zĕbûb* — attested in Targ, *kdybb'* "like a fly" — is in agreement with the masculine singular verb *yab'îš* ("causes to turn rancid") and is an appropriate parallel for the singular noun *siklût* "foolishness," whereas the plural noun "flies" poses a grave syntactical problem.

<*a bowl of*>. The form *yabbîaʿ* in MT is problematic. It appears to be related to the root *nbʿ* "to burst forth, spring forth, gush." Hence, it is usually assumed to mean "to bubble" and, hence, secondarily, "to ferment." The verb is assumed to be asyndetically linked to the preceding: "causes to turn rancid (and) ferments." Some scholars invoke Arabic *baġaġa* or *baġġa* "to emit, effervesce" (so Driver, "Problems and Solutions," pp. 231–32), but the existence of this verb in Hebrew is highly questionable. The word is omitted in Symm, Targ, and Vulg, perhaps because it was perceived to be redundant. Accordingly, it is frequently deleted as an explicatory gloss or some sort of a dittography (so Barton, Galling, Lauha). There is some indication, however, that the word is taken as a noun instead of a verb. Thus, Syr has *m'n'* "vessel" and LXX has *skeuasia* "preparation," perhaps an inner Greek error for *skeuos* "vessel" (so Horst in *BHS*). It is possible that the original text may have had *gābîaʿ* "cup, bowl." The confusion of *yod* and *gimel* is not surprising, since the two were graphically similar in several scribal hands from the third century B.C.E. on (e.g., *byt* "house" for *bgt* "in Gath" read by LXX in 2 Sam 21:22). Hence we read *gbyʿ*, instead of *ybyʿ* in MT.

perfumer's oil. Hebrew *šemen rôqēaḥ*. The identical term is attested several times in Ugaritic, *šmn rqḥ* (*KTU* 1.41.21; 1.148.21; 4.91.5; cf. also 4.31.2). An Aramaic equivalent, *rqḥ zy mšḥ* "perfume of oil," is found in a fragmentary text from Saqqara in Persian period Egypt (see Segal, *Aramaic Documents*, No. 45b.5). The perfume appears to be an item of great value. Cf. also Hebrew *qĕṭōret rōqaḥ maʿăśēh rôqēaḥ* "perfumed incense, product of a perfumer" (Exod 30:35; see also 30:25, 29; 37:29). The "perfumer's oil" is really an ointment concocted with various aromatic spices.

outweighs wisdom and honor. The earliest translators apparently had trouble with the meaning of the verse. LXX reads *timion oligon sophias hyper doxan aphrosynēs megalēn* "a little wisdom is more honor than the great glory of folly," apparently reflecting Hebrew *yqr ḥkmh m'ṭ mkbwd sklwt gdwlh*. Vulg has *pretiosior est sapientia et gloria parva et ad tempus stultitia* "wisdom and glory are more precious than small and short-lived folly," reflecting Hebrew *yqrm ḥkmh kbwd sklwt m'ṭ*. We should probably not take *yāqār* to mean "precious," however. Rather, the adjective may be used here in the sense of "weighty" (so Rashbam). The meaning is found in Postbiblical Hebrew and in Aramaic (see Jastrow, *Dictionary*, pp. 592–93).

2. *to their right . . . to their left*. The mind of the wise is supposed to be antithetical to that of fools; "right" and "left" simply indicate opposite sides. In Gen 24:49, "right" and "left" are used in connection with decision-making; the idiom "to the face the right or the left" means "to decide what to do." Quite possibly, too,

"right" and "left" here have ethical connotations. That is, "right" signifies what is good, honorable, and favorable, while "left" refers to what is bad, weak, and unfavorable (cf. Gen 48:12–20; Matt 25:31–46). Thus, in Jon 4:11 the inhabitants of Nineveh are said to have been incapable of distinguishing "between their right hand and their left" (*lōʾ-yādaʿ bên-yĕmînô liśmōʾlô*) — that is, they could not tell what is good from what is bad. In Postbiblical Hebrew, the denominative verb *hiśmĕʾîl* "to go left" can have the meaning "to go wrong" or "to make the wrong use," and the Hiphil verb *hêmîn* "to go right" may mean "to do the right thing" (*b. Šabb.* 63a; 88b). Cf. English what is "right" and what is "sinister" (from the Latin word meaning "left") and French *droit* and *gauche*.

3. *when fools.* Both *Ketib* (*kĕśehassākāl*) and *Qere* (*kĕśessākāl*) are possible. The meaning of the text is unchanged in either case. One may conjecture, however, that the reading of *Ketib*, which does not syncopate the definite article and, therefore, has the more difficult reading, is original. Some Hebrew MSS and LXX support *Qere*, however.

their minds are deficient. Hebrew *libbô ḥāsēr.* Despite the frequency of the idiom *ḥăsar lēb* "lacking sense" (Prov 6:32; 7:7; 9:4, 16; 10:13; 11:12; 15:21; 17:18; 24:30), we need not take *libbô* as the object (so Ginsburg; Hertzberg). That *libbô* "his heart" might be construed as the subject here should hardly be surprising, given the fact that *lēb* is personified so frequently in this book (see Notes and Comment at 1:16 and 2:3). So Targ interprets: *lbyh ḥsyr mn ḥkmtʾ*, lit. "his heart is lacking from wisdom."

they tell everyone they are fools. Hebrew *wĕʾāmar lakkōl sākāl hûʾ* may be translated literally either as (1) "*and* he says to everyone that he is a fool" (so RSV) or (2) "*but* he says of everyone, 'He is a fool!'" (NEB: "calls everyone else a fool"; NAB: "he calls everything foolish"). Either the fool reveals his own folly readily, or he readily judges others to be fools. And each interpretation has its supporters among commentators, both ancient and modern (see Whitley, *Koheleth*, p. 84). The translation adopted here attempts to preserve the ambiguity of the Hebrew, with a slight tilt (evident in the translation of the conjunction *wĕ-* as "and") in favor of the first view. This ambiguity may have been intended by Qohelet himself. Perhaps in Qohelet's view, those who are wise in their own eyes, who regard everyone else as fools, show themselves to be real fools by their conduct. This seems to be the understanding of the Syriac translators.

4. *temper.* For this meaning of *rûaḥ*, see Prov 16:32; Judg 8:3; and Notes at 7:8.

calmness. The Hebrew word *marpēʾ* may be multivalent. If the root is *rpʾ* ("to heal"), the word may have to do with reconciliation and forgiveness. See the use of *rpʾ* in Ps 60:4 (Eng v 2); 103:3; Hos 7:1; 2 Chron 7:14. Thus, *marpēʾ* is used of soothing/healing speech (Prov 12:18; 15:4; 16:24). But *marpēʾ* may also bear some meaning of the root *rph* ("to relax"); it may connote calmness (see Prov 14:30). It is unnecessary to limit the range of meaning to one root or the other, for there may be some semantic overlap between the two. Even within a single book, Jeremiah, both *marpēʾ* (14:19) and *marpēh* (8:15) occur, with no apparent difference in meaning. In Jer 8:15, *marpēh* may mean both "calm" and "healing" (so NEB "respite"; NJPS "relief"; NRSV "healing"), and in Jer 38:4 *mĕrappēʾ* is

attested where *mĕrappeh* is expected. In other Semitic languages, too, *rp'* may
have the same wide semantic range. Thus, in Arabic, the verb may mean either
"to mend, effect reconciliation, appease" or "to treat with gentleness, soothe"
(Lane, *Arabic-English Lexicon*, Part 3, p. 1117). It is likely, therefore, that *marpē'*
in Ecclesiastes means both "calmness" (remaining calm) and something like
"soothing" or "pacification." Fox is correct, therefore, in saying that it is a near-
synonym of *naḥat* "calmness" in 9:17 (*Contradictions*, p. 266). It is not only
calmness in the sense of composure (so NASB and JB; NAB: "mildness"), however, but also in the sense of pacification or soothing. One must remain calm in
a dangerous situation (see 8:3), but one should also try to calm the angry one
down (see Prov 16:14; Sir 20:28b). Both forms of calmness are needed in an
overheated situation.

5. *under the sun.* See Notes at 1:3.

a veritable mistake. The preposition *k* in *kišgāgâ* is not meant to indicate a lack
of reality, thus "*like* a mistake" or "*as if* a mistake," as some of the ancient versions
have it (so LXX *hōs*; Aq and Theod *homoiōs*; Vulg *quasi*). Rather, it is to be taken
as the *kap̄ veritatis* (see GKC §118.x; Joüon-Muraoka §133.g).

stemming from. The form *yōṣā'* is the feminine participle formed on analogy
with III-weak verbs (see Notes at 2:26); otherwise we should expect *yōṣē't*.

the proprietor. See Notes at 7:19.

6. *The simpleton.* The Hebrew word *hassekel* is a *hapax legomenon*. The ancient versions either assumed the word to be *hassākāl* "the fool" (cf. 2:19; 7:17;
10:3 [twice], 14), or they took *hassekel* to be used in the concrete sense. Indeed,
most interpreters take *hassekel* to be no different in meaning from *hassākāl*. The
parallelism of "the fool" (or "folly") and "the rich" seems awkward, however.
Hence, some commentators emend the word to read *haśśekel* "the clever" (so
Ibn Ezra; Kimḥi). Others take *'ăšîrîm* to mean not the wealthy, but those who are
"rich in eloquence and wisdom" (so Jerome). Still others disregard the Masoretic
punctuation — with the disjunctive accent on *rabbîm* — to read *rabbîm wa'ăšîrîm*
"the *noble* and the rich" (so NEB), which, it is assumed, provides a better contrast
with *hassekel:* i.e., the fool is set in high places // the nobles and the rich abide
in low estate (so Lauha).

There is no need to emend or repunctuate the text. In contrast with *'ăšîrîm*,
the word *hassekel* "the fool" refers to someone who is a social outcast. In this
case, the *sekel* is the one who is thought to be mentally deficient (cf. *libbô ḥāsēr*
"his mind is deficient" in 9:3 and *lō'-yāda' lāleket 'el-'îr* "he does not know the
way to town" in 10:15), a half-wit, who is not expected to succeed in society.
In the Akkadian texts, the *saklu* "simpleton" (the equivalent of Hebrew *sekel*) is
regularly associated with the outcasts of society; it is associated with *sakku* "half-
wit," *samû* "inept," *ḫasikku* "deaf," *la mudû* "ignoramus," *isḫappu* "rogue," and
so forth (see *CAD* XV, p. 80). Indeed, the simpletons are described as people
who do not belong to "the old families" and whose appointment to high office is
regarded as an irregularity (see *ABL* 1103:6; 437 rev. line 15, both cited in *CAD*
XV, p. 80). Unsophisticated, uncultured simpletons (the adjective *saklu* in Akkadian means "uncouth") are not expected to rise to the top in society. Qohelet

is, thus, speaking of a topsy-turvy world in which the incompetent are in positions of power and influence, whereas the elite are in lowly positions. The author probably has in mind the "offender" whose action caused much damage (9:18), or the proprietor one who is responsible for the error mentioned in the preceding verse. In any case, the Hebrew noun *hassekel* corresponds to what one may call today, whether in seriousness or in insults, "the moron" or "the idiot." And Qohelet might have used the term *hassekel* in the same derisive way that we do when we speak of incompetent people being where they ought not be: the "morons" are in charge! Cf. also 10:16, where the king is said to be a *na'ar*, i.e. either "a lad" or "a servant" (see Notes and Comment at 10:16). The normal order of things has been disrupted.

great heights. If MT is correct in its punctuation, the absence of the definite article with the adjective, *rabbîm*, must be regarded as a peculiar feature of late Hebrew, where the definite article on the adjective or participle is occasionally omitted, even though the noun that it qualifies is definite (cf. *haggepen nokrîyâ* "the wild vine," Jer 2:21; *haggôyîm rabbîm* "the many nations," Ezek 39:27; *happeša' šōmēm* "the transgression that desolates," Dan 8:13; *haššiqqûṣ mĕšōmēm* "the abomination that makes desolate," Dan 11:31). The same phenomenon is evident in Postbiblical Hebrew, where we find expressions like *hm'rkh gdwlh* "the great pile" (*m. Tamid* 2:4). See, further, Segal, *A Grammar of Mishnaic Hebrew,* §377. There is no need, therefore, to emend or repoint the text.

the rich. In contrast with "the simpleton" (*hassekel*), "the rich" simply means the wealthy upper class (cf. Isa 53:9; Jer 9:22 [Eng v 23]; Mic 6:12). Wealth is really not the issue, but the presumed status of these people. The rich are expected to be in the ruling class (see Prov 22:7; Mic 6:12). See also 10:20, where *'āšîr* "rich" is associated with *melek* "king."

low estate. Or "humiliation" (cf. Ps 136:23). The meaning of *šēpel* in our passage is not entirely clear, however. Perhaps it refers to the demotion of those who were once powerful. Cf. Isa 26:5, "for he has brought low those who dwell on high (*yōšĕbê mārôm*)."

7. *on horses.* Two Hebrew MSS (Kennicott nos. 18, 167) add *rkbym* "riding" after *'bdym*, probably an explicatory plus. I prefer the shorter reading. D. N. Freedman, however, argues plausibly that the reading of the majority of witnesses is erroneous. He contends that original *rkbym* was lost by haplography (note the similar *-ym* ending of *'bdym*). Freedman's reconstruction yields a better balance between the two cola. It may also be noted that the three verbs *yšb* (v 6), *rkb* (v 7), and *hlk* (v 7) are also used together in Judg 5:10. In any case — whether we take the longer or shorter reading — the meaning of the text is unaffected.

Foreign to the Levant, horses were very expensive to acquire and maintain. Hence, they were used largely for military purposes. In the Persian period, horses were also used by the imperial government for couriers (Esth 8:10, 14). Donkeys and camels were ordinarily used for transportation of ordinary citizens, whereas horses were used to carry only kings and nobles (see Esth 6:8–9; 2 Chron 25:28). Ownership of horses was a mark of wealth and power (cf. Deut 17:16). Horses were a status symbol. So one reads in one of the Amarna letters: "the messenger of the king of Akka is honored more than [my] messeng[er], f[or they fur]nished [h]im with a horse" (*EA* 88:46–48; translated in W. L. Moran, *The Amarna Letters* [Baltimore: Johns Hopkins University, 1992], p. 161). Certainly slaves were not expected on horses.

8. *pit.* The word *gûmmāṣ* is probably an Aramaic loanword (Wagner, *Aramäismen*, p. 52). It is a *hapax legomenon* in Hebrew. Similar versions of the proverb are found elsewhere, although the noun is not *gûmmāṣ*, but *šaḥat* (Prov 26:27, Ps 7:16 [Eng v 15]) or *śîḥâ* (Ps 57:7 [Eng v 6]). The author has in mind the hunter who digs a pit as a trap for animals (see Jer 18:22; 48:43–44; Sir 27:26). Since these pits were camouflaged, the hunters had to be extremely careful, for they themselves were the most vulnerable to their traps.

one who breaks down. The reference is to one who dismantles a *gādēr* (see Isa 5:5; Ps 80:13 [Eng v 12]), hence one should not translate "breaks *through* a wall" (RSV). Note that in Eccl 3:3, *liprôṣ* "breaking down" is the opposite of *libnôt* "building up."

wall. The Hebrew word *gādēr* here is not a "hedge," as in Hos 2:8 (Eng v 6), but a stone fence (cf. Prov 24:31; Num 22:24), which may be built up (Mic 7:11) or broken down (Isa 5:5; Ps 80:13 [Eng v 12]; Prov 24:31). See also *DNWSI* I, p. 215. Such stone fences, still ubiquitous in Palestine today, are made of unhewn stones that are piled up. They were built to protect vineyards, orchards, and gardens. Snakes may lurk between the stones in such walls, so one who removes the stones becomes vulnerable to snakebites. Even city walls or residential walls are known to harbor snakes in the nooks and crannies (see Amos 5:19).

9. *quarries.* The Hiphil of *ns'* may mean "to quarry" (1 Kgs 5:31 [Eng v 16]) — i.e., to remove stones from a *massā'* "quarry" (1 Kgs 6:7). Although the Bible does not often mention the quarrying of stones, we know from the number of quarries found in Israel that quarrying activities must have been quite extensive (see Y. Shiloh and A. Horowitz, "Ashlar Quarries of the Iron Age in the Hill Country of Israel," *BASOR* 217 [1975], pp. 37–47).

be injured. It has been observed that Hebrew *'ṣb* may be related to different roots in Proto-Semitic: *'ṣb, *'ḍb, or *ǵḍb. I. Kottsieper is probably correct to note that the verb here is related to Proto-Semitic *'ḍb "to cut, pierce" ("Bedeutung der Wz. *'ṣb* und *skn*," pp. 213–22). Cf. Arabic *'aḍaba* "to cut, pierce, break, injure" (Lane, *Arabic-English Lexicon*, Part 5, pp. 261–62). In any case, the injury here is certainly physical (cf. *'aṣṣĕbôtām* "their wounds," Ps 147:3).

be endangered. The verb *sākan* occurs with this meaning only here in the Hebrew Bible, but it is widely attested in Postbiblical Hebrew and Aramaic (see Jastrow, *Dictionary*, p. 991). Some have argued for a more specific meaning, suggesting a denominative verb related to the noun *sakkîn* "knife" in Prov 23:2 (Driver, "Problems," p. 239), hence the meaning "to cut oneself." But, while the noun *sakkîn* "knife" is found in Postbiblical Hebrew and in Aramaic, the verb is not attested anywhere. Kottsieper ("Die Bedeutung der Wz. *'ṣb* und *skn*," pp. 220–23) cites Ugaritic *sknt* "image" (*KTU* 1.4.I.42), from which he argues for a verb meaning "to engrave, to cut into." The precise meaning and etymology of Ugaritic *sknt* are far from clear, however. Deut 19:5 gives an instance of the danger that a woodcutter faced: the ax head may slip off and hit someone.

10. *implement.* Hebrew *barzel* often refers to instruments of iron, specifically iron tools for cutting wood (Deut 19:5; 2 Kgs 6:5–6; Isa 10:34) — i.e., ax, hatchet, or the like.

is blunt. MT *qēhâ* (Piel perfect 3 ms), if correctly vocalized, should be taken as transitive but interpreted impersonally: thus, "one has blunted the implement" means the same thing as "the implement has been blunted." Other scholars maintain that the Piel verb has an intransitive meaning in this particular case. It must be noted, however, that the verb is not attested elsewhere with this meaning in Piel. We should perhaps vocalize the verb as *qāhâ* (Qal perfect 3 ms) or, better, take the form to be an adjective, *qēheh*, a form widely attested in Postbiblical Hebrew for iron implements (see Jastrow, *Dictionary*, p. 1321). LXX *ekpesē* "fall off" does not reflect Hebrew *npl*, as Ginsburg suggests (*Coheleth*, p. 431), but rather, a meaning of *qhh* known in Postbiblical Hebrew (*y. Ber.* IX, 13ª; *Deut. Rabb.* section 2). The Greek translator(s) may have been thinking of the slipping of the ax head, as described in Deut 19:5.

one does not sharpen it first. Hebrew *wĕhûʾ lōʾ-pānîm qilqal* is difficult. Commentators have long assumed that *pānîm* here means "edge" on the basis of Ezek 21:21 (Eng v 16) where, in reference to a sword, it is said: *ʾānâ pānayik mûʿādôt,* lit. "wherever your face is directed" (NRSV: "wherever your edge is directed"). Hence, *wĕhûʾ lōʾ qilqal* is usually translated as "(its) edge is unsharpened" (so NIV), or the like. The sword in the Ezekiel passage is personified, however, so one cannot argue from that text alone that *pānîm* in Hebrew has the meaning "edge." The text simply refers to the direction that the personified sword may take (so NJPS: "whither are you bound?"). Hebrew *pānîm*, in fact, never refers to the tip of a blade; *peh* "mouth" may be used for the edge of an iron implement, but not *pānîm*, lit. "face." One should, therefore, assume that *pānîm* in our passage is used adverbially, in place of the more common *lĕpānîm* "before" (cf. Ezek 2:10; 1 Chron 19:10; 2 Chron 13:14; see also examples in Postbiblical Hebrew cited in Jastrow, *Dictionary*, p. 1189). One may compare here the usage of *rōʾš* "[at the] beginning" in Judg 7:19, where *rōʾš* is used adverbially in place of the expected form *lĕrōʾš* (so in Lam 2:19). Cf. also Akkadian *pānû* "earlier, earliest, before" (*AHW*, pp. 822–23). So Vulg translates *et hoc non ut prius* "and it is not as before." Failure to understand this irregular usage of *pānîm* led to the confusion in the ancient versions, some of which omit the negative altogether (LXX, Syr), while others read *lw* in its place (MSSᵒʳ). The reading in MT should be retained.

As for the form *qilqal*, one may take it to be a denominative verb related to *qālāl* "burnished" (Ezek 1:7; Dan 10:6). It is possible, however, to vocalize the verb as a passive, *qulqal*, and take *hûʾ* as referring to the implement (so Driver, "Problems," p. 232): thus, "but it (the implement) has not been sharpened first."

exert more force. Hebrew *waḥăyālîm yĕgabbēr*, lit. "one increases power." Compare the idiom *gābĕrû ḥayil* "increase in power" (Job 21:7).

It is an advantage. Disregarding the disjunctive accent on *hkšyr* and taking *wĕyitrôn hakšîr ḥokmâ* as a verbless clause, with the infinitive used in place of a noun (see Waltke-O'Connor §36.2.1), lit. "an advantage is to make wisdom appropriate." Cf. A. Frendo ("The 'Broken Construct Chain' in Qoh 10,10b," pp. 544–45), who reads: "the advantage of wisdom is success."

to appropriate. Lit. "to make suitable"—assuming the reading *hakšîr* (the Hiphil inf. cs.) with *Ketib*, instead of *hakšēr* (Hiphil inf. abs.) with *Qere*. The Hiphil of *kšr* does not occur elsewhere in the Bible, but in Postbiblical Hebrew it occurs frequently in the sense of "to permit, adapt, make appropriate, make fit, enable." Cf. Jastrow, *Dictionary*, p. 677. One may also compare Imperial Aramaic *kšyr* "suitable, appropriate" and the verb *kšr* "to be suitable" (see Segal, *Aramaic Texts*, Nos. 26.7, 14; 48.1–2, 6–7). Here in Ecclesiastes the point is that one should apply wisdom properly. In other words, it is an advantage to use wisdom correctly. Instead of the Hiphil infinitive absolute (*hakšēr*), many Hebrew MSS and, presumably, the *Vorlage(n)* of LXX, Symm, and Syr assume the definite article + substantive: "the successful one." Since the Hiphil of *kšr* does not occur elsewhere in the Hebrew Bible, it is easy to see how scribes might have interpreted the form in terms of what is common. MT is the *lectio difficilior* and, therefore, not to be emended.

11. *If a snake that cannot be charmed bites.* There are two ways to interpret Hebrew *'im-yiššōk hannāḥāš bĕlô'-lāḥaš*. The Masoretic punctuation—with a disjunctive accent on *hannāḥāš* (thus, "if a snake bites without a charm")—assumes that the snake bites *before* a charm is effected. It is also possible, however, that the expression *bĕlô'-lāḥaš* "without charm" refers to the snake itself, rather than to the situation or the bite. If so, we should disregard the disjunctive accent on *hannāḥāš* and read the noun with the following words: thus, *hannāḥāš bĕlô'-lāḥaš* "a snake without charm"—a snake for which no charm is effective. The reference is, then, to deadly snakes, those for which charms are of no use. Jer 8:17 refers to certain poisonous snakes for which there is no charm (*'ên-laḥaš*), while Ps 58:5–6 (Eng vv 4–5) refers to snakes that do not heed the sound of the charmer, cannot be charmed. Cf. Akkadian *ṣēri la šiptim* "a snake without charm" (*Sumer* 13, p. 93, lines 1, 3), by which is meant a snake that cannot be warded off by incantations. An Aramaic letter from the Persian period refers to a person who almost died of snakebite, but we do not know how death was averted in that case (*TAD* I, 2.5.8).

charmer. It is curious that the charmer is not simply called *mĕlaḥēš*, as elsewhere in the Bible (*mĕlaḥăšîm* in Ps 58:6 [Eng v 5]), or *ḥwbr nšwk* (Sir 12:13), but *ba'al hallāšôn*, lit. "the master of the tongue." The designation may be of the snake charmer as one who is ordinarily able to repress the dangerous tongues of snakes (cf. Job 20:16; Ps 140:4 [Eng v 3]). It is more likely, however, that the reference is to the charmer as an expert of incantations. We should perhaps compare Hebrew *ba'al hallāšôn* "master of the tongue" with Akkadian *bēl lišāni*, lit. "master of the tongue," which in Neo-Assyrian and Standard Babylonian texts refers to anyone who is skilled in a foreign language, and note that *lišānu*, lit. "tongue," may be used of spells and prayers (see *CAD* IX, pp. 211, 215). In this case, the *ba'al hallāšôn* is perhaps one who is conversant with snake incantations (cf. KJV: "a babbler"), perhaps incantations against snakebites.

12. *The words from the mouth of the wise bring favor.* This verse is usually interpreted to mean that the words of the wise will bring favor upon themselves. The expression "words from the mouth of the wise" in this verse, however, also recalls "the words of the wise" in 9:17 and, by extension, also the words of the wise commoner in 9:13–16 (see *dĕbārāyw* in 9:16). In the case of that wise commoner, it seems that the words of the wise did not win any favor, even as it is suggested in 9:11 (*lō' layyōdĕ'îm ḥēn* "favor does not belong to the clever"). One cannot, therefore, interpret 10:12 apart from the reality identified at the beginning of the passage, namely, 9:11–18. For Qohelet, it is true that the wise may win favor (so 10:12), but there is no guarantee that they will (so 9:11, 17). By the same token, the words of fools may destroy them, but then again the fools may be heard over the wise.

the lips of fools consume them. The plural form for "lips" (instead of the more common dual form), appears only in late texts (Ps 45:3; 59:8; Cant 4:3, 11; 5:13; Isa 59:3). Moreover, the verb *tĕballĕ'ennû* is singular even though the subject (*śiptôt*) is plural, perhaps because it was understood that the mouth was intended (but see GKC §145.n). "Mouth," whether literal or figurative, is elsewhere the subject of the verb *bl'* (Num 16:30, 32; Prov 19:28; cf. Jer 51:44). For the juxtaposition of *ḥn* "favor" and *śptwt* "lips," one may compare the saying in the Aramaic *Proverbs of Ahiqar*: *ḥn gbr hymnwth wśn'th kdbt śpwth* "truthfulness brings one favor, but the lies of one's lips bring hatred" (see text in *TAD* III, 1.1.132).

13. *irrationality.* See Notes at 2:12.

14. *multiplies words.* See Notes at 6:11.

No one knows what will happen. Some Hebrew MSS, LXX, Symm, Syr, SyrH, and Vulg read *mšhyh* "what has happened," instead of *mh-šyhyh* in MT, which is supported by Targ. The use of the imperfect *lō' yēda'* makes it unlikely that the past is meant (unless one also emends *lō' yēda'* to read *lō' yāda'*). Nor is it true that people do not know what has happened.

hereafter. Hebrew *mē'aḥărāyw* may refer generally to the future but also, as elsewhere, to death (see Notes at 6:12). The translation here preserves that ambiguity. Cf. also 9:12.

15. *The toil of fools wearies them.* The Hebrew text is difficult for two reasons: (1) the lack of coordination between the apparent masculine gender of *'āmāl* and the feminine verb *tĕyagge'ennû*, and (2) the lack of coordination between the plural noun *hakkĕsîlîm* and the singular object suffix attached to the verb. In the first place, since *'āmal* is elsewhere always masculine, the verb *tĕyagge'ennû* would suggest either a textual corruption of some sort or that *'āmāl* in this one instance is feminine. Many scholars emend the verb to the masculine form, *yyg'nw* (Ehrlich, Hertzberg, Galling, Zimmerli, Lauha). But it is difficult to see, then, why anyone would have read *tyg'nw*, the more problematic reading that is attested in all but one Hebrew MS. The *taw* cannot be explained as a mechanical error of some sort. Fox has proposed to read *'ml hksyl myg'nw*, explaining the *taw* as a sort of dittograph of either *mem* or *yod* (*Contradictions*, p. 270). Clearly

tygʿnw is the more difficult — and probably correct — reading. Whitley proposes to take the verb *tygʿnw* as an example of the *taqtul* masculine imperfect, such as we find in Ugaritic (*Kohelet*, pp. 86–88). This obviates any need to emend the text to an easier reading. Yet the existence of the *taqtul* imperfect in Hebrew is doubtful (see the detailed discussion in Schoors, *Pleasing Words*, pp. 80–85).

It is perhaps easiest to assume that *ʿāmāl* is treated as a feminine noun here (see BDB, p. 765); nouns that are generally treated as masculine are occasionally treated as feminine (e.g., *maḥăneh* in Gen 32:9; *hāmôn* in Job 31:34; *mûsār* in Prov 4:13). One should not, therefore, be hasty to emend the text to an easier reading. As for the tension between the noun *hakkĕsîlîm* and the object suffix attached to the verb, the textual witnesses are divided: LXX[B] and Syr take the pronominal suffix to be plural, whereas LXX[ASP], Targ, and Vulg assume the noun to be singular. The singular noun is supported by the singular verb *yādaʿ* in the parallel line. Whitley argues that *hakkĕsîlîm* is really a noun with an old case-ending and the enclitic *mem* (*Koheleth*, p. 8), but it would be odd to find such archaisms in so late a book. It is easiest to follow Ginsburg (*Coheleth*, p. 440) in assuming the distributive use of the object suffix and the singular verb *yādaʿ* in the parallel line (see GKC §145m).

for. The particle *ʾăšer* may be translated as causal (so Symm) or resultative, depending on how one interprets the idiom that follows.

they do not know the way to town. Hebrew *lōʾ-yādaʿ lāleket ʾel-ʿîr*, lit. "he does not know to go to town." This is probably an idiom referring to the incompetence of fools (cf. v 3; so Fox, *Contradictions*, p. 269). This verse may provide some clue as to the extent of urbanization in Palestine during Qohelet's time. In an urbanized society, the city is the center of commercial and social intercourse. The way to the city is, therefore, common knowledge; everyone except the most stupid and incompetent knows the way to town.

COMMENT

The words *šabtî wĕrāʾōh* "further I saw" (or, literally, "I turned and saw") at the beginning of 9:11 signal a new literary unit. In the face of the common fate of death for all people (9:1–6), the author calls for enjoyment of life while it is still possible (9:7–10). Now he turns to observe that everything in life is subject to chance. The larger literary unit may be divided into three sections, each introduced by "I have observed": 9:11–12; 9:13–10:4; 10:5–15. The common thread through all three sections is the notion that everything in life is precarious. At the beginning of the unit, the author says that human beings do not know their time (9:12). At the end of the passage, the point is reiterated that human beings do not know what will happen (10:14). This reference to human lack of knowledge thus frames the literary unit.

Time and Incidence (9:11–12)
In 9:11–12, Qohelet makes the point that there are no prescribed rules that can guarantee success. Things do not always work out as people might expect. Neither the swift nor the valiant can be assured of victory. The author appears to

have in mind the able-bodied people — the fast and strong — who are always expected to win. Heroes are always expected to triumph. But the expected may not happen. So, too, the intellectual elite — the wise, the intelligent, the learned — will not necessarily have an advantage over others in terms of their livelihood, wealth, or favor. This is not to say that they will fail, or that they do not generally have an "edge" over others in life (compare Prov 3:16), only that there is no guarantee. There is no assurance of success for those who are physically able, nor for those who are intellectually gifted.

The problem is that people do not control time (9:11). By the curious expression "a timely incident" (literally "a time and an incident") the author means an accident, perhaps a fatal accident. The verb for the happening of this incident (*yiqreh* "befall") is related to the word *miqreh* "fate" in 9:2–3 (also 2:14–15; 3:19). Accidents happen. No one can predict when something tragic may happen that will put an end to one's ability to enjoy life, achieve one's goals, or fulfill one's potential. Indeed, no one knows when the ultimate misfortune, namely death, may come. This is the one "incident" from which nobody escapes. Every person has his or her own inevitable time — that is, the time of death — but no one knows when that will be (9:12; 10:14; see also 7:17). This "incident" is "timely" only in the sense that it will happen in time, but the timing is utterly unpredictable. In such a world, all mortals are like fish and birds that wander about innocently. All of a sudden they may be caught, without any distinction as to their species or their readiness. The trap may spring and the net may be cast or hauled up at any time. It is not as if only the fully mature will be caught, but anyone at all. Everything is subject to chance. That is precisely why the author urges people to enjoy life at every opportunity (see *kol-ʿēt*, literally, "at every time" in 9:8).

Truisms and Reality (9:13–10:4)

The introductory words "this, too" indicate that there is both continuity and discontinuity with the preceding verses. What follows is a further observation about wisdom. Whereas in 9:11 there is only a general remark that the wise, the clever, and the learned are not assured of success, the author turns now to a specific example that illustrates the fact that wisdom will not necessarily get one ahead. The case concerns an unnamed little town. We do not know if this example was taken from a historical incident well-known to Qohelet's audience (but is lost to the modern reader), or if it is merely an anecdote that has no specific historical basis (compare 4:13–16). Attempts to locate the story in history have not been successful; and they are not necessary. Qohelet uses the story to illustrate a point about how the effectiveness of wisdom is also subject to chance. The anecdote begins with the invasion of a certain "little town" by a "great king," who surrounded the city and built a "great siege-work" — possibly a movable assault tower (see Notes above) — against it. One notes immediately the contrast between what is small and what is great, and the ironic fact that the anecdote about this "little town" allows Qohelet to make an observation that he calls "great" (9:13).

In the midst of this town was a wise person, who just happened to be a commoner. And we are told that this wise commoner might have saved the city

321

through his wisdom. The text says nothing about how the town might have been saved through wisdom. One can only speculate. The "omniscient narrator" alone knows that the town might have been saved and how it might have been saved, if only this wise commoner had been given the opportunity to do so. But no one gave thought to that sage, which is quite a remarkable omission, given the fact that the town was in such dire straits and the fact that there were only a few persons in it. It is apparent that the sage was disregarded because of his status as a commoner. Certainly in this instance favor did not belong to the wise (see 9:11 and contrast 10:12). Qohelet then cites a traditional saying that "wisdom is better than might" (compare Prov 21:22), but he observes immediately that this truism is negated by reality: "but wisdom is despised" (9:16). The general truth of the saying is contradicted by the reality of that particular situation. People may say that wisdom is better than might, but when they are confronted with a threat from the mighty, they may not think the cliché to be sufficiently practical. Even if it is generally true that wisdom is better than might, wisdom may not prevail for some reason or other. Everything is subject to chance. In this particular anecdote, although there was wisdom available in the little town, it was disregarded, as issues of class and status apparently got in the way (compare Sir 13:21–23). Thus, we have a "true-but" observation in v 16: it may be generally *true* that wisdom is better than might, *but* the reality may relativize the saying.

Interpreters have long observed that 9:17 stands in direct opposition to 9:16, if both are taken at face value. One notes, however, that in 9:16, the phrase "their words are not heeded" states the reality that relativizes the rule that wisdom is better than might. In the story of the little town, the words of the wise — the sage who happened to be a commoner — were not heeded. The principle did not work in that case. Then in 9:17, Qohelet returns to a general principle, namely, that the words of the wise uttered calmly are heard more readily than the ranting of a ruler among fools. Although the text does not say so explicitly, the reader knows that this axiom about the words of the wise is also relativized by the example in 9:13–16: the words of this particular wise person were not heeded. Having stated the reality in 9:16, the author is simply returning to the principle once again in 9:17, but he repeats key terms in v 16 to highlight the contradiction. The *unheeded* words in v 16 stand in contrast to the *heeded* words in v 17. One is supposed to remember the reality mentioned in v 16, even as one reads v 17. The contradiction is deliberate. It is a contradiction between the principle and the reality, the rule and the exception.

The author contrasts the calm words of the wise in 9:17, not with the loud rantings of fools in general, but specifically with the "ruler among fools" — that is, the one who rules over fools (those of the little town!) and is the chief of them all. In context, one sees this "ruler" set over against the wise commoner, who is to be regarded among the wise who speak wise words calmly. Thus, the general principle is that the calm words of the wise, even a commoner, should be heeded more than the shout of fools, even a ruler. But that principle was apparently contradicted in reality, presumably because the wrong words — that of the "ruler among fools" — were heeded. The principle did not work in that instance.

The contradiction between the general principle and the reality is further brought out in 9:18, in another "true-but" observation: it may be generally *true* that wisdom is better than weapons of war, *but* the presence of a single "offender" destroys much good. In context, it is difficult to separate the "offender" (RSV: "the bungler") from the "ruler" just mentioned. In fact, 9:17 serves to link the two "true-but" observations, one in 9:16, the other in 9:18. The reader is supposed to evaluate the two "true" sayings in the light of the contradictions of them in reality. The point is that wisdom may be better in principle, but in reality it all depends on the circumstances and the choices that people make. Wisdom may be negated by folly; much good may be negated by a single bungler.

We do not know the full story of the siege of the little town. What we do know is that wisdom apparently did not carry the day. On the contrary, the words of the wise commoner were not heeded. Instead, a single "offender" (presumably the ruler) managed to destroy much good. Any advantage that wisdom may have over folly has been negated by a single fool. This observation prompts the author to quote a proverb about the contaminating effect of a single negative element: a fly — he means a single fly — that dies in a pot of perfumer's ointment destroys the entire content of that pot (10:1a). The fly is a symbol of the devastating effect that a single foolish person could have on the rest of the community. Or, as we may say in English, "one rotten apple spoils the whole barrel." A single bad thing can destroy much good. So Qohelet judges that "a little folly outweighs wisdom and honor" (10:1b). A little folly in a little town may be just too much!

For the author, there is obviously a tension between wisdom and folly. He states it graphically: "the mind of the wise is to the right, the mind of the fool is to the left" (10:2). The wise and the fool are not of the same mind, as it were. In the ancient Near East, "right" and "left" may simply indicate opposites, sometimes with the connotation that they are poles in a moral dilemma. In the Hebrew Bible, "right" and "left" often denote the options that one has in life's journey — one may turn this way or that, or one may go straight along the way (see Gen 24:49; Num 20:17). For the Deuteronomists, the straight way of adherence to God's commandments is the proper choice in life; one must turn neither to the left nor to the right in that imaginary journey (Deut 5:32; 17:11, 20; Josh 1:7; 23:6; 1 Sam 6:12). In Proverbs, the straight way is extolled, while deviations to the left or to the right are equated with turning to evil (Prov 4:25–27). The author may have had the imagery of the journey in mind, for he says, "yea, even on the way, when fools travel, their mind is deficient" (10:3). By their conduct, fools show just who they are. They may talk as if others are fools, but by their conduct tell all that they are the real fools (see Prov 12:23; 13:16). Perhaps Qohelet still has in mind the fate of the little town and the choices that people made therein: they did not heed the voice of the wise commoner (9:14–16) and, instead, allowed the ranting of the "ruler among fools" to prevail, so that this single bungler prevented a positive outcome (9:17–10:1). Perhaps the author means that this ranting "ruler among fools" is so stupid that he does not even know that he is showing himself to be a fool (10:3).

The author concludes the section with a piece of practical advice: if the wrath of the ruler flares up, one must remain in one's place, for calmness eliminates great offenses (10:4). This advice may be compared and contrasted with that in 8:3, where one is told not to be so overwhelmed and intimidated by the king's presence that one is not able to respond properly. There is no need to linger unnecessarily before a dangerous authoritarian, especially after an order has been issued. Defiance evident in one's countenance (8:1) or in one's slowness to respond (8:2–3) will do one no good. Given that situation, one should calmly leave. In 10:4, however, the advice is not to leave but to stay. Obviously leaving might be dangerous in this situation, when the temper of the ruler is rising. Calmness allays great offenses. The author is diplomatically ambiguous here (see Notes above). He means that one should remain calm and try to work things out. At the same time, he is saying that one should try to calm the angry ruler down before one can proceed. Calmness is needed all around to avert the danger. Perhaps Qohelet means that words uttered in calmness may still be heeded after all, and that wisdom may still be better than might. It seems clear that this verse is linked to the preceding sayings, since the indefinite "*a* ruler among fools" in 9:17 is now called "*the* ruler" in 10:4. But whereas in the preceding verses the expected advantage of calmness is subverted in reality, here the advice is that one must, nevertheless, preserve calmness. The point is that, given the right decisions, the principle stated in 9:17 may still work. There is no guarantee that calmness will be effective in every case, but it may still be effective. The principle may not work every time. But then again, it may work some of the time. Wisdom may, indeed, be better than might when one is dealing with the wrath of the ruler. The calm words of the wise may be better than rantings of fools. The wise may yet win favor. The general principle may be contradicted by reality time and again, but it may yet be effective. There are no guarantees, there are risks, but things do work out sometimes. One must simply live with the fact that everything in life is subject to chance.

Problems Large and Small (10:5–15)

Beginning in 10:5, the author speaks of a veritable mistake, an inadvertent error, stemming from the presence of "the proprietor." It is not clear, however, what the error is or precisely whom he means when he speaks of *haššallîṭ* "the proprietor" (10:5). Perhaps he has in mind one of the powerful proprietors of his generation (see Notes at 7:19). Or the author may be thinking of the ruler, the "offender" (*ḥôṭeʾ*, literally "one who misses the mark") mentioned in 9:18. Whether or not this "proprietor" is to be identified with the bungling ruler, the point is the same: one cannot count on those in positions of power (compare 9:11, 17–18). Something seriously wrong must have happened in the land, and Qohelet seems to blame it on those who are in charge.

In any case, he goes on to paint a picture of a society in turmoil. The "simpleton" (*hassekel*) is set in high places, while the rich are in low estate (10:6). What he means is that the incompetent — "the idiot" (see Notes above) — is promoted. Perhaps he has in mind the bungling ruler in 9:17–18, or "the proprietor" who is responsible for the foul-up. Certainly one is reminded here of the arrogant fool who is so mentally deficient that he does not even know his way around (see 10:3, 15). "Idiots" like these are being promoted. Meanwhile, those who are expected to be in positions of influence are not. Perhaps he means that members of the ruling class have actually been demoted — that is, made to sit in lowly places.

Things do not always pan out, as one might expect (see 9:11). So people who are not supposed to be in power are riding horses, the ancient equivalent of the luxurious foreign vehicles of transport, while the people of the ruling class are going about on foot like abject slaves. Things are not turning out according to expectations.

Such were the socioeconomic conditions of Qohelet's world (see Introduction, pp. 23–36). It was a society in turmoil. The government could not be trusted to rule efficiently, for it was losing control. There was apparently a significant turnover in the bureaucracy, as incompetent "idiots" were promoted to high offices, while members of the ruling elite were brought down. The economy was clearly unstable. Perhaps as a result of excessive speculation and foreclosures in that period, those who were once rich and powerful suddenly found themselves in want, even as their subordinates came unexpectedly into positions of wealth and power. It is true that there are no guarantees that things will turn out as expected (9:11). The world seems to have gone mad; the normal order of things seems to have been turned upside down.

In ancient Near Eastern literature, such reversals are part and parcel of descriptions of the breakdown of order in the cosmos and in society (see R. C. van Leeuwen, "Proverbs 30:21–23 and the Biblical World Upside Down," *JBL* 105 [1986], pp. 599–610). The motif of a topsy-turvy world is present in the Egyptian pessimistic texts. In *The Complaint of Khakheperre-Sonb* (*AEL* I, pp. 145–49) we read also of a land in turmoil, a land where changes are taking place rapidly, and "order is cast out." Those who used to shine are brought down; those who used to issue orders are now like those who receive orders, and everyone seems resigned to the hopeless situation. No one seems to know what would happen next and there is nothing on which one could count (compare Qoh 10:14). A similar state of affairs is found in *The Admonitions of Ipuwer* (*AEL* I, pp. 149–62). The poor and the rich seem to have traded places. In that topsy-turvy world, those who once could not even afford sandals have suddenly become wealthy. The rich become poor while the poor become wealthy, the rich lament while the poor rejoice, princes work while slaves own property. Those who were once rich and powerful are expelled from their positions. Likewise, in *The Prophecies of Neferti* (*AEL* I, pp. 139–45), one reads of a land in turmoil, where order has been cast out, where the great have been overthrown, and nobles have to rob to live, while beggars become rich. It is a world that has been turned upside down. This is the sort of society depicted in Ecclesiastes. There seems to be no order in society or in the cosmos. It is the sort of society that produced "pessimistic literature" or made such works popular.

There is lack of certainty not only among the various strata of society (10:5–6), but also for individuals in their daily chores (10:8–9). Everything is precarious; everything is subject to chance. Citing a well-known saying, the author speaks of the danger involved when one digs a pit (10:8a). What he has in mind here is the practice of excavating pits as traps for animals, pits that were then camouflaged with a net (see Prov 26:27, Pss 7:16 [Eng v 15]); 35:7; 57:7 [Eng v 6]; compare Ezek 19:8; Ps 140:6 [Eng v 5]; Isa 24:17–18). Since these excavators ventured into the areas where such traps were most likely to be made and the traps were camouflaged, they themselves were the most vulnerable to them. They may fall into the traps that are set for animals. They may, indeed, fall into the pits that they themselves have dug.

By the same token, one who dismantles a stone wall is vulnerable to snakes that may be nesting among the stones in the wall. The wall here refers not to the residential wall or city wall, but to the low stone fences built to define the areas of an orchard or a vineyard (Num 22:24; Isa 5:5). Such walls usually consisted of unhewn stones that were piled up with no mortar. One imagines, therefore, a farmer breaking down such an old wall (see Prov 24:31) in order to use the stones to build a new one. An element of danger is inevitable in that chore. The hunter who digs the pit and the farmer who dismantles stone fences both face dangers. Likewise, one who quarries stones runs the risk of physical injury, and a woodcutter is susceptible to certain dangers that come with the job, as evident in Deut 19:5.

All these are what we call today "occupational hazards." The point is that accidents happen in all walks of life. Accidents may happen in one's daily chores. Neither the rich and powerful (10:6–7), nor the ordinary worker (10:8–9) can be exempt from the dangers in life. At a macro-level, there are dangers when society is in transition: social, economic, political forces may bring about unexpected changes in the midst of which one may become victimized. Even the most powerful and economically secure may lose their positions. In other words, the race does not belong to the swift, nor does victory belong to the valiant. So, too, the wise and clever are not guaranteed wealth or livelihood. At a micro-level, there are dangers even in the mundane routines of life. Accidents can happen anywhere and at any time. At all levels there are risks. Risks are part of life's realities. Everything in life is subject to chance.

Based on these observations about the precarious nature of society and of daily life, the author draws two conclusions. The first (10:10) is apparently derived from the image of people working with sharp implements; he probably has in mind people who quarry rocks or cut wood (10:9). The second (10:11) refers to people who may be bitten by snakes lurking in the crevices of a stone wall, or, perhaps, in the pit (10:8). Qohelet first speaks of problems that may be remedied through the application of wisdom (see 10:4): if the implement is blunt, then one should sharpen it first. Knowing the risks that accompanied the tasks of quarrying stone or cutting wood, for instance, one should make sure that the tools are properly prepared. A little precautionary measure in the routine helps one reduce the danger of accidents. It does not prevent accidents, but the risks may be significantly reduced. So the author concludes in 10:10b that there is advantage to the proper use of wisdom — despite the fact that wisdom's effectiveness is also subject to chance. The appropriation of wisdom may save one from some life-threatening situations (see also 10:4). Risks can be reduced with a little common sense, as it were. This is practical wisdom.

Yet, it appears that there are problems for which there are simply no remedies. If one is dealing with a dangerous snake, a snake charmer may be summoned as a precautionary measure. But if the snake bites before it is charmed, or if the snake is of a species that simply cannot be charmed, then there is no advantage in having a snake charmer (v 11). Sometimes accidents just happen, no matter how careful one tries to be. Wisdom may have its advantage, but wisdom guarantees one nothing.

The author uses a peculiar term for the "charmer" here. There is a technical term in Hebrew, a more common term that the author could have used (see the Notes at 10:11). But he does not choose that designation. Instead, he uses an expression that may be translated literally as "the master of the tongue." This expression has no parallel elsewhere in the Hebrew Bible, but it is not inappropriate. In Akkadian, a similar expression (*bēl lišāni* "master of the tongue") may be used of someone who is an expert in foreign languages. Qohelet is probably referring to the charmer as an expert in the language of magic and incantation. By referring to the one who is supposed to provide remedies for snakebites as "the master of the tongue," however, the author is already setting the reader up for his comments on the verbosity of fools in 10:12–15. At the same time, he may be alluding to the verbosity of the wisdom teachers, those who are ever ready to offer catchy advice on how to handle every situation in life. It is true that wisdom may have an advantage in many situations (10:10), but there are times when the magic formulas of these "charmers" are really of no use, either because they come too late (like the snake biting before it is charmed), or simply because there are no solutions to the problems (like the snake for which there is no effective charm).

It appears, then, that Qohelet juxtaposes two conclusions that, at least on the verbal level, appear to be contradictory: 10:10b affirms the advantage of wisdom; 10:11b denies it. Both statements are, in fact, equally true. On the one hand, the practical application of wisdom is a good thing, even a necessary thing for coping with life's problems. On the other hand, it is true that there are problems in life that are beyond the ken even of the experts. Some accidents may be attributed to the lack of wisdom, but others cannot be so explained. Sometimes people are just caught, like fish in the sea (see 9:12). One must cope with risks in life as best one can, but risks cannot be eliminated altogether. That's the way life is.

The contrast in 10:12 between the words of the wise and the words of fools recalls a very similar contrast in 9:17. Moreover, the repeated mention of the fool and of folly in 10:12–15 parallels a similar repetition in 9:17–10:3. Certainly one may think of the ranting of the "ruler among fools" in 9:17 in the light of Qohelet's more general assessment about the futility of foolish words here in 10:12–14. Such fools talk excessively, but they know nothing (see 6:10–12). In truth, human beings do not know "their time" (9:12). And they do not know what will happen (10:14).

Qohelet speaks in 10:3 of the mental deficiency of fools who "even on the way" show that they are incompetent. Now he concludes that the toil of these fools wearies them so much that they do not even "know the way to town" (v 15). Whatever else the idiom "to go to town" may have meant (see the Notes on 10:15), the mention of a "town" seems to point back suggestively to the reference to the "little town" at the beginning of the literary unit. If Qohelet has in mind the "ruler among fools" mentioned in 9:17, and if the "ruler" is someone from that little town, then Qohelet's conclusion is all the more biting: one who is ready to shout advice concerning the town, in the end does not even "know the way to town"!

II.B.3. LIVING WITH RISKS (10:16–11:6)

[16]Alas for you, O Land, whose king is a minor and whose princes feast in the morning! [17]Fortunate are you, O Land, whose king is a noble and whose princes feast on time — with fortitude and not with carousing!

> [18]Through slothfulness the beam-work collapses;
> through slackness of hands the house crumbles.
> [19]For merriment food is prepared,
> also wine that gladdens the living;
> And money preoccupies everyone.

[20]Even in your intimacy do not disparage a king, nor in the bedroom disparage a rich person, for a bird of the sky may carry the utterance and a winged creature may report any matter.

> 11 [1]Release your bread upon the waters;
> after many days you may find it.
> [2]Give a portion to seven, and even to eight;
> you do not know what misfortune may come upon the land.
> [3]If the clouds become full,
> they will pour rain on the land.
> And if a tree falls whether in the south or in the north,
> the place where the tree falls, there it will be.
> [4]One who watches the wind will not sow;
> and one who looks at the clouds will not reap.

[5]Just as you do not know how the life-breath gets [into] the fetus in the belly of the pregnant woman, so you do not know the action of God, the one who does everything. [6]Sow your seeds in the morning, and at evening do not let your hand go, for you do not know which will succeed, the one or the other, or if both will be equally good.

NOTES

10 16. *Alas for you.* See Notes on *'î-lô* "alas for him" in 4:10.

O Land. LXX and Syr reflect Hebrew *'yr* "city," instead of *'rṣ* "land," but this is probably due to the influence of the preceding verse, which ends with *'el-'îr.*

minor. Hebrew *na'ar* may mean either "youth" or "servant." The latter meaning is suggested by the contrast with *ben-ḥôrîm* "noble" in the next verse and by the fact that *ḥôrîm* itself is contrasted with *'ebed* "servant" in Sir 10:25. Hence, most recent English translations render the word as "servant" (NIV; NAB; NRSV), "slave" (NEB; REB), or "lackey" (NJPS); contrast KJV: "child." Yet, it is difficult to separate the use of *na'ar* here from the account of Solomon's dream at Gibeon, where the king marveled that he had been favored, even though he was only a *na'ar*, who did "not know to go out or come in" (1 Kgs 3:7). In order to be able to govern effectively, then, he asked for wisdom, which would presumably compensate for his disadvantage as a *na'ar*. The assumption is that a *na'ar* is ordinarily without wisdom and unqualified to rule. In that passage *na'ar* cannot refer to Solomon's social status; it must refer to his youthfulness. In any case, it appears that a *na'ar*, whether it means "youth" or "servant," was not normally expected to be in a position of responsibility (cf. Isa 11:6; Jer 1:6–7). It was simply against convention for a *na'ar*, either as one who is not yet of age or as one who is not of the right status or character, to be king (cf. Isa 3:4, 12). The word *na'ar* in our passage is clearly a term of denigration. In Prov 1:4, the *na'ar* is equated with *pĕtā'îm* "naive ones." A *na'ar* is one who has yet to acquire knowledge and discretion, a youngster. While it is true that *na'ar* here is contrasted with the *ben-ḥôrîm* "noble" in v 17, it is also suggestive that the activities of the princes in v 19 are set over against the princes of v 17, who feast *bigbûrâ*, lit. "with manliness." That is, a *na'ar* is one who is immature. To preserve the multivalence of the word in this context, therefore, I translate it as "minor," understanding the word both in the sense of someone who is a minor in age and someone who is of minor status, that is, a lackey.

feast in the morning. The verb *yō'kēlû* in this context means more than ordinary eating; it means having a banquet or simply indulging in pleasure (cf. 1 Kgs 4:20; 18:42; Isa 21:5; Jer 16:8; Amos 6:4; Job 1:4). There is obviously nothing wrong with eating in the morning *per se* (cf. Exod 16:12, 21), but carousing in the morning is viewed as an indiscretion (see Isa 5:11–12, 22–23; Acts 2:13–15). These people were ready to indulge themselves even in the morning and were, thus, incapable of doing their duties. The wisdom tradition does not denounce drinking, just drinking in excess and during inappropriate times (see, e.g., Prov 31:5–7; Sir 31:27–31).

17. *fortunate.* Hebrew *'ašrêk*. In Judahite Hebrew we should expect *'ašrayik* for earlier **'ašrayk* (cf. the form with 2 ms suffix, *'ašreykā*; with 3 ms suffix, *'ašrāyw* or *'ašrêhû*; etc.). The consonantal text suggests a southern (Judahite) spelling (*'šryk*), but the pronunciation — *'ašrêk* — may be a remnant of northern Hebrew pronunciation.

noble. Hebrew *ben-ḥôrîm*, lit. "son of freeborn ones." It is clear that the *ḥôrîm* belonged to the elite in Israelite society (cf. 1 Kgs 21:8, 11; Isa 34:12; Jer 27:20; 39:6; Neh 2:16; 4:8, 13; 5:7; 6:17; 7:5; 13:17), but it is unclear if their status was a birthright or if it was one that had to be achieved. The designation *ben-ḥôrîm* may be compared with Aramaic *br ḥrn* "noble" mentioned in the Aramaic *Proverbs of Ahiqar* (see *TAD* III, 1.1.216). Cf. also *ḥwry hyhwdym* "Judaen nobles" and *ḥwry yhwdh* "nobles of Judah" in the Elephantine letters (see *TAD* I, 4.7.19; 4.8.18). In Sir 10:20 (Text B), *ḥwrym* is contrasted with *'bd* "servant, slave."

on time. Hebrew *bā'ēt* by itself occurs elsewhere only in Sir 11:20 (Text A), where it has the same meaning. Otherwise, the form is always *bĕ'ittô* "in its time" or "in its season" (Deut 11:14; 28:12; Jer 5:24; Ps 1:3; etc.). The reference here is to the due time or appropriate time, as in Pss 104:27 and 145:15, where *'ēt* also refers to the proper time for eating. Suggestive in this regard is Sir 31:28, where one reads: "Gladness of heart and rejoicing of the soul is wine drunk *on time* and moderately." Although Text B has *b'tw* "in its time," a marginal gloss has *b't* "on time" and the Greek has *en kairō* "on time."

with fortitude. Hebrew *gĕbûrâ*, usually translated as "strength, power," may also be taken to mean, lit., "manliness" (cf. Symm: *andragathias*). Thus, one reads in Jer 51:30, "their manliness (*gĕbûrātām*) has dried up, they have become like women" (cf. also Isa 3:25; Judg 8:21). It is also possible that the *gĕbûrâ* mentioned so frequently in annalistic texts of the Bible (1 Kgs 15:23; 16:5, 27; 22:46; 2 Kgs 10:34; 13:8, 12; 14:15, 28; 20:20; 1 Chron 29:30; Esth 10:2) should be compared with the references to the "manly deeds" or "manliness" of the king mentioned frequently in the Hittite annals, which were frequently composed to defend the king against innuendoes about his incompetence. Thus, in the face of criticisms about his lack of qualifications as king, especially his immaturity, Mursilis II gave an account of his *LÚ-natar* "manliness" (see Götze, *Die Annalen des Muršiliš*, p. 20; the term *LÚ-natar* may be used of the male genitalia, as well as "manly deeds"). In the context of our passage in Ecclesiastes, however, this "manliness" is manifested in self-control, as opposed to drunkenness. Syr correctly understands this word, translating it as *bkšyrwt'* "with propriety." Since *gĕbûrâ* is associated not only with physical strength, but also with rightness, goodness, wisdom, and understanding (see *TDOT* II, pp. 369–70), a translation like "maturity" or "fortitude" is appropriate.

carousing. Hebrew *šĕtî* is a *hapax legomenon*, but it is a variant form of *šĕtiyyâ*, which occurs in Esth 1:8 and frequently in Postbiblical Hebrew. One may compare the interchangeability of the forms *bĕkî* and *bĕkiyyâ* "weeping" (the latter form attested in Postbiblical Hebrew) or *šĕbî* and *šibyâ* "captivity." Cf. Ethiopic *sĕtay* "drink, drinking, beverage," but also *sĕtyat* "drinking" (Leslau, *Comparative Dictionary of Ge'ez*, p. 518). LXX (followed by SyrH) apparently reflects Hebrew *bšt* "shame." This is an easier reading, however; *bšty* is an unexpected form, which may explain why it was "corrected." Targ has *bḥlšwt* "with weakness/laxity," which is probably interpretive. Syr (*bmšt'* "in feasting") is also interpretive of the reading in MT.

18. *slothfulness.* Hebrew *'aṣaltayim*, with what appears to be a dual ending, is a *hapax legomenon*. The form is identified in GKC §88.b as the dual form of the

adjective 'āṣēl, and some commentators accept this. Yet, the presence of a dual adjective form in Hebrew is without parallel. Unless what we have here is a loan-word, it is better to vocalize the word as *'aṣlātayim, a dual form of the noun 'aṣlâ "slothfulness," attested in Prov 19:15. In any case, troubled by the use of the dual adjective form, some commentators suggest reading 'ṣlt < > ymk (instead of 'ṣltym ym), assuming a dittography of yod and mem, and vocalizing the substantive either as 'aṣlût to parallel šiplût (e.g., Bickell, Zimmerli), or as 'aṣlat (e.g., Graetz, Fox). Otherwise, the dual form is usually explained as "the dual of intensity," comparable with the ending of common nouns like ṣohŏrayim, mayim, and 'ārābayim, as well as many place names (so Delitzsch, Hertzberg, Gordis). But these endings are little understood and they are, in any case, capable of other explanations (see Joüon-Muraoka §91.f–h; GKC §88.c, d). Moreover, as Fox observes, one should find a warning against *any* laziness at all, not just a double portion of laziness (*Contradictions*, p. 271), or one might add, more intense laziness. It is more likely that the author is thinking of a pair of slow hands (so Ibn Ezra). The dual form thus anticipates šiplût yādayim in the parallel line (so NAB: "when hands are lazy . . . when hands are slack"). We may note in this connection that the related adjective eṣlu in Akkadian is always used of hands and feet, as is the verb eṣēlu (see CAD IV, pp. 341, 350).

collapses. Hebrew yimmak, lit. "sink." It is unclear if the author means that the beam-work of the roof has sagged, partially caved in, or completely collapsed. The basic meaning of the root mkk in classical Hebrew and Aramaic is "to be low, to sink low," but in Ugaritic it appears to have the meaning "to collapse, to fall," or the like (cf. Aramaic mmkmk bmylwy "to crush with his words" in *Targ. Neof.* Gen 44:19). Thus, one reads in KTU 1.2.IV.17: 'z ym lymk ltnǵṣn pnth lydlp tmnh "Yamm was strong, he did not *collapse*, his joints did not wobble, his frame did not crumble."

the house. If this saying is merely a proverb, "house" here is meant literally. Through slothfulness, one's property would be ruined (cf. Prov 6:6–11; 20:4; 21:25; 24:30–34). There is a fragmentary Akkadian wisdom text that may reflect this attitude: a fool would soon become impoverished and soon ruin his house through neglect (see BWL, p. 99, lines 8–18). It is also possible, however, to hear the saying as a subtle criticism of the political establishment. If so, the word "house" may refer not just to the literal house of the lazy fool, but also to the royal "house." Hebrew bayit "house" may, of course, be used in this sense (1 Sam 20:16; 2 Sam 7:11; 1 Kgs 12:26; 13:2; Isa 7:2, 13; etc.). This meaning of "house" is also attested in Ugaritic (bt [m]lk itbd! "the dynasty is ruined," KTU 1.14.I.7–8), Phoenician (see KAI 24.5–6, 16; 26.A.16), Aramaic (e.g., KAI 215.2, 3, 5, 7, 9), and Akkadian (see CAD II, pp. 293–94).

crumbles. The root dlp here has traditionally been taken to mean "drip," and hence, "leak." That is certainly a possible meaning of dlp. The verb is used that way in Job 16:20 ("my eye drips tears"). The occurrence of ydlp in Ugaritic in the same context as ymk "collapsed" (KTU 1.2.IV.17), however, has led several scholars to maintain that Qohelet's usage of dlp may be understood in the light of Ugaritic (so NEB: "the rafters collapse . . . the house crumbles away"). Since *ydlp* in Ugaritic is associated with the verb *ynǵś* "wobbled" (presumably related to Arabic *naǵaḍa*), *ydlp* in Ugaritic is taken to mean "quivered" or "crumbled" (cf. Akkadian *dalāpu* "to disturb, shake"). This meaning of *dlp* is attested in Ps 119:28, where *dālĕpâ napšî mittûgâ qayyĕmēnî kidbārekā* means "My soul crumbles from grief // raise me up according to your word." See W. Moran, "A Note on Ps 119:28," *CBQ* 15 (1953), p. 10, and J. C. Greenfield, "Lexical Notes I," pp. 208–9.

19. *food is prepared.* Hebrew *'ōśîm leḥem*, lit. "(people) prepare food." LXX[BP] and Syr add "and oil," but that reading appears to be expansive; the additional element is not in LXX[AC], SyrH, Theod, Vulg, or Targ. The idiom *'āśâ leḥem* (cf. Ezek 4:15) corresponds to Aramaic *'bd lḥm* "to prepare food (for a feast)" (Dan 5:1). It is roughly synonymous with the more common idiom *'āśâ mišteh* "to prepare a banquet" in Gen 21:8. The subject of the participle *'ōśîm* is nonspecific (see GKC §116.t; cf. Exod 5:16). If this saying is read as a proverb, which one must do if it is read apart from its context, the subject of *'ōśîm* must be people in general: food is prepared for merriment (cf. Syr: "bread and wine are made for merriment, and oil makes life merry") — that is, people generally prepare food for enjoyment. This is how the verse is understood in JB: "We give parties to enjoy ourselves, wine makes us cheerful, and money has an answer for everything." But it is also possible to take the saying as an implicit criticism of the rulers. In that case, the unspecified subject would be the princes mentioned in v 16: they (the princes) prepare food for merriment (cf. LXX) — that is, all they do is prepare to feast (so NJPS: "they make a banquet for revelry").

also wine that gladdens the living. That is, wine that makes mortals happy. Hebrew *wĕyayin yĕśammaḥ ḥayyîm* may be translated simply as "wine gladdens the living." But, with Ibn Ezra, we should probably take *wĕyayin yĕśammaḥ ḥayyîm* here as an asyndetic relative clause (see Joüon-Muraoka §158.d), comparable with similar expressions found elsewhere in the Bible: *wĕyayin yĕśammaḥ lĕbab-'ĕnôš* "and wine that gladdens the human heart" (Ps 104:15); *tîrôšî haśśammĕah 'ĕlōhîm wa'ănāšîm* "my new wine that gladdens gods and mortals" (Judg 9:13). Thus, *wĕyayin yĕśammaḥ ḥayyîm* "even wine that gladdens the living" may be understood as the second object of *'ōśîm*. This interpretation finds some support in LXX[B], where wine is the object of the participle. So, too, Vulg and Targ take wine as the second object of *'śym*. By contrast, LXX[SAC] have *oinos*, taking "wine" as nominative.

preoccupies. The verb *ya'ăneh* may be taken as Qal or Hiphil. The ancient versions are confused: LXX has *epakousetai* and Vulg *obediunt*, both assuming *'nh* to mean "answer, respond" (or as the causative "cause to respond"); but Syr (*m'n'*) apparently takes *'nh* to mean "to afflict." If this whole saying is read as a proverb, we should take it to mean that money "answers" everything. It is, then, an affirmation of money's value, along with other things to be enjoyed by humanity. It is perhaps the sort of saying quoted by people in defense of the enjoyment of life (cf. Ps 104:14–17; Sir 31:27–31). Perhaps it was originally a drinking song, as some have suggested (Galling, Lauha). But if the saying is taken as a criticism of the elite (see the Comment below), we should take the verb as the Hiphil "to preoccupy": they (the rulers) are constantly preparing feasts and drinking the choicest wine, and they are all preoccupied with money! Here, as elsewhere in Qohelet, the root *'nh* is multivalent (see Notes at 1:13).

20. *even.* It is clear that *gam* here is emphatic (see Podechard; Hertzberg).

intimacy. The most obvious meaning of *maddā'* is "knowledge" (2 Chron 1:10–12; Dan 1:4) or "intelligence" (Sir 3:13). Hence many commentators take the word to refer, by extension, to "thoughts." If so, it is argued, v 20 should be rendered as follows: "Do not disparage the rulers even in your thoughts" (see NRSV; NIV; NAB). Such a sense of *maddā'* ("thought") would be unique, however; the word never has this meaning anywhere else. In the Qumran documents, *bmd'w* is attested three times, but there it means "with his knowledge," that is, *deliberately* or *knowingly* (1QS 6.9; 7.3, 5). The word means either "knowledge" or "intelligence," but not "thought" (for which we expect *mahăšābâ*). Thus, *bĕmaddā'ăkā* would not mean "don't think about it" (so Fox and many others), but "don't know it." The latter meaning makes little sense, however. Moreover, our passage suggests that one's disparagement of the authorities even in one's own *maddā'* will be picked up and reported. If *maddā'* means "thoughts" (LXX: *syneidesis* "consciousness") that would be impossible. Gordis is apparently aware of this problem, for he feels compelled to elaborate that what is in one's thoughts (*maddā'*) may be revealed when one is asleep or in an unguarded moment (*Koheleth*, p. 329). Accordingly, one ought not even have such thoughts, because the thoughts may be accidentally expressed out loud. But that is unrealistic advice. The fact that Qohelet is even mentioning the possibility suggests that they are already thinking about it, and what's more, if they are not, he is putting the idea in their heads!

It is possible to take "knowledge" in this context as having sexual connotations, as the root *yd'* so often does. If so, *maddā'* would refer literally to a place of "knowing" in the sexual sense (the *maqṭāl* pattern indicating a noun of place), thus a synonym for the bedroom (so *KBL*, p. 497). Accordingly, *md'* has sexual connotations in Targ of 1 Sam 25:22, where *yd' md'* "one who knows knowledge" refers to one who is a male adult. NASB reflects this understanding of the noun, for it reads: "in your bedchamber (*bĕmaddā'ăkā*) . . . in your sleeping rooms (*ûbĕhadrê miškābĕkā*)."

Still others follow Perles in emending the word to *maṣṣě'ăkā* "your couch" in light of the parallelism with "your bedrooms" (see Perles, *Analekten* I, pp. 71–72; so Zimmerli, Lauha). But all the textual witnesses attest to the substantial accuracy of the consonantal text. The emendation is purely conjectural. D. Winton Thomas has proposed that the word should be vocalized as *mōdā'ăkā* and relates it to Arabic *mawdû'* "rest, repose" ("A Note on בְּמַדָּעֲךָ in Eccles. X.20," p. 177). This is followed by some translators (so NEB: "in your ease"; REB: "when you are at rest"). Better is Dahood's proposal to relate the word here to Akkadian *mudû* "friend" ("Canaanite Words in Qohelet 10:20," pp. 210–12). Cf. *mōdā'* "relative" (Ruth 2:1 [*Qere*]; Prov 7:4).

There is, in fact, no need to emend or repoint the text. In the light of the parallelism with "your bedrooms," we should translate the word as "intimacy," or the like. The root *yd'* may, of course, refer to intimate knowledge of someone or something. In the Qumran Scrolls, *yd'* is sometimes used of the knowledge of secret and esoteric things: *sôd* "secret" and *rāz* "mystery" are often the objects of the verb (see *TDOT* V, p. 481). Indeed in one instance, the noun *md'* refers to esoteric knowledge: "in the eyes of all those who know . . . these are the wonders of knowledge (see 4Q181, Fragment 2, lines 5–7). By translating the noun as "intimacy," we preserve the multivalence of the word in this context. What Qohelet has in mind is the information that one shares with intimate ones (so NJPS) or with those who are "in the know," as it were. Perhaps what he is thinking of here are not only the things that are private or secret, but also the things that are supposed to be cryptic or subversive, things that one only tells to those who are trusted friends.

may carry. A few Hebrew MSS read *ywlk* (instead of *ywlyk*, the imperfect), but the jussive makes no sense. We may assume that *ywlk* merely reflects a defective spelling.

winged creature. Ketib has the definite article, but not *Qere*; both readings are possible. Hebrew *ba'al hakkĕnāpayim*, lit. "possessor of wings," may refer to any winged creature—probably a bird, but possibly also an insect. In Prov 1:17, *ba'al kānāp* refers to a bird, but Ugaritic *b'l knp* refers to a god (*KTU* 1.46.6). Cf. also Hebrew *ba'al haqqĕrānayim* "the one who possesses two horns" (Dan 8:6, 20) and Ugaritic *b'l qr nm wdnb* "the one who possesses two horns and a tail," referring to a deity (*KTU* 1.114.20). In any case, the saying reminds one of the proverbial "little bird" that tells one secrets (as in "a little bird told me so") or the saying that "walls have ears." What one considers safe to say may not, in fact, be kept secret. In the Aramaic *Proverbs of Ahiqar* one finds a similar warning:

> [My] son, do not c[ur]se the day until you have seen [nig]ht,
> Do n[ot] let it come upon your mind,
> since their e[yes] and their ears are everywhere.
> As regards your mouth, watch yourself;
> Let it not be [their] prey.
> Above all watchfulness, watch your mouth,
> and against him who [is listening] harden (your) heart;
> for a word is a bird and one who releases it is without sens[e].

> (see *TAD* III, 1.1.80–82)

may report. Curiously, this verb is taken as the jussive in *Qere*, whereas *yôlîk* earlier in the verse is left untouched. Both forms should be read as imperfects.

11 1. *Release your bread upon the waters.* Hebrew *šlḥ 'l-pny hmym* means "to let float on the surface of the waters." The Piel of *šlḥ* may mean either "to send" or "to release, let go" and *'al-pĕnê hammayim* means specifically "on/upon the surface of the waters" (Gen 1:2; 7:18; Exod 32:20; Isa 18:2; Hos 10:7; Prov 8:27; Job 24:18; 26:10). Isa 18:2 is commonly cited because of the proximity of *haššō-lēaḥ* and *'al-pĕnê-mayim*, but it is clear there that *'al-pĕnê-mayim* means "upon the waters" (not "overseas," or the like). In Postbiblical Hebrew, too, the expression is used of objects floating on water (*m. Ohol.* 8:5; *Para* 9:6; *Beṣa* 5:2; see Fox, *Contradictions*, p. 275). Clearly, *šālaḥ ʿal-pĕnê hammayim* "to release *upon* the waters" should not be confused with *hišlîk ʾel-hammayim* "to throw *into* the waters" (see Exod 15:25). In any case, this verse in Ecclesiastes does mean that one should send merchandise abroad, as it has commonly been suggested. Apart from the meaning of the idiom *šālaḥ ʿal-pĕnê hammayim* ("to release upon the waters"), it must be observed that the presence of a resumptive pronoun at the end of the verse (*timṣāʾennû* "you may find *it*") makes it unlikely that merchandise is meant. Furthermore, if *leḥem* is a metaphor for foreign investment (i.e., merchandise), one should not expect merely to find "it" after many days. One expects to find more than "it"; one expects a profit. If *leḥem* means merchandise, one must interpret the object pronoun to have an unspecified referent, like profit or wealth: that is, send your "bread" overseas, and in time you will find "it." That seems unnecessarily cryptic. We should take *leḥem* to mean "bread." What the author has in mind here is not the thick loaf that surely would not float ("upon the waters"), but one of the variety of flat breads common in the Middle East, perhaps something like the *rāqîq* "wafer" mentioned in the Bible (Exod 29:23; Lev 8:26; 1 Chron 23:29). The verse is not about foreign investments, but about liberality.

after many days. Hebrew *kî-bĕrob hayyāmîm.* It is possible that *kî* here may be motivational: thus, *"for* after many days you will find it" (so NJPS; RSV; NIV). This translation is appropriate, if one interprets the verse to be a call to invest abroad (so NEB). If, however, the point is that spontaneous deeds like the release of bread upon the waters may, despite the odds, yield benefits, then one should take the particle *kî* as a weakened asseverative and leave it untranslated (see Joüon-Muraoka §164.b). The finding of the bread after many days is not the reason for releasing it, although there remains a possibility that all is not lost in the releasing of the bread. For the various alternatives, see Michel, *Eigenart*, pp. 207–8; Ellermeier, *Qohelet* I/1, p. 255.

2. *Give a portion.* The idiom *nātan ḥēleq,* lit. "give a portion," occurs elsewhere in Josh 14:4, 15:13, and Eccl 2:21, in the context of the distribution of property. The noun *ḥēleq* may, however, refer to a share of anything, including wealth (Gen 14:24; 1 Sam 30:24) and food (Hab 1:16; Deut 18:8). The latter meaning is particularly suggestive in light of the preceding verse about releasing bread upon the waters. It must be noted that *nātan ḥēleq lĕ* always means to "give a portion *to*," as in Josh 14:4, *lōʾ-nātĕnû ḥēleq lalwiyyîm* "they did not give a portion to the Levites." In Postbiblical Hebrew, too, the preposition *lĕ-* in this idiom indicates the recipient of the portion: *tĕnû lî ḥelqî* "give me my portion" (see *Sipre Deut.* 312; cf. also *m. Peʾa.* 5:5). The idiom does not mean "to divide a portion among," as many translations and commentaries have it (so NEB). Hence, we should not interpret this verse to mean that one ought to spread the risk around to minimize loss in case of a disaster (Podechard, Whybray). The point, as in v 1, is liberality.

to seven, and even to eight. This is a numerical saying, so the numbers are not to be taken literally (compare Prov 6:16; 30:15–33; Amos 1–2; Sir 25:7; etc.).

The numbers "seven" and "eight" together signify a fairly large, though indefinite, number. So in Mic 5:4 (Eng v 5), frequently in Ugaritic (see the examples cited in *RSP* II.530, pp. 345–46), and in the Phoenician inscription from Arslan Tash (*KAI* 27.17–18). Dahood gives other examples from the Levant ("Canaanite-Phoenician Influence," pp. 212–13), but he goes too far to try to establish Canaanite-Phoenician influence on Qohelet; the seven-eight formula is used to refer to multiplicity or substantiality as far afield as in the various Chinese languages. The numerals simply indicate a large number: various and many. The point of the verse is, again, liberality.

you do not know. Hebrew *kî lōʾ tēdaʿ.* The *kî* is, again, ambiguous. Depending on one's interpretation of the verse, it may be taken as motivational ("for"), concessive ("even though"), emphatic ("indeed"), or, as in v 1, a weakened and untranslatable asseverative. It is most likely that *kî* has a concessive force here ("although"). If so, the point is that one should give generously, *even though* misfortunes may occur.

3. *If the clouds become full, they will pour rain.* The Masoretic punctuation suggests that *gešem* "rain" is the object (accusative of material) of *yimmālĕʾû*. So KJV reads: "If the clouds be full of rain, they empty *themselves* upon the earth" (NIV, without any indication of emendation, reads: "If clouds are full of water, they pour rain upon the earth"). Thus, too, LXX and Syr take *gešem* "rain" as the object of the first verb. Such an interpretation assumes that the second verb, *yārîqû*, is intransitive: they become empty (KJV: "they empty *themselves*"). It is true that *yārîqû* may be parsed either as Qal (intransitive) or Hiphil (transitive), but the former would be unique. It is easier, therefore, to assume a disjunctive accent on *heʿābîm* "clouds" and take *gešem* as the object of *yārîqû* (cf. Zech 4:12; Mal 3:10; see also Jastrow, *Dictionary*, p. 1463): "they pour out rain." The Niphal of *mlʾ* may occasionally omit explicit mention of the object (Exod 7:25; Ezek 26:2; 27:25; 2 Kgs 10:21; Job 15:32; Eccl 1:8; 6:7), so *yimmālĕʾû heʿābîm* simply means "the clouds become full (i.e., saturated)."

north . . . south. As Fox notes, "north . . . south" is a merism for "anywhere" (*Contradictions*, p. 275).

there it will be. The final verb in v 3 is to be analyzed as the Qal imperfect of *hwh*, with the confusion of III-Weak and III-*Alep* roots, a common phenomenon in late Hebrew (cf. Biblical Aramaic *tehĕwēʾ* "shall be" in Dan 2:40; *lehĕwēʾ* "be" in Dan 2:20). See also the form *hōweh* in 2:22. The vocalization of MT is, however, most peculiar. We should expect *yihweʾ* or *yehweʾ* (for *yihweh*), but not *yĕhûʾ*. The Masoretic form may, in fact, be a conflation of two variants: *šām hûʾ* (cf. *qāṭōn wĕgādôl šām hûʾ* "the small and the great are there," Job 3:19) and *šām yihyeh*. Indeed, four MSS read *šām hûʾ* "there it is," which means essentially the same thing as *šām yihweʾ*. The consonantal text of Codex Leningrad (and most MSS) is undoubtedly correct, but some scribes failed to understand the peculiar spelling of *hwh* and so generated the conflate reading.

5. *just as.* Codex Leningrad and most MSS read *kaʾăšer.* Against this, three Hebrew MSS, LXX, Aq, and SyrH read *bʾšr;* but the correlation of the word with

kkh "thus" in v 5b favors the reading of the majority of Hebrew MSS: "just as you do not know (*ka'ăšer 'ênĕkā yôdēa'*) . . . so you will not know (*kākâ lō' tēda'*)."

how the life-breath gets. Hebrew *derek hārûaḥ* refers to the mysterious behavior of the *rûaḥ*. In conventional wisdom, *derek* is sometimes used of the way something behaves or works. Thus, the wonders of nature are expressed in terms of the various "ways" (Prov 30:18–19). As for the meaning of *rûaḥ* here, Targ and LXX correctly interpret it to mean "life-breath" and not "spirit." The author is speaking here of the mystery of the origin of life in a human being.

[into] the fetus. Codex Leningrad has *ka'ăṣāmîm* "as (the) bones/body-frame," which is supported by LXX and Vulg. But this reading is exceedingly problematic. Those who follow it take *kĕ-* to have a conjunctive function like *ka'ăšer*, thus assuming two comparisons: "just as the life-breath . . . (just) as the bones" (so Hertzberg). But as Gordis notes, if two comparisons had indeed been intended, one should expect a copula, *wĕka'ăṣāmîm* (*Koheleth*, p. 332). There is no evidence for the copula, however. We should probably emend to read *ba'ăṣāmîm* with over forty Hebrew MSS and Targ (*bgwp* "in the body") and assume a graphic confusion of *bet* and *kap* (so Ehrlich). The Hebrew noun *'eṣem* may mean not just "bone," but also, especially in the plural, "body-frame" or even "body" (Lam 4:7; Isa 66:14; Prov 3:8; 15:30; 16:24). Likewise, in Akkadian, *eṣemtu* (*GÌR.PAD.DU*) may refer either to "body-frame" or "body" (see CAD IV, esp. p. 343). The meaning "body" is secured by a text that says, *šamnam eṣemtī ula ulabbak* "I cannot rub *my body* with fine oil" (TCL 1 9:8–9). It is clear that *eṣemtu* in this context cannot refer to bones. Even more interesting is an incantation for a woman in labor: *līṣâ nabnītu GÌR.PAD.DU (eṣemtu) aḫītum binût amēlūti arḫiš littasamma* "let a living creature, a body-frame, a human form, come forth quickly (from the womb)" (*BAM* 248, ii.55 = *KAR* 196). The *eṣemtu* in this case refers to the body-frame of a fetus. So, too, *'ăṣāmîm* in our passage probably refers to the body of the fetus that is in the mother's belly. The point is that no one knows how or when the life-breath enters the body of the fetus and somehow gives it life. The enlivening of the fetus is doubly wondrous, since this "body" is itself in the body of another.

in the belly of the pregnant woman. Since *bĕbeṭen hammĕlē'â* is apparently a construct chain, one should take *hammālē'â* as a substantive, "the full one," hence, "the pregnant one." This is the interpretation of LXX, Vulg, and Syr. This usage of *mālē'â* is attested in Mishnaic Hebrew (m. Yebam. 16:1; cf. Ruth 1:21). It is also attested at Qumran (see Qimron, *Hebrew of the Dead Sea Scrolls*, p. 92). The choice of this word is probably part of a wordplay with *yimmālĕ'û* in v 3. When the clouds are "full" (*yimmālĕ'û*), one expects rain, even though one knows nothing of what the wind (*rûaḥ*) might do; when a woman is "full" (*mālē'â*), one expects a child to be born, even though one knows not how, when, or even if the life-breath (*rûaḥ*) might enter the fetus.

6. *in the morning . . . at evening.* The pair, *babbōqer . . . lā'ereb* does not mean "from morning *till* evening," for which one should expect *mibbōqer . . . lā'ereb* (Job 4:20). Nor does it mean "in the morning . . . till the evening," which would

be expressed by *mibbōqer . . . ʿad-bōqer*. Rather, as Fox has argued (*Contradictions*, p. 277), the pair together means "at any time" or "regularly" (see Gen 49:27; Ps 90:6; 1 Chron 23:30. Cf. *lbqr . . . lʿrb* (Ezra 3:3; 1 Chron 16:40).

your hand. Many Hebrew MSS read a dual, *ydyk* "your hands."

equally. Hebrew *kĕʾeḥād*, lit. "altogether," occurs only in Late Biblical Hebrew (Isa 65:25; Ezra 2:64; 3:9; 6:20; 2 Chron 5:13) and in the Mishnah (*Bek.* 7:4; cf. also *kĕʾaḥat* in *Kil.* 1:9). It is probably a calque from Aramaic *kḥdh/kḥdʾ* (Dan 2:35; Targ on Gen 13:6; see also *TAD* II, 1.1.6).

COMMENT

The new unit is marked by a shift in mood from the author's reflection (9:11–10:15) to a direct address of the audience (10:16–11:6). Yet, the observation that everything in life is precarious is continued; the sense of danger conveyed in 9:11–10:15 still pervades. Two sections are discernible within the unit, the first concerns risks in the political realm (10:16–20); the second is about risks in the economic realm (11:1–6). Across these two sections of the passage, however, are some suggestive links. The fate of the "land" is of concern in the first section (twice in 10:16–17), as it is in the second (twice in 11:2–3). The whole passage begins with the slothfulness of rulers "in the morning" (10:16), and it ends with a summons to diligence "in the morning" (11:6). Likewise, we find a reference to the "slackness of hands" in 10:18, but in 11:6 there is a call not to "let your hand go." Thus, we have two sections that are intended to be read together. The passage appropriately follows the preceding unit (9:13–10:15), which concerns the precarious nature of everything in life. Now the author, ever the pragmatist, turns to give some practical advice on how to live in such a world so filled with risks.

Risks in the Political Realm (10:16–20)
This section is framed by the references to the political elite in 10:16–17 (the king and princes) and 10:20 (the king and the rich). The *inclusio* poses a problem for the interpreter, however, for the author appears to begin with explicit and implicit criticisms of the political establishment (10:16–17), but he ends with a warning not to engage in criticism of the powerful (10:20). The end of the section appears to contradict the beginning. Moreover, it is not easy to see how the middle portion (10:18–19) fits the framework.

It is clear that the two declarations in 10:16–17 belong together, although one is stated negatively (v 16) and the other positively (v 17). The vilification of the rulers is explicit in 10:16. The king is said to be a *naʿar* "minor." It is not clear, however, if the text is referring to the king's youth or to his social status; both meanings are possible in Hebrew (see Notes above). If the reference is to the king's youth, one may note that there are similar polemics against pretenders to royal thrones elsewhere in the ancient Near East. So the Hittite king, Mursilis II, was slandered by his enemies, who said: "[Mursilis] who now sits upon his father's throne is a youth and he is not able to defend the land of Hatti and its borders" (see Götze, *Die Annalen des Mursilis*, 20). Likewise, Nabonidus of Babylon charged that one of his rivals, Labashi-Marduk, tried to take the throne while he was still a minor and had not yet "learned how to behave" (*ANET*[3], p. 309). References to a ruler's youth became part and parcel of political rhetoric, used in attacks on the ruler's legitimacy. In the royal apologies, however, the rulers sometimes dealt with the charges head on and, indeed, deliberately pointed to their own youth as a sign of their divine calling. Thus, Nabopolassar, who had usurped the Babylonian throne, admitted that he was "a son of a nobody," but he also insisted that the gods had chosen him in his youth (S. Langdon, *Die neubabylonischen Königsinschriften* [VAB 4; Leipzig: Hinrich's, 1912] p. 66).

The Hebrew word *na'ar*, however, may be used in the sense of a "servant." If so, the saying in v 16 intends to contrast such a one of low estate with one who is high-born, a *ben-ḥōrîm* "noble" (so v 17). The text seems, therefore, to echo earlier comments about the social upheaval in the land (see the Comment on 10:6–7). Conventional wisdom expresses horror over this kind of upheaval, and it is said that the land cannot tolerate "a servant when he becomes king" (Prov 30:22). So the insult in 10:16 is either that the king is immature, or that he is a parvenu, a nobody. Whether one takes the *na'ar* to be literally a "youth" or a "servant," the point is that incompetent people have gained ascendancy (compare 9:17–18; 10:5–6). And other leaders, too, have proven themselves unqualified by their indiscretion. They feast at inappropriate times; they carouse early in the morning (see Isa 5:11; Acts 2:15). These "minors" seem to be primarily interested in revelry at all hours of the day. The same point about proper conduct is made in 10:17, although there it is stated positively, namely, that dignified and responsible leaders do behave appropriately: "they feast on time, with fortitude and not with carousing." The flip side of the truth of 10:16 is stated in 10:17. By pointing to what responsible conduct is like, any actual immaturity and incompetence is revealed as such. Whereas the criticism in 10:16 is explicit, it is only implicit in 10:17.

There is insufficient information for us to speculate about the precise historical background of what is said. We do not know who the king and rulers were; nor do we have any information about the nobles. We do not know if there was such a king who was literally or practically immature, or if he was a parvenu. Commentators have sometimes tried to be specific in their identification of these figures, but they have failed to convince. Comments about the proper conduct of rulers are, in fact, typical of didactic literature throughout the ancient Near East. Indeed, it has long been argued that much of ancient Near Eastern wisdom literature, at least in the case of Egypt, grew out of the court schools that were intended to train youngsters to be rulers and bureaucrats. So what we have in 10:16–17 are precisely the kinds of things that one might expect to find in textbooks of the court schools. Indeed, one may compare the teachings here to admonitions given to King Lemuel in Prov 31:4–5.

If these comments were directed at actual leaders in Qohelet's time, as many scholars have surmised, then one may note the subtlety of presentation. They are couched in terms of typical sapiential comments. They are also presented in a balanced way, with a negative comment (10:16) and a positive one (10:17). And they are addressed to the land rather than to the rulers and aristocrats themselves. They are aimed at the rulers and aristocrats, but they are presented in such a way that their originators may deny culpability as to their political intent. Indeed, what we may have here is a parody of subversive political comments in Qohelet's time. The perpetrators were apparently taking jabs at the political establishment, but they were doing so through what they thought were the safe havens of sapiential forms. They were criticizing the rulers and aristocrats, but pretending that they were only proffering disinterested wisdom teachings.

In 10:18–19 we have two other examples of political commentary in the guise of neutral proverbs. At first blush, these appear to be typical wisdom sayings. Thus, 10:18 teaches that discipline is essential to ensure stability: "through slothfulness the beam-work collapses; through slackness of hand the house crumbles." This seems no different from the typical sapiential admonition against laziness (see Prov 6:6–11; 20:4; 21:25; 24:30–34). And 10:19 may be interpreted positively as an affirmation of life's pleasures and rewards: food is meant to be eaten, wine makes people happy, and "money answers everything" (see Notes). In isolation from a specific context both proverbs seem innocuous enough. One should, of course, be diligent and careful, but one should enjoy life's pleasures. The original saying could well have been a drinking song, lyrics in praise of life's pleasures (so Galling, Lauha).

It is also possible, however, to hear in these sayings an implicit criticism and threat of the political elite. The "house" in 10:18, then, would not refer simply to any house, but may have political overtones (so Hertzberg, Lohfink), particularly if one interprets the saying within the context of the political framework that the section provides. That is, if we assume that these sayings have to do with kings, princes, and the rich (10:16–17, 20), the proverbs take on different meanings. Isolated from its context, one finds the proverb to be totally innocent, but heard in the context of sayings pertaining to the king and princes, "house" has different nuances. The word "house" may be interpreted in the sense of a "dynasty," a usage found in the Bible and elsewhere in the Levant. Thus, the proverb becomes both a criticism of the political establishment and, perhaps, even an implicit threat: through negligence the "house" is in danger of collapse! The rulers who eat and drink at all times of the day (10:17) are responsible for the demise of their own domain.

By the same token, 10:19 could be taken as a criticism of the lifestyles of those in power. In this negative reading, 10:19c may be taken to mean that money keeps everyone—that is, everyone of the ruling classes—preoccupied. Thus, 10:19 can be read as an affirmation of pleasure—perhaps that was the original use of the saying—but it can also be taken as an indictment of the lifestyle of the rich: all they do is prepare food for parties, including the most intoxicating wine, and they are all preoccupied with money. The text is capable of both a positive and a negative reading. The proverb may not be so innocent after all. The vilification of the ruling class in 10:16–17 is, in fact, continued in 10:18–19.

It must be admitted that the criticisms, apart from 10:16, are not obvious. Indeed, were it not for 10:20, one would not even interpret them negatively at all. They are negative only when read or heard in certain contexts. They are "inside jokes," as it were, capable of one interpretation when uttered publicly, but have another meaning for those "in the know." They are furtive political comments disguised as innocuous wisdom teachings. And that, indeed, is what Qohelet is concerned about. Even such cryptic and private criticisms will become known, presumably to those from whom one intends to keep the secret. There are risks in taking on those in positions of power, so one must be careful not to talk subversively even in subtlety or in the privacy of one's bedroom (compare also Mic 7:5–6; Luke 12:3). Indeed, through unexpected agents the secret may be leaked: "for a bird of the sky may carry the utterance and a winged creature may report the matter."

Here the allusion may be to the ubiquitous presence of spies. The Greek historians wrote of various government informants during the Persian period known as "the eyes and ears of the king" (Xenophon, *Cyropaedia* VIII.ii.10; Herodotus I.114). From Elephantine in Egypt, where a Jewish community existed during the Persian period, comes a letter mentioning the presence of such agents of the Persian government: "magistrates, police, and 'listeners' who are appointed in the province" (see the text in *TAD* I, 4.5.9). The term translated as "listeners" (*gwšky*) is an Old Persian loanword and probably refers to the Persian government agents known as "the king's ears." A cognate of that word in Armenian (*gušak*) means "informer." Circulating among the Jews of the same Jewish community in Egypt is the wisdom text known as the *Proverbs of Ahiqar*, which warns one to be careful with what one says because "there are eyes and ears everywhere" (see Notes above). A word is like a bird, according to this text, that the fool releases. Qohelet is probably issuing a similar warning to his audience. They are engaging in subversive talk, perhaps disguising their criticisms as common wisdom teachings. But Qohelet warns that such activities are dangerous. Indeed, there are "eyes" and "ears" everywhere, and what is said in private or within an inner circle may be leaked to the authorities. There are dangers everywhere. There are dangers in the political realm, but there are some things that one can do, or rather, *not do*, to minimize the risks.

Risks in the Economic Realm (11:1–6)

The first two verses in Chapter 11 have been interpreted in various ways. A common assumption among recent commentators is that they concern the wisdom of sound economic planning: together these verses, it is believed, constitute commercial advice (so Gordis, Zimmerli, Crenshaw, Murphy, and others). According to this view, 11:1 advocates investment abroad, and 11:2 concerns the diversification of one's investments in case of disasters. The translation of NEB reflects this perspective: "Send your grain across the seas, and in time you will get a return. Divide your merchandise among seven ventures, eight maybe, since you do not know what disasters may occur on earth."

It is evident, however, that several questionable interpretive moves are required to make the text fit the theory. Thus, in the translation of NEB, *leḥem* "bread" is interpreted to mean "grain," *'al-pĕnê hammayim* "upon (or 'on the surface of') the waters" is taken to mean "across the seas," the object pronoun "it" at the end of the verse ("you shall find *it*") is interpreted as profit (instead of its obvious antecedent "bread"). The *leḥem* "bread"/"grain" is then taken to refer to "merchandise." The idiom "give a portion to" is interpreted to mean "divide portions among," and the unspecific "seven" and "eight" are taken to refer to seven or eight *ventures*. Other commentators take "seven" and "eight" to refer to different vessels that carry the merchandise abroad: do not put all your merchandise on the same vessel — in case something happens that may destroy all your investments.

Thus, these two verses are taken to be encouraging foreign investment (because it will bring higher yield) and the diversification of one's investments to hedge against bad times. In short, take the risk of investing abroad, but do not put all your eggs in the same basket (so Gordis). If 11:1 is about investment, however, it is not sound economic advice, for the author seems to say that one may eventually recover what one puts out: "in many days you will find it." One should get back *more* than one's capital outlay and not just "find it" after many days! Moreover, the Hebrew verb "to find" is never used of commerce. It is true that *leḥem* may refer to grain (Isa 28:28; Prov 30:23), but the Hebrew in this verse suggests that the *leḥem* is allowed to float on the surface of the waters. It is doubtful, too, if "bread" is ever used in the sense of general merchandise anywhere in the Bible. Prov 31:14 is sometimes cited as evidence for such a usage of the word, but in the context of Proverbs 31 the capable wife-mother (*'ēšet ḥayil*) is only said to bring food for her family *like* merchant ships. The point is that this wife/mother brings *food* from afar, even as the ships bring merchandise from afar.

Furthermore, the Hebrew at the beginning of 11:2 does not mean "divide the merchandise *among*," but "give a portion *to*" (see Notes above). Most importantly, the idea of an economic plan, in this case foreign investments and diversification of one's risk, certainly contradicts everything Qohelet says. Instead, he persistently calls for spontaneous actions without too much anxiety about calculated consequences. The point of the sayings (11:1–2), then, is not that one must be shrewd in economic planning, but that people ought to take some chances, even if they do not know what will happen.

Regarding the saying in 11:1, H. Lewy notes that there are remarkably similar proverbs in Greek, Turkish, and Arabic, as well as in Goethe's writings (see "Parallelen zu antiken Sprichwörtern und Apophthegmen," *Philologus* 58 [1899], pp. 80–81). Unpublished when Lewy wrote is an even more striking parallel found in the Egyptian *Instruction of Ankhsheshonq*, the only extant witness from the Ptolemaic period, but the composition of which is undoubtedly earlier:

> Do a good deed and throw it in the water;
> when it dries you will find it.

> (19,1; see *AEL* III, p. 174)

In this proverb, as in most of the examples cited by Lewy, instead of releasing bread upon the water, as we have it in Ecclesiastes, one is exhorted to do good or perform a good deed and discard it in the water.

It appears, then, that to release the bread on the waters is to take the risk of a spontaneous good deed. The bread that is mentioned in this regard probably refers to one of a variety of lightweight, flat breads common in the Levant. In any case, releasing bread upon the water is a metaphor for doing good without expecting rewards: one should throw away a good deed, as it were — just let it go — without expecting a return. Indeed, this is how the earliest interpreters understood the metaphor (so the Targum, *Qoh. Rabb.*, *b. Yebam.* 121a, Gregory Thaumaturgos).

This is also the understanding of the proverb quoted in a long Arabic tale cited by H. F. von Diez (*Denkwürdigkeiten von Asien* I, [Berlin: Nicolaischen Buchhandlung, 1811], pp. 106–16). According to this story, a certain Mohammed the son of Hassan, threw bread daily upon the water and inadvertently saved the life of a caliph's adopted son. The prince had almost drowned downstream but had managed to climb onto a rock, where he had been stranded. He was sustained by the bread that floated daily down the river. Mohammed was subsequently rewarded for his spontaneous deeds, thus confirming for him the truth of the proverb that he had learned as a youth: "Do good, cast your bread upon the waters; one day you will be rewarded." Or, as the Turkish version of the proverb has it: "Do good, cast bread into the water; if the fish does not know it, God will" (quoted by von Diez, *Denkwürdigkeiten*, p. 115).

The Medieval Jewish commentators Rashi and Rashbam, likewise, understood the casting of bread as acts of liberality that may be unexpectedly beneficial to the doer. As Martin Luther explained it, the Hebrew expression means "share your food, which the Lord has given you . . . [t]he fact that you have been generous with others will not perish, even though it seems to perish" (*Luther's Works*, Vol. 15; [ed. J. Pelikan; St. Louis: Concordia, 1972], p. 171). Goethe puts it like this: "Why do you want to find out where generosity flows! Throw your bread into the water! Who knows who will enjoy it" (*West-östlicher Divan* [ed. H. A. Maier; Tübingen: Niemeyer, 1965], p. 111).

Qohelet's point seems clear: one ought to take some risks in doing good, for even in those seemingly frivolous deeds one may find some surprising rewards. It is not that one must put out something to get back more later on, nor that one should give in order to receive. Rather, all may not be lost in spontaneity. One should throw away a good deed and not worry about the consequences, for the consequences of human actions are often contrary to expectations.

The same point is made in 11:2, which is, again, about liberality. One should give freely — not just to a few, but indeed to many (see Notes above) — even if one does not know what terrible things may happen in the future. Presumably terrible tragedies may strike; the economy may collapse. No one knows if or when a misfortune may happen. Generosity ought not be kept in abeyance in anticipation of possible tragedies ahead. There are risks to be sure, but one cannot refrain from doing good just because of the possibility that bad things may happen in the future.

Qohelet intends for 11:1 to be read with 11:2 (Galling, Hertzberg). On the one hand, he says that a person cannot anticipate a positive outcome from a spontaneous act of liberality. One may do something without thinking much about it and, yet, all is not lost in that spontaneous act (11:1). On the other hand, he says that one ought to not expect a negative outcome from one's generosity. One should not stop giving generously because hard economic times may come in the future (11:2). In the first instance one may unexpectedly regain what one has given up before (11:1). By the same token, one cannot know what bad things may happen in the future (11:2). In any case, one should be generous. Qohelet is a realist. He does not promise that liberality will be rewarded. He does not say that those who give generously will *not* face economic hardships later on. He does, nevertheless, urge the risk of liberality. People cannot live life always wondering about what will happen — either anticipating a good outcome (11:1) or fearing a negative outcome (11:2).

A couple of aphorisms are introduced in 11:3, which give the initial impression of contradicting what is said in 11:1–2. The two sayings in 11:3 seem to suggest that there is a certain amount of predictability in nature: when clouds are saturated, it will rain; when a tree falls in any direction, there it will be. Scholars sometimes contend that Qohelet's advice in 11:3–4 is that we must watch nature to learn how to predict it. But that is only the first impression that Qohelet wants to give, for he quickly emphasizes the impossibility of knowledge — three times in the next two verses!

The impression of human ability to know in 11:3–4 is but another of Qohelet's rhetorical setups. That initial impression dissipates like mist when one reads the sayings in 11:3–4 in context, noticing that the sayings are sandwiched between comments about what people cannot know (11:2, 5–6). Qohelet, again, first gives the impression that nature is dependable, perhaps even citing commonly recognized aphorisms, only to conclude the opposite. He does not, in fact, think nature is so utterly predictable — certainly not to the extent that one can live by observing it (see Comment at 3:1–15). He has already argued in 11:1–2 that no one can predict what things, whether good or bad, will happen (v 2: "you do not know"). He will reinforce that argument in 11:5 ("you do not know").

Indeed, neither the clouds nor the winds are perceived in the wisdom tradition as being understandable (see Job 36:29). As for the wind, it is the ultimate symbol of things that are unpredictable (see the Comment at 1:14). To be sure, one may know something about natural law (for instance, when the clouds are saturated it will rain). But one has no control over the event; one does not know when the rain will come.

The author is, in fact, pointing to "the *inevitability* of the natural process" (Whybray). When a tree is uprooted it will fall and it makes no difference whether it falls in one direction or another. The point is not that one must depend on one's observation of nature, despite the fact that saturated clouds do generally bring rain and trees will fall when they are uprooted. On the contrary,

344

one cannot count on the reliability of "natural laws." Nature may give one the impression of predictability, but it is in fact not completely predictable. Certainly the natural phenomena are beyond human control. And so one cannot read the signs of nature before one acts. The NJPS translation conveys the meaning of the passage well: "if one watches the wind, one will never sow; and if one observes the cloud, one will never reap" (compare also NEB).

Qohelet is thinking here of farmers who are constantly postponing what needs to be done for fear of inclement weather. There are those who will not sow for fear that the wind might be too strong, and there are those who will not reap for fear that the rain might ruin their harvest. They are reluctant to take any risk at all because they are looking for perfect conditions. They want to watch nature, as if human knowledge about nature were so completely reliable. But Qohelet insists that one may have to be more spontaneous and take some risks. Despite some signs of reliability, nature is still a mystery. Too much care in planning may be crippling, for the timing of nature is beyond human ability to control.

The point is further clarified in 11:5. Human beings do not really know how nature works. In 11:4 Qohelet uses the Hebrew word *rûaḥ* to mean "wind," and he uses the same word in 11:5, except that in the latter verse he means human breath. He uses the verb *yimmālě'û* "become full" to speak of the cloud's saturation in 11:3, and then in 11:5 he uses the word *hammĕlē'â* — literally "the full one" — to speak of the pregnant mother. He could have used other words for the woman (such as *'ēm* "mother," *hārâ* "pregnant woman"), but he does not. He uses this word: *hammĕlē'â* "the full one." Thus, vv 3–5 are linked by catchwords and are probably meant to be interpreted together. When the clouds are "full" one knows that it will probably rain, but one does not know what the wind might do. The result is beyond human control. By the same token, when a woman is "full," one knows that an infant will probably be born, but one knows nothing about the mysteries of the life-breath — how, when, or even *if* the life-breath might enter the body of the fetus (see 6:3–5). The result is beyond human control. If the *rûaḥ* as wind is mysterious and unpredictable, so is the *rûaḥ* as the breath of life. No one knows how the *rûaḥ* behaves. It is all a mystery.

A similar analogy drawn between the wind's unpredictable ways and the mystery of birth is taken up in the New Testament in Jesus' discourse on spiritual rebirth: "the wind blows where it chooses, and you hear the sound of it, but you do not know where it comes from or where it goes. So it is with everyone who is born of the Spirit" (John 3:8). The way of the *rûaḥ* "wind/life-breath" is an utter mystery: you cannot know it. The result of its activity is beyond human control.

Just so, no one really will ever know how God works (11:5b). The consequences are beyond human control. This is finally the point that Qohelet wants to emphasize — not the unpredictable wind or the mysteriousness of life-breath, but the ways of God, who is the one who makes everything happen. The wind and the life-breath are only analogies through which the author points to the unpredictable and mysterious ways of God. The text is deliberate in its comparison: "just as you *do not know* . . . so *you will not know*" (11:5). Qohelet moves from the elements of nature, to the wonders of life coming into being, and ultimately to theology: wind is unpredictable (11:4), the life-breath is a mystery (11:5a), and God is inscrutable (11:5b).

Qohelet's message is that one cannot have all the consequences calculated to the last detail before one proceeds with what needs to be done. He returns to the issue of timing and propriety broached at the beginning of the literary unit (10:16). The expression "in the morning" occurs in 10:16 and 11:6; the reference to slackness of hand in 10:18 is answered by the charge not to let go of the hand in 11:6. Or as it is said in the Aramaic *Proverbs of Ahiqar*: "Harvest any harvest and do any work" (*TAD* III, 1.1, col. 9, line 127).

Certainly the exhortation to be spontaneous (11:1–6) does not mean that one should relinquish diligence and propriety. Spontaneity does not mean that one should carouse "in the morning" (10:16) or show "slackness of hands" (10:18). Rather, Qohelet says "sow in the morning, and at evening do not let go your hand" (11:6). What he means by this is not that people should work all the time, or work long hours (see the Notes). Morning and evening are not times when one must or should work; they are times when one *may* work. They are not mandatory times for work. Rather, they are permissive times. One may do what one feels should be done at *any* time — as the need or the opportunity arises, even though no one knows what the outcome will be every time. The reader must interpret the end of the unit together with its beginning. Qohelet says one ought to take risks and be responsive to opportunities, yet be diligent and responsible at the same time. What he advocates in the face of all the risks is to maintain a balance between responsibility and spontaneity.

II.B.4. CONCLUSION (11:7–12:8)

11 ⁷Light is pleasant,
>   and it is delightful for the eyes to see the sun.
> ⁸If one should live many years,
>   let one rejoice in them all,
>   and remember that the days of darkness may be many;
>   all that comes is vanity.
> ⁹Rejoice, O youth, while you are young,
>   let your heart delight you in the days of your prime.
>   Follow the ways of your heart and what your eyes see;
>   and know that on account of all these,
>   God will bring you into judgment.
> ¹⁰Remove vexation from your heart,
>   and banish unpleasantness from your body,
>   for youth and the dawn of life are vanity.
12 ¹Remember your creator in the days of your prime,
>   before the days of unpleasantness come and years arrive,

when you will say, "I have no pleasure in them";
²before the sun darkens, even the light,
   and the moon and the stars,
   and the clouds return with the rain;
³at the time when those who watch the house tremble,
   and valiant men convulse;
 those who grind stop because they are diminished,
   and those who look through the windows grow dim;
⁴the double-doors in the street-bazaar are shut,
      while the sound of the mill drops;
   the sound of the birds rises,
      and all the daughters of song come down low —
⁵even from on high they see terror on the way;
      the almond becomes revolting, the locust droops,
         and the caper comes to naught;
 Yea, the human goes to the grave,
      and the mourners march in the street-bazaar;
⁶before the silver tendril is smashed,
      and the golden bowl is crushed;
   the jar is broken at the spring,
      and the vessel is crushed at the pit.
⁷Dust returns to the earth where it had been,
      and the life-breath returns to God who gave it.
⁸Vanity of vanities, says Qohelet, everything is vanity!

NOTES

11   7. *Light is pleasant.* The *waw* at the beginning of the verse is disjunctive. We need not, however, take the *waw* to be emphatic (see Ellermeier, *Qohelet*, I/1, pp. 303–6). It introduces a new theme and, therefore, need not be translated. Cf. the introductory *waw* in 3:16; 4:4; 8:10; 12:1. Note also the *waw* introducing both parts of the epilogue (12:9, 12). The adjective *mātôq* means literally "sweet," but here it is used in the sense of "pleasant," as in *mĕtûqâ šĕnat hāʿōbēd* "the worker's sleep is pleasant" (5:11 [Eng v 12]). The word is a synonym of the parallel term, *ţôb* "delightful, pleasant, good." One notes, too, that the Akkadian equivalent of the word, *matqu* "sweet," is glossed in lexical texts as *ţābu* "good, delightful, sweet" (see the references in *CAD* X/1, p. 413).

to the eyes. The form *laʿênayim* shows virtual doubling of the ʿ*ayin*, as in 1 Sam 16:7, instead of compensatory lengthening (BL, §31.g). See Notes on *lĕyaʾēš* at 2:20.

to see the sun. The idiom means "to be alive." Cf. *lĕrōʾê haššāmeš* "to those who see the sun" (7:11); *šemeš lōʾ rāʾâ* "has not seen the sun" (6:5). See also Pss 49:20 (Eng v 19); 58:9 (Eng v 8); Job 3:16. One may also compare the saying in the *Gilgamesh Epic*: "May my eyes see the sun so that I may have my fill of light" (Gilg M 13; cf. Gilg X i 13). Scholars cite Euripides: "Sweet it is to see the light"

(*Iphigenia in Aulis*, I.1218). This parallel does not, however, prove that the saying in our passage is borrowed from the Greek.

8. *If.* The force of *kî 'im* is unclear. Although elsewhere in the book *kî 'im* may be exceptive (3:12; 5:10; 8:15), here one should probably understand *kî* as a weakened asseverative and leave it untranslated (see Joüon-Muraoka §164.b). The presence of *kî* connects this verse to the preceding.

let one rejoice . . . and remember. The verbs *yiśmaḥ* and *wĕyizkōr* should both be interpreted as jussives. They anticipate the imperative forms *śĕmaḥ* "rejoice" (11:9) and *zĕkōr* "remember" (12:1). We should not, therefore, follow Ellermeier (*Qohelet*, I/1, pp. 303–6) in taking these verbs as indicative (so also Lauha).

in them all. We are to understand "rejoice in them all" as "be happy in (i.e., during) all of them" rather than "be happy about them" or "enjoy all of them." The preposition *bĕ-* is temporal; it indicates the times when one should enjoy, not the object of enjoyment. Cf. the use of the same preposition in the next verse: *śĕmaḥ bāḥûr bĕyaldûteka* "rejoice, O youth, in your youth" = "rejoice, O youth, when you are young" // *bîmê bĕḥûrôteka* "in the days of your prime."

remember that the days of darkness may be many. Lit. "remember the days of darkness, that they may be many." The anticipation of the object is typical of Qohelet's style (cf. 9:11; 10:3). The "days of darkness" refers not to death (Gordis) or Sheol (Barton), but to a time of gloom and misery (see Job 3:4–5; 15:23; Amos 5:18). Cf. *kol-yāmāyw baḥōšek yōʾkēl wĕkāʿas harbēh wĕholyô wĕqāṣep* "all his days he consumes in darkness, and much vexation, sickness and anger" (5:16 [Eng v 17]), where the days of darkness are the gloomy and miserable days in one's lifetime. The expression is also clarified in 12:1 as *yĕmê hārāʿâ* "the days of unpleasantness." The author probably has old age in mind (so Ehrlich), but not only that; he is thinking of all the difficult times that may come in the future. The reference to darkness, however, anticipates the darkening of the luminaries in the sky in 12:3, a reference to the end of human existence. For Qohelet, the darkness does not come only at the end of one's life, it may begin to dominate even when one is alive (see Comment at 5:16 [Eng v 17]): one's days of darkness may begin even when there is still light!

all that comes. Most commentators take *kol-šebbāʾ* "all that comes" to mean the future, after death. Whybray, for instance, interprets the expression thus: "'that which will happen afterwards': that is, the future (after death)" (*Ecclesiastes*, p. 161). For Qohelet, however, everything is *hebel*—not just what comes after death; all the experiences of life, and life itself, are *hebel*; they are all ephemeral and beyond human ability to control. It is unlikely that the author is talking about what comes after death, about which he insists no one knows anything (see 3:21; 10:14). Moreover, whenever Qohelet refers to future happenings, he uses the expression *meh šeyyihyeh / mah ššeyyihyeh* "whatever will be" (see 3:22; 8:7; 10:14), *mah-yyihyeh* "what will be" (6:12; 11:2), or *šeyyihyeh* (1:9, 11; 2:18), but never *kol-šebbāʾ* "all that comes." The term *šebbāʾ* appears twice in the book, both times referring to people coming into existence (5:14–15 [Eng vv 16–17]). Cf. also 6:4, *bahebel bāʾ ûbaḥōšek yēlēk* "[the stillborn infant] comes in vanity and goes in darkness"; *šeyyābôʾ* "(someone) who comes" (2:12). In the introduction to the book (1:4), the author speaks of generations of people going (*hōlēk*) and coming (*bā'*) while the earth stands *lĕ'ôlām*. He speaks now of all that comes (*bā'*), referring to anyone who comes. At the end of this passage (in 12:6), he speaks of humanity going (*hōlēk*) to the "house of eternity" (*bêt 'ôlāmô*). It makes sense to take *kol-šebbā'* in 11:8 as referring to anyone who comes — or any generation that comes — into existence. The point is that every human, like anyone or anything else on earth, is *hebel*. Nothing is permanent, so one who has come into this world better enjoy while there is still time.

vanity. See Notes at 1:2.

9. *while you are young.* We should read *bĕyaldûtekā* with the Ben Ḥayyim edition of the Rabbinic Bible and some MSS (so Kennicott nos. 18, 77, 157, 166), instead of *bĕyaldûtêkā* in Codex Leningrad and numerous other MSS. Certainly the correct forms should be *bĕyaldûtekā* // *bĕḥûrôtêkā* (cf. 12:1), instead of *bĕyaldûtêkā* // *bĕḥûrôtekā*, as we have it in BHS. It is possible to take the preposition *bĕ-* as indicating the object of the enjoyment (so Ehrlich: "enjoy your youth"), but the parallelism with *bîmê bĕḥûrôtêkā* "in the days of your prime" suggests that the expression is temporal: "in your youth" = "while you are young" // "in the days of your prime." Cf. *byldwty* "in my youth" (b. Ḥull. 24b) and *byldwtk* "in your youth" (b. 'Abod. Zar. 52b). Given the fact that a *bāḥûr* "youth" is addressed, we should probably interpret *yaldût* not as "childhood" (NASB) or "boyhood" (NEB). The term *yaldût* may be used of a young adult, as in b. 'Abod. Zar. 52b, cited above (see Notes at 4:13). The *bāḥûr* refers to a male in the prime of life (the choice period), someone eligible for military service.

let your heart delight you. The verb is to be parsed as the Hiphil imperfect of *ṭwb* (thus, **wĕyĕṭîbĕkā > wîṭîbĕkā*), rather that the Hiphil of *yṭb*. The choice of the root *ṭwb* recalls the use of *ṭôb* in 11:7. In any case, we should not emend the text to read the Qal imperfect, as Ehrlich, Galling, and others have done (cf. NASB: "let your heart be pleasant"; NAB: "let your heart be glad"). The idiom is not the same as *yîṭab lēb* "the heart will be glad" in 7:3, where there is no direct object of the verb. Here we have a direct object, so the Hiphil is correct. The heart is the active (personified) subject here, as it is in 2:1–3.

in the days of your prime. The form *bĕḥûrôtekā* is unique to Ecclesiastes (see also 12:1). Elsewhere in the Bible, we find the masculine plural form, as in Num 11:28. But one may compare the use of the unique form *nĕ'ûrôt* "youth" in Jer 32:30 for the more common noun *nĕ'ûrîm*. In any case, the noun here and in 12:1 is abstract (cf. BL §61.y.α); it must not be confused with *bahûrîm/bahûrôt* (with the virtual doubling of *ḥet*) "young people" (see Joüon-Muraoka §136.h.Note 2).

Follow the ways of your heart. Hebrew *wĕhallēk bĕdarkê libbĕkā*, lit. "walk in the ways of your heart." The idiom may be compared with Egyptian *šms-ib* "follow the heart" = "follow one's desire" = "enjoy" (cf. also the idiom *swt nt šms-ib* "places of following the heart" = "places of enjoyment" (see WbÄS IV, pp. 483–84). After the phrase "follow the ways of your heart," LXX adds *amōmos* "blamelessly" and, instead of "and what your eyes see" (*ûmar'ê 'ênêkā* in MT), it reads: *kai mē en horasei ophthalmōn sou* "and not in the sight of your eyes" (although the negative particle is omitted in some Greek witnesses). These moves indicate that the injunction to follow one's heart did not sit comfortably with everyone in antiquity, perhaps because it appeared to contradict Num 15:39 ("do not search after your own heart and your own eyes"). The discomfort is evident in Targ, as well: "walk in humility with the ways of your heart and be careful with what your eyes see that you do not see evil. . . ." The Egyptian parallels, however, show that the point here is enjoyment. The idiom has nothing to do with how one makes ethical decisions (i.e., whether one follows one's heart or obeys divine orders).

and what your eyes see. See Notes at 6:9 on *marʾēh ʿênayim* "what the eyes see" (cf. also 5:10 [Eng v 11]). *Ketib* has the plural form *mrʾy*, but *Qere*, followed by numerous MSS, LXX, Vulg, and Syr assume the singular, *mrʾh*, as in 6:9. The evidence in Targ is mixed (Sperber has the singular, but Lagarde has the plural). The plural form is never used in this sense elsewhere (although it is attested with a different meaning in Nah 2:5; Song 2:14); but its occurrence here may have been derived secondarily through the influence of *bĕdarkê*: thus *bĕdarkê // bĕmarʾê*. In either case, the meaning of the text is not affected. The point is to enjoy what is present before one's eyes.

and know. The conjunction may be translated as "and" or "but," depending on one's interpretation of the verse. Those who take this line to be an editorial gloss, a caveat by an orthodox editor, interpret it to mean "but" (Galling, Lauha, Zimmerli). That is, it may be interpreted as qualifying the call to enjoy: follow your heart, *but* know that one must not exceed the bounds of what God approves, for God will bring you into judgment. The similarity of this line with 12:14a (in the epilogue) raises for these scholars the possibility that this gloss was supplied by the epilogist. Qohelet, however, does speak of God's judgment in the present (see Comment at 3:17), and it is possible that the epilogist in 12:14 is simply reiterating or slightly reinterpreting the point that Qohelet makes in 11:9. The line should not be deleted.

10. *vexation.* See Notes at 1:18. In 5:16 (Eng v 17), the days of darkness are said to contain "much vexation (*kaʿas*), sickness, and anger."

banish unpleasantness. The noun *rāʿâ* "unpleasantness" is antithetical to what is *ṭôb* "delightful, pleasant, good" (see 11:7; cf. also *wîṭîbĕkā* in 11:9). It refers to one's experience of pain and misery. The reference anticipates *yĕmê hārāʿâ* "the days of unpleasantness" in the next verse, 12:1. One should try to avoid pain and misery, for there will come a time when it will no longer be possible to avoid such unpleasantness. One may compare the injunction here with Sir 30:21–25, esp. the Greek text in v 23: *kai lypēn makran apostēson apo sou* "and remove grief far from you."

the dawn of life. The noun *šaḥărût* occurs only here in Hebrew. The ancient versions are confused about its meaning. Vulg has *voluptas* "desire," apparently relating the noun to the verb *šḥr* "to seek, search." LXX (*anoia* "want of understanding") and Syr (*lʾ ydʿtʾ* "no knowledge") probably also reflect the same exegesis — that is, since *šḥr* in Prov 1:28 and 8:17 is used of the search for wisdom, the noun *šaḥărût* is interpreted to mean a lack of wisdom or a lack of knowledge. Clearly, the translators of these ancient versions did not think that "blackness" was an appropriate meaning. One version of Targ (see Lagarde), however, reads: "youth and the darkness of hair are vanity." Here the word *šaḥărût* is taken to mean "blackness of hair," a metaphor for youth and, thus, a term against *sêbâ* "gray hair" = "old age" (so BDB and most modern commentators). Support for this interpretation may be found in the Talmud (*b. Ned.* 30b), where *šḥwry hr*š* "black-headed" is contrasted with *qrḥyn* "bald" and *bʿly śybwt* "gray-haired" (see Salters, *Studies in the Versions,* pp. 234–35). So NJPS translates: "youth and black hair are fleeting." One may also relate this word to *šaḥar* "dawn" and note the close association of *yaldûtekā* "your youth" and *mišḥār* "dawn" in Ps 110:3, although that text is uncertain as it stands in MT. The noun *šaḥărût* may be related to Arabic *šaḥr* "first period or stage of youth," which is a metathesized form of the more common noun *šarḥ* "the prime and best period of youth" (Lane, *An Arabic-English Lexicon,* Part 4, pp. 1515, 1531). Whatever the etymology, it is difficult to believe that the audience would not have connected the word with dawn. The noun *šḥrt* appears with the meaning "dawn" on the Moabite Stone (*KAI* 181.15).

vanity. See Notes and Comment at 1:2.

12 1. *your creator.* BHS has *bôrě'êkā*, apparently a plural, but many MSS read the singular form *br'k/bwr'k* "your creator." The former is, however, the *lectio difficilior*; the latter may represent an attempt to correct the text. The form is sometimes explained as the "plural of majesty" (so Delitzsch), but in Isa 43:1 we find the form *bōra'ăkā* "your creator" used of the deity; the "plural of majesty" is not used there. It is better not to interpret the form as a plural, but as the result of the frequent confusion in late Hebrew of III-*'Alep* and III-Weak roots (see Notes at 2:26). The form is, thus, comparable with the participle *'ōśeh* "maker" (used of God), which is also attested with a pronominal suffix (see Isa 54:5; Ps 149:2; Job 35:10). There is no need to emend the text or to interpret the form as a plural of majesty. The more serious problem is with the meaning of the word.

All the ancient versions understand the form (either reading *bwr'k* or *bwr'yk*) to mean "your creator," but not all commentators agree that "your creator" is best suited to the context, especially since the deity is always called *'ĕlōhîm* in Ecclesiastes. Hence, instead of *bôrě'êkā* or *bôra'ăkā*, various alternatives have been proposed. These include: (a) *běrû'êkā* "your well-being" or "your health" (Ehrlich); (b) *boryāk* "your vigor" (Zimmermann); (c) *bě'êrêkā* or *bôrêkā* "your well" (Graetz), a metaphor for one's wife, as in Prov 5:15; (d) *bôrěkā* "your pit," a synonym for the grave (Galling).

None of these explanations is entirely satisfactory. Only *bwr'k/bwr'yk* is supported by the textual witnesses. If the consonantal text is correct, as all the witnesses attest, it is difficult to think that something other than "creator" is the primary meaning. Certainly by the time one gets to the end of the passage (12:7), with its allusion to the creation of humanity (Gen 2:7; 3:19), it is difficult not to think of the creator. The author may indeed intend to evoke other connections in using this word. Given his penchant for wordplays, it seems likely that he might have intended his audience to hear more than one meaning in the word. An early interpreter, Rabbi Akabya ben Mahallalel (first century C.E.), is said to have understood the text just so (*m. 'Abot* 3:1; *Qoh. Rabb.* on 12:1; *Lev. Rabb.* section 18). Said the rabbi: "Consider three things and you will not come into the power of sin: Know whence you came; where you are going; and before whom you are destined to give an accounting." Rabbi Akabya's interpretation is based on three different Hebrew words: *b'rk* "your source" (from whence you came), *bwrk* "your pit" (whither you are going), and *bwr'k* "your creator."

Since the context has to do with the enjoyment of life in one's youth (see 11:7–10), we may surmise that anyone first hearing the exhortation, might easily have assumed that Qohelet meant *bôrĕkā* "your cistern." If so, the hearer might recall the proverb "drink water from your own cistern (*bôrekā*), streams from your own well (*bĕ'ērekā*)," particularly since the passage in Proverbs continues to say, "let your fountain be blessed, and rejoice in the *wife of your youth*" (Prov 5:15, 18; cf. Song 4:15). But it is possible that the author also intends for one to think of death. If not in 12:1, certainly by the time one gets to v 6, with its mention of the shattering of the pots at the pit (*habbôr*), the grave comes to mind. In sum, the primary meaning is creator: the word is *bôrĕ'ĕkā* "your creator," but it is also appropriate to think of enjoyment (*bôrĕkā* "your cistern" = "your wife") and/or death (*bôrĕkā* "your pit").

before. Hebrew *'ad 'ăšer lō'*, lit. "until when not," means "before" (so Symm *prin*; Vulg *antequam*). Cf. also the common Mishnaic idiom *'d šl'* "until not when" = "before" (*m. Mak.* 2:4; *Ter.* 1:3). See Brockelmann, *Syntax*, §174; Segal, *A Grammar of Mishnaic Hebrew*, §513. The phrase appears at strategic points in the poem (vv 1b, 2a, 6a).

the days of unpleasantness. Hebrew *yĕmê hārā'â* refers to a time of suffering and misery including especially, but not limited to, old age. See *yôm rā'â* "time of adversity" in 7:14 (cf. Prov 16:4; Pss 27:5; 41:2 [Eng v 1]; Jer 17:17, 18; 51:2). It is equivalent to *yĕmê hahōšek* "the days of darkness" in 11:8. It may also be observed that *hārā'â* "unpleasantness" stands in contrast to what is delightful (*ṭôb*) in 11:7. The text is referring to a time when one can no longer put away unpleasantness. The unpleasantness is the unpleasantness that one tries to get rid of when one is still young enough to do so (see 11:9). Gregory Thaumaturgos, however, begins his eschatological interpretation here; instead of the plural *yĕmê hārā'â* "days of unpleasantness," he has *tēn tou theou megalēn hēmeran kai phoberan* "the great and terrible day of God," words which recall Joel 3:4 (Eng 2:31); Mal 3:22 (Eng 4:5); Zech 1:14–18. See Jarick, *Gregory Thaumaturgos' Paraphrase of Ecclesiastes*, p. 289.

when you will say. The particle *'ăšer* is probably temporal, not "of which (you will say)."

"I have no pleasure in them." There is some ambiguity about the translation of this phrase, depending on how one interprets the suffix in *bāhem*. If the suffix refers to the *šānîm* "years" (a feminine plural, but see 2:6, 10; 10:9; 11:8), we should translate "I have no pleasure in them" (i.e., I have no pleasure during this period because I am too old). This is probably the correct interpretation, since *šānîm* is the closest antecedent. If, however, the suffix refers to "the days of your youth" in 12:1a, then one should translate the phrase as "I had no pleasure in

them" (i.e., I did not have pleasure back then, when I could have, and now it is too late).

2. *before.* See Note on *'ad 'ăšer lō'* above (v 1). The introduction of another *'ad 'ăšer lō'* clause suggests that the author is moving to another scene, beyond the depiction of old age in v 1.

the sun darkens, even the light. The light refers to the light of day. In the Hebrew Bible, the light of day is not equated with the sun, nor is the brightness of the day thought to be derived from the sun. The distinction between "light" and "sun" is made in Genesis 1, where light is called "day" (Gen 1:4) and it existed before the luminaries of the sky were made (Gen 1:14–18). In Isa 30:26, the light of the sun is compared with the light of day and in 2 Sam 23:4, the rising sun and the morning light are named side by side. The terms do not refer to the same thing. In any case, the mention of the sun and the light echoes 11:7, where we have *hā'ôr* "light" in parallelism with *haššemeš* "the sun." The darkening of the luminaries in the sky signifies the end of human life (Isa 5:30; 13:10; Ezek 32:7–8; Amos 8:9; Joel 2:2, 10; 3:4 [Eng 2:31]; 4:15 [Eng 3:15]; Job 3:6; Matt 24:29; Mark 13:24–25). In the inscription discovered at Tell Deir 'Allā, one reads of a similar vision of the end of life brought about by the gods (Hoftijzer and van der Kooij, *Deir 'Alla*, Combination I, lines 3–7). The call is issued in the divine council to a deity to cover the heavens with clouds and to set darkness in the sky instead of light. Qohelet uses such eschatological language to speak of the end of human life; it is as if the whole cosmos is coming to an end. Moreover, one must not fail to see the contrast between this passage, the last passage in the body of the book, and the introduction of the book. In 1:5, the sun rises and sets, only to rise again. The sun shines (*zāraḥ*) and, even if it sets at the end of the day, it will rise to shine again. But here, in the final mention of the sun, it is darkened, along with the light of day, even the moon and the stars. For the Targumists, the allegory of old age begins here: the sun signifies the brightness of the face, the light refers to the light of the eyes, the moon corresponds to the beauty of the cheeks, and the stars are the pupils of the eyes.

the moon and the stars. Busto Saíz ("Estructura," p. 22) wants to eliminate *wĕhayyārēaḥ wĕhakkôkābîm* on metrical grounds, but there is no textual evidence for doing so. It may be that the author added the moon and the stars deliberately to emphasize the sheer darkness. Even the lesser luminaries (cf. Gen 1:16), those of the night, are darkened.

the clouds. The coming of the clouds (*he'ābîm*) is another eschatological element. In Ezek 32:7, the clouds cover the sky and darken the luminaries. In the Deir 'Allā inscription, the clouds ('*bn* = Hebrew '*bym*) also darken the heavens. Thus our text is not just describing an approaching storm, as scholars commonly suggest; it is describing a time of doom (see Ezek 30:3). The imagery is ultimately derived from the myth of the divine warrior's march to battle, which is accompanied by dark rain clouds (see 2 Sam 22:12 = Ps 18:12; Judg 5:4; Isa 19:1; Job 36:29; 37:19).

with. It is awkward to translate the preposition *'aḥar* as "after," as if the clouds come temporally after the rain. In descriptions of the divine warrior's march, rain sometimes accompanies the clouds (see Ps 77:18–19 [Eng vv 17–18]; cf. also 1 Kgs 18:44; Job 26:8). The notion of a cloud coming after the rain does not make sense and is without parallel. One should probably translate the preposition as "with," as in Ruth 1:15, where *šûbî 'aḥărê yĕbimtēk* (lit. "return behind your sister-in-law") really means "return with your sister-in-law." M. Dahood ("Hebrew-Ugaritic Lexicography," *Bib* 44 [1963] pp. 292–93) has argued that in Ugaritic *aḥr* is juxtaposed with *'mn* "with" (e.g., *KTU* 1.24.32–33), so that the preposition in Ugaritic and in several passages in the Bible may mean "with." Yet, it must be admitted that the meaning of *aḥr* in Ugaritic is not without controversy. The assessment of D. Pardee in this regard is properly judicious: "the word *aḥr* (and Hebrew *'aḥar*) itself seems more often to connote 'immediately after' (whence the occasional legitimacy of translating 'with') than is the case with English 'after' which refers to any time or distance after, with no connotation of proximity or distance. This, of course, does not imply that *aḥr* (*'aḥar*) indicated any other position than 'after, behind'" ("The Preposition in Ugaritic," *UF* 7 [1975], p. 252). Pardee allows, however, that quite often the translation "with" reflects the English idiom better than "after" or "behind." That is certainly the case in our passage. From the standpoint of a human looking toward the sky, the clouds are literally *behind* the rain; *'aḥar* indicates the spatial relationship of the clouds to the rain from the perspective of someone standing on the ground and looking up. In English, however, we render this preposition as "with" (so NRSV; NEB), rather than "after" or "behind."

3. *at the time when.* Hebrew *bayyôm še-*, lit. "on the day when." See Song 8:8; cf. also *bayyôm 'ăšer* (Deut 27:2; 2 Sam 19:20 [v 19]; Mal 3:21 [Eng 4:3]; Esth 9:1). So Vulg has *quando* "when." As Fox has observed, this clause connects vv 3–5 to v 2 (*Contradictions*, p. 301). The expression "at the time when," thus, elaborates on what happens when the day darkens. Moreover, this "time" is expressed by the singular noun *yôm*, whereas the time of youth and old age are both expressed by the plural, *yĕmê* "days of" (11:8, 9; 12:1) and *šānîm* "years" (11:8; 12:1). The author has clearly moved beyond the periods of youth (v 1a) and old age (v 1b) to speak of the end-time. In the present context, therefore, the events of vv 3–5 should not be interpreted as referring to old age. Rather, they should be interpreted in the light of the eschatological rhetoric of v 2: all these things happen when the luminaries of the sky darken, when the light of day is extinguished. The "day" here sounds very much like "the great and terrible day of YHWH" (Joel 3:4 [Eng 2:31]; cf. Zeph 1:14–15).

those who watch the house. The expression probably refers to the caretakers of the house (cf. 2 Sam 15:16; 16:21; 20:3). These are not just servants, however, but people with authority over the house in some way. They are put in charge of the house. In the light of the parallelism with *'anšê heḥāyil* "valiant men," we should probably think of these *šōmĕrê habbayit* as those who guard the house, that is, the watchmen of the house (LXX: *phylakes tēs oikias* "guards of the house"). In Postbiblical Hebrew *šwmr* means "guard, watchman, trustee" and *šwmrh* is a "guardhouse" (see Jastrow, *Dictionary*, pp. 1536–37). One may compare the Hebrew expression *šōmĕrê habbayit* with Punic *šmr mḥṣb* "guardian/

watchman of the quarry," in an inscription from Malta (*KAI* 62.7; cf. Punic *ḥgrt šmrt* "guardhouse" in *KAI* 81.4). In Punic we often get the expression *šmr wnṣr* "to protect and guard" (see *DNWSI* II, p. 1167). In this expression the verb *nṣr* is cognate to Akkadian *naṣāru*, as in *bītam naṣāru* "to guard/protect the house" and *nāṣiru* "guard" (*CAD* XI/2, pp. 35, 48). The term makes sense literally; one need not interpret these "watchmen" as an allegory for the limbs of the body (so Targ) or the ribs (so the Talmud in *b. Šabb.* 152a).

tremble. The Hebrew verb means to tremble *in terror* (see Esth 5:9; Hab 2:7; Sir 48:12; cf. the Aramaic in Dan 5:19; 6:2) and the related noun *zw'h* refers to terror (Deut 28:25; Isa 28:19). The nouns in Hebrew and Aramaic are most frequently associated with earthquakes, but also tempests. Similarly, too, Arabic *zā'a* refers to vehement shaking and *za'za'at* means "calamity, adversity" (Lane, *Arabic-English Lexicon*, Part 3, pp. 1229–30). The text in Ecclesiastes is describing the fearful reaction of those who guard the house. It does not refer to the weakness of old age or the dilapidation of an old house. If the shaking caused by weakness were meant, one should expect the root *mwṭ*, rather than *zw'*.

valiant men. The term is used of people who are trustworthy (Gen 47:6; Exod 18:21, 25; 1 Sam 31:12 // 1 Chron 10:12; 1 Kgs 1:42; 1 Chron 26:8) or brave (Ps 76:6 [Eng v 5]; Judg 3:29). Soldiers are often called *'anšê (he)ḥayil* (Judg 20:44, 46; 2 Sam 11:16; 23:20; 24:9; Jer 48:14; Nah 2:4). These men are dignified, brave, or strong. Again, the literal meaning makes sense; one need not interpret the term as an allegory for the limbs or bones of the body, as is sometimes done. Even the brave are cowed on that terrible day.

convulse. In the light of the parallelism, we should take the verb to mean either "cower" (i.e., crouch in fear) or "convulse." For the latter meaning, we may compare the Aramaic noun *'wyt* "convulsion" (so in *b. Ḥul.* 60a; *Giṭ.* 70d; see Jastrow, *Dictionary*, pp. 1049–50). The related verb *'wh* is used of terror in the face of impending doom (Isa 21:3). The point of the verse in Ecclesiastes seems clear: even the dignified and brave are terrified of what is happening. Those who interpret the text as an allegory, take the verb to mean that the bones are crooked or that the legs are bent.

those who grind. The word *haṭṭōḥănôt* may refer either to people (women) who work the mills (see Judg 16:21; Num 11:6) or to the molar teeth. For the latter meaning, one may compare Arabic *ṭāḥināt* "grinders" = "molar teeth" (see Lane, *Arabic-English Lexicon*, Part 5, p. 1832). This is one of the places where the physiological interpretation has appeal, for in old age one's teeth do become few. Yet, a purely physiological interpretation is inadequate, since v 4 speaks of the reduction of the noise at the mill — unless, of course, one interprets the "mill" as the mouth and the noise as the sound of chewing.

stop. The verb *bāṭēl* is a *hapax legomenon* in the Hebrew Bible, but it is attested in Postbiblical Hebrew. It may mean to cease altogether, or to suspend activity. The related Akkadian verb *baṭālu* may refer to the interruption of work due to the shortage of labor, tools, or other supplies, or the stoppage of delivery of goods (*CAD* II, pp. 174–76). Commentators are sometimes troubled by the suggestion that the women stop work because they have become few in number.

Under normal circumstances, one should expect the few remaining millers to work even harder (so Podechard). Crenshaw suggests, therefore, that it is the members of the house that have become few (i.e., the verb *mi'ēṭû* "diminish" is impersonal) and, therefore, less food needs to be produced (*Ecclesiastes*, p. 186; "Youth and Old Age in Qoheleth," p. 9 note 34). But why do the women stop work? Why do they not merely reduce their workload and produce less? Fox proposes that the women have become few because the rest have gone to join the funeral (*Contradictions*, pp. 302–3). If the women were dying out, Fox surmises, they should easily have been replaced by others. The common assumption among commentators seems to be that the diminishing takes place over a period of time. But the point may be that some have died *suddenly*. Qohelet is describing what is happening *bayyôm še-* "on the day when" (v 3a). Everything is happening suddenly. That is why they cannot be replaced. The women stop work because something terrible is suddenly happening and some of the number have already disappeared. The imagery of sudden disappearance of workers belongs to the general description of the end-time. See the eschatological scene in Matt 24:40–41 and Luke 17:34–35, where some of the "women who work the mills" (*alēthousai*, cf. LXX) suddenly disappear, while others remain on earth.

diminished. The verb *mi'ēṭû* should probably be taken to mean that the subjects have diminished (cf. *b. Ḥul.* 60b; *Sanh.* 17a) — either the teeth become few, or the millers, for some reason, become few in number. It is possible that verb may be interpreted to mean that the millers are reducing their output (cf. *m. 'Abot* 4:10; *Ta'an.* 1:7, where the verb is used of economic transactions), but if that were the case, one should expect an object for the verb. We should, therefore, probably take the Piel verb here as resultative.

those who look through the windows. Elsewhere in the Hebrew Bible, the feminine participle *rō'ôt* always refers to the eyes (Gen 45:12; Deut 3:21; 4:3; 11:7; 28:32; 2 Sam 24:3; 1 Kgs 1:48; Isa 30:20; Jer 20:4; 42:2); only here in Eccl 12:3 is there any ambiguity. With the additional *bā'ărubbôt* "through the windows," however, we should understand "those who look" to be women (Judg 5:28; 2 Sam 6:16 = 1 Chron 15:29; 2 Kgs 9:30; Prov 7:6; Song 2:9). The motif of women who look through the window belongs to a literary convention, often used to express the dashed hopes of the women (see S. Abramsky, "The Woman Who Looked Out the Window," *Beth Mikra* 25 [1980], pp. 114–24 [in Hebrew]).

grow dim. The verb is used of eyes in Lam 5:17 and Ps 69:24 (Eng v 23; cf. *b. Ber.* 16b). One may also compare the saying in the Aramaic *Proverbs of Ahiqar: 'ynyn ṭbn 'l y'kmw* "may good eyes not be dimmed (lit. 'be darkened')" (*TAD* III, 1.1.157). If the reference to "those who look through the windows" is to women, we should understand the text to mean that their eyes have grown dim through grief (see Lam 5:17), perhaps on account of their loved ones who do not return or of dashed hopes.

4. *double-doors in the street-bazaar.* Hebrew *dĕlātayim baššûq* refers to the gates leading into the *šûq* "street-bazaar," perhaps the city gates (cf. Deut 3:5; Josh 6:26; 1 Sam 23:7; Isa 45:1; Jer 49:31; Sir 49:13), rather than to the doors of the houses on the street. If all the doors of the houses on the street were meant, one should

expect the plural form *dĕlātôt* instead of the dual *dĕlātayim*. For the idiom *dĕlā-tayim bĕ-* "the double-doors at," one may compare *šĕʿārîm bāʿîr* "the city gates" (lit. "the gates at the city") in Prov 1:21 and *šaʿar šalleket bamsillâ* "the Shalleket Gate of the Highway" (lit. "the Shalleket Gate at the Highway"), the name of the gateway to the thoroughfare (1 Chron 26:16). So *dĕlātayim baššûq* means the "double-doors in the marketplace." It must be remembered, too, that the *šûq* is not only a street, but also a center of commercial and social intercourse, like the *ḥûṣôt* "streets" = "street-bazaars" mentioned in 1 Kgs 20:34 (note that Syr and Targ take the streets here to be referring to the *šûq*) and the *ḥûṣ* "street" in Prov 1:20 (// *rĕḥōbôt* "squares"). The existence of the *šûq* in Cisjordan is known from the second millennium B.C.E., as attested in one of the Amarna letters from Tyre (*EA* 150:33). In Akkadian, the *sūqu* "street" is a vibrant center of commercial and social activities; it was the equivalent of the marketplace, where people gathered for business and gossip, and where religious processions and funerals were conducted (see *CAD* XV, pp. 401–6; W. Röllig, "Der altmesopotamische Markt," *WO* 8 [1976], esp. pp. 291–92). The word *šwq* also occurs in Palmyrene, in reference to a market (*CIS* II, 3932.5). At all events, there is no doubt that a center of lively activities is meant, except that the place is closed for some reason. Cf. LXX *en tē agorā* "in the bazaar." The picture one gets in our passage is that all regular commercial and social activities have come to a stop, except and perhap *because of* the funeral mentioned in v 5.

while the sound of the mill drops. Hebrew *bišpal qôl haṭṭaḥănâ*, lit. "while the sound of the mill becomes low." The preposition *bĕ-* is temporal and *šĕpal* is the Qal infinitive construct of the stative verb *špl* (see GKC §45.c). Milling was an indispensable chore and very much a part of domestic life. As K. van der Toorn observes, "[t]he scraping sound of grinding stones was as characteristic of a habited home as the light of the lamp" (*ABD* IV, pp. 831–33). The silencing of the mills, then, like the closing of the double-doors to the *šûq*, is an ominous sign: the regular economic and social activities cease, and even the indispensable domestic activities stop. It is unclear if domestic mills or commercial mills are in question here. The noun *ṭaḥănâ* occurs only here in Hebrew. In the Aramaic papyri from Saqqara, *ṭḥnt* refers to commercial mills run by hired hands (see Segal, *Aramaic Texts*, No. 20.5).

the sound of the birds rises. The meaning of the phrase *wĕyāqûm lĕqôl haṣṣippôr* is disputed. The subject of *yāqûm* is most often assumed to be unspecific (so NRSV: "one rises up at the sound of a bird"). But that is based on the supposition that this passage is an allegory of the travails of old age; in that case, the unspecified subject is the aged person. According to this interpretation, the aged are so sensitive that the slightest sound causes them to be awakened. As Fox notes, however, if that were the meaning, one would expect the verb to be from *qwṣ* or *ʿwr*, but not *qwm* (*Contradictions*, pp. 303–4). Moreover, it is not self-evident that the senses of the aged are so keen. On the contrary, the aged may sleep more readily and become oblivious to low noises when they sleep. Certainly the sound of birds should not be enough to rouse them. As the Egyptian *Instruction of Ptahhotep* has it in its litany of problems facing the aged, "He (the aged man) goes to sleep, being in discomfort all day long" (*sdr.n.f hdr rʿ nb*; see *Papyrus Prisse*, line 4; alternatively, one may emend *hdr* to *hrd* — so Lichtheim reads: "[childlike] one sleeps all day" [*AEL* I, pp. 63, 76]).

A few scholars have proposed to emend our text in Ecclesiastes slightly and redivide the consonants to read *wĕyiqmal qôl haṣṣippôr* "the sound of the bird fades" (so Zapletal; Wildeboer; Strobel). So, too, NEB translates: "the chirping of the sparrow grows faint." But it is doubtful if the Semitic root *qml* has this meaning. The root occurs only twice in Hebrew, in Isa 19:6 and 33:9, and to judge from both contexts and the cognates, the root probably means "to be infested (either with insects or with mold)" (cf. *HALAT*, p. 1036). The Hebrew verb *qml* does not mean "to fade" or "to grow faint." Certainly it could not be used with "sound" as the subject.

Podechard emends to read *wydwm qwl hṣpwr* "the sound of birds falls silent" (*L'Ecclésiaste*, p. 459), while Ginsberg prefers to read *wyq(w)l qwl hṣpwr* "and the voice of the bird becomes faint," citing Ugaritic *ql* "to fall" ("Koheleth 12:4," p. 100). Hertzberg takes the text to mean "one rises to the sound of the bird," suggesting that one's voice becomes high-pitched, like that of birds (*Prediger*, p. 212). Still others take "bird" as the subject, but are compelled to take *lĕqôl* as an infinitive: "the bird begins to voice" (so Taylor, *The Dirge of Coheleth*. 19–20; Fox, *Contradictions*, p. 304). But *qôl* is never used as an infinitive in classical Hebrew or Aramaic. Moreover, such a translation ignores the contrast between the low sound of the mill (*qôl haṭṭaḥănâ*) in v 4a and the easily audible sound of the bird (*qôl haṣṣippôr*) in v 4b. Indeed, the contrast appears to be between the noise of the mill, which has dropped (*špl*), and the noise of the birds, which has risen (*qwm*). In short, *špl* is contrasted with *qwm*, and *qôl haṭṭaḥănâ* is deliberately contrasted with *qôl haṣṣippôr*.

It is possible to take the phrase *lĕqôl haṣṣippôr* as the subject, in which case the *lamed* may be compared with the *lamed* that occasionally appears before the subject in Late Biblical Hebrew (see 1 Chron 28:1; 2 Chron 7:21; see Joüon-Muraoka §125.1). Alternatively, one may assume the "asseverative-*lamed*," an example of which is found in 9:4. If so, the text would mean, lit. "it rises, indeed, the sound of birds." The *lamed* calls attention to the sound of the birds; it focuses on what happens when the mills are silent — the sound of the birds increases. The noun *haṣṣippôr* here is collective (so also in Hos 11:11; Pss 8:9 [Eng v 8]; 148:10), as the parallelism with "the daughters of song" suggests. It is also used generically here for all kinds of birds, and not specifically of the sparrow (*contra* Driver, "Problems," p. 233). The word *ṣippôr* may refer to birds of prey (Ezek 39:4). The author is probably thinking not of birds singing in joy, as is commonly assumed, but either of birds hooting ominously or of birds of prey making a commotion when they sense death or when they move into a depopulated place. Like the fading sound of the mill, the rising sound of the birds is a sign of death. Taylor thinks of birds of evil omen and associates the sound with the mournful noises of these birds (*Dirge of Coheleth*, pp. 20–23). In the Akkadian texts, the sounds of various birds are associated with mourning: so *bakkītu* "crier" and *lallartu* "wailer" both may refer to mourners or to birds (see *CAD* II, pp. 34–35; IX, p. 48).

daughters of song. Since the expression *běnôt haššîr* "the daughters of song" occurs in parallelism with *haṣṣippôr* "the birds," one thinks in the first instance of birds in general. It is pertinent to note in this connection that there is a species of birds known as *běnôt (hay)ya'ǎnâ* in the Bible (Mic 1:8; Isa 13:21; 34:13; 43:20; Jer 50:39; Job 30:29). Together with jackals, hyenas, and other unsavory creatures, these birds are often portrayed as moving into an area after it has been destroyed; they occupy places where the human population has been annihilated. In Mic 1:8, these birds are associated with mourning. There, as in Isa 13:21, LXX translates the name of the bird as *seirenes* (cf. English "sirens"), a word which elsewhere in classical Greek may refer to a singing bird (Liddell-Scott, *Lexicon*, p. 1588; cf. also 1 Enoch 19:2). Whatever its true etymology, it appears that *ya'ǎnâ* in this designation was assumed to be derived from *'nh* "to sing," so that *běnôt ya'ǎnâ* may have been understood as "daughters of the one that sings," or the like (cf. *rěnānîm* "criers" in Job 39:13, which Vulg interprets as *struthio* "ostrich," the normal translation for Hebrew *bat hayya'ǎnâ*). It is possible, therefore, that "the daughters of song" in our passage may be a euphemism for birds associated with death and mourning. This does not mean that the phrase "daughters of song" here refers specifically to the *běnôt ya'ǎnâ*, but that it refers to all kinds of hooting birds (note *kol-*) like the *běnôt ya'ǎnâ*.

Dahood cites Ugaritic *bnt hll snnt*, which he translates as "daughters of joyful noise, swallows" ("Canaanite-Phoenician Influence," p. 215). He is followed by Fox, who takes the expression "daughters of song" in our text to refer to mourning women (*Contradictions*, p. 304). The epithet *bnt hll snnt* occurs several times in Ugaritic, always in reference to the birth goddesses, the Kotharātu (see *KTU* 1.17.II.26–27, 31, 33–34, 36, 38, 40; 1.24.6, 41). It is not clear, however, why these goddesses are called *bnt hll snnt*, nor do we know what the epithet means. The Ugaritic epithet is not helpful for the interpretation of our text.

More pertinent is the inscription from Tell Deir 'Allā, where several birds are mentioned, including one that squawks or shrieks (*ḥrpt* related to Arabic *ḥrp* "to be sharp"?) and one whose voice "sings" (Combination I, lines 7–9; see the translation of Hackett, *Deir 'Allā*, pp. 29, 46–48). It is difficult to identify the various species of birds in this text. Nor can one ascertain what each bird is doing. The birds are accompanied by various animals, including the hyena, also doing strange things. Baruch Levine is probably correct that what we have in this text from Deir 'Allā is a "depiction of desolation and wilderness, with birds shrieking and wild animals feeding freely. The implication is that where domestic animals had formerly been tended, wild animals now reign" ("The Plaster Inscription from Deir 'Alla," in *The Balaam Text from Deir 'Alla Re-evaluated* [ed. J. Hoftijzer and G. van der Kooij; Leiden: Brill, 1991], p. 60). A similar scene is evident in our text: the birds are noisily moving into a place of desolation.

come down low. If the expression "daughters of song" refers to professional wailers (so Fox), *šḥḥ* indicates a mourning posture — either they are bent down low or they are sitting on the ground (Pss 35:14; 38:7 [Eng v 6]; 44:26 [Eng v 25]; Isa 29:4; Lam 3:20). But if one understands "the daughters of song" as birds of some sort, the verb may mean that they are swooping down low and ready to attack the corpses. In this regard, one notes that *šḥḥ* is used of a lion crouching down low and waiting to attack its prey (Job 38:40). It is also possible to relate the verb here to one of the activities of the raven in the *Gilgamesh Epic*: *ikkal išaḥḥi itarri ul issaḥra* "it eats, it preens (?), it soars (?), it does not turn around" (Gilg XI 154). In light of the reference to the sound of the birds in the parallel line, one might be tempted to follow Sawyer in repointing the verb to read *wĕyāśîḥû* "and (the daughters of song) chatter" ("The Ruined House," p. 527). There is no need to do so, however. Indeed, the next verse suggests that the birds are in flight ("from on high"). So "come down low" (i.e., swooping down) makes sense. It may be observed that the verb here is 3 mp, whereas the subject—the *bĕnôt yaʿănâ*—is feminine plural. This lack of coordination is a characteristic of colloquial language, which is also passed on to literary Hebrew of the late period (see GKC §135.o, 144.a, 145.p, t, u).

5. *even from on high they see*. Assuming that the consonantal text is correct, but vocalizing the verb as *yirʾû* "they see" (so eighty-one MSS, LXX, SyrH, Copt, and Symm), instead of *yîrĕʾû* "they are afraid" (so numerous MSS, Vulg, Syr). Thus the line reads, lit. "even from a high (place) they see." The interpretation of the text as "they are afraid" is due to the influence of *wĕhathattîm* "terror" in the parallel line: *yrʾ* "to be afraid" is seen as the verb that naturally goes with "terror." Many commentators interpret the verse to mean that the aged are afraid of heights and face terrors on the road—that is, they fear to climb to high places and to walk long distances (so JB; NEB). But such translations overinterpret the Hebrew. The aged are not mentioned in the text. Moreover, it seems strange that the subject is specified in 12:4b, only to be followed immediately by a clause with the unspecified subject, which one is expected to know is referring to the aged. The most natural subject of the verb is, in fact, *bĕnôt haššîr* "the daughters of song" in the preceding line—that is, those who come swooping down. The plural subject, then, is entirely appropriate; one must not emend the text to read the singular (so Galling, Lauha). Nor should this line be deleted on metrical grounds (so Busto Saíz, "Estructura," p. 22).

terror on the way. The *waw* is explicative or emphatic. There is no need, therefore, to delete it as a dittography (so one MS and many commentators). Indeed, it is the apparent redundancy of the *waw* that has caused the verb *yrʾw* to be interpreted incorrectly as "they are afraid," since the verb is then thought to be parallel to *hathattîm* "terror." One may compare the idiom here with *tirʾû ḥătat wattîrāʾû* "you see a terror (i.e., a calamity) and were afraid" in Job 6:21. The word *hathattîm* occurs only here in classical Hebrew, but its meaning is clear. The form may suggest something like repeated terror. Perhaps the text means that they (the birds from on high) notice the panic of a community facing death. The birds literally see the calamities from on high and they come swooping down. The noun *hathattîm* is related to the noun *mĕhittâ* "terror, ruin," a word used of destroyed human habitats in Ps 89:41–42 (Eng vv 40–41).

becomes revolting. Reading with *Ketib* (*wyn's*) and taking the verb as a Hiphil: *wĕyan'ēṣ*, lit. "and [the almond] causes one to revile/be repulsed." Many commentators prefer to read with *Qere*: *wĕyānēṣ*, assuming *nṣṣ* "to blossom." This reading ("blossom") is supported by LXX, SyrH, Syr, and Vulg. But the explanation of the *'alep* in *Ketib* as merely orthographic (so Gordis and others) is unconvincing; all the examples cited are Middle-Weak, rather than geminate roots, and in each case the *'alep* indicates *ā* not *ē*. It is doubtful if *'alep* ever indicates a long vowel in a geminate verb. The reading of *Ketib* is probably correct, although it may not be the only reading intended by the author.

Scholars who take the passage as a depiction of the woes of old age assume the text to be saying that the almond nut has become unpalatable to the aged: the almond is "despised." The word *šāqēd* "almond," however, may refer either to the nut (Gen 43:11; Num 17:23) or to the tree (Jer 1:11). If the former is meant, the point is that the nut that is regarded as one of the choice fruits of the land (see Gen 43:11) will become repulsive. One can only speculate if that means the nut has become rotten or if the nut is despised because it cannot be eaten by the aged, whose "grinders" have become few (see 12:3). The almond tree may be meant, however. If so, the point is that the tree that is so appreciated for its lovely blossoms, somehow becomes revolting. Almond trees are known for their beauty; they do not look bad even when the blossoms fall off. Yet, they are susceptible to extreme cold and to a variety of fungal diseases that may cause the tree to rot and become unsightly. The rare sight of a repulsive-looking almond tree is, thus, an ominous sign.

In this connection, one may note that Akkadian *nâṣu* (from *na'āṣu*) may be used of something that is revolting to look at: "if the appearance of the house is repulsive (*nāṣ*)" (CT 38, 14:4, 22; see *AHW*, p. 758). In a lexical text cited in *CAD* XI/2, p. 53, the word is listed with other terms for "trembling." Although one cannot be certain of its meaning, one may conjecture that it means "shuddering," or the like.

In any case, it is possible that the author of our text intends a wordplay, substituting the verb *yan'ēṣ* "it becomes revolting" (causes one to shudder?) for the expected form *yānēṣ* "it blooms." The two verbs are homonyms: the almond blooms (*yānēṣ*), but it will become revolting (*yan'ēṣ*). It is easy to see how such a wordplay might have generated the genuine variants now reflected in the different witnesses.

Alternatively, one may posit that the verb was originally *yānēṣ* "blossom." If so, the imagery here may at one time have been an allegory for old age, as many commentators have suggested: the white blossom of the almond tree is a figure for the white hair that one gets in old age. A Sumerian wisdom text, likewise, uses allegory to describe the white hair of old age: "My black mountain has produced white gypsum" (B. Alster, *Studies in Sumerian Proverbs* [Mesopotamia 3; Copenhagen: Akademisk, 1975], p. 93, line 28). One Talmudic passage cites an allegory for old age, where the white hair of the aged is likened to a mountain covered with snow (*b. Šabb.* 152a). The allegorical meaning, however, lies only in the background, as the author now speaks not of the white blooms of the almond tree, but of its decay. Along with other eschatological signs, the almond tree will become revolting. If this reconstruction is correct, the original text had *yānēṣ* "blooms" (appropriate when the text was used as an allegory of old age), but it was subsequently read as *yan'ēṣ* "becomes repulsive" (when the text was read eschatologically). The presence of the *'alep* is, in fact, a clue as to the interpretive process.

the locust. Mentioned between almond and caper, it seems most likely that *ḥāgāb* "locust," properly "grasshopper," refers not to the insect but to some kind of plant. The word "locust" in English refers to a wide variety of plants throughout the world, most of which have pods that apparently remind one of the insect (see *The Oxford English Lexicon*, VIII, pp. 1093–94). In the Levant, too, this association between the insect and certain types of trees seems to have been made. Indeed, the Greek word *akris* "locust," used normally of the insect, may have referred to pods of the carob tree, as well. It has long been argued that the "locusts" eaten by John the Baptist (Matt 3:4) may, in fact, have been such "locust" pods. There is ample evidence, however, that the insect was consumed by people in the Levant in ancient times, as many bedouin do even today. So the locusts consumed by John the Baptist may have been the insect, after all. Nevertheless, it is significant that many interpreters in antiquity assumed the "locusts" to be legumes. This is an interpretation of *akris* "locust" found in the apocryphal Gospel to the Ebionites and followed by Athanasius, Chrysostom, and others (see the citations in Lampe, *Patristic Greek Lexicon*, p. 65). It appears that even in Levantine antiquity, "locust" was recognized as a term used for a kind of plant. It makes sense to think that *ḥāgāb* refers to a plant, perhaps the carob tree (*ḥārûb*), whose pods remind one of locusts. In any case, *ḥāgāb* "locust" in our passage has traditionally been taken figuratively, as referring to a part of the body (so Targ and *Qoh. Rabb.* assume that the locust refers to the ankle that becomes swollen in old age). In the Talmud it is said that *ḥāgāb* refers to one's *'gbwt*, a reference to the male sexual organ (*b. Šabb.* 152a; cf. *šîr 'ăgābîm* "love-song" in Ezek 33:32; *'ăgābātāh* "her lust" in Ezek 23:11; the verb *'gb* meaning "to have [sexual] desire"). And this is a possible interpretation at the allegorical level, one accepted by Rashi and Ibn Ezra (see Levy, *Qoheleth*, p. 135).

droops. The meaning of the verb *yistabbēl* is uncertain because one cannot be sure what *ḥāgāb* refers to. The root *sbl* "to carry (a load), be laden" occurs in the Qal and Piel, but nowhere else does it occur in the Hithpael. Arabic *sabala* is often cited as a cognate, from which the meaning "to drag" is derived. Those who take *ḥāgāb* "locust" to refer literally to the insect, think of the insect laden with food and dragging itself along. Those who allegorize the text, think of some part of the body being a burden — perhaps it is laden with water, or the like (so Targ: "your ankles will be swollen"). The verb in Arabic is also commonly found with the meaning "to let down," "to drop down," or "to hang down" (Lane, *Arabic-English Lexicon*, Part 4, pp. 1301–3). Thus, the verb *sbl* here may mean that the dead locust tree droops — from the weight of the pods. If the passage is taken as an allegory of old age, as it may have been originally, and the "locust" is understood as a figure for the old man's sexual organ, the root is especially appropriate, for it may suggest the man's lack of virility. In this connection, one should note that Arabic *musbil* means "penis" — named because of its pendulous nature (so Lane) — and *musabbal* refers to "an ugly old man." Many Hebrew MSS read *wystkl* "they become foolish," but that is clearly the easier reading. The text may have meant originally that in old age one becomes impotent, but in its present context, it has to do with the death of nature: the locust droops — that is, it languishes.

caper. Hebrew *'ăbîyyônâ* occurs only here in the Bible, but it is attested in the Mishnah and Talmud, where it refers to the fruit of the caper bush (see *m. Ma'aś.* 4:6; *y. Ber.* 36:1, 26). LXX translates the word as *kapparis* (cf. Vulg, Syr), which in the Levant would probably refer to the genus *kapparis spinosa.* Several varieties of the *kapparis* family were (and still are) thought to have medicinal values. They were also reputed to have been stimulants for the appetite (so Plutarch, *Symposia* VI.ii.4) and thought to have worked as aphrodisiacs, a view assumed in Targ and *Qoh. Rabb.* It is sometimes argued that the noun *'ăbîyyônâ* is related to the root *'bh* "to want, be willing, consent," and hence the translation of the word as "desire" (RSV: "desire fails"; KJV: "desire shall fail"). But Hebrew *'bh* is not to be confused with *'wh* the normal root for words indicating sexual desire. Any association of the noun with sexual desire is a function of interpretation, not definition.

comes to naught. The verb *tāpēr* is very problematic. The form, as pointed in Codex Leningrad, appears to be the Hiphil of *prr* "to break, frustrate, make ineffectual, bring to naught," or the like. If the caper signifies some kind of a stimulant, then the point is that the caper berry fails to be effective: instead of stimulating desire, it only "frustrates" (cf. Gilbert, "La description de la vielliesse," pp. 105–6). The caper does no good. So Targ may not be far off in its interpretation: "and you will be prevented from having intercourse." This solution makes sense, if one interprets this passage as an allegory for the troubles of old age: when one grows old, stimulants may have no effect. But, as in the other images in this verse, there seems to be another level of meaning. The allegorical meaning is superseded by another level of signification. Some of the ancient versions take the verb to indicate that the fruit is scattered or dispersed (so LXX, SyrH, Copt, and Symm; but Aq has *karpeusei*, perhaps reflecting Hebrew *tpr<h>* "bears fruit," a reading that assumes a haplography of *he'*). What is meant, then, is that the fruit has split open and the seeds are scattered. Not a few commentators, therefore, prefer to repoint the verb as a passive. But it is not clear how that image fits with the others in the verse, images of the death of vegetation. Perhaps we should take the root *prr* to mean "to fall off, drop off." One may compare Ugaritic *prr* "to break, break from" (*KTU* 1.15.III.30; 1.19.III.14, 28), which is related to Arabic *farra*, a verb that in the causative stem may mean "to fall off, to shed." If this interpretation is correct, the Hiphil of the root in Hebrew may also mean "to shed, to cause to fall off." The point, then, is that the caper bush is defoliated (cf. the apocalyptic vision in Rev 6:12–13). So all three images in this verse may have to do with the death of plants when the end-time comes: the almond becomes revolting, the locust droops, and the caper is defoliated. Nature comes to an end.

Yea, the human goes. The *kî* marks the culmination of the long sentence beginning in v 2. It gives the reason for all the gloom that one encounters in the poem. It becomes apparent now that the sky darkens, light is dimmed, all domestic, economic, and social activities cease, even nature dies, because of this: the human is going to eternal darkness. This is an eschatological vision. In this case it is not an individual who dies, but *hā'ādām* "humanity." Unlike the reference to the going and coming of generations in 1:4, here it is humanity that goes to "the eternal house."

grave. Hebrew *bêt 'ôlāmô*, lit., "his eternal house." R. F. Youngblood has argued recently that *bêt 'ôlām* should be interpreted not as grave but as "dark house" (lit. "house of darkness"), so that *hōlēk . . . 'el bêt 'ôlāmô* is comparable with *baḥōšek hôlēk* in 2:14 and *ḥōšek yēlēk* in 6:4 ("Qohelet's 'Dark House,'" pp. 211–27). The term is, however, widely attested in the Levant (see *DNWSI* I, p. 161). Although no influence can be established, there can be little doubt that the Semitic expression is the semantic equivalent of Egyptian *pr n nḥḥ* or *pr n ḏt* "house of eternity," meaning the grave (see *WbÄS* I, p. 514). Diodorus Siculus informs us that the Egyptians called their graves *aidioi oikoi* "eternal houses."

The sense of finality evident in our passage is also present in the Deir 'Allā inscription, where one reads: *y'br 'l byt 'lmn* "he will go over to the 'House of Eternity'" (Combination II, line 6; see Hackett, *Deir 'Allā*, pp. 58–59). That destination is further defined in that text as the place where one who goes (*hlk*) will not ascend. The netherworld, the place of perpetual darkness.

march. The verb *sābĕbû* here means "march"—i.e., be in a ritual procession (see Ps 48:13; Josh 6:3, 4, 7, 14, 15).

6. *before.* Hebrew *'ad 'ăšer lō'* (see Notes at v 1). Basically from vv 2–5 we have one long sequence introduced by *'ad 'ăšer lō'*. Now we have another sequence, introduced the same way. This is the concluding strophe of the poem.

the silver tendril. Hebrew *ḥebel hakkesep* is usually taken to mean "a silver cord" and it is thought to be a metaphor for life: i.e., the cord of life is broken. The word *ḥebel*, however, may refer to anything that is long and twining. The Arabic cognate *ḥabl*, usually meaning "cord," is used of various parts of a plant (stalk, shoot, branch), and *ḥabalat* refers to grapevine or a stock of the grapevine (see Lane, *Arabic-English Lexicon*, Part 2, pp. 504–6). Hebrew *ḥebel* may refer to a "lot" or a "portion," perhaps originally meaning an offshoot of the whole, perhaps even a "branch." In Job 39:3, the word is understood in the sense of an "offspring" (*yaldêhen* "their children" // *ḥeblêhen* "their offspring").

Since the parallel term in our verse, *gullat hazzāhāb* "golden bowl," probably refers to a receptacle for oil at the end of a lampstand (see Note below), we should understand "the silver tendril" as a part of the lampstand or, by extension, the lampstand itself. It may be observed that lampstands in the Levant were often stylized as trees, probably representing the tree of life. An example of a lampstand from Tell Beit Mirsim shows three branches at the top of the pedestal on which the receptacle was supposed to rest, and this is confirmed by a fragmentary piece from Tell en-Naṣbeh, with a bowl cradled by the three branches (see R. H. Smith, "The Household Lamps of Palestine in Old Testament Times," *BA* 27

[1964], pp. 23–24, fig. 11). The pedestal and its branches together symbolized the tree of life. The *ḥebel* in Eccl 12:6, then, may refer to such a stand or a part thereof (a branch?). One may compare the usage of singular *qāneh*, lit. "reed," which is used of a branch of the lampstand or collectively for all the branches—the "branch-work" (Exod 25:31; 37:17). The singular form *qāneh*, thus, may refer to a single branch of the lamp or to the whole lampstand, the central shaft and all the branches of it. So, too, the *ḥebel* may refer to a single part of the lampstand, or to the whole lampstand. The "golden bowl," which contained the oil, was simply set on top of these branches or tendrils of the stylized tree. Alternatively, the bowl could have had a protrusion at the bottom of it, by which it was attached to a cylindrical stand or a cylindrical branch of the stand. An example of such lamps from the Persian period has been uncovered (see Ruth Amiran, *Encyclopedia Biblica* V, col. 924; Stern, *Material Culture*, p. 128, fig. 202).

To be sure, these artifacts are ceramic, not metal as our text has it, but it is likely that the ceramic ones were modeled after more elaborate and expensive metal ones, a practice mentioned in Wis 15:9. In any case, metal (particularly bronze) lampstands are attested elsewhere in the Levant. There is no need, therefore, to posit that Eccl 12:6 indicates that the lamp was hung by the silver cord (so Galling and others), for which we have no archaeological evidence whatsoever. What is indicated in Eccl 12:6, then, is the destruction of the lamp—both the stand and the receptacle—the symbol of light and life (cf. Job 18:5–6; 21:17; Prov 13:9; 20:20; 24:20). One may note the symbolism in Job 21:17, which involves a suggestive wordplay with *ḥilleq ḥebel*, ordinarily meaning "divide a portion": "how often is the lamp of the wicked extinguished . . . (and) he destroys the tendrils (*ḥăbālîm*) in his anger?"

is smashed. Reading with Qere and forty-four MSS, *yērāteq*, instead of Ketib, which has *yrḥq* "be distant" or "be removed." LXX has *anatrapē*, lit. "is overthrown," which is usually explained as an inner-Greek error for *anarragē* or *aporragē* (so McNeile), both said to reflect Hebrew *yēnāteq* "snapped." A number of scholars argue, therefore, that *yntq* is original (so Euringer), even though not a single Hebrew MS has *yntq*. Nor can one be certain that the *Vorlage* of LXX had *yntq*. It is possible that Greek *anatrapē* reflects Hebrew *yrtq*, incorrectly interpreted as a Hiphil, meaning "to hit (with the fist)" and hence, "to fight back, rebel" (see Jastrow, *Dictionary*, p. 1504). Cf. also the noun *marteq* "a blow"; Aramaic *martôqā'* "a blow with a fist." The verb *rtq* "to knock" is attested in Jewish Aramaic (see *DNWSI* II, pp. 1088–89). Hence, *yrtq* must be interpreted to mean "broken" or "crushed" (i.e., struck by a blow). Vulg has *rumpatur*, Syr *ntpsq*, and Symm *kopēnai*—all reflecting *yrtq* "is broken" or "is crushed." Thus, the ancient versions for the most part reflect Hebrew *yrtq*. In sum, the alternatives are *yrḥq* or *yrtq*, but not *yntq*, which has no support. The confusion between the first two arose in part because of the graphic similarity of *ḥet* and *taw*. The former (*yrḥq*) makes no sense at all in the context; the latter is probably correct. The point is that the lamp pedestal, in the form of a stylized tree, is smashed (*yērāteq*)—that is, struck with a hard blow.

golden bowl. The "golden bowl" here refers to the receptacle at the end of the lampstand (see Zech 4:2–3). Our text suggests that the receptacle for the oil is detachable from the extension ("tendril" or "branch") that connects it to the stand: the bowl is made of gold, but the tendril of silver. One thinks here either of the bowl cradled by the tendrils or branches of the lampstand, as in examples found at Tell en-Nasbeh and Tell Beit Mirsim, or the kind of receptacle that has a protrusion at the base of it by which it is attached to a cylindrical stand or to one tendril of the lampstand (see Notes on "the silver tendril" above). In the example mentioned in Ecclesiastes, the bowl and its attachment are made of different metals. In any case, the lamp in this passage is not unlike the *mĕnôrâ*, which is usually mentioned in cultic contexts, but is also mentioned once as being in a private home (2 Kgs 4:10) and is archaeologically attested in domestic contexts (see Smith, "Household Lamps," pp. 9–11).

crushed. The Qal imperfect verb here may be taken as impersonal: "one crushed" = "(it) is crushed" (Joüon-Muraoka §155.b.Note 2). There is no need, therefore, to emend the text to read *tērōṣ* (i.e., the Niphal imperfect), as some commentators have suggested (e.g., Lauha, Hertzberg). As typical of many geminate verbs, the Qal imperfect of *rṣṣ* is vocalized as if it were a Middle-Weak root (cf. *yārûṣ*, an imperfect form of *rṣṣ* in Isa 42:4; *'ārûṣ*, an imperfect of *rṣṣ* in 2 Sam 22:30; *yāšûd*, the imperfect of *šdd* in Ps 91:6; and so forth).

the jar is broken at the spring. The shattering of pots may have been a funerary custom. It is noteworthy that broken pots have been found in Jewish tombs from the second temple period and those found in sealed contexts often indicate that they were already broken before or at the time when they were placed (see R. Hachlili and A. Killebrew, "Jewish Funerary Customs During the Second Temple Period, in the Light of the Excavations at the Jericho Necropolis," *PEQ* 115 [1983], p. 121). Commenting on the large number of sherds found at such tombs, P. Bar-Adon conjectures that they may have symbolized death ("Another Settlement of the Judean Desert Sect at 'Ain el-Ghuweir on the Dead Sea," *BASOR* 227 [1977], p. 20). Broken earthen vessels and fragments of them have also been found in some coffins from the Persian period. Those discovered at Shechem are all, curiously, broken at the neck of the vessel before being deposited in the coffin (see E. Stern, "Achaemenian Tombs from Shechem," *Levant* 12 [1980], pp. 100–2). These sherds can hardly be funerary offerings, as some scholars have posited. Rather, they are a testimony to an ancient funerary custom that is still practiced in Israel among the Jews from North Africa and Persia. According to the ritual today, pots are shattered at a funeral, either at the house of the dead or at the burial site. This is supposed to symbolize the end of life and the fact that the mortal is a "broken sherd."

Since mortals were viewed as earthen vessels made by the divine potter (cf. Isa 29:16; 64:8; Jer 18:6; Gen 2:4b–7), it is likely that the shattering of earthen vessels during a funeral represented the end of life. So in Ps 31:13 (Eng v 12), death is likened to the breaking of a vessel (see also Jer 22:28). One wonders, too, if the shattering of earthen jars by Gideon and his soldiers in Judg 7:15–23 might have some symbolic, rather than strategic, significance (cf. Ps 2:9; Isa 30:14; Jer 48:38; Hos 8:8; Lam 4:2). Perhaps the smashing of the jars symbolized the certainty of death for the enemy. As a passage in the Talmud says regarding the breaking of pots: "their breaking is their death" (*b. B. Qam.* 54a). One may further surmise that the throwing of the sherds into the grave represented the return of the body to the earth. If, indeed, such a custom lies in the background of our passage, it is particularly ironic that the ritual in this case took place at the "spring," a veritable symbol of life.

vessel. Dahood ("Canaanite-Phoenician Influence," pp. 213–14) is surely correct that *glgl* here does not mean "wheel" for drawing water (see NAB: "the broken pulley falls into the well"). Waterwheels were known in the Levant from the ninth century B.C.E. onward, but they were not commonly used; they were limited to palaces and the like. At ordinary wells, buckets were simply lowered directly or, in case of large buckets, lowered from the side, over time leaving abrasion grooves on the walls of the wells. In any case, from all that we know, waterwheels in the ancient Near East were large and sturdy contraptions, unlikely to be "crushed at the pit." It seems likely, therefore, that the noun here refers not to a waterwheel (a pulley), but to a vessel of some sort. This is suggested already by the parallelism of the noun here with *kad* "pitcher." We should perhaps vocalize the noun in question as **golgōl* (from earlier **gulgul*), a noun related to *gullâ* "basin, bowl" and *gulgōlet* "skull." It refers, perhaps, to a globular vessel. In Akkadian, *gulgullu* and *gulgullatu*, usually meaning "skull," are also names of cooking pots, and *gullu* and *gullatu* also refer to various vessels (see *CAD* V, pp. 128–29). Dahood calls attention to the word *glgl* inscribed in Punic on a vase (*RES* 907). Cf. also Ugaritic *gl*, which refers to a drinking vessel (*KTU* 1.14.II.18–19, IV.1–2; cf. Akkadian *gullu*).

at the pit. Perhaps "into the pit." The expression '*el-habbôr* is not a little curious. One expects '*al-habbôr* (cf. '*al-habbôr* "at the pit" in Isa 24:22), as in '*al-hammabbûa*' "at the spring." Perhaps we are to interpret the Hebrew to mean that the fragments of the vessel are thrown *into* the pit (so also '*el-habbôr* "into the pit" in Gen 37:22). It is not amiss to observe that *bôr* is not only a cistern/well, a source of "living waters" (cf. Gen 26:19), but also the grave (see Isa 14:19; Prov 28:17; Ps 30:4 [Eng v 3]; cf. the references to the dead as *yōrĕdê bôr* "those who go down to the pit" in Pss 28:1; 143:7; Isa 38:18; Ezek 26:20; 32:25, 29, 30). The double meaning of the word *bôr* is evident in Jeremiah's prophecy (Jer 2:13). The parallelism of *habbôr* with *hammabûa*' "the spring" does not necessarily mean that *habbôr* must refer to the cistern or well. Qohelet is probably referring to the custom of shattering earthen vessels at a funeral, a ritual symbolizing the return of the body to the earth, a subject that he touches on in the next verse.

7. *returns.* For the use of the jussive in place of the expected imperfect, see GKC §109.k. Alternatively, read *wĕyāšūb*, the defective spelling for *wĕyāšûb*. Cf. *yābî'* in 12:14.

life-breath. The *rûaḥ* in this context is synonymous with the *nišmat ḥayyîm* "breath of life" in Gen 2:7. This is the last mention of the *rûaḥ* in Ecclesiastes. In its first occurrence of the word, *rûaḥ* is the wind blowing around and around, only to return to its circuits (*wĕ'al-sĕbîbôtāyw šāb hārûaḥ*, 1:6). Now, in the final poem, the restless and unpredictable *rûaḥ* "returns," not to its rounds but to God who gave it. Even as the sun has set forever (see Notes at 12:2), so too, the *rûaḥ* returns to its source. The world as humans know it has come to an end.

8. *Absolute vanity.* See Notes and Comment at 1:2.

COMMENT

The first issue in the interpretation of this passage is its beginning. A number of scholars prefer to make 11:7–8 the conclusion of the preceding unit (so Hertzberg, Michel, Zimmerli). We have seen, however, that 11:6 properly ends the unit that begins with 10:16: "in the morning" in 11:6 recalls "in the morning" in 10:16; "do not let go of your hand" in 11:6 is contrasted with "slackness of hands" in 10:18. The attention to diligence and responsibility in 11:6 balances the reference to irresponsibility and sloth in 10:16–19. Thus, 11:6 belongs with the preceding literary unit.

Whybray (*Ecclesiastes*, p. 161) does not link 11:7–8 to the preceding passage, but he isolates those two verses from what follows on the grounds that they are stylistically different and, specifically, that the verses that follow use imperatives. But 11:7–8 shows close vocabulary and thematic ties with the verses that follow (see Witzenrath, *Süß ist das Licht*, pp. 20–28; Backhaus, *Zeit und Zufall*, pp. 303–17). The exhortations in 11:7–8 to be happy and to remember are reiterated by imperatives in 11:9 and 12:1:

"let one rejoice" (11:8a)	"rejoice" (11:9)
"and (let one) remember" (11:8b)	"remember" (12:1)

Moreover, the themes of light and darkness link 11:7–8 with the rest of the passage; the mention of light and the sun in 11:7 is matched by the reference to the darkening of the sun and the light in 12:2. One notes, too, the recurrence of certain expressions for time: "years" (11:8a; 12:1c), "days" (11:8b; 11:9; 12:1a, 1b), "before" (12:1b, 2, 6). The mention of "delight" (*ṭwb*) to the eyes (11:7) is reinforced by the call in 11:9 to let the heart "delight" (Hiphil of *ṭwb*) oneself, and "what the eyes see" in 11:9 recalls the eyes' seeing of the sun in 11:7. The references to "delight" are matched by the mention of its opposite, *rāʿâ* "unpleasantness," in 11:10 and 12:1.

Despite several textual and interpretive problems, it is clear that the passage as a whole is a carefully-constructed cohesive unit; there is a certain structural symmetry evident in the whole poem and within its component parts (see Witzenrath, *Süß ist das Licht*, pp. 5–7; Busto Saíz, "Estructura," pp. 17–25). Indeed, 11:7–8 may be seen as the "overture" (so Ravasi) to Qohelet's grand finale.

The passage consists of two sections: 11:7–10 and 12:1–8. The first section emphasizes the present; it is a call to enjoy while it is still possible to do so — while there is still light, as it were. The second half of the passage is about what happens when it is too late — when the light begins to dim and is finally extinguished altogether. Here Qohelet may have reworked an old composition about old age and impending death, and he elevates the issue to a cosmic level, so that it is not only the demise of an individual that is in focus but of humanity in general. There is a movement evident in the whole passage, from youth to old age and death, from the dawn of life to the return of the body to the earth and the life-breath to God. This passage is Qohelet's conclusion to the book and, as such, it parallels the preface (1:2–11). At the beginning of the book, one gets the impression that there is much activity in the cosmos: generations go and come, the sun rises and sets, the winds blow hither and thither, the streams keep flowing into the sea. To be sure, all the movements are routine and the point is made that "there is nothing new under the sun" (1:9). People come and go, but the world remains as always (*lě'ôlām*). Nevertheless, life goes on, and the movements of nature indicate that life goes on. But now, at the end of the book, all activities seem to grind to a halt. The sun and other luminaries of the sky darken, the daily chores cease, the doors of the street-bazaar are closed, nature seems to come to an end, and the human body returns to the earth, while the life-breath (*rûah*) returns to God. Qohelet's point is poignantly made: for all its limitations, existence does provide one with opportunities for joy. So one better enjoy while one can, for there will be an end to it all.

The hand of an editor is evident in 12:8, where Qohelet is mentioned by name (in addition to the superscription, 1:1, and the epilogue, 12:9–14, see also 1:2; 7:27). The summary-judgment echoes the very beginning of the book; it stands as the last verse of the concluding passage, even as the similar saying in 1:2 stands as the first verse of the introductory passage. Thus, the book is framed by the summary-judgment that everything is absolute *hebel* "vanity" (see Comment at 1:2). This is not to say that 12:8 is simply tacked on to 11:7–12:7, without any consideration for its unity with the rest of the passage. Indeed, the mention of *hebel* "vanity" appropriately ends the second half of the passage, even as the mention of *hebel* "vanity" ends the first half— 11:10 (see Ravasi, *Qohelet*, p. 332; Ogden, "Qoheleth XI,7–XII,8," p. 29).

Enjoy While There Is Still Time (11:7–10)

Qohelet begins with an affirmation of existence: "Light is pleasant and it is a delight to see the sun." Light and the sun are metaphors for life in the ancient Near East (see Job 3:16; 33:28, 30; Pss 36:10 [Eng v 9]; 56:14 [Eng v 13]). This is evident in the *Gilgamesh Epic*, where the protagonist says: "Let my eyes see the sun, that I may be sated with light!" (see *ANET*[3], p. 89). For Gilgamesh, the alternative to seeing light is the darkness of the netherworld. In another text, known as *The Descent of Ishtar*, the netherworld is known as the "Land of No Return" where those who enter are deprived of light; they see no light and dwell perpetually in darkness (*ANET*[3], p. 107; compare Job 10:21–22). Clearly, light is life, darkness is death. But the ancients knew well that it was not only in the netherworld that there is darkness; people who live in misery and gloom are also said to be in darkness (see Comment at 5:16 [Eng v 17]). Thus, it can be said that there are many "days of darkness," even in life. As Lohfink observes, the pleasantness of light is not automatically experienced by everyone who is alive; one must do something to experience it (*Kohelet*, pp. 80–81).

So Qohelet urges people to live to the full (11:8): "if one should live many years, let one rejoice in them all." He exhorts people to enjoy to the full and at every opportunity (see 9:8), because one knows that the "days of darkness" will be many. The experience of light can be threatened. The threat is not only from death and the darkness of the netherworld, but also from gloom and misery in this world. For Qohelet, darkness may dominate one even before death!

The injunction in 11:8 to "remember" (*yizkōr*) the gloomy days to come seems to contradict 5:19 (Eng v 20), where the author says that people should *not* "call to mind" (*yizkōr*) too much the days of life, presumably referring to the fact that one's lifetime includes days of gloom. Remembering seems to be capable of two effects for the author: it may prompt one to enjoy while one is able to do so (11:8), or, if it is overdone (*harbēh* "too much"), it may cause one not to enjoy the present (see Comment at 5:19 [Eng v 20]). So first he says one should not remember (5:19 [Eng v 20]), but now he says "let one remember." In a similar manner, Deutero-Isaiah uses the verb "remember" (*zkr*) in two ways, both in reference to past events. On the one hand, the poet says one must not remember the past because God is doing wondrous new things in the present (Isa 43:18). On the other hand, one must remember the past, because the past is a testimony to the consistency of God's acts (Isa 46:8). For the exilic poet, memory may have two effects: it may make one nostalgic and blind one to the possibility of new miracles (a negative effect), or it may cause one to trust the deity (a positive effect). If memory causes one to be despondent in the present, so that one cannot see new possibilities, one should not remember; but if memory serves the present well and enhances faith, then one should remember. Remembrance of events in the past should help one live in the present.

So, too, Qohelet speaks of memory for the sake of the present. In 5:19 (Eng v 20) he says one should not call to mind the days of life, because doing so can spoil the possibility of enjoyment in the present. At the same time, he says in 11:8 that one should remember that there will be hard times, for then one may be prompted to be happy. Unlike Deutero-Isaiah, he is not thinking of the remembrance of past events, but of the days to come. Remembering can have a future dimension (compare "remember the end" in Sir 7:36; 41:3). Yet, there is, in fact, no contradiction between the two perspectives in the book. In 5:19 (Eng v 20), the problem is that people do remember too much (*harbēh*), and so they are enjoined *not* to do so. The author is both a realist and a pragmatist. He knows that misery is a reality of life, and he is aware that most people know that there are going to be difficult times. But Qohelet also believes that that recognition need not be crippling. On the contrary, that knowledge may make one appreciative of what pleasures one can discover here and now. The present is what matters, for anyone who comes into existence is only here for a fleeting season: "all that comes is vanity" (11:8).

Then the author turns to address an imaginary audience, a youth, although everyone is meant to overhear that exhortation: "Rejoice, O youth, while you are young, and let your heart delight you in the days of your youth; follow the ways of your heart and what your eyes see" (11:9a–b). The call to enjoyment is reminiscent of an Egyptian tomb inscription, known as *The Song of Antef*, which includes the injunction to "follow the heart" while one is yet alive (II.v.26; see Fox, "A Study of Antef," p. 407). The idiom "follow the heart" occurs also in *The Instruction Ptahhotep*, a text that begins with a series of complaints about the infirmities of old age (*AEL* I, p. 66).

Commentators are sometimes troubled by the expression "and let your heart delight you" in our passage (11:9). So the text is frequently emended or interpreted to mean "let your heart be pleasant" (so NASB) or "let your heart be glad" (so NAB). This difficulty stems from a failure to recognize that the heart is personified here as, indeed, the language of following the ways of the heart also implies. The heart acts as if it were a separate entity (see Comment at 1:16); it is here capable of giving pleasure.

Another instance where the heart functions independently is in 2:1–3, a text that has many points of contact with 11:7–10. In the former passage, it is the heart that causes one to have joy (*śimḥâ*) and experience delight (*rĕʾēh ṭôb*, literally "see good"). In the latter, it is the heart that causes one to have delight (the verb is from *ṭwb*). In 2:2, the heart leads ("my heart conducted by wisdom and did not lead by folly"); in 11:9, the injunction is to follow the heart — obviously the heart also leads.

The links between 2:1–3 and 11:7–10 also prompt one to consider the apparent tension between the two. One passage seems to cast doubt on the significance of joy (2:1–3), the other calls for joy (11:7–10). Yet, there is no real contradiction between the two. The point of 2:1–3 is that joy is ephemeral because life is ephemeral — the days of one's life are numerable (see Notes at 2:3). That does not mean that one should not enjoy at all; it only means that joy, like everything else, is fleeting. The injunction in 11:9 to enjoy is made precisely because life is ephemeral. However many years one may live, the human life span is, nevertheless, limited. In other words, the days of pleasure are numerable. So one should enjoy whenever possible. Enjoyment is urged, but nowhere does the author imply that enjoyment is anything but a fleeting thing, *hebel* "vanity."

So insistent is Qohelet on enjoyment that he puts it in theological terms: "know that for all these God will bring you into judgment" (11:9c). This line is sometimes regarded as a pious gloss, an orthodox corrective to Qohelet's emphasis on enjoyment. According to this view, Qohelet says "enjoy yourself," but an orthodox glossator adds a caveat: "*but* recognize that you are called into account" (so Galling, Zimmerli, Lauha). Yet, the remark in 11:9c is not incongruous with the author's perspective. For him, the enjoyment of life is both the lot of humanity (a "portion," see Comment at 2:10) and a gift of God (2:24–26; 3:10–15; 5:17–19 [Eng vv 18–20]; 9:7, 9). Human beings are supposed to enjoy life to the full because that is their divinely assigned portion, and God calls one into account for failure to enjoy. Or, as a passage in the Talmud has it: "Everyone must give an account before God of all good things one saw in life *and did not enjoy*" (*y. Qidd.* 4:12; emphasis added). For Qohelet, enjoyment is not only permitted, it is commanded; it is not only an opportunity, it is a divine imperative.

When It Is Too Late (12:1–8)
The continuity of this half of the literary unit with the first is suggested by the
call to remember (12:1), which is paired with the call to enjoy in 11:9, even as
the exhortation to enjoy and remember are paired in 11:8. The themes of light
and darkness in 11:7–10 are continued in 12:1–8. Specifically, light and sun are
paired in 11:7, as they are in 12:2. Neither the extent of the section, nor its connection with the preceding passage is seriously questioned. There is also wide
consensus that the end of life is at issue. The controversies on this section of the
unit are less about its literary unity or its general purpose and more about the
interpretation of specifics. And there are two flashpoints in the debate:

1. What or who is one called to remember in 12:1: the creator or something
   else?
2. How should one read 12:2–6: allegorically, literally, or figuratively?

The most lively debate revolves around the second of these issues, namely, the
proper handling of 12:2–5. The earliest interpreters took these verses as an allegory about the woes of old age (so the Targum, Midrash, and Talmud). In this
approach, the dimming luminaries are various parts of the face, the trembling
guards are the limbs of the body and the convulsing men are the limbs or the
bones, the diminishing "grinders" are the teeth, those who look out the window
are the eyes, the closing of the doors are the clogging of the orifices of the body
(referring either to deafness or constipation) or the closing of the lips (the mouth
is silent), and so forth. Along similar lines, 12:5b is taken to be descriptive of old
age: the almond tree is said to be in bloom (see Notes), and the whiteness of the
tree when it is in bloom is thought to represent white hair; the caper-berry, which
is supposed to have been a stimulant of some sort, is thought to be ineffective
when one becomes old. Such interpretations, at least for 12:3–5, are still common among commentators (so Lauha, Zimmerli, Barucq). Yet, despite the fact
that there are parts of the text that are amenable to an allegorical interpretation
(e.g., 12:3b, 5b), there are other parts that need not (12:3a, 4a) or even cannot
(e.g., 12:5a) be so interpreted. The allegorical approach cannot be applied consistently through the text. Nor do interpreters agree on the "correct meaning" of
each part of the supposed allegory.
   While the allegorical interpretation has persisted, some modern scholars take
the descriptions to be literal. Thus, Gilbert argues that trembling, bending,
blindness, and so forth, describe the literal physiological conditions of old age
("La description de la vielliesse," pp. 103–4). Others think the scene is a house
or an estate falling into disrepair, which is a metaphor for death (Witzenrath,
Süß ist das Licht, pp. 44–50) or the failure of human efforts (Sawyer, "The Ruined House," pp. 519–31). The description is literal, it is assumed, but the intent
is symbolical. Still others argue that the verses describe the approach of a rain-
storm, again, a metaphor for death (so Ginsburg, *Cohelet*, pp. 457–68; Leahy,
"The Meaning of Ecclesiastes 12,1–5," pp. 297–300). Loretz takes the passage to
be describing a dark and wet winter's day (a metaphor for old age), which is

followed by the rejuvenation of nature in spring (*Qohelet*, pp. 189–93). The point, then, is that human beings only grow old and die; unlike nature, they do not experience this rejuvenation. Some scholars contend that there are elements that seem to describe a community in mourning during a funeral (so Anat, "The Lament on the Death of Humanity," pp. 375–80, and Fox, *Contradictions*, pp. 286–89). For Fox, the passage may be read at different levels — literal, symbolic, and allegorical ("Aging and Death," p. 42). Indeed, the interpretations are many and varied, but no one approach is entirely satisfying.

Recognizing the complexity of the text, Sawyer has proposed that the section (12:3–5) was originally a literal depiction of a house in disrepair, but the original text was subsequently reworked and given an allegorical meaning ("Ruined House," pp. 519–31). According to Sawyer, Qohelet wrote a parable of a ruined house to illustrate the futility of human efforts, but that parable was later allegorized. In other words, the text as we have it does not represent the work of Qohelet but of later interpreters. Yet, an allegorical interpretation cannot be sustained throughout the passage, as Sawyer himself admits; nor can the original text with its literal meaning be recovered, although Sawyer attempts to do so. If the text as we have it was meant to be read as an allegory, the revisers failed badly. Nevertheless, Sawyer's observations about the tensions between the apparent allegorical and the literal elements in the text are appropriate. Parts of the poem, indeed, sound allegorical. One wonders if the compositional process had not been the reverse of what Sawyer suggested: the allegorical elements might have come first. This would explain why we only get a hint of the allegory here and there. If so, there is no reason why Qohelet himself could not have been the one who reworked the old materials to suit his purposes. The author may have taken an old composition about aging, one that included some allegorical elements but need not be entirely allegorical, and he gave it a new twist in a new context. One may compare the litany of complaints about old age in *The Instruction of Ptahhotep*, even though that text is not an allegory, but a literal description. I would translate the passage as follows:

Agedness is here, old age has befallen,
Feebleness has come, weakness is arriving.
Being in discomfort, one sleeps all day long.
Eyes are dim, ears are deaf.
Strength wanes, for my heart is weary.
The mouth is silent; it cannot speak.
The mind is finished, it cannot remember the past,
The bones hurt all over.
Good has become bad; all taste is gone.
What old age does to all people is a terrible thing.
The nose is blocked up, it cannot breathe.
It is debilitating to stand or to sit.

(*Papyrus Prisse*, I, lines 3–10)

A similar view of old age is found in *The Tale of Sinuhe*:

Would that my body were young (again),
For old age has befallen,
Misery has overtaken me.
My eyes are heavy,
My arms weak,
My feet fail to follow,
The heart is weary.
Death draws near to me!

(my translation; *Papyrus Berlin* 3022, lines 167–70)

The original piece used by the author might have mixed the literal (perhaps something like one of the above descriptions of old age) with the metaphorical. Such a mixing, as Fox has suggested, is evident in the following Sumerian text about the effects of old age:

The old man answered the king:
(I was) a youth, (but now) my luck, my strength, my personal god,
and my youthful vigour have left my loins like an exhausted ass.
My black mountain has produced white gypsum.
My mother has brought in a man from the forest, he gave me captivity.
My mongoose which used to eat strong smelling things
    does not stretch its neck towards beer and butter.
My teeth which used to chew strong things can no more chew strong things.
My urine used to flow (?) in a strong torrent,
    (but now) you flee (?) from my wind.

(Alster, *Studies in Sumerian Proverbs*, p. 93, lines 27–33)

In this example, the literal statements about youthful energy, teeth, and urine are mixed with the metaphors like the black mountain that produced white gypsum (representing the graying head) and the mongoose which does not smell well anymore (representing the nose). So, too, Qohelet may have used an old composition that included a literal description of old age, along with metaphorical or allegorical references. We are not able, however, to recover the original piece. Only here and there do we get a hint of what *might* have been.

Whatever the original composition was that the author used — whether a written text or an oral piece known to the audience — it is clear that there is now another level of meaning. The text as it stands in Ecclesiastes is no longer about old age, nor is it about the death of the individual *per se*. Rather, as Fox has convincingly argued, there is also a cosmic and universal dimension in the depiction of the disaster that lies ahead (*Contradictions*, pp. 289–98). In this he is anticipated in some ways by Gregory Thaumaturgos and other early and medieval exegetes (see Leanza, "Eccl 12,1–7," pp. 191–207).

Qohelet begins with the injunction to remember (12:1), but the object of remembering is disputed. Without emendation, one should take the word to mean, first and foremost, "your creator." If so, the mention of the creator anticipates the allusion to the fact of creation in 12:7, where the mortal is said to be returned to the dust and the life-breath to God. The use of an epithet for the deity is admittedly irregular in Ecclesiastes. The deity is always simply referred to as *hā'ĕlōhîm* "God." But the choice of this epithet may have been intended as a wordplay, for Hebrew *bôrĕ'êkā* means "your creator," but it is also a near homonym for "your cistern" (*bôrĕkā*) and "your pit" (*bôrĕkā*). A number of commentators have argued that the author is continuing the thought in 11:7–10 and thinking of the enjoyment of one's wife (compare 9:9), since *bôr* "cistern" is used elsewhere as a metaphor for one's wife: "Drink water from your own cistern (*bôrĕkā*), flowing water from your own well (*bĕ'ērĕkā*)" (Prov 5:15). The passage from Proverbs is suggestive, for it goes on to say "let your fountain be blessed and rejoice in *the wife of your youth*" (Prov 5:18). At the same time, one may also think of *habbôr* "the pit" mentioned in 12:6, a word which may have reference to the grave. Given Qohelet's penchant for wordplay, it should hardly be surprising that a word is chosen that may be multivalent. The call to remember in 12:1 may point back to the call for enjoyment while one is able (11:7–10), but it also points forward to the scene of death at the end of the passage (12:6b) and to the creator who gave and will receive the life-breath of mortals (12:7).

The expression "the days of your youth" in 12:1a stands in contrast with "the days of unpleasantness" (*yĕmê hārā'â*) in 12:1b. The latter probably refers to old age, for the days of youth are said to come *before*. These "days of unpleasantness" are "the days of darkness" mentioned in 11:8, a period of misery and gloom. One presumes that when those days arrive, one will no longer be able to banish misery — unpleasantness (*rā'â*) — from one's body, as one is able to do in one's youth (11:10). When that time comes, those who did not enjoy themselves will realize that it is too late (12:1c), because it is no longer possible to enjoy all of life's pleasures. In the *Instruction of Papyrus Insinger*, written in Demotic, one is urged not to let the body suffer, for there are unpleasant days ahead. When old age comes, it may be too late to enjoy life's pleasures:

> He who has passed sixty years, everything has passed for him.
> If his heart loves wine, he cannot drink to drunkenness.
> If he desires food, he cannot eat as he used it. [*sic*]
> If he desires a woman, her moment does not come.

(XVII, lines 11–14, AEL III, p. 199)

From the Bible we have the testimony of Barzillai the Gileadite, who told King David, when the latter invited him to reside in Jerusalem, "I am eighty years old. Can I discern what is pleasant and what is not? Can your servant taste what he eats or what he drinks? Can I listen to the voice of singing men and singing women?" (2 Sam 19:36 [Eng v 35]). *If* this is the time with which Qohelet is concerned in the verses that follow (12:3–5), the view that the poem is about old age makes sense.

The author, however, seems to change direction; 12:2 is probably about old age, but in 12:3, the author moves on. This transition is indicated by the introduction of another "before"-statement: "before the sun darkens, even the light, and the moon and the stars, and the clouds return with the rain" (12:2). It is important to observe that the mention of "the sun" together with "the light" echoes 11:7. One should not, therefore, take the verse to be about inclement weather, but rather, about the end of life itself—since 11:7 is about being alive. After a cursory allusion to old age, the text is moving on to something more terrible than old age. The luminaries of the sky darken. Something more ominous than a storm is in view. Indeed, of all the references in the Bible to the darkening of the heavenly luminaries and of the light of day, not one refers to a rainy day. Rather, as Lohfink observes (*Kohelet*, p. 84), the language of the darkening luminaries belongs to the rhetoric of eschatology and description of the demise of the world (Isa 5:30; 13:10; Amos 5:8; 8:9; Mic 3:6; Job 3:9; 18:6; Joel 2:10; 3:4 [Eng 2:31]; 4:15 [Eng 3:15]; Matt 24:9; Mark 13:24; Luke 23:45; Acts 2:20). In an inscription from Tell Deir 'Allā on the east bank of the Jordan, there is a vision of cosmic disaster ordained by the gods of the divine council, and the first sign of the disaster that "Balaam son of Beor" saw was the darkening of the sky through a rain cloud and the withholding of light (see Notes above).

The threat suggested by our text is, therefore, far more cosmic and universal than old age or the death of an individual. The imagery is eschatological. That accounts for the absolute terror that the text depicts. It is not amiss to observe, too, that this is the final reference to the sun in the book. Thirty-five times the sun is mentioned; but here, in its final appearance, the sun is darkened. In the opening passage of the book, one finds the sun shining; it sets routinely, only to rise again (1:5). The activity of the sun does not change anything; nothing new is brought about. Yet, the sun shines and shines again. But now, in Qohelet's final words, the sun is darkened—along with other sources of brightness, whether of day or of night. All lights are dimmed. We can harbor no illusions about the sheer darkness that Qohelet intends for us to see.

The events that will happen are introduced by the temporal clause, "on the day when" (12:3). These are events that will accompany the darkening of the sky and of day; the heavens darken *when* all the things described in the verses to follow come to pass. One notes that whereas the period of old age is referred to as "days" (12:1b) or "years" (12:1c), the ominous signs that will happen are said to be "at the time" (literally "on the day"), as if all will happen on a single, decisive day. It is for good reason that some early interpreters connected this "day" with the end-time, the "great and terrible day of YHWH" (see Leanza). The language here is eschatological; it is reminiscent of various passages depicting the end-time.

We do not know if there was originally another meaning for the trembling of the guards of the house and the convulsing of the valiant men (12:3b). If there is an allegorical level of meaning, it is not immediately evident. Interpreters have speculated that the guards of the house and the valiant men refer to a person's arms (the guards) and the legs (the valiant men), or the limbs (the guards) and the bones (the valiant men). Accordingly, the point is that the limbs tremble when one is old — one becomes weak in old age. But it is not clear why the limbs should be called "guards *of the house*," nor is it clear why "valiant men" should refer to legs or to bones. Moreover, the Hebrew verb used for trembling is one that describes terror, not weakness (see Notes above). In any case, in its present context, following the ominous darkening of the sky, there are men who are terrified. They tremble (out of fear) and they convulse (or "cower"). It seems that even those who are supposed to be strong and dignified are terrified by something. The scene is reminiscent of passages about imminent destruction brought about by the deity, the mere threat of which causes even the brave and powerful to tremble in terror (Exod 15:14–15; Isa 13:6–8; Amos 2:13–15). In one NT vision of the end-time, the darkening of the sky is accompanied by the experience of great terror even by kings and military commanders, the rich and the strong (Rev 6:12–17).

If it is true that an older composition about the woes of old age lies behind the present form of the text, it is in 12:3b that the connection with old age is most apparent. The ones who grind — "the grinders" — stop because they are diminished. The text has traditionally been interpreted to mean that the teeth of an old person become few. It so happens that in Arabic, the word *ṭāḥināt* "grinders" (cognate of Hebrew *ṭōḥănôt* "grinders") also refers to molar teeth. But there is nothing allegorical about this saying. The statement, if that is what it means, is literally true; the old literally cannot chew (or at least cannot chew well) anymore, because their teeth have become few.

The parallel line, too, may have referred to old age, if *rō'ôt* ("those who look") refers to the eyes. It is true that one's eyes become dim with age. Importantly, the verb for the dimming occurs elsewhere in connection with the eyes (Ps 69:24; Lam 5:17). But in its present context, any reference or allusion to the physiological conditions of the aged fades into the background.

Following the mention of the guards of the house and the valiant men, those who grind must be understood as women who work the mills (Exod 11:5; Isa 47:2; Job 31:10). These women stop their grinding. The suddenness of the event is implied by the fact that the few women who remain are not able to work harder and cover for those who have disappeared. We do not know why the women who work the mills are diminished. We can only surmise that a large number of them suddenly die or are forced to abandon their indispensable work. We know only that some of the women who work the mills are suddenly gone, but others remain. One is reminded of the description of the end-time in the NT: "Then two will be working in the field; one is taken and one is left. Two women will be grinding at the mill; one is taken and one is left" (Matt 24:40–41; Luke 17:34–35). In this NT passage, the Greek word for the women who work the mills is *alēthousai*, precisely the translation of the Septuagint for Hebrew *ṭōḥănôt* "those who grind." There is no warning when the end-time comes, it seems, and there is no time to react on that decisive day: "*on that day*, anyone on the housetop who has belongings in the house must not come down to take them away; and likewise anyone in the field must not turn back" (Luke 17:31; compare Matt

24:17–18). This is why the grinding stops — because there is sudden death. The scene is eschatological; it is totally consistent with the darkening of the luminaries in the sky in v 2 (see also Matt 24:29).

As for "those who look out the window," we can only conjecture that these are wives and mothers who long for their loved ones to return. The motif of women who look out of the window is a literary convention used to depict the dashed hopes of mothers, wives, and lovers (see Abramsky, "The Woman Who Looked Out of the Window," pp. 114–24). Like Sisera's mother, who looked out the window, longing in vain for her son to return (Judg 5:28), these women presumably also wait in vain. They are like Michal, who looked out of the window only to see her hopes for the house of Saul dashed (2 Sam 6:16–23). They are like Jezebel, who looked out of the window (2 Kgs 9:30), only to see her hopes dimmed. Perhaps their vision become blurry because of grief (see Lam 5:17). Perhaps they "darken" because there is no more hope. In any case, something terrible is happening.

The activities stop not only at home, but also in the public places. The double-doors of the street-bazaar are closed. The reference here is to the street-bazaars that were common in antiquity and are still found everywhere in the Middle East. They are still known by the Hebrew name *šûq* ("shuq") or Arabic *sûq* ("suq"). The street-bazaar was and is the center of economic and social activities in the city. The closing of the doors leading into the *šûq*, therefore, means the cessation of lively commerce and social intercourse.

This dwindling of activity is further suggested by the silencing of the noises of the mill. Since in antiquity bread had to be baked daily, the sound of grain being milled was an assuring sign of life. So, too, Jeremiah associated the sound of the mill with other salutary sounds: "I shall banish from them the sound of joy and the sound of gladness, the voice of the bridegroom and the voice of the bride, the sound of the millstones and the light of the lamp" (Jer 25:10). The sound of the mill was a sound of life. By contrast, the silencing of the mill was ominous. It was equated with putting out the light, a sign of death. According to Rev 18:22–23, the decisive destruction of "Babylon" in the end-time is symbolized by the throwing of a great millstone into the sea and, it is said, the end of the city will be indicated by the fact that the sound of the millstone will no longer be heard and the light of the lamp will shine no more. Thus, the silencing of the mill is a terrible sign. The end is at hand. The point in 12:4a, then, is that all economic and social activities are suspended (the doors of the marketplace are closed), and even life-sustaining activities are stopped (the sounds of the mills drop). Something disastrous is happening.

In contrast to the lowering sound of the mill, the sound of birds is increased (see Notes): the decrease of one noise is replaced by the increase of another. We do not know precisely what is meant by "sound of the birds," or if the author has particular birds in mind. At all events, the increase in the sound does not seem benign. The lowering of the salutary sound of the mill is accompanied by the increase in the unsavory sound of the birds. Perhaps we are to think of the encroachment of the birds, as hitherto inhabited land becomes depopulated. The deathly silencing of a ruined human habitat is replaced by the increasing cacophony of the place's new inhabitants. The same chapter in the book of Revelation that refers to the silencing of the millstone and the extinguishing of the lamp in the final destruction of "Babylon" also speaks of the city becoming "a haunt for every vile and despicable bird" (Rev 18:2). The sound of life-sustaining activities (the mill) is replaced by the sound of the desolation of human life (the birds). Something terrible is happening.

In the vision of impending cosmic disaster in the inscription from Tell Deir ʿAllā, following the depiction of the darkening skies, there is a peculiar sequence involving several birds. Though fragmentary and difficult to interpret at critical points, the text clearly refers to birds squawking at one another and, indeed, the voice of vultures sings, while other birds apparently attack one another (Combination I, lines 7–9). Wild animals, too, are mentioned. Significantly, one reads later in the inscription of someone crossing over into "the House of Eternity" (*byt ʿlmn*), the same term used for the grave in our poem (12:5). Perhaps the birds in this passage of Ecclesiastes are equally symbolic of death. Like the birds in the Deir ʿAllā inscription, they are noisily moving in where the human population is on the verge of extinction.

The silencing of the mill is followed immediately and emphatically by the increased noise of the birds. And the "daughters of song," the poet continues, "come down low." If these "daughters of song" are birds, as the parallelism suggests, one imagines the birds swooping down to their new haunt in the face of the depopulation of the human habitat. In that case, the "daughters of song" would be like the *běnôt yaʿănâ*, which may have been understood in popular etymology as "daughters of one that sings" (see Notes above). Curiously, these birds are associated with mourning (Mic 1:8) and they inhabit all kinds of unsavory places that cannot sustain human life (Isa 13:21; 34:13; Jer 50:39; Zeph 2:14). The poet is referring to all kinds of birds, but one presumes in the context that the audience would think probably of birds like the *běnôt yaʿănâ*, literally "daughters of the one that sings." Apparently these creatures recognize the vulnerability of the remaining population, for "even from on high" they sense the terror down below (12:5a). That explains why they "come down low."

The meaning of 12:5b is unclear. As it stands, the text is capable of different interpretations. This is one of the places in the passage where it makes sense to interpret the text as an allegory of old age. Or, to put it differently, this is one of the places where the old allegorical meaning is nearer to the surface than elsewhere in the present text. Thus, the text may be taken to mean that the almond tree is in bloom, with the white blossoms signifying white hair. As for the locust, it probably does not refer to the insect, but to a plant, perhaps a carob tree (see Notes above). Thus, taking this verse allegorically, one tradition of interpretation understands the "locust" to refer to the male sexual organ (Rashi, Ibn Ezra, *b. Šabb.* 152b). If that is correct, one may interpret the drooping of the locust (a tree named for the drooping carob pods that resembled locusts) to be an allusion to impotence. The caper, which was reputed to be a stimulant, is said to "come to naught" or "become ineffective." Perhaps instead of stimulating one's appetite, it only frustrates (see Notes above).

Thus, at the allegorical level, all three plants may refer to the woes that an old man faces: the hair becomes white, the penis droops, and the caper does not help one's libido. Qohelet uses these images, perhaps with a wink of an eye at his knowing audience, but he means more than the woes of old age. The verb which may be translated as "blossom" (originally *yānēṣ*) may also be heard as "become revolting" (*yān'ēṣ*). Perhaps the author alters the text of the original composition a little to secure the new meaning in the new context. What he means is that the almond tree, which is well-known for its beauty, becomes exceedingly ugly. Perhaps it is withered. This is a rare sight and a sign of disaster. Moreover, the locust tree literally droops. The caper plant "comes to naught." Perhaps it is defoliated. It appears that all three plants are dead or dying. The scene here reminds one of the languishing of nature in the face of impending doom (see F. M. Cross, *Canaanite Myth and Hebrew Epic* [Cambridge, Massachusetts: Harvard, 1973], pp. 174–77). One may compare the death of nature here with the scene in Isa 34:4, although our passage is not nearly as cosmic:

> The heavens roll up as a scroll,
> And all their host languishes,
> As the leaf falls from the vine,
> and as leaves falling from the fig tree.

Similar descriptions of the languishing of nature are found elsewhere (Amos 1:2; Nah 1:4; Hab 3:17). In Canaanite mythology, one reads of the cessation of life and fertility when Mot, deified Death, becomes triumphant. All life ceases, nature dies.

The climax of the passage is reached in 12:5c. There lies the explanation for all the gloom in the preceding verses: "because the human is going to the grave and the mourners process in the street-bazaar." All the levels of meaning are brought together in this explanation. The metaphors of old age in the original composition, some of which are lost to us but others are still barely discernible, culminate in this march to the grave.

Apparently, the author has superimposed on the metaphors of old age another level of signification, drawing upon the imageries of cosmic doom, to depict the end of human existence. Hence, the sky darkens, every natural light is extinguished, all activities — domestic, economic, and social — cease, and nature dies. The poet takes the reader slowly from one scene to another: from the home, to the city and its street-bazaars, to the road, and eventually to the countryside. Everywhere there are signs that something terrible is happening. But only at the end of the passage does the reader realize what it is that the signs of the preceding verses portend. As Fox puts it: "[The author] audaciously invokes images of general disaster to symbolize death; more precisely — the death of you, the reader, to whom Qohelet is speaking when he addresses his youth, his ostensive audience"

(*Contradictions*, p. 293). The reader has been drawn inexorably towards this inevitable end (so Ravasi, *Qohelet*, p. 339). Unlike the opening chapter of the book, there is no thought of generations coming and going while the earth remains *lĕ'ôlām* "as always" (1:4). Rather, here humanity goes to the *bêt 'ôlām*, literally "house of eternity." This "house of eternity" is, as the inscription from Tell Deir 'Allā has it, the place where the one who goes (*hlk*) will not rise again (Combination II, lines 6–7; see Hackett, *Deir 'Allā*, pp. 28, 30). This land of no return is the netherworld, a land of perpetual darkness, from which one cannot turn back. The end is so permanent; it is so dark.

The finality of death is reinforced by a series of metaphors. The first is the destruction of the "silver tendril" and the "golden bowl" (12:6a). The silver tendril in this case probably refers to a part of the lampstand and, by extension, to the lampstand itself; it refers to the branch or branches of a stylized tree of life, which the typical lampstand symbolized (see Notes above). In some examples uncovered by archaeologists at Tell Beit Mirsim and Tell en-Nasbeh, the receptacle for the oil is a bowl cradled by the branches of a stylized tree. In one example from the Persian period, there is a protrusion at the bottom of the lamp, apparently so that the lamp may be fitted into a cylindrical lampstand or a branch of the lampstand (see Notes above). In any case, our example here is a lampstand with silver tendril and a golden bowl (compare Zech 4:2–3). Whatever the case may be, in our text, the tendril and the bowl are made of different materials: one is of silver (the tendril), the other of gold (the bowl). The point of our text is that the whole lamp, perhaps in the form of a stylized tree of life, is destroyed. The symbol for the light of life is destroyed.

Lamps are among the most common finds in Levantine tombs from various periods; by one estimate, they account for 25 to 50 percent of the vessels found in tombs (see Smith, "Household Lamps," p. 12). Presumably the lamps were included in the tombs because they symbolically helped the dead cope with the darkness of the netherworld. Qohelet, however, describes the complete destruction of this elaborate and resilient lamp. Even the stand made of silver will be smashed and the bowl made of gold will be crushed. He leaves no doubt about the absolute darkness at the end of life: humanity's lamp will be extinguished forever (compare 2 Sam 21:17). There can hardly be a stronger symbolic denial of immortality.

Moreover, the author speaks of the shattering of various pots (12:6b). This metaphor may have been taken from a funerary custom. Such a custom may help explain the number of sherds and broken pots found in the tombs, particularly those discovered in sealed contexts, where it is clear that they were placed only after they had been broken (see Notes). The pots may have been smashed at funerals — a custom still evident among some Jews today — to symbolize death. Since the human body is likened to an earthen vessel (compare 2 Cor 4:7), we may conjecture that the breaking of earthen pots at the funeral is symbolic not only of death, but of the return of the body to the earth: dust to dust. In our text, the pots are broken at the fountain, the source of life, and crushed at the pit, perhaps here meaning the grave (see Notes above). So the author speaks of the return of the body to the earth: "dust returns to the earth where it had been, and the life-breath returns to God who gave it." Here the text alludes to creation (Gen 2:7; 3:19), but the point is that the end of the human creature will come. In the end, Qohelet returns once again to his conviction that everything originates from and ends in the hand of God (so Zimmerli). He has spoken repeatedly of God's giving (1:13; 2:26; 3:10–11; 5:17–18 [Eng vv 18–19]; 6:2; 8:15; 9:9) and of God's gift (3:13; 5:18 [Eng v 19]). Now, in this grand finale, he stands with tradition in affirming that the life-breath belongs to God. In the end, the life-breath returns to its source (Ps 104:29–30; Job 34:14–15; Isa 42:5; Ezek 37:5). Unlike the restless wind (*rûaḥ*) in the preface to the book (1:2–11), the wind that blows every which way, around and around (1:6), the *rûaḥ* here returns not to its many rounds, but to God. Qohelet is describing the end of human life. True to traditional Hebrew anthropology, he believes that life is possible only because of the life-breath that God gives; apart from that life-breath, the body is only dust. The author is not making a distinction here between body and soul, a distinction foreign to Hebrew thought. In 3:21, the author refuses to speculate about the different destinations for the human life-breath, as opposed to that of animals. No one knows, he says, if one is going up and the other is going down. He says simply that at death the life-breath returns to God. Qohelet means the life-breath of every mortal who expires. And that return to God is neither up nor down. It is simply returned to God.

The final verse of the passage echoes the first verse of the introductory passage (1:2–11). Thus, whereas the introductory passage begins with the assertion that all is absolute *hebel* "vanity," that same assertion concludes the closing passage. Clearly, 1:2 and 12:8 together form a framework for the entire book. This verse is also appropriate as the conclusion to the passage, for it recalls the mention of *hebel* "vanity" in 11:8, 10. The point is that everything is ephemeral and beyond human control. All that comes into existence is fleeting (11:8), for however long one may live, the human life span is limited. Youth, too, is not lasting. It is not something that one can hold on to forever (11:10). As the poem in 12:1–7 shows, everything—humanity and all that goes with it—is ultimately *hebel*: nothing lasts, nothing is within the grasp of humanity.

EPILOGUE (12:9–14)

[9]Additionally, because Qohelet was a sage, he constantly taught the people knowledge. He listened and deliberated; he edited many proverbs. [10]Qohelet tried to find felicitous words and he wrote words of truth rightly. [11]The words of the sages are like goads; like implanted pricks are (the words of) the mentors of the assemblies—they are applied by a certain herder. [12]Beyond them, my child, beware. There is no end to the excessive production of writings; excessive talking wearies the body. [13]End of the matter; everything has been heard. Fear God and

keep his commandments, for every human being is to be so. [14]Surely God will bring every deed to judgment for everything hidden, whether good or evil.

NOTES

12 9. *Additionally, because Qohelet was.* The *waw* on *wĕyōtēr* does not necessarily link this verse to the preceding; it introduces a new subject matter (cf. the use of *waw* in 3:16; 4:4; 8:10; 11:7; 12:1). Moreover, the disjunctive accent on the word suggests that this word is syntactically separate from the rest of the sentence. Thus, *yōtēr* is to be interpreted either as a noun meaning "an addition" (or, as we may say, "postscript/addendum"), or a substantive used adverbially, meaning "additionally" (see GKC §118.q). The translation *kai perisson* in LXX probably reflects the former interpretation — otherwise one should expect *kai perissōs*.

A number of commentators, however, prefer to disregard the punctuation and take *wĕyōtēr šehāyâ* as one accentual unit. Gordis cites two texts from the Talmud: *ywtr mmh šh'gl rwṣh lynq hprh rwṣh lhynyq* "more than (the fact that) the calf wishes to suck, the cow wishes to suckle" (*b. Pesaḥ.* 112a) and *ywtr mšh'yš rwṣh lyś' h'šh rwṣh lhnś'* "more than (the fact that) a man wishes to marry, a woman wishes to be married" (*b. Yebam.* 113a). On the basis of these examples, Gordis argues that the verse means that Qohelet was *more than* a sage: "Not only was Koheleth a sage himself, but he also taught the people knowledge" (*Koheleth*, pp. 351–52). It is supposed, then, that the author of the epilogue means that Qohelet was more than a professional teacher in a wisdom school, whose clients were the elite of society. In this view, the instruction of the general public was thought to be extraordinary for a sage, whose audience was generally the upper class (so also Lohfink). Yet, the sages in Israel, whatever one may assume about their social location, surely did not regard teaching of the public as something extraordinary (cf. Sir 37:23). Public instruction was not what one did "besides being a sage" (so JB). One reads, for instance, of personified Wisdom teaching in the streets, in the markets, and at the city gates. Personified Wisdom calls out from the top of city walls and at the thoroughfares (Prov 1:20–21; 8:1–3). In Israel, public teaching was not contradictory to the task of the sages, but integral to it. In the words of personified Wisdom (Prov 8:4): "Unto you, O people (*'îšîm*) I call out, my cry is to humanity (*bĕnê 'ādām*)." The sages were supposed to teach the public, even humanity in general, and not just the elite. Moreover, the idiom in the two Postbiblical Hebrew texts cited by Gordis is properly *yōtēr min*, not *yōtēr še-* as we have in our text. It is the *min* that makes the expression comparative, not the *še-*. One can cite many examples of this idiom: e.g., *ywtr mmny* "more than me" (Esth 6:6); *ywtr mmny* "greater than I" (*y. Ber.* IV.7d); *ywtr md'y* "more than enough" and *ywtr mkšy'wr* "more than the proper amount" (*b. Mo'ed Qat.* 27b). That very idiom (*yōtēr min*) is found in Eccl 12:12, where *wĕyōtēr mēhēmmâ* means "beyond them."

As for the particle *še-* in *šehāyâ*, one should take it not as relative but as causal (see the use of *še-* in 8:14; Song 1:6; 5:2; cf. also the use of *'ăšer* in 4:9; Joüon-Muraoka §170.e).

a sage. The word is used here in the technical sense of someone who is a wisdom teacher (Jer 18:18; Prov 1:6; 22:17; 24:23) and not just the generic sense of a wise person. This does not necessarily imply, however, that Qohelet was a *professional* teacher in a "wisdom school" (cf. Fox, *Contradictions*, pp. 330–32).

constantly. The adverb *'ôd* here indicates persistence (cf. Gen 46:29; Ps 84:5 [Eng v 4]; Ruth 1:14).

the people. LXX[BSAP] (supported by SyrH) have *ton anthrōpon*, while Aq, Symm, some Greek MSS (supported by Copt) read *ton laon*, which is what one expects for Hebrew *hā'ām*. Greek *ton anthrōpon*, however, does not necessarily reflect *hā'ādām* in the *Vorlage*, as is commonly assumed (so Graetz, who wants to emend accordingly). Hebrew *'am* is translated by Greek *anthrōpos* a number of times in LXX (Job 12:2; Isa 36:11; 44:7). In either case, the general public is meant and not just a specific community at a point in time.

listened. Or "paid attention." Hebrew *'izzēn* is most readily identified as a denominative verb related to *'ōzen* "ear." All the ancient versions assume some association with ear, taking the word either as a noun or a verb (see Euringer, *Masorahtext*, pp. 131–32). It is true that elsewhere in Hebrew the verb is always in Hiphil, not Piel as we have it here, but there is considerable semantic overlap between the Hiphil and the Piel, and many Hebrew verbs are attested in both stems, without any discernible difference in meaning. A number of commentators, however, take the verb to mean "he weighed," assuming a denominative verb from *mō(')zĕnayim* "scales" (e.g., Hertzberg, Podechard, Murphy). So also NRSV, NAB, JB. In modern Western cultures one speaks of "weighing" words in the sense of evaluating them or testing them, but it cannot be assumed that the idiom was also present in the ancient Near East. Such a usage of *'zn* is unattested anywhere else in Hebrew: *'zn* never means "to weigh (words), to evaluate." The verb for weighing something, even when used with the noun *mō(')zĕnayim* "scales," is always *šql* (Jer 32:10; Ezek 5:1; Job 31:6), and the verb is never used with words as the object. Indeed, the noun *mō(')zĕnayim* is properly related not to the root *'zn* but to *yzn*, Proto-Semitic **wzn* (Arabic *wazana* "to weigh"). The noun is attested in Ugaritic, where it is spelled as *mznm*, presumably with the original **w* contracted. This root is unrelated to the verb *'izzēn* "to hear."

The point in this verse is that the sage listened attentively (lit. "gave ear") to the traditional sayings (cf. Job 33:1; 34:1–2). In this connection, it is important to note the significance of the ear in the wisdom tradition and the frequent association of wisdom with the willingness of the ear to hear (Prov 2:2; 4:20; 5:1, 13; 15:31; 18:15; 20:21; 22:17; 25:12; Job 29:11; 34:3; Sir 3:29; 6:33–35). In Akkadian, *uznu* "ear" is a metaphor for wisdom and the expression *uznu rapaštu* (lit. "wide ear") means "intelligent" (see *AHW*, p. 1448). The epilogue thus makes the point that Qohelet was wise. He was truly a *ḥākām* because he not only taught the general public, he also listened. LXX has *kai ous exichniasetai kosmion parabolōn* "and (the) ear traces (the) ordering of parables," apparently reflecting Hebrew *w'zn ḥqr tqn mšlym*, with the *waw* omitted before *ḥqr* (see MT).

deliberated. The verb *ḥqr* means not only to search out, but also to examine carefully in order to understand (Prov 25:2; Sir 44:5) or to investigate if some-

Ethics: Coping with Risks and Death

thing is true (Job 5:27). Job 32:11 is especially suggestive because it juxtaposes '*zn* with *ḥqr*: "I paid attention (*'āzîn*) to your understandings, while you deliberated over (*taḥqĕrûn*) the words."

edited. Several Hebrew MSS, Syr, and Aq have the conjunction before the verb (thus, *wĕtiqqēn*), but this reading may be secondary. The meaning of *tiqqēn* here is unclear. Elsewhere in the book (1:15; 7:13), the verb means "to straighten" that which is crooked. So this verb is sometimes taken to mean "to correct" (i.e., to "straighten out") or the like (thus JB: "he emended many proverbs"). In Postbiblical Hebrew the verb has an interesting range of meanings besides "to straighten" or "to repair": "to fix in place, set in order, prepare, establish, introduce, improve" (Jastrow, *Dictionary*, pp. 1691–92). In Sir 47:9, *tyqn* may mean "he arranged" (music). Creativity may be implied. In Akkadian, the verb *tuqqunu* means "to order, to bring to order" (*AHW*, p. 1323), also a possible nuance of the verb in Hebrew. This meaning is conveyed by LXX, which has *kosmion* "ordering" (i.e., reading either *tōqen* or *tĕqūn*). The Greek translators apparently understood Qohelet's work to be editorial: he collocated the proverbs — i.e., he gave them order (so NAB: "arranged many proverbs"). But this is true only in the sense that there are some proverbs that Qohelet placed within a new interpretive framework. He did not merely rearrange things; he placed them in their new contexts and gave them new meanings (see Comment at 1:15). His editorial task was, thus, not a mechanical one, but hermeneutical, as it were. The Hebrew verb may include some element of renovation (repairing, improving) and innovation (creating, composing). Perry (*Dialogues*, p. 172) seeks to preserve the dual aspect of composition (writing) and correction (righting): "righting many proverbs."

many proverbs. The point is simply that Qohelet was a sage — the typical sage worked with many proverbs (cf. 1 Kgs 5:12 [Eng 4:32]; Prov 1:6).

10. *felicitous words.* The Hebrew word *ḥēpeṣ* here may refer not only to what is aesthetically pleasing but also what is apt and timely (see Notes at 3:1). C. Dohmen argues that the term means instructions about life ("Der Weisheit letzter Schluß?" pp. 14–15). One cannot, however, separate *ḥēpeṣ* from its association with enjoyment, a connotation the word has elsewhere in the book (5:3 [Eng v 4]; 8:6; 12:1).

and he wrote. MT has *wktwb* (*wĕkātûb*), which is also supported by LXX, *kai gegrammenon* "and what is written." But a few Hebrew MSS have *wktb* (see de Rossi), interpreting the verb as active, "and he wrote." Aq, Symm, Syr, and Vulg all translate the word as a finite verb in the past tense, "and he wrote." This does not necessarily mean, however, that their *Vorlage(n)* had the Qal perfect 3 ms form. Rather, they may be interpreting the form (*ktwb*) as an infinitive absolute used in place of a finite verb, as in 4:2; 8:9; 9:11. This is probably correct. Thus, we should not emend to read *wĕkātab*, as is commonly done. Rather, one should repoint the word to read *wĕkātôb*. Perhaps an early variant had the word spelled defectively (i.e., *wĕkātōb*) and, hence, we find the translation in Aq and other witnesses.

rightly. Fox takes *yōšer* as a bound form (thus *yōšer dibrê 'ĕmet* "the most honest words of truth"), citing *qōšṭ 'imrê 'ĕmet* in Prov 22:21 as a syntactical parallel. But

385

the Proverbs text cited is notoriously problematic: the unique and morphologically strange form *qōšṭ* need not be interpreted as a construct form and is not interpreted so by the Masoretes or the ancient versions. It is easiest to interpret *qōšṭ* as an adverbial accusative (see GKC §118.m). As for the meaning of *yōšer*, one may compare the expression *'imrê yōšer* "right words" in Job 6:25 (cf. Ps 25:21, where we have *yōšer* "rightness" // *tōm* "integrity"). It is not amiss to note that the noun *yšr* "rightness" in Ugaritic may be a synonym of *ṣdq* "legitimacy": *mtrḫt yšrh* "his rightful bride" // *att ṣdqh* "his legitimate wife" (*KTU* 1.14.I.13). A similar parallelism is found in a Phoenician inscription: *mlk ṣdq* // *mlk yšr* "a legitimate king" // "a rightful king" (*KAI* 4.6–7). The point in our text, then, is the legitimacy and correctness of Qohelet's words. Most commentators, however, detect a certain defensiveness in this verse. Hence, there is a tendency to interpret *yšr* as "honesty." The meaning, of the verse, then, is supposed to be as follows: it is true that what Qohelet wrote is aesthetically pleasing, *but* what he wrote is straightforward and honest (so NEB: "He chose his words to give pleasure, but what he wrote was the honest truth"). Or, as Barton puts it, Qohelet "never sacrificed matter to form" (*Ecclesiastes*, p. 197). Underlying this interpretation is an assumption that the ancient readers were somehow suspicious of literary artistry, and so one must point out that there is substance and sincerity behind the forms. So this verse is seen as an apology for the artistry. It is doubtful, however, if the ancients perceived a tension between artistry and truth. Certainly in the wisdom literature throughout the ancient Near East there is no such dichotomy. Indeed, truth is always expected to be conveyed elegantly (see *The Eloquent Peasant, AEL* I, pp. 169–84). Words of truth are expected to be conveyed with artistry. The sincerity of Qohelet is surely not in question. Indeed, *yōšer* implies not so much honesty or straightforwardness (in contrast to the supposed crookedness of rhetorical artistry), as correctness and legitimacy. The entire verse is, in fact, an endorsement of Qohelet's aptitude as a sage. It claims that he was a bona fide sage precisely *because* he chose felicitous words and rightly (rightfully?) wrote them.

11. *the words of the sages.* The expression *dibrê ḥăkāmîm* "the words of the sages" occurs in 9:17, where it refers generally to the advice of wise people, with a possible allusion to the "wise commoner" who could have saved the little city from destruction (see 9:13–16). It is also attested in Prov 1:6 (// *wĕḥîdōtām* "and their riddles") and 22:17 (// *da'tî* "my knowledge" — i.e., Woman Wisdom's knowledge). The term does not appear to have a technical meaning, as some have suggested. It is a reference to wisdom teachings in general and not to a specific corpus (like the book of Proverbs), although the teachings of Qohelet are certainly at issue here.

like goads. Despite the inexplicable presence of the *Mûnaḥ* on the first syllable and the spirantized *bet*, we should probably vocalize the noun as *dorbōnôt* (not *dārĕbōnôt*) and compare the singular form *dorbān* (see HALAT, p. 221; cf. *qorbān*). In light of the form *dorbān*, however, we expect *dorbĕnôt*; but the second vowel is confirmed by some thirty MSS that read *drbwnwt*. The noun *dorbān* in 1 Sam 13:21 is associated with various sharp metal implements. In Mishnaic Hebrew, the noun may refer to the iron tip of a *malmēd* "goad" (*m. Kelim* 9:6;

25:2) and, by extension, to the goad itself (*b. Ḥag.* 3b). Dahood ("Phoenician Background," p. 282) cites Ugaritic *drb*, which occurs with "knives" and "spear" (*KTU* 4.385.8). Whitley accepts this cognate and cites Arabic *dariba* "to be sharp" (*Koheleth*, p. 102). But, while Arabic *drb* does correspond to Ugaritic *drb*, it should correspond to Hebrew *zrb not *drb*, unless the Hebrew is a loanword from Aramaic (so BL §61.sθ). But if the word is of Aramaic origin one should expect the -*ān* ending instead of -*ôn*. It is more likely that the word is related not to Arabic *dariba* "to be sharp," but *dariba* "to be(come) accustomed, habituated," a verb frequently associated with the training of animals (Lane, *Arabic-English Lexicon*, Part 3, pp. 866–67). Thus, the word is related in meaning to *malmēd* "prod" (i.e., a training tool), a word associated with the verb *lmd* "to learn."

like implanted pricks. The form *maśmĕrôt* — with the *śin* — is simply an alternate spelling for the more common *masmĕrôt* (Jer 10:4; cf. 2 Chron 3:9) or *masmĕrîm* (Isa 41:7). We presume that *maśmĕrôt*, like *masmĕrîm*, is masculine plural. A *masmēr* may refer not only to a nail but to any kind of nail-like object (see Jastrow, *Dictionary*, p. 809). We should think here of spikes or nails implanted at the end of sticks to be used as prods (so Rashbam: "like nails driven firmly and inserted into the ends of sticks"). Technically, an ox-goad (*malmēd*) consists of a wooden handle with a specific type of iron tip (*dorbān*) properly set. But there were probably also improvised prods, made with pieces of wood, with nails or the like implanted in them (cf. Fox, *Contradictions*, pp. 324–25). Cf. NJPS: "like nails fixed in prodding sticks"; NAB: "like fixed spikes."

the mentors of the assemblies. Hebrew *ba'ălê 'ăsuppôt*, lit. "the masters of the assemblies" or "the masters of the collections." The expression is unique in the Bible, but it is attested in the Talmud, where it refers to the members of the Sanhedrin (*b. Sanh.* 12a; *y. Sanh.* X.28a; cf. *Num. Rabb.* 14). The latter is also the interpretation of Targ (*rbny-snhdryn* "the masters of the Sanhedrin") and Vulg (*magistrorum consilium* "the council of masters"). If this interpretation is correct, one may assume from the parallelism with *dibrê ḥăkāmîm* "words of the wise" that "(words of) the members of the assemblies" is meant. We are not sure, however, if the term refers generally to the scholars of the community (i.e., the sages) or if a formal assembly is meant.

Alternatively, *'ăsuppôt* may be understood not as "assemblies" of people but as "collections" (of wisdom sayings). Thus, the word is rendered by the Greek translators as *synagmatōn* "collections" (so LXX^SA). If this is the meaning of *'ăsuppôt*, then *ba'ălê* may be understood as experts, thus, "experts of the collections" (so Fox [*Contradictions*, p. 324], who compares the Mishnaic Hebrew expressions *b'ly mqr'* "experts in Scripture" and *b'ly 'gdh* "experts in Aggadah").

they are applied. The passive subject of *nittĕnû* may be the words of the wise, or the goads and nails. Since the agent of the action is the herder, it is more likely that the goads and pricks are meant, rather than the words. Fox notes that the verb *ntn* in Deut 15:17 means "to stick (something) in" (*Contradictions*, p. 326). Likewise, the verb here refers to the sticking of goads and pricks into the ox, which is a metaphor for one who hears the words of the wise.

a certain herder. Hebrew *rō'eh 'eḥād*. Interpreters have variously identified the herder here with Moses, Solomon, Qohelet, or God. The dominant view in most modern commentaries is that God is the herder. This verse is, thus, seen as a defense of the wisdom tradition as having divine authority. Although Wisdom itself is said to be from God (Prov 2:6; 1 Kgs 3:12, 28), nowhere else are the very words of the wise considered to be given by God (see Fox, *Contradictions*, pp. 325–26). Fox argues, instead, that the reference here is not to anyone in particular, but to "any herder." In this context, the word *'eḥād* does not mean a single herder. The emphasis is not on oneness. Rather, the word is used here as the equivalent of an indefinite article or it may even be used in the sense of "some" or "any" (see Joüon-Muraoka §137.u–v; GKC §125.b). So, too, Aramaic *ḥd* may mean "someone" or "a certain (one)" (Sokoloff, *Dictionary*, pp. 187–88), or it may appear as an indefinite article (see *TAD* III, 1.1.38; 2.1.52). Any herder would use whatever it takes to move the herd in the desired direction. Cf. Jer 3:15, "I will give you herders (*rō'îm*) after my own heart, and they will pasture (*rā'û*) you knowledgeably and skillfully."

12. *Beyond them.* Fox (*Contradictions*, pp. 326–27) maintains that a disjunctive accent should be placed on *wĕyōtēr*, as in v 9, and he interprets the verse to be a warning against the sayings of the wise. But the idiom *yōtēr min* is well attested in Postbiblical Hebrew (see Notes at v 9). The warning is simply not to go *beyond* the words of the wise, in this case, the words of Qohelet. The epilogue in the *Instruction to Kagemni*, too, ends with a warning not to exceed what is said: "All that is written in this book, heed it as I said it. Do not go beyond what has been set down" (*AEL* I, p. 60). According to the epilogue in this Egyptian text, those who received the instruction of the sage read it "as it was written" and "it was more beautiful upon their hearts than anything that was in the entire land (*wn.in nfr st ḥr ib.sn r ḫt nbt nty m t3 pn r dr.f*; *Papyrus Prisse* II, lines 13–14; cf. the reference to the felicity and rightness of Qohelet's words in 12:10). Thus, the warning not to go beyond the words of the text is formulaic: it is an affirmation of the completeness and sufficiency of the text. The Akkadian treaty texts, too, often end with such a testimony to the text's completeness and sufficiency. These are similar to the so-called "canonical-formula" found in the Bible (cf. Deut 4:2 and 13:1 [Eng 12:32]; M. Fishbane, "Varia Deuteronomica," *ZAW* 84 [1972], pp. 349–52). At the end of the Apocalypse of John one reads: "I warn every one who hears the words of this book; if anyone adds to them, God will add to that person the plagues described in this book, and if anyone takes away from the words of the book of this prophecy, God will take away that person's share in the tree of life and in the holy city, which are described in this book" (Rev 22:18–19). The point of the warning is the sufficiency of the text. The sages have adequately given their instructions and there is, therefore, no need to go beyond them.

my child. Hebrew *bĕnî*, lit. "my son." By addressing the reader as *bĕnî*, lit. "my son," the author calls to mind the narrative situation assumed in much of the wisdom literature of the ancient Near East: the parent-child instruction (see Fox, "Frame-Narrative," p. 99). Thus, the Sumerian *Instructions of Shuruppak* is presented as lessons offered by Shuruppak to his son (*BWL*, pp. 92–94). The epilogue in the Egyptian text called the *Instruction of Anii* is framed as a dialogue between a father and his son, where the son is exhorted to pay attention to the instructions of the sage, even though they are difficult to understand, and the father praises the words of the sage (*AEL* II, pp. 144–45). The epilogue in the *Instruction to Kagemni* also assumes this narrative situation. It depicts an old vizier calling his children together for instruction, and he warns them not to go beyond what has been set down (*AEL* I, p. 60). This parent-child situation is also assumed in the book of Proverbs, where the recipient of instructions is addressed as *běnî* "my child" (1:8, 10, 15; 2:1; 3:1; etc.).

There is no end to the excessive production of writings. Hebrew *ʿăśôt sěpārîm harbēh ʾên qēṣ*, lit. "the making of writings excessively is without end." The construction may be compared with Isa 9:6 (Eng v 7): *lěmarbēh hammiśrâ ûlěšālôm ʾên-qēṣ* "of the increase of authority and of peace there is no end." In any case, *harbēh* is adverbial, as it is in the parallel line (lit. "talking excessively") and in 7:16–17. It is not clear what precisely *ʿăśôt sěpārîm* "the production of writings" refers to. Is it the composition, the compilation, or the copying of texts? M. Fishbane makes the interesting observation that the verb *ʿśh*, lit. "to make," is similar to Akkadian *uppušu* (the D stem of *epēšu* "to make"), a term used frequently in colophons together with other terms of scribal activities (*Biblical Interpretation in Ancient Israel* [Oxford: Clarendon, 1985], p. 31). The term itself may mean either "to draw up (a document)" or "to copy" (see *CAD* IV, pp. 224, 231). The Aramaic expression *ʿbd spr*, the equivalent of Hebrew *ʿśh spr*, occurs once in the Aramaic letters from Elephantine, where it means "to prepare a document" (*spr znh zy ʾnh ʿbdt* "this document which I prepared," see Kraeling, *Aramaic Papyri*, pp. 238–39, Papyrus 9, line 22; but the verb is *ktb* "to write" in line 27). One may presume that the preparation means or includes composition, but the expression is unique among the texts from Elephantine; elsewhere we find the expression *ktb spr* "to write a document" (e.g., Kraeling, *Aramaic Papyri*, 2.14; 14.25; 4.42; 8.4; 10.10–11; 11.12, 15.1). Cf. Ezra 7:10, where *laʿăśôt* is used for the composition or compilation of the Torah.

As in the Aramaic texts from the Persian period, Hebrew *sěpārîm* refers to written texts. The traditional translation "books" is anachronistic, however, for it strictly refers to sets of written pages. Such "books" were not in use till the early centuries of the common era. In the Persian period, substantive texts were written on papyri or leather scrolls—as we see in the Aramaic documents from Elephantine and Wadi Daliyeh. In any case, by the phrase *ʿăśôt sěpārîm*, the author merely means the writing and compilation of written texts.

excessive talking. MT *wělahag* is often explained on the basis of Arabic *lahija* "to be devoted, dedicated." This Hebrew word is not attested in other contexts, however. The ancient versions all seem to assume some form of the root *hgh* (LXX *meletē* "practice"; Vulg *meditatio* "meditation"). This verse is quoted in the Talmud (*b. Erub.* 21b), where it is also explained in terms of *hgh*. *Qoh. Rabb.* also interprets the word to mean *lahăgôt* "to talk about." A number of scholars, therefore, emend the text to *lhg <wt>* (so Perles, *Analekten* I, p. 29). It is difficult, however, to explain the loss of -*wt*. The infinitive absolute of *hgh* is attested as *hāgōh* and *hāgô*, but the infinitive construct is not attested anywhere. It is easier to assume a haplography of *h* and read *lhg* <*h*> and note that there are examples of infinitives of III-Weak verbs with final *h* instead of *t*: *hěyēh* (Ezek 21:15); *rĕ'ōh* (Gen 48:11); *qěnōh* (Prov 16:16); etc. (see GKC §75.n). The word here means "talking" (so Pss 37:30; 38:13 [Eng v 12]; 71:24; Isa 59:3; Prov 8:7); the root is often parallel to *dbr* "to speak." The warning is similar to what is in the epilogue of the *Instruction to Kagemni*: one must not go beyond what is *written* (the writings) and one must heed the instruction as the sage has *spoken* it (AEL I, p. 60). In our text, the words of the wise in general, and of Qohelet in particular, are authoritative. There is no need to go beyond them in writing or in talking, for "everything has been heard." The parallelism of *spr* and *hg* in Ugaritic is also suggestive: *dbl spr* "innumerable" (beyond recounting) // *dbl hg* "unspeakable" (*KTU* 1.14.II.37–38). In any case, this verse is not a polemic against the production of books or erudition. Nor does it have reference to the closing of the canon.

13. *End of the matter.* This is a closing formula typically placed at the end of a literary corpus. It is similar to the expression *sôpā' dî-millĕtā'* "the end of the matter" in Dan 7:28. Cf. also Talmudic Aramaic *swp dpswq* "the end of the verse," *swpyh dspr'* "the end of the book" and *swp hlkt'* "the end of the *halakah*" (see Sokoloff, *Dictionary*, p. 371). For other concluding formulas in the Bible, see Job 31:40, Jer 51:64, Ps 72:20, and Sir 43:27. Barton thinks the absence of the definite article on *dābār* indicates that this phrase is a technical expression marking the end of the editor's work (*Ecclesiastes*, p. 200). This assessment may be correct. We should also compare the usage of *dābār* here with *dābār* in Deut 4:2, where the singular noun refers generally to Mosaic legislation: "You shall not add to the *dābār* which I am commanding you." By analogy, we understand *dābār* in this epilogue of Ecclesiastes to refer generally to Qohelet's teachings. The formula indicates the completeness of the book—beyond that one must not go.

everything has been heard. The form *nišmā'* may be parsed as the Qal imperfect 1 cs ("let us hear"), the Niphal participle ("what is heard"), or the pausal form of the Niphal perfect 3 ms ("has been heard"). LXX (followed by Copt) and Syr assume an imperative ("hear!"), an easier reading that anticipates the two imperatives in the next line. Vulg takes the form to be the Qal imperfect: *audiamus* "let us hear." In any case, this phrase is a variation of the closing formula. In fact, *sôp dābār* "end of the matter" and *hakkōl nišmā'* "all has been heard" are phrases in apposition to one another.

Fear God and keep his commandments. There is nothing in the text that requires the subordination of this phrase to the preceding, as is implied in some translations (so NJPS: "when all is said and done: Revere God. . . ."). Rather, v 13a marks the end of the original epilogue; v 13b begins a gloss (see Comment below).

for every mortal is to be so. Hebrew *kî-zeh kol-hā'ādām*, lit. "this is all humanity." The expression is problematic. It is probably elliptical, like *'ammĕkā nĕdābôt* "your people are willingness" = "your people are willing" (Ps 110:3); *wa'ănî tĕpillâ* "and I (am) prayer" = "and I am a person of prayer" (Ps 109:4); *'ănî šālôm* "I peace" = "I am a person of peace" (Ps 120:7); *tĕmôl 'ănaḥnû* "we are yesterday" = "we are of yesterday" = "we are fleeting" (Job 8:9). Whitley proposes to read *zh kl <l> h'dm* "this is the principle of humanity" (*Koheleth*, p. 105), but it is unnecessary to alter the text.

14. *for everything hidden.* The preposition *'al* indicates the basis of divine judgment. One may compare 11:9, *'al-kol-'ēlleh yĕbî'ăkā hā'ĕlōhîm bammišpāṭ* "for all these, God will bring you into judgment."

COMMENT

There is wide consensus among scholars that 12:9–14 is an appendix of some sort. The unit falls outside the framework marked by the nearly identical statements in 1:2 and 12:8 that everything is absolute "vanity." The text itself begins with *wĕyōtēr* "additionally" or "an addition/postscript" (v 9). Moreover, these verses refer to Qohelet in the third person, whereas the first-person style is typical of the rest of the book—except for the superscription (1:1), the editorial framework (1:2; 12:8), and an editorial comment in 7:27. Most importantly, this appendix appears to look back at the book and reflect on the work of Qohelet. Modern scholars agree, therefore, that 12:9–14 constitutes additional material.

There is no consensus, however, on the unity of these verses. A few scholars (e.g., Hertzberg) discern three different hands in these verses: vv 9–11, v 12, vv 13–14. Some see two editions (Podechard, Galling, Zimmerli), vv 9–11, vv 12–14. Those who take the view of multiple editions, whether two or three, see the first (vv 9–11) as sympathetic toward Qohelet. In this view, the first edition of the epilogue, namely, 12:9–11, is supposed to come from the hand either of the compiler or a disciple of Qohelet. The rest of the passage is thought to be an implicit criticism of Qohelet (v 12) and an attempt to answer it with a more orthodox perspective (vv 13–14). Those who see a single epilogist at work generally detect an apologetic undercurrent: Qohelet's point of view is defended (vv 9–11), but then, quickly placed within a more orthodox theological framework (vv 13–14). In any case, the majority of scholars regard 12:9–14 as coming from some editor or editors—some person or persons other than the author of the book.

Fox has argued, however, that neither the third-person reference nor the retrospective style of the epilogue is indicative of different authorship ("Frame-Narrative," pp. 85–106). For him, the epilogist is the narrator of the entire book and the narrator's persona is Qohelet. In support of his thesis, Fox cites a number of Egyptian texts, as well as the books of Deuteronomy and Tobit. Typically, says Fox, the first-person narrative of a story is framed by third-person retrospection, often evaluating and extolling the work of the principal figure in the main narrative. One may observe further that the epilogue of the Egyptian text known as the *Instruction to Kagemni* is particularly suggestive not only because of its third-person retrospective style, but also because it includes a comment on the reliability of the sage's teachings and a warning not to go beyond them:

Then he said to them: "All that is written in this book, heed it as I have said it. Do not go beyond what has been set down." Then they placed themselves on their bellies. They recited it as it was written. It seemed good to them beyond anything in the whole land. They stood and sat accordingly.

(AEL I, p. 60)

Admittedly, this Egyptian parallel proves nothing about the origin of the epilogue in Ecclesiastes or its unity. One still cannot be certain if the narrator of the epilogue is the very author of the entire book, as Fox would have it. It is possible that an editor might have been responsible for compiling the words of Qohelet and framing the composition. Nevertheless, Fox has successfully shown that the third-person retrospective style does not necessarily mean that there was an epilogist who was reacting to Qohelet's views and correcting them in some way. Indeed, the epilogue may contain the same views as the body of the text, although those views are articulated in a different voice, whether of the author or an epilogist/compiler.

The epilogue in Ecclesiastes begins by identifying Qohelet as a sage who taught the general public. Then it proceeds to itemize what Qohelet did: he listened, he deliberated, he edited many proverbs (v 9). The point can hardly be that Qohelet was responsible for a specific genre of wisdom literature or, even less, of the book of Proverbs (so Barton and others). Only a small amount of what Qohelet wrote or worked on falls in the category of proverbial sayings. Rather, the assertion is that his work was typical of a sage (compare 1 Kgs 5:12 [Eng 4:32]; Prov 1:6).

The epilogue praises Qohelet's use of felicitous words, a reference to the aptness and aesthetic quality of his sayings. Precision and elegance of speech are qualities valued in the wisdom tradition throughout the ancient Near East (see, for instance, Prov 15:23; 16:24). Qohelet is also commended for being correct in speaking *dibrê 'ĕmet* "words of truth" — reliable words (compare Ps 132:2). A similar commendation of the author is found in the epilogue of the Egyptian *Instruction of Anii*, where the sage who wrote the instructions is said to be a learned man, "a man who is a master, whose strivings are exalted, whose every word is chosen" and whose "words please the heart" (AEL II, p. 146). Interestingly, the epilogue of this Egyptian wisdom text also shows an awareness that the words of the sage might be difficult to understand and to follow, as the words of Qohelet are. Hence the epilogue in the *Instruction of Anii*, though in the form of a debate between father and son, serves as an apology for the efficacy and sufficiency of the sage's words. The "son" is urged to take the words of the instruction seriously, for they come from a true sage who chose his words carefully and presented them in a pleasing manner. A similar move is evident in the epilogue in Ecclesiastes: the reader is urged to pay attention to the words of Qohelet because he was a learned sage, whose words had been carefully crafted and correctly written.

From the words of a particular sage (vv 9–10), the text turns to the words of sages in general (v 11). Yet, there is no doubt that the teachings of Qohelet are in view. The expression "the words of the sages" does not appear to be a technical term. As in 9:17 (also Prov 1:6; 22:17), it refers simply to the advice of the wise. These teachings are said to be "like goads" and "like implanted pricks." The term "goads" refers properly to the tip of an ox-goad; it occurs only one other time in the Bible, in 1 Sam 13:21, but it is attested several times in Postbiblical Hebrew. The word "pricks" is less certain, but given the herding imagery and the parallelism, one may conjecture that improvised prods are meant — that is, sticks with pricks embedded in them. The next expression, *baʿălê ʾăsuppôt*, literally "masters of the assemblies" or "masters/owners of the collections," is also ambiguous. The first meaning is attested in the Talmud and it is the interpretation favored by the Targum and Vulgate (see Notes). The second is a possible meaning, but there is no evidence for it. Hence, we should probably take the term to refer to teachers or scholars in the community or in the congregations. It is the teachings of these sages and mentors, then, that are compared with goads and pricks. And they — these goads and pricks — are applied by a herder. Clearly the herding imagery is still in effect, and so the herder must refer to any teacher of wisdom. The point is that goads and pricks do not come upon one accidentally, without someone using these implements. Rather, one always knows that they are applied deliberately by some herder or other. The imagery of a herder using goads and pricks implies that there is some pain involved. The lesson may be difficult to learn, but the pain is necessary. This point of view is nothing new. The sages of the ancient Near East always assumed that good instructions may be painful for the learner, but some pain is necessary before one truly learns (see Comment at 1:18). The words of the wise may hurt; they are not what one may choose to hear. Yet, in the end, they are better for one's well-being (compare 7:5). Interestingly, the epilogue in the *Instruction of Anii*, which recognizes the difficulty of learning the sage's lessons, also uses the imagery of animals learning to behave: "Say: 'I shall do like all the beasts,' Listen and learn what they do" (*AEL* II, p. 144).

The epilogue in Ecclesiastes proceeds to advise against excess. The meaning of the advice is, however, not immediately evident. Commentators do not agree on what it is that one is asked not to exceed or why one must not do so. A number of scholars have argued that the text evidences a certain "canon consciousness." According to this view, the epilogist was reacting against the secular literature or various contemporaneous writings that are deemed to be substandard. As Crenshaw would have it, the epilogist is "warning against an open attitude toward the canon" (*Ecclesiastes*, p. 191). Fox, on the other hand, holds that it is the wisdom writings against which one is warned: "Writing is praiseworthy, but there is no point in overdoing it" (*Contradictions*, p. 327). The warning is probably formulaic, however. It is intended to establish the authority of the text or texts in question. In this case the warning is not to exceed "the words of the wise," referring specifically to the teachings of Qohelet.

It is important to note a similar warning in the conclusion of the *Instruction to Kagemni*: "Do not go beyond what is set down" (*AEL* I, p. 60). The epilogue in the *Instruction to Kagemni* warns one not to go beyond what is written ("all that is written in this book") and what is said ("as I said it"). So, too, the epilogue of Ecclesiastes warns in v 12 against going beyond what is written (i.e., the books) and what is said (i.e., talking). The point is that everything intended by the author has been laid out; there are no accidental omissions and no superfluous materials. So there is no need to go beyond the text (or to hold back its teachings) — either in writing or in speaking. The intent of the warning is the same as the so-called "canonical formula" found in Deut 4:2; 13:1 (Eng 12:32); Sir 42:21; Rev 22:18–19. It serves to establish the complete reliability of the text in question (for the ancient Near Eastern background, see Fishbane, "Varia Deuteronomica, pp. 349–52). The occurrence of the "canonical-formula" in Deuteronomy did not rule out other books from consideration. Neither did the formula at the end of the book of Revelation set the limit of the canon. In each case, the formula was intended only to assert the complete reliability of the respective text for its purpose and to ensure the integrity of the text in its preservation. The dogmatic usage of the formula (that is, as establishing a canonical corpus) was not attested for centuries (see W. C. van Unnik, "De la règle *mēta prostheinai mēta aphelein* dans l'histoire du canon," *Vigilae Christianae* 3 [1949], pp. 1–36). So, too, the epilogue in Ecclesiastes warns one not to go beyond the teachings of sages, meaning here the words of Qohelet, but the warning was not intended to be canon defining. The epilogue in Ecclesiastes functions in a similar manner to the epilogues in the Egyptian wisdom texts like the *Instruction of Anii* and the *Instruction to Kagemni:* it serves as an apology for the rest of the book, giving the book a stamp of legitimacy. It asserts that everything that the author meant to say has been said.

At the very end of the epilogue in the *Instruction to Kagemni*, a colophon states: "It is finished." Similar notations are found at the end of other Egyptian wisdom texts (see *AEL* I, pp. 76, 144, 169, 182, 191; II, p. 162; III, p. 213). So, too, v 13a probably marks the end of the book: "end of the matter; everything has been heard." Barton makes the interesting suggestion that the book originally ended at just this point; what comes after that is an additional comment of a later editor (*Ecclesiastes*, p. 199). This may be correct. Egyptian wisdom texts also end in such terse colophonic notations. It may be noticed, too, that there are no syntactical clues that link v 13b to 13a (see Notes above); so it appears that vv 13b–14 are simply tacked on at the end.

While the fear of God is a notion present in the teachings of Qohelet (3:14; 5:6 [Eng v 7]; 8:12–13), the call to obey God's commandments is not. Qohelet does speak of one who keeps the commandment (*šōmēr miṣwâ*) in 8:5, but there the command of a human despot seems to be at issue. The charge to keep God's commandments in the epilogue, therefore, is an additional dimension to the teachings of Qohelet. Even Fox, who argues vigorously for the unity of the whole epilogue, concedes that "[t]he attitude expressed here is close to the traditional Wisdom epistemology, except insofar as it assumes a revelation of God's commandments" (*Contradictions*, p. 328).

The perspective at the end of the epilogue seems to be different from the rest of the book. It is true that Qohelet speaks of divine judgment in 3:17, but there he does not say how the deity will judge. The author is troubled by the injustice that prevails in the world, but he says simply "God will judge" in the same way that he affirms "God will seek the pursued" in 3:15 (see Comment at 3:17). For Qohelet, everything is in the hand of a mysterious God. He does not speak of

God's judgment in the future, as in a judgment day, only of a deity who reserves the right to judge at any time and in any way. In 11:9, Qohelet says that God brings people into account, but there the context is a call to enjoy life while one is able. Enjoyment is a divine imperative for which one is accountable. Although the phraseology in 12:14 is partly similar to what we find in 11:9, the content is quite different. Here in 12:14 the accountability is specifically for keeping God's commandments. God will bring every deed into judgment (v 14). As Murphy observes, it is ironic that the word used here is *ma'ăseh* "deed," since the word is used elsewhere in the book for God's inscrutable activities and for events that transpire in human life. But now, observes Murphy, "the 'work' or 'deed' (human) is here associated too easily to divine judgment" (*Ecclesiastes*, p. 126). It is probable that an eschatological judgment is meant in 12:14, for the text suggests that everything hidden will be revealed, whether good or bad.

It must be said that the perspective in vv 13b–14 is not contradictory to the rest of the book. Nowhere does Qohelet, or the writers of Proverbs for that matter, deny the importance of obedience to divine commandments. Nor is the possibility of an eschatological judgment explicitly rejected. Yet, the final remark in the epilogue does put a different spin on Qohelet's work by associating the fear of God with obedience to the commandments. G. T. Sheppard has called attention to a similar conjoining of the injunctions to fear God and to keep God's commandments throughout Ben Sira ("Epilogue to Qoheleth," pp. 182–89). Sir 1:26–30 may be cited as an example of how the injunctions are combined:

> If you desire wisdom, keep the commandments,
> and God will supply it to you;
> For the fear of God is wisdom and learning,
> and fidelity and humility are his delight.
> Do not be disobedient to the fear of God;
> Do not approach him with a duplicitous heart.
> Do not be a hypocrite before others,
> keep watch over your lips.
> Do not exalt yourself lest you fall,
> and bring dishonor upon yourself.
> God will reveal your secrets
> and cast you down in public,
> because you did not come in the fear of God
> with your heart full of guile.

Since Ben Sira also manifests a conscious linking of the role of wisdom and the authority of the Torah (see Sir 2:16; 15:1; 19:20; 24:1–34), Sheppard argues that the end of the epilogue in Ecclesiastes "represents a fairly sophisticated theological interpretation of sacred wisdom in relation to an authoritative Torah" ("Epilogue to Qoheleth," p. 187). In a later essay, Sheppard proposed that "the final statements of the epilogue belong either to Ben Sira's period or later and may have played a constructive role in the canonization of the book" ("Canonization: Hearing the Voice of the Same God Through Historically Dissimilar Traditions," *Ex Auditu* 1 [1985], p. 108). But it must be admitted that the link between Wisdom and the Torah is not all that clear in the epilogue of Ecclesiastes. The text does not explicitly link Wisdom and Torah. But even if the author of vv 13b–14 did intend to associate Wisdom and Torah, we cannot date that redaction to the time of Ben Sira. Already in the time of Ezra-Nehemiah, the expression "the wisdom of your God" appears to have been interchangeable with "the Torah of your God" (Ezra 7:14, 25). It is not only in the time of Ben Sira that such a linkage was possible. Indeed, the perspective of the redactor is not far different from Deuteronomy, where obedience to divine commandments is defined as wisdom: "keep them and do them; for that will be your wisdom and your understanding" (Deut 4:6).

Without contradicting Qohelet, then, the redactor calls attention to an important dimension to be considered when all is said and done: that it is possible to hold the perspective of sages like Qohelet together with the central tenets of Israelite faith. Radical Wisdom in the end need not be seen as contradictory to the call to obedience. And, indeed, it is the possibility of such a hermeneutical move that assured the acceptance of Ecclesiastes into the canon (see *b. Šabb.* 30b).

INDEX OF AUTHORS

◆

INDEX OF SUBJECTS

◆

INDEX OF SCRIPTURAL AND OTHER REFERENCES

◆

409

INDEX OF FOREIGN WORDS

◆

ekklēsiastēs 95
mēden agan 254
mesotēs 254
paradeisos 128
tychē 135

HITTITE

LÚ-natar 330

PERSIAN

paridaiḏa 128

PHOENICIAN/PUNIC

glgl 367
nḥt 213
ʿqrt 160
šmr mḥsb 354
tḥt šmš 16, 105

SYRIAC

dngr rwḥʾ 238
mlk 134
pišrā 277

UGARITIC

aḥd 180
aḫr 354
atryt 231, 234
uḫry 231, 234
uḫryt 231, 232, 234
bnt hll 359
gl 367
dlp 331
drb 387
hg 163, 390
ḫšt 15, 140
ḥtbn 260
yḥd 180
ktr 137
ktrt 137
mdnt 130
mkk 331
mtk 127

sglt 130
sknt 316
spr 390
ǵlm 163
ʿml 135
prr 363
šmn rqh 312
št 131
tkḥ 286
ṯn 180
ql 358

HEBREW

ʾzn 384
ʾeḥād 180
ʾănî 17
ʾēt 17
ʾet-nirdāp 165–166
bwr 297
bêt hāsûrîm 31, 184
bêt ʿôlām 54
bĕnôt ya ʿănâ 359
baʿal hallāšôn 318
gābōah 203–204
dlp 331
hebel 42–43, 44–46, 101–102, 112–113
hôlēlôt 133
hršʿ 166
zōh 17–18, 126
zwʿ 355
zĕmān 13, 159
ḥbl 196–197
ḥebel 364–365
ḥāgāb 362
ḥwš 139
hôteʾ 25, 141–142, 157, 311
ḥākām 37, 60, 67
ḥēleq 24, 58, 132, 133
ḥōpen 180
ḥpṣ 159
ḥēpeṣ 159
ḥesrôn 122–123, 148
ḥešbôn 22, 260–261, 271
ṭaḥănâ 13
yāṣāʾ 255
yitrôn 103–104
kšr 137
kišrôn 137
limšôk 127
maddāʿ 333
mkk 331
màlʾāk 196
maʿăneh 209, 223–224
mĕṣûdâ 309
māṣôr 309
mĕṣûrâ 309

māqôm qādôš 285
miqreh 135
marpeʾ 313
marpēh 313
miskēn 183, 310
mišlaḥat 282
mērôṣ 307
mrr 261
mātûn 237
mātan 237
mattānâ 237
naḥat 213
nĕkāsîm 209
naʿar 329
sĕgullâ 130
sekel 314
skn 316
sākan 316
ʿôlām 163, 172–173
ʿim 135
ʿāmāl 104
ʿinyān 121
ʿṣb 316
ʿqr 160
pardēs 12, 37, 128
pēšer 277
pitgām 12, 286
ṣēl 22
qbr 284
rûaḥ 59, 282, 367
rĕʿût rûaḥ 121
raʿyôn rûaḥ 121
šʾp 107
šiddâ wĕšiddôt 131
šûq 356–357
šaḥărût 350
škḥ 286
šlṭ 13, 136
šallîṭ 14, 28–29, 256, 257, 293
šēm 234
šĕtî 330
taḥat haššemeš 104–105